D1589011

THE BFI COMPANION TO CRIME

BR/CR/113.

The
BFI Companion
to Crime

Edited by
Phil Hardy

Foreword by
Richard Attenborough

CASSELL

First published in 1997 by
Cassell
Wellington House
125 Strand
London WC2R 0BB
and the
British Film Institute
21 Stephen Street
London W1P 2LN

The British Film Institute exists to promote
appreciation, enjoyment, protection and development of moving image culture in and throughout
the whole of the United Kingdom. Its activities
include the National Film and Television Archive;
the National Film Theatre; the Museum of the
Moving Image; the London Film Festival; the
production and distribution of film and video;
funding and support for regional activities; Library
and Information Services, Stills, Posters and
Designs; Research, Publishing and Education; and
the monthly *Sight and Sound* magazine.

British Library Cataloguing-in-Publication Data
A catalogue record for this book is available from
the British Library.

ISBN   0 304 33211 9
       0 304 33215 1 pbk

Cover design by Jamie Tanner

Design and typesetting by Ronald Clark

Printed and bound in Great Britain by
Butler and Tanner, Frome, Somerset

FRONTISPIECE Richard Attenborough as
Pinkie in *Brighton Rock*

Foreword

by Richard Attenborough

There have always been crime stories. However, modern society has developed a particular enthusiasm for tales of robbery and murder. Quite why this is so we can leave the sociologists to discuss. What is evident is that from the earliest days of the cinema, stories of crime and criminals have been among the most popular with audiences the world over.

One of the things which this book pays particular attention to is the wealth of crime films in the non-English speaking countries. Here are films from Russia, Japan, Brazil, France, Africa, Italy and elsewhere, some of them obviously drawing on American models, others trying to develop new forms adapted to their own societies. But of course it is Hollywood which dominates, especially from the early 1930s, when a combination of social and technical factors gave birth to the gangster film. The growth of organised crime that was the result of prohibition, and the introduction of sound (making possible the vivid reproduction of the screaming car tyres, wailing sirens and chattering machine-guns that are inseparable from the genre), gave rise to a new kind of story that had all the immediacy of today's newspaper headlines, and was as likely as not drawn from them.

British cinema was not far behind Hollywood in its enthusiasm for such material, and in the 40s and 50s particularly made a number of tough, realistic and imaginative crime films, as well as some affectionate parodies such as *The Ladykillers*. This is where I, as an actor, had a small part to play in the evolution of the British crime movie.

When I started out, screen criminals were required to look tough and worldly, so my somewhat cherubic features made it very unlikely that I would ever be asked to play such a character. But, to my great joy, very early in my screen acting career the Boulting Brothers elected to cast me as Pinkie, the evil boy gangster in *Brighton Rock* – a part I had played at the Garrick Theatre in 1943. It would be a long time before I was offered such a good part again. Indeed, the next time I played a criminal – albeit a sympathetic one in *Seance on a Wet Afternoon* – I was sixteen years older, by no means cherubic and wore a large false nose.

Moralists have always been quick to condemn the cinema for its supposedly unhealthy stimulation of fantasy and antisocial impulses, especially among the young. Crime films especially have been condemned, as mere blueprints for action on the part of delinquent youth. But at its best the crime film can offer a unique insight into the darker recesses of the soul and the undergrowth of society, bringing to the surface truths about ourselves and others which it would be more comfortable to conceal.

10 Rillington Place, a factual movie in which I played mass killer John Reginald Christie, was made in 1970 with the express aim of defeating an attempt in Parliament to re-instate capital punishment. (Christie's simple lodger, Timothy Evans, had been found guilty of a murder committed by his landlord and had been hanged in error.) Finding sufficient sympathy and insight to create Christie on the screen, despite his catalogue of truly nauseating crime, was without doubt the most difficult task of my entire acting career. But capital punishment was not brought back, then or afterwards, and I do believe that the film may well have swayed both public and political opinion at that time.

British film has contributed much to the crime genre over the years and has usually done so, I feel, in the mature and responsible fashion of such recent examples as *Mona Lisa*, *Dance with a Stranger* and *Let Him Have It*.

This is a book which focuses squarely on the cinema itself, on its achievements and significance during its hundred-year-old history. It celebrates the great and the good among the thousands of crime films that have been made. It documents the rich variety of milieux and topics which crime films have explored, and it provides the essential historical background of such key institutions as the FBI, the mafia and the yakuza. Perhaps most valuably of all, it gives full credit to those writers whose imaginations provided the essential motive power for so many wonderful films. Cornell Woolrich, David Goodis, Jim Thompson and Eric Ambler, not to mention the more celebrated Raymond Chandler, Dashiell Hammett and of course Graham Greene all have their honoured place in the pantheon of great criminal minds.

This book is dedicated to the memory of Julian Symons, poet, critic, novelist and man of letters.

Acknowledgments

Every editor says it and every editor is right to do so, so here we go again. The contributors listed opposite are the creators of this book. Without them it would not have existed. That said, I take full responsibility for the finished product. Among the contributors I would like to single out Kim Newman, who wrote more than anyone, got the words in on time – and was the last to be paid. It's always been a pleasure working with Kim. I'd also like to thank Ed Buscombe, who handled the transition from commissioning editor to copy editor with great élan and a degree of patience that was very helpful. Thanks also to Millie Simpson for picture research.

The illustrations have all come from the production companies listed on page 24 with the following exceptions:
Frontispiece – Richard Attenborough Productions Limited;
Pages 12 above, 71 right, 72 left, 80 left, 82 below right, 85 above right, 119, 151 above, 161 above right, 167 left and right, 183, 208 below right – The Hulton Getty Picture Collection;
Pages 78 above, 169 above left, 204, 260 right, 342 – Mary Evans Picture Library;
Pages 122 above and below – PolyGram;
Colour pages 1 (all four), 2 below right, 3 above left and above right, 4 above and below right and below left – Moviestore.

Contributors

AW: Adrian Wootton is Head of the National Film Theatre and Director of the London Film Festival. He is also founder of the crime and mystery festival, Shots in the Dark.

DM: David McGillivray is a screenwriter (*House of Whipcord, Satan's Slave*), playwright, critic and author of *Doing Rude Things*.

EB: Edward Buscombe is the editor of *The BFI Companion to the Western*.

JL: Jack Lodge is a free-lance researcher and author and a specialist on silent cinema.

KN: Kim Newman is the editor of *The BFI Companion to Horror*, author of *The Night Mayor* and other novels and the critical studies *Nightmare Movies* and *Wild West Movies*.

MP: Mike Phillips is an author and Arts Foundation Fellow for Crime Fiction. His latest novel is *The Dancing Face*.

PW: Paul Willemen is Professor of Film at Napier University, Edinburgh, and is co-author of *The Encyclopaedia of Indian Cinema* and the author of *Looks and Frictions* and other works.

TP: Tim Pulleine works on the *Guardian* and is a critic, journalist and frequent contributor to Aurum Film Encyclopaedias.

TV: Tise Vahimagi works for BFI Library and Information Services and is the author of *British Television: An Illustrated Guide*.

Introduction

The history of crime is as old as the human race. All known societies have had rules or laws, and there have always been people to break them. But crime as a subject for art and entertainment has not always exerted the same fascination as it has done in the west for the past hundred years or so. The reasons why crime is so prominent on our television and cinema screens and in our newspapers and popular fiction are various and deep-seated, and would require investigation in a book very different from the present volume. What is attempted here is something different, a survey and a classification of the main types and examples of crime fiction in the cinema.

The book does not offer a formal definition of what constitutes a crime film. To an extent, the definition proceeds by exclusion. Obviously all crime films have narratives in which crimes are committed; but then so do films in other genres. Horror films and Westerns are replete with crimes, but they have their own domain (and their own volumes in this series). What in general *The BFI Companion to Crime* covers is the history of a genre, however loosely formed, which sociologically has its origins at a certain period in Europe in the late nineteenth century which saw the formation of an organised police force and the professionalisation of both the forces of law and the criminal. This gave rise to a literature, of which Sir Arthur Conan Doyle is the first great exponent, in which the process of investigation is paramount (in a way that it is not in previous fiction about notable crimes, for example *Macbeth*). Typically, this investigation is not merely a matter of detecting the crime and the criminal; it also involves an understanding of the motive. It therefore has a psychological, and ultimately a social, dimension.

The crime film, though developed from these early works of fiction, was not best suited to the minutiae of detection as practised in literary works. But what it could provide par excellence was both a comprehensive depiction of a criminal milieu in all its shocking but fascinating detail, and an insight into the mind of the criminal himself (rarely, for sound sociological reasons, herself). What then arose both in Europe and America during the 1920s were a series of representations of daring criminals (Fantômas, Dr Mabuse) and striking and highly popular recreations of the criminal underworld. From these films have developed virtually everything that is treated in this book, and later developments such as prison movies, juvenile delinquent films, films about serial killers or terrorists are only refinements of this initial staking out of the terrain.

It is appropriate, therefore, that the longest entry in this book is devoted to Sherlock Holmes. Conan Doyle's creation confronts mysterious murders and elaborate conspiracies (which though they often have their origins in a far-flung corner of the globe are violently played out in England, hub of

LEFT Rod Steiger, *Al Capone*

ABOVE Sir Arthur Conan Doyle
RIGHT Basil Rathbone, Nigel Bruce, *The Hound of the Baskervilles*

Empire and heart of the world). Holmes is called in to rescue reputations, state secrets and damsels in distress. At the same time he is clearly a figure of his times. Amidst the swirling fog of London, with the ever-present clip-clop of a hansom cab audible in the background, he is a Victorian super-man, who when bored turns to drugs, the violin or the classification of tobacco ash. And as in all complex mythology there is more to Holmes than Holmes. He is ministered to by a faithful landlady and a devoted friend, competes with an even more insightful, but infinitely lazier, broth-er, Mycroft, and in Professor Moriarty is set against the only villain capable of (possibly) besting him.

Sherlock Holmes may not have been the first consulting detective, nor even the most complete one, but he is the most long-lived. He is also the most written-about character by those other than his creator. Torn from Conan Doyle's care, Holmes has attracted a vast number of other authors intent on adding to the canon. Following the lapse of copyright in 1974, there was a flood of Holmes material in which Holmes meets historical characters like Freud, Bram Stoker, Teddy Roosevelt and, most often, Jack the Ripper.

Reaching out for a hero

However, to those used to seeing Holmes on film – where he arrived in *Sherlock Holmes Baffled*, a one-minute trick film made between 1900 and 1903, and was outwitted by a Wellsian Invisible Man – such changes were commonplace. From as early as the mid-1940s, producer-director Roy William Neill set Holmes against the Axis powers, helping unmask deep-cover Nazi spies, recovering stolen secret weapons and making Churchill-ian pronouncements on the course of World War II. It is this flexibility that is Holmes's greatness. For, although his success and longevity are unique, as a creation he is not. Rather he is one of many, albeit more successful than most, representatives of a world order on the cusp of change, as the USA replaced Great Britain as the leading nation in the world, as metal replaced wood at sea, the gun the sword on land (just as later the Model T would replace the hansom and the tank the horse), as man took to the air and the terrible cost of modern warfare made its presence felt. At the end of *His Last Bow* (1917), Conan Doyle knowingly spoke of this in the famous 'East Wind' speech he gives Holmes:

'There's an east wind coming, Watson.'

'I think not, Holmes. It is very warm.'

'Good old Watson! You are the one fixed point in a changing age. There's an east wind coming all the same, such a wind as never blew on England yet. It will be cold and bitter, Watson, and a good many of us may wither before its blast. But it's God's own wind none the less.'

If Conan Doyle saw his character bound to a particular time, others embraced the future with its new mechanics of death and power willingly. As Doyle was ending the career of his detective, other writers were spinning equally elaborate tales as the industrialisation of culture led to an explosion of cheap serialised fictions in Europe and in the US. The requirements of the genre (easily consumable, action-based narratives organised around a central, imagination-grabbing figure to ensure ongoing sales) combined with the social tensions of the period (the immense dislocations wrought by modernisation) to produce a series of superheroes (detectives and adventurers) and supervillains such as Holmes, Fantômas and Mabuse.

Consider Dr Mabuse. The Luxembourg writer Norbert Jacques devised the figure of Mabuse, using the name of a sixteenth-century Flemish painter, as a modernised version of both Holmes and his central antagonist Moriarty. A protean figure, Mabuse fuses within himself the megalomania of a feudal lord and the threat incarnated by the lower-class, upstart entrepreneur: Mabuse is a gambler (like the aristocrats) and a pseudo-scientific entertainer (Mesmer and Rasputin rolled into one). And yet Mabuse is a significant advance on Holmes/Moriarty. While for Conan Doyle's character the accumulation of wealth, or simply making a living, were rather distasteful activities, for Mabuse the accumulation of financial power is the key to everything else, making him into a thoroughly modern figure – in one respect. Yet at the same time Mabuse like Holmes is a backward-looking figure. He uses the most modern of technologies – and indeed the films by Fritz Lang about the character are as much about how Mabuse controls the world by controlling people's perception of it – and yet despite the grandeur of his dreams the extent of his world is hardly any greater than Sax Rohmer's Fu Manchu. Both characters dream of world domination, but it is the energy with which they pursue it that is modern. If Moriarty is a conspirator, they are criminals, but criminals caught in an idealised, nightmare world. What is missing is the humdrum reality of crime, crime not as a conspiracy but as a matter of fact.

The evolution of the gangster film

From this perspective, the final inter-title of D. W. Griffith's *The Musketeers of Pig Alley* (1912) is highly revealing. After a shot of a hand passing some banknotes to a cop through a half-opened door, the title 'Links in the Chain' appears. Jump forward twenty-five years and that inter-title is writ

Clive Brook, *Underworld*

large in the gangster film, which began in the late 20s and early 30s with stories about the effects of prohibition, ripped from the front pages of the nation's newspapers (and often written for the screen by former reporters). Whereas Holmes and Mabuse confronted and created elaborate conspiracies, suddenly in the 20s crime in the USA became organised in a way it had never been. Where before it had been piecemeal and artisanal, after the arrival of prohibition it became systematic and on an industrial scale. With it came a new kind of crime film, the gangster film.

An early example of this is *Underworld* (1927), which (like *Scarface*, 1932) was written by former reporter Ben Hecht. The film features the rise-and-fall scenario that would be oft repeated and, like so many later films, was clearly grounded in reality and featured characters based on real gangsters. Yet at the same time, if one compares it to *Little Caesar* (1930) or *The Public Enemy* (1931), it is clearly a transitional film. The ending of *Underworld*, in which Bancroft remains behind to die in a volley of police bullets while Evelyn Brent and Clive Brook escape via a secret passage, looks backwards to Victorian melodrama and the world of Sherlock Holmes and Fantômas.

If prohibition and the events of Chicago provided the factual basis of the gangster film genre, its popularity stemmed in no small part from its articulation of the complex feelings generated in the USA by the Depression. As Robert Warshaw puts it in his seminal essay 'The Gangster as Tragic Hero' (1948): 'The gangster is the "no" to the great American "yes" which is stamped so large over our official culture.' Warshaw's essay highlights a central truth about 30s gangster films and their reception. Let down themselves by established official society, audiences during the Depression cheered on the gangsters (often folk heroes in real life as well as on the screen), sharing with them, if only in spirit, the delight of putting on

RIGHT Edward G. Robinson, William
Collier Jr., *Little Caesar*

RIGHT James Cagney, Edward Woods,
The Public Enemy

evening dress and mixing with those to whom such trappings were a birthright. In this the appeal of the gangster film was like that of the musical in which the little people put on a show and finally win the approval of those in charge, but only after fierce opposition, with the added bonus of the immediate translation of one of their number from supporting role to star. There is a further similarity between early musicals and gangster films: the central role of energy in both, be it flashing legs, tapping feet, blazing machine-guns, or car chases. (It is no accident that the intensely dynamic James Cagney was a star of both.) It is this energy and social climbing (both features of displaced sexuality) that make the early gangster an optimist figure and at the same time a tragic one, doomed because his energy can never be enough to save him from destruction.

This manic energy can be seen in virtually all early gangster films. Consider *Little Caesar* and *The Public Enemy*. Each within their rise-and-fall scenario highlights different aspects of the energetic drive to success. These films set the template for the genre throughout the 30s. Changes would take place: in the wake of the popularity of federal agent Melvin Purvis after the shooting down of Dillinger in 1934 law officers would share the stage with gangsters (for example *'G' Men* in 1935); and as the genre became well-established twists would be offered to ring the changes, resulting in kids' gangster pictures (the Dead End Kids), gangsters on the range (a common feature of late 30s Western series), and the comedy gangster film, for example John Ford's *The Whole Town's Talking* (1935), with Edward G. Robinson.

The lethargy that was *film noir*

By the beginning of the 1940s the gangster as a figure had lost much of his power. He was no longer a mirror of the times. In particular, America's entry into the war in 1941 had resulted in significant changes in the posi-

Lana Turner, John Garfield, *The Postman Always Rings Twice*

tion of women, which made their portrayal as mere girlfriends or molls problematic. Traditional models for sex and gender relations came increasingly into conflict with the realities of a world where women were taking over men's jobs while their husbands were away fighting. In short, women became more active. The classic example of this is *Mildred Pierce* in 1945. A simple role reversal that follows from this change is that of seducer and seduced (*The Postman Always Rings Twice*, 1946). Another feature of the crime films of the 40s is that women are not only *femmes fatales*, preying on confused males, but often the active party seeking to clear their partner's name (*Phantom Lady*, 1944). It is also worth noting that masculine energy is not a common feature of *film noir*, surely the most languid of sub-genres. In *film noir* the way a (wo)man held a cigarette was as important as the way (s)he held a gun. In the same way the rise-and-fall narrative, a plot in which energy was essential, is little found in *film noir* (and when it is it is ironically book-ended by flashbacks, as in *Mildred Pierce*). The rise-and-fall structure is replaced by that of the investigation, often in a present time that is seemingly stretched to fill the running time of the film as in *The Big Clock* (1947), leaving the central character, as it were, trapped in a ceaseless present in which time is forever running out.

Another example of how dramatically the landscape of the crime film changed during the 40s can be seen in the changing in the contrast between the over- and underworlds. In its straightforward version, as in private-eye films and a number of *films noirs* of the 40s, corruption ruled and the two worlds sat (all too easily) side by side, with representatives of each world often having a role within the other world as well. Thus the police were expected to be corrupt and the man running the local night-club was expected to be a criminal (*The Big Sleep, Murder My Sweet*). Increasingly, however, what came to be at issue was not the group and society but the individual and a divided self. For just as the war brought about a radical change in the cultural pattern of life in America, so the

RIGHT Garry Owen, Joan Crawford, *Mildred Pierce*

RIGHT Humphrey Bogart, Lauren Bacall, *The Big Sleep*

influx of European émigrés increased the speed of dissemination in American intellectual life of the ideas associated with Sigmund Freud. As psychology and psychoanalysis found their way to Hollywood in the late 40s they provided writers and directors with the image of an over- and underworld within a single person (consciousness and the unconscious). Two chapter headings from Parker Tyler's *Magic and Myth of the Movies* (1947), 'Finding Freudians Photogenic' and 'Schizophrenia à la Mode', wittily sum up the impact of Freudian ideas on Hollywood. But notions of the double and of divided identity also came in via artists steeped in the Romantic tradition and through those who had worked in German expressionist cinema in the 1920s. This influence was to surface first in the horror film of the 30s, and then in 40s *film noir*. John Huston's *The Maltese Falcon* (1941), adapted from Dashiell Hammett's novel and one of the earliest *films noirs*, is a convenient starting-point from which to examine changes in the narrative strategies of the crime film and the emergence of *noir* as the dominant form of the genre throughout the decade. The central plot – the recovery of an obscure object of value – harks back to plots from Victorian times and earlier (Wilkie Collins's *The Moonstone* is an obvious example) and in Sydney Greenstreet's grotesque Gutman there is a character very similar to Collins's Count Fosco. The film's hero, Sam Spade, is neither saint nor sinner but a vulnerable and emotional man whose rejection of seductive villainess Mary Astor sums up the battered would-be romantic heroism of the private eye to perfection: 'You'll never understand me, but I'll try to explain. When a man's partner is killed he's supposed to do something about it. It doesn't make any difference what you thought of him, he was your partner and you're supposed to do something about it.' The speech marks the transition from the frenetic edginess of the Cagney characters of the 30s to the crumpled and world-weary charm of the

RIGHT Farley Granger, Robert Walker,
Strangers on a Train

Bogart characters of the 40s. And then there is Astor herself, a strong, manipulative woman playing at being vulnerable, seen in a mix of gleaming close-ups and a network of shadows that prefigure her journey to gaol. At the centre of this rich mixture are the notions of indulgence, represented by Astor and Greenstreet, against which Bogart guards himself, and doubleness, in which the characters can be seen as alternatives of each other. The one thing *noir* that is missing is a flash-back. The use of flash-backs was to become a staple item of *film noir*, in which one of its major purposes was to deny the possibility of progress. Hence the decline of the rise-and-fall scenario. By suggesting that looking back, as in that marvellously titled film, Jacques Tourneur's *Out of the Past* (1947), was the dominant experience, the hope of the future is forever tarnished. In such a world, pools of light obscured as much as they revealed.

To see how significant a change the arrival of *film noir* was one only has to look at a minor outing like Robert Siodmak's *Phantom Lady* (1944). The plot is simplicity itself: a man convicted of killing his wife is to be executed in eighteen days. His secretary believes him to be innocent and sets about proving him to be so by finding a missing lady who can supply him with an alibi. She does so and wins his love. What is noteworthy from the outset is that the circumstantial evidence that Alan Curtis is guilty is accompanied by a strong sense that he wanted to kill her, that she deserved to die (she was having an affair), and that her murderer (his 'friend' Franchot Tone, described as a schizophrenic artist), is in a real sense Curtis's double, someone acting out his repressed desires (which of course is the theme of Hitchcock's *Strangers on a Train*). Having the potential to commit murder or act violently is a common feature of *film noir* (for example, Nicholas Ray's *In a Lonely Place*, 1950). For most of *Phantom Lady* Curtis is removed from his world, and in the same way Ella Raines spends the whole film discovering another world. Two sequences in particular stand out. In the first she follows a possible witness from her world to his, through gloomy, narrow streets that bring to mind a classical Greek rather than criminal underworld. The second is even more extreme. Posing as a prostitute, Raines goes to a late-night jazz session which climaxes with an orgiastic drum solo, highlighted by expressionist lighting and dramatic camera angles, which visually confirms the power of sex (and along the way explains why Tone killed Curtis's wife). Nothing could show more clearly how Freudian notions of a divided self, with upper and lower worlds competing for control, had imposed itself as a world-view.

Crime writers and Hollywood (and the country house)

One significant way in which, despite these changes, the 50s saw a continuation of practices evolved earlier, particularly in the USA, was in the importance of the crime writer to the crime film. With a few exceptions like Zane Grey, very few genre writers had their names above the titles of Hollywood films. But of the waves of writers who flooded to Hollywood in the wake of the coming of sound, it was the crime writers who were most successful. Where the likes of Scott Fitzgerald sank under the weight of expectations and William Faulkner needed the special protection of such as Howard Hawks to allow him to use Hollywood rather than be abused by it, large numbers of crime writers, many of whom had started as reporters, found steady and useful employment in Hollywood. Even in Britain, crime novelists found it entirely feasible to mix film and literary work, for example Graham Greene and Eric Ambler. A partial list of crime writers who became successful screenwriters includes W.R. Burnett, Steve Fisher, David Goodis, Jonathan Latimer, Elmore Leonard and Daniel Mainwaring. These writers, several of whom wrote non-crime scripts as well as crime films, are celebrated in this book as significant participants in the film-production process. They were not merely 'sources', as so many novelists were, nor did their work merely consist in adapting their own original novels.

Of course this did not mean that their relationship with the studios was particularly affable. Consider the case of James M. Cain. His seventeen-year stay in Hollywood as a screenwriter (1931–48) was not a success. During it he only secured writing credits on three films. Raymond Chandler, who scripted *Double Indemnity* (1944) and had a similarly difficult relationship with his paymasters, reportedly said Cain's major failing was that his dialogue read well but did not speak well. Cain was very critical of Hollywood's treatment of writers. He denounced the film of *Mildred Pierce* for the changes made from his novel and set up the short-lived American Authors' Society to seek better deals for authors from the studios. Another writer who suffered at the hands of Hollywood was Patrick Hamilton. *Hangover Square* (1945) bore little relationship to the novel of the same name. But in general crime writers did well in Hollywood. Unlike most other forms of literary production, crime fiction actually had a status as low as, or even lower than, the movies. Crime writers didn't have to bear the stigma of slumming that seemed to so have affected Fitzgerald and other literary types. And crime stories, with their emphasis on action and on the solid details of contemporary urban life, seemed especially well adapted to the screen.

This would not necessarily apply to all types of crime fiction. In the late

20s and early 30s, as the gangster film was getting started in the USA, in Britain (and to an extent in the USA) what has been called the Golden Age of Detective Fiction was well underway. In this the puzzle was king and the detective novel was conceived not as an exploration of character or milieu but as a mental battle between writer and reader. Accordingly rules were invented and organisations such as the Detective Club became as much legislators as a social club for practitioners. Occasionally, the rules were broken – as when Agatha Christie had the murderer turn out to be the narrator – but the effect was only to underline their importance, seen most dramatically in Ellery Queen's 'Challenge To The Reader'. Printed formally late in the book it signified that the reader had all the information needed to solve the crime and it was now time to pit one's wits against Ellery Queen. (For more on this see Julian Symons's definitive study of the evolution of the crime novel, *Bloody Murder*, 1985). Such puzzles were inherently uncinematic, with their avoidance of action and concentration on the hidden moment. It is noticeable that relatively few such novels were transformed to the screen, and when they were the motor force of the film was often a nostalgic look back on a golden age. This is particularly so with Agatha Christie. Another feature of these Anglo-American detective novels was their conservatism; for a detailed, and very funny, account of British crime writers of this ilk see Colin Watson's *Snobbery With Violence* (1971). In these novels, when the murderer was uncovered the world was returned to rights with everything back in its proper place again and the butler on hand to pour out the sherry. This runs counter not only to the prevailing social tone of Hollywood, but to the powerful currents of social and personal upheaval within both crime novels and crime films.

Crime films as social and political comment

This current is particularly visible outside the USA and Britain. In countries as disparate as Spain, Japan and France crime films (and novels, for example those of Maj Sjöwall and Per Wahlöö in Sweden) have regularly highlighted social issues and changing mores. This is even more so in places (for example Latin America) where politics is often extra-parliamentary. *Aç kurtlar* (1969), *Adieu poulet* (1975), *Affaire Blum* (1948), *Agent trouble* (1987), *O Amuleto de Ogum* (1974), *Apartado de correos 1001* (1950), *Buta To Gunkan* (1961) and *Camada negra* (1977) are all examples of films with a strong social and political dimension. Of course, similar films were also made in the USA and Britain – one only has to think of *Bonnie and Clyde* (1967) and *The Long Good Friday* (1979) – but despite their power to shock, their troubles with censorship and the debates about violence they raised, these two films were the exception. Moreover when such films were made the protests about them were generally either apolitical or political with reference to a specific irritation in the country. Elsewhere such films were often the only means of expressing social dissent.

Once upon a time in America

Following the return of organised crime on the back of war-provision profiteering in the USA, the gangster sub-genre once more dominated the crime film. But the new gangster films had different themes and motifs from those of the 30s. In the earlier decade it was the supply of liquor in

ABOVE *Aç kurtlar*

Lee Marvin, *Point Blank*

Chicago's East Side that was at issue. In the 50s the fate of a nation was under threat externally from the Russians, or internally from the mafia, in films whose stories were taken not from the front pages of the nation's newspapers but from the Kefauver Commission on Crime. Another feature ushered in by the 50s was the slew of biographies of American criminals, each presenting a jaunty version of the Depression. They included such varied items as *Al Capone* (1959) and *The Rise and Fall of Legs Diamond* (1960) and climaxed with *Bonnie and Clyde* (1967). However, these were ultimately less significant than films like *The Enforcer* (1950) and the quickie *Inside the Mafia* (1959), inspired by the accidental discovery in 1957 of a major mafia meeting in Apalachin. By the 1960s crime in the USA was habitually described as 'organised' and run by businessmen, so much so that by the time of *Point Blank* (1967), crime boss Keenan Wynn could yell in genuine exasperation at Lee Marvin, who, gun in hand, is demanding repayment of money owed him, 'But I don't have any cash. I don't carry it', leaving Marvin with nothing to do but shoot up the telephone in exasperation. Equally significant was Sam Fuller's *Underworld U.S.A.* (1960). Many critics have pointed out that for Fuller warfare and its organisation was a controlling metaphor for life; Fuller uses military imagery in other films, notably *Pickup on South Street* (1953) and *House of Bamboo* (1955). But it is the totality with which it is followed through, the vision of the syndicate and the FBI gazing down on battleground America from their military eyries, that makes its use so powerful in *Underworld U.S.A.* Nowhere is this better expressed in the film than in its military talk – 'There'll always be people like us. As long as we keep the books and subscribe to charities we'll win the war,' says syndicate leader Robert Emhardt – and its imagery: behind FBI man Larry Gates as he describes the activities of the syndicate are numerous military plaques giving the sequence the feel of a military briefing.

The publication of a trio of best-selling books, Peter Maas's *The Valachi*

RIGHT Al Pacino, *The Godfather*

RIGHT Robert De Niro, *The Godfather Part II*

Papers (1968), about the testimony of mafia informant Joe Valachi, Gay Talese's *Honor Thy Father* (1969), an inside account of life in the Bonanno family, and Mario Puzo's novel *The Godfather* (1969) brought the mafia directly to the attention of America. Deriving directly from the last of these came the first of Francis Ford Coppola's Corleone Family Chronicles, *The Godfather* (1972), which spawned the sequels *The Godfather Part II* (1974), *The Godfather Part III* (1990). These established the compelling ground rules of the mafia movie. Henceforth, there would forever be a patriarch in a darkened room spouting assassination orders, family-first philosophy and pasta recipes; the scheming underlings, relatives and hangers-on trying to get ahead in the family; unhappy marriages punctuated by the occasional burst of machine-gun fire; lyrical music and sharp suits; the intersection of showbiz gossip (Frank Sinatra anecdotes) and political history (mafia involvement in anti-Communist intrigues, especially around the time of the Cuban revolution); and a nostalgic feeling that murder and extortion were more dignified and bearable when carried out by wise, folksy Italians than by a newer breed of dope-crazed, kill-happy psychopaths of the manner of Andy Robinson, the killer in *Dirty Harry* (1971).

That film introduced the other major theme of the era, rogue cops and police corruption. Ironically as the mafia films expanded their scope to deal with real politics and the building of Las Vegas, the police corruption films seemed to narrow down, refining their focus on individuals (for example *Serpico*, 1973). The financing and building of Las Vegas featured in so many films it was almost as though the contrast between the building of the gaudy casinos and then their population by tawdry customers surrounded by slot machines and fistfuls of cash was an ironic version of the Westward movement. These films also told of the transformation of the desert into a garden, one of the great themes of the Western and particularly of those

Westerns directed by John Ford, but the outcome was a very different garden from that envisaged by the first pioneers.

These films were directly concerned with social issues, largely with the dreams of over- and underground America and tensions within the two warring families/camps, but in the 1980s there emerged a number of films called 'neo-*noirs*', films which took as their dominant influences the *films noirs* of the 40s. (For an extended discussion of this development see the third edition of *Film Noir* by Alain Silver and Elizabeth Ward, 1992.) These new films also drew from the novels of 40s writers. Two in particular found fame again, Jim Thompson and David Goodis. Displaying a pessimistic, satirical and deeply cynical world view, populated by psychopaths, losers and vicious professional criminals, Thompson's lean and mean writing was some of the most innovative and extreme of its era. Classic films from his novels include *The Killer Inside Me* (1976), *The Getaway* (1973), *Pop. 1280* (1964, filmed 1981) and *The Grifters* (1990). Goodis, though he had worked as a screenwriter and had his novels filmed in the 50s, was by the late 70s largely forgotten in the USA – he wasn't even given an entry in Chris Steinbrunner and Otto Penzler's seminal *Encyclopedia of Mystery & Detection* (1976). These films are largely character-based, about the doomed rather than the successful, their dreams of wealth and their complicated stratagems for achieving it.

Reservoir Dogs (1991) was such a film. However, where those films in great part looked back, and *Reservoir Dogs* could be seen as a variant on *The Asphalt Jungle* (1950), a caper film gone horribly wrong, it had a sense of style and conviction that marked it out as radically different from what had gone before. If anything the film, and its follow-up *Pulp Fiction* (1994), was a descendant of *Mean Streets* (1973) with the difference that all sense of control about the characters was gone. In *Mean Streets* the De Niro character is the loose cannon that sparks off the plot, but he pales beside the Tim Roth character of *Pulp Fiction*, just as *Mean Streets'* Harvey Keitel for all his freneticism has a secure sense of society in contrast to *Pulp Fiction*'s John Travolta, who can only innocently wonder about the odd thread that connects the events of his life, and follow the rules to the letter, but to no avail.

These gangster film are deeply pessimistic and very violent. Even a film like *Heat* (1995) which uses far finer brushstrokes to depict its two central loners as they circle each other endlessly in search of some kind of meaning to their lives, is deeply sad. Like countless cops and crooks before them, the film's two 'heroes' test themselves by how well they perform their job, living by rules as quaint as the Western's mythic cliché of 'A man's gotta do what a man's gotta do.' In contrast to this, the space between what a person is and does is central to Jodie Foster's performance in *The Silence Of The Lambs* (1990), where her success is the double one of coming to understand herself and catching a killer. This refusal to immerse oneself in a job (while executing that job with great competence) is seen at its best in Frances McDormand's performance as the police captain in *Fargo* (1996). Literally carrying the future within her, she sorts out problems with ease, whether it be her anxious bird-painter of a husband or the whereabouts of a pair of volatile killers. The contrast between her and the Travolta character in *Pulp Fiction* could not be greater. He may know about the threads of

Al Pacino, *Serpico*

life – the name of a Big Mac in France – but he cannot bring them together like McDormand, who knows that what matters is warmth and food, love and babies.

*   *   *

When considering where to draw the line as regards which films count as crime films, I have tended towards inclusion rather than exclusion. Thus the book includes many films which are on the borders of the genre: parodies, works of science fiction such as *Blade Runner*, films such as *Psycho* which are also seminal to the modern horror film. It includes surveys of all the major sub-genres (heist movies, caper films, boxing films, etc.) and other related topics, whether historical (Prohibition) or generic (nightclubs, lawyers, corpses). It does not provide career summaries for film-makers; crime films, unlike say the Western or the horror film, have not lent themselves to specialisation of the sort which identifies a film-maker with a particular genre (with the possible exception of Alfred Hitchcock). On the other hand there are many fiction writers who are closely identified with the genre, and these have their own entries when their work has been a significant source for the cinema. By and large the field of reference is restricted to the cinema, and television productions are only noted in passing.

Abbreviations are as follows: *p* producer; *d* director; *s* scriptwriter; *orig* author of the original story, novel or play; *c* camera; *m* music; *lp* leading players; COL Columbia; FOX 20th Century-Fox; MGM Metro-Goldwyn-Mayer; PAR Paramount; REP Republic; RKO Radio-Keith-Orpheum; U Universal; UIP Universal-International; WB Warner Bros. All films are American unless otherwise indicated (GB = Great Britain). Dates of films in general refer to the date of copyright, which may differ from the release date. The companies listed in the credits are usually the original production companies; for the US majors these are also usually the distributors. All stills are courtesy these companies. Running times are in minutes, except that for silent films the length is usually given in feet or metres. Films are given their original language titles, with British release titles given afterwards. Words in **bold** indicate that the reader may find further significant information on this topic under its own entry.

ABOVE Faye Dunaway,
Bonnie and Clyde

RIGHT Cathy Tyson,
Bob Hoskins, *Mona Lisa*

ABOVE Sharon
Stone, *Casino*

RIGHT Miranda
Richardson,
*Dance with a
Stranger*

ABOVE Al Pacino, *Scarface*

ABOVE Michael Douglas, *Black Rain*

BELOW Marlon Brando, *The Godfather*

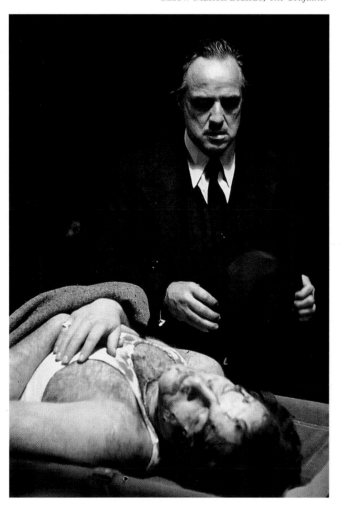

BELOW Richard Roundtree, *Shaft*

ABOVE Clint Eastwood, *Dirty Harry*

ABOVE Joe Pesci, Ray Liotta, Robert De Niro, *Good fellas*

ABOVE Catherine Rouvel, Jean-Paul Belmondo, Alain Delon, *Borsalino*

LEFT Gary Kemp,
The Krays

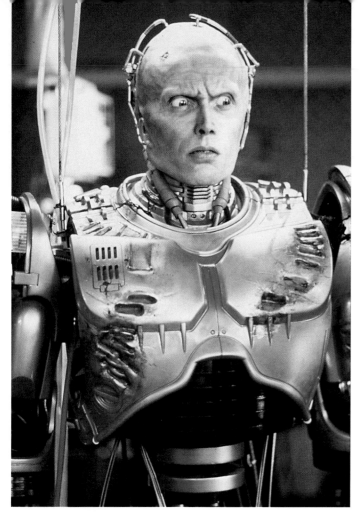

ABOVE Peter Weller, *RoboCop II*

ABOVE Jack Nicholson, *Batman*

BELOW Jamie Lee Curtis, *Blue Steel*

ABOVE Christopher Lloyd, *Who Framed Roger Rabbit*

ABOVE Jean-Paul Belmondo, *À bout de souffle*

A

À bout de souffle/Breathless

Godard's first feature inaugurated cinematic modernism in Europe and became the standard bearer of the French New Wave. Very successful at the box office, its freewheeling approach to cinematic language caused a critical sensation. The plot, adapted from a 1956 François Truffaut script, is a mere narrative skeleton involving a journey, crime, money and desire. Michel Poiccard (Belmondo) steals a car in Marseille and drives to Paris to collect a Pay off. On the way, he shoots a traffic cop. In Paris, he steals money from women and moves into the room of Patricia Franchini (Seberg), an aspiring journalist. He steals another car, has long discussions with Patricia who is now pregnant, and tries to collect his money from an elusive paymaster. The police are on his tracks and eventually, with Patricia's help, shoot him dead in the streets. The film is a testament to Godard's love of cinema for its own sake, and especially the Hollywood B movie. He films with obvious delight the encounter between locations, sounds and actors' bodies, cut together in impulsive, staccato rhythms. The colloquial dialogues, stuffed with comments about life and cinema, also introduced a new tone in French cinema. The censors removed a scene where Eisenhower meets De Gaulle on the Champs Elysées in the background while Belmondo and Seberg walk along, thus setting a political context for the movie's cynically selfish figures. Godard's approach emerged from his involvement with a group of critics congregating around the vigorously polemical magazine *Cahiers du cinéma*, many of them acting in and otherwise contributing to the film. Jean-Pierre Melville, an independent film-maker defended by the journal, played the role of a celebrated novelist, while Godard cast himself as the informer. It was remade in Hollywood as *Breathless* (1983). PW

1960/France/89m/Imperia Films-S.N.C./ *p* Georges de Beauregard/*d*/*s* Jean-Luc Godard/*c* Raoul Coutard/*m* Martial Solal, Mozart/*lp* Jean-Paul Belmondo, Jean Seberg, Daniel Boulanger, Roger Hanin, Henri-Jacques Huet.

Abashiri Bangaichi Fubuki No Torso/The Man from Abashiri Jail: Duel in the Snow Storm/A Story from Abashiri Prison: Duel in the Snow

The long-running Abashiri series directed by Ishii and starring Takakura as the tough but sentimental mother-obsessed gangster started in 1965 and proved so popular that there were over twenty instalments using the same basic plot and characters. *Abashiri Bangaichi Koya No Taiketsu* (1966) used a western genre setting as the horse-riding hero settles a range war; A*bashiri Bangaichi Hokkai-Hen* (1965) saw Takakura unwittingly driving a truck full of drugs across country, while *Shin Abashiri Bangaichi* (1968) is a standard revenge drama. This episode, more spectacular and odder than most, has Takakura serving time for multiple murder, arson, theft and spying. Thus having established his credentials as a hard man, the movie lurches into quasi-gothic prison scenes with secret passageways and the hero taking the place of a condemned man in order to escape and avenge his father, a wealthy businessman accused of spying for the Russians. The accuser (Nakatani) then takes over the business along with the hero's girl-friend. When Takakura finds him, he discovers another gang has kidnapped their shared girl-friend. The two unwilling companions track down the kidnappers in the snow-clad mountains and finally confront each other. The plot is merely an excuse to get from one scene to the next, while the stylised settings and the familiar motifs and gestures are choreographed into an almost abstract play between contrasting spaces and atmospheres. This was the tenth film in the series and came closest to the spirit of Feuillade's serials so beloved by French surrealists. PW

1967/Japan/87m/Toei/*d*/*s* Teruo Ishii/*p* Koji Shundo, Wataru Yabe/*s* Akira Murao/ *c* Yoshio Nakajima/*m* Masao Yagi/*lp* Ken Takakura, Ichiro Nakatani, Tatsuo Umemiya, Nobotu Ando, Hayato Tani.

Absence of Malice

This powerful drama has Field's idealistic reporter being duped by Federal task force chief Balaban into printing a story which implies that the innocent Newman, who happens to be the son of a mobster, is connected with a Jimmy Hoffa-like disappearance. Although Newman eventually gets even with Field, after her wayward journalism has led to tragedy, the strong story raises multiple questions about the intrusion of privacy and the press's right to publish what is 'technically' the truth. TV

1981/116m/Mirage Enterprises/*p*/*d* Sydney Pollack/*s* Kurt Luedtke/*c* Owen Roizman/

ABOVE Paul Newman, *Absence of Malice*

m Dave Grusin/lp Paul Newman, Sally Field, Bob Balaban.

Aç kurtlar/The Hungry Wolves

Güney, Turkey's most distinguished director, had scripted and starred in dozens of features before he turned director in 1967 with *Benim Adim Kerim*, and went on to make a series of powerfully cinematic films (some directed by proxy while he was gaoled by the regime of the time: notably *Sürü/The Herd*, 1978 and *Yol*, 1982). *Wolves* was shot while he was doing his military service in Anatolia and tells of a brigand and his gang living in the snowy mountains, terrorising the villages and pursued by the police. The revenge plot and the imagery as well as the acting style recalls Sergio Leone's Westerns except that Güney infuses the proceedings with a less cynical, more lyrical and rebellious atmosphere, portraying the brigand as a fiercely proud character who becomes an outlaw because social conditions left him no other option of living by his particular code of honour. In the end, he is gunned down. Some sources give the production date as 1967, before *Seyyit Han* (1968), his equally 'Western' style story of a man who is tricked by a wealthy landowner into shooting his bride. That film also has a remote rural setting and a particularly harrowing ending: the hero, clad in a black coat, is challenged to a duel by his rival on the day of his wedding and has to shoot a basket placed on the ground between them, not knowing that his beloved has been buried up to her neck in the ground with the basket covering her head. PW

1969/Turkey/72m/Güney Film/p/d/s Yilmaz Güney/c Ali Ugur/m Necip Saricioglu/lp Yilmaz Güney, Hayati Hamzaoglu, Sevgi Can, Enver Güney, Türkan Agrak.

The Accused

This is an example of an American film using the crime genre as a way of dramatising important social questions. The issue here is a woman's right to say no; that is, to be free to determine if and when to engage in sexu-

ABOVE Jodie Foster, Kelly McGillis, *The Accused*

al activity. At the beginning of the film a young woman, Sarah (Foster), runs screaming into the road after being gang-raped in a bar. In flashback we see the rape, in considerable detail. Inevitably the scene is titillating, but it is the brutality of the men assaulting Sarah that remains in the mind. The strength of the film is that it doesn't depend on easy sympathy for Sarah. We see that she had too much to drink in the bar and danced provocatively in front of a group of men. Indeed the assistant D.A. assigned to the case (McGillis) initially considers it unwinable because of Sarah's past. But the film decisively rejects any notion that she 'asked for it'. EB

1988/110m/PAR/p Stanley R. Jaffe, Sherry Lansing/d Jonathan Kaplan/s Tom Topor/c Ralf D. Bode/m Brad Fiedel/lp Kelly McGillis, Jodie Foster, Bernie Coulson, Leo Rossi, Ann Hearn.

Across 110th Street

Alone among early 70s black-themed crime pictures, this dares to adopt the downbeat tone of **Chester Himes**'s Harlem novels with their complex interlocking of black and white and cop and crook. Three black petty crooks, excluded from Harlem's organised crime, hold up a group of accountants as they are collecting a huge take from the area which is to be conveyed to the white downtown mafia. During the heist Benjamin opens fire, gunning down black and white mobsters and a black policeman. Two sepa-

LEFT *Aç kurtlar*

rate salt-and-pepper investigations of the crime start. An ageing, wearily corrupt strong-arm cop (Quinn) is partnered by a college-educated black detective (Kotto) while the nervously sadistic mafia enforcer (Franciosa), barely tolerated in the mob because he is a godfather's son-in-law, is shepherded around Harlem by a pair of self-aware black hoods who stand by without comment as he runs out of control, treating one of the heist men (Fargas) to castration and crucifixion in one of the film's many moments of extreme (and often-censored) violence. With compromised, desperate characters and dishonest but credible motivations, *Across 110th Street* is among the most merciless of crime movies. Along the way it does more than **Serpico** to expose a routinely corrupt NYPD. KN

1972/102m/Film Guarantor-UA/*p* Ralph Serpe, Fouad Said/*d* Barry Shear/*s* Luther Davis/*orig* Wally Ferris/*c* Jack Priestley/*m* J.J. Johnson/*lp* Anthony Quinn, Yaphet Kotto, Anthony Franciosa, Paul Benjamin, Ed Bernard.

Actors

As early as the 17th century actors were called 'rogues and vagabonds' and this stigma is hard to refute three hundred years later. The Production Code was created in the USA in 1934 specifically because of the immoral and criminal behaviour of actors. However, censorship only held back the tide. The regular use of actors as characters in films about crime says as much about the acting fraternity as about the cinema's need for glamorous settings. Actors are murdered in *The Studio Murder Mystery* (1929), *The Strangler* (1932), *Death at Broadcasting House* (1934), *Ladies in Retirement* (1941), *The Falcon*

ABOVE Actors: Gloria Swanson, *Sunset Blvd.*

ABOVE Yaphet Kotto (left), Burt Young, *Across 110th Street*

in Hollywood (1944), *Tall Dark and Dead* (1952), *The Whole Truth* (1958), *Sugar Cookies* (1972), and *Special Effects* (1984). *Sweet Saviour* (1971) and *Helter Skelter* (1976) are inspired by the murder of Sharon Tate. Actors plot or carry out murder in *The Man Who Cried Wolf* (1937), *The Velvet Touch* (1948), **Sunset Blvd.**, *Sudden Fear* (1952), *What Ever Happened to Baby Jane?* (1962, TVM 1991), *The Flesh and Blood Show* (1972), *Theatre of Blood* (1973), and *Madhouse* (1974). In *Men Are Not Gods* (1937), *The Brighton Strangler* (1945), *A Double Life* (1947) and *Yukinojo Henge/An Actor's Revenge* (Japan 1963) actors are maddened by the parts they are playing. Actors are terrorised, stalked or kidnapped in *Mad Love* (1935), *A Face in the Fog* (1936), *Dangerous Intruder* (1945), *The Fan* (1981), *Overexposed* (1990), *The Body-*

guard (1991), and *A House in the Hills* (1993). *Victims for Victims: The Theresa Saldana Story* (TVM 1984) is based on the true story of the stalker who attacked the eponymous actress. A drama student is involved with a suspected murderer in *Stage Fright*. Since the 80s many struggling or unemployed actors have been embroiled in crime: *L'Addition* (France 1983), *Body Double* (1984), *Dead of Winter* (1987), *True Identity* (1990), *Off and Running* (1991), *Every Breath* (1993), *Boca a boca* (1994). In *The Morning After* (1986) an alcoholic actress wakes up with a corpse beside her. Murders are committed or investigated in theatres in *Four Hours to Kill* (1935), *The High Terrace* (1956), *Murder Most Foul* (1964), *Theatre of Death* (1966) and *Deliria/Stagefright* (Italy 1987). *What's the Matter with Helen?* (1971) is set in a drama school. Among the

ABOVE *Affaire Blum*

few actors who are wrongly accused of murders, or help to solve them, are those in **Murder!**, *The Feathered Serpent* (1934), *Twelve Good Men* (1936), *Portrait of Alison* (1955) and *Without a Clue* (1988). In the latter, **Sherlock Holmes** is revealed to have been a second-rate actor. Actors murdered in real life include (chronologically): Thelma Todd (disputed), Lewis Stone (indirectly), Marilyn Monroe (disputed), Ramon Novarro, Sharon Tate, Sal Mineo, Onslow Stevens, Bob Crane, Victor Kilian, John Lennon, Dorothy Stratten, John Belushi, Peter Arne, David Huffman, George Rose, Rebecca Schaeffer, Tupac Shakur, Jack Nance and Barry Evans. DM

Adieu poulet/So Long Copper

Granier-Deferre's movie is about political gangsterism. The plot was based on an actual killing during an election campaign investigated by an Inspector Javilliey. A fly-posting thug (Brosset), part of the right-wing law-and-order party headed by Lardatte (Lanoux), beats a leftist to death and kills a policeman in the process. The experienced Inspector Verjeat (Ventura) and his assistant Lefevre (Dewaere) of the Rouen police are assigned the case but their investigation gets snarled up with electoral shenanigans and the smooth Lardatte uses his influence to protect his thug. When the inspector exposes the politician by allowing a conversation

between Lardatte and the murdered boy's irate father to be put on a public address system, Verjeat is threatened with a posting to another town. Lefevre arranges for Verjeat to be accused of corruption, thus preventing the transfer. When Verjeat finds that the thug has turned on his own party boss and Lardatte appeals for police help, the inspector simply leaves his office, telling his mate: 'Adieu poulet', roughly meaning 'Goodbye copper' and allowing the viewer to think that he is leaving the force disgusted by its craven subordination to politicians. The moral of the story is that the pure and honest coppers have their hands tied by a corrupt society which badly needs cleaning up by a robust leader. Energetically realised by a solidly mainstream director noted for his Georges Simenon adaptations (notably *Le Chat*, 1970 and *La veuve Couderc*, 1971), the film is notable for the pleasant interplay between the granite-faced Ventura and the volatile Dewaere. It also has a brief appearance by the silent film star Eve Francis. This film signalled the end of post-1968 politically critical crime movies, with the demonising of left and right political groups and casting the loveable and honest police as the beleaguered defenders of democracy. PW

1975/France/94m/Ariane-Mondex/
p Georges Dancigers/*d* Pierre Granier-Deferre/*s* Francis Véber/*orig* Raf Vallet [Jean Laborde]/*c* Jean Collomb/*m* Philippe Sarde/*lp*

Lino Ventura, Patrick Dewaere, Victor Lanoux, Julien Guiomar, Françoise Brion.

Affaire Blum/The Blum Affair

One of Brecht's theatre collaborator's first films in East Germany recounts a story that happened in 1926. When an accountant is murdered by a fascist activist, the 'patriotic' judges try to blame a Jewish entrepreneur for the killing. Stemmle had tried to make the film in Munich, but nobody wanted to produce it there. The East German studio, which had achieved some success with Germany's first post-war feature, Wolfgang Staudte's *Die Mörder sind unter uns* (1946), and with Kurt Maetzig's denunciation of anti-Semitism *Ehe im Schatten* (1947), agreed to produce the film. DEFA continued examining and denouncing fascist currents at work in Germany in Staudte's *Rotation* (1949). PW

1948/Germany/102m/DEFA/*d* Erich Engel/
s Robert Adolf Stemmle/*c* Friedle Behn-Grund, Karl Plintzner/*m* Herbert Trantow/
lp Gisela Trowe, Arno Paulsen, Maly Delschaft, Blandine Ebinger, Ernst Waldow.

L'Affaire Dominici/The Dominici Case

In this, the 68-year-old Gabin's last major performance, he plays with great dignity an old peasant accused of mass murder. The real case dates back to the summer of 1952 when an English family (father, wife and daughter) came to Dominici's farm near Lurs to visit the site where, during the war, their son appeared to have died. In the night, as the family camped by the side of the road, shots rang out. The next morning, the English parents were found, shot to death; their daughter was lying a bit further away, her brains bashed in. The film recounts the events and then concentrates on the 15-month-long investigation conducted by a police inspector (Crauchet) who discovers that one of Dominici's sons (Lanoux) had found the daughter in the morning, still alive. He had simply gone away and left her to die, for which he received a derisory sentence. Dominici's two sons eventually accuse their father of having killed the entire family. He confesses, but with an improbable story, boasting that he had been making love with the English woman and that her husband had caught them. The film clearly brings out the culture clash between the illiterate peasant clan and the judicial forces which arrested and condemned the authoritarian patriarch on circumstantial (though very convincing) evidence. As to who exactly (the father, one or both of the sons) committed the murders, the film, like the court case, sheds no conclusive light. PW

1973/France/105m/Rochat-Giroux/*p* Claude Giroux, Eric Rochat/*d*/co-s Claude Bernard-Aubert/*co-s* Daniel Boulanger, Louis-Emile Galey/*c* Ricardo Aronovich/*m* Alain Goraguer/*lp* Jean Gabin, Victor Lanoux, Gérard Darrieu, Gérard Depardieu, Jeanne Allard.

Agent trouble/Trouble Agent

Mocky's ecological thriller suggests that 'the authorities' in collusion with a water company simply murder a busload of tourists to hush up the accidental contamination of the drinking water in an Alpine region. This proposition is worked out in the form of a thriller with a passer-by (the pop singer Novembre) who discovers a bus full of corpses and, intrigued by the television news bulletin which gives a false account of the event, sets out to try and make money out of his discovery. He is shot by a mysterious agent of the state (Bohringer) but his aunt, a museum employee (Deneuve, wearing a red wig and glasses), continues the investigation with the help of her ex-lover (Arditi). She survives only because the killer has a heart attack while pursuing her through the snow-covered mountains. Mocky, a cinephile who likes to evoke the classic Hollywood masters

in his movies, achieved a moody looking thriller with quirky, stylised performances, sometimes recalling Jacques Tourneur's **Nightfall**. He also plays the role of a sinister state official in the film. PW

1987/France/90m/AFD-Koala-Canal Plus-FR3/*p* Maurice Bernart/*d*/s Jean-Pierre Mocky/*orig* Malcolm Joseph Bosse *The Man Who Loved Zoos* (1974)/*c* William Lubtchansky/*m* Gabriel Yared/*lp* Catherine Deneuve, Richard Bohringer, Tom Novembre, Dominique Lavanant, Pierre Arditi.

Al Capone

This painstaking attempt at historical reconstruction follows the rise and fall of Capone (Steiger) up to his arrest for income tax evasion. However, the use of a twenty-year montage made by Warners for **The Roaring Twenties** points to the problems accompanying this difficult blend of documentary and fiction. The ugliness and corruption of Capone's career unravel without sentiment or weasel justification, but Steiger's bravura performance draws as much on the history of the 1930s gangster epics as it does on a reconstruction of Capone's mannerisms. As a result the film becomes a vehicle for Steiger's acting and charisma, as well as a tribute to the starring roles taken by others in **Little Caesar** and **Scarface**. MP

1959/105m/AA/*p* John Burrows, Leonard

ABOVE Rod Steiger, *Al Capone*

Ackerman/*d* Richard Wilson/*s* Malvin Wald, Henry F. Greenberg/*c* Lucien Ballard/*m* David Raksin/*lp* Rod Steiger, Fay Spain, Nehemiah Persoff, Martin Balsam, Murvyn Vye.

Alcohol

Bootleg liquor and contraband brandy have gone the way of all flesh in the crime film. Indeed, the host no longer seems to offer the guest 'Scotch?' before getting down to business. The one constant during a century of cinema is the alcoholic cop/lawyer/reporter seeking redemption. Even in 1992, it is not just heroin and crack, but booze too, that draws the *Bad Lieutenant* (1992) to his kismet. Similarly in 1996 Dustin Hoffman was as troubled by booze as drugs playing the lawyer seeking redemption in *Sleepers*. The illegal trafficking of alcohol during the Prohibition era in the US (1919–33) is an element in most gangster films of the period, and fuels the entire plot of **Scarface**, in which the hoodlum rises from, in the words of trade paper *Variety*, 'bodyguard for an early district beer baron to the booze chief of the whole city.' Later the Prohibition era was the setting for *Call Northside 777*, then a succession of gangster films at the turn of the 60s about the likes of Dutch Schultz and Legs Diamond. *Boulevard du rhum* (1971) is an alcohol route from Mexico. *A Slight Case of Murder* (1938), re-made as *Stop, You're Killing Me* (1952), is about a gangster trying to adapt to the end of Prohibition. The same period features in **Once Upon a Time in America**. There is unlicensed alcohol manufactured in *Late at Night* (1946), *White Lightning* (1973) and *Moonshine County*

ABOVE Alcohol: the end of Prohibition in *Once Upon a Time in America*

Express (1977), and alcohol smuggling in *The Night Hawk* (1938), *Whisky Galore!* (1948), *Brandy for the Parson* (1951) and *My Death Is a Mockery* (1952). It is usual in such films for the audience to identify with the wrongdoer. Perhaps inspired by their creators' personal habits, the private eyes of the 40s are never far from a whisky glass, but such weakness is endearing. Dipsomania is addressed in *The Lost Weekend* (1945), but it was many years later that popular heroes were required to come to terms with their problem. In *The Girl Hunters* (1963), Mickey Spillane has to be rescued from a drunken binge. So does Warren Oates in *Chandler* (1971). Alcohol abuse can be counted on to bring bad guys to a sticky end. Drunken drivers always cause accidents that kill themselves or others. **To the Public Danger** (1948) specifically concerns drunken driving. Drunken slobs deserve what they get. In *Reckless* (1935) dancer Jean Harlow is accused of murdering her drunken husband. Pub landlady Googie Withers really does poison hers in *Pink String and Sealing Wax*. Good guys who over-imbibe can be implicated in crimes they didn't commit, as in *Fall Guy* (1947), *The Morning After* (1986), *Physical Evidence* (1988), and *Shakes the Clown* (1990). In *This Man Is News* (1938), *Come Fill the Cup* (1951) and *Appointment with a Shadow* (1958) drunken newspaper men pull themselves

together to fight crime. Alcoholic father Michael Redgrave saves his son from the gallows in **Time without Pity**. Alcoholic barrister James Mason returns to court in *Stranger in the House* (1967). DM

Alibi/The Perfect Alibi

Alibi was the first dialogue picture released by United Artists. Griffith is the daughter of a police sergeant. She loves Morris, a gangster, but is sure that he is going straight, and marries him. They go to a theatre, Morris sneaks out in the interval, and commits a murder, with Griffith as his alibi. Toomey, a cop, joins the gang as an undercover agent, and is also killed by Morris, who proves when eventually cornered to be a coward. West, whose small output included notable crime films in *The Bat* (1926) and its sound remake, *The Bat Whispers* (1930), used the new medium of sound to the full in *Alibi*, which is replete with the sounds of whistles, the banging of night-sticks, the rattle of a machine gun, running feet, and birds singing in lyrical counterpoint to the excitement. There is also an excess of dialogue – but in 1929 few film-makers could resist the temptation. Less successful was what critic Carlos Clarens has called the 'ritual terrorising of the hood' in the two vivid third-degree sequences in which criminals are literally threatened with death unless they speak.

ABOVE Eleanor Griffith, *Alibi*

Morris had made a few films as a child actor, but this was his first important adult role. A tough and forceful character, he subsequently played the sympathetic crook **Boston Blackie**. JL

1929/8167ft/UA/*p*/*d*/*co-s* Roland West/*co-s* C. Gardner Sullivan/*orig* John Griffith Wray, J. C. Nugent, Elaine S. Carrington *Nightstick*/ *c* Ray June/*lp* Chester Morris, Harry Stubbs, Mae Busch, Eleanor Griffith, Regis Toomey.

Ambler, Eric (1909–)

Between 1935 and 1940 Ambler wrote six novels which helped redefine the modern thriller. Beginning with *The Dark Frontier*, these stories, set in the shadowy world of eastern European politics between the wars, are as remarkable for their political maturity and prescience as for their writing. Ambler's masterpiece is *The Mask of Dimitrios* (1939), which in its plot as much as its cynical exposé of the connections between crime and *realpolitik* anticipates **The Third Man**, as well as much of le Carré. During the war, working with the Army Kinematograph Service along with such film-makers as Carol Reed and John Huston, Ambler developed his abilities as a screenwriter and producer, and in the post-war British cinema wrote a number of successful films, of which *The Cruel Sea* is today the best known. He continued to write thrillers, two of which, *The Light*

ABOVE Alcohol: Renée Houston, Alec McCowen, Michael Redgrave, *Time Without Pity*

of Day (1962) and *Dirty Story* (1967), feature Arthur Abdel Simpson, a disreputable Anglo-Egyptian addicted to dubious get-rich schemes. Ambler had no direct involvement with any of the films made from his thrillers and appears to have been disappointed with all of them. *Uncommon Danger* (1937) was filmed as *Background to Danger* (1943) by Raoul Walsh, with George Raft. *Journey Into Fear* (1940) was filmed under that title in 1943, notionally directed by Norman Foster, but a product of Orson Welles's Mercury company, starring Joseph Cotten and Dolores Del Rio. (A remake in 1976 starred Zero Mostel and Shelley Winters.) Jean Negulesco directed **The Mask of Dimitrios**, with Zachary Scott, Sydney Greenstreet and Peter Lorre. *Hotel Reserve* (1944) was a British version of *Epitaph for a Spy* (1938), with James Mason. Peter Ustinov, who had also been with Ambler in the AKS, starred as Arthur Abdel Simpson in **Topkapi**, a version of *The Light of Day*. In 1985 Ambler published his autobiography, slyly entitled *Here Lies Eric Ambler*. EB

The American Cop Movie

Though the everyday life of a beat copper was the stuff of cinema as early as Edwin S. Porter's *The Life of an American Policeman* (1905), the cop film took far longer to coalesce than the cowboy movie or the gangster film. The predominant image of the police in the silent era was as the knockabout buffoons of the Keystone Kops series, Charlie Chaplin's *Easy Street* (1917) or Buster Keaton's *Cops* (1922). In early talkies, the regular police tend to be marginalised with sleuths, gangsters and 'supercops' from the **FBI** taking centre stage. While the police procedural variation on the classic mystery remains popular in detective fiction and has reached television via the ingenious inquiries of Columbo, Wexford and Morse, few big-screen policemen have ever been called upon to do serious deduction.

After World War II, the crime movie became more realistic. **Dick Tracy**, an FBI man in 30s serials, reverted to a police detective in 40s B-films. The squadroom cop came to the fore in tough-talking, straight-arrow plain-clothes heroes like Dana Andrews in **Laura**, Brian Donlevy in **Kiss of Death**, Victor Mature in **Cry of the City** and Scott Brady in **He Walked by Night**. It is notable, however, that in these films, whether reflected in billing or not, the main interest is in the law-breakers, played by Clifton Webb, Richard Widmark, Richard Conte and Richard Basehart. The cop subgenre was defined by **The Naked City** in America and **The Blue Lamp** in Britain. Both grew out of national traditions established during the war, the semi-documentary American spy thriller and the patriotic British war film, and both spawned key television series, *The Naked City* (1958–63) and *Dixon of Dock Green* (1955–76), that further defined the police procedural tradition, a mixture of crime drama, soap opera and social document.

In America, this strain was exemplified by Jack Webb's *Dragnet*, as a radio series (1949–56), two TV shows (1952–59, 1967–70) and several film spin-offs (1954, 1969, 1987), mixed in with such imitations and rivals as *Highway Patrol* (1955–59), *The Lineup* (1954–60) and *87th Precinct* (1961–2), which presented ordinary cop heroes, famously clipped and unemotional in Webb's concept of the deliberately colourless Sergeant Joe Friday, who stand outside the world of crime, looking in with pity and disapproval. This evolved, via a more humanist approach to the inevitable tainting of the cop who works on a daily basis with criminals and violence, into the cop operas of policeman-turned-novelist **Joseph Wambaugh** (*The New Centurions/Precinct 45, Los Angeles Police*, 1972, *Police Story*, 1973–80, *The Blue Knight*, 1973, *The Choirboys*, 1977, *The Onion Field*, 1979, **The Black Marble**) and the neo-realist tradition of *Kojak* (1974–8), *Hill*

ABOVE Eric Ambler

Street Blues (1981–7), *Cagney and Lacey* (1982–8), *Law and Order* (1990–) and *NYPD Blue* (1992–). In Britain, a similar evolution can be traced from *Dixon* through *Z Cars* (1962–78), *Softly, Softly* (1966–76), *The Sweeney* (1975–8), *Law and Order* (1978), *Prime Suspect* (1991) and *Between the Lines* (1992–) on television and in movies *The Long Arm/The Third Key* (1956), *Gideon's Day/Gideon of Scotland Yard* (1959), **Hell Is a City**, *All Coppers Are . . .* (1971) and *The Offence* (1973). These present an increasingly disenchanted, cynical look at law enforcement, though *The Bill* (1985–) and *Heartbeat* (1992–) almost return to cosiness, just as America has continued to churn out Jack Webb-style endorsements of the staunch men in blue, *T.J. Hooker* (1982–5) and *Hunter* (1984–91).

While the image of a police force consisting of a squadroom full of regulars working together is the backbone of most TV cop series, the cinema prefers to deal with the lone figure of the rogue cop, usually an out-of-time throwback. The rogue cop has a personal grudge against the criminals he is pursuing, may or may not have a partner who gets killed during the investigation, and is almost invariably forced outside the law, finally cracking the case while on suspension. This character appeared in embryo – played by Dana Andrews in **Where the Sidewalk Ends**, Van Heflin in **The Prowler**, Steve Cochran in *Private Hell 36* (1954) and Robert Taylor in *Rogue Cop* (1954) – as a doomed *noir* protagonist who might surrender to his own criminal urges. Gradually, he became – played by Edmond O'Brien in *Between Midnight and Dawn* (1950), Glenn Ford in **The Big Heat**, Cornel Wilde in **The Big Combo** and Glenn Corbett in **The Crimson Kimono** – a tormented but heroic figure in line with the gunslinger of the Western.

Kirk Douglas in **Detective Story** prefigures the lonely, embittered, compromised and violent cop hero who came to the fore in the 60s. Amongst these were Richard Widmark in **Madigan**, Frank Sinatra in **The Detective**, Clint Eastwood in **Coogan's Bluff, Dirty Harry**, *The Gauntlet* (1978) and **Tightrope**, Gene Hackman in **The French Connection**, Donald Sutherland in **Klute**, Anthony Quinn in **Across 110th Street**, Robert Blake in **Electra Glide in Blue**, Al Pacino in **Serpico** and *Cruising* (1980), Burt Reynolds in *Hustle* (1975), Mel Gibson in *Mad Max* (1979) and *Lethal Weapon* (1987), Nick Nolte in **48Hrs.**, Roy Scheider in **Blue**

ABOVE The American Cop Movie: Anthony Quinn, *Across 110th Street*

Thunder, Mickey Rourke in **Year of the Dragon,** Dennis Quaid in **The Big Easy**, Peter Weller in **Robocop**, Steven Seagal in *Above the Law/Nico* (1988), Bruce Willis in **Die Hard**, Don Johnson in *Dead Bang* (1990), Michael Douglas in **Black Rain**, Jamie Leigh Curtis in **Blue Steel**, Theresa Russell in *Impulse* (1990), Harvey Keitel in *Bad Lieutenant* (1992) and Takeshi Kitano in **Sono Otoko, Kyobo Ni Tsuki/Violent Cop**. Alongside this tradition has emerged a mirror image in which rogue cops are monstrous villains, notably Robert Z'Dar in *Maniac Cop* (1988), Richard Gere in *Internal Affairs* (1990), Nick Nolte in *Q&A* (1990), Robert Patrick in *Terminator 2: Judgment Day* (1991) and Ray Liotta in *Unlawful Entry* (1992).

However, the spirit of the Keystone Kops was not completely exorcised, with almost every major comedian and most of the minor ones getting into uniform for at least one cop comedy: Laurel and Hardy in *The Midnight Patrol* (1933), Will Hay in *Ask a Policeman* (1939), George Formby in *Spare a Copper* (1941), Bob Hope in *Off Limits/Military Policemen* (1953), Abbott and Costello in *Abbott and Costello Meet Dr Jekyll and Mr Hyde* (1953), the Carry On gang in *Carry On Constable* (1960), Norman Wisdom in *On the Beat* (1963), Peter Sellers as Inspector

Clouseau in **The Pink Panther** and sequels, Chevy Chase in *Foul Play* (1978), Cannon and Ball in *The Boys in Blue* (1983), Steve Guttenberg in **Police Academy** and sequels, Linda Blair in *Night Patrol* (1985), Eddie Murphy in **Beverly Hills Cop** and sequels, Meg Tilly in *Off Beat* (1986), the Comic Strip crowd in *The Supergrass* (1986), Leslie Nielsen in **The Naked Gun** and TV series and sequels, Dan Aykroyd in *Loose Cannons* (1989), Arnold Schwarzenegger in **Kindergarten Cop** and Sylvester Stallone in *Stop or My Mom Will Shoot* (1992). KN

American Gigolo

This is another look at the seedy underside of American life from Schrader, who in *Hardcore* (1979) detailed the murky depths of the **pornography** business. Again sex is for sale, only this time the people have more money. Gere is Julian, a cultivated young man who makes his living sleeping with the wealthy women of Southern California. When one of his clients is murdered he is accused of the crime. The only way he can prove his innocence is to persuade the wife of a senator with whom he is conducting an affair that she admit in court that he was with her at the time of the murder. Schrader successfully involves us in the mechanics and minutiae of Julian's life, coolly observing him working out, choosing a tie, carefully selecting a potential client in a smart club. Less successful is the relationship between Julian and the senator's wife (Hutton). While we are convinced by the film's detached portrayal of the loneliness and emptiness that no amount of material comforts can assuage, Julian redeemed by the love of a good(ish) woman is less convincing, and a less interesting character. EB

1980/117m/PAR/p Jerry Bruckheimer/

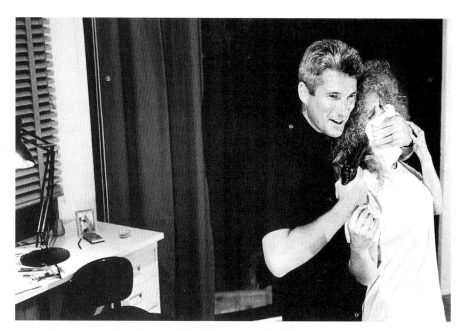

ABOVE The American Cop Movie: Richard Gere, *Internal Affairs*

RIGHT Sylvia Sidney, Phillips Holmes, *An American Tragedy*

d/s Paul Schrader/*c* John Bailey/*m* Giorgio Moroder/*lp* Richard Gere, Lauren Hutton, Hector Elizondo, Nina Van Pallandt, Bill Duke.

An American Tragedy

Paramount initially commissioned a script of Theodore Dreiser's famous novel from Sergei Eisenstein, who was clearly attracted by its social critique. Predictably, though Dreiser liked his treatment, Eisenstein fell out with Paramount, and the project passed to Sternberg, who was less interested in Dreiser's aesthetic realism and social commentary than in using the novel's plot to explore the destructive potential of sexual desire. Visually the film has many characteristic Sternberg touches, especially in the scenes on the lake, with shimmering light reflected on the water producing a luminous image of the lures that lead to murder. Holmes is the young hero desperately trying to escape his working-class origins. Initially he scrambles up the social ladder through his own efforts and a succession of happy accidents, but his liaison with the daughter of wealthy socialites (Dee) is threatened by the pregnancy of his factory-girl lover Roberta (Sidney), whom he resolves to murder. Once on the lake he lacks the courage to go through with his plan to kill her, but in an accident she drowns. He is arrested and condemned to death for murder. In 1951 the novel was again filmed, as *A Place in the Sun*. EB

1931/95m/PAR/*d* Josef von Sternberg/ *s* Samuel Hoffenstein/*c* Lee Garmes/*lp* Phillips Holmes, Sylvia Sidney, Frances Dee, Irving Pichel, Frederick Burton.

O amuleto de Ogum/The Amulet of Ogum

When Cinema Novo petered out in the late 60s, its pioneer and Brazil's most innovative director, dos Santos, made this gangster film fusing avant-garde aesthetics and popular culture. Under duress, a blind balladeer (Macale) tells about the young Gabriel (Sant'Anna), whose mother (Ribeiro) performs the appropriate umbanda ritual and gives her son an amulet making him invulnerable as long as she remains alive. The boy is sent to Caixas to join the gang of Severiano (Soares) but the mobster's mistress (Rocha) takes a shine to the boy and gets him to join a rival gang. Severiano sends

two hoods to kill the boy's mother. Although they fail, Gabriel believes her to be dead and goes to confront Severiano in his luxury residence. After a spectacular action sequence, the two kill each other but Gabriel comes alive again when his mother arrives on the scene. Dos Santos provides a critique of Cinema Novo's refusal to engage with popular culture and particularly of Glauber Rocha's *Barravento* (1962), which he had edited. In that film, umbanda was equated with superstition and backwardness whereas dos Santos now seeks to convey the positive energy in the way poor people devised strategies of survival. The mother is a metaphor for Brazil's poor: wanting her son to do well but ultimately threatened by the very people she hoped would lift them out of poverty. However, the metaphoric dimen-

sion never becomes didactic and the film adopts the tone and pace of popular ballads, both lurid and lyrical, with a freewheeling energy driving the action as well as the humour. With this extraordinary film, dos Santos pioneered a new direction in cinema, opening the door to contemporary Brazilian masters like Carlos Reichenbach and J.P. de Andrade. PW

1974/Brazil/112m/Regina Filmes-Embrafilme/*p/d/co-s* Nelson Pereira dos Santos/*orig* Francisco dos Santos/*co-s* Helio Silva, Jose Cavalcanti/*m* Jards Macale/ *lp* Jofre Soares, Annecy Rocha, Ney Sant'Anna, Maria Ribeiro, Jards Macale.

Anatomy of a Murder

A great critical and financial success for Preminger, *Anatomy of a Murder* is one of the director's most masterful exercises in ambiguity. Gazzara plays an army lieutenant indicted for the murder of a bartender. His defence is that the victim had beaten and raped his wife (Remick). Stewart is the small-town lawyer who defends him. Stewart learns that dislikeable Gazzara has a history of violence, and that his wife has frequently been unfaithful. Much of the action takes place in the courtroom as Stewart tries to defend what appears an increasingly weak case. Eventually he finds evidence that seems to support Gazzara's version of events, though the audience is left in uncertainty about the real merits of the case. Gazzara is acquitted on the grounds of temporary insanity, and disappears without paying Stewart's bill. The film attracted notoriety because of the explicit language used to describe the evidence of rape. Preminger later brought a court case to prevent the film's television screenings being constantly interrupted by commercials. He lost. EB

1959/160m/COL/*p/d* Otto Preminger/*s* Wendell Mayes/*c* Sam Leavitt/*m* Duke Ellington/*lp* James Stewart, Lee Remick, Ben Gazzara, Eve Arden, George C. Scott.

And Then There Were None

This is the first and best version of Agatha Christie's four times filmed novel, *Ten Little Niggers* (1939, retitled *Ten Little Indians* in subsequent editions). In 1965 it was filmed as *Ten Little Indians*, and again under this title in 1989. The third version, in 1974, was under the title *And Then There Were None*. Oddly none of the films was set in the same place. The first version is set on an isolated island, the 1965 film in the Swiss Alps, the 1974 one in a hotel in Persia, the last in Africa. Scripted by Nichols from Christie's own 1943 stage adaptation (which changed the ending of the novel), René Clair's version follows the murder, one after the other, of the guests at a house party, most of whom have a guilty secret. The carefully judged script gives the strong cast ample opportunities for their cameo roles. Particularly successful are Huston, Fitzgerald and Hayward. Director Clair, better known for films like *Le Million* and *A nous la liberté* (both 1931), gives the film a slightly fantastical feel. PH

1945/97m/FOX/*p* Harry M. Popkin/*d* René Clair/*s* Dudley Nichols/*c* Lucien Andriot/*m* Mario Castelnuovo-Tedesco/*lp* Walter Huston, Barry Fitzgerald, Louis Hayward, Roland Young, C. Aubrey Smith, Judith Anderson.

Angel Face

This is one of Preminger's last films before becoming an independent producer, undertaken as a favour to Howard Hughes, who had Simmons under contract. Mitchum becomes chauffeur to a wealthy family and falls for the beautiful daughter (Simmons), who hates her step-mother and murders her by tampering with the brakes of her car. Mitchum and Simmons are tried for murder, but a clever lawyer tells them to get married, to play on the jury's sympathy, and so gets them off. When Mitchum tries to abandon Simmons after the trial, she drives them both off a cliff to their death. Simmons is compelling as the spoiled rich daughter. Mitchum, fascinated, knows she is deadly but cannot tear himself away. As so often in the American crime film, wealth is associated with corruption. Mitchum, who starts out as an ambulance driver, has his integrity guaranteed by his poverty. But integrity is ultimately powerless against the manipulations of high-class *femme fatale* Simmons. EB

1952/91m/RKO/*p/d* Otto Preminger/*s* Frank Nugent, Oscar Millard/*c* Harry Stradling/*m* Dimitri Tiomkin/*lp* Robert Mitchum, Jean Simmons, Mona Freeman, Herbert Marshall, Leon Ames.

Angela Markado

Brocka's rape-revenge film transcends the genre's exploitative conventions. Adapting a popular sex-and-violence comic strip by Carlo Caparas, the plot has the heroine being abducted and sexually abused for days by a group of thugs in a deserted warehouse. Before they let her go, they tattoo their names on her back. In order to overcome the ordeal, she sets out to kill the rapists one by one. She catches up with the last one on Manila's rubbish dumps at night, with smoke and fire emanating from the refuse as she completes her revenge in a deliriously hellish setting. Brocka manages to give the rapists some individuality as the heroine finds each of them in their daily lives, sometimes with a family of their own, so that some of the social conditioning that created such men becomes clearer, which in some ways increases the horror since the rapists are not psychotic sex maniacs but ordinary men rendered brutally callous by life in Manila. As a mainstream commercial movie,

ABOVE Louis Hayward, Roland Young, Walter Huston, June Duprez, Barry Fitzgerald, *And Then There Were None*

this is one of the most intense rape-revenge films made. PW

1980/Philippines/90m/Four Seasons/*p* Peter L. Gan/*d* Lino Brocka/*s* Jose F. Lacaba/*orig* (comic strip) Carlo J.Caparas/*c* Conrado Baltazar/*m* Jerio Soriano/*lp* Hilda Koronel, Johnny Delgado, Rez Cortez, Ruel Vernal, Tonio Gutierrez.

Angels with Dirty Faces

In this imitation of *Dead End* (1937), the tearaways of the earlier picture reunite for the first of many follow-up outings under various names (the Dead End Kids, the East Side Kids, the Bowery Boys). A better picture than William Wyler's stagebound, message-heavy drama, this is also a far more seminal movie. While the professionals from Warner Bros. provide the snappy dialogue and criminal bit-players, Curtiz directs with semi-gothic flair and sublimates the story of kids who hang around the fringe of organised crime to a more interesting, more often imitated, plot. Because one escapes from the cops while the other is caught after a prank, two boys from the same slum background grow up to have very different lives: Cagney becoming a flashy hoodlum and O'Brien a mild but two-fisted priest. Cagney gives the subtlest of his 'good gangster' portrayals, his sharp clothes and sneering manner showing exactly how his Rocky could have grown out of the kind of ragged junior tough played by Halop or Gorcey, and finally (in one of the great melodramatic reversals of the 30s gangster cycle), persuaded by O'Brien that he has to stop seeming a hero to the kids, opting not to go to his execution with grim defiance but to be dragged screaming and kicking to the electric chair he has earned by knocking off treacherous fellow gangster Bogart. 'ROCKY DIES YELLOW' scream the headlines, cueing a last-minute change of heart from the kids and O'Brien's touching tribute to 'the boy who couldn't run as fast as I could', a sequence so sentimental it shouldn't work but which, played without the hand-wringing any other studio would have insisted on, emerges as a powerful emotional and social statement. KN

1938/97m/WB/*p* Sam Bischoff/*d* Michael Curtiz/*s* John Wexley, Warren Duff/*c* Sol Polito/*m* Max Steiner/*lp* James Cagney, Pat O'Brien, Humphrey Bogart, Ann Sheridan, George Bancroft.

O anjo nasceu/An Angel Is Born

Bressane was part of the Sao Paulo-based generation of 'Udigrundi' (Underground) film-makers. Santamaria is a gangster who believes an angel will come and absolve him of his crimes. In the belief that the worse his crimes, the sooner the angel will arrive, he goes on a rampage of merciless violence, half-heartedly assisted by Urtiga. In the end, Santamaria loses any sense of reality and goes insane, identifying himself with the awaited angel. The style is fragmented, raw and frenzied conveying a sense of desperately frustrated anger bordering on religious mania set incongruously in one of Sao Paulo's most violent districts. Bressane's next film, **Matou a familia e foi ao cinema** developed the theme of Camus's *L'Etranger* (1942). PW

1969/Brazil/82m/Julio Bressane Producoes/*p*/*d*/*s* Julio Bressane/*c* Thiago Veloso/*m* Guilherme Vaz/*lp* Hugo Carvana, Milton Goncalves, Norma Benguel, Carlos Guimar, Neville d'Almeida, Maria Gladys.

Apartado de correos 1001/Post Office Box 1001

This film, together with Iquino's **Brigada Criminal**, launched the Spanish crime movie genre. It was able to bypass Spain's strong censorship because the genre was regarded as too blatantly imitative of American and French models to be pertinent to the Spanish situation. However, the film, and its successors, did have an element of social relevance through their negative depictions of father-son relationships, implying a critique of Franco as the father of the nation. Here the Catalonian director features two police inspectors investigating the murder of a young woman in the streets of Barcelona. Through the discovery of a journalist with a personal post box, the inspectors track down a corrupt post-office worker who is a drug addict, and thus uncover a drugs racket. The climactic chase of the chief racketeer is effectively staged in a fairground. The film attempts to combine elements of the Warner Bros. crime film (previously distributed by the producer, Emisora Films) with overtones of neorealist-style location shooting. Salvador went on to make further films in the genre, notably *Han matado a un cadaver* (1960). PW

1950/Spain/86m/Emisora Films/*d* Julio Salvador/*s* Julio Coll, Antonio Isasi/ *c* Federico Larraya/*m* Ramón Ferrés/*lp* Elena Espejo, Conrado Sanmartìn, Tomás Blanco, Manuel de Juan, Carlos Muñiz.

ABOVE James Cagney, *Angels with Dirty Faces*

Aru Koroshiya/A Certain Killer/The Hitman

This odd story features Shiozawa (Ichikawa), a former kamikaze pilot turned professional assassin out of disillusionment with the decline in moral standards amongst Japan's leading citizens. A gang boss, Kimura (Koike), hires him to kill a corrupt politician, which he does with spectacularly cool efficiency. A couple planning a drugs deal (Nogawa and Narita) hire Shiozawa but they fall foul of Kimura, his boss. In the ensuing fight, Kimura is killed and Shiozawa walks away, leaving his share of the drugs profits to his untrustworthy associates, signifying that financial gain was never his motivating force. Released in the same year as Melville's **Le Samouraï**, Mori's picture bears some resemblance to the French classic, especially in the way it concentrates on the killer's professionalism: his meticulous preparations, the precision of his gestures and his impassive demeanour. Mori was mainly an action director, having filmed some of Kurosawa's samurai scripts and having launched the Zatoichi blind swordsman series. His pace in this film is too fast and only fitfully approaches the smouldering intensity of Melville's films. Masumura, one of the scenarists, went on to direct his own yakuza pictures, **Daiakuto** and *Shibire Kurage* (1970), while Mori made a sequel, *Aru Koroshiya No Kagi* (1967) based on another Fujihara novel, *Kesareru Otoko*. PW

1967/Japan/82m/Daiei/*p* Hiroaki Fuji/*d* Issei Mori/*s* Yasuzo Masumura, Yoshihiro Ishimatsu/*orig* Shinji Fujiwara *Zenya c kazuo Miyagawa*/*m* So Kaburagi/*lp* Raizo Ichikawa, Yumiko Nogawa, Mikio Narita, Asao Koike, Mayumi Nagisa.

Ascenseur pour l'échafaud/Lift to the Scaffold/Elevator to the Gallows/Frantic

Malle's first solo feature is an atmospheric thriller with burnished low-lit interiors, released before the New Wave broke through with Truffaut's *Les Quatre cents coups* (1959) and Godard's **À bout de souffle**. The plot has a conventionally murderous love triangle: Julien Tavernier (Ronet) kills his boss (Wall), the husband of his mistress, Florence (Moreau), making it look like suicide. However, he forgets to remove the rope with which he climbed from an upper floor of the building to the window of his boss's office and he has to return to retrieve it. While in the elevator, a night watchman turns off the electricity and Julien is stuck. His mistress wanders the streets of Paris believing her lover has left her after the killing and a couple of teenagers steal Julien's car. They find a gun in his glove compartment and use it to kill some German tourists in a motel, which puts the police on the trail of Julien. Immensely successful at the time, the film is a little too mechanical to be genuinely suspenseful. But Decaë's *noir* cinematography, including the hallucinatory drive by the joyriders through the night, and the controlled but sensuous acting of Moreau and Ronet ensure the movie's continuing power, enhanced by the score, improvised during one single screening, by the Miles Davis quintet. PW

1957/France/89m/Nouvelle Editions de Films/*p* Jean Thuillier/*d*/co-s Louis Malle/*co-s* Roger Nimier/*orig* Noël Calef/*c* Henri Decaë/*m* Miles Davis/*lp* Jeanne Moreau, Maurice Ronet, Georges Poujouly, Jean Wall, Félix Marten.

Los ases de contrabando/Contraband Aces

Like Roger Corman's exploitation quickie, *Cocaine Wars* (1986), Duran's action picture about drug traffickers interrupts its endless

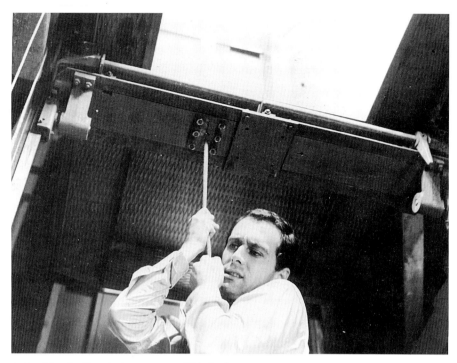

ABOVE Maurice Ronet, *Ascenseur pour l'échafaud*

chases with sudden eruptions of violence and anti-drug sermons as the protagonists confront each other before resuming the chase. The cast is headed by Mexico's leading action star, Goyri, behaving like a cross between Charles Bronson and Clint Eastwood. The only novelty of this routine cops and traffickers plot is that the latter are presented more sympathetically than the former, which says something about the film's target audiences. PW

1986/Mexico/92m/Hermanos Tamez/*p* Orlando Tamez G., Guadalupe E. Viuda de Tamez, Hugo Tamez/*d* Fernando Duran/*s* Carlos Valdemar/*orig* Matilde Rivera, Felipe Morales/*c* Agustin Lara/*lp* Sergio Goyri, Rebecca Silva, Gregorio Casals, Humberto Herrera, Juan Valentin.

The Asphalt Jungle

Based on W.R. Burnett's hard-boiled novel, *The Asphalt Jungle* finds odd moments of consolation in the sleazy and devious world it observes, for example in Hayden's dogged if dim heroism, or in a little cameo of injured innocence by Marilyn Monroe. But for the most part this is *noir* of the blackest kind, which fully earns the bleak oxymoron of its title. The film was enormously influential, almost single-handedly creating **the caper movie**, in which an assortment of individuals gather together to plan, organise and commit a robbery. In this case the leader is the meticulous Doc (Jaffe) and Calhern the bent lawyer who intends to double-cross him. In the event the robbery goes wrong. Dix (Hayden) discovers the lawyer's plot and foils it. He is rewarded in the final sequences of the film; when fleeing the grimy underworld of the city, the sun comes up as he drives into the country, and he finally achieves release through death. EB

1950/112m/MGM/*p* Arthur Hornblow Jr/*d* John Huston/*s* Ben Maddow, John Huston/*c* Harold Rosson/*m* Miklos Rozsa/*lp* Sterling Hayden, Louis Calhern, Jean Hagen, James Whitmore, Sam Jaffe.

Assalto ao trem pagador/Attack on the Pay Train/The Train Robbers

Amongst the first group of films marking the arrival of Brazil's Cinema Novo. Farias uses 'the great train robbery' plot not to generate suspense but to diagnose the state of things in Rio de Janeiro at the time. He concentrates on the leader of the gang, Tiao Medonho (Gomes), a disaffected middle-class suburbanite who teams up with Carioca robbers to attack the mail train in Central Brazil in 1960. The gang divides the spoils and each member seeks to indulge his dreams of an easier life. When the police close in, Medonho cracks and is about to betray his gang when his tougher (because lower-class) accomplices shoot him and he dies in hospital. His wife eventually tells the police where the money is hidden. PW

1962/Brazil/102m/Farias-Richiers/ *p/d/co-s* Robert Fariasco/*co-s* Luiz Carlos Barreto, Alinor Azevedo/*c* Amleto Daisse/ *m* Remo Usai/*lp* Eliezer Gomes, Luiza Maranhao, Reginaldo Farias, Ruth de Souza, Grande Otelo.

L'Assassin habite . . . au 21/The Murderer Lives at No 21

This was the directorial debut of Clouzot, best known for his controversial career under German occupation (Continental Films was a German company) and for the major post-war successes *Le Salaire de la peur* (1952) and **Les Diaboliques**. Based on a Belgian crime writer's novel, although also remarkably similar to Alexander Hall's *The Amazing Mr Williams* (1939), this is a rather academically directed effort following the investigation of Inspector Wenceslas Worobeïtchik *aka* Commissaire Wens (Fresnay) into a series of Parisian murders claimed by a Mr Durand. Sent by an informer to the Pension des Mimosas (in tribute to Jacques Feyder's 1935 film, *Pension Mimosas*), Wens has three suspects: Colin (Larquey), a macabre doll-maker, Linz (Roquevert), a crusty retired soldier, and Lalah Poor (Tissier), a circus illusionist. It turns out that all three work together as a group. Wens is flanked by his scatty lover (Delair) who constantly embarrasses him but helps to rescue the inspector in the end. The film follows on from a previous Steeman adaptation, *Le Dernier des six* (1941), scripted by Clouzot but directed by Georges Lacombe, and Clouzot again turned to Steeman's novel *Légitime défense* for his celebrated film *Quai des Orfèvres* (1947). Other Inspector Wens films include Maurice Cammage's last film, finished by his assistant, *L'Ennemi sans visage* (1946) based on *Monsieur Wens et l'automate*, starring Jean Tissier; E. G. De Meyst's Belgian film *Les Atouts de Monsieur Wens* (1946) starring Werner Degan as the inspector; Roger Blanc's *Mystère à Shanghai* (1950) based on *La Nuit du 12 au 13*, with Maurice Teynac in the title role; the first episode of Verneuil's *Brelan d'as* (1952), starring Raymond Rouleau; and Yvan Govar's Belgian co-production *Que personne ne sorte* (1963), based on *Six hommes à tuer*, starring Philippe Nicaud as Wens's son. PW

1941/France/84m/Continental/*p* J.A. Liote/*d/co-s* Henri-Georges Clouzot/ *co-s* Stanislas-André Steeman/*c* Armand Thirard/*m* Maurice Yvain/*lp* Pierre Fresnay, Suzy Delair, Pierre Larquey, Noël Roquevert, Jean Tissier.

L'Assassinat du père Noël/The Murder of Father Christmas

With the German occupation of France, film production came to a halt until this German-controlled company summoned established French film-makers to come and work for it. This, Continental's first production, is set in the mountains near Chamonix in a village where each year the genial old Cornusse (Baur), a storyteller who also makes beautiful globes of the world, plays Father Christmas. Two plots are developed: a love story between Cornusse's daughter (Faure) and a mysterious baron who always wears one glove (Rouleau), and a whodunit about the robbery of a treasure kept in the church and the murder of the Father Christmas who guards it. The villain is a stranger whose accomplice is the village pharmacist. In the end, the village returns to normal and the lovers get together. With spectacular mountain scenes and an atmosphere combining village romance with elements of a thriller, the film was full of allegorical phrases and motifs devised by the dialogue writer, Charles Spaak, suggesting that France would one day wake up from the oppressive circumstances that had befallen it. It is one of the few adaptations of Pierre Véry's work on which the author did not collaborate. PW

1941/France/105m/Continental/*p* François Carron/*d* Christian-Jaque/*co-s* Pierre Véry from his novel/*co-s* Charles Spaak/*c* Armand Thirard/*m* Henry Verdun/*lp* Harry Baur, Renée Faure, Raymond Rouleau, Robert Le Vigan, Fernand Ledoux.

Assault on Precinct 13

In revenge for a SWAT ambush, a multiracial street gang go on a random murder raid, gunning down a little girl and then pursuing her father to the decommissioned police station where he seeks refuge. Inside the station, a black cop (Stoker) has to forge an alliance with a convicted murderer (Joston) to mount a defence against the almost supernaturally vicious and persistent gang. Following his science fiction debut, *Dark Star* (1974), Carpenter here carves out his postmodern generic territory, borrowing plot elements and incidents from Westerns (*Dragoon Wells Massacre*, 1958, *Rio Bravo*, 1959) and horror films (*The Birds*, 1963, *Night of the*

ABOVE Sam Jaffe, Sterling Hayden, Anthony Caruso, James Whitmore, *The Asphalt Jungle*

LEFT *Assault on Precinct 13*

Living Dead, 1968) to transform the familiar landscape of the urban crime-action drama into a multi-faceted myth informed by a Hawksian sense of community – with Zimmer especially cool in the Angie Dickinson role, and Joston and Stoker exchanging clipped wisecracks in extremis. The razor-sharp editing, effective electronic music and Carpenter's visual skills make this one of the cinema's most efficient suspense machines, as flavoured by characterisation as it needs to be but primarily designed to shred nerves and deliver periodic shocks. The film is not part of the subsequent cycle of realistic youth gang pictures that includes *Colors* (1988) and *Boyz N the Hood* (1991). KN

1976/91m/CKK/*p* J.S. Kaplan/*d*/*s*/*m* John Carpenter/*c* Douglas Knapp/*lp* Austin Stoker, Darwin Joston, Laurie Zimmer, Nancy Loomis, Charles Cyphers.

At the Villa Rose

The first of three versions of A. E. W. Mason's detective story, Maurice Elvey's film is the best. Although Elvey's sound films were largely routine, in the silent period he was a master of calm, unhurried pacing, and blessed with a superb eye for effective locations. *At the Villa Rose* is set in Monte Carlo, and the excellent surviving print does full justice to Elvey's atmospheric sense. Cameraman Paul Burger makes a notable contribution. A rich woman is murdered in her home, and her companion vanishes. The case is solved by Mason's French detective, Hanaud, who quickly works out that the

woman was killed for her jewels and then, when the thieves could not find them, they kidnapped the companion to make her talk. The script's originality is that once Hanaud has established this we are taken in a lengthy flashback through the history of the crime. One contemporary critic did not like this 'standing the story on its head', as he called it, and it was indeed a daring ploy, but it works well. Arundell is a smoothly effective Hanaud, and Burton outstanding as a very sympathetic character who is far from what he seems. A 1930 version was directed by Leslie Hiscott, with Austin Trevor as

Hanaud, and in Walter Summers' 1939 film Hanaud was played by Keneth Kent. The 1930 version was made simultaneously in French, directed by Louis Mercanton and René Hervil. JL

1920/GB/7038ft/Stoll/*d* Maurice Elvey/ *s* Sinclair Hill/*orig* A.E.W. Mason/*c* Paul Burger/*lp* Teddy Arundell, Langhorne Burton, Manora Thew, Kate Gurney, Joan Beverley.

Ato do violencia/Act of Violence

Written by Machado, a professor of philosophy, and directed by an experienced editor, this feature was based on the case of Francisco da Costa Rocha. Also known as

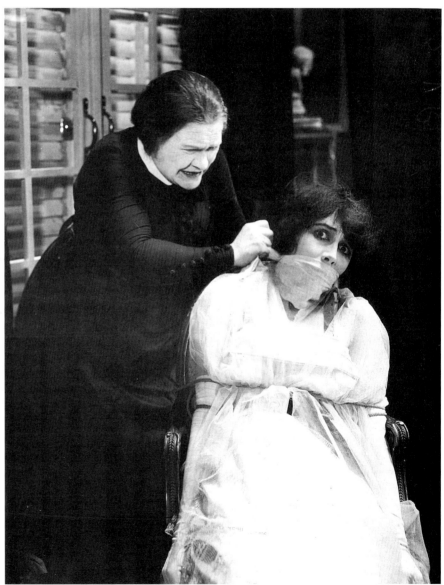

ABOVE *At the Villa Rose*

'Chopped Chico' he strangled two women between 1966 and 1976 apparently for no discernible reason. The film tells of Antonio (Leal Maia), a quiet, ordinary man of normal intelligence who strangles a woman in Sao Paulo while making love and cuts her body into pieces. Some years earlier, he had committed a similar murder but had been released for good behaviour and because the psychiatrists couldn't find anything wrong with him. Arrested, he declares to the press that he has no idea why he committed the murders. The film suggests Antonio is simply incapable of experiencing love, hate or guilt. He is emotionally dead. Shot like a thriller by the director's brother, the film has an atmospheric score by the jazz guitarist Gismondi. PW

1980/Brazil/112m/Linxfilm-Embrafilm/ *d*/*co-s*/*co-p* Eduardo Escorel/*co-p* Cesar Memolo Jr/*co-s* Roberto Machado/*c* Lauro Escorel Filho/*m* Egberto Gismondi/*lp* Nuno Leal Maia, Selma Egrei, Renato Consorte, Eduardo Abbas, Liana Duval.

B

Baby Face Nelson

This is one of several masterly, cheap little films turned out by Siegel in the late 1950s. It is loosely based on fact, tracing the rise and fall of a gangster who was briefly the FBI's Public Enemy No. 1 in the 1930s. Rooney is brilliantly cast as the diminutive Baby Face, a small bundle of nervous energy with a big chip on his shoulder. In an accelerating crescendo of violence, the film follows Baby Face as he blasts his way through a series of armed robberies. In the course of his career he briefly joins with John Dillinger (Gordon), and the latter's death is one of the film's set pieces. Baby Face cares only for his girl-friend Sue (Carolyn Jones). By the end she is repelled by his increasing sadism and paranoia; cornered by the FBI and grievously wounded, Baby Face in effect commits suicide. The film started a brief cycle over the next two or three years of film biographies of historical criminals, including **Machine Gun Kelly**, *The Bonnie Parker Story* (1958), **Pretty Boy Floyd** and **The Rise and Fall of Legs Diamond**. A remake under the same title, starring C. Thomas Howell as Baby Face, appeared in 1995. EB

1957/85m/UA/*p*/Al Zimbalist/*d* Don Siegel/ *s* Irving Shulman, Daniel Mainwaring/*c* Hal Mohr/*m* Van Alexander/*lp* Mickey Rooney,

ABOVE Jack Thompson, Carol Burns, *Bad Blood*

Carolyn Jones, Sir Cedric Hardwicke, Leo Gordon, Ted De Corsia, Anthony Caruso.

Bad Blood

Shot on location in the Koiterangi Valley near Hokitika on the west coast, the actual site of the events dramatised in the movie, the film tells the story of a dairy farmer Stan Graham (Thompson in his best screen role). A loner with a quick temper who has married a brash outsider (Burns), he keeps him-

self from his neighbours whose antagonism triggered his paranoia. It explodes when four policeman come to see him. He shoots them, triggering New Zealand's biggest ever manhunt. The film's other outstanding feature is the landscape as shot by Australian cinematographer Hansen. PW

1981/New Zealand/114m/Southern Pictures-New Zealand Film Commission/*p* Andrew Brown/*d* Mike Newell/*s* Andrew Brown/

orig Howard Willis *Manhunt: The Story of Stanley Graham*/*c* Gary Hansen/*m* Richard Hartley/*lp* Jack Thompson, Carol Burns, Dennis Lill, Donna Akersten, Martyn Sanderson.

The Bad Seed

Based on the play by Maxwell Anderson, which itself was adopted from William March's novel, this is a study of eight-year-old McCormack as the innocent-faced murderess who is responsible for a series of homicides. A similar character would appear in another genre two decades later as the devil-child in the .Omen movies. Director LeRoy, unfortunately, remains too close to the stage presentation – even bringing his cast on at the end to take a bow after the final curtain – rather than allowing Rosson's camera to describe the rather morbid drama. TV

1956/127m/WB/*p*/*d* Mervyn LeRoy/*s* John Lee Mahin/*c* Hal Rosson/*m* Alex North/*lp* Nancy Kelly, Patty McCormack, Henry Jones.

Badlands

In Nebraska in 1958, 19-year-old Charles Starkweather murdered the family of his 13-year-old girl-friend Caril Fugate and took to the road with her on a crime spree which finally left ten dead. The inspiration for several exploitation movies (*The Sadist*, 1963, *The Thrill Killers*, 1965), the incident is here faithfully filmed, though the locale is shifted to South Dakota and the principals are renamed Kit Carruthers and Holly Sargis. Holly (Spacek) narrates their exploits in dry fan-magazine/teenage-diary prose, while Kit (Sheen) is a blankly mysterious force, unmoved even by his own homicidal rage. His only apparent motive is a need to escape obscurity by building his own legend. This he does by erecting a mound of stones to mark the historic site of his own arrest and acting according to some inexplicable soldier's code which requires him to be polite to people he kills. Accordingly, *Badlands* is curiously passionless, suggesting Kit and Holly don't even have a sexual relationship, each so locked in their own fantasies they cannot connect with each other, let alone their innocent bystander victims (when they dance in the open to 'Love Is Strange' they don't even look at each other, much less touch). Sheen and Spacek rigorously refuse to be the glamorous figures their characters believe themselves to be. Like *The Honeymoon Killers* (1968) and **Henry Portrait of a Serial Killer**, the film gives no 'explanation'of purposeless crimes, though its depiction of the divide between the characters' Eisenhower-era rural aimlessness and the romantic lies of popular culture (represented by songs, magazines and movies) suggests a gap between aspiration and achievement at the heart of the killing spree. KN

1973/95m/Pressman-Williams/

p/*d*/*s* Terrence Malick/*c* Brian Probyn/*m* George Tipton/*lp* Sissy Spacek, Martin Sheen, Warren Oates, Alan Vint, Ramon Bieri.

Bajo la influencia del miedo/Gangsterismo en el deporte

After his indulgent but successful Johnny Carmenta movies (**El reino de los Gangsters**, *Gangsters contra Charros*, both 1947; *El Charro del Arrabal*, 1948), the ageing Orol again cast himself as an Italianate mobster, Tony Carpio. Framed by his wife Marbella, the torch singer Kalia the Egyptian (Carmina), together with a night-club owner (Alcocer), Carpio avenges himself by becoming a notorious gang boss and fights with his wife's new associate, El Bronco (Martinez), for control over the boxing rackets. He finances his operations by pretending to make a film at a bank and robbing it for real. In the end, Carpio is jailed again but this time his wife will be waiting for him, suitably repentant, on his release. An example of Orol's camp approach is a scene where some hoods machine gun their opponents without damaging the glazier's shop behind them. PW

1954/Mexico/102m/España Sono/*p*/*d*/*s* Juan Orol/*c* Agustin Martinez Solares/*lp* Juan Orol, Rosa Carmina, Arturo Martinez, Victor Alcocer, Jose Pulido.

La Balance/The Nark/Dime Dropper

Set in the Belleville area of Paris amongst petty crooks and bent coppers, Swaim's film is notable for the way it alternates between ogling Nathalie Baye, playing Nicole, a prostitute, and the physical brutalities inflicted on the body of her pimp, Dédé (Léotard) by the cops. The film opens with the killing of an informer (the eponymous 'balance') and the cops have to find a new one. Enter Dédé, who finds himself caught between a nasty cop (Berry) and an even nastier villain, Massina (Ronet). Dédé is made to infiltrate Massina's gang but the police's plans go awry costing the lives of innocent bystanders and with disastrous consequences for Dédé as well as for his girl-friend. Although less stylised than his first feature, *La Nuit de Saint-Germain-des-Prés* (1977), Swaim's second film strenuously labours to achieve a fashionable 'grittiness': cops wear blue jeans and tote walkmans, locations are strewn with rubbish, the dialogue is peppered with exotic slang phrases, the sound track sports elec-

ABOVE Martin Sheen, Sissy Spacek, *Badlands*

ABOVE Philippe Léotard (centre), *La Balance*

tronic, jazzy pop, etc. Swaim, a former American anthropology student and maker of countless advertising commercials, claimed the film was meticulously researched and showed the 80s Paris cops as they really are: thugs who make a small-time pimp look sympathetic. The movie was outgrossed at the French box office only by *E.T.* that year. PW

1982/France/102m/Les Films Ariane-Les Films A2/*p* Georges Dancigers, Alexandre Mnouchkine/*d*/*s* Bob Swaim/*c* Bernard Zitzermann/*m* Roland Bocquet/*lp* Nathalie Baye, Philippe Léotard, Richard Berry, Maurice Ronet, Christophe Malavoy.

La banda de los tres crisantemos

This was made by Iquino, the director of numerous pot-boilers including crime melodramas (*Al margen de la ley*, 1935; **Brigada criminal**; *Aborto Criminal*, 1973) and Italo-Hispanic Westerns. In this gangster picture he tries to combine elements of the western with traditional Depression-era Chicago iconography in a story about three machine-gun wielding hoods (Reed, Martin and Duque). They come up against one of the trio's uncles (Sancho), an ex-cop now sheriff in a small Texas town. The film's main interest is in its unacknowledged theme: the repressed homosexuality of the three heroes evident in their many strutting and preening

scenes, which alternate with them showing aggression towards each other. PW

1970/Spain/86m/IFI España/*p*/*d*/*s* Ignacio Ferres Iquino/*c* Antonio L. Ballesteros/*m* Enrique Escobar/*lp* Dean Reed, Daniel Martin, Luis Duque, Angel del Pozo, Fernando Sancho.

La Bande à Bonnot/Les Anarchistes ou la bande à Bonnot

Bonnot was a troublesome turn-of-the-century 'anarchist' who had terrorised Paris and was tracked by the police to his farm, The Red Nest, at Choisy-le-Roi, where, after a siege, Bonnot's friends were gunned down and he was captured and later guillotined. Very soon, the Eclair company made quasi-documentary films on the subject called *Bandits en automobile*, which included *L'Auto grise* and *Hors la loi* (both 1912). The films were banned in many French cities after a campaign organised by Edouard Herriot, the mayor of Lyon and later president of France. A few years later, in Mexico, a similar story was filmed about a local gang formed by ex-revolutionary soldiers, called *El automovil gris* (1919), including shots of their execution. Shortly before May 1968, Fourastié followed his flawed *Un choix d'assassins* (1967) with a reinterpretation of the Bonnot gang's adventures, partly in answer to a book by Bernard Thomas which had depicted them as delin-

quents. Fourastié's film opens with Bonnot (Cremer) pushing a wounded man out of his car and coldly finishing him off. This is followed by the title, in red letters, 'Les Anarchistes', with the Bonnot reference in the subtitle. Then the film goes back to the beginning when Callemin *aka* Raymond-la-Science (the popular Belgian singer Brel), an anarchist agitator advocating direct action, joins Bonnot. Together with some friends and opportunists, they embark on a career of hold-ups. Achieving enormous notoriety, the group is eventually ambushed and killed. The film flopped. Audiences expecting a nostalgic piece were confronted with a Gallic **Bonnie and Clyde** and were shocked to hear lines such as: 'I never killed any people; only a cop and a banker, and they aren't human.' However, the film also disappointed left-wing audiences with its refusal to distinguish between banditry and legitimate violence against the state. PW

1968/France, Italy/110m/ Intermondial Film-Kinesis Film-Mega Film/*p* J. P. Guibert/*d*/*co-s* Philippe Fourastié/*co-s* Pierre Fabre, Rémo Forlani, J. P. Beaureneau, Marcel Jullian/*c* Alain Levent/*lp* Bruno Cremer, Jacques Brel, Annie Girardot, Jean-Pierre Kalfon, Anne Wiazemski.

O bandido da luz vermelha/The Red Light Bandit

With a title evoking Caryl Chessman, one of the US's most infamous murderers whose stays of execution were legendary, Sganzerla's apocalyptically energetic and carnivalesque movie became the most famous title in the Sao Paulo Udigrundi (Underground) film movement which followed the Cinema Novo period in Brazil. The dense, fragmented and meandering narrative tells of a psychopathic burglar and killer in Sao Paulo known as the Red Light Bandit because he always carries a red lantern and has long conversations with his victims. He contemptuously evades the police and freely spends his loot until he comes into contact with the crime boss of the notorious Boca do Lixo quarter. Betrayed by a gangster, he is chased through the city and kills his mistress before committing suicide. When the police chief arrives on the scene, he electrocutes himself in the trap he had set for the bandit. The film abounds with references to Cinema Novo films as if to settle accounts with the preceding film generation (especially with Glauber Rocha) and deploys a complex, ironic soundtrack which at times overlays three or four different pieces of music ranging from Beethoven to folk songs and American hits. The off-screen narration is conducted in metallic voices evoking radio announcers which, in Robert Stam's words, 'sometimes declaim the hero's prowess, so that the film becomes a self-mocking advertisement of itself.' PW

1968/Brazil/92m/ Cordeiro-Reis-Sganzerla/ *co-p/d/s/m* Rogerio Sganzerla/*co-p* Jose da Costa Cordeiro, Jose Reis/*c* Peter Overback/ *lp* Paulo Villaca, Helena Ignez, Jose Marinho, Roberto Luna, Ezequiel Neves.

Barker, Arizona Clark (1880–1935)

Matriarch of a family of thugs, kidnappers and heist men, 'Ma' Barker was gunned down with her remaining son Fred in a shoot-out with the **FBI**. She had already lived through the suicide of her eldest, Herman, and the long-term incarceration of her sons Arthur and Lloyd. She has proved one of the most popular figures in the gangster movie, though Roger Corman's **Bloody Mama**, with Shelley Winters in the lead, remains the sole Barker film to take a historical approach and use actual names. Claire Trevor plays the role in 'Ma Barker and Her Boys', an episode of *The Untouchables* that gave offence to J. Edgar Hoover by spuriously accrediting the downfall of the Barker Gang to the Department of Justice's Eliot Ness, perhaps prompting the inclusion of the climax of her career as an incidental in **The FBI Story**. Hoover's stage-managed but still-

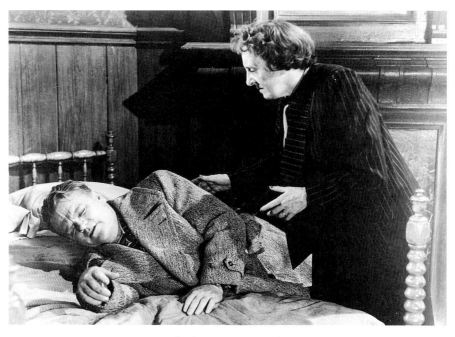

ABOVE James Cagney, Margaret Wycherly (Ma Jarrett), *White Heat*

bungled (he forgot the handcuffs) arrest of the last surviving Barker gang member, Alvin 'Creepy' Karpis (Brad Dexter), was dramatised in **The Private Files of J. Edgar Hoover**.

Under her own name, Ma has been played by Jean Harvey in *Guns Don't Argue* (1957), Lurene Tuttle in *Ma Barker's Killer Brood* (1960) and Eileen Heckart in *The FBI Story: The FBI Versus Alvin Karpis, Public Enemy Number One* (1974). Otherwise, Ma Barker has been represented, with a sex change, as Pa Stark (Charles Middleton) in *Dick Tracy Returns* (1938); as Ma Webster (Blanche Yurka) in *Queen of the Mob* (1940), made at a time when the FBI were still sensitive about gunning down a little old lady and so requested the film-makers depart from the facts to lay the guilt elsewhere; as Ma Grisson (Lilly Molner) or Grissom (Irene Dailey) in *No Orchids for Miss Blandish* (1948) and **The Grissom Gang**; as Ma Gentry (Ida Lupino) in 'The Ma Gentry Gang' (1974), an episode of the TV series *The Manhunter*; and, most notably, as Ma Jarrett (Margaret Wycherly), cuddling middle-aged mama's boy killer James Cagney in her lap in **White Heat**. Before taking the role seriously in *Bloody Mama*, Winters appeared on the *Batman* TV show as Ma Parker, 'The Greatest Mother of Them All'. Barker also inspired Boney M's disco hit 'Ma Baker'. The success of Corman's film encouraged him to produce a slew of self-imitations in which the bloodthirsty, incestuous and perverted Barker brood gradually transform into sympathetic, free-spirited rebels: *Big Bad Mama* (1974) and *Big Bad Mama II* (1987), with Angie Dickinson, Jonathan Demme's *Crazy Mama* (1975), with Joan Blondell and Cloris Leachman, and *Daddy's Boys* (1988). KN

LEFT Lurene Tuttle, *Ma Barker's Killer Brood*

Barton Fink

This satire on Hollywood mores contains one of the more startling recent portraits of a crazed criminal. Turturro plays the eponymous hero, a left-wing writer in the 1930s who is hired by Hollywood to write a wrestling picture. The studio boss (Michael Lerner) is a cigar-chomping philistine who advises Turturro to get advice from the studio's most illustrious, if drunken, screenwriter, played by John Mahoney as an outrageous parody of **William Faulkner**. Turturro spends most of his time holed up in a seedy hotel waiting for inspiration. And in the next room is Goodman's salesman, whose apparent and richly tedious normality hides a truly paranoid personality. The film ends with the hotel turned into an inferno as Goodman sets fire to it, a scene which can be read as an allegory of the Holocaust, but can equally well be a simple illustration of the vision behind all of the Coens' films: that crime and chaos lurk beneath even the most banal and bland exteriors. EB

1991/117m/Circle/p Ethan Coen/d Joel Coen/s Ethan Coen, Joel Coen/c Roger Deakins/m Carter Burwell/lp John Turturro, John Goodman, John Mahoney, Judy Davis, Michael Lerner.

Basic Instinct

This was one of the first mainstream Hollywood films to treat sex explicitly. It opens dramatically: a couple heave to a climax, whereupon the woman reaches for an ice pick and kills her partner. The victim's girlfriend is Catherine (Stone), psychologist turned successful novelist. Anyone close to Catherine has died in mysterious circumstances, the details described or predicted in her books. Catherine is brainy, rich, sexy and provocative, up to tricks like spreading her legs in front of a roomful of cops to reveal herself. The detective in charge, Nick (Douglas), falls hard, but her next book is based on him, and he's faced by the big question – is she a criminal genius killing for kicks, or is she being set up? The script twists and turns and the direction keeps step, focusing on the sexual and psychological undercurrents between the two stars. Sharon radiates sexuality and Douglas is a brilliant foil. MP

1992/122m/Carolco/p Alan Marshall/d Paul Verhoeven/s Joe Eszterhas/c Jan De Bont/m Jerry Goldsmith/lp Michael Douglas, Sharon Stone, George Dzunda, Jeanne Tripplehorn, Dorothy Malone.

Batman

The May 1939 issue of *Detective Comics* featured the debut of the Batman, caped and cowled *alter ego* of Bruce Wayne, orphaned multi-millionaire and self-made superhero.

ABOVE Adam West, Burt Ward, *Batman*

The creation of Bob Kane and Bill Finger, Batman was a cross between Zorro and **The Shadow**, while his distinctive outfit was inspired by the villain of the movie *The Bat Whispers* (1930) and by Leonardo da Vinci's sketch of a bat-winged flying machine. Batman was given his own comic book in 1940, the first issue of which marked the arrival of The Joker, a villain modelled on Conrad Veidt in *The Man Who Laughs* (1928) and who would become the series' most regular bad guy. Batman's original dark violent and frightening appearance was quickly toned down. Bruce Wayne adopted Dick Grayson, a circus orphan who became Robin, a name prompted by the popularity of Errol Flynn's Robin Hood (with whom the Boy Wonder shared a typeface) and the strip became more humane and humorous. In the 40s, Wayne turned into a pipe-smoking father-figure, while Batman and Robin developed a strand of good-humoured wise-crackery. In response to this the villains became more grotesque. Taking their cue from Chester Gould's *Dick Tracy* and his collection of scarred, bizarre, eccentric and nicknamed nemeses, Kane, Finger and their associate Jerry Robinson came up with Selina Kyle (the Catwoman), ex-District Attorney Harvey Dent (Two-Face), Edward Nigma (The Riddler) and Oswald Chesterfield Cobblepot (The Penguin). Supporting characters like butler Alfred Pennyworth and Commissioner James Gordon, and accoutrements like the Batcave, the Bat-signal and the Batmobile were also established in the 40s. Columbia made two minor serials featuring Batman and Robin, Lambert Hillyer's *Batman* (1943), with Lewis Wilson and Douglas Croft in baggy tights up against Japanese secret agent Dr Daka (J. Carrol Naish), and Spencer Gordon Bennet's *Batman and Robin* (1949), with Robert Lowery and John Duncan up against The Wizard. While Superman appeared on radio as early as 1938, Batman had to wait until 1992 and the BBC for whom Bob Sessions played the role in *Superman on Trial, Batman: The Lazarus Syndrome* and *Batman: Knightfall*. In the 50s in keeping with the spirit of the times the comic was further bowdlerised. The Joker stopped killing people and became a prank-playing nuisance, and Batman acquired a 'family' with the appearance of Batwoman, Batgirl, Bat-Mite (a sprite modelled on Superman's frequent pest Mr Mxyztplk). The stories were also often science-fiction inclined.

From 1966 to 1969, the character was

even more changes. Frank Miller Jr's *The Dark Knight Returns* (1986), a limited run comic book later repackaged as a 'graphic novel', is set in a near future when a 55-year-old Bruce Wayne is lured out of retirement into a futuristic Gotham City overrun by mutant street gangs. Miller uses the superhero format to raise the issues of vigilantism and neurosis that have always been implicit in the stories. The success of this more complex *Batman* led to several other attempts to play with the character. These include Miller and artist David Mazzucchelli's *Batman: Year One* (19867) which covers Bruce Wayne's (and Jim Gordon's) first weeks on the streets, in a Chandlerish tale of crooked cops and a rotten city, Alan Moore and Brian Bolland's *The Killing Joke* (1988) and Jim Starlin, Jim Aparo and Mike DeCarlo's bathetic *A Death in the Family* (1988). In this Jason Todd – Dick Grayson's replacement as Robin – is killed by the Joker (after a poll of comics readers said they who wanted him out of the way), although a new, even more irritating, Robin was soon found in Tim Drake.

Tim Burton's **Batman** led to the excellent animated TV series *Batman* (1992). The success of the series led to a feature, *Batman: Mask of the Phantasm* (1993), loosely derived from *Batman: Year Two*. Martin H. Greenberg edited *The Further Adventures of Batman* (1989), *The Further Adventures of the Joker* (1990), and other follow-ups. These anthologies were followed by a series of paperback original novels by the likes of Craig Shaw Gardner, author of the *Batman* movie novelisations, the most noteworthy of

revitalised by the *Batman* TV series produced by William Dozier. This took a camp approach, devised by Dozier and scenarist Lorenzo Semple Jr, with Adam West and Burt Ward stiffly straight-laced as the Dynamic Duo while special guest villains like Frank Gorshin (The Riddler), Burgess Meredith (The Penguin), Cesar Romero (The Joker), Vincent Price (Egghead), Julie Newmar (Catwoman) and Victor Buono (King Tut) relished strange costumes, awful jokes and nefariously stupid schemes. Along with Nelson Riddle's superorchestrated score, the slimline Cadillac Batmobile and the animated sound effects balloons, these villains gave the series a peculiar charm. There was a movie spin-off directed by Leslie H. Martinson in 1966, and two animated TV series (1973 and 1977–8), plus an animated special *The Challenge of the Superheroes* (1979)

with the voices of West and Ward. After the show was cancelled, Dennis O'Neil became the writer-in-chief of the comics and, with artists Neal Adams and Dick Giordano, set out to restore some of the dark feel of the 40s. Dick Grayson was packed off to college, Bruce Wayne got a Richard Chamberlain haircut and became more brooding and unapproachable, the Batman costume lost its mod 60s look and became again a sinister long-eared silhouette, and the Joker resumed killing people. Batman stories of this period feature supernatural and horrific incidents, and new characters introduced include the Man-Bat, a werewolf character whose wings and batface aren't a costume, and R'as al-Ghul, a Fu Manchu-style master villain whose daughter fell in love with the Caped Crusader.

In the 80s, the character went through

Batman – Michael Keaton (left)
Jack Nicholson (below) as the Joker

which is Lansdale's excellent *Batman: Captured by the Engines* (1991).

Batman's darker shadings make him a more adaptable, interesting character than Superman, just as the irascible Donald Duck has always had a wider appeal than squeaky-clean Mickey Mouse. Perhaps the key to Batman's longevity is that he can be played in so many different ways – as the fop-cum-brute of the earliest strips, as the father-figure detective of the Batman and Robin team, as the light-hearted square of the TV series, as Frank Miller's obsessive vigilante, as the whinging reactionary of *A Death in the Family* (in which the Joker is working for the Ayatollah Khomeini), as the stone-faced straight man of Keith Giffen and J. M. DeMatteis' relaunch of the *Justice League of America,* as the lonely monomaniac of Neil Gaiman and Dave McKean's *Black Orchid* (1988), or as Burton's bewildered Bruce Wayne in search of an identity to make him safe in the dark. KN

Batman

Tim Burton signals his approach to the world of *Batman* with his vision of Gotham City as a tainted Metropolis of neon and steam which resembles a 40s vision of a hellish future, populated by unwary victims and criminals. The film sees Batman (Keaton) and the Joker (Nicholson) as dramatic antitheses. The Joker is created partially due to Batman's frightening him into falling into a vat of chemicals, and the young Jack Napier, who will become the disfigured criminal, is the mugger who kills Bruce Wayne's family and triggers off the neuroses that lead young Bruce to become the fearsome Batman. Through Nicholson, Burton works cruel humour in the vein of his *Beetlejuice* (1988), as a joy-buzzer is used to reduce a gangland figure to a smoking skeleton, or a museumful of classical pieces is desecrated ('I am the world's first fully functional homicidal artist') with only a nastily surrealistic canvas of dismembered human carcasses spared the spray paint. Keaton manages to bridge his usual bumbling image (unable to tell Basinger the truth during a tense confrontation, he mumbles 'I'm Batman' over and over behind her back as she answers the door) and the obsessional quality necessary for the Caped Crusader. Throughout, everyone agrees that there must be something wrong with anyone who dresses up in a bat suit to fight crime.

The sequel is even more committed to Expressionism, taking the series further into gothic realms with a despairing tone that undercuts any cape-swinging action. While Keaton's Batman is top-billed, after being given second place to Jack Nicholson's Joker on *Batman*, he is again a supporting player, his familiar trauma given far less weight than the appalling pressures which create a pair of further grotesques, Danny DeVito's spherical Penguin, modelled after Werner Krauss's Dr Caligari, and Michelle Pfeiffer's schizophrenic Catwoman, a ditzy loser reincarnated as a PVC pervert. The hints of a romance between Batman and Catwoman, carried through in fetishist clashes of leather and rubber outfits as the strangest SM relationship in mainstream cinema, signalled by the potent image of Catwoman licking Batman's face from chin to cowl, threaten to reconcile their fractured personalities but remain hauntingly unfulfilled. The final outing to date saw Batman, as a result of polls taken by Warner that showed audiences found the series too dark, edging closer to his 60s television persona with the difference that this time the KER-POWS were created with state-of-the-art special effects. Once again Batman played support, this time to Tommy Lee Jones's Two-Face and Jim Carrey's ever-elastic Riddler. KN

1989/126m/WB/*p* Jon Peters, Peter Guber/ *d* Tim Burton/*s* Sam Hamm/*c* Roger Pratt/ *m* Danny Elfman/*lp* Jack Nicholson, Michael Keaton, Kim Basinger, Michael Gough, Billy Dee Williams.

Batman Returns/1992/127m/WB/ *co-p/d/* Tim Burton/*co-p* Denise DiNovis, Daniel Waters/*s* Daniel Waters/*c* Stefan Czapsky/*m* Danny Elfman/*lp* Michael Keaton, Danny DeVito, Michelle Pfeiffer, Christopher Walken, Michael Gough.

Batman Forever/1995/120m/WB/*p* Tim Burton, Peter MacGregor-Scott/*d* Joel Schumacher/*s* Lee Batchler, Janet Scott Batchler, Akiva Goldsman/*c* Stephen Goldblatt/*m* Elliot Goldenthal/*lp* Val Kilmer , Jim Carrey, Tommy Lee Jones, Michael Gough, Michael Murphy.

Beat Girl/Wild for Kicks

On the surface this is an exploitation quickie in which Hills is a disturbed daughter who briefly flees home, into which her father (Farrar) has introduced a 'wicked (and decidedly youngish) stepmother' (Adam), for the horrors of Soho, thus allowing the audience a glimpse of the young at raucous play and the opportunity to 'tut, tut'. In fact *Beat Girl* is more measured and interesting. In Soho, the vitality of which is pointedly contrasted with the barrenness of Farrar's designer house, Hills discovers that Adam has a past – as a stripper no less – and finds in Faith (in his first screen role) an unlikely support. Hills attempts to recreate Adam's past in the form of an impromptu striptease at a party at her house. This fails and she is implicated in a murder, whereupon 'Daddy' comes swiftly to her rescue. Thus the family is restored and improved and sexuality put in its place. If this message seems both repressive and exploitative, Gréville's direction is far more restrained, emphasising not excess but a desire for control on behalf of its young protagonists, notably Faith whose cool demeanour is central to the tone of the film. PH

1960/GB/85m/Willoughby/*p* George Willoughby/*d* Edmond T. Gréville/*s* Dail Ambler/*c* Walter Lassally/*m* John Barry/*lp* David Farrar, Noelle Adam, Christopher Lee, Gillian Hills, Adam Faith, Shirley-Ann Field.

Bedraget I doden/Gar el Hama/ A Dead Man's Child/The Illusion of Death

After the popular terrorist drama *Dodsflugten* (1911), Schnedler-Sørensen made this slightly more sophisticated thriller about a banker, the evil James Pendleton (Lagoni) who covets the estate of Countess Wolfenhagen (Beumann) and her fiancé, Baron Sternberg (Seeman). Rebuffed by the Countess, Pendleton hires the nasty Oriental Gar el Hama (Hertel) to drug the heroine with a poisoned rose, inducing a death-like state, allowing the villain to rob the tomb and abduct the heroine to Constantinople. The Baron hires a detective called Newton (Zangenberg) and after a chase across Europe culminating in spectacular shots on a moving train, a happy ending is secured. The interiors were filmed in deep focus and deployed almost expressionistic lighting effects. Like most Danish crime films the story was set in England. The same team continued the adventures of the Oriental master criminal in *Dr Gar el Hama II* (1912) where he is pursued by a character called Dr Watson, played by Robert Schyberg. PW

1911/Denmark/50m/Nordisk/*p* Ole Olsen/ *d* Eduard Schnedler-Sørensen/*s* Ludvig Landmann/*c* Alex Graatkjaer/*lp* Aage Hertel, Edith Beumann, Henry Seeman, Otto Lagoni, Einar Zangenberg.

The Bedroom Window

With *The Bedroom Window* William de Mille attempted what might seem impossible in the silent cinema, a classical detective story with a complicated murder, assorted suspects, and a highly individual detective. He succeeded, simultaneously developing plot and character in the way he had learned in the theatre. A wealthy man is murdered, his daughter's suitor (a young Ricardo Cortez) is arrested, and a popular mystery writer (Wales) solves the crime, pinning it on the family lawyer (Edeson). And after all that, there is a final surprise. The dead man's secretary (McGregor), who has been around most of the time looking a likely suspect and a little frightened, wins McAvoy. With no more than the usual allowance of titles to help him, de Mille manages the story with perfect clarity and elicits convincing characterisations from the cast, in particular from Wales, who makes the writer not the eccentric she could so easily have been, but an acute and plucky woman. JL

1924/6550ft/Famous Players-Lasky/
d William de Mille/*s* Clara Beranger/*c* L.Guy Wilky/*lp* Ethel Wales, May McAvoy, Malcolm McGregor, Ricardo Cortez, Robert Edeson.

Best Seller

Dennehy is the **Joseph Wambaugh**-like

former cop turned writer who is approached by sinister hit-man Woods to research a book which will expose a ruthless industrialist (Paul Shenar) for whom Woods used to carry out contract killings. As the duo move around the locations of these previous crimes the purpose of it all starts emerging. Director Flynn maintains the dramatic pace as well as the central characters' psychological aspects as uneasy partners in this absorbing thriller. TV

1987/110m/Orion/*p* Carter De Haven/
d John Flynn/*s* Larry Cohen/*c* Fred Murphy/*m* Jay Ferguson/*lp* James Woods, Brian Dennehy, Victoria Tennant.

La Bête humaine/The Human Beast/Judas Was a Woman

Renoir's adaptation of Zola's 1890 novel transformed the writer's naturalist tract into a piece of poetic realism with *noir* overtones. Denise Leblond-Zola, Zola's daughter, received a credit for the alterations she and the producers made to Renoir's script. Séverine (Simone Simon, who returned from Hollywood to play the part) wants her lover, the locomotive engineer Lantier (Gabin), to kill her stationmaster husband, Roubaud (Ledoux), a jealous and brutal man who already killed her earlier lover/pimp. Lantier is a rough but honest working-class

ABOVE Jean Gabin, Simone Simon, *La Bête humaine*

man proud of his skills and status as an engineer and he cannot bring himself to do the deed. In a fit of exasperated frustration he strangles his beloved instead and then commits suicide by throwing himself off a fast moving train. Renoir achieved masterfully dramatic shots on the speeding train, only the final jump being filmed against a transparency in the studio. Renoir himself made a cameo appearance as Cabuche, a poacher. The film was a major success on its release just before the outbreak of war, but when re-released shortly afterwards, Renoir was forced to cut one of his favourite shots: the camera closely roaming across Severine's murdered body evoking a sense of violence, guilt and desire all wrapped into one complex image. Fritz Lang's remake, *Human Desire* (1954), had its own moments but Hollywood was far more censorious about exploring the potential for lust and violence within ordinary people. PW

1938/France/100m/Paris-Film-Production/
p Robert and Raymond Hakim/*d/s* Jean Renoir/*co-s* Denise Leblond-Zola/*c* Curt Courant/*m* Joseph Kosma/*lp* Jean Gabin, Simone Simon, Fernand Ledoux, Julien Carette, Colette Régis.

Beverly Hills Cop

Murphy plays Axel Foley, a Detroit cop whose friend, a small-time crook, is murdered. He discovers the friend had been working for Victor Maitland (Berkoff) an art

ABOVE Jean Gabin, *La Bête humaine*

dealer in Beverly Hills, so Foley decides to go out there to do some freelance sleuthing. This allows fast-talking, streetwise Foley to interrelate with the laid-back, straight-laced police department of LA's ritziest suburb, whose initial hostility he charms away. Without too much trouble Foley discovers Maitland is smuggling in dope under cover of his art business. The plot is paper-thin, a rickety vehicle for Murphy's slick repartee, but the jokes are just about good enough for him to carry it off. Murphy in 'La-La' land has something in common with Clint Eastwood in the Big Apple in **Coogan's Bluff**, but Murphy's attempt to be action-man in the final shoot-out doesn't convince. The film has just enough racial edge to avoid charges of a sell-out, but not enough to offend white audiences. Its success led to *BHC II* (1987) and *BHC III* (1994). EB

1984/105m/PAR/*p* Don Simpson, Jerry Bruckheimer/*d* Martin Brest/*s* Daniel Petrie Jr/*c* Bruce Surtees/*m* Harold Faltermeyer/*lp* Eddie Murphy, Lisa Eilbacher, Steven Berkoff, Judge Reinhold, Ronny Cox.

Beyond a Reasonable Doubt

Lang's last American film is a highly effective thriller which gives a new twist to the idea that justice is blind. The law is shown to be doubly an ass, prepared to convict an innocent man, and then to acquit a guilty one. At the end justice is done, but only because Fate takes a hand. A writer (Andrews) conceives a plot to demonstrate that capital punishment is wrong since the law can make mistakes. He and a publisher, also his prospective father-in-law, concoct false evidence to implicate him in the murder of a stripper, intending to reveal the truth in court. Unfortunately, before the case can come to trial the publisher is accidentally killed. Andrews is therefore convicted of the crime and sentenced to death. Evidence then appears confirming his innocence; but at the last moment his fiancée discovers that Andrews did in fact commit the crime after all, and was using the 'false evidence' story to conceal his guilt; he is led away to execution. Andrews's peculiarly distant screen personality is admirably suited to the role of the rather calculating hero, and makes plausible the twist that reveals him as a murderer. The opening scene, in which Andrews watches an execution, was replaced for the

British release with a mere recounting of what he has seen. EB

1956/80m/RKO/*p* Bert Friedlob/*d* Fritz Lang/*s* Douglas Morrow/*c* William Snyder/*m* Herschel Burke Gilbert/*lp* Dana Andrews, Joan Fontaine, Sidney Blackmer, Philip Bourneuf, Shepperd Strudwick.

Beyond Reasonable Doubt

Scripted by Yallop on the basis of his own book-length exposé of one of New Zealand's most controversial trials, Laing's effective documentary-style thriller starts with the discovery in 1970 of a crying baby in an isolated, blood-stained farmhouse. The parents of the child are missing and the opinionated Inspector Hutton (Hemmings) suspects the mother's father. When the parents' corpses are discovered, Hutton ruthlessly hunts down another farmer, Arthur Thomas (Hargreaves), and plants evidence to secure the conviction obtained after a sensational court case. When Hutton's tampering is discovered later on, he again manipulates the case and Thomas is convicted at the retrial in 1973. In 1979, Thomas received a pardon and, a year later, was paid $1 million in compensation, although his wife had by then divorced him. PW

1980/New Zealand/115m/Endeavour-New Zealand Film Commission/*p* John Barnett/

d John Laing/*s* David Yallop/*c* Alun Bollinger/*m* Dave Fraser/*lp* David Hemmings, John Hargreaves, Tony Barry, Martyn Sanderson, Grant Tilly.

Bezzerides, A[lbert] I[saac] (1908–)

Bezzerides is a novelist-screenwriter whose largely unknown background is something of a mystery in itself. However, based on his track record as a genre screenwriter, Bezzerides's experience appears to lie in the world of haulage truckers. His novel *The Long Haul* became the basis for Raoul Walsh's *They Drive by Night* (1940), with George Raft and Humphrey Bogart toughing it out in the trucking business, and his later novel *Thieves' Market* became Jules Dassin's hard-hitting drama of trucking corruption in **Thieves' Highway**, from Bezzerides's own screenplay. The engrossing manhunt melodrama **On Dangerous Ground** was scripted by Bezzerides from a Gerald Butler novel which, with its narrative power, gave Ida Lupino and Robert Ryan, the latter as a bitter New York cop, some excellent scenes together. **Kiss Me Deadly**, a Bezzerides script from the Spillane novel, has so many wonderful things going for it that the screenplay almost becomes lost in the shuffle for appreciation. However, Bezzerides was there when the excellent things were developed. TV

Bianyuan Ren/Man on the Brink

Cheung graduated from Super-8 films to TV where he made a wide variety of programmes including episodes for the crime series *CID* before turning director with *Dian Zhi Bingbing* (1979) and *Bianyuan Ren*. This concerns a cop (Chan) who infiltrates a triad gang. Cutting himself off from his family for two years while establishing a reputation as a tough guy, he maintains a rather fraught relationship with an older cop (Kam) who sports yakuza-type tattoos on his body. The homoerotic overtones of the relationship and of the petty gangsters' life-style in general are echoed in the film's misogyny, which also provides the dramatic resolution: Ah Fen (Fung), the only woman involved in the story, hysterically attacks and kills the hero believing him to be a real gangster. Cheung's visual style is clearly influenced by Japanese action films although it remains more conventional than the work of his fellow director, writer and cameraman, Peter Yung (**Xing Gui/The System**). PW

1981/Hong Kong/100m/Century/*p* Peter K. Yang [Yang Qun]/*d*/*s*/*c* Alex Cheung [Cheung Kwok-ming]/*lp* Eddie Chan, Kam Hing-yin, Callan Leung, Ada Fung [Fung Oi-chi], Law Chung.

The Big Clock

A fine corkscrew plot, loaded with novel twists and turns as well as some superb characterisations, sees stressed crime magazine editor Milland (famed for his exposé of criminals) placed in the position of having to cover his own tracks while trying to run down the real murderer of his boss's mistress; Milland was the unknown man sighted at the murder scene. Laughton is the domineering publishing tycoon whom Milland toils for and who is responsible for having him start the publicised manhunt. Director Farrow moves the suspenseful story along at a breathless pace. The film provided the basis of *No Way Out* (1987) starring Kevin Costner. It was based on the 1946 novel by Kenneth Fearing. TV

1947/95m/PAR/*p* Richard Maibaum/*d* John Farrow/*s* Jonathan Latimer/*c* John Seitz/*m* Victor Young/*lp* Ray Milland, Charles Laughton, Maureen O'Sullivan, George Macready.

The Big Combo

This and **Gun Crazy** are Lewis's masterpieces. Ostensibly a straightforward gangster picture, with detective Cornel Wilde on the

ABOVE Cornel Wilde, Jay Adler, *The Big Combo*

trail of mobster Richard Conte, it is a heady brew of sex and sadism. Wilde is also in pursuit of the beautiful Susan (Jean Wallace), who gets her kicks by slumming with Conte. One of the most famous scenes has two of Conte's hoods, fairly obviously homosexual, torturing Wilde by playing deafening noises through an earpiece. The scene has the visceral impact of the notorious ear scene in **Reservoir Dogs**. *The Big Combo* also has one of the most bravura displays of *noir* lighting in any crime film from cinematographer John Alton. The final sequence, a shoot-out in an aircraft hangar, turns to positive advantage the low budget and minimal sets, making an almost purely abstract play of light and dark. The film has a terrific David Raksin score and a pleasing gallery of memorable character actors, including Lee Van Cleef, Earl Holliman, Ted De Corsia and Whit Bissell. EB

1954/89m/Allied Artists/*p* Sidney Harmon/*d* Joseph H. Lewis/*s* Philip Yordan/*c* John Alton/*m* David Raksin/*lp* Cornel Wilde, Richard Conte, Brian Donlevy, Jean Wallace, Robert Middleton.

The Big Easy

This police corruption drama alternates investigation with sexual jousting between pushy homicide cop Quaid and visiting assistant D.A. Barkin, the latter turning up in the plot's New Orleans setting to investigate possible corruption in the force. The cocky Quaid and the sexy Barkin hit it off as the attracting opposites, while Beatty's homicide chief, John Goodman's detective, and Marc Lawrence's mafia boss supply the background character colour. TV

1986/108m/Kings Road Ent/*p* Stephen Friedman/*d* Jim McBride/*s* Dan Petrie Jr/*c* Affonso Beato/*m* Brad Fiedel/*lp* Dennis Quaid, Ellen Barkin, Ned Beatty.

The Big Heat

Dave Bannion (Ford) is disturbed and suspicious after the suicide of colleague Duncan, especially when a girl who talks to him is murdered. He's taken off the case, but continues digging, and a bomb planted in his car kills his wife. Bannion resigns from the police force and goes looking for revenge. He blames gang boss Mike Lagana (Scourby), but there's no evidence until Debby (Grahame) comes forward to identify his wife's killer. Based on the novel by **William P. McGivern**, the film follows Bannion as the good man whose lust for vengeance fuels his descent into the hellish underworld of organised crime and corrupt politicians. In this it is remarkably similar to Lang's Western *Rancho Notorious* (1952). The film fixes its moral focus on the victims, and on the obligation of witnesses to speak out, reflecting public interest in the Senate crime investigations at the start of the decade. Grahame is powerful as the moll who fights back after she's mutilated by Marvin's sadistic killer. MP

1953/89m/COL/*p* Robert Arthur/*d* Fritz Lang/*s* Sydney Boehm/*c* Charles Lang/ *m* Daniele Amfitheatrof/*lp* Glenn Ford, Gloria Grahame, Jocelyn Brando, Alexander Scourby, Lee Marvin.

The Big Knife

This is perhaps the most melodramatic picture ever made about Hollywood. Charlie Castle (Palance) is the unbalanced and alcoholic star who, disillusioned with his career, blames his agent for the kind of parts he is getting. Producer Stanley Hoff (Steiger) is not prepared to let him go, and blackmails him with threats that he will reveal the star's involvement in a fatal drunk-driving accident. After a witness to the accident is murdered by the producer's assistant, Charlie sinks further into alcoholic depression, and when his wife leaves him he cuts his wrists in the bath. Based on a play by Clifford Odets, this is an example of how far the crime film dominated Hollywood at this time. Even a film about the picture business itself fell naturally into a noirish melodrama of skulduggery among the moguls. Palance and Steiger, losing no opportunity to chew the scenery, have a tremendous time spitting

ABOVE Lauren Bacall, Humphrey Bogart, *The Big Sleep*

out the pieces. Their final confrontation is an epic battle of egos. EB

1955/111m/UA/*p*/*d* Robert Aldrich/*s* James Poe/*c* Ernest Laszlo/*m* Frank DeVol/*lp* Jack Palance, Ida Lupino, Rod Steiger, Wendell Corey, Jean Hagen.

The Big Sleep

Less effective as a **Philip Marlowe** movie than **Murder My Sweet**, this sticks faithfully to its source novel (simply omitting the sex, drugs and pornography MacGuffin, thus rendering an already complex plot impenetrable) until the last reel, which exposes a conventionally rotten hood (Ridgely) as the villain rather than the hophead nymphomaniac at the heart of Chandler's nasty pattern of murder and corruption. Bogart's hardboiled Marlowe extends his own image rather than that of Chandler's hero, and the crackle of sexual tension in his relationship with the girl in the case (Bacall) is obviously intended to follow the romantic teaming in Hawks's *To Have and Have Not* (1944), a similarity underlined by reshooting of their scenes after previewing to play up the erotic banter. Nevertheless this remains a classic private eye movie, deploying Chandler's picturesque supporting cast to exceptional effect: Vickers's rich tramp is not allowed to

LEFT Jack Palance, Ida Lupino, *The Big Knife*

be the killer, but she's still a formidable slut as she tries to sit in Marlowe's lap while he's standing up; Waldron's General Sternwood, pickled in alcohol in his oppressively hot greenhouse amid the orchids he loathes, reminiscing about his wild life; Cook in his definitive weasel loser role, forced to drink poison by a blankly malevolent hood (Steele); and Malone as the provocative bookstore clerk who offers Marlowe clues and an afternoon's solace. Famously impossible to follow, this is less a jigsaw than a mystery tour: individual setpieces in which Bogart's Marlowe bests one or more strange characters are strung together on a trail that has been deliberately obscured. Realising the arbitrary guilt assigned by Chandler to his characters and also blunting the sting of the author's undoubted misogynous streak, Hawks turns out a movie that, like his Western *Rio Bravo* (1958), serves almost as a parody of its genre, its storyline simply an excuse for visual and verbal pleasures. KN

1946/113m/WB/*d*/*p* Howard Hawks/ *s* William Faulkner, Jules Furthman, Leigh Brackett/*c* Sid Hickox/*lp* Humphrey Bogart, Lauren Bacall, Martha Vickers, John Ridgely, Dorothy Malone, Bob Steele, Charles Waldron, Elisha Cook Jr.

Black Hand

This outing treats the activities of the turn-

ABOVE Chester Morris, *Boston Blackie's Rendezvous*

of-the-century Italian crime society, the Black Hand, among New York's Italian immigrants and a lone Italian-American's (Kelly) fight against them. It has all of the expected mafia-style gangster action associated with the genre (extortion, bombings, assassinations), an interesting change of type for Kelly, and an excellent performance from Naish as an Italian-American NYC policeman also out to get the murderous society. The character was based on Lt Joseph Petrosino who, before his 1909 assassination, was among the first to recognise the existence of the American mafia. Petrosino was later played by Ernest Borgnine in the 1960 biography *Pay or Die*. TV

1950/92m/MGM/*p* William H. Wright/ *d* Richard Thorpe/*s* Luther Davis/*c* Paul C. Vogel/*m* Alberto Colombo/*lp* Gene Kelly, J. Carrol Naish, Teresa Celli.

The Black Marble

Wambaugh's police-as-fallible-human-beings story (once again) deals with the uncomfortable partnership of troubled cop Foxworth, having transferred from homicide, and Prentiss as they investigate the theft of Babcock's prize showdog. The Foxworth-Prentiss teaming eventually allows some romantic moments between the action, while Stanton's bumbling dognapper is a delight between his moments of (offscreen) cruelty. More lightweight in tone than director Becker's previous Wambaugh outing with *The Onion Field* (1979). Wambaugh's screenplay is based on his own novel. TV

1980/113m/Avco Embassy/*p* Frank Capra Jr/ *d* Harold Becker/*s* Joseph Wambaugh/ *c* Owen Roizman/*m* Maurice Jarre/*lp* Robert Foxworth, Paul Prentiss, Harry Dean Stanton, Barbara Babcock.

Black Rain

This is another variation on the theme of a cop pursuing a crook into a city he doesn't know or understand, in the manner of **Coogan's Bluff** and **Beverly Hills Cop**. Douglas and Garcia are New York detectives sent to escort a Japanese gangster back to Osaka. No sooner do they arrive than they lose their prisoner, and the rest of the movie is spent chasing him through the bewildering underworld of a high-tech city inhabited by dangerous yakuza. In an effort to make Douglas interesting he's given a less than squeaky-clean record, and sexual interest is supplied in the form of Capshaw, a blonde American bargirl who knows her way around. But it is the city that is the most important character. Osaka is, rather like Los Angeles of **Blade Runner**, a nightmarish vision of the future, a totally artificial environment constructed of cold steel and glaring neon. EB

1989/126m/PAR/*p* Stanley R. Jaffe, Sherry Lansing/*d* Ridley Scott/*s* Craig Bolotin, Warren Lewis/*c* Jan De Bont/*m* Hans Zimmer/*lp* Michael Douglas, Andy Garcia, Ken Takakura, Kate Capshaw, Yusaku Matsuda.

Blackie, Boston

One of the several would-be, wise-cracking amateur detectives and defender of damsels in distress that populated series movies of the 40s, Boston Blackie was first brought to the screen by Bert Lytell in *Boston Blackie's Little Pal* (1918). Created by Jack Boyle, Blackie's former occupation as a jewel thief identifies him as being inspired by E. W. Hornung's **Raffles** whose first screen appearance was in 1905. By 1941, when he was brought to the screen for the first of 14 outings by Chester Morris, that connection was only evident in the character of Arthur Manleder, Blackie's friend, a rich bungler in the manner of Hornung's Bunny. In the series Morris was aided by Runt (mostly played by George E. Stone), a loyal but not-so-clever ex-thief, and harried by Inspector Farraday (Richard Lane). For the most part the films were formulaic with Blackie forever being accused of a crime and having to find the real villains to prove his own innocence, but the first in the series that Robert Florey directed, *Meet Boston Blackie* (1941), was swiftly paced. Even better was the atmospheric *Boston Blackie's Rendezvous* (1945), in which Morris is in search of Steve Cochran's escaped homicidal maniac who in turn is menacing Nina Foch's dance-hall girl. It was directed by Arthur Dreifuss. The last outing in the series was *Boston Blackie's Chinese Venture* (1949). Other actors who played Blackie prior to Morris were Lionel Barrymore (*The Face In The Fog*, 1922), David Powell (*Missing Millions*, 1922), William Russell (*Boston Blackie*, 1923), Forest Stanley (*Through The Dark*, 1924) and Raymond Glenn (*The Return Of Boston Blackie*, 1927). Morris and Lane reprised their characters for the NBC radio series (1944) while Richard Kollmar was Blackie in a syndicated radio series in 1945. Kent Taylor was television's Boston Blackie (1951–53). The character has no connection with Boston. PH

Blackmail

This was Hitchcock's first sound movie and is often claimed as the first British talkie. More

accurately it is Hitchcock's first 'part sound' movie. To make matters even more complex, two versions exist, one silent, the other 'part sound' with Joan Barry speaking off camera while the German actress Ondra pantomimed the words. This latter version is the one most commonly screened. More significantly, though the film was clearly conceived of as a silent movie, the arrival of sound marked a decisive shift in the intensification process that subsequently became central to Hitchcock. Sound allowed for new methods of dramatic construction, as when Hitchcock cuts from Ondra's shriek to a shot of the charwoman finding the body (a sequence repeated in *The 39 Steps*, 1935), or when, after the murder, the conversation at Ondra's family breakfast table is seen subjectively from her point as the repetition of the one word 'knife', the implement with which she killed Ritchard's would-be rapist. The film is created in three acts. The first shows the detective Longden routinely doing his job, catching criminals. He then has a row with Ondra who first attracts and then suffers the attention of Ritchard's artist, a cen-

ABOVE Alfred Hitchcock, John Longden, Anny Ondra, *Blackmail*

BELOW Cyril Ritchard, Anny Ondra, *Blackmail*

tral feature of many later films in which women are tormented by others. Equally importantly, the screen relationship between the detective and the artist suggests less the famous transference of guilt – a key Hitchcock theme – than a transference of desire, with Ritchard attempting what Longden cannot admit he feels. This element of transference would never be so clearly stated in Hitchcock until **Frenzy**, the director's uneasy return to Britain (and the British theme of repression). The third act neatly further parallels Longden with Calthrop's blackmailer (who saw the murder), both of whom 'want' Ondra and introduces the first example of Hitchcock's oft-essayed metaphorical contrast of the public and the private, with the chase of Calthrop by Longden around the roofs of the British Museum. PH

1929/GB/96m/British International Pictures/ p John Maxwell/d/co-s Alfred Hitchcock/co-s Benn W. Levy, Charles Bennett/orig Charles Bennett/c Jack Cox/lp Anny Ondra, John Longden, Charles Paton, Sara Allgood, Donald Calthrop, Cyril Ritchard.

Blackout

This film follows the French trend of translating *films noirs* into glossy advertising imagery in the manner of **Diva** and **La Balance**. It is set in a nameless city's Chinatown and echoes Wenders' **Hammett**, featuring a private eye, Werner (Scheele) who seems to be a fusion of **Sam Spade**, **Philip Marlowe** and **Mike Hammer**. Corpses are fished out of rivers, cops and hoods both persecute the hapless hero, local VIPs are in cahoots with the mafia, sexy women send the sleuth on dangerous errands, a long-suffering, wisecracking secretary mothers the tough guy, etc. The result is a studio-bound pop video version of urban sleaze as the background for a string of clichés. PW

1985/Norway/88m/Norsk Film-Esselte Video-Kodak Film/*p* Anders Enger/*d*/*co-s* Erik Gustavson/*co-s* Erik Ildahl/*c* Kjell Vassdal/*lp* Henrik Scheele, Elisabeth Sand, Tommy Kørberg, Ramon Gimenez, Per Bronken.

Blade Runner

An ambitious, partially-successful science fiction rethinking of *film noir*, *Blade Runner* presents a teeming, rainswept future city that is a mutation of the world of 40s Hollywood movies and underlines the traditional alienation of its trench-coated detective (Ford) by stranding him in a case which causes him finally and literally to doubt his own humanity. Detailed to track a group of runaway 'replicants' (superhuman androids) in a decaying Los Angeles, Ford gradually realises his quarries have been unjustly treated by their manufacturer, created for slave labour with a built-in life expectancy of only a few years. In traditional Chandler fashion, the mystery provides an excuse for a tour of a corrupt world, from streets overrun with armoured cars, colourful hustlers and a bombardment of adverts to highrise pyramids of power where heartless executives decide the fates of millions. Although enormously influential in its image of the future (in movies, written science fiction and such ephemera as rock videos and TV commercials), none of several available cuts make the kind of hallucinatory sense attained by the most intricate of the *noirs* it apes. The novel is less pretentious and much funnier. KN

1982/WB/118m/*p* Michael Deeley/*d* Ridley Scott/*s* Hampton Fancher, David Peoples/*orig* Philip K. Dick *Do Androids Dream of Electric Sheep?*/*c* Jordan Cronenweth/*m* Vangelis/*lp* Harrison Ford, Rutger Hauer, Sean Young, Edward James Olmos, Daryl Hannah, M. Emmet Walsh.

Blake, Sexton

Essentially a clean-cut, simple-minded and 'manly' **Sherlock Holmes**, Blake first appeared in 'The Missing Millionaire', a novella by Harry Blyth (1852–98) in the *Halfpenny Marvel* magazine in 1893. However, in his longevity and two-fisted attitude, Blake is closer in spirit to Nick Carter than Holmes, and his boy assistant Tinker is more a precursor of Robin than a cousin of Watson. In the *Marvel*'s stablemate *Union Jack*, Blake pursued evil-doers even more singular than Holmes's foes. These included Zenith the Albino, the Fu Manchu-like Prince Wu Ling of the Brotherhood of the Yellow Beetle and Waldo the Wonder Man. Blake's adventures continued through the transformation of the *Union Jack* into *Detective Weekly* in 1933, and then to the *Sexton Blake Library* series of novellas, which lasted until 1963. Subsequently, Blake

ABOVE Harrison Ford, *Blade Runner*

adventures appeared as hardback and paperback originals, though the character has seemed retired since John Garforth's TV tie-in *Sexton Blake and the Demon God* (1978). Among over 200 hands who have contributed nearly 4,000 stories (over 1600 novels, 1500 novelettes and nearly 1000 short stories and serials) to the Blake canon are William Murray Graydon, John Creasey, Arthur Maclean, Wilfred McNeilly, Jack Trevor Story, Jack Adrian and Martin Thomas.

Blake probably made his film debut in *Sexton Blake* (1909), an adaptation of Graydon's *Five Years After* (1906) directed by and starring Douglas Carlile. Carlile returned in *The Council of Three* (1909), *Lady Candale's Diamonds* (1910), *The Jewel Thieves Run to Earth by Sexton Blake* (1910) and *Sexton Blake v Baron Kettler* (1912). A typical exploit found Blake exposing a spy ring of bus drivers commanded from a tower in Epping Forest by an evil entomologist. In 1914, Charles Raymond directed Philip Kay as Blake in *The Mystery of the Diamond Belt* (adapted from a contemporary serial by Lewis Carlton, who also played Tinker), *Britain's Secret Treaty* and *The Kaiser's Spies*, with Blake dividing his time between the war effort and ordinary crooks. In 1915, Raymond recast Harry Lorraine and Bert Rex as Blake and Tinker for *The Great Cheque Fraud*, *The Thornton Jewel Mystery* and *The*

LEFT Rutger Hauer, *Blade Runner*

Stolen Heirlooms. Douglas Payne and Neil Warrington were Blake and Tinker in *The Further Exploits of Sexton Blake: The Mystery of the SS Olympic* (1919), directed by former-Blake Lorraine. Payne returned, partnered by George Bellamy as Tinker in *The Dorrington Diamonds* (1922). Langhorne Burton and Mickey Brantford were Blake and Tinker, with Mrs Fred Emney as Mrs Bardell, in a 1928 *Sexton Blake* series of six interlinked two reelers. There were also parodies: 'Bexton Slake' in *The Would-Be Detective* (1913), Fred Evans in *Sexton Pimple*, and Wally Bosco as 'Sherlock Blake' in *I Will, I Will, I Will* (1919).

In the 1930s, George Curzon, partnered by Tommy Sympson as Tinker and Marie Wright as Mrs Bardell, starred in three Blake films: *Sexton Blake and the Bearded Doctor* (1935), Alex Bryce's *Sexton Blake and the Mademoiselle* (1935) and, most notably, George King's *Sexton Blake and the Hooded Terror* (1938). The last is probably the best Blake film, pitting Curzon's wooden heroics against the flamboyant villainy of Tod Slaughter as a kindly stamp collector who moonlights as the Hooded Terror, mastermind of an international criminal organisation known as the Black Quorum. David Farrar took over the role for two films directed by John Harlow: *Meet Sexton Blake* (1944) and *The Echo Murders* (1945). Geoffrey Toone was a stolid Blake in *Murder on Site Three* (1958), with Richard Burrell as Tinker, from W. Howard Baker and Jack Trevor Story's *Crime is My Business* (1958). Leslie Norman's *Mix Me a Person* (1962), a courtroom drama with Adam Faith unjustly accused, is based on a Sexton Blake novel, Story's *Nine O'Clock Shadow* (1958), but the Blake role was rewritten, à la Story's revised novel *Mix Me a Person* (1959), as a lawyer played by Anne Baxter.

Also active on the stage and the radio, Blake has perhaps best been served by television. Laurence Payne and Roger Foss starred as Blake and Tinker in *Sexton Blake*, a 1967–71 series which boasts such bizarre plot devices as Valentine Dyall as a mad undertaker who believes he is King Arthur reborn. Also interesting is the serial, *Sexton Blake and the Demon God* (1978), scripted by Simon Raven. Unlike Blake's blandly contemporary film exploits, both series choose a 1920s setting and emphasise the semi-supernatural aspects of the sleuth's wilder adventures. KN

Blind Alley

Morris is the escaped-convict killer who, with associates, holes up in the home of psychology professor Bellamy and makes prisoners of his family and guests (in **The Desperate Hours** style). The story of Morris's killer career is then told through flashback as Bellamy psychoanalyses the criminal to uncover the subconscious basis for his mania. For a moderate Columbia *film noir*-ish programmer this yarn has a few interesting twists in its telling. It was remade by Rudolph Maté as *The Dark Past* (1948). TV

1939/68m/COL/*p* Fred Kohlmar/*d* Charles Vidor/*s* Phillip MacDonald, Michael Blankfort, Albert Duffy/*c* Lucien Ballard/*m* Morris Stoloff/*lp* Chester Morris, Ralph Bellamy, Ann Dvorak.

Blind Date/Chance Meeting

With the thriller **Time without Pity**, the gangster film **The Criminal** and the science fiction film *The Damned* (1963), the detective film *Blind Date* is the best of Losey's pre-*The Servant* (1963) British movies. The puzzle is as technical as any created during Detective Fiction's 'Golden Age' – it revolves about the victim not being who she seems to be – but whereas then the solution was all important, in the film Presle's guilt is established virtually by accident. More importantly what is at stake is not whodunit but the complex relationships of the suspects and Baker's policeman to the supposed victim. The wife of Flemyng's upper crust diplomat, Presle begins the game of love in the afternoon with Kruger's naively youthful artist, intending to frame him for the murder of Flemyng's mistress whom she impersonates for his (Kruger's) benefit before killing her. Found in the murdered woman's flat, Kruger paints an idealistic picture of a woman wanting love, in contrast to policeman Baker who sees the victim as someone who was 'a taker not a giver'. Yet quickly all is not what it seems. Thus, Baker is shown to be independent of authority – he rejects the idea put to him that Flemyng, though the murdered woman is his mistress, must not be involved and that Kruger fits the bill as the murder suspect – yet prurient – most visibly in the sequence in which he fondles the murdered woman's underwear. Similarly Kruger is naive to the point of a lack of concern about his being found guilty – asked why he washed his hands in the flat (which he had not previously visited) he replies 'to smell the soap' – yet as an artist he has a sus-

taining identity that is not at risk. The murder investigation gives the film a cooler structure than in Losey's previous British films, pointing the way forward to the director's collaboration with screenwriter Harold Pinter on *The Servant* in which repression would replace eruption as the hallmark of a Losey film. PH

1959/GB/95m/Independent Artists/*p* David Deutsch/*d* Joseph Losey/*s* Ben Barzman, Millard Lampell/*orig* Leigh Howard/*c* Christopher Challis/*m* Richard Rodney Bennett/*lp* Hardy Kruger, Stanley Baker, Micheline Presle, Robert Flemyng, Gordon Jackson, Jack MacGowran.

Bloch, Robert (1917–94)

Since Alfred Hitchcock's successful 1960 filming of the novel **Psycho**, Robert Bloch has been almost exclusively associated with this single credit. However, his lasting reputation is built on a considerable body of work in the horror, science fiction and thriller genres. An early disciple of H.P. Lovecraft, Bloch's first stories were in the vein of cosmic horror opened by the sage of Providence. However, in the 40s, Bloch found his own voice, most notably with the short story 'Yours Truly, Jack the Ripper' (1943), several times adapted for radio and television, in which the Whitechapel Murderer is at large in contemporary America. In his mix of supernatural themes and matter-of-fact settings (plus his use of gruesome humour), Bloch was to prove influential on the school of horror later represented by Richard Matheson, EC comics, *The Twilight Zone* and Stephen King. In addition to *Psycho*, his thrillers (many dependent on pop psychology and twisted mystery) include *The Scarf* (1947), *The Kidnapper* (1954), *The Will to Kill* (1954), *The Dead Beat* (1960), *Firebug* (1961), *The Couch* (1962) and *Night of the Ripper* (1984). His autobiography is typically entitled *Once Around the Bloch* (1993).

After *Psycho*, Bloch came into demand as a screenwriter, specialising in mysteries with a *grand guignol* twist like *The Cabinet of Caligari* (1962), loosely from the 1919 film, *Strait-Jacket* (1964), *The Night Walker* (1964), *The Psychopath* (1965) and *The Deadly Bees* (1966). More recently, Bloch was most active as a novelist, producing the Lovecraft-influenced *Strange Eons* (1978), two sequels to *Psycho* (*Psycho 2*, 1982, *Psycho House*, 1990) unrelated to the continuing film series, and, in collaboration with Andre Norton, a follow-up to Stevenson's *The Strange Case of Dr Jekyll and Mr Hyde*, *The Jekyll Legacy* (1991). KN

Blood Simple

Visser (Walsh) is a private detective hired by Texas bar owner Julian Marty (Hedaya) to kill his wife Abby (McDormand) and her lover Ray (Getz). He fakes the hit with photographs and winds up killing Marty instead. Ray discovers the body and assumes that Abby has done the murder. In a fever of anxiety for her he takes the body out to a field to bury it, but finds himself being buried instead. Typical of a new wave of *noir* derivations, the script draws on a database of **James M. Cain**'s stories, but is more concerned with style than with moral issues or nuances of character, in a nightmare world of brutality and battery in which violence is a flashy, empty, and seemingly pointless statement. Hedaya manages to be both repulsive and sympathetic in the role. MP

1984/97m/River Road/*p* Ethan Coen/*d* Joel Coen/*s* Ethan Coen, Joel Coen/*c* Barry Sonnenfeld/*m* Carter Burwell/*lp* John Getz, Frances McDormand, Dan Hedaya, M. Emmet Walsh, Samm-Art Williams.

ABOVE Alan Ladd, *The Blue Dahlia*

Bloody Mama

Typically, Corman opted not simply to imitate **Bonnie and Clyde**, but to deconstruct Arthur Penn's approach to the outlaw myth. He one-ups Penn's stylised beautiful people and jarring mix of slapstick, lyricism and violence by presenting a truly demented vision of a criminal family dominated by matriarch Kate 'Ma' **Barker** (Winters), who is capable of performing 'I Didn't Raise My Boy to Be a Soldier' without irony, but also beds her sons, drives them to increasing feats of depravity and finally drags them down with her in a holocaust-cum-shootout. Corman's Barkers, like his Ushers, are incestuously self-destructive and archetypally American. The sons are torn between a monstrously dominant mother and an absent father, replaced, in the film's most extraordinary sequence, by kidnapped and blindfolded businessman Hingle, whose quiet insolence inculcates in Ma's Number One Son (Stroud) a desperate need to look him in the eyes. With a strong and strange supporting cast (De Niro as a glue-sniffing loser, Walden and Dern as sadistic homosexuals) and Winters in a career-justifying role as the horrifying and yet somehow touching Ma, this is a far less distanced account of Depression-era outlaws than *Bonnie and Clyde*. Its authentic rawness and nastiness resists nostalgia, emphasising a genuine awareness of the horrible consequences of casual murder-sprees, a refusal to look down on its characters for their tragic lack of vision, and a black comic glee that goes beyond Penn's banjo-picking knockabout to make challenging sequences of the violent highlights. Typically, Corman capitalised on the success of this imitative movie by presiding over an entire sub-genre of follow-ups: Martin Scorsese's **Boxcar Bertha**, Steve Carver's *Big Bad Mama* (1974), Jonathan Demme's *Crazy Mama* (1975) and Joe Minion's *Daddy's Boys* (1988). KN

1970/90m/AIP/*p/d* Roger Corman/*s* Robert Thom/*c* John Alonzo/*m* Don Randi/ *lp* Shelley Winters, Pat Hingle, Don Stroud, Diane Varsi, Bruce Dern, Robert De Niro, Robert Walden.

The Blue Dahlia

Johnny Morrison (Ladd) returns from the war with a few buddies, who include Buzz (Bendix), a damaged hero with a steel plate in his head, intolerable headaches and amnesia. Johnny's wife is in the middle of a party, and an affair with another man. He

ABOVE Anne Baxter, *The Blue Gardenia*

leaves her, but when she's murdered he's the chief suspect. Making his escape by kidnapping Joyce (Lake), he sets out to clear his name. The plot encapsulates the fear and disillusion surrounding the rehabilitation of World War II veterans. In this role Ladd's frozen, passionless air suggests an emotional damage which parallels Bendix's wound. The Navy Department objected to the ending where it turns out Bendix has murdered the wife out of loyalty to his friend, and Chandler changed it. This makes little difference to the overall impact. Chandler's script was Oscar-nominated, and it's tight, witty, grim *noir*, with his characteristic anger lurking not too far below the surface. MP

1945/96m/PAR/*p* John Houseman/*d* George Marshall/*s* Raymond Chandler/*c* Lionel Lindon/*m* Victor Young/*lp* Alan Ladd, Veronica Lake, William Bendix, Howard Da Silva, Doris Dowling.

The Blue Gardenia

Adapted from a short story by **Vera Caspary**, whose novel formed the basis for **Laura**, *The Blue Gardenia* is both a murder mystery and a 'woman's picture'. The heroine (Baxter) is a disoriented woman, recently jilted, who impulsively goes on a blind date with a philanderer (Burr), only to have him found dead in her apartment and to become the prime suspect for the killing. A journalist (Conte) who is pursuing the case

comes to her aid and helps her clear her name. A modest production, evidently filmed in only twenty days, this is an undeservedly neglected work. Not only does it adumbrate a concern with media ethics, touched on in **You Only Live Once** and central to **While the City Sleeps**, but the narrative is organised, even by Langian standards, with exemplary concentration, and the adoption of a female protagonist serves to refine the director's continuing preoccupation with the figure of the judicial victim.
TP

1953/90m/WB/*p* Alex Gottlieb/*d* Fritz Lang/ *s* Charles Hoffman/*c* Nicholas Musuraca/ *m* Raoul Kraushaar/*lp* Anne Baxter, Richard Conte, Ann Sothern, Raymond Burr, Jeff Donnell.

The Blue Lamp

A landmark in the history of the British crime film, *The Blue Lamp* introduced P.C. George Dixon (Warner), a deferential representative of the authority that the British police force represented well into the 70s, and, in the character of Tom Riley (Bogarde), the violent juvenile delinquent who would dominate British thrillers of the 50s. Bogarde is the leader of a gang of delinquents who when refused help by the criminal underworld turn to armed robbery, in

ABOVE Bruce Seaton, Dirk Bogarde, *The Blue Lamp*

the course of which Dixon is shot. When he dies police and underworld unite to track down Bogarde. But, if the film is rooted in reality – a voice-over at the beginning describes the unsettling effects of the war on modern youth – the attempt to suggest an

unconscious but cohesive community, with even the 'underworld' holding to the same values as the police – seen most memorably in the racetrack sequence where, in the manner of **M**, crooks and police join together to capture Bogarde – remains highly idealistic. More successful is the depiction of the police as a large family, within which new recruit Mitchell (Hanley) finally finds his place. First he becomes a surrogate son to Warner, then is jolted into manhood by his 'father's' death and finally is seen giving directions to a stranger, thus repeating the opening scene in which Warner did the same. Less satisfactory is the film's rejection of the 'sexuality' that Bogarde's gun-fondling youth represents. Unlike the demented characters of **Gun Crazy** who are linked by their attraction to guns, Bogarde's gun fetish seems imposed from without rather than developing from within the character. Moreover, whereas restraint is the order of the day for most of the film – the classic example being the sequence where Hanley tells Warner's wife of Warner's death – the depiction of Bogarde almost suggests that sexuality itself is threatening. This goes someway to explaining why, despite his death in the film, P.C. Dixon and his cheery 'Ev'ning all' was so warmly taken to the collective British heart in the BBC TV series *Dixon Of Dock Green* (1955–76) starring Warner and overseen by Dixon's creator

ABOVE Dirk Bogarde (with mask), Doris Yorke, *The Blue Lamp*

Blue Steel—Bob le flambeur

Willis. Willis also wrote several books about the character. PH

1950/GB/82m/Ealing/*d* Basil Dearden/ *p* Michael Balcon/*s* T. E. B. Clarke/*orig* Jan Read, Ted Willis/*m* Ernest Irving/*c* Gordon Dines/*lp* Jack Warner, Dirk Bogarde, Jimmy Hanley, Robert Flemyng, Peggy Evans, Bernard Lee.

Blue Steel

This uses the woman in jeopardy format, rather in the manner of the slasher films that Curtis made her name in, to explore issues of sexism in the macho world of contemporary policing. Curtis is the rookie cop who shoots a stick-up man in a late-night corner store. Unknown to her the crook's gun is pocketed by a Wall Street dealer who happens to be present. Curtis gets into trouble with her unsupportive superiors because she has apparently shot an unarmed man. Meanwhile bodies start turning up, shot with the missing gun. The audience knows fairly early on that the dealer (Silver) is a serial killer; the tension derives from the fact that he begins an affair with Curtis, who of course is ignorant of his deeds. Will she discover what he is before he decides to dispose of her? Curtis manages to be vulnerable without being feeble, and stout-hearted while remaining sexy. Silver's character is much less clearly defined. But this is a starkly realist cop picture, not the nether-world of Bigelow's previous film, *Near Dark* (1987). EB

1990/102m/Vestron/*p* Edward R. Pressman, Oliver Stone/*d*/*co-s* Kathryn Bigelow/*co-s* Eric Red/*c* Amir Mokri/*m* Brad Fiedel/*lp* Jamie Lee Curtis, Ron Silver, Clancy Brown, Elizabeth Peña, Louise Fletcher.

Blue Thunder

This aerial action picture stars a top secret anti-terrorist helicopter complete with artillery and all manner of high-tech surveillance gadgetry. Veteran LA police helicopter pilot Scheider, his boss Oates, and villain McDowell (the latter involved in a anti-US military conspiracy) play second lead to the title chopper's special effects destruction display. The climactic half-hour in which airborne Scheider and McDowell play a hide-and-seek aerial game among the city's towering buildings is stunning in a cartoon action style way. TV

1983/108m/COL/*p* Gordon Carroll/*d* John Badham/*s* Dan O'Bannon, Don Jakoby/ *c* John A. Alonzo/*m* Arthur B. Rubinstein/

ABOVE Jamie Lee Curtis (centre), *Blue Steel*

lp Roy Scheider, Malcolm McDowell, Warren Oates, Candy Clark.

Blue Velvet

Small town USA, before Civil Rights, Vietnam, and street corner drugs. The idyll is subverted when college student Jeffrey (MacLachlan) finds a severed human ear in a disused lot. Aided by naive schoolgirl Sandy (Dern), he sets out to solve the mystery. Fixating on night-club singer Dorothy Valens (Rossellini), he breaks into her apartment and witnesses her in a bout of violent sado-masochistic sex with Frank Booth (Hopper). Subsequently he clinches with the masochistic Dorothy himself and is tormented by Frank, who is holding her husband and child prisoner to ensure her compliance. Touted as exposing the seamy side of suburban life, the film's plot makes it incredible as social commentary. It is the characters, their performances and the juxtaposition of archaic would-be goodness with vicious and perverted exploitation that gives the film its peculiar charge. Rossellini glows with rotten sweetness, and the heart of the film is a graphic depiction of the unstated and hidden sexual exploitation of the movies and Hollywood itself. MP

1986/120m/DEG/*p* Fred Caruso/*d*/*s* David Lynch/*c* Frederick Elmes/*m* Angelo Badalamenti/*lp* Kyle MacLachlan, Isabella Rossellini, Dennis Hopper, Laura Dern, Dean Stockwell.

Bob le flambeur

Melville's caper film was written in 1950, abandoned after seeing **The Asphalt Jungle** and rewritten, in Melville's words, as a comedy of manners in 1955, when it was shot partly in the director's own studio. Bob (Duchesne), the central character of the story, set in the Paris of 1935, is an ex-crook and inveterate gambler in the casino of Deauville. He has a young male admirer, Paulo (Cauchy), and he gives shelter to Anne (Corey) to save her from prostitution. The two young people fall in love. After a losing streak, Bob meticulously organises the hold-up of the casino, news of which reaches his friend, Inspector Ledru (Decomble). On the actual day, Bob starts gambling and, winning big money, forgets all about the caper, which goes badly wrong and costs Paulo's life. Bob is arrested by Ledru, having won the sum the robbery was meant to yield. The real interest of the film is in Melville's captivating *mise en scène*: his orchestration of bodies in movement in the city's dangerous and lonely spaces, enhanced by Decaë's coolly sensuous lighting and fluid camera. Melville also called it his love letter to Paris, which was followed by a love letter to New York, *Deux hommes dans Manhattan* (1959). PW

1956/France/100m/ O.G.C.-Studios Jenner-Play Art-La Cyme/*p*/*d*/*co-s* Jean-Pierre Melville/*co-s* Auguste Le Breton/*c* Henri Decaë/*m* Eddie Barclay, Jo Boyer/*lp* Isabel

Corey, Roger Duchesne, Daniel Cauchy, Guy Decomble, André Garet.

Body and Soul

As usual in the movies, boxing becomes a metaphor for life, for the struggle between good and evil. Charlie (John Garfield) is a young man from a poor neighbourhood who sees the fight game as a way to get on in life. As he becomes successful he moves away from the family and girl-friend who had sustained him, preferring the company of those who flatter him and who want a share in his career. Eventually it suits their interests for him to throw a fight and Charlie is faced with a choice: either to follow orders and take the money, or to turn back to those who he still knows have his true interests at heart. The boxing scenes are achieved with conviction, and the film carries a powerful social charge, with a meaty central performance by Garfield (who himself had a very rough upbringing), some hard-hitting scripting by Polonsky, and gritty camerawork by James Wong Howe. In the 1950s Garfield, Rossen and Polonsky were all victims of the witchhunt against left-wing film-makers, which effectively ruined all their careers. EB

1947/105m/UA/p Bob Roberts/d Robert Rossen/s Abraham Polonsky/c James Wong Howe/m Hugo Friedhofer/lp John Garfield, Lilli Palmer, Hazel Brooks, Anne Revere, William Conrad.

Body Heat

Kathleen Turner's first starring role was as a *femme fatale* in this homage to the likes of **Double Indemnity**. Matty is married to a rich but boring businessman. She amuses herself in a steamy love affair with Ned (William Hurt), a lawyer in a sleepy little town in Florida. Once she's got him in up to his neck, panting for more, it's easy enough to entice him into her scheme to murder her husband and collect the insurance money. Lawrence Kasdan presses all the right stylistic and narrative buttons: pools of light in the inky darkness, crickets chirping, ceiling fans circulating, dialogue full of innuendo or menace; a wilful woman, a weak man, some hoods who soon demonstrate that the principals are out of their depth when it comes to real criminal intent. But as with Kasdan's Western, *Silverado*, there's a feeling that the cleverness with which the originals are being imitated has become an end in itself, that the film is merely an exhibit, not a living thing powered by real emotions. EB

1981/113m/WB/p Fred T. Gallo/ d/s Lawrence Kasdan/c Richard H. Kline/ m John Barry/lp William Hurt, Kathleen Turner, Richard Crenna, Ted Danson, Mickey Rourke.

Boileau and Narcejac

Pierre (originally named Prosper) Boileau (1906–) and Pierre Ayraud (1908–), the lat-ter adopting the pseudonym Thomas Narcejac, are the most prolific and famous French crime-writing team. Boileau is reportedly the one with the outlandish and romantic imagination, while Narcejac is better known as the team's stylist as well as an accomplished theorist of the crime novel. Having established themselves each in his own right before becoming co-authors (they collaborate by correspondence) and rising to fame in the 1950s, they became immensely popular and their work was often used as the source for somewhat macabre thrillers in film and television. Boileau had his first success in the 1930s with a series of **Sherlock Holmes** pastiches featuring Inspector André Brunel, while Narcejac wrote more classical thrillers in the 1940s. In his *Esthétique du Roman Policier* (1947), Narcejac criticised North American thrillers for abandoning what he regarded as the genre's key: the exploration of the darker sides of reason, substituting instead physical action and an underlying sense of conformism. Boileau responded to Narcejac's analysis and together they set out to demonstrate how it should be done. The result was *Celle qui n'était plus* (1952), adapted by Clouzot as **Les Diaboliques**. They continued with *Les visages dans l'ombre* (1953; filmed by David Eady as *Faces in the Dark*, 1960), *D'entre les morts* (1954; filmed by Alfred Hitchcock as **Vertigo**), *Les Louves* (1955; filmed by Luis Saslavsky in 1956), *Le Mauvais Oeil* (1956), *Les Magiciennes* (1957; filmed by Serge Friedmann in 1959), *L'Ingénieur aimait trop les chiffres* (1958), *A Coeur perdu* (1959; filmed by Etienne Périer as *Meurtre en 45 tours* in 1960), *Maléfices* (1961; filmed by Henri Decoin in 1961), *Madonne* (1962; filmed by Sergio Gobbi in 1968), *Les Victimes* (1964), *Et mon tout est un homme* (1965), *Le train bleu s'arrête treize fois* (short stories, 1966, also a television series), *La mort a dit: peut-être* (1967), *La Porte du large* and *Delirium* (both 1969), *Les Veufs* (1970), *Manigances* (short stories, 1971) and many others. The duo also contributed a number of film scripts, some original, some adapted from other writers, for Georges Rouquier's *SOS Noronha* (1956) and *Un témoin dans la ville* (1958), Geza Radvanyi's *Douze heures d'horloge* (1958), Georges Franju's *Les yeux sans visage* (1959) and *Pleins feux sur l'assassin* (1960), Gérard Oury's *Le crime ne paie pas* (1961) and so on. While their contemporaries in the late 1940s and 1950s were fascinated by an imaginary America, Boileau and Narcejac are credited with having helped to create the template

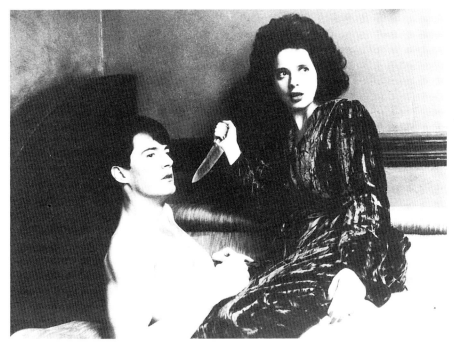

ABOVE Kyle MacLachlan, Isabella Rossellini, *Blue Velvet*

ABOVE George Murphy, Howard Da Silva, Charles McGraw, *Border Incident*

for an indigenously French subgenre of the *policier*, combining the domestic melodrama and the thriller genres, mostly via stories set in the provinces (few of their novels are set in Paris, although Boileau was firmly rooted in Pigalle), stressing the mental-psychological dimension of coolly calculated and diabolically engineered crimes revolving around the greed, corruption and, above all, the hypocrisy of the indigenous bourgeoisie. PW

See also **Policier**.

Bonfire of the Vanities

Costing over $45 million and based on Tom Wolfe's best-seller, this De Palma production collapsed under the weight of its own reputation. Hanks is the unsympathetic Wall Street mover who, with his mistress (Griffith), is involved in a hit-and-run accident that accelerates into a legal and political circus. The enigmatic Willis comes into the fray as an alcoholic newspaperman who makes a personal success out of telling the story of Hanks's misfortune. An overlong story populated by obnoxious people and, for the most part, by events that remain (to the viewer) happily someone else's problem. TV

1990/125m/WB/*p*/*d* Brian De Palma/ *s* Michael Cristofer/*c* Vilmos Zsigmond/ *m* Dave Grusin/*lp* Tom Hanks, Bruce Willis, Melanie Griffith.

La Bonne Année/Happy New Year

Lelouch returned to the crime genre (he had made *Le Voyou* in 1970) to contrast the cynical 1970s with the 'innocent' mid-60s, when he had an international hit with the love story *Un homme et une femme* (1966), bemoaning the intervening emergence of 'women's liberation'. Prior to his release on New Year's eve from a 6-year prison sentence, Simon (Ventura) watches Lelouch's earlier film. He locates his former lover, Françoise (Fabian), who has become a cold and calculating woman who selects her own lovers, and his ex-partner in crime, Charles (Gérard), to obtain his share of the loot from a jewel robbery, shown in flashback. In the end, a disillusioned but rich Simon resigns himself to living with the intellectually superior Françoise. Expertly acted by Ventura and shot entirely with a portable camera, the film exudes a sense of sour nostalgia for the time when women allegedly were happy to conform to men's pubertal fantasies. PW

1973/France/115m/Les Films 13-Rizzoli Films/*p*/*d*/*co-s* Claude Lelouch/*co-s* Pierre Uytterhoeven/*m* Francis Lai/*lp* Lino Ventura, Françoise Fabian, Charles Gérard, André Falcon, Silvano Tranquilli.

Bonnie and Clyde

Bonnie and Clyde did for the gangster movie what *Butch Cassidy and the Sundance Kid*

(1969) would later do to the Western, focusing on the free-spirited but doomed outlaw activities of two beautiful, stylish people who can't quite bring themselves to have a sexual relationship. Beatty's alienated, impotent, pin-striped Clyde Barrow and Dunaway's awkwardly aware, 60s cover girl-beautiful, beret-and-skirt Bonnie Parker are, within and without the frame of the film, fashion-setting icons of cool. They constantly pose for pictures or strike attitudes copied from movies. With soft-focus cinematography and fast-picking banjo score, evoking the hard times of the Depression for jokey nostalgia (as when the gang try to hold-up a bank only to find it has gone out of business), the film is at its best when the comedy is subtly darkened. The sudden switch from slapstick to splatter as a bungled robbery turns violent when a bystander is shot in the face is much less unnerving than the scene in which the desperadoes hijack nervous Gene Wilder's car and take the quivering young man and his date on a wild ride which Wilder somehow finds as exhilarating as it is scary. Influential in its treatment of specific historical crimes (and triggering a wave of direct imitations like Roger Corman's **Bloody Mama**) as well as in its self-consciously ironic take on gangster chic and use of explicit violence, *Bonnie and Clyde* remains an attitude rather than a film. KN

1967/111m/WB/*p* Warren Beatty/*d* Arthur Penn/*s* David Newman, Robert Benton/ *c* Burnett Guffey/*m* Charles Strouse/ *lp* Warren Beatty, Faye Dunaway, Michael J. Pollard, Gene Hackman, Estelle Parsons, Denver Pyle.

Border Incident

US and Mexican immigration authorities join forces and go undercover to catch a gang running illegal Mexican immigrants into California, where unscrupulous employers pay them starvation wages. It's a tense and tough picture, with a particularly brutal scene in which the gang murder George Murphy by ploughing him into a field. Da Silva enjoys himself as the sneering Parkson, leader of the gang, equally contemptuous of the authorities and his own men. Politically ahead of its time in its sympathetic treatment of the exploited Mexicans (Montalban and Murphy as the Mexican and American heroes are given equal time and weight), the film is also one of the masterpieces of *noir* photography. John Alton knew no equal in the use of low-key lighting, and in a film

ABOVE Jean-Paul Belmondo, Alain Delon, *Borsalino*

hired the consummately professional action director Deray for the film and François de Lamothe, set designer for **Le Samouraï**, provided the exuberantly fetishistic art direction. The movie started a new fashion in headgear in Paris. Michel Nerval made a crude parody of this pastiche, starring an aged Darry Cowl, *Les Borsalini* (1979). PW

1970/France, Italy/126m/Adel-Marianne-Mars/*p* Alain Delon/*d/co-s* Jacques Deray/*co-s* Jean-Claude Carrière, Claude Sautet, Jean Cau/*orig* Eugène Saccomano *Bandits à Marseille/c* Jean-Jacques Tarbes/*m* Claude Bolling/*lp* Alain Delon, Jean-Paul Belmondo, Michel Bouquet, Catherine Rouvel, Françoise Christophe, Arnoldo Foà.

The Boston Strangler

From the director of **Compulsion**, which was about the Leopold and Loeb case, this movie, based on the psychopathic career of Albert DeSalvo, was far more influential than it seemed at the time. In it Fleischer pioneered the tactics later used in TV docudramas like *Helter Skelter* (1976), *Fatal Vision* (1984), *Out of the Darkness* (1985), *The Atlanta Child Murders* (1985), *The Deliberate Stranger* (1986), *The Case of the Hillside Stranglers* (1989) and *To Catch a Killer* (1991). Distinguished actors play figures in the case with dignified restraint and the 'story'

which takes place largely at night director Anthony Mann gives him his head. EB

1949/93m/MGM/*p* Nicholas Nayfack/*d* Anthony Mann/*s* John C. Higgins/*c* John Alton/*m* André Previn/*lp* Ricardo Montalban, George Murphy, Howard Da Silva, James Mitchell, Alfonso Bedoya.

Borsalino

The late 1920s Marseille criminals Carbonne and Spirito were the models for this highly lucrative encounter of France's two male superstars in 1930s costume having fun with the buddy-movie genre. The chaotic comedy plot, stuffed with set pieces, has Siffredi (Delon) emerge from prison to find his girl

Lola (Rouvel) in the arms of Capella (Belmondo). After some physical interaction between the two men, they begin to prefer each other's company and set out to conquer Marseille's underworld. They eliminate the reigning hoods (Bollet, Foà and Bouquet) one after the other, culminating in a shootout in a sumptuous gambling club. The duo realise the town isn't big enough for the both of them and Capella plans to leave with Lola but he is gunned down under the very eyes of his bosom buddy. The grief stricken Siffredi disappears, never to be seen again . . . until the sequel, *Borsalino & Co* (1974). Delon

RIGHT Tony Curtis, *The Boston Strangler*

advances in fits and starts which simulate the messy actual progression of the real-life events. The film contains a moving (if questionable) performance from Curtis as a basically decent man as puzzled by the atrocities he has committed as anyone else, and cleverly adopts split-screen techniques to suggest the gradual accumulation of detail presented in Frank's best-selling journalistic account. Though there are some strangely comic sequences – an attempt by psychic Peter Hurkos (George Voskovec) to solve the case, the reactions of cops on the case to the kinks of their suspects – the tone is mainly sober and intense to the point where resemblance to a thriller fades. KN

1968/116m/FOX/*p* Robert Fryer/*d* Richard Fleischer/*s* Edward Anhalt/*orig* Gerold Frank/*c* Richard H. Kline/*m* Lionel Newman/*lp* Henry Fonda, Tony Curtis, George Kennedy, Mike Kellin, Murray Hamilton, Hurd Hatfield.

Le Boucher/The Butcher

Chabrol immediately followed his successful **Que la bête meure** with this intense thriller again starring Yanne and Audran, the director's wife and star of **La Femme infidèle**. These three films constitute the highlight of France's contribution to the thriller genre. After soldiering for 15 years to escape his domineering father, Popaul returns to his village in the Perigord and takes over the butcher shop. He falls in love with the school teacher, Hélène (Audran), but she isn't ready for a relationship yet and their love remains unconsummated. Then two gruesome sex murders happen and Hélène finds out Popaul is the maniac but she remains quiet about it. In the end,

ABOVE Barbara Hershey, Barry Primus, *Boxcar Bertha*

locked in her school, she is confronted by Popaul and his butcher's knife. However, he uses it on himself and confesses his love for her as she drives him to hospital where he dies. Taking his cue from Hitchcock, about whom he wrote a book, Chabrol uses a lighter as the trigger of the suspense: Hélène gives it to Popaul, then finds it next to a corpse and puts it in her purse, where Popaul notices it, which prompts him to go and see Hélène in the school. Yanne and Audran's wonderfully subtle performances are matched by the sensuous cinematography and Chabrol's mischievously misanthropic yet romantic direction. PW

1970/France, Italy/94m/La Boétie-Euro-International/*p* André Genovès/*d*/*s* Claude Chabrol/*c* Jean Rabier/*m* Pierre Jansen/*lp* Jean Yanne, Stéphane Audran, Antonio Passalia, Roger Rudel, Mario Beccara.

Boxcar Bertha

This was one of the cycle of movies about Depression-era criminals which followed the box-office triumph of **Bonnie and Clyde**, and whose depiction of outlawry was

LEFT Jean Yanne, Stéphane Audran, *Le Boucher*

deemed to chime in with the then current counter-culture values. Set in Arkansas, it tells the story of Bertha Thompson (Hershey), who mounts a vendetta against the railroad company which caused her father's death. Of her three male cohorts (Carradine, Primus, Casey), the first two have been her lovers, but it is to Carradine, a radical union activist rejected by union officialdom, that she forms a commitment. They stage a string of successful robberies, causing the railroad to bring in ruthless manhunters. This leads to the death of Primus and the arrest of the other two men, with Bertha left to drift into prostitution. In an epilogue, she is reunited with Carradine, only for the railroad's thugs to seize him and crucify him on a boxcar. Scorsese's first Hollywood venture, the picture has a quickfire surface, and cleverly juggles moods between humour, lyricism and bursts of savage action. John Carradine puts in an imposing cameo appearance as the cynically imperturbable railroad baron. TP

1972/88m/A-I/*p* Roger Corman/*d* Martin Scorsese/*s* Joyce H. Corrington, John William Corrington/*c* John Stephens/*m* Gib Guilbeau, Thad Maxwell/*lp* Barbara Hershey, David Carradine, Barry Primus, Bernie Casey, John Carradine.

Boxing

There have been crime films dealing with baseball (*Eight Men Out*, 1988), horse racing (*Dead Cert*, 1974), soccer (*The Arsenal Stadium Mystery*, 1939) and American football (*The Last Boy Scout*, 1991), but no sport has been as associated with illegality in the cinema as often as boxing. Major films include *The Champ* (1931), *Iron Man* (1931), *Kid Galahad* (1937), *The Crowd Roars* (1938), *Golden Boy* (1939), *Killer McCoy* (1947), *Champion* (1949), *Right Cross* (1950), *The Ring* (1952), *The Square Ring* (1955), *The Square Jungle* (1955), **The Harder They Fall**, *The Great White Hope* (1970), *Rocky* (1976), *Penitentiary* (1979), *Streets of Gold* (1986), *Homeboy* (1988) and *Diggstown/Midnight Sting* (1992), which feature fixed fights, corrupt gamblers, broken-down losers, short-lived champions, brutal beatings in and out of the ring, smelly locker rooms, punch-drunk ex-pugs, manipulative managers and a general air of sleaze, desperation and misery. The international glitz of the later *Rocky* sequels is atypical. That said, the concluding *Rocky V* (1991) has the hero returning to the Philadelphia slum he came from.

Somebody Up There Likes Me (1956) is unusual in that it depicts boxing as a positive influence, showing the redemption of small-time hood Rocky Graziano (Paul Newman) when he capitalises on his talent for pugilism. This is similar to the path followed by Sylvester Stallone's Rocky when the revitalising of his career in *Rocky II* (1978) means that he does not have to take a job as a strong-arm man for a loan shark. More familiar are the trajectories of John Garfield in **Body and Soul**, Robert Ryan in *The Set-Up* (1949) and Stacy Keach in *Fat City* (1972), whose careers are compromised by criminals and who go out as losers even if they win. Garfield wins the fight he is supposed to throw and defiantly goes to his probable death after the credits, while Ryan is so hopeless his manager doesn't even bother to tell him he is supposed to lose and, after a brief moment of glory when he wins his third-rate bout, is hunted down and killed by gangsters. In *Triumph of the Spirit* (1989), Willem Dafoe, who does his boxing in a concentration camp, hardly seems to have things *worse* than any other screen pug. The patron saint of these losers is Marlon Brando's Terry in **On the Waterfront**, who 'coulda been a contender' and whose mumbled big speech is powerfully and ironically

RIGHT Boxing: Robert De Niro, *Raging Bull*

reprised by Jake LaMotta (Robert De Niro) in *Raging Bull* (1980). The best movie about the inhumanity of the fight game, *Raging Bull* is unique in its concentration on the degrading violence that takes place inside the ring rather than any criminal activities that go on in the boxing world. A rare ex-pug hero is Tom Berenger in *Fear City* (1984), who uses his pugilist skills to confront a psychopathic kung fu killer. *Hard Times/The Streetfighter* (1975), *Bloodsport* (1987) and *Gladiator* (1991) take place in the world of illegal, no-rules, no-gloves boxing. All climax with excessively violent slug-fests. KN

Brannigan

With *McQ* (1974) and this film, made in London, Wayne briefly switched away from the Westerns which dominated the latter phase of his career and into cop movies. Both pictures bear the thematic influence of the Clint Eastwood vehicles **Coogan's Bluff** and **Dirty Harry**, a wholly appropriate influence given that Eastwood had just assumed Wayne's box-office mantle. The plot concerns a 'maverick' protagonist seeking to confront the potential disparity between law and justice. Wayne is the Chicago cop who arrives to extradite a drug

ABOVE Unknown, William Hartnell, Richard Attenborough, Nigel Stock, *Brighton Rock*

trafficker (Vernon), only to find that he has apparently been kidnapped by rival mobsters, and thus sets out on his own unofficial course of investigation. Superficially it is well managed, with set pieces staged in Piccadilly Circus and on London Bridge, but plausibility is not the movie's strong suit, either in details of plotting or in the anomaly of Wayne at his age being one of Chicago's finest. Similarly cavalier is the attitude to London geography, whereby a flat in a side street behind the Albert Hall can boast a panoramic view of the Thames. TP

1975/111m/UA/*p* Arthur Gardner, Jules Levy/*d* Douglas Hickox/*s* Christopher Trumbo, Michael Butler, William P. McGivern, William Norton/*c* Gerry Fisher/*m* Dominic Frontiere/*lp* John Wayne, Richard Attenborough, Judy Geeson, John Vernon, Mel Ferrer.

Brigada criminal

Together with the Catalonian Julio Salvador's **Apartado de correos 1001**, who set his action in Barcelona, Iquino's film, set in Madrid, inaugurated a Spanish version of *film noir*. Like Salvador, Iquino resorted to extensive location shooting to tell of Fernando, a fresh graduate from the police academy who stumbles upon a bank robbery. His chief regards him as too inexperienced to investigate the crime and assigns him to a case of petty larceny in a garage. Fernando obeys his chief but finds that, coincidentally, his garage assignment leads him to the boss of the hold-up gang. The moral of the story is that success can be achieved by strictly obeying one's hierarchical superiors. The merit of the film is in its style: fast-paced, atmospherically shot in Madrid's streets with a climax set on a building site, which yields powerful images but also highlights the point about obedience and nation-building. Iquino went on to produce another cop film, *Los agentes del Quinto Grupo* (1954), directed by Ricardo Gascón, and the thriller **El ojo de cristal**, directed by Antonio Santillán. PW

1950/Spain/77m/IFI/*p*/*d*/*co-s* Ignacio F. Iquino/*co-s* Juan Ladó, Manuel Bengoa/*orig* José Santugini/*c* Pablo Ripoll, Antonio García, Pedro Rovira/*m* Augusto Alguero/*lp* José Suarez, Alfonso Estela, Manuel Gas, Soledad Lance, Pedro de Córdova.

Brighton Rock/Young Scarface

Like Howard Hawks's Scarface, Greene and Attenborough's Pinkie is more than a mere monster: he is a man obsessed, a man whose fixation fuels his frenetic activity and gives him power over others. Pinkie's fears of the fires of hell and his knowledge that he is damned enable the adolescent to dominate his gang of racecourse thieves and woo Marsh's innocent waitress (who, unwitting, could send him to the gallows). This dynamic centre gives added weight to Waxman's splendid depiction of the seedy, purgatorial splendour of post-war Brighton. The simple plot has Attenborough and his gang first chase and then kill Wheatley, who killed their former boss, only for their plan that his death look like suicide to be thwarted by Baddeley's tart with a heart of gold and Marsh's put-upon waitress. Attenborough, with evident distaste, courts Marsh, then marries her while Baddeley chases after the pair attempting to make the love-lorn Marsh see sense. To escape Attenborough proposes a suicide-pact to Marsh, with no intention of killing himself, only for the police, led by Baddeley to arrive at the last minute. Attenborough is splendid as the adolescent gang-leader who rules through a bizarre mix of tantrums and native wit, as is Marsh as the Madonna on the half-shell and Baddeley as an avenging angel who delivers the film's chilling message: 'People don't change. It's like those sticks of rock, bite one all the way down, you'll still read Brighton. That's human nature'. Greene's description of the film's end – Marsh goes home after Attenborough's death, still in love with him and intending to prove his love for her by playing the disc he has cut, on which he told her he declares his love for her but in fact denounces her as a bitch – as being 'the

ABOVE Richard Attenborough, *Brighton Rock*

worst horror of all' has been much quoted. But its meaning remains unclear: certainly Marsh's Rose is the only character in the film who is granted the possibility of change and growth. PH

1947/GB/92m/Associated British/*p* Roy Boulting/*d* John Boulting/*s* Graham Greene, Terence Rattigan/*orig* Graham Greene/ *c* Harry Waxman/*m* Hans May/*lp* Richard Attenborough, Hermione Baddeley, William Hartnell, Carol Marsh, Alan Wheatley, Harcourt Williams.

The Brink's Job

The robbery of the Brink's headquarters in Boston in 1950 netted a then-record $2.7 million and for a while became a *cause célèbre*. Surprisingly, given the commercial success of Friedkin's realist **The French Connection**, this film treats the planning and execution of the heist in terms of broad (if not very funny) comedy. The band of professional criminals responsible are shown as bungling incompetents, whose success is due more to luck than judgment, and it is unsurprising that little suspense is generated along the way. By this account, nemesis belatedly descends on the robbers when one of the more unbalanced of their number (Oates) is arrested on an unrelated charge and proceeds to spill the beans. Leonard plays a cartoon version of FBI chief J. Edgar Hoover, who lost no time after the robbery in proclaiming it the work of Communists. TP

1978/103m/U/*p* Ralph Serpe/*d* William Friedkin/*s* Walon Green/*c* Norman Leigh/ *m* Richard Rodney Bennett/*lp* Peter Falk, Peter Boyle, Warren Oates, Gena Rowlands, Sheldon Leonard.

Brother Orchid

This light-hearted gangster story produced in the familiar Warner Bros. fashion stars Robinson as a 'reformed gangster', not too distant from his earlier role in *A Slight Case of Murder* (1938). Here, Robinson abdicates as a mob boss, leaving Bogart to take over, and when he decides to return to assume control he barely survives Bogart's assassination attempt. Recuperating in a monastery, he begins to enjoy the monks' quiet way of life. The story builds to Robinson (now known as Brother Orchid) rallying some visiting ranchers in defeating Bogart's protection gang. Ann Sothern as Robinson's ditzy moll delivers some clever comic moments. TV

1940/88m/WB/*p* Mark Hellinger/*d* Lloyd Bacon/*s* Earl Baldwin/*c* Tony Gaudio/

m Heinz Roemheld/*lp* Edward G. Robinson, Ann Sothern, Humphrey Bogart, Donald Crisp.

The Brotherhood

This merits a small footnote in movie history as the first Hollywood film, barring movies with period settings such as *Pay Or Die* (1960), to allude to the mafia by name. Otherwise, despite prestigious credits, this vehicle for Kirk Douglas, which ends on the masochistic note seen in some of the actor's more notable roles, is a pedestrian affair. The episodic narrative focuses on relations between Douglas and his younger brother, woodenly played by Cord. Contrary to generic expectations, the older man is only too glad to welcome his sibling into the executive ranks of the mafia's New York operations, but Douglas's pursuit of a personal vendetta against a fellow board member turns him into an outcast. He flees to Sicily, but Cord is sent after him. When the brothers come face to face, Douglas, knowing full well the risk to Cord's family if he disobeys instructions, insists that the sentence be carried out. TP

1968/98m/PAR/*p* Kirk Douglas/*d* Martin Ritt/*s* Lewis John Carlino/*c* Boris Kaufman/ *m* Lalo Schifrin/*lp* Kirk Douglas, Alex Cord, Luther Adler, Susan Strasberg, Eduardo Ciannelli.

The Brothers Rico

Among the 50s crime movies predicated upon the activities of a nationwide crime syndicate, *The Brothers Rico* is distinctive in demonstrating the pervasiveness of its criminal empire through the paradoxical principle of near-invisibility. In keeping with this, the movie's style is for the most part almost eerily understated and matter-of-fact, with virtually no overt violence until the end, and the effect is underscored by the casting as the syndicate kingpin of the smoothly avuncular Larry Gates, an actor more readily associated with lawyers or family friends. The narrative turns on Eddie (Conte), a successful businessman whose bygone debt to the 'organisation' is called in when he is enlisted to find his missing brother. Too late, he realises that this is to enable the mob to rub out his brother, a potential witness against them. In the source novel (by Georges Simenon) Eddie bows to the inevitability of this discovery, but in the film he becomes an avenger, eluding the syndicate's ubiquitous agents and finally putting paid to Gates in a shoot-out amid the

emblematic surroundings of Eddie's mother's home in New York's Little Italy. TP

1957/92m/COL/*p* Lewis J. Rachmil/*d* Phil Karlson/*s* Lewis Meltzer, Ben Perry/*c* Burnett Guffey/*m* George Duning/*lp* Richard Conte, Dianne Foster, Larry Gates, James Darren, Kathryn Grant.

Brown, Fredric (1906–72)

A newspaper man turned mystery writer and science fiction writer (to alleviate, he is reported as saying , the 'too real' aspects of detective fiction) Brown wrote briefly for Alfred Hitchcock's television series in the 50s. There his clever, tricksy plots were highly valued. In the main, however, his novels were too odd for Hollywood. *Crack-Up* (Irving Reis, 1946), based on his short story *Madman's Holiday*, has a typical Brown plot. An art expert is drugged and given false experiences so that his expertise will not be trusted by the authorities and thus allow a gang to get away with substituting forgeries for masterpieces at the art gallery he works at. More brutal and direct is **Screaming Mimi**, a variant on the beauty and the beast myth with Phil Carey and Anita Ekberg. Jean-Pierre Mocky directed an intriguing version of *Knock Three-One-Two* (as *L'Ibis rouge*, 1975), the story of a liquor salesman who watches a killer as he terrorises a city. PH

Brute Force

'No women, no crooked district attorneys' was Don Siegel's admiring response to first reading the script of his *Riot in Cell Block 11* (1954), and though *Brute Force*, the most significant and influential post-war prison movie prior to Siegel's film, does not take the commercial risk of excluding women from its cast, their presence is confined to a series of flashbacks. While these may, strictly speaking, be extraneous, their predominantly sentimental tone helps to point up the romantic liberalism which underpins Brooks's screenplay. The narrative centres on a plan to break out by a group of convicts (Lancaster and Duff prominent among them) working in the 'drainpipe', a construction project outside the jail, and on the brutal manipulation of the inmates by the sadistic captain of the guard (a chilling portrayal by Cronyn). Dassin described the episode in which Cronyn interrogates and beats a prisoner as having been shot to resemble a love scene. The violent climax, depicting the thwarting of the escape, was in its day considered extreme, and culminates

ABOVE Jack Overman, John Hoyt, Whit Bissell, Jeff Corey, Burt Lancaster, *Brute Force*
BELOW *Brute Force*

in the nihilistic image of the potential gate to freedom jammed shut by the force of a truck which one of the escapers has in desperation used to try to smash through it. TP

1947/95m/U/*p* Mark Hellinger/*d* Jules Dassin/*s* Richard Brooks/*c* William Daniels/*m* Miklos Rozsa/*lp* Burt Lancaster, Hume Cronyn, Howard Duff, Yvonne De Carlo, Ann Blyth.

Buchan, John (1875–1940)

Buchan was a diplomat – he was appointed governor-general of Canada – publisher – he was a partner in Thomas Nelson & Son and was responsible for publishing E.C. Bentley's *Trent's Last Case* in 1913 – and writer. Most of Buchan's literary output was biographical and historical writing but it is the rough vigour of his adventure stories that he is remembered for. His most enduring creation is Richard Hannay, introduced in *The 39 Steps* (1915) and the hero of *Greenmantle* (1916) and *The Three Hostages* (1924). Hannay also appears in *Mr Standfast* (1919). A 'man's man' – he was based on Buchan's military idol, Edmund 'Tiny' Ironside, later a Field-Marshal – in the novels Hannay criss-crosses

ABOVE John Buchan

Europe in service of the British Empire but it is in the Scottish Highlands, observed by Buchan with precision and detachment rather than sentimentality, that he is most at home and at risk. Hannay's values are nationalistic and right-wing. *The 39 Steps* was filmed memorably by Hitchcock with Robert Donat as Hannay in 1935, less successfully in 1959 with Kenneth More. In 1978 it was filmed with Robert Powell, for the first time being set, as was the novel, during World War I. Powell also starred in the UK tele-series *Hannay*. PH

Bugsy Malone

Parker's feature debut, this is an engaging tale of gang warfare. The twist is that all the cast are children and their splurge, i.e. machine-guns, fire a creamy mush, instead of bullets. The movie holds fast to the conventions of the genre – the **night-club** as Fat Sam's HQ, the dandified dress of the combatants, the use of headlines and news flashes to propel the story, and even the opening sequence with its weary voice-over – thus confirming how flexible genres can be when joshing rather than **parody** is the name of the game. Similarly, as several critics have noted, the plot could have been borrowed from a wayward Warners 30s film. Fat Sam (Cassisi) and Dandy Dan (Lev) are the rival gangleaders seeking control of New York, Tallulah (Foster) the gangster's moll, Blousey Brown (Dugger) the ingenue dreaming of a Hollywood career and Bugsy (Baio) the pragmatic dreamer. On occasion the plot's

shenanigans are given too glossy a treatment – as when the film dawdles at Dandy Dan's – but the cast eschew sentimentality as does Paul Williams in the catchy songs he wrote for the film and sings. The undoubted stars are the imported Americans, Baio and Foster. A mark of the film's success is the exasperation it evokes in many parents who have sat through the video too many times with their children, its translation to the London stage and the numerous TV commercials that have borrowed its central idea. PH

1976/GB/93m/*p* Alan Marshall/*d/s* Alan Parker/*c* Michael Seresin, Peter Biziou/ *m* Paul Williams/*lp* Scott Baio, Jodie Foster, Florrie Dugger, John Cassisi, Martin Lev, Paul Murphy.

ABOVE Jodie Foster, John Cassisi, *Bugsy Malone*
BELOW Prepare to be splurged: *Bugsy Malone*

ABOVE Dan Duryea, *The Burglar*

Bullitt

When a Chicago hood-turned-witness is exploited for publicity by an attention-seeking Assistant D.A. (Vaughn) and killed by ex-associates, this cues conflict between the cop (McQueen) who was guarding the dead man and the D.A., with justice and individual cool set against expedience and corporate creepiness. Adapted from a solid but conventional 1963 police procedural, *Bullitt* set the tone for the cop movies of the 70s and into the 80s. The hero is a lonely man of integrity, virile with his vacuous girl-friend (Bisset), with a commitment to frontier values that shades into neurosis and semi-vigilante tactics, a man well on his way to becoming Clint Eastwood's Lieutenant Harry Callahan. The setting is a San Francisco filmed by Fraker with all the tricks of *nouvelle vague* then filtering into Hollywood through counterculture movies like *The Graduate* (1967) and *Petulia* (1968). Also symptomatic of the time and the style are Lalo Schifrin's jazzy, endlessly imitated TV-theme-tune-style score and Vaughn's pre-Watergate villain, marked as less worthy than McQueen because his suits are squarer. The set piece of the film is the car chase around the hills and freeways of San Francisco that has little to do with the plot but which serves, like the grittier automotive action of **The French Connection**, as a talking point to bring people into cinemas and as the most potent set of images they would take out. KN

1968/113m/WB/*p* Philip D'Antoni/*d* Peter Yates/*s* Alan R. Trustman, Harry Kleiner/ *orig* Robert L. Pike *Mute Witness*/*c* William A. Fraker/*m* Lalo Schifrin/*lp* Steve McQueen, Robert Vaughn, Jacqueline Bisset, Don Gordon, Robert Duvall, Simon Oakland.

The Burglar

The only screen adaptation of a **David Goodis** novel to be scripted by the author, *The Burglar* was a low-budget production marking the directing debut of Paul Wendkos, and has a stylistic self-consciousness which suggests it was intended as a 'calling card' to the industry. Downbeat as well as offbeat, the picture opens with an elaborate sequence of a jewel robbery at the home of a rich eccentric, then centres on the mutual dependence between the ageing criminal (Duryea) who has masterminded it and his young ward (Mansfield), daughter of his mentor. An attempted double-cross by Duryea's lover (Vickers) and a crooked policeman leads to the latter taking Mansfield hostage; the scene shifts to out-of-season Atlantic City, where the pier and amusement arcades provide suitably expressionistic surroundings for the descent of nemesis, and at the final fade-out Duryea is dead and his adversary in police hands. Soon afterwards, Wendkos made *The Case Against Brooklyn* (1958), an adept example of the factually-based crime exposé. TP

1956/90m/COL/*p* Louis W. Kellman/*d* Paul Wendkos/*s* David Goodis/*c* Don Malkames/ *m* Sol Kaplan/*lp* Dan Duryea, Martha Vickers, Jayne Mansfield, Mickey Shaughnessy, Stewart Bradley.

Burma, Nestor

An anarchic, vulgar, slang-speaking private eye invented by the novelist Léo Malet, writing also under the pen-name Frank Harding. Burma, the hero of France's first private eye novels, was intended as a transposition of the American *Black Mask Stories*. The first of the novels appeared under the German occupation and was filmed by Jacques Daniel-Norman as **120 rue de la gare**, starring René Dary as Burma, except that, unlike Burma, Dary smoked cigarettes instead of a pipe, for fear of reminding audiences of Maigret. The next film was by the celebrated theorist and historian of the cinema, as well as a co-founder of the French *cinémathèque*, Jean Mitry: *Enigme aux Folies-Bergères* (1959, starring Frank Villard). Unfortunately, the film is utterly devoid of interest and remained Mitry's sole feature film. Burma appeared again in Bob Swaim's *La Nuit de Saint Germain-des-Prés* (1977, starring Michel Galabru) and in Jean-Luc Miesch's *Nestor Burma Détective de choc* (1982, starring Michel Serrault and with a guest appearance of Léo Malet as a newspaper vendor). Burma provided the template for many popular argot-spouting figures in French *policiers*, including the popular San Antonio series. PW

Burnett, W[illiam] R[iley]
(1899–1982)

The author of **Little Caesar**, **High Sierra** and **The Asphalt Jungle**, Burnett was with **Raymond Chandler** and **Dashiell Hammett** one of the most important influences on the development of the US crime movie. In addition, unlike Chandler and Hammett whose importance primarily rested on their novels and stories, Burnett was a hugely successful screenwriter. He also wrote two influential Western novels. Burnett's importance rests not on his prose, which Julian Symons has described as being pedestrian, with Edward G. Robinson's playing of Rico in *Caesar* giving the figure 'style and colour lacking in the novel', but in the seminal models he provided and the enduring icons of the genre. *Caesar* was the first American gangster novel. Equally importantly the action was seen from the gangster's point of view. Written in ringing 'American' so much so that the first UK edition required a three-page glossary, Burnett's tale of the rise and fall of a tough Chicago gangster ushered in a wave of gangster films. *High Sierra*, with its elegiac, forlorn sense of 'rushing to death' (as one of the characters says), signalled the end of a particular era of gangster films and pointed forward to *film noir*. *The Asphalt Jungle* was equally significant. It introduced the **caper film**, signalling the end of the simple free enterprise of Chicago gangsterism and the arrival of crime as a corporate activity ruled by time and complex planning. Following the success of *Caesar* Burnett (who wrote 18 crime novels between 1929 and 1968) turned to scriptwriting. His first was the minor *The Finger Points* (1931) co-written with Monk Saunders. More significant was **Scarface**, to which he contributed. Most of Burnett's scripts, notably *High Sierra*, were co-written with others, initially from his own stories and novels but later also derived from the works of others. In 1942, with Albert Maltz, he adapted Graham Greene's *A Gun For Sale* as **This Gun for Hire**. For Raoul Walsh, a regular director of his scripts, he adapted **Eric Ambler**'s novel *Uncommon Danger* as **Background To Danger** (1943). Other screenplays by him include *The Racket* (1951), *Captain Lightfoot* (1954) from his own story, the Western *Sergeants 3* (1962) and the prisoner of war movie, *The Great Escape* (1963). Other significant films from Burnett's novels and stories include the Westerns *Law and Order* (1932), which treated Wyatt Earp and the Clantons as policemen and gangsters, from the novel *Saint Johnson* (1930), *Dark Command* (1940), from the 1938 novel of the same name, and *Yellow Sky* (1948), plus the gangster comedy *The Whole Town's Talking* (1935) and *Dr. Socrates* (1935). A mark of the influence of *The Asphalt Jungle* is that the film was

RIGHT *Buta To Gunkan*

remade three times, as a Western, *The Badlanders* (1958), as the exotic heist film, *Cairo* (1963) and as the blaxploitation actioneer *Cool Breeze* (1972). Similarly *High Sierra* was remade by Raoul Walsh as a Western (*Colorado Territory*, 1949) and later in 1955 with a script by Burnett as *I Died a Thousand Times*. PH

Buta To Gunkan/Hogs and Warships

This, Imamura's fifth feature, combines a documentary realism with an acute sense of the grotesque, a mixture that would become the hallmark of his work. In the slums near a US naval base shortly after World War II people try to survive through prostitution, petty larceny and racketeering. The local mob, forced to close its brothel, turns to raising pigs fed on the base's waste products. When the gang splits into rival groups, one lot try to truck the pigs to the slaughterhouse while the others try to prevent it. When the young hero (Nagato) learns that he has been set up as a scapegoat in a deal between the rival groups, he releases the

pigs into the streets and starts emptying his machine gun wildly, destroying the neon facades of the red light district before, mortally wounded, he crawls into a toilet to die. Although melodramatic in places, the film has an operatic visual flair, allowing a wall-size photograph of a US destroyer to dominate the scope screen and creating a hallucinatory tragi-comedy as the pigs rampage through the narrow city streets, crushing people to the accompaniment of a machine gun battle. The film conveys a sense of pent-up anger, neatly summarising the intolerable conditions of life in a scene where a group of ruffians realise that the stew they are eating contains the remains of one of their victims whose corpse couldn't be disposed of in any other way. PW

1961/Japan/108m/Nikkatsu/*p* Yukihara Moriyama/*d*/*co-s* Shohei Imamura/*co-s* Hisachi Yamauchi/*c* Shinsaku Himeda/*m* Toshiro Mayuzumi/*lp* Hiroyuki Nagato, Jitsuko Yoshimura, Mitzi Mori, Tetsuro Tamba, Takeshi Kato.

C

Cain, James M[allahan]
(1892–1977)
Cain's tales of tortured, mostly proletarian, passion written with ragged economy and psychological insight were an enduring influence on the development of the American crime film. Major films from his novels include **Double Indemnity** (story 1943), **Mildred Pierce** (novel 1941), **The Postman Always Rings Twice** and **Ossessione** (novel 1934), *Serenade* (novel 1937, film 1956) and *Slightly Scarlet* (1956, novel *Love's Lovely Counterfeit*, 1942). Ironically his 17-year stay in Hollywood as a screenwriter (1931–48) was not a success; he only secured writing credits on three films. Moreover, Cain was very critical of Hollywood's treatment of writers. He denounced the films of *Mildred Pierce* and *Love's Lovely Counterfeit* for the changes made from his novels and set up the short-lived American Authors' Society to seek better deals for authors from the studios. Raymond Chandler, who scripted *Double Indemnity*, reportedly said Cain's major failing *qua* Hollywood was that his dialogue read well but did not speak well. A former journalist, in the 20s Cain started writing stories, which led to his joining Paramount as a screenwriter. Then came the enormous success of *Postman*. Though in

part motivated by its Depression setting, Cain, unlike Theodore Dreiser, was little interested in social criticism. His characters were more elemental. Generally written from the protagonist's point of view his novels were tales of men tempted and then twisted inside out by strong sensual women – often food, violence and sex were linked in key scenes, such as the murder of the husband in *Postman*. Forcefully written, particularly for the period, the novels now seem mannered in comparison to the work of **Jim Thompson**. Certainly several of the later ones (e.g. *Butterfly*, 1947, filmed 1981) are lesser works, well researched but little imagined. What remains powerful are the strong plotlines, which survive the element of fantasy behind the central situations, and their sense of despair, even when this is given a sentimental edge (as in *Serenade*, possibly his most personal novel; he wanted a career as an singer and married an opera singer). That said the number of versions of *Postman* testify to the strong appeal of the central situation, while *Mildred Pierce* is a chilling insight into the self-help ethos of the American psyche. PH

Call Northside 777
This straddles the *noir* and semi-documentary traditions of the late 40s. When reporter McNeal (Stewart) covers the story of a washer-woman who has saved for ten years to put up a reward for information leading to the release of her unjustly imprisoned son Frank Wiecek (Conte), the soft-soap hack transforms the son into a crusading hero. Stewart's battle is not to identify the cop killer whose crimes Wiecek is paying for but to pierce the police bureaucracy which refuses to reconsider its obvious mistake. The case hinges on Wanda Skutnik (Garde), who identified Wiecek in a line-up, and the search for Wanda leads McNeal through a characteristic *noir* montage of seedy bars to an archetypal slum apartment by the elevated railway, where the embittered perjuress refuses to take back her testimony. When the documentary strain takes over, a wildly implausible sequence shows a photograph blown up to such an extent that the date on a newspaper is legible, providing crucial evidence that demolishes the case against Wiecek. There are homilies about the basic soundness of the American judiciary system, but the film remains deeply suspicious not only of the shaky procedures used to jail Wiecek but of the complacent, nervously secretive refusal of anyone to take his appeal

seriously. Hathaway underlines the futility by allowing through the genuinely realist touch that the prisoner's wife didn't stand by him all these years and has divorced him and remarried. KN

1948/111m/FOX/*p* Otto Lang/*d* Henry Hathaway/*s* Jerome Cady, Jay Dratler/*orig* James P. McGuire/*c* Joe MacDonald/*m* Alfred Newman/*lp* James Stewart, Richard Conte, Lee J. Cobb, Helen Walker, Betty Garde.

Camada negra/Black Brood/Black Litter
A brutal film shot shortly after Franco died although written before then, this tells of Tatin, a young fascist (Alonso) who obeys the teachings of his mother (Ponte) and wants to join a right-wing gang presented as a choral group. Wanting to prove his Spanish manhood, the boy finally tries to rape his girl-friend, an unmarried mother (Molina), but ends up bashing in her head with a rock, accompanying every blow with the nationalist shout: For Spain! Having lived up to his mother's expectations, he then officially becomes a member of the fascist organisation. The film was released after the 1977 elections and was vigorously attacked by Franco loyalists, who bombed cinemas and threatened other mayhem. Although an attempt to show the workings of a typical fascist mentality, the film-maker was carried away by his obvious anger and couldn't resist melodramatic sensationalism. PW

1977/Spain/82m/El Iman/*p*/*co-s* José Luis Borau/*d*/*co-s* Manuel Gutierrez Aragon/*c* Magi Torruella/*m* José Nieto/*lp* José Luis Alonso, Maria Luisa Ponte, Angela Molina, Joaquin Hinojosa, Manuel Fadon.

The Canary Murder Case
This was the first film to feature author S.S. Van Dine's debonair crime solver **Philo Vance**. It stars Powell, who would go on to appear in two more Vance films for Paramount, *The Greene Murder Case* (1929) and *The Benson Murder Case* (1930). This outing presents a story about a merciless blackmailer, an unconventional Brooks as the singing star 'canary' of the title, who is murdered by one of the three prominent men she was blackmailing. Powell solves it cleverly by staging a poker game with the suspects in order to psychologically probe the murderer. The original production was silent but was reworked for sound with the entire cast

ABOVE James M. Cain: Fred MacMurray, Barbara Stanwyck, *Double Indemnity*

dubbing their voices (except for Brooks, who was dubbed by Margaret Livingston). TV

1929/80m/PAR/*d* Malcolm St. Clair/ *s* Florence Ryerson, Albert S. Le Vino, titles Herman J. Mankiewicz/*c* Harry Fischbeck/ *lp* William Powell, Louise Brooks, Jean Arthur, Eugene Pallette.

Cap Canaille

One of the few French crime movies directed by a woman, Berto, who was also one of France's finest actresses. She had worked with Jean-Luc Godard (*Le Gai savoir*, 1968) and her co-director Roger had helped to direct *British Sounds* and *Pravda* (both 1969). Together, they made the gritty semi-documentary *Neige* (1981) about the depressingly callous and dim-witted milieu of petty drug pushers and users in Pigalle. This, their second joint venture, chronicles the underworld milieu of Marseille, where powerful crime syndicates control both the politicians and the police. The plot begins with one of the many forest fires that are started to destroy tracts of land in order to free them for speculative development. The fire destroys the property of Paula (Berto), whose family is part of the gangster milieu.

RIGHT Gregory Peck, Robert Mitchum, *Cape Fear*

Set on revenge, she wants to find the arsonist. She is assisted by a cynical journalist (Bohringer) and an ambitious local cop (Crépon). The film's often hand-held camera, orchestrated by another former Godard collaborator, Lubtchansky, roams through the narrow streets of Marseille exploring its violence-prone bars, its harbour and so on, in an exuberant celebration of the joys of film-making, apparently shared by the cast. The climax sees Paula in a car at the bottom of the sea while her lover (Chesnais) sails away, high above her. PW

1982/France, Belgium/103m/Babylone-Top N1-ODEC-F3/*p* Ken and Romaine Legargeant/*co-d/co-s* Juliet Berto, Jean-Henri Roger/*co-s* José Varela, Claude Vesperini, Boris Bergman/*c* William Lubtchansky/*m* Elisabeth Wiener/*lp* Juliet Berto, Richard Bohringer, Patrick Chesnais, Jean-Claude Brialy, Bernadette Lafont.

Cape Fear

Psycho Max Cady (Mitchum) is released from prison after serving six years for rape. He heads straight for the Florida town where lives Sam Bowden (Peck), the witness whose evidence put him away. Sam is a lawyer and a respectable family man, whose friend Sheriff Dutton (Balsam) tries to harass Max when he shows up, but Max fakes a beating and threatens a lawsuit. Then he begins a war of nerves against Sam, his wife Peggy (Bergen) and his daughter Nancy (Martin).

ABOVE James Stewart, Richard Rober, *Call Northside 777*

He poisons their dog, and makes obscene calls, until Sam, at the end of his tether, decides to set a trap which will get rid of him once and for all. The direction is focused round Mitchum's frightening performance as

and the mission-that-could-shorten-the-war combat film. A visionary criminal mastermind/Broadway producer/mid-level officer conceives a robbery/show/military action and convinces the mob/backers/the army to underwrite the operation. Variously-skilled experts are assembled, often with much conflict, and put through a period of training that turns them into a tightly-knit team. In the climax, the plan is put into action, despite inevitable last-minute hitches that have to be overcome (e.g. the substitution of the talented unknown for the established star who has broken her leg in the stereotypical *42nd Street*, 1933). This leads to a clean getaway/an applauding audience/victory, with the heist generally ending in an ironic defeat unheard of in the parallel sub-genres. The inter-link of generic strains is underlined by combat movies like *The Secret Invasion* (1964) and *The Dirty Dozen* (1967), in which daring military actions are carried out by criminals, and crime movies like **House of Bamboo**, **The League of Gentlemen** and *Thunderbolt and Lightfoot* (1974), with disillusioned ex-army men using military skills in daring robberies. The musical connection is demonstrated by comedies like **The Ladykillers** and *The Producers* (1968) in which show business is used as a cover for the planning of a robbery or the staging of a Broadway musical is itself a form of crime.

Max, which makes De Niro's reprise in the 1991 remake seem mannered and superficial. Peck is rock solid, as the lawyer forced to compromise his law and order principles in order to defend himself. The result is a scary, roller coaster ride of terror. MP

1961/105m/Melville-Talbot/*p* Sy Bartlett/ *d* J. Lee Thompson/*s* James R Webb/*c* Sam Leavitt/*m* Bernard Herrmann/*lp* Robert Mitchum, Gregory Peck, Polly Bergen, Lori Martin, Martin Balsam.

The Caper Film

This term was applied retrospectively to dramas from about 1950 onwards in which professional crooks plan and execute a clever, daring but (the censors insisted) ultimately unsuccessful robbery, usually of cash or jewels. Often the thieves fall out, or make one fatal error that leads to their arrest. Although the word 'caper' was first used in a film title, *The Big Caper*, in 1956, it was largely unknown in Europe until the late 60s, by which time a new style of caper film had gained popularity. This had a much stronger element of romantic comedy and often a fantastic plot involving the theft of a price-

less objet d'art. As a result of the abandonment in the USA of the Production Code, the thieves almost always get away with the loot. The caper movie shares its story structure with the putting-on-a-show musical

RIGHT The Caper Film: *The Italian Job*

ABOVE The Caper Film: John Cazale, Al Pacino, *Dog Day Afternoon*

The caper movie is featured in embryonic form as an incidental in gangster films like **Little Caesar** and Westerns like *Jesse James* (1939), which necessarily have to show a few robberies but never get more complicated than having a hood stick up some swells with a gun and collect their jewels or a gang stop a train and blow a safe. The embryo develops in *film noir*, as meticulously-staged robberies interrupt stories of betrayal like musical production numbers, in **The Killers**, **Criss Cross**, **White Heat** and **The Burglar**. Gradually, the heist itself rather than the doomed gangsters assumes narrative centre stage in *Armored Car Robbery* (1950), **The Asphalt Jungle**, **Touchez pas au grisbi**, **Rififi**, *A Prize of Gold* (1955), **The Killing**, *Odds Against Tomorrow* (1959), *The Day They Robbed the Bank of England* (1960) and *A Prize of Arms* (1961). Influenced perhaps by *The Treasure of the Sierra Madre* (1948), these films tend to follow a successful robbery with murderous feuding in the criminal community, individual greed overcoming collective action to set up a finale in which the loot is rendered useless and, like the gold in *Sierra Madre*, often blows away on the wind, as in the spoof *It's a Mad Mad Mad Mad World* (1963).

The sub-genre proper evolved when these films took a lighter turn in order to capitalise on the natural sympathy audiences feel for robbers, producing first the endear-

ing comedy of **The Lavender Hill Mob**, with its mix of dreamy Alec Guinness amateurism and Sid James non-threatening criminality, and then a run of serious but glamorous pictures (*5 Against the House*, 1955, *Seven Thieves*, 1960, *Assault on a Queen*, 1966) which soon gave way to such glossy, stylish fantasies as **Ocean's Eleven**, which with its self-mocking stars and flip punchline might be considered the first real caper movie. The sub-genre, which owes much to the concept of the gentleman thief found in a run of films from *Raffles* (1930) and *Arsène Lupin* (1932) through **To Catch a Thief** and **The Pink Panther**, gelled with a run of films including **Topkapi**, *Gambit* (1966), *How to Steal a Million* (1966), **The Thomas Crown Affair**, *The Biggest Bundle of Them All* (1968), *Grand Slam* (1968), **Las Vegas 500 milliones/They Came to Rob Las Vegas**, *Duffy* (1968), **Le Clan des Siciliens/The Sicilian Clan**, *$/The Heist* (1972), *Cops and Robbers* (1973), *The Thief Who Came to Dinner* (1973), *Lady Ice* (1973), *The Bank Shot* (1974), *Inside Out/The Golden Heist* (1975), *Diamonds* (1975), *L'Année sainte/Holy Year* (1976), *Perfect Gentlemen* (1978), *Rough Cut* (1980) and *How to Beat the High Co$t of Living* (1980).

Hudson Hawk (1991) is a throw-back to this frivolous tradition in which the protagonists are less likely to end up shot dead amid the swirling banknotes, often through 'joke' endings like those of *Dead Heat on the Merry-Go-Round* (1968) and **The Italian Job** in which the heist is pulled off but a twist of fate renders the effort futile. With the victory of style over morality, hoods in the likes of **The Hot Rock/How to Steal a Diamond in Four Uneasy Lessons** and *A Man, a Woman and a Bank* (1979) are even allowed to get away scot-free with their well-earned loot. The instant decadence of the form was demonstrated by hybrids like the science fiction caper movie (*Diabolik/Danger: Diabolik*, 1968), the Western caper movie (*The War Wagon*, 1967, *The Great Bank Robbery*, 1969), the war caper movie (*Kelly's Heroes*, 1970) and the period caper movie (*Harry and Walter Go to New York*, 1976, *The First Great Train Robbery/The Great Train Robbery*, 1979). While a typical *noir* heist man might be a thuggish prole played by Sterling Hayden in the pursuit of a vaultful of grubby used bills, a caper movie protagonist tends to be a well-dressed, impeccably cool character played by Robert Redford, Warren Beatty, Steve McQueen or

RIGHT Al Capone

James Coburn, assisted in high-fashion outfits by Candice Bergen, Goldie Hawn, Melina Mercouri or Audrey Hepburn as they go after fabulously sparkling jewels. Similarly, while the thieves of the 40s and 50s are defeated by petty quarrels and ironic fate, their 70s and 80s successors are more likely to be thwarted by a complex society where institutionalised corruption and ruthlessness is set against their minor efforts. There have been films based on real-life heists like the Boston Brink's armoured car hold-up (*Brink's: The Great Robbery*, 1976, **The Brink's Job**) and the British Great Train Robbery (*The Great St. Trinian's Train Robbery*, 1966, *Robbery*, 1967, *Buster*, 1988, *Prisoner of Rio*, 1988), though it is revealing that the majority of these adopt the jokey tone of the comic caper film rather than go along with the grimness of *Odds Against Tomorrow*. Perhaps the ultimate critique of the caper movie is another based-on-fact film, Sidney Lumet's **Dog Day Afternoon**, which features not the meticulously-planned, coolly-executed heists of the likes of *Perfect Friday* (1970) and *11 Harrowhouse* (1974) but an ill-thought-out, grossly-bungled bank job by a character in search of a sex change. KN

Capone, Al (1899–1947)

Many sources, usually with a vested interest in making him seem alien, state his birthplace was Castel Amaro, Italy, but Alphonse Capone (*not* Caponi) was born in Brooklyn, New York. As Katherine Gerould wrote in *Harpers Monthly* in 1931, 'it is not because Capone is different that he takes the imagination: it is because he is so gorgeously and

ABOVE Vince Barnett, Paul Muni, *Scarface*

LEFT The real Al Capone

typically American'. When a teenager, he was wounded in a bar-fight and acquired parallel scars on his left cheek which lead to the nickname 'Scarface'. In 1921, Capone went to Chicago to work for gang-leader Johnny Torrio, a New York friend, and rose to power during the early days of Prohibition. Upon taking control of the city's underworld, Capone become a national public figure, noted for public flamboyance and private brutality. The press and public, under unpopular dry laws, proved remarkably tolerant of the Big Fellow, who was always ready with a grand gesture or a quote ('I've been spending the best years of my life as a public benefactor . . . 90% of the people of Cook County drink and gamble and my offence has been to furnish them with those amusements'). Though profligate enough to contract in his teens the venereal disease which would kill him, Capone was outspoken about his devotion to family values, and supported a cadre of worthless male relatives, while doting on his sainted mother Theresa, saintly wife Mae and long-suffering son Albert Francis.

By 1927, when he was still in his 20s, Capone's annual net profits (from bootlegging, protection racketeering, prostitution and sundry 'legitimate' businesses into which he forced his way) had reached an esti-

mated $60 million, making him one of the most successful self-made men of the century. Among the underworld enemies Capone murdered, bested or outlasted were the Genna Brothers, Dion O'Banion, Hymie Weiss, Roger Touhy and Bugs Moran. Though the St Valentine's Day Massacre, which took place in 1928, did not serve to eliminate Moran himself, it wiped out most of his lieutenants. Ultimately Capone was undone because his high life-style and unashamed criminality was such a severe rebuke to the authorities that President Hoover was driven to order an end to his reign.

Insulated from conventional law enforcement by widespread corruption among the politicians (notably Mayor 'Big Bill' Thompson) and prohibition agents of Chicago, Capone was nevertheless harried by various concerned groups, including the vigilante commission known as the Secret Six, and targeted by federal law enforcement agencies, including the so called 'Untouchables', a squad of prohibition agents commanded by **Eliot Ness**. In 1929, he was convicted of carrying a concealed pistol; while he served his short sentence, his tax records were investigated. In 1931, Capone was sentenced to an eleven-year term for income tax evasion, a blatant miscarriage of justice in that

he was given an unduly harsh punishment for the comparatively minor crimes of which he could be convicted, rather than for the undoubtedly major crimes, including several murders which he had personally committed, in which he was involved. After serving some time in the Atlanta Penitentiary, where his influence was able to win him a soft life, he was transferred to the newly-opened Alcatraz Island. There he was unpopular with fellow convicts. In 1939, Capone was released from jail, suffering from syphilis.

Virtually all gangster films of the 30s borrow some element of Capone's life and legend. In **Little Caesar** he is represented both by the central character of petty hood-on-the-rise Cesar Bandello (Edward G. Robinson) and by the Big Boy (Sidney Blackmer), the ultimate crime boss of the city, while in **The Public Enemy**, he is the offstage but all-pervasive 'Schemer Burns', arranging for the death of the Hymie Weiss-like Tom Powers (James Cagney). *The Front Page* (1931), set in a deeply corrupt but unidentified Chicago, is similarly permeated with the Capone atmosphere. Howard Hawks's **Scarface** uses most of the Capone story in its account of the rise of Tony Camonte (Paul Muni), a scar-faced vulgarian who assassinates a Colosimo-type (Harry J. Vejar), edges out a Torrio figure (Osgood Perkins), arranges a St Valentine's Day Massacre, demonstrates his love of opera, tries to pass in high society, surrounds himself with hood bodyguards and shames his decent immigrant family.

Other Capones-à-clef include Wallace Beery in **The Secret Six**, trapped by firm vigilante action; Ricardo Cortez in *Bad Company* (1931), involved in the first-ever screen St Valentine's Day Massacre; Paul Lukas in *City Streets* (1931); a bulky lookalike seen only from the rear and referred to as 'Number One' in *The Finger Points* (1931), an account of the career of Jake Lingle, a newsman on Capone's payroll who was rubbed out before talking with the tax investigators; Jean Hersholt in *Beast of the City* (1932); Edward Arnold in *Okay America* (1932), offering, as did Capone, to help solve a case similar to the Lindbergh kidnapping; C. Henry Gordon in **Gabriel over the White House**, as perhaps the most racist of the Italian caricatures in the genre; John Litel in *Alcatraz Island* (1937); Edward G. Robinson in *The Last Gangster* (1937), in which an immigrant crime boss emerges from jail a different man, though not, of course, maddened by syphilis; Barry Sullivan in *The Gangster* (1947), sporting a Capone-style scar; Edmond O'Brien in *Pete Kelly's Blues* (1956); Lee J. Cobb in **Party Girl**, re-enacting a famously horrific incident in which Capone climaxed a black-tie testimonial speech by battering to death three traitors at the table; by both George Raft, carrying out yet another St Valentine's Day Massacre, and Nehemiah Persoff, as 'Little Bonaparte', in **Some Like It Hot**; and Al Pacino, spoofing Capone and Richard III, as Big Boy Caprice in **Dick Tracy**.

In 1947, the Breen Office refused to give a seal of approval to a proposed film of Westbrook Pegler's biography of the recently deceased Capone. This ruling prompted Joseph H. Lewis to adapt an article entitled 'He Trapped Capone' into **The Undercover Man**, a contemporary-set but otherwise fact-based account of the Internal Revenue's war on Capone, who is represented by the Big Fellow (Ralph Volkie). Lewis drew on Elmer L. Irey's just-published *The Tax Dodgers: The Inside Story of the T-Men's War With America's Political and Underworld Hoodlums* (1948), but interest in Capone was really revived by Eliot Ness and Oscar Fraley's *The Untouchables* (1957), an autobiographical account of the case against Capone which prompted Frank J. Wilson, with Beth Day, to add to

the shelf of anti-Capone memoirs with *Special Agent: A Quarter Century with the Treasury Department and the Secret Service* (1965). *The Untouchables* became a two-part television pilot with Robert Stack as Ness, theatrically released as *The Scarface Mob* (1959), with Robert Stack's grim and dedicated Ness pitted against Neville Brand's Capone. Brand's Capone reappeared in a cameo in *The George Raft Story/Spin of a Coin* (1961), complimenting Ray Danton's Raft on his role in *Scarface* and saying 'next time, you play me, huh?' After remaking *Scarface* in 1983 with Al Pacino as an 80s Cuban reincarnation of Muni, Brian De Palma remade *The Scarface Mob* as **The Untouchables**, with Kevin Costner as a straight-arrow Ness, Billy Drago as an ahistorically killed-off Nitti and Robert De Niro as a blubbery, opera-loving, baseball bat-wielding Capone. This eventually prompted a revival of the TV series (1992–), with William Forsythe, nearer in age than most screen Capones, cast as Big Al.

Richard Wilson's **Al Capone** is the first major screen biography. Jason Robards was Capone in Roger Corman's **The St. Valentine's Day Massacre**, while Ben Gazzara took the role in Steve Carver's Corman-produced *Capone* (1975). American television has offered many Capones: Louis Giambalvo in *The Gangster Chronicles/Gangster Wars* (1981), Thomas G. Waites in *Verne Miller/Gangland: The Verne Miller Story* (1987), Vincent Guastaferro, with Anthony LaPaglia in the title role, in *Frank Nitti: The Enforcer* (1988), Ray Sharkey, with Keith Carradine as a dedicated fed, in *The Revenge of Al Capone* (1989), and Eric Roberts, with Adrian Pasdar as the gangster's lawman brother, in *The Lost Capone* (1990). Jose Calvo blusters as a rare comic Capone in the lowbrow Italian comedy *Due Mafioso contro Al Capone* (1966), and bitpart Capones include Titus Welliver in *Mobsters* (1991) and Nicholas Turturro in *Young Indiana Jones and the Mystery of the Blues* (1993), a feature-length episode of the *Young Indiana Jones Chronicles*.

The inspiration for many novels in the 30s and 40s – *Little Caesar*, *Scarface* and *Gabriel Over the White House* are based on novels and, of course, Bertold Brecht's *The Resistible Rise of Arturo Ui* is as concerned with Capone as Hitler – Capone has recently started to figure in fiction under his own name, notably in Max Allan Collins' *True Detective* (1983), Stuart Kaminsky's *You Bet Your Life* (1978), Neil Gaiman and Dave McKean's *Violent Cases* (1987), Howard Browne's *Pork*

City (1988) and Kim Newman and Eugene Byrne's science fiction 'USSA' series. Among the major biographies of Capone are Fred D. Pasley's *Al Capone: The Biography of a Self-Made Man* (1930), John Kobler's *Capone: The Life and World of Al Capone* (1971) and Robert J. Schoenberg's *Mr Capone* (1992). KN

Carter, Nick

Created by publisher Ormond G. Smith and author John Russell Coryell, Nick Carter made his first appearance in 'The Old Detective's Pupil' in *New York Weekly* in 1886. Like Sexton Blake in Britain, Carter flourished for over a century in adventures written by many and varied authors. Frederic Day was the most prolific of Carter's chroniclers, writing nearly 500 novellas between 1892 and 1913, but other authors to produce Carter adventures include William Wallace Cook and Martin Cruz Smith. After a burst of early silent activity that included seven outings between 1908 and 1915 and the serial *Nick Carter* (1921) starring Tom Carrigan, the cinema has somewhat neglected Carter. Walter Pidgeon took the part in Jacques Tourneur's *Nick Carter,*

ABOVE Nick Carter: Donald Meek, Walter Pidgeon, *Phantom Raiders*

Master Detective (1939) and *Phantom Raiders* (1940) and George B. Seitz's *Sky Murder* (1940). Pidgeon's sleuth is barely differentiated from the contemporary **Saints**, **Falcons** and **Lone Wolves**, but Donald Meek makes a lasting impression as a beekeeping, surprisingly bright-for-a-stooge sidekick. Tourneur's films are disappointingly prosaic, but *Sky Murder* is fast and fun, and all three use intriguing up-to-date settings (passenger planes, luxury liners). Less effective is the serial *Chick Carter, Detective* (1946). Eddie Constantine starred in a few French films of the 1960s (*Nick Carter va tout casser*, 1964, *Nick Carter et le trefle rouge*, 1965) but the sleuth was not presented in a manner appropriate to his stature and was indistinguishable from Constantine's outings as **Lemmy Caution**. Subsequently, Carter has been played by Robert Conrad in Paul Krasny's *The Adventures of Nick Carter* (1972), a failed TV pilot with a turn-of-the-century setting, and Michal Docolomansky in Oldrich Lipsky's charming Czech spoof *Adela jeste nevecerela/Nick Carter in Prague* (1977). KN

Casino

A definitive account of the American criminal experience, this offers a complex but totally lucid account of both the mechanics and the psychology of organised crime. The film centres on Ace Rothstein (De Niro), a bookie who in the 1970s works his way up to become the mob's key man in Las Vegas, organising with meticulous care the skimming of vast sums of money off the top of legitimate gambling businesses. His desire for total control is frustrated by his marriage to Ginger (Stone), a hooker who is unable to shake herself free of her pimp (Woods) and who later, undermined by drugs, has an affair with Ace's long-time associate Nicky (Pesci), who turns against him. Nicky eventually places a bomb under Ace's car, a scene which comes at the beginning of the film. As we later discover, Ace survives, but by this time things are changing. Big business has moved into Vegas and entrepreneurs like Ace aren't needed any more. EB

1995/178m/U/*p* Barbara DeFina/*d* Martin Scorsese/*s* Nicholas Pileggi, Martin Scorsese/*c* Robert Richardson/*m* (editor) Bobby Mackston/*lp* Robert De Niro, Sharon Stone, Joe Pesci, James Woods, Don Rickles.

Caspary, Vera (1899–1987)

Caspary's best book was the hugely successful **Laura**, which with wit and intelligence

ABOVE Eddie Constantine, *Alphaville une étrange aventure de Lemmy Caution*

plays the trick of having the detective fall in love with the murder victim and then save her from a second murder attempt. Elegantly written from multiple viewpoints, the novel, like most of Caspary's work, is essentially a character study in the guise of a mystery. The character of Waldo Lydecker was based on Alexander Woolcott. Caspary first wrote for and then edited magazines in the 20s before turning to novels in 1929 with *The White Girl*, the story of a black Chicago girl who passes for white in New York. Her novels were not great successes and in the 30s after her play *Blind Mice* (written with Winifred Lenihan) was filmed as *Working Girls* (1931) Caspary turned to screenwriting. Most of her screenplays were for women's films, often like her novels using mystery plots as a means of character investigation. *Stranger Than Truth* (1946) was set in the world of magazine publishing while *The Husband* (1957) took as its central idea a wife's fears that her husband is homicidal. Films from her novels and stories include *The Night Of June 13* (1932), *Scandal Sheet* (1938), *Bedelia* (1947), **The Blue Gardenia** and *Les Girls* (1957). She was also responsible for the initial adaptation of *A Letter To Three Wives* (1949). PH

Catchfire

Hopper is the professional killer who is hired to track down and eliminate Foster, an accidental witness to a mob killing. However,

when he does finally catch up with her he wants to keep her for himself. The background to this disjointed picture is that the film was made originally in 1988 under the title *Backtrack* and directed by Hopper. Following post-production problems over Hopper's three-hour cut, the Director's Guild gave it a 'Alan Smithee' credit, and it was recut (with a 1989 copyright) to the present length. TV

1991/98m/Vestron Pictures/*p* Dick Clark, Dan Paulson/*d* 'Alan Smithee'(Dennis Hopper)/*s* Rachel Kronstadt Mann, Ann Louise Bardach/*c* Ed Lachman/*m* Curt Sobel/*lp* Dennis Hopper, Jodie Foster, Dean Stockwell, Vincent Price.

Caution, Lemmy

Created by **Peter Cheyney** for his first crime novel, *This Man is Dangerous* (1936, filmed by Jean Sacha as *Cet homme est dangereux*, 1953, the second Lemmy Caution movie), Caution is an FBI agent best known in film under the craggy features of the American crooner Eddie Constantine. The film that set the tone was Bernard Borderie's **La Môme vert-de-gris** (from the novel *Poison Ivy*) in which Caution foils a gang of gold bullion hijackers. Constantine, speaking French with a heavy American accent, which only added to his rugged charm, played the agent as a wise-cracking, philandering brute given to casual, nonchalant violence, constantly smoking and hankering after a good glass of whisky. Constantine went on to play Nick Carter in the same vein as well as another Cheyney creation, Slim Callaghan. In one film, Henri Verneuil's *Brelan d'as* (1952), John Van Dreelen played the role of Lemmy Caution. Other Caution titles include: Bernard Borderie's *Les Femmes s'en balancent* (1954), Pierre Chevalier's *Vous pigez?* (1956), Borderie's *Comment qu'elle est* (from the novel *I'll Say She Does*) and *Lemmy pour les dames* (both 1961) as well as *A toi de faire, mignonne* (from the novel *Your Deal, My Lovely*, 1963). The strangest Caution film was Godard's *Alphaville une étrange aventure de Lemmy Caution* (1965), in which Constantine's mythic stature was given full rein. Michel Audiard created a French version of Caution called Georges Masse (played on the screen by Raymond Rouleau), an investigative journalist whose exploits were filmed from 1949 onwards, adapted by Audiard himself and directed by André Hunebelle: *Mission à Tanger* (1949), *Méfiez-vous des blondes* (1950) and *Massacre en dentelles* (1951). Ironically this French imitation in fact preceded the appearance of Caution on the screen in 1952. In the US, Caution made a television appearance in *Dangerous Agent* (1968). PW

Le Cave se rebiffe/Counterfeiters of Paris

After the success of Becker's **Touchez pas au grisbi**, French commercial cinema developed its own version of the New Wave's obsession with Hollywood B movies: the French *série noire* adaptations of novels by Simenon, Le Breton and the like generally starring Gabin and featuring the dialogues of Michel Audiard. This forgery caper comes at the tail end of the series when the initial energy had evaporated into mannerisms. Maréchal (Gabin), alias 'le dabe'. is persuaded to come out of his retirement breeding horses in Caracas to organise a major forgery coup in Paris. Together with the draughtsman Mideau, alias 'le cave' (Biraud in his breakthrough film) and the latter's wife (Carol in her last major role) he outsmarts his accomplices and they take off with all the loot. Simonin, Audiard and Gabin later worked together on the hit *Mélodie en sous-sol* (1963). PW

1961/France, Italy/98m/Cité Films-Compagnia Cinematografica Mondiale/*p* Jacques Bar/*d*/*co-s* Gilles Grangier/*co-s* Albert Simonin, Michel Audiard/*orig* Albert

Simonin (1954)/*c* Louis Page/*m* Michel Legrand, Francis Lemarque/*lp* Jean Gabin, Maurice Biraud, Martine Carol, Bernard Blier, Françoise Rosay.

La caza/The Hunt

This was the first of a long series of collaborations between Querejeta and Saura. Three middle-aged Franco supporters indulge in the caudillo's favourite sport, hunting. Carefully avoiding over-explicit political symbols (which had caused his previous film, *Llanto por un bandido*, 1963, to be mutilated by the censor), Saura uses the poisonous interactions between the three now comfortably middle-class 'comrades' from the Civil War to depict a society rotten with malice and repression, exploding into murder and sadism, leaving the fourth member of the rabbit-hunting party, a member of the next generation, becoming dimly aware of the festering, decades-long corruption that led to the massacre. PW

1965/Spain/88m/Querejeta/*p* Elias Querejeta/*d*/*co-s* Carlos Saura/*co-s* Angelino Fons/*orig* C. Saura/*c* Luis Cuadrado/*m* Luis de Pablo/*lp* Ismael Merlo, Alfredo Mayo, Jose Maria Prada, Fernando Sanchez Polack, Emilio Gutierrez Caba.

120 rue de la gare

The first screen adaptation of a Malet novel, featuring the first French private eye, **Nestor Burma** (Dary), although, to avoid confusion with Maigret (then portrayed by Albert Préjean), Malet agreed that his hero would not have to smoke a pipe. The convoluted plot has Burma witness the shooting of his partner on a railway platform and he sets out for Lyons to solve the case. This involves a mysterious woman who turns out to be the daughter of a gangster presumed long dead, various attempts on the detective's life and his reluctant partnership with an enthusiastic secretary, Hélène (Desmarets) until he finds that at the eponymous address in Paris, the dead gangster had hidden a hoard of jewels to take care of his daughter. The film was successful but Dary refused to repeat the role because his female partner, the delightful Desmarets, was a head taller than the hero. Burma reappeared on the screen 30 years later in Bob Swaim's *La Nuit de Saint-Germain-des-Prés* (1977) and again in Jean-Luc Miesch's *Nestor Burma, Détective de choc* (1982). PW

1945/France/90m/Sirius/*p* Georges Bernier/*d*/*s* Jacques Daniel-Norman/*orig* Léo

Malet/*c* Henri Tiquet/*m* Vincent Scotto/*lp* René Dary, Sophie Desmarets, Gaby Andreu, Jean Parédès, Albert Dinan.

Le Cercle rouge/The Red Circle

Melville's penultimate film works like clockwork but lacks the intensity of his masterpieces, **Le Samouraï** and **Le deuxième souffle**. The heist movie involves obsessive relationships between five men (diluting the impact of any single one of them): Inspector Matteï (Bourvil, cast against type and excellent in his last role) in search of a hood who gave him the slip on a train, Vogel (Volonté); Corey (Delon), who teams up with Vogel to stage a daring jewel robbery; Jansen (Montand), the alcoholic ex-cop turned gunman; and Santi (Perier), a suave night-club owner and a grass. The lives of the protagonists relentlessly work out their personal logic, drawing them together until they meet in a deserted house for the climactic shootout with the police. The English version, although supervised by Melville, renders the proceedings even more mechanical with the suppression of material filling out the character of the dogged cop, Matteï, who might just as easily have been a gangster, just as Jansen who is a gangster used to be a cop. The badly graded English release prints destroyed much of Melville's surreal pictorialism and only a few scenes recall the director's bravura style: the encounter between Delon and Volonté in a barren field, the silhouettes of men in hats and coats moving through the streets profiled against deliriously coloured skies. PW

1970/France, Italy/150m/Corona-Selenia/*p* Robert Dorfmann/*d*/*s* Jean-Pierre Melville/*c* Henri Decaë/*m* Éric de Marsan/*lp* Alain Delon, André Bourvil, Yves Montand, Gian Maria Volonté, François Périer.

C'est arrivé près de chez vous/Man Bites Dog

This is a straight-faced grotesque comedy disguised as a typical television documentary-gone-wrong on a quirky personality. The quirky subject, living in the provincial Walloon town of Namur, happens to be a brutal serial killer, Ben Patard (Poelvoorde), who helpfully demonstrates his professional skills by killing people on camera, accompanying his actions with explanatory comments. As is customary in such television programmes, the eccentric subject is regarded affectionately by the film crew, who give him ample opportunity to hold forth on

ABOVE Keye Luke, Warner Oland, *Charlie Chan at Monte Carlo*

Wong series with Boris Karloff (and Keye Luke for one film) as a Chinese policeman whose popularity never matched Chan or Moto. Winters is introduced in *The Chinese Ring* (1947), a remake of *Mr Wong in Chinatown* (1939). Victor Sen Yung and Keye Luke return to the series in their old roles in *Charlie Chan in Black Magic* (1944). Other titles included *The Jade Mask* (1945) and *The Red Dragon* (1945).

Most Fox Chans are excellent little mysteries, enlivened by the presence of such luminaries as Ray Milland, the young Rita Hayworth (billed as Rita Cansino in *Charlie Chan in Egypt*), Boris Karloff (a splendid amnesiac baritone in *Charlie Chan at the Opera*), George Zucco (keeping disembodied criminal brains alive in *Charlie Chan in Honolulu*), Cesar Romero (the flashy magician of *Charlie Chan at Treasure Island*), Leo G. Carroll, Lon Chaney Jr, Victor Jory and Lionel Atwill. Of course, the charm of the movies lies in Chan's imitable aphorisms ('Murder like potato chip: cannot stop at *just one*', 'Hasty deduction like hole in water: easy to make', 'Perfect case like perfect doughnut: have hole') and witty irrelevancies ('Fortunately, assassination of French language not major crime', 'Silence is golden, except in police station'), but the entries in which the screenwriters emphasised the mysterioso or bizarre elements also have many picturesque twists and creepily camp moments. Among the best are Louis King's *Charlie Chan in Egypt*, where x-rays reveal a newly-exhumed three-thousand-year-old mummy has a bullet in its heart, and the killer is disguised as a curse-fulfilling living statue; H. Bruce Humberstone's *Charlie Chan at the Opera*, for Karloff's extravagant performance and a witty mock opera provided by Oscar Levant; Eugene Forde's *Charlie Chan on Broadway*, with a nicely contrived plot device involving a night-club photographer whose snaps are vital clues; *Charlie Chan at Treasure Island*, directed by Norman Foster, which has murders committed during Romero's magic acts and a plot involving astrology and prediction; Herbert I. Leeds's *Charlie Chan in City in Darkness* (1939), set in Paris the night before the Germans march in, in which the butler really does turn out to be the killer, albeit a sympathetic one since the victim was a quisling supplying arms to the Nazis; Foster's *Charlie Chan in Panama*, about espionage in the canal zone, which features Chan's purchase of the panama hat which became part of his trademark costume; Lynn Shores's *Charlie Chan at the Wax Museum*, set

from *The Chinese Parrot*). At this point Fox increased the rate of production from one film to three or four a year and brought in a host of new writers (Seton I. Miller, Phillip MacDonald, Robert Ellis, Philip Wylie, John Larkin) to supplement Biggers's comparatively slender output. In this phase, Chan was much given to globe-trotting, appearing in *Charlie Chan in London* (1934); *Paris; Egypt and Shanghai* (1935), *Honolulu* (1938), *Reno* (1939), *Panama* (1940) and *Rio* (1941). The detective also had a taste for a variety of popular entertainments, as demonstrated by *Charlie Chan at the Circus, the Race Track, the Opera* (1936), *the Olympics, Broadway* (1937), *Monte Carlo* (1938), *Treasure Island* (1939) and *Charlie Chan at the Wax Museum* (1940).

While on his 1935 trip to Paris, Oland's Chan is joined by Keye Luke as Number One Son Lee Chan, whose Sino-American antics ('Gee whiz, Pops!') provide usually unnecessary comic relief and occasionally surprising bits of useful detecting assistance. In *The Black Camel*, Chan is seen at the breakfast table with his wife and ten children before happily escaping from domestic bliss into the peace and quiet of a murder investigation; in *Charlie Chan's Chance*, Mrs Chan presents her husband with Number Eleven; and, in *Charlie Chan at the Circus*, a Chan family outing is depicted. Luke was later joined, and

eventually replaced, first by Layne Tom Jr, as either Charlie Chan Jr (*Charlie Chan at the Olympics*), Tommy Lee Chan (*Charlie Chan in Honolulu*) or Willie Chan (*Charlie Chan's Murder Cruise*, 1940), and then by Victor Sen Yung (first seen in *Charlie Chan in Honolulu*) as Number Two Son Jimmy Chan. Oland appeared in sixteen Chans for Fox, and died in 1938 while the studio was preparing the script for *Charlie Chan at the Fights/Charlie Chan at the Arena*. With typical Hollywood invention, the property was reworked slightly to emerge as *Mr Moto's Gamble* (1938), in which Peter Lorre's Japanese sleuth is partnered by Luke's Lee Chan, and Moto is polite enough to express admiration for the rival oriental detective.

Sidney Toler was brought in to replace Oland. The eleven films he appeared in from 1938 to 1942 are the best of the Chans. By this time Fox had the business of B-picture production down pat, and imaginative directors like Norman Foster were brought in. Fox ended the series in 1942 and the rights eventually passed to Monogram, where Toler starred in eleven films on much reduced budgets, commencing with *Charlie Chan in the Secret Service* (1944). Toler died in 1947 and undistinguished Roland Winters came in for eight further films, with plots sometimes lifted from the studio's earlier Mr

during a live broadcast from a chamber of horrors and featuring much by-play with plastic surgery and gangland slayings; and Harry Lachman's *Castle in the Desert*, with clever use of the San Simeon-like setting.

Chan's next screen outing was on television with *The New Adventures of Charlie Chan* (1957), a run of 39 half-hour episodes filmed in England with J. Carrol Naish (exposed as the killer by Oland in *Charlie Chan at the Circus*) as Chan and James Hong as Number One Son Barry Chan. In the meantime, Chan was played on radio by Walter Connolly, Ed Begley and Santos Ortego.

Dennis Lynds revives the character in his novel *Charlie Chan Returns* (1974), but other attempts at bringing back Chan have been desultory. The Saturday morning limited animation series *The Amazing Chan and the Chan Clan* (1972–4), with the voice of Keye Luke as Chan, and Leslie Martinson's TV pilot *Charlie Chan: Happiness is a Warm Clue* (1970), with Ross Martin, are both dreadful, with the unsold pilot not even aired until 1978. The campy tone of these outings is echoed in Robert Moore's *Murder By Death* (1976), scripted by Neil Simon, in which Peter Sellers's Sidney Wang is criticised by Truman Capote for omitting prepositions from his aphorisms, and Clive Donner's *Charlie Chan and the Curse of the Dragon Queen* (1981), with Peter Ustinov's Chan and Richard Benedict's half-Jewish Number One Grandson unable to raise so much as a smile and even Angie Dickinson's cockatoo-

ABOVE Raymond Chandler

plumed villainess not getting much of a look-in. Since then, despite a strange homage in Wayne Wang's *Chan is Missing* (1982), the screen's premier oriental detective has been resting. KN

Chandler, Raymond [Thornton]
(1888–1959)

Born in Chicago and famous for his Los Angeles-set crime fiction, Raymond Chandler was educated at Dulwich College, London.

Like Dashiell Hammett, a major influence, Chandler turned to writing comparatively late in life, after failing in the California oil business. Having made a reputation in pulps like *Black Mask* and *Dime Detective Magazine* in the 30s, he cannibalised early stories (which feature protagonists Ted Carmady and John Dalmas) into his first novels, *The Big Sleep* (1939) and *Farewell, My Lovely* (1940), which introduced his narrator-detective hero **Philip Marlowe**, the hero of all his subsequent novels, *The High Window* (1942), *The Lady in the Lake* (1943), *The Little Sister* (1949), *The Long Goodbye* (1953) and *Playback* (1958). Though he felt constrained by the private-eye genre – often planning 'crossover' projects – Chandler never broke away to attempt anything else, though *The Poodle Springs Mystery*, a fragment later completed by Robert B. Parker, attempts to stretch Marlowe's format by marrying him off and playing up the bitter social satire of Californian mores that had always been part of the appeal of his novels. Outside his fiction, Chandler's major works were essays for *Atlantic Monthly*, including 'The Simple Art of Murder' (1944), in which he outlines the qualities of Marlowe and his world in the famous 'mean streets' passage, and 'Writers in Hollywood' (1945) and 'Oscar Night in Hollywood' (1948), characteristic exercises in biting the hand that feeds, which complain bitterly about his treatment by the studios.

He did an uncredited draft of **The Lady in the Lake** and *Playback* is based on an unproduced screenplay (which did not feature Marlowe), but Chandler's major work in Hollywood was adapting other writers' novels. Twice he found himself a middle-man between a visionary *auteur* and a minor classic of the crime novel, when he assisted Billy Wilder in his 1944 adaptation of James M. Cain's **Double Indemnity** and Alfred Hitchcock in his 1951 version of **Patricia Highsmith**'s **Strangers on a Train**. While the former benefits enormously from such Chandlerian devices as voice-over narration and hard-boiled banter and indeed stands as his most notable Hollywood credit, the latter (on which his contributions were mainly rewritten by Czenzi Ormonde) finds his personality almost obliterated by Hitchcock, aside from the peculiarly fascinated distaste director and writer share for flirtatious elder

LEFT Humphrey Bogart as Raymond Chandler's Philip Marlowe in *The Big Sleep* with Lauren Bacall

ly women which, in Chandler's case, is almost certainly due to his lengthy marriage to a woman eighteen years his senior. In both cases, subsequent remakes (*Double Indemnity*, 1973, *Once You Kiss a Stranger*, 1969) and imitations (**Body Heat**, **Throw Momma From the Train**) have chosen to follow the scripts Chandler part-authored rather than return to the original novels. Chandler's other screen credits include Irving Pichel's soap opera *And Now Tomorrow* (1944) and Lewis Allen's gothic mystery *The Unseen* (1945), from novels by Rachel Field and Ethel Lina White. His only produced original screen story is **The Blue Dahlia**, a mystery blandly directed by George Marshall with Alan Ladd and Veronica Lake in the leads, but with an interesting supporting psychotic from William Bendix as a shell-shocked serviceman driven mad by 'that monkey music', jazz. KN

Charles, Nick and Nora

'Is your husband working on a case?' asks a dithery admirer of urbane supersleuth Nick Charles (William Powell) in W. S. Van Dyke's *The Thin Man* (1934). 'Yes,' replies chic and devoted wife Nora (Myrna Loy), 'a case of Scotch.' However, when a mysterious thin man (Edward Ellis) is murdered, no one else can solve the crime and, egged on by Nora and their dog Asta, he gets out his junior detective fingerprint kit and magnifying glass and goes to work. The mystery, extracted from **Dashiell Hammett**'s only slightly less flippant 1934 novel, is hardly mystifying, but *The Thin Man* remains a delight primarily because of fast-paced wisecracks and the way Powell and Loy play off each other, moving the film away from hard-boiled whodunit towards the sophisticated run of cocktail-fuelled marital comedies that were to proliferate in the mid-1930s. MGM retained Powell and Loy for a further five adventures between 1936 and 1947. Unusually, with the stars and the original director returning regularly and without the sweatshop production schedule of the **Charlie Chan** or **Saint** series, the *Thin Man* films maintained the quality at least until Van Dyke's *After the Thin Man* (1936), *Another Thin Man* (1939) and *Shadow of the Thin Man* (1941), before tailing off slightly in Richard Thorpe's *The Thin Man Goes Home* (1944) and Edward Buzzell's *Song of the Thin Man* (1947).

Powell and Loy became so identified with the roles there have been no subsequent attempts to use the characters in the cinema.

ABOVE Nick and Nora Charles: William Powell and Myrna Loy

However, Peter Lawford and Phyllis Kirk took the parts in *The Thin Man* (1957–9), an adequate television series, Craig Stevens and Jo Ann Pflug starred in a dreadful TV movie *Nick and Nora* (1975), and the latter title was also used for a famously disastrous flop Broadway musical in 1991. David Niven and Maggie Smith parodied the Charleses as Dick and Dora Charleston in *Murder By Death* (1976). Most husband-and-wife sleuth teams and not a few husband-and-wife sit-com characters owe a deal to Nick and Nora, most blatantly Richard and Frances Lockridge's Mr and Mrs North and Francis Durbridge's Paul and Steve Temple. The Norths appeared in *Mr and Mrs North* (1936) and many subsequent novels, plus a 1941 movie with William Post and Gracie Allen. The Temples originated in a 1938 radio serial and novel entitled *Send for Paul Temple*, starred in three films (*Calling Paul Temple*, 1948, *Paul Temple's Triumph*, 1950, *Paul Temple Returns*, 1952) and a television series with Francis Matthews and Ros Drinkwater. The most recent Nick and Nora clones have been Robert Wagner and Stefanie Powers in *Hart to Hart* (1979–85), a television series which even partners the detectives with an Asta-imitation dog. Hammett, down on his luck, created a radio series named *The Fat Man*, which was filmed in 1951. KN

Charley Varrick

Washed-out stunt pilot Charley Varrick (Matthau), self-styled 'last of the independents', assembles a little team of professionals and stages a smalltime robbery, only to pick, by accident, an obscure New Mexico bank that happens to be used as a mafia drop, thus walking away with three-quarters of a million dollars. Confident of his ability to evade the FBI, Varrick, stuck with a jittery Vietnam vet (Robinson) as his only surviving partner, is less certain he can escape the mob, who have assigned Molly (Baker), a maroon-suited, pipe-smoking good ole boy sadist, to track him down. After the initial heist, during which Charley's wife (Farr) shockingly shoots a deputy sheriff in the head and is herself killed, the film follows Charley and Molly as they dance around each other, Molly violently pressuring minor hoods, Charley setting up an elaborate mechanism which will allow him to escape scot-free with most of the money. *Charley Varrick* is cool and cynical, yet less in love with glossiness than such heist movies as **The Thomas Crown Affair**. Vernon is the sharp-suited businessman who stands for the pastel-and-chrome corporate values Charley is in revolt against. Siegel, relaxing slightly after the more gruelling **Dirty Harry**, has the grouchily charming Matthau rather than the grim Clint Eastwood as a hero, and very slightly guys the central characters, taking slightly guys the central characters, taking the violent edge off their actions with wry quips. The picture is especially strong on the details of minor crime: Molly has to put up in an authentically tacky rural motel-cum-brothel, and Varrick, in an acidly funny scene, has to procure passports from an extremely mercenary underworld photographer (North). KN

1973/111m/U/p/d Don Siegel/s Howard Rodman, Dean Riesner/orig John Reese *The Looters*/c Michael Butler/m Lalo Schifrin/ lp Walter Matthau, Joe Don Baker, Felicia Farr, Andy Robinson, John Vernon, Sheree North.

The Chase

Based on a typical **Cornell Woolrich** story (the 1944 novel *The Black Path of Fear*), this outing features Cummings's chauffeur and Morgan's gangster's wife on a paranoia-ridden run to Havana away from gangster-husband Cochran. The result is highly suspenseful until the screenplay resorts to the cop-out device of having a it's-all-been-a-dream insert. Nevertheless, newcomer Cochran is impressive as the handsome, suave killer whose hobby is racing his car against speeding trains to near-misses at railway crossings. Planer's photography adds to the film's dark, appropriately smothering atmosphere. TV

1946/86m/UA/p Seymour Nebenzahl/ d Arthur Ripley/s Philip Yordan/c Franz F. Planer/m Michel Michelet/lp Robert Cummings, Michele Morgan, Peter Lorre, Steve Cochran.

The Chase

Bubba (Redford) escapes from prison, back to his Texas hometown, where he's a local hero from the wrong side of the tracks, and his former best friend (James Fox) is now the local squire uneasily hitched to Bubba's ex-girl-friend (Fonda). Unfortunately Redford has returned during a political convention when the local bums are lubricated with corn liquor and the urge to kill, and Bubba seems the perfect candidate. The sheriff (Brando) keeps the peace, torn between a bullying bigwig (Marshall) and his duty. The script, by Hellman from a play by Horton Foote, features her characteristic preoccupation with small-town secrets, snobbery and sexual dysfunction. MP

1965/133m/COL/p Sam Spiegel/d Arthur Penn/s Lillian Hellman/c Joseph La Shelle/ m John Barry/lp Marlon Brando, Jane Fonda, Robert Redford, E.G. Marshall, Angie Dickinson.

Chase, James Hadley

(René Raymond, 1906–85)
A prolific writer, Chase is best remembered for *No Orchids For Miss Blandish* (1939, first filmed 1948) and its (at the time) shocking mix of sex and violence. The plot is similar to that of **William Faulkner**'s *Sanctuary* (1931). Like Peter Cheyney, Chase had his greatest success in France where several of his novels were filmed. Despite, like most of his novels, being set in the US, the film of *No Orchids* was decidedly British in feel and theme. An heiress is kidnapped, made love to by a gangster and in turn falls for him. Accordingly, despite the cut-price depiction of the US complete with phoney British American accents, *No Orchids* was a simple tale of class warfare, given an added edge by the emphasis on sex and violence which caused a public outcry. The film (like the novel before it) was a huge hit in the UK and in Europe; however, in the US there was as much comment about the American accents as the sex and violence. The novel was filmed again by Robert Aldrich as **The Grissom Gang** with a Depression setting which gave greater resonance to the story. The only other substantial film derived from a Chase novel is *Eve* (novel 1945, film *Eva* 1962) which is completely reworked by Joseph Losey. In the 50s and 60s several Chase novels were filmed in France. These include *Voici le temps des assassins* (1956, from

LEFT James Hadley Chase with starlet Tania Beryl

ABOVE Robert Cummings, *The Chase* (1946)

More Deadly Than The Male, 1946), *L'Homme à l'imperméable* (1957, from *Tiger by the Tale*, 1954), *Une Manche et la belle* (1957, from *The Sucker Punch*, 1954), *Fais-moi confiance* (1960, from *You Find Him, I'll Fix Him*, 1956), *Tirez la chevillett* (1963, from *Come Easy – Go Easy*, 1960) and *Trop petit mon ami* (1969, from *The Way the Cookie Crumbles*, 1965). PH

The Cheaters

Shot as a silent film in 1929 after **The Far Paradise**, some sound scenes were added later to increase distribution opportunities but at the expense of the film's dramatically visual rhythm. The film has a remarkably similar story to that of the earlier one. When the Dr Mabuse-like gang lord and swindler Bill Marsh (Greenaway) is released from prison after twenty years he seeks revenge on the man who betrayed him (Faulkner). His daughter Paula (Lorraine) falls in love with her father's arch enemy's son (Bambach), eventually reforms and, freed from Greenaway's evil influence, marries her beloved. The movie evokes the super-criminal serials with secret passages and sophisticated gadgetry at Marsh's headquarters. The film's visual sophistication, with elegant camera movements and well-judged close-ups, is remarkable. The McDonagh sisters not only directed, produced and wrote the film; Phyllis also took care of the art

direction. PW

1930/Australia/MCD/*co-p*/*d*/*s* Paulette McDonagh/*co-p* Phyllis McDonagh/*c* Jack Fletcher/*lp* Marie Lorraine, Arthur Greenaway, John Faulkner, Josef Bambach, Nellie McNiven, Elaine de Chair, Frank Hawthorne.

Children

The issue of children and crime is as emotive in the cinema as in life, with much of the power of such varied films as *Oliver!* (1968), **Taxi Driver** and *Pixote* (1981) coming from the depiction of children entrapped in an adult-generated web of crime and corruption, rarely if ever benefiting personally from their misdeeds, traded like cattle by adult 'protectors' and relied upon by the film-makers to underline their arguments with appeals to sentimental feelings for big-eyed urchins. The amorality and instinctive criminality of children is a disturbing subject rarely addressed by the cinema. *Pixote, Mixed Blood* (1985) or *Boyz N the Hood* (1991), which have Third World or urban American settings, approach the realism of *Los Olvidados* (1950). However, most treatments of the child criminal are heavily influenced by Dickensian sentiment, whether in the junior con women of *Paper Moon* (1974) and *Curly Sue* (1991) or the goodhearted tearaways of *Les Quatre Cents Coups/The Four Hundred Blows* (1959), **Bugsy Malone**, *That Sinking Feeling* (1979), *The People Under the Stairs* (1991), *Terminator 2: Judgment Day* (1991) and *Life With Mikey/Give Me a Break* (1993). Even

ABOVE Children: *Bugsy Malone*

more fantasised are films, from *Emil and the Detectives* (1931) through **Hue and Cry** to *Home Alone* (1990), in which resourceful children trap comic, ineffectual adult crooks. In an occasional strain, typified by *Whistle Down the Wind* (1961) and **Kindergarten Cop**, childish innocence misinterprets criminality and hard-bitten crooks and cops are redeemed, if not reformed, by their involvement with waif-like kids.

The most frequent use of children in crime cinema is in the passive role of victim, where their innocence and helplessness is too often used as an easy way of making villains seem despicable, though the effect varies between the crimes of the compulsive child-killers and molesters of **M**, *Never Take Sweets from a Stranger* (1962), *The Atlanta Child Murders* (1985), *A Nightmare on Elm Street* (1985) and *Olivier Olivier* (1991) and the incidental child-slaying of indiscriminate killers in *The Crimes of Stephen Hawke* (1937), *C'era una volta il West/Once Upon a Time in the West* (1968), **Dirty Harry**, **Assault on Precinct 13**, *Communion* (1976), **Manhunter** and *Rampage* (1986).

LEFT Children: Jodie Foster, *Taxi Driver*

The crime of kidnapping, which stereotypically uses children as a leverage to extort money from their parents, is less likely in the movies to involve children than teenagers or adults, though *The Lindbergh Kidnapping Case* (1976) dramatises the precedent-setting crime and the odd thriller, like both versions of *The Man Who Knew Too Much* (1934, 1954) and **Tengoku To Jigoku/High and Low**, use child-kidnapping as a MacGuffin. Child abduction, a modern form of the fairytale device of being stolen by the gypsies, has become an increasingly frequent plot device, as evidenced by such agonised soaps as *Without a Trace* (1983), *The Stranger Within* (1990), *In a Stranger's Hand* (1991) and *Baby Snatcher* (1991). Perhaps the most-used child-involved crime plot is that in which a child witnesses a crime and is either disbelieved in a variation on the story of the boy who cried wolf (**The Window**, *Invaders From Mars*, 1953, *The Boy Cried Murder*, 1966, *Eyewitness/Sudden Terror*, 1970, *The Boy Who Cried Werewolf*, 1973, *Cloak and Dagger*, 1984) or is pursued and menaced by a criminal the kid can identify (*Blind Alley/Perfect Strangers*, 1984, **Witness**, *Lady in White*, 1988). KN

ABOVE Jack Nicholson, *Chinatown*

Chinatown

Set in 1937, but overshadowed by congealed crimes dating back to the founding Los Angelenos, *Chinatown* is the archetypal retro-chic private eye movie. It digs into the origins of the world of **Raymond Chandler** and Ross MacDonald, combining a nostalgia for clean-lined cars and snappy suits with an ironic awareness of genre convention and a Watergate-era cynicism about a conspiracy-laden society. J.J. Gittes (Nicholson), a smart but sleazy detective, investigates the supposed adultery of a water department official, only to uncover both a massive confidence scheme to make a profit out of bringing water to the desert city, and a tangled web of incest and violence. Both circles of evil emanate from Noah Cross (Huston), a craggy robber baron who could be the fancy-waistcoated villain of many a Western grown rich and old, and who has systematically starved the community of water while fathering by rape a child by his own daughter Evelyn (Dunaway). Haunted by an unspecified earlier incident ('talking about the past bothers everyone who works in Chinatown') from his earlier life as a cop, Gittes tries to step in and save the heroine and her daughter-sister. Way out of his depth, his nose brutally slit by a bow-tied weasel played by Polanski himself, Gittes is

finally drawn back to the terrifyingly mnemonic title locale to watch another set of tragedies, as Evelyn is shot dead and her daughter-sister delivered into the still-lecherous embraces of Noah. A multi-layered masterpiece, perhaps the perfect synthesis of *auteur* director and director-proof script/star package, *Chinatown*, along with **The Long Goodbye** and **Night Moves**, took the private eye to his ultimate conclusions, demystifying the trench-coated knight errant by revealing how powerless he is against prevailing social and spiritual evil from which he just barely abstains. There are no mysteries or surprises in these films, just weary confirmations that things are as bad as they seem. An influence on retro pictures like *Farewell, My Lovely* (1975) and *The November Plan* (1976, from the TV series *City of Angels*) and also such stranger mutations as **Blade Runner** and **Who Framed Roger Rabbit**, *Chinatown* entered the popular culture enough for Noah Cross to figure at the centre of the web of David Thomson's mosaic novel *Suspects* (1985), thence to reappear in Thomson's *Silver Light* (1990) and Eugene Byrne and Kim Newman's *'Ten Days That Shook the World'* (1991). A long-planned sequel, *The Two Jakes* (originally to be directed by Towne, with Evans cast as the second Jake) finally appeared in 1990, directed by

star Nicholson, with Gittes embroiled in a post-war real estate scam involving Harvey Keitel and the now-grown-up daughter-granddaughter (Meg Tilly) of Noah Cross. With all its emotional development dependent on the already past-haunted first film, *The Two Jakes* is a strange failure, longwinded but gorgeous, an imitation art movie made by Hollywood professionals, whereas *Chinatown*, made by a European artist, is one of the great achievements of a self-aware popular culture. KN

1974/130m/PAR/*p* Robert Evans/*d* Roman Polanski/*s* Robert Towne/*c* John A. Alonzo/*m* Jerry Goldsmith/*lp* Jack Nicholson, Faye Dunaway, John Huston, Perry Lopez, John Hillerman, Darrell Zwerling.

Christie, Agatha [Mary Clarissa] (1890–1976)

Christie was one of the best-selling authors in the world, the writer of the longest-running play in the history of London's West End (*The Mousetrap*, 1954, adapted from the novelette *Three Blind Mice*, 1948), the creator of two of the best known series characters in detective fiction (**Hercule Poirot** and **Miss Marple**) and one of the most significant writers in the history of detective fiction. However, though several of her books were filmed (and her characters formed the basis of a number of television series), her major role in cinema and television has been to provide stories and backdrops for nostalgic costume dramas in which a gallery of stars charm their way through a wafer-thin plot. The classic example of this is **Murder on**

ABOVE Agatha Christie

ABOVE June Duprez, *And Then There Were None*, adapted from an Agatha Christie novel

the manner of pieces on a Cluedo board. In so doing she found new ways to twist and turn the reader: making the most likely suspect first 'proved' to be innocent and then turn out to be the guilty party after all; having a group of people rather than an individual responsible for a murder; having the narrator as the murderer; having a murderer pretend to be a serial killer to hide an obvious motive for his killing one of the victims, and so forth. The ingenuity and complexity of her puzzles in great part explains the limited impact she and other Golden Age detective writers had on the crime film. In novels it was relatively easy to hide away the little clues to the unfolding mystery. Crime novelist and critic H.R.F. Keating has singled out one such 'hidden' clue: 'Does she need to establish that the butler is short-sighted (and so did not see the person he swore he had)? Poirot makes great play over asking whether a date had been torn off a wall-calendar. The butler crosses the room to give him his answer. Poor deluded readers puzzle away about the significance of the dates while the true clue has been quietly dropped into their laps.' On paper perfect, but on the screen, where there is less time available for dialogue and hidden observation and where there is a need for characters rather than ciphers and for action rather than explanation, the puzzle plot is less powerful. Indeed it only works when it could be attached either to a strong central character (in the manner of **Sherlock Holmes**) or to the costume drama sense of nostalgia as in *Murder on the Orient Express*.

Christie's other series detectives included the fantastic Harley Quin, who made his appearance in the short-story collection *The Mysterious Mr Quin* (1930), and Parker Pyne, who first appeared in *Parker Pyne Investigates* (1934). Both characters only ever appeared in short stories. Tuppence and Tommy Beresford, who first appeared in *The Secret Adversary* (1922) which was the first of her novels to be filmed (in Germany as *Die Abenteuer GmbH*, 1928), saw Christie broaden her scope to include espionage. Other films which derived from her novels and stories included the courtroom drama *Witness for the Prosecution* (1957, story 1948). Christie as a character featured in *Agatha* (1979) which detailed her well-documented disappearance in 1926, reportedly caused by the death of her mother and the impending break-up of her first marriage. Christie was played by Vanessa Redgrave. PH

the Orient Express (from the 1934 novel), with Albert Finney as Hercule Poirot. Less successful was *The Mirror Crack'd* (1980, from the 1962 novel), which attempted the same thing with Angela Lansbury as Miss Marple and a cast that included Elizabeth Taylor, Kim Novak, Rock Hudson and Tony Curtis. The UK television series starring David Suchet as Poirot (1989–91) and Joan Hickson as Miss Marple (1984–92) were similarly constructed with an eye on a past golden age.

Christie's novels, commencing with *The Mysterious Affair At Styles* (1920), which introduced Poirot, are generally considered as ushering in what critics have called the Golden Age of Detective Fiction. The best of her novels include *The Murder of Roger Ackroyd* (1926), *Lord Edgware Dies* (1933, filmed 1934), *The ABC Murders* (1936, filmed as *The Alphabet Murders*, 1965) and *Ten Little Niggers* (1939, filmed as **And Then There Were None** in 1945 and 1974 and as *Ten Little Indians* in 1965 and 1989). In them Christie proved herself the mistress of puzzle construction as the centrepiece of the detective novel. As a result, with the exception of her detectives, the characters in the novels became mostly ciphers whom she moves around the rooms of the country house in

The City Gone Wild

Encouraged by the success of **Underworld**, Paramount made this vigorous Chicago gangland melodrama, paving the way for the famous 1930s films of organised crime. Meighan is the criminal lawyer, forever getting his clients acquitted on a technicality; Standing is his opponent, the District Attorney. But Meighan and Standing are friends out of court, and love the same girl (Milner). Standing is killed when he discovers the identity of 'the man upstairs', who is Milner's father. Meighan abandons his practice and becomes the D.A. who saves Milner from disgrace when a slighted gun-moll (none other than Brooks) reveals all. The film appears lost. It was praised at the time for its authentic sets and details, and for the novelty of the plot. One touch that *Variety*'s reviewer enjoyed was that each of the two main hoodlums (Kohler and Martin) was accompanied by a girl carrying a loaded gun in her handbag. Kohler's girl was Brooks, playing the deliciously titled 'Snuggles Joy'. JL

1927/5408ft/PAR/*d* James Cruze/*s* Jules Furthman/*c* Bert Glennon/*lp* Thomas Meighan, Marietta Milner, Wyndham Standing, Fred Kohler, Louise Brooks.

City that Never Sleeps

In this would-be clone of **The Naked City** the locale is Chicago rather than New York and the earlier film's laconic voice-over commentary is reductively imitated in the shape of a folksy narration (spoken by cowboy actor Chill Wills) supposedly provided by the conscience of the city itself. Other drawbacks are that the film's studio sequences suffer from the makeshift production values that marred some other Republic pictures of the time, and is burdened by an over-detailed plot. The double stranded plot, which takes place over one night, features a police officer (Young) poised to give up his wife and job to run off with a striptease dancer (Powers) and the hunt for a killer on the run. When the latter guns down the policeman's father it precipitates a predictable change of heart. Talman as the killer and Arnold as his first victim, a corrupt lawyer who has found Talman in flagrante with his young wife, provide compensation for the colourless playing of the leads. TP

1953/90m/REP/*p/d* John H. Auer/*s* Steve Fisher/*c* John L. Russell Jr./*m* R. Dale Butts/*lp* Gig Young, Mala Powers, Edward Arnold, Marie Windsor, William Talman.

ABOVE Alain Delon, Jean Gabin, Lino Ventura, *Le Clan des Siciliens*

Le Clan des Siciliens/ The Sicilian Clan

Adapted from a novel by the man who invented the word 'rififi', Verneuil's hit film starred three of France's male superstars. Gabin is the boss of the Manalese family, Ventura a tenacious and laconic cop and Delon the psychotic killer who also doubles as the romantic lead. The plot has Sartet (Delon) sprung from a prison van by the Manalese family in order to help set up a big jewellery heist in Rome, which also involves links with the US mob. The highlights include the spectacularly shot landing of an aeroplane on a US motorway and Delon viciously battering a live eel to death on a rock, watched by his shaken but excited lover (Demick). After the successful heist, the Manalese clan's boss has to execute Sartet for seducing his daughter-in-law and the cops round up all the criminals. Verneuil, fresh from a failed attempt to break into Hollywood with *The Battle of San Sebastian* (1967), had the good sense to let the accomplished film actors carry the movie, as he had done with his major hit starring Gabin and Delon, *Mélodie en sous-sol* (1963). The film benefited from some unplanned publicity. During the shooting, Delon became implicated in the Markovic murder case and the papers had front-page pictures of the star in handcuffs. The film, also released in an English language version in the US, became a massive hit on its release in 1969, eclipsed only by **Borsalino** shortly afterwards. PW

1968/France/124m/Fox Europa-Les Films du Siècle/*p* Jacques Éric Strauss/*d/co-s* Henri Verneuil/*co-s* José Giovanni, Pierre Pelegri/*orig* Auguste Le Breton/*c* Henri Decaë/*m* Ennio Morricone/*lp* Jean Gabin, Lino Ventura, Alain Delon, Irina Demick, Amedeo Nazzari.

A Clockwork Orange

Almost uniquely in the cinema, this approaches the problem of crime not from the point of view of its causes (here, a combination of urban and moral decay) but in an attempt to assess methods of dealing with unrepentant criminals. In the future, Alex (McDowell), a bowler-hatted juvenile delinquent jailed after a childish sexual violence spree, earns parole by submitting to a treatment which turns him into a brown-suited good citizen, nauseated at the thought of sex or violence and, incidentally, classical music. On his release, the former thug is promptly and symmetrically victimised by all the people he has earlier assaulted, the most horrifying discovery being that his old gang of violent stooges have found their ideal place in society by joining the police. Exploited by the state and by intellectual dissidents as a symbol of liberation or repression, Alex is finally unscrambled, and prepares to cut loose again. In this satirical dystopia, Kubrick ambiguously celebrates the ape-like primitivism of Alex, who resembles the bone-wielding missing link of *2001: A Space Odyssey* (1968), set against the hypocrisies of corrupt and mealy-mouthed factions intent on using his life to make abstract points. KN

1971/GB/137m/WB/*d/p/s* Stanley Kubrick/*orig* Anthony Burgess/*c* John Alcott/*m* Walter Carlos/*lp* Malcolm McDowell, Patrick Magee, Michael Bates, Miriam Karlin, Adrienne Corri, Aubrey Morris.

Coeur de Lilas

This features one of Gabin's last appearances as a villain. A businessman is found murdered and one of his employees (Delaître) is arrested, even though the distinctive glove of a well-known cabaret artiste known as Cœur de Lilas (Romée) is found next to the corpse. Inspector Lucot (Luguet) disguises himself as an unemployed mechanic and gets to know the beautiful singer. Her ex-lover and probably pimp (the story and the imagery allow both interpretations), Martousse (Gabin) makes his presence felt and when the incognito inspector takes Cœur de Lilas for a weekend in the country, Martousse follows

them and reveals to her that her new lover is a police inspector seeking to incriminate her. She is devastated and goes to give herself up for the murder of the businessman. The film, her last, is devoted to the romantic image of Romée. She committed suicide a year later. PW

1931/France/90m/Fifra/*d/co-s* Anatole Litvak/*co-s* Dorothy Farnum, Serge Veber/*orig* Charles-Henry Hirsch, Tristan Bernard/*c* Curt Courant/*m* Maurice Yvain/*lp* Marcelle Romée, André Luguet, Jean Gabin, Madeleine Guitty, Carlotta Conti, Marcel Delaître.

Cohen and Tate

Eric Red scripted **The Hitcher**, an ingenious cross between road movie and chiller, and something of the same mix of genres is present in this, his directorial debut, although here they are contained within an ostensibly more realistic framework. The eponymous characters (Scheider, Baldwin) are professional killers detailed to kidnap a small boy (Cross) who has witnessed a gangland affray. The Texas-set action begins with their assault on the safe house where he and his family are being kept by the authorities, and covers the single night of the threesome's (inevitably unfinished) journey back to Houston. The stark compression of the nar-

ABOVE Wilkie Collins

rative, in which only the first and last sequences occur in daylight, invites comparison with the crime movies of such directors as Phil Karlson and Don Siegel; in particular the latter's **The Lineup** comes to mind in the contrast between the two killers, the older man resigned and taciturn, the younger one febrile and increasingly jittery. The movie is somewhat reliant in its earlier passages upon dialogue, but when the action develops it is succinctly managed, and there is a gripping sequence in which cool nerve and a capacity for improvisation enable the killers to negotiate an extensive police roadblock. TP

1988/85m/Nelson/*p* Antony Rufus Isaacs, Jeff Young/*d/s* Eric Red/*c* Victor J. Kemper/*m* Bill Conti/*lp* Roy Scheider, Adam Baldwin, Harley Cross, Cooper Huckabee, Suzanne Savoy.

Collins, Wilkie (1824–89)

Collins was the author of both *The Moonstone* (1868, first filmed 1915), called by T.S. Eliot 'the first, the longest, and the best of modern English detective novels', and of **The Woman in White** (1860, first filmed 1917) which mixed grotesquerie (Count Fosco's bulk) and thrills (with Marian Holcombe forever in danger) in a shifting plot in which Fosco's crime is only unravelled by hard detective work. The two novels can be seen as standing at the head of two different traditions of crime writing. *The Moonstone* is more purely

LEFT *A Clockwork Orange*

one of detection; it even includes the first of many country houses and introduces in Sergeant Cuff a characterful detective. The novel was successfully adapted for television in the UK in 1996. *The Woman in White* is more thrilling. Moreover in Marian Holcombe it has a strong character who seeks to redress a social wrong as well as expose a crime – this was even more the case in the equally fine *No Name* (1862), which features an even stronger-minded heroine, and in *The Law and the Lady*. The movies drew more from the second tradition.

The Woman in White was filmed in 1929 and 1940 (as *Crimes at the Dark House* with Todd Slaughter giving a typically bravura performance as the evil Percival Clyde). The best version is the 1948 film with Sydney Greenstreet as Count Fosco, the engine of Glyde's scheming. Collins, who with his close friend Charles Dickens was much interested in amateur theatricals, wrote dramatic versions of both novels. Many of his other novels and stories have a mystery element. The most interesting from our perspective is *Armadale*, whose anti-heroine Lydia Gwilt is surely the first *femme fatale* in the modern sense. PH

Colors

In a **Joseph Wambaugh**-like scenario, Duvall and Penn are, respectively, vet and rookie partners attached to the LA street gang unit who, despite the characters' conflicting police procedure personalities, end up creating more individual problems than they are assigned to solve. Nevertheless, the high-speed visual action is impressive, as is the relentless on-the-edge score by Hancock. TV

1988/120m/Orion/*p* Robert H. Solo/*d* Dennis Hopper/*s* Michael Schiffer/*c* Haskell Wexler/*m* Herbie Hancock/*lp* Sean Penn, Robert Duvall, Maria Conchita Alonso.

Coma

Adapted from Robin Cook's 1977 novel, this updates the anti-medical unease of Frankenstein or Burke and Hare themes into a high-tech hospital environment. Doctor Bujold suspects that certain patients in the hospital where she works have died due to deliberate malpractice. With little help from her thuggish intern boyfriend (Douglas), she proves her sinister superior (Widmark) has established a repository of comatose semi-corpses, ready to donate organs to wealthy invalids for a huge fee. Crichton, himself a doctor

and a novelist, expertly surrounds the suspense movie mechanisms of the plot with a profoundly eerie hospital setting, a strip-lit, white-on-white nightmare that serves the same function as the unholy convent of the gothic novels, entrapping the heroine in an inhuman system where robed acolytes perform ritual sacrifices, and the supposedly noble cause of medicine is perverted into a crass capitalist conspiracy. The influence of *Coma* can be seen in *The Cradle Will Fall* (1983), *Terminal Choice* (1985), *B.O.R.N.* (1988), *Dead Ringers* (1989) and *The Ambulance* (1991). KN

1978/113m/MGM/*p* Martin Erlichman/*d/s* Michael Crichton/*orig* Robin Cook/*c* Victor J. Kemper, Gerald Hirschfeld/*m* Jerry Goldsmith/*lp* Genevieve Bujold, Michael Douglas, Elizabeth Ashley, Rip Torn, Richard Widmark, Lois Chiles.

Comics

Despite many attempts at translating comic strips (carried, usually in daily instalments, by newspapers) and books (published usually on a monthly schedule) to the cinema and, latterly, television, few crime-fighters of the comics have made the grade in the movies – with the exceptions of **Dick Tracy** and **Batman**. Among comics characters who have featured in live-action adaptations, often chapterplays or disposable TV series, are aerial daredevils Ace Drummond,

Blackhawk, Smilin' Jack, Tailspin Tommy and Bruce Gentry; superheroes Superman, the Flash, Captain America, Wonder Woman, the Human Target, the Incredible Hulk, the Teenage Mutant Ninja Turtles and the Crow; and girl reporters Brenda Starr and Friday Foster. Among rare comics-derived films to concentrate on law enforcement are the serials *Radio Patrol* (1937), *Secret Agent X-9* (1937), *Red Barry* (1938), *King of the Royal Mounted* (1940) and *Congo Bill* (1948). Even these, with the exception of the car-based *policier*, *Radio Patrol*, owe more to Western, espionage or jungle genres than to what is usually understood by the crime movie. KN

Compartiment tueurs/ The Sleeping Car Murders

The first film adapted from a Japrisot novel, this is a stylistic exercise modelled on Hollywood's 40s thrillers by Konstantinos Gavras *aka* Costa-Gavras, best known for his political melodramas *Z* (1969), *Etat de siège* (1973) and *Missing* (1982). The people who occupied a particular compartment on the Marseille-Paris train are being killed one after another. Inspector Grazzi (Montand), suffering from a cold that plays havoc with his Marseille accent, and his assistant, Jean-Loup (Mann) investigate. It turns out that Jean-Loup, with an accomplice (Trintignant), committed the murders and after a spectacu-

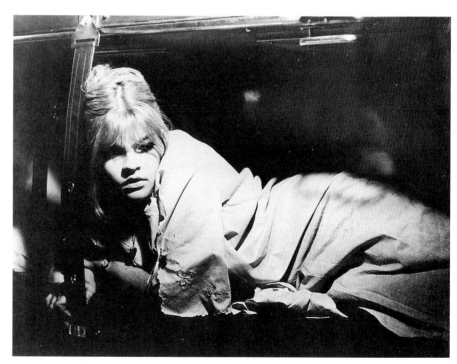

ABOVE Catherine Allégret, *Compartiment tueurs*

to refer to them as 'a couple of powder boys'. But the emphasis rests more on a grippingly detailed account of the closing of the judicial net around the perpetrators of the crime, which itself remains unseen. The concluding courtroom scenes are rescued from any threat of anti-climax by the quality of Welles's intervention as the defending lawyer, and the eloquence of his (successful) plea against capital punishment is all the greater for being made in the context of his clients' unequivocal guilt. TP

1959/103m/FOX/*p* Richard D. Zanuck/ *d* Richard Fleischer/*s* Richard Murphy/ *c* William C. Mellor/*m* Lionel Newman/ *lp* Bradford Dillman, Dean Stockwell, Orson Welles, E.G. Marshall, Diane Varsi.

Con Men (and Women)

The confidence man, whose literary and mythic roots stretch from the *Canterbury Tales* and Brer Rabbit to Melville's *The Confidence Man* (1857) and Grant Allen's *An African Millionaire* (1898), is a familiar film character. Confidence tricks generally involve the working-out of a pleasantly intricate plot and stereotypically have as victims unsympathetically venal and rich characters. Accordingly, the con man is rarely the screen villain; even Stavisky, who ruined many people in France in the late 20s by selling forged government bonds, is represented by attractive performers like Dustin Hoffman in *Papillon* (1973) and Jean-Paul Belmondo in *Stavisky. . .* (1974). The archetypal con man movie is **The Sting**, in which handsome swindlers Paul Newman and Robert Redford stage an elaborate charade in order to cheat a deeply nasty gangster (Robert Shaw) out of money he didn't earn. The set-up, which establishes Shaw's misdeeds, is a moral get-out clause that allows the audience, who see some (but crucially not all) of the inside workings of the sting, to enjoy watching a crime being committed. Similar in tone are the comic and romantic adventures of Janet Gaynor and Douglas Fairbanks Jr in *The Young in Heart* (1938), Charles Coburn and Barbara Stanwyck in *The Lady Eve* (1941), Clark Gable in *Honky Tonk* (1941), Robert Preston in *The Music Man* (1962), David Niven and Marlon Brando in *Bedtime Story* (1964), Joanne Woodward and Henry Fonda in *A Big Hand

for the Little Lady/Big Deal at Dodge City* (1966), George C. Scott and Michael Sarrazin in *The FlimFlam Man* (1967), Richard Attenborough and David Hemmings in *Only When I Larf* (1968), Zero Mostel and Gene Wilder in *The Producers* (1968), James Garner and Lou Gossett in *Skin Game* (1971), Sid Caesar in *Barnaby and Me* (1977), Anthony Quinn and Adriano Celentano in *The Con Artists* (1977), Jackie Gleason and Mac Davis in *The Sting II* (1983), Michael Keaton in *The Squeeze* (1987), Michael Caine and Steve Martin in *Dirty Rotten Scoundrels* (1989), Jim Belushi and Alysan Porter in *Curly Sue* (1991), Eddie Murphy in *The Distinguished Gentleman* (1993) and Mel Gibson in *Maverick* (1994). These are loveable scoundrels with a mile-wide soft streak; their crimes don't hurt anyone and, more often than not, their caper falls down at the last, dumping them back in the small-time.

A less prolific strain are more realistic con men. These include Richard Widmark's night-club tout in **Night and the City,** Anthony Quinn and Richard Basehart in *Il bidone/The Swindle* (1955), Tony Curtis's 'press agent' in **Sweet Smell of Success,** Paul Newman's pool player in *The Hustler* (1961), Ryan and Tatum O'Neal in *Paper Moon* (1973), Jodie Foster and Gary Busey in *Carny* (1980), Joe Mantegna in *House of

lar chase across Paris, he kills himself. The surviving love interest is provided by Bambi (Allégret) and Daniel (Perrin). The conventional plot structure is enlivened by some well-observed acting, especially by Signoret as an ageing actress and Piccoli as a nervous victim. But Costa-Gavras's real merit is in the way he conveyed a sense of joyful virtuosity in the *mise en scène* and the use of the CinemaScope screen, pleasures manifestly shared by the cast and by the famous names making cameo appearances (Arnoul, Lafont, Gélin and Dauphin). The film was also released in a dubbed version. PW

1965/France/95m/PECF/*p* Julien Derode/ *d/s* Costa-Gavras/*orig* Sébastien Japrisot/ *c* Jean Tournier/*m* Michel Magne/*lp* Yves Montand, Simone Signoret, Pierre Mondy, Catherine Allégret, Jacques Perrin, Michel Piccoli, Jean-Louis Trintignant.

Compulsion

Names and some details have been altered, but this film, drawn from Meyer Levin's novel, unmistakably derives, as did **Rope**, from the case of the 'thrill killers' Leopold and Loeb in 1920s Chicago. On this occasion the period and locale are retained, and the film, commandingly shot in black and white CinemaScope, conjures up the Jazz Age to vivid effect. Censorship precluded direct recognition of the homosexual relationship between the murderers (Dillman and Stockwell), although the sardonic D.A. is allowed

ABOVE Rufus, Michel Bouquet, *Un Condé*

Games (1987), John Cusack and Anjelica Huston in **The Grifters**, Michael Biehn and Nicolas Cage in *Deadfall* (1993). These live from petty scam to petty scam and often suffer when caught out and their intellectual money-making schemes are rewarded with brutal beatings.

The most frequently-used movie con involves impersonating the missing heir (*The Texan*, 1930, *Branded*, 1950, *Paranoiac*, 1964, *What's a Nice Girl Like You . . .?*, 1971, *The Stranger Within*, 1991, *The Addams Family*, 1992), the most ambitious variant being Samuel Fuller's *The Baron of Arizona* (1950), based on the true story of the attempts of James Addison Reavis (Vincent Price) to convince the US government that he was legally entitled to ownership of a vast tract of Western territory. KN

Un Condé/The Cop/Blood on My Hands

Boisset's brutal but stylish thriller became a *cause célèbre* when the French Government, remembering the police's enthusiastic actions against the demonstrators in May 1968, succeeded in delaying the film's release for a few months. Pierre Vial-Lesou, the son of a policeman and the author of **Le Doulos**, wrote this portrait of a callous and violent cop. Inspector Favenin (Bouquet) has to

clear up some gangland killings. He does his job with brutal efficiency, torturing and killing his way towards the necessary confessions. He also keeps quiet about the gangsters' connections with right-wing politicians and cops, including his own boss (Celi). Boisset has Bouquet play the lead as a sinister, obsessive bureaucrat dressed in black, carrying out orders and doing what he perceives to be his duty. Since being a policeman is a 'dirty job' it can only be done in a dirty manner, according to Favenin. The government's attempts to suppress the suggestion that policemen torture and kill, as well as being in cahoots with gangsters and corrupt politicians, only helped to promote the film. Boisset continued with cop-corruption movies such as *Le saut de l'ange* (1971). PW

1970/France, Italy/98m/Stephan-Empire/ *p* Véra Belmont/*d*/*co-s* Yves Boisset/ *co-s* Claude Veillot/*orig* Pierre Vial-Lesou *La mort d'un condé*/*c* Jean-Marc Ripert/ *m* Antoine Duhamel/*lp* Michel Bouquet, Françoise Fabian, John [Gianni] Garko, Michel Constantin, Rufus, Henri Garcin.

Condores no entierran todos los dias/Condors Don't Die Everyday

In the mould of **Scarface**, this ambitious film by ex-documentarist Norden chronicles

the rise and fall of an asthmatic petty criminal and fanatic Catholic. Ramirez is Leon Maria Lozano who became a notorious political and underworld mobster in 1948 during a period known as La Violencia when about 180,000 Colombians were killed as the conservatives sought to cleanse the country of its liberal opponents. The paid assassins were called 'los pajaros' (the birds), with Lozano, their leader, as The Condor. Ramirez achieves a chillingly brutal portrait of a small entrepreneur who murders his way to the top with support from the Conservative Party machine. Unfortunately, much of his performance gets lost amid the endless gun battles although the final burning of The Condor is impressively staged. PW

1984/Colombia/90m/Procinor-Focine/ *p*/*d*/*co-s* Francisco Norden/*co-s* Duni Kuzmanich, Antonio Montana, Carlos Jose Reyes/*orig* Gustavo Alvarez Gardeazabal/ *c* Carlos Suarez/*lp* Frank Ramirez, Isabelle Corona, Victor Morant, Leon Maria Lozano, Santiago Gardia.

Coogan's Bluff

A key movie, this literally transferred Eastwood's Western image into an urban police setting and set the agenda for the cop movies of the next twenty-five years. Deputy Walt Coogan (Eastwood) turns up in New York to claim a hippie prisoner (Stroud) he is supposed to escort back to Arizona for trial, only to find the man has escaped from the hospital. The big city cop (Cobb) and social worker (Clark) with whom he clashes treat Coogan much as the New Yorkers in *Midnight Cowboy* (1968) treat Joe Buck, making fun of his boots and hat and anachronistic John Wayne values, but Coogan sets out to track down the fugitive. Trailing Stroud through hippie hang-outs like the Pigeon-Toed Orange Peel Club as if he were tracking an outlaw in the desert, Coogan's direct and marginally illegal methods constantly bring him into conflict with the tired and bureaucratic legal system. Finally, the film has it both ways: Coogan gets his man, proving he is a real hero not a ridiculous imitation, but his dead-right values have softened enough for him to show sympathy for his captive. Eastwood and Siegel set the ground rules for their masterpiece, **Dirty Harry**, while the cowboy-cop-out-of-water theme was reprised directly for the TV series *McCloud* (1971–5) and, in increasingly bizarre disguises, in *The French Connection II* (1975), **Brannigan**, *Cruising* (1980), **Beverly Hills Cop**, **Red Heat** and **Black Rain**. KN

RIGHT Corpses: *Sweeney Todd* (1928)

1968/94m/U/*p*/*d* Don Siegel/*s* Herman Miller, Dean Riesner, Howard Rodman/ *c* Bud Thackery/*m* Lalo Schifrin/*lp* Clint Eastwood, Lee J. Cobb, Susan Clark, Tisha Sterling, Don Stroud, Betty Field.

Cop

This moody, psychological drama, based on the **James Ellroy** novel *Blood on the Moon* (1984), follows LAPD detective Woods, another cop with his marriage on the rocks, on the hunt for a serial killer. The killer has some sort of mysterious connection to feminist bookstore owner Warren, a complicated lady whose equally complicated past may be surfacing via Woods' hunted killer. The film marked a decisive shift from **Joseph Wambaugh**'s view of cops as fallible humans to Ellroy's bleaker view of cops as psychotics. This is perfectly caught in the final moment when Woods simply kills the killer. TV

1988/110m/Atlantic/*p* James B. Harris, James Woods/*d*/*s* James B. Harris/*c* Steve Dubin/*m* Michel Colombier/*lp* James Woods, Lesley Ann Warren, Charles Durning.

Cornered

This solid thriller stars Powell, in his second film away from his song-and-dance portrayals, as a Canadian pilot hunting the wartime collaborationist who was responsible for his French wife's death. Set mainly in post-war Argentina, Powell's excellent tough guy with a fine delivery of cynical dialogue is on a par with his above-average Marlowe in the earlier **Murder My Sweet**. The anti-Fascist mood running throughout the film here, concerning the uncovering of pro-Nazis in the Argentine, was to be expected given the leftist names behind the production. The film, perhaps, represents one of the mid-1940s *film noir* high points. The story and adaptation was by John Wexley. TV

1945/102m/RKO/*p* Adrian Scott/*d* Edward Dmytryk/*s* John Paxton/*c* Harry J. Wild/ *m* Roy Webb/*lp* Dick Powell, Walter Slezak, Micheline Cheirel.

Corpses

With **Family Plot** Hitchcock proudly proclaimed that he had made a suspense thriller without a body. The innovation failed to catch on. Whether dragged from the lake, or hanging from a makeshift noose, or collapsing into the detective's arms with a knife in its back, the corpse is part of the mythos of the movie mystery, its surprise appearance often providing the most exciting thrill. One of the most ridiculous clichés, the perambulating corpse, has been used for comic effect since the early 30s and still turns up in TV movies. (An innocent discovers a dead body, which has disappeared by the time an authority figure has arrived to inspect it. Later it turns up somewhere else.) Variations on this theme are *The Plot Thickens* (1936),

ABOVE Corpses: Véra Clouzot, Simone Signoret, Paul Meurisse, *Les Diaboliques*

The Cotton Club

Seven Sinners (1936), *The Mad Miss Manton* (1938), *The Lady in the Morgue* (1938), *One Body Too Many* (1944), *Campus Sleuth* (1948) and *Les Bricoleurs* (1962).

Clouzot's **Les Diaboliques** put the perambulating corpse in a more frightening context, a plot to drive a victim insane. This highly influential thriller has inspired three remakes – the telefilm *Reflections of Murder* (1974), another made-for-TV film *House of Secrets* (1994) and *Diabolique* (1996) – and many imitations, among them *Taste of Fear* (1961), *Nightmare* (1963), *The Curse of the Living Corpse* (1963), *Lo Spettro* (1963), *Hush . . . Hush, Sweet Charlotte* (1964), *Games* (1967) and *The Corpse* (1969). A dead body is constantly moved from place to place throughout **The Trouble with Harry**, *Loot* (1970) and *Weekend at Bernie's* (1989). The problem of corpse disposal is dealt with in *Angela* (1954), *Dilemma* (1962), *Eating Raoul* (1982) and **Shallow Grave**, but the most preposterous solution (bodies are hidden in a rocket blasted into space) is in *Spaceways* (1953). It is probable that corpses have been dumped in cars more than any other movie location.

Body-snatchers feature in *The Greed of William Hart* (1948), *Corridors of Blood* (1958), *The Flesh and the Fiends* (1959) and *Burke & Hare* (1971). In exploitation movies from the 70s onwards, psychopathic killers sometimes collected together the corpses of their victims, or embalmed them. In *Blind Terror* (1971) Mia Farrow is unable to see that she

ABOVE Leonard Cimino, unknown, Raymond St. Jacques, Godfrey Cambridge, *Cotton Comes to Harlem*

is surrounded by the dead bodies of her family. Among the most celebrated corpses in film history are the ones whose throats are slashed by *Sweeney Todd* (1928), and again by *Sweeney Todd, The Demon Barber of Fleet Street* (1936); Joe Gillis, who still manages to narrate the plot of **Sunset Blvd.**; and Mrs Bates, whose mummified remains are revealed in the unforgettable climax of **Psycho**. DM

The Cotton Club

This film is probably best known for its production problems. William Kennedy, author of a couple of classic crime novels, *Legs* (1975) and *Ironweed* (1983), was brought in late in the day by Coppola to reshape a script that had originated with Mario Puzo, author of **The Godfather**. As a result, costs rocketed and only at the last moment did Coppola agree to direct to salvage the production. Set in the famous New York night spot in the 1920s and 1930s, the story has Gere as a young musician who saves mobster Dutch Schultz from death. He is given a job at the Cotton Club and is drawn into its world of glamour and crime. Hines is a black dancer at the club, where the audiences are all-white. Their lives intersect in a complex saga that takes in the gang wars between Irish, Jews and Italians for control of the underworld, and its connection to Hollywood, where Gere ends up playing George Raft-type roles. The result is an effectively mounted panorama of the site where gangland and show business meet that never quite achieves the mythical dimension of *The Godfather*. EB

ABOVE Diane Lane, Richard Gere, *The Cotton Club*

1984/127m/Orion/*p* Robert Evans/*d* Francis Ford Coppola/*s* William Kennedy, Francis Ford Coppola/*c* Stephen Goldblatt/*m* John Barry/*lp* Richard Gere, Gregory Hines, Diane Lane, Lonette McKee, Bob Hoskins.

Cotton Comes to Harlem

This funky and endearing comedy thriller inspired the more exploitative **Shaft**, setting off the 70s wave of blaxploitation pictures. *Cotton Comes to Harlem* sets Chester Himes's unconventional, jive-talking black cops Coffin Ed Johnson (St Jacques) and Grave Digger Jones (Cambridge) on the trail of a bogus reverend (Lockhart) mounting a 'Back to Africa' scam, and of a large sum of money concealed in a cotton bale. Updating Himes's violent 1964 thriller into a jokey romp, scored by Galt MacDermot of *Hair*, Davis lightens the tone and dilutes the cynicism of the novel, in which Johnson and Jones are as corrupt as everyone else but much more dangerous, with amiable performances from engaging leads. The villain (Cannon) is forced to black up to go undercover in Harlem and is sniffed out while hiding in a lumberyard by a cool black who claims 'I smell a honky in the woodpile'. The film was successful enough to warrant a sequel, Mark Warren's *Come Back Charleston Blue* (1972), from Himes's novel *The Heat's On* (1966), but Coffin Ed and Grave Digger retired from the screen only to reappear, as minor characters

played by Stack Pierce and George Wallace, in Bill Duke's *A Rage in Harlem* (1991), from Himes's *For Love of Imabelle* (1957). KN

1970/97m/UA/*p* Samuel Goldwyn/*d*/*cos* Ossie Davis Jr/*co-s* Arnold Perl/*orig* Chester Himes/*c* Gerald Hirschfeld/*m* Galt MacDermot/*lp* Raymond St Jacques, Godfrey Cambridge, Calvin Lockhart, Judy Pace, Redd Foxx.

Courtrooms

The workings of the judicial system, enacted with a theatricality that extends even to climactic, impassioned speeches and, in some courts, wigs and costumes, have been a dramatist's gift. The courtroom drama has been one of the cinema's most popular (and under-documented) genres throughout the century, apart from a period from the mid-60s to the mid-70s, when public appetite was sated by television shows about lawyers, including *The D.A.* (1971–2); *Owen Marshall, Counselor at Law*, (1971–2) and *Petrocelli* (1974-6). In the archetypal courtroom drama a person wrongly accused of a crime is represented by an attorney or counsel, who discovers the truth, sometimes with the aid of a private eye, and then forces the true culprit to confess on the stand. The character whose name is synonymous with this process, which unfailingly culminates in an emotional confession, is **Perry Mason**.

ABOVE Courtrooms: Raymond Burr as Perry Mason

Warren William is Mason in the character's first screen appearance, *The Case of the Howling Dog* (1935), and other actors to have played him included Ricardo Cortez and Donald Woods, but it was Raymond Burr in a long-running television series (1957–66) and many television movies (1985 to Burr's death in 1993) who is most closely associated with Mason. Probably the most famous melodrama with a courtroom setting was *Madame X*, in which a mother charged with murder is unknowingly defended by her son. This was filmed seven times between 1906 and 1981. A more disturbing inversion of this plot was *The Music Box* (1989), in which Jessica Lange defends her father against the charge that he was a war criminal. Memorable courtroom scenes occur in *A Free Soul* (1931), re-made as *The Girl Who Had Everything* (1953); **Fury**; *They Drive by Night* (1940); *Roxie Hart* (1942); and *The Enforcer/Murder Inc.* (1950). Among the many murder mysteries gradually unravelled in court, the most commercially successful is undoubtedly **Agatha Christie**'s *Witness for the Prosecution* (1957, US TVM 1982). Until recently, films beginning with a tragic incident and ending in court regularly expressed

ABOVE Courtrooms: Joanne Whalley-Kilmer, *Scandal*

ABOVE Courtrooms: David Hemmings, *Beyond Reasonable Doubt*

some social concern. Examples of this are *An American Tragedy*, *State's Attorney* (1932), *They Won't Forget* (1937), *London Belongs to Me* (1948), *Trial* (1955), **Anatomy of a Murder**, *The Young Savages* (1961) and *The Boys* (1962). *Outrage* (1950), directed by Ida Lupino, was the first film to present the ordeal of a rape victim from a female perspective. Rapists also came to trial in *Town without Pity* (1961), *Lipstick* (1976), *Rape and Marriage: The Rideout Case* (TVM 1980), and **The Accused**. In many adaptations of real-life cases, a miscarriage of justice, particularly the misapplication of capital punishment, is criticised. Examples of this include *Yield to the Night* (1956), *I Want to Live!* (1958), **In Cold Blood**, **10 Rillington Place**, **Beyond Reasonable Doubt**, *The Thin Blue Line* (1988), *Let Him Have It* (1990), *In the Name of the Father* (Ireland, GB, US 1993). A real case is also the source of **Compulsion**, **Dr. Crippen**, *The Lawyer* (1970), **Violette Nozière** and *Honor Thy Father and Mother: The True Story of the Menendez Murders* (TVM 1994). The vicissitudes of the jury room were the focus of *Justice est faite* (1950) and *The Last Man to Hang?* (1956) before the definitive treatment of the subject in *12 Angry Men* (1956). In *Trial by Jury* (1994) a jury member influences others to find a guilty defendant innocent. Corrupt lawyers, commonplace from *The Mouthpiece* (1932) and *Crime without Passion* (1934), have been ousted in recent years by corrupt judges, as

in *. . .And Justice for All* (1979), *The Star Chamber* (1983), *Suspect* (1987) and **Presumed Innocent**. *Sleepers* (1996) featured a corrupt lawyer with a difference: he wanted revenge for being sexually abused as a teenager while in a remand home, to ensure the freedom of his friends who murdered their abuser and to incriminate other abusers who gave testimony in the case. Nonetheless the film has time for two traditional items of the courtroom drama, the public confession and the burnt-out lawyer who grasps his/her opportunity for a comeback. This figure is also seen in *The Verdict* (1982), *True Believer* (1988) and *The Client* (1991). The unethical lawyer/client relationship, introduced in **The Paradine Case**, returned with *Storyville* (1992), *Guilty As Sin* (1993), **Jagged Edge** and *Body of Evidence* (1992). DM

El Crack/The Crash/The Crack

German (Landa) is a private eye who is dating a psychotherapist (Casanova) and is a father-figure to her daughter. Hired to find the daughter of a dying landowner, he finds that she is a prostitute and a runner for a New York drugs syndicate. When, quoting Fritz Lang's **The Big Heat**, the daughter is blown up in his car, the charismatic sleuth goes to Manhattan and kills the villains and comes home in time for Christmas with his girl-friend. Intended as an exercise in the 50s *film noir* style, it is romantic rather than

threatening. Indeed the atmospheric cityscapes and quaint-looking fade-outs in fact recall the French versions of the genre. It was immensely successful at the Spanish box office, and Garci made a sequel, *El Crack II* (1983) with the same characters. It was set in a homophobic atmosphere and lacked the humour of the first instalment. In between the two thrillers, Garci had made *Volver A Empezar* (1982), a sentimental tale partly designed for export to the US where it won the Oscar for best foreign film. PW

1981/Spain/130m/Nickel Odeon-Acuarius/ *p* Francisco Hueva, Carlos Duran/*d*/*co-s* Jose Luis Garci/*co-s* Horacio Valcarcel/*c* Manuel Rojas/*m* Jesus Gluck, Udo Juergens/ *lp* Alfredo Landa, Maria Casanova, Miguel Angel Rellan, Jose Bodalo, Raul Fraire.

Crane, Bill

Created by **Jonathan Latimer**, Crane featured in the short-lived Universal Crime Club series in the 30s. All the films were adapted from the Crime Club novels published by Doubleday, Doran. Ironically Latimer had nothing to do with the films; it was only after the series ended that Latimer turned to screenwriting. Moreover, though the films faithfully reproduced Crane's hard drinking, they toned down the blunt wisecracking and loose sexual attitudes of the novels. All three films were drawn from Latimer novels and featured Preston Foster as Bill Crane. They were *The Westland Case* (1937, from *Headed for a Hearse*, 1935), *Lady in the Morgue* (1938, novel 1936), the best of the series which took much of its dialogue from the novel, and *The Last Warning* (1938, from *The Dead Don't Care*, 1938). Other novels featuring Crane are *Murder in The Madhouse* (1935) *Red Gardenias* (1939). PH

Le Crime de Monsieur Lange/The Crime of Monsieur Lange

Not a massive success on its release in 1936, this was the first of Renoir's 'popular front' movies made when the Comintern abandoned its divisive class-against-class policy in favour of a broad left coalition against the rise of fascism throughout Europe. Many collaborators of the left-wing theatre October Group (Prévert, Kosma, Brunius and a dozen others) worked on this story designed to show how capitalism worked. The film is set mostly in a courtyard surrounded by a print works and the dwellings of its labourers. Lange (Lefèvre) is the author of a dime novel series featuring Arizona Bill (in homage to the character played by France's

he was not responsible for any of the scripts of the 10 films, all featuring Warner Baxter as the Crime Doctor, made between 1943 and 1949. In the initial film Dr Robert Ordway was a respected psychiatrist threatened with blackmail when a prisoner whose parole is rejected reveals that Ordway has a criminal past, but subsequent outings focused on the traumas affecting others. Interestingly as the series did this, matching at series level the growing general interest in psychology in Hollywood, reviewers at the time spoke of the series' using horror elements in its plots. A good example of this is the third series outing, *Shadows in the Night* (1944) in which Nina Foch's recurring dream of a hooded woman calling for her to drown herself is revealed to be literally an illusion. William Castle directed four of the films, *Crime Doctor's Warning* (1945), *Crime Doctor's Manhunt* (1946), *Just Before Dawn* (1946) and *Crime Doctor's Gamble* (1947). PH

Crime Does Not Pay

Launching with *Buried Loot* in 1935, Loew's Inc/MGM began this series of one- and two-reel subjects which covered just about all forms of crime and criminal elements, enhanced with production values enjoying the use of Metro's standing sets and quality stock footage. The series was, in its way, a minor public showcase for various law enforcement branches (most of the entries were introduced by an 'MGM Crime Reporter' who set the scene or presented a legal agent to the audience) as well as a way of fulfilling the industry's civic obligations. While the series employed young up-and-coming actors such as Robert Taylor and Van Johnson, it also served as something of a practice ground for directors such as Jacques Tourneur (*Think It Over*, 1938), Fred Zinnemann (*While America Sleeps*, 1939; *Help Wanted*, 1939; *Forbidden Passage*, 1941), and Joseph Losey (*A Gun in His Hand*, 1945). Tourneur's 1939 feature, *They All Come Out*, actually started out as one of the two-reelers but was expanded on commission by the Justice Department as a federal prison documentary. During World War Two the series-subjects became spies and saboteurs, alongside the usual thieves and felons. The series, after some twelve years and 46 short subjects, came to a close with Joseph Newman's *The Luckiest Guy in the World* in 1947. Screenwriter John C. Higgins, who later made his name as a writer of crime films for

popular silent cinema cowboy, Joë Hamman). The factory boss, Batala (Berry), pockets the profits and absconds with the company's cash. The workers then form a collective and manage to make the enterprise profitable, at which time the boss turns up again, disguised as a priest, and once more starts appropriating the fruits of the workers' labour. Lange realises that there is no alternative but to kill the publisher in order to keep the enterprise going. When Lange and his lover are arrested, she explains the reasons for his crime and they are released. Renoir's style echoes the political themes: the film starts with individuals confronting each other, then the camera frames groups of people as the solidarity between the workers increases. In addition, because most of the action takes place in a courtyard,

Renoir adopted a very fluid camera style and deep-focus shooting, achieving startlingly beautiful and intimate imagery as the camera peers through doors and windows, showing how public events impact on private spheres. PW

1935/France/84m/Obéron/*p* André Halley/ *d*/*co-s* Jean Renoir/*co-s* Jacques Prévert/ *orig* Jean Castanier/*c* Jean Bachelet/*m* Jean Wiener/*lp* René Lefèvre, Jules Berry, Florelle, Nadia Sibirskaïa, Sylvia Bataille.

The Crime Doctor

Created by playwright Max Marcin (1879–1948) for radio in 1940, the Crime Doctor was translated to film in *The Crime Doctor* (1943). Although Marcin wrote the scripts for the radio series (which ran until 1947)

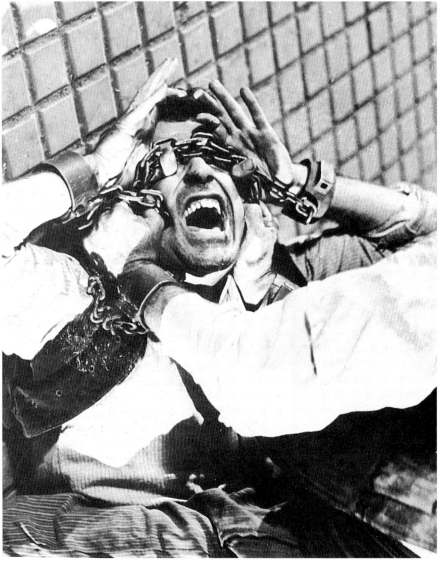

ABOVE *El crimen de Cuenca*

Anthony Mann, including **T-Men** and **Raw Deal**, supplied several original stories and scripts to the series between 1936 and 1942. TV

Crime et châtiment/Crime and Punishment

This was the first major adaptation of Dostoevsky's 1867 novel since Wiene's *Raskolnikov* (1923). It was followed a year later by Sternberg's adaptation in Hollywood. The subject lent itself beautifully to Chenal's predilection for combining urban locations with stylised studio sets, giving his films an air of brooding romanticism with elements derived from expressionism as well as from surreal poetry. Here, the emphasis is on the cat and mouse game the investigator,

Porphyre Petrovitch (Baur), plays with the youthful murderer Raskolnikov (Blanchar), bringing out the contemporary relevance during the rise of fascism of Raskolnikov's belief that superior people may be recognised by their ability to kill without remorse. The two main actors give excellently judged performances while the sets designed by Aimé Bazin and Eugène Lourié enhance the cinematic impact of the movie. It remained the best version of the novel in spite of many further adaptations (Hampe Faustman's *Brott och straff*, 1945; Fernando de Fuentes' *Crimen y castigo*, 1950; Georges Lampin's *Crime et châtiment*, 1956, and Lev Kulidz-hanov's *Prestuplenie i nakazanie*, 1969). PW

1935/France/110m/Général/*p*/co-s Christian

Stengel, Vladimir Strizhevski, Marcel Aymé/*d*/co-s Pierre Chenal/*c* René Colas, Joseph-Louis Mundviller/*m* Arthur Honegger/*lp* Pierre Blanchar, Harry Baur, Madeleine Ozeray, Alexandre Rignault, Lucienne Le Marchand.

Crime of Passion

This offering capitalised upon Stanwyck's well-established image of female ruthlessness, initially embodied here, as so often before, in the ambivalent image of the career woman. She plays a go-getting journalist who impulsively opts for marriage to a homicide detective (Hayden). Dissatisfaction with suburban domesticity soon sets in and she embarks on the dangerous game of seducing her husband's superior (Burr) in order to pressure him into hastening Hayden's preferment. Mounting complications leave Burr dead at her hands and at the ironic ending the dismayed Hayden is obliged to arrest his own wife. A cast adroitly chosen from the extraordinarily rich gallery of supporting players available to Hollywood movies of the time provides the prime satisfaction in the film. TP

1957/85m/UA/*p* Herman Cohen/*d* Gerd Oswald/*s* Jo Eisinger/*c* Joseph La Shelle/*m* Paul Dunlap/*lp* Barbara Stanwyck, Sterling Hayden, Raymond Burr, Fay Wray, Royal Dano.

ABOVE Barbara Stanwyck, *Crime of Passion*

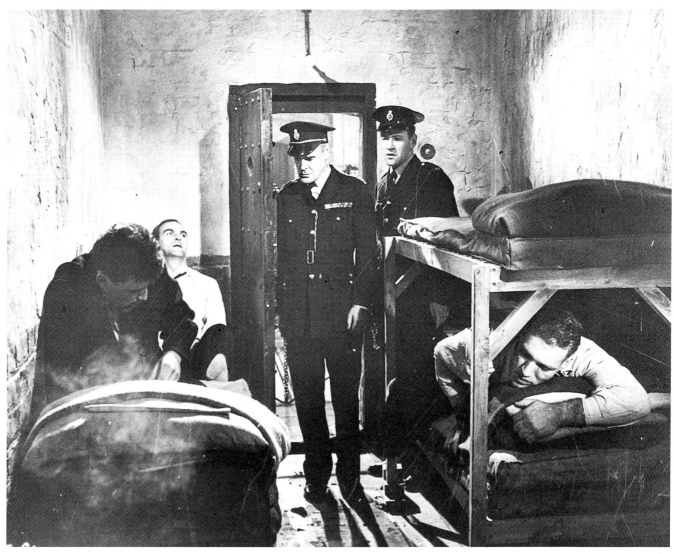

ABOVE (centre) Stanley Baker, Patrick Magee, Edward Judd, *The Criminal*

El crimen de Cuenca/
The Cuenca Crime

In 1913, two shepherds (Cervino and Dicenta) from the Cuenca region were arrested and tortured by the police, aided and abetted by the whole village of Osa de la Vega and especially by the local politician, Contreras (Rey), until they confessed to murdering a fellow shepherd and to a robbery. This graphically recounts the suffering of the two victims. Eventually, the alleged murder victim turns up eight years later in another village, exposing the monstrous behaviour of the police and of the politician as well as of the magistrate who presided over the trial. When the case is re-tried, three men implicated in the brutalities inflicted on the shepherds commit suicide. The Spanish military establishment seized the film and sued the director and the producer for defamation. When the film was finally released in 1981, it became a box office success and established the reputation of Miro who later became minister of cinema. PW

1979/Spain/94m/Incine-Jet/*p* Alfredo Matas/*d*/*co-s* Pilar Miro/*co-s* Salvador Maldonado/*c* Hans Burmann/*m* Anton Garcia Abril/*lp* Jose Manuel Cervino, Daniel Dicenta, Amparo Soler Leal, Hector Alterio, Fernando Rey.

The Criminal/The Concrete Jungle

A film that looks forward to **The Hit** in its account of a man's preparation for and confrontation with death, *The Criminal* benefits greatly from Baker's performance in the title role. In prison Baker's simple attitude of superiority is enough to save him from suffering at the hands of either Magee's sadistic warder or the liberal hand-wringing of the prison governor (Willman). Assured and seemingly non-neurotic, in prison Baker seems to be a unique Losey hero, a man overcoming his circumstances through endurance. But once out, Baker's mask slips and he admits his own humanity via his needs, for love – of Saad – and luxury – the proceeds of the racecourse robbery that resulted in his going to prison. Whereas Wanamaker (whose role on the outside parallels that of Magee inside the prison) is merely greedy in a feral manner, Baker needs his cloak of assurance to survive. Accordingly the end is all the more powerful, with Baker stripped of all his defences, and dying, scrabbling in the snow for his ill-gotten gains, just another man fearful of death. Krasker's cinematography, which edges towards expressionism rather than sober British realism, and Johnny Dankworth's jazzy score are well used by Losey to further intensify the feel of self-destruction that suffuses the film. PH

1960/GB/97m/Merton Park/*p* Jack Greenwood/*d* Joseph Losey/*s* Alun Owen/ *c* Robert Krasker/*m* Johnny Dankworth/ *lp* Stanley Baker, Sam Wanamaker, Patrick Magee, Margit Saad, Jill Bennett, Noel Willman.

The Criminal Code

This is only a marginal addition to the prison reform movies of the early 1930s, such as *The Big House* (1930) and **I Am a Fugitive from a Chain Gang**. Hawks is less interested in the sociological aspects of prison life than in the opportunity for another dramatisation of all-male relationships within a closed society. A young man (Holmes) is wrongly imprisoned for legitimately killing in self-defence. In jail he is forced into joining with his fellow convicts against an oppressive regime presided over by Huston as the manipulative warden, even though Huston offers Holmes special favours, making him his chauffeur. Karloff is impressive

ABOVE James Shigeta, *The Crimson Kimono*

as the taciturn hard man who murders the prison's stool pigeon. Holmes witnesses the murder, but he refuses to break the criminal code by testifying to the authorities, and is put in solitary until Karloff eventually confesses. The film was remade as *Penitentiary* (1938) and *Convicted* (1950), and a clip of Karloff's performance appears in Peter Bogdanovich's **Targets**. EB

1930/97m/COL/*p* Harry Cohn/*d* Howard Hawks/*s* Seton I. Miller, Fred Niblo Jr./ *c* James Wong Howe, Ted Tetzlaff/*lp* Walter Huston, Phillips Holmes, Constance Cummings, Mary Doran, Boris Karloff.

The Crimson Kimono

One of Fuller's most striking melodramas, typically combining a crime story with social analysis. With location shooting in Little Tokyo in Los Angeles, the film has a genuine feel for the culture clash which is at the heart of its social commentary. The film is also strongly marked by Fuller's characteristic love of extremes of emotion, with for example tender scenes of piano-playing clashing with sudden outbreaks of violence. Charlie (Corbett) and Joe (Shigeta) have been friends since they were in the Korean War together and Joe saved Charlie's life by providing blood for a transfusion. Fuller uses this as a metaphor for their common humanity, which overrides their racial difference – Joe is a Nisei, or Japanese-American. Now they are detectives together in the Los Angeles police. In the course of investigating the murder of a stripper they meet a beautiful woman. Each falls for her and she reciprocates the feelings of Joe. Charlie is jealous of their relationship and Joe interprets his negative feelings as a racist reaction against a Nisei associating with a Caucasian. In the course of a Kendo contest Joe's anger gets the better of him and he seriously hurts Charlie. The murderer of the stripper turns out to be another woman motivated by jealousy, and the solving of the crime causes both detectives to reflect on their own triangular relationship. EB

1959/82m/COL/*p/d/s* Samuel Fuller/*c* Sam Leavitt/*m* Harry Sukman/*lp* Victoria Shaw, Glenn Corbett, James Shigeta, Anna Lee, Paul Dubov.

Criss Cross

Practically a blueprint for *film noir*, *Criss Cross* is one of Siodmak's finest achievements. Lancaster plays Steve, a role which has something in common with his part in

ABOVE Anna Lee, *The Crimson Kimono*

Siodmak's earlier film **The Killers**. The break-up of his marriage to Anna (De Carlo), related largely in the flashback mode which, in *film noir*, so often expresses a sense of inevitable fate, has left his life without purpose. She is now involved with Dundee, a gangster (Duryea). When Dundee catches them together, they pretend Steve is planning a robbery for which he needs Dundee's help. Dundee is suspicious, and plans to double-cross Steve. Though wounded in the robbery, Steve escapes, but Anna runs out on him. Finally Steve and Anna are tracked down by Dundee, who kills them both before the police arrive. The treacherous but beautiful Anna exerts a deadly fascination over the doomed hero, enmeshed in a web of bluff and deceit. The staging of the robbery is a bravura piece of film-making, with a brilliant use of light and shadow, expressive of the excitement that Steve cannot renounce. EB

1948/88m/UI/*p* Michel Kraike/*d* Robert Siodmak/*s* Daniel Fuchs/*c* Frank Planer/ *m* Miklos Rozsa/*lp* Burt Lancaster, Yvonne De Carlo, Dan Duryea, Stephen McNally, Richard Long.

Crossfire

Despite the excellent cast, and certain noirish elements of *mise en scène*, this film obstinately refuses to escape the preachy tones of a message picture. But there are some pleasing elements in the depiction of seedy city life, particularly in the performance of Grahame as a good-time girl. Four army men meet up in a club with Samuels (Levene) and his girl-friend. They are invited back for a drink by the couple. Montgomery (Ryan), an aggressive racist, discovers the man is a Jew and beats him to death. The police suspect one of the other men, and Montgomery then kills one of his friends in order to avoid being caught. But eventually a trap is set and he is captured. The case against anti-Semitism is unnecessarily weighted by having the victim turn out to be a war hero. The producer, Adrian Scott, went to prison as one of the Hollywood Ten. In Richard Brooks's original novel the victim is a homosexual. EB

1947/85m/RKO/*p* Adrian Scott/*d* Edward Dmytryk/*s* John Paxton/*c* J. Roy Hunt/*m* Roy Webb/*lp* Robert Young, Robert Mitchum, Robert Ryan, Gloria Grahame, Sam Levene.

Cry Danger

Cry Danger contains marked elements of fatalism, made all the stronger by being set in motion by the jaunty pugnacity of Powell's screen persona. At its centre lie the efforts of an ex-con (Powell), framed for robbery, to clear his name and that of his still-jailed associate. Conrad is the racketeer behind the original chicanery. This fatalism is initially belied by the offhand briskness which characterises both writing and direction. Another factor in the equation is the use of everyday locations in downtown Los Angeles, with a key setting provided by the trailer park where Powell hides out. The fatalistic dimension comes more to the fore in the depiction of Powell's partner's wife (Fleming), who had once been his own lover and now becomes his ostensible helpmate. It transpires, though, that she has been in on the crooked dealing all along, has procured part of the robbery proceeds, and is using Powell in a bid to get the rest. But even this reversal is ultimately shrugged off by the protagonist in a movie (Parrish's first as director) whose quickfire surface may reflect his earlier distinguished career as a film editor. TP

1951/79m/RKO/*p* Sam Wiesenthal, W.R. Frank/*d* Robert Parrish/*s* William Bowers/ *c* Joseph Biroc/*m* Emil Newman, Paul Dunlap/*lp* Dick Powell, Rhonda Fleming, William Conrad, Richard Erdman, Jay Adler.

Cry of the City

The story of *Cry of the City* has something in common with the 1930s Warner crime melodrama **Angels with Dirty Faces**, in which James Cagney is a gangster and Pat O'Brien plays his childhood friend, a priest. But instead of the sociological certitudes of the 1930s, *Cry of the City* offers the baroque and disturbed sensibility of *noir* at its best, in which the city itself becomes a metaphor for the dark night of the soul. Martin Rome (Conte) is a crook recovering in hospital from a shoot-out with the police. Candella, a policeman (Mature), who grew up with Rome in New York's Little Italy, suspects Rome of being involved in a jewel robbery. Rome escapes and for the rest of the picture Candella pursues him through the night-time streets of New York. Eventually he tracks him down in a church and is forced to shoot him when Rome will not surrender. In a scene of memorably perverse eroticism, Conte, wounded and on the run, has his shoulders rubbed by a hugely fat masseuse; as she coaxes information from him on the whereabouts of the jewels, her fingers tighten around his neck. EB

1948/96m/FOX/*p* Sol C. Siegel/*d* Robert Siodmak/*s* Richard Murphy/*c* Lloyd Ahern/ *m* Alfred Newman/*lp* Victor Mature, Richard Conte, Fred Clark, Shelley Winters, Betty Garde.

Cul-de-sac

As a follow-up to **Repulsion**, Polanski was allowed to make this black comedy influenced by Harold Pinter and Samuel Beckett. Set on the island of Lindisfarne, the film follows a squabbling married couple, the shrill, mincing George (Pleasence) – who spends most of the film in a night-dress like Deneuve's from *Repulsion* – and sulky Teresa (Dorléac). Their endless round of sex games and self-abuse is interrupted by the arrival of a frog-voiced American gangster Richard (Stander) and his badly-wounded sidekick Albie (MacGowran), who, their Volkswagen stranded on a causeway with the waters rising, are waiting not for Godot but the similarly tardy master criminal Katelbach. The crooks take over and terrorise the couple while settling into the isolated abbey-turned-farm, but the tables are more or less turned

ABOVE Lionel Stander, Françoise Dorléac, Donald Pleasence, *Cul-de-sac*

by the arrival of some of George's friends, which forces Richard to pretend to be a butler. The result is a cruel movie, like Polanski's Polish debut feature *Knife in the Water* (1962), with an unhealthy marriage at its centre and a supporting cast of effete snobs and violent thugs. KN

1966/GB/111m/Compton/*p* Gene Gutowski/ *d*/*co-s* Roman Polanski/*co-s* Gérard Brach/ *c* Gilbert Taylor/*m* Komeda/*lp* Donald Pleasence, Françoise Dorléac, Lionel Stander, Jack MacGowran, William Franklyn, Jacqueline Bisset.

Cutter's Way/Cutter and Bone

The film follows two oddball losers whose friendship is tested when thirtyish gigolo Richard Bone (Bridges) tells one-eyed, crippled, embittered Vietnam vet Alex Cutter (Heard) that the man he glimpsed late at night stuffing something that has turned out to be the massively-abused corpse of a young girl into a trash can might be J.J. Cord (Elliott), a self-made oil billionaire who comes to represent everything evil and poisonous about the United States. Cutter first tries to involve Bone in a vaguely-formulated blackmail plan and then proceeds on a solo mission of symbolic vengeance, as much against what Cord stands for as the man himself. The strangely hopeful finale sees Cutter and Bone invade Cord's mansion during a party. Cutter makes a bizarrely heroic charge through the grounds on a white horse, prompting Bone to confront the ambiguously guilty Cord and, manipulating Cutter's dead hand on a gun, shooting him. Passer's film is, like *Citizen Kane* (1941) and **Chinatown**, an examination of the secret crimes upon which America itself is founded, before opting for a fairy tale finish in which the monstrous dragon of J.J. Cord is slain. KN

1981/109m/UA/*p* Paul R. Gurian/*d* Ivan Passer/*s* Jeffrey Alan Fiskin/*orig* Newton Thornburg *Cutter and Bone*/*c* Jordan Cronenweth/*m* Jack Nitzsche/*lp* Jeff Bridges, John Heard, Lisa Eichhorn, Ann Dusenberry, Stephen Elliott, Arthur Rosenberg, Nina Van Pallandt.

D

Daiakuto/The Evil Trio/ The Big Bastard

The erratic but at times brilliant Masumura collaborated again with scenarist Ishimatsu (with whom he wrote Issei Mori's **Aru Koroshiya**) on this cynical story. Yoshiko (Midori) is blackmailed by her gangster lover (Sato) into seducing a pop singer (Kuraishi) who is then blackmailed as well. The singer's manager (Uchida) enlists the lawyer Tokuda (Tamiya) to solve the problem. The lawyer persuades Yoshiko to kill her greedy lover, assuring her that he will obtain her acquittal, which he does. When Yoshiko learns she had been manipulated into murdering her lover, she blackmails the lawyer into handing over his astronomic fee. The woman, at first a victim, emerges as the strongest character of all, neatly turning the tables on the men who sought to use her. The director's style remained as flamboyant as in his first gangster movie, **Futekino Otoko**, but his narratives and characters have become far more cynical. In his next films he would explore violent sexual obsessions (*Moju, Jotai*, both 1969) before returning to more gangster and action films with *Denki Kurage*, Yakuza Zessho and *Shibire Kurage*, all 1970). PW

1968/Japan/93m/Daiei/*p* Yukisuke Seki/*d*/ *co-s* Yasuzo Masumura/*co-s* Yoshihiro Ishimatsu/*orig* Masaya Maruyama, Akutoku Bengoshi/*c* Setsuo Kobayashi/*m* Tadachi Yamanouchi/*lp* Mako Midori, Jiro Tamiya, Kei Sato, Tomoo Uchida, Isao Kuraishi.

A dama do cine Shanghai/The Lady from the Shanghai Cinema

As the title suggests, Prado's *film noir* exercise evokes the Hollywood thrillers of the 40s and 50s. A real estate agent goes to see a film in the Shanghai Cinema and finds that the beautiful and alluring heroine of the film is sitting next to him. He is drawn into the world of this archetypal *femme fatale* and winds up being asked to kill her husband. The film's fascination derives less from the acting or the plot than from the wonderfully expressionist colour cinematography of nocturnal scenes in seedy rooms and luridly lit flats and streets seen through windows. Prado's characters are reduced to enigmatic figures moving through a deliriously stylised world, but the film avoids the trap of advertising slickness or pop-promo gimmickry by a palpable delight in the combination of cinematic rhythms and atmospheres. PW

1987/Brazil/115m/Star Films-Raiz Producoes Cinematograficas/*p* Assuncao Hernandes/*d*/*s* Guilherme de Almeida Prado/*c* Claudio Portioli, Jose Roberto Eliezer/*m* Hermelino Neder/*lp* Maite Proenca, Imara Reis, Antonio Fagundes, Jose Lewgoy, Jorge Doria.

RIGHT Miranda Richardson, *Dance with a Stranger*

Dance with a Stranger

An account of the life of Ruth Ellis, the last woman hanged in Great Britain, this docu-drama, produced for British television, is the most powerful film in a run of British retro-crime drama-documentaries: *Prick Up Your Ears* (1987), *Personal Services* (1987), *Buster* (1988), *White Mischief* (1988), **Scandal**, *Chicago Joe and the Showgirl* (1990), *Let Him Have It* (1991). Like most of the cycle, the film avoids tabloid sensationalism by stressing points of law, class issues, double-edged nostalgia and self-conscious 'quality' in performance and writing. Hanged in 1955, and already the inspiration for *Yield to the Night* (1956), Ellis (Richardson) is a fading good-time girl whose shooting of her diffident aristocratic lover (Everett) is a reaction to entrapment in a class system which has warped her aspirations. Ellis's unconfined sexuality is a threat which the Establishment, represented both by Everett's worthless snob friends and the machinery of the law, must eradicate. Made with the unimaginative competence that too often passes for excellence in Britain, the film benefits from the extraordinary performance of Richardson, red-lipped and peroxided, fiercely cutting through aptly dull surroundings. KN

1984/GB/101m/Goldcrest/*p* Roger Randall Cutler/*d* Mike Newell/*s* Shelagh Delaney/*c* Peter Hannan/*m* Richard Hartley/*lp* Miranda Richardson, Rupert Everett, Ian Holm, Jane Bertish, Stratford Johns.

Dark City

Heston made his Hollywood debut in this film, and the impact of his performance, efficient but hardly memorable, echoes that of the production as a whole. Heston's cynical gambler, tied up with underworld operators, has his better feelings aroused after he is confronted by the widow (Lindfors) of a fellow card-player who has died in suspicious circumstances, and his ensuing investigation leads to the unmasking of a deranged killer, an unnerving figure as played by the hulking Mike Mazurki. However, both the working out of the story and its screen treatment have a rather half-hearted air and the action is punctuated a little too often by songs from Scott in the token role of the gambler's love. Heston recalls in his memoirs that he mastered a number of card-playing techniques, such as one-handed dealing, only to be told by a technical advisor that a real gambler would avoid using them so as to conceal his professional standing. TP

1950/98m/PAR/*p* Hal B. Wallis/*d* William Dieterle/*s* John Meredyth Lucas, Larry Marcus/*c* Victor Milner/*m* Franz Waxman/*lp* Charlton Heston, Lizabeth Scott, Viveca Lindfors, Don DeFore, Jack Webb.

The Dark Corner

'I got a feeling something's closing in on me, I don't know what,' says Stevens's luckless private detective during *The Dark Corner*, and the movie is an ingeniously developed treatment of the 'double jeopardy' premise. Stevens emerges from jail after being set up by his treacherous ex-partner (Kreuger), only to be caught up in what proves to be a first attempt to goad him into killing Kreuger, then to frame him for Kreuger's subsequent murder. The motivating figure is Clifton Webb as an epicene art dealer, whom Kreuger has cuckolded, and with fitting irony his schemes are ultimately stymied by his wife, who shoots him in revenge for her lover's death. The movie's narrative momentum is boosted by heavily shadowed lighting. The effective casting, with Webb trailing echoes of **Laura**, includes Bendix as 'White Suit', the art dealer's hired thug, who meets his fate when pushed by his displeased employer from a skyscraper window. TP

1946/99m/FOX/*p* Fred Kohlmar/*d* Henry Hathaway/*s* Jay Dratler, Bernard Schoenfeld/*c* Joe MacDonald/*m* Cyril Mockridge/*lp* Mark Stevens, Lucille Ball, Clifton Webb, Kurt Kreuger, William Bendix.

Dark Passage

David Goodis's novel makes for an interesting if flawed thriller. Halfway through the story, Vincent, on the run from prison after being wrongly convicted of the murder of his wife, undergoes radical plastic surgery in order to change his identity. What for a novel is mere description is a problem for a film. Do you cast two actors as the hero, one before and one after? The film daringly opts for another solution, which is to keep the hero's face hidden from the camera for about two-thirds of the film, during the 'before', and only show him as 'after'. It's daring because since the hero is played by Humphrey Bogart, the audience expect to see his face. In the event the device is remarkably effective (setting up in the audience's mind the curious thought of what did Bogey look like *before* he had his face done?). The story is complicated by familiar figures from the world of *film noir*, including

a petty crook, who attempts to blackmail the hero and falls to his death from a window, and the hero's dead wife's friend, a viperous Moorehead, whose false evidence had resulted in his conviction. Eventually Vincent finds happiness with Lauren Bacall. EB

1947/106m/WB/*p* Jerry Wald/*d*/*s* Delmer Daves/*c* Sid Hickox/*m* Franz Waxman/*lp* Humphrey Bogart, Lauren Bacall, Bruce Bennett, Agnes Moorehead, Tom D'Andrea.

Dead Calm

Kennedy-Miller Productions, who had come to prominence with their Mad Max series, produced this woman-in-jeopardy movie derived from the novel (published in 1963) that Orson Welles had been trying to film since 1968 as *The Deep* or *Dead Reckoning*. John (Neill) and his wife Rae (Kidman), traumatised by a car crash which killed their young son, are becalmed on a cruise with their yacht Saracen when Hughie (Zane), a frantic escapee from the sinking Orpheus, rows over to them with wild tales about what happened on his ship. John then rows to the Orpheus to investigate and discovers gruesome scenes but is trapped on the sinking ship while Hughie tries to rape and then terrorise Rae, who shoots him with a harpoon. However, according to the post-*Halloween* (1979) convention, the corpse refuses to lie down and has to be killed time and again. PW

1988/Australia/96m/Kennedy-Miller/*co-p*/*s* Terry Hayes/*co-p* Doug Mitchell, George Miller/*d* Phillip Noyce/*orig* Charles Williams/*c* Dean Semler/*m* Graeme Revell/*lp* Sam Neill, Nicole Kidman, Billy Zane, Rod Mullinar, Joshua Tilden.

Dead Men Don't Wear Plaid

A short-attention-span movie, but still an amusing spoof on 1940s thrillers, in which private detective Martin interacts with cleverly integrated clips from various black-and-white films. There is not really much of a story, but the multiple scenes in which Martin appears to banter with the likes of Humphrey Bogart and James Cagney or kiss Ava Gardner are fun for film buffs. But even then the nostalgia vapour wears off pretty soon. TV

1982/89m/U/*p* David V. Picker, William E. McEuen/*d* Carl Reiner/*s* Carl Reiner, George Gipe, Steve Martin/*c* Michael Chapman/*m* Miklos Rozsa/*lp* Steve Martin, Rachel Ward, Reni Santoni, Carl Reiner

Death Wish

A key film in the vigilante cycle, this mutates the interesting ambiguity of cop movies like **Dirty Harry** into an uncomfortable lynch mob attitude. A crowd-pleasing espousal of instant justice is thinly disguised with attempted discussion of the issues later raised by the Bernie Goetz case. Pacifist architect Paul Kersey (Bronson), unhinged by the gang rape of his wife (Lange) and daughter (Tolan), takes to the New York streets with a gun, taking a Western-style individual stand by shooting muggers who come after him. The film was success enough to prompt Winner and Bronson to return in the entirely meretricious *Death Wish 2* (1982) and *Death Wish 3* (1985), with J. Lee Thompson stepping in for *Death Wish 4: The Crackdown* (1987) and Allan Goldstein wringing the stone dry with *Death Wish 5: The Face of Death* (1994). The sequels strip away any of the character traits Kersey exhibits in the original and turn him into a superhuman terminator, boasting in *Death Wish 3* that his gun is bigger than Dirty Harry's. The vigilante cycle also threw off a horde of cheap imitations (*Boardwalk*, 1979, *The Exterminator*, 1980, *Vigilante*, 1982, *Fighting Back*, 1982) and a sex-reversal sub-cycle (*I Spit On Your Grave*, 1980, *Sudden Impact*, 1983, *Handgun*, 1983, *The Ladies Club*, 1986) of which by far the most interesting is **Ms .45**. Winner imitated *Ms .45* with the mediocre British-set *Dirty Weekend* (1993). KN

1974/PAR/92m/*co-p*/*d*/ Michael Winner/ *c-op* Hal Landers, Bobby Roberts/*s* Wendell Mayes/*orig* Brian Garfield/*c* Arthur J. Ornitz/ *m* Herbie Hancock/*lp* Charles Bronson, Hope Lange, Vincent Gardenia, Steven Keats, Kathleen Tolan, Jeff Goldblum.

Deewar/The Wall/I'll Die for Mama

After the dacoit-action hit *Sholay* (1975), Chopra directed Bachchan in this gangster movie which confirmed the actor as the Hindi cinema's undisputed superstar of the 70s and eventually led to a brief career as a member of parliament. The story, told in flashback, recounts how Vijay (Bachchan), the son of a docker, rebels against the prevailing corruption by making a career as a criminal while putting his younger brother Ravi (Kapoor) through school. Ravi becomes an honoured policeman and eventually has to confront his wayward brother and shoot him. The wounded Vijay manages to drag himself to a temple where he gives evidence of religious feelings and is rewarded by dying

ABOVE Charles Bronson, *Death Wish*

in the arms of his forgiving mother. Emotionally, the film is on the side of the tough gangster brother who beats up and kills the real villains with immense gusto, but the mother-fixation displayed by both brothers, equated with respect for religion and tradition in the face of urban materialism and corruption, turns the film into an oedipal drama with the two siblings vying with each other to become mother's favourite little man. A substantial part of the film's seductiveness comes from the script's use of Bombay vernacular language. The main character was modelled on the real-life gangster Haji Mastan Mirza, a media celebrity as public enemy number one. PW

1975/India/174m/Trimurti/*p* Gulshan Rai/ *d* Yash Copra/*s* Salim-Javed/*c* Kay Gee/ *m* R.D. Burman/*lp* Amitabh Bachchan, Shashi Kapoor, Neetu Singh, Nirupa Roy, Parveen Babi, Manmohan Krishna.

The Depression

At the end of the 20s, a combination of social and political factors sent the American economy into a reverse from which, despite the economic programs of President Franklin Roosevelt, it did not fully recover until World War II. Crime is intrinsic to the Depression movie, whether exemplified by the violence of **The Night of the Hunter** and **Bloody Mama** or the hand-to-mouth survival of *Paper Moon* (1973) and *The Journey of Natty Gann* (1986), suggesting that it was impossible to survive inside the law in the period, a theme most explicitly dealt with in Lewis Teague's *The Lady in Red* (1979), in which the heroine is driven into prostitution and bank-robbery after childhood on a dirt-poor farm and a spell in a nightmarish sweatshop.

Whereas crime in the 20s was typified by flamboyant urban figures like Al Capone, Arnold Rothstein and Charlie Luciano, the famous crooks of the Depression era were rural bandits who, like Jesse James a generation earlier, gained a certain measure of popularity by preying on the banks and mortgage companies perceived to have benefited from the toil of the starving masses. Thus **John Dillinger**, **Bonnie and Clyde**, **Pretty Boy Floyd**, **Ma Barker** and even certifiable maniacs like **Baby Face Nelson** became the subject of Robin Hood legends.

The socially conscious cinema of the 30s is weighed down by the issues of the Depression, which even affect such frothy confections as *The Gold Diggers of 1933* (1933) and *Hallelujah, I'm a Bum* (1933), comedies like *Modern Times* (1935) and *It Happened One Night* (1936) and outright fantasies like *King Kong* (1932), which may climax with Fay Wray in satin atop the Empire State Building but opens with her in rags stealing an apple from a street stall. Social problem movies like **I Am a Fugitive from a Chain Gang** and *Wild Boys of the Road* (1933) directly address the headlines of the era, and the deprivation which drives the heroes of these films to crime is also a factor in the archetypal gangster scenarios, **The Public Enemy**, *Dead End* (1937), **Angels with Dirty Faces**, **The Roaring Twenties**. There is often an ambiguous contrast between flashily doomed get-rich-quick hoodlums played by Cagney and Bogart and their trodden-down but stubbornly honest families, whose survival beyond the end credits to long lives of ethnic poverty perhaps confirms the gangster's characterisation of them as 'suckers' rather than, as presumably intended, the vital importance of staying on the right side of the law.

Common film images of the era include urban soup kitchens, rural shacks, hoboes in patched overalls, miserable faces, chain gangs and pan-handlers. The ever-present desperation (suggested in the Gold Diggers films by the thin line between girls walking the streets looking for jobs and girls walking the streets as a job) indicates that the

ABOVE The Depression: *The Grapes of Wrath*

Depression created a swelling class of the marginalised, a listless army of the homeless and unemployed existing outside the protection of society. In film terms, the key Depression personality is Henry Fonda, a decent man driven outside the law by economic circumstances, widespread injustice and blind fate in **You Only Live Once**, *Jesse James* (1939) and *The Grapes of Wrath* (1940), all of which deal explicitly or obliquely with

ABOVE The Depression: Paul Muni, *I Am a Fugitive from a Chain Gang*

ABOVE The Depression: The Dead End Kids (Gabriel Dell, Huntz Hall, Bernard Punsley), *Angels with Dirty Faces*

Deprisa deprisa—Desperate

attitudes common in the immediate aftermath of the Depression, whereby the individual outlaw is seen as heroic when compared with entrenched government or business interests. However, Fonda later played the prototypical Pa Walton in *Spencer's Mountain*, which preaches the virtues of family self-sufficiency as a cure for the country's economic ills. Henry Fonda's son Peter appeared in *Easy Rider* (1968), which revived the Depression genre of the road movie, while his daughter Jane starred in an explicit recreation of the 30s social injustice genre in *They Shoot Horses, Don't They?* (1969). *Grapes of Wrath* co-star John Carradine fathered David and Keith, similarly iconic Depression outlaws in **Boxcar Bertha**, *Emperor of the North Pole* (1973), *Thieves Like Us* (1974) and *Bound for Glory* (1976), part of a cycle, initiated by **Bonnie and Clyde**, in which a connection was seen between the outlaws and hoboes of the 30s and the radicals and dropouts of the 60s. KN

Deprisa deprisa/Fast, Fast

Saura's film extends a long line of teenage delinquent movies (including Juan Fortuny and Victor Merenda's *Delincuentes,* 1956 and Jose Antonio de la Loma's *El ultimo viaje,* 1973). Here, a group of Madrid teenagers rampage through the city's suburbs committing armed robberies, consuming drugs and driving cars at high speed to the accompaniment of disco music and loud, rather inane dialogues. Saura shot the film in sequence and took great pains to get the language and accents right, even rehearsing every scene on video in order to achieve a sense of documentary realism. PW

1980/Spain, France/98m/Querejeta-Les Films Molière-Consortium Pathé/*p* Elias Querejeta, Toni Molière/*d/s* Carlos Saura/ *c* Teo Escamilla/*lp* Jose Antonio Valdelomar, Jose Maria Hervas Roldan, Jesus Arias Aranzeque, Berta Socuellamos Zarco.

Dernier atout

The first feature by Becker, the author of classics like *Casque d'or* (1952), **Touchez pas au grisbi** (1954), *Les Aventures d'Arsène Lupin* (1956) and *Le Trou* (1959). Just released from captivity during the war, Becker wanted to make a film that reminded him of the Hollywood films he loved and which were no longer available in occupied France. The

comedy thriller is set in an imaginary Latin American country, and shot on the French Riviera. Two top cadets from the police academy are sent out on a practical test: solve the murder in a luxury hotel of a gangster. The daring Clarence (Rouleau) starts an affair with a rival gang boss's daughter, Bella Score (Balin) and infiltrates the gang. The more calculating and precise Montès (Rollin) follows up clues. The paths of the two aspirant detectives cross via a radio and Montès comes to Clarence's rescue when the latter is discovered by the crafty gang boss, Rudy Score (Renoir). Clarence and Montès graduate *ex aequo* from the academy and Bella is let off because she assisted the police. PW

1942/France/105m/Essor Cinématographique Français/*p* Jean Gehret/ *d* Jacques Becker/*s* Maurice Aubergé, Louis Chavance, Pierre Bost/*c* Nicolas Hayer/*m* Jean Alfaro/*lp* Raymond Rouleau, Mireille Balin, Pierre Renoir, Georges Rollin, Noël Roquevert.

Descente aux enfers/Descent into Hell

Based on David Goodis's *The Wounded and the Slain* (1955), this is a story about a blocked and boozy crime writer, Alan Kolber (Brasseur), who takes a vacation with his wife Lola (Marceau) in Haiti. Their marriage is rekindled when Kolber, in self defence, cuts the throat of a mugger. Lola acknowledges violence in her own past when she fought off a rapist, and together the couple

then dispose of the odd duo (Bakaba and Dubois) who try to blackmail Alan for the killing. PW

1986/France/90m/Partners Productions-La Cinq/*p* Ariel Zeitoun/*d/co-s* Francis Girod/ *co-s* Jean-Loup Dabadie/*orig* David Goodis/ *c* Charlie Van Damme/*m* Georges Delerue/*lp* Claude Brasseur, Sophie Marceau, Sidiki Bakaba, Marie Dubois, Hippolyte Girardot.

Desperate

This is the most satisfying of the several B-pictures made by Anthony Mann prior to his graduation to bigger projects after **T-Men**. *Desperate* gains from the high standard of production values which graced even second features at RKO, as well as from a screenplay that is both eventful and tightly constructed. In fact the linear progression of the narrative might be said to anticipate Mann's later Westerns such as *Winchester '73* (1950). The scenario offers a variant on the 'couple on the run' motif, with newlyweds Brodie and Long going into hiding after Brodie has been duped into taking part in a robbery staged by a psychotic criminal (Burr). Brodie then becomes the victim of an attempt to frame him for the killing of a policeman by Burr's younger brother during the raid. The episode in which Brodie is beaten by Burr's men illuminated only by a swinging overhead light possesses an emblematic force, and Burr's performance offers a further reminder that until claimed by the TV role of Perry Mason

he had a prime place in cinema's rogues gallery. TP

1947/73m/RKO/*p* Michael Kraike/ *d* Anthony Mann/*s* Harry Essex/*c* George E. Diskant/*m* Paul Sawtell/*lp* Steve Brodie, Audrey Long, Raymond Burr, Douglas Fowley, Jason Robards Sr.

The Desperate Hours

Glenn (Bogart) breaks out of prison with his kid brother Hal (Martin) and Kobish, a huge mental defective (Middleton). They hide out in the suburban home of Dan Hilliard (March), while Glenn awaits a call from his girl-friend. In the meantime Glenn threatens and bullies Hilliard, his wife Eleanor (Scott), his daughter Cindy (Murphy) and his young son Ralphie (Eyer). The police eventually track them down and surround the house, while, inside, there's a duel of wills between Bogart's angry cynicism and March's stubborn integrity. The story, by Joseph Hayes, first saw life as a novel, then as a Broadway play with Paul Newman as Glenn. The script is finely honed, suspenseful, the drama flowing naturally from the moral conflict between March and Bogart, in his penultimate role. The story marks a transition in the American perception of crime as an invasive disruption of the comfortable certainties of the American dream. MP

1955/112m/PAR/*p* William Wyler/*d* William Wyler/*s* Joseph Hayes/*c* Lee Garmes/*m* Gail Kubik/*lp* Humphrey Bogart, Fredric March, Arthur Kennedy, Martha Scott, Gig Young, Dewey Martin, Mary Murphy, Robert Middleton, Richard Eyer.

Despues del gran robo/After the Great Train Robbery

With utter disregard for the facts of the UK's so-called Great Train Robbery, this Barcelona-based comedy shows the robbers as a bunch of homicidal maniacs trying to kill each other in a winter holiday resort, upsetting the local Spanish middle-class tourists. Alternatively, the film could be read as a wry critique of Fascist Spain's policy of providing a haven for criminals on the run to the inconvenience of its citizens. Spain also produced a parody of **Ocean's Eleven**, *La pandilla de los once* (1962). PW

1965/Spain/77m/Isasi/*p* Antonio Isasi, Isasmendi Lasa/*d*/*co-s* Miguel Iglesias/ *co-s* Noel Claraso, M.Cusso/*c* Juan Gelpi/ *m* Juan Duran Alemany/*lp* Rafael Alonso, Elena Duque, Carlos Lemos, Manuel Gallardo, Antonio Duran, Maria Jose Nadal.

The Detective

This is an ambitious attempt to use a **Raymond Chandler**-style two-strand mystery to social ends, as a couple of separate cases (the mutilation-murder of a homosexual, the suicide of a corrupt land speculator) converge. The detective is finally forced to realise he has been part of a corrupt system which has executed the first victim's unstable lover for a crime he did not commit and covered up the guilt of the actual murderer, who is, of course, the neurotic suicide (Windom), a man who has confessed 'I felt more guilty about being a homosexual than a murderer'. Sinatra gives a rare committed performance, and the film attempts an all-embracing portrait of a rotten city. Though its lavender underworld sequences have dated badly, the collection of crooked and compromised cops, from time-serving chief (Meeker) to fag-bashing beat cop (Duvall), remain strikingly effective portraits. Roderick Thorp's sequel novel was filmed as **Die Hard**, in which Joe Leland became super ordinary man John McClane. KN

1968/114m/FOX/*p* Aaron Rosenberg/ *d* Gordon Douglas/*s* Abby Mann/*orig* Roderick Thorp/*c* Joseph Biroc/*m* Jerry Goldsmith/*lp* Frank Sinatra, Lee Remick, Ralph Meeker, Jacqueline Bisset, Robert Duvall, William Windom.

Detective Story

A day in the life of a busy precinct, focused around Detective Jim McLeod (Douglas), who is a rigid and old-fashioned moralist, full of rage and with an almost uncontrollable streak of violence. He beats up a suspected abortionist Dr Schneider (Macready), and when Lieutenant Monahan (MacMahon) investigates he discovers that Schneider once operated on McLeod's wife Mary (Parker). The script is based on a play by Sidney Kingsley and stays confined to the grimy, realistic precinct house set. Accordingly, the major characters have no prettifying touches, and the portrait of a cop heading for the edge is unsentimental and, for the time, startling. The parade of deadbeats and victims who move through the set provide a backdrop to McLeod's mindset and a compendium of contemporary Method acting, which gives the slender plot variety and pace. The resulting network of storylines along with the direction, which wheels smoothly round the claustrophobic set, prefigures Steven Bochco's multi-layered treatment of cop stories, most notably in the *Hill Street Blues* teleseries. MP

1951/105m/PAR/*p*/*d* William Wyler/*s* Philip Yordan, Robert Wyler/*c* Lee Garmes/*m* none/ *lp* Kirk Douglas, Eleanor Parker, William Bendix, Cathy O'Donnell, George Macready, Horace MacMahon.

Detektive/Detectives

In the wake of Schlöndorff's **Mord und Totschlag**, critic and short film-maker Thome made this stylishly vacant movie about two men (Bohm and Lommel) who decide to be detectives. They save a young woman (Berben) from her gangster admirer and are hired by an entrepreneur who plans something nasty for his ex-lover. The detectives as well as their client come to a sticky end. The film is noteworthy mainly as the cinephile Thome's feature debut. The acting feels improvised, the actors not seeming to care what the next scene will be, but the film is not about characters, but about harsh though glossy harsh urban spaces dedicated to consumption, filmed with stark contrasts and many neon lights. Director Wim Wenders hailed Thome's work, especially his next feature *Rote Sonne* (1969), as a genuine German adaptation, rather than imitation, of Hollywood's 1940s and 1950s films by Howard Hawks or Fritz Lang. PW

1969/Germany/91m/Eichberg/*p* Carol Hellman/*d* Rudolf Thome/*s* Max Zihlmann/ *c* Hubs Hagen, Niklaus Schilling/*m* Kristian Schultze/*lp* Iris Berben, Marquard Bohm, Ulli Lommel, Chrissie Mahlberg [Uschi Obermeier], Elke Hart [Elke Haltaufderheide].

Detour

This near-legendary *film noir* was produced on a minuscule budget, and it shows. But such is the force and conviction of the direction that we are swept along on this roller-coaster ride to a dead end. Al (Neal) is a piano player and his girl-friend (Savage) a singer in New York. She leaves to try her luck in Hollywood. He follows later. While hitchhiking to LA. he is picked up by a man in a big car who is carrying a lot of money. As Al is driving, the man falls asleep and later proves to have died from natural causes. But in the course of lifting the body, Al unfortunately gives the dead man a severe head wound. Fearful he will be blamed for murder, Al decides to drive on. He picks up a woman, who then discovers the dead man is heir to a fortune. She concocts a plan for Al to impersonate him and collect the money. But in a bizarre accident Al strangles her with a phone cord. Now doubly an apparent

ABOVE Ann Savage, Tom Neal, *Detour*

closest friend Paul (Pellegrin) is tortured by sadistic cops (the most unpleasant moments were removed on the advice of the censors), he kidnaps the nastiest cop (Frankeur), forces him to confess the trickery and then murders him. Gu, believing he has restored his reputation, goes to meet his mob but in a spectacular shoot-out on a stairway, everyone gets killed. Inspector Blot (Meurisse), out of respect for Gu's integrity, drops his nasty colleague's written confession at the feet of a journalist. The movie of epic proportions sustains a unique level of visual inventiveness throughout, including a hypnotically paced bravura sequence detailing what many consider the best filmed hold-up in film history, an eerie chase through a desolate quarry and elaborately choreographed interplays between camera and actors in desolate, lonely spaces. Melville also introduced little character touches that obviate the need for elaborate dialogues, like the professional killer who takes pride in removing the telescopic sight from his rifle before shooting a policeman. The all-male world of the gangsters is complemented by Melville's most sensitive portrayal of a heterosexual relationship, between Gu and his girl-friend Manouche (played by the TV personality Fabrega). Melville often commented on his love of Hollywood, but with this film (and,

murderer Al is left pondering the cruel twists of fate. The plot and its improbable coincidences may strain the audience's incredulity, but Ulmer is so successful in creating a claustrophobic atmosphere, a world in which we know that what can go wrong will go wrong, that disbelief is suspended. EB

1945/68m/PRC/*p* Leon Fromkess/*d* Edgar G. Ulmer/*s* Martin Goldsmith/*c* Benjamin H. Kline/*m* Leo Erdody/*lp* Tom Neal, Ann Savage, Claudia Drake, Edmund MacDonald, Tim Ryan.

Le Deuxième Souffle/
Second Breath

After four years of silence, Melville, the French *noir* cinema's most accomplished stylist, filmed this adaptation of Giovanni's novel, first published in 1958. The story is a typical gangster tragedy about an ageing villain, Gu Minda (Ventura), who is tricked by the police into betraying his accomplices of a magnificently staged hold-up. When Gu's

RIGHT Véra Clouzot, Simone Signoret,
Les Diaboliques

in colour, with **Le Samouraï**), he by far outclassed his models. PW

1966/France/150m/Les Productions Montaigne/*p* Charles Lumbroso/*d/co-s* Jean-Pierre Melville/*co-s/orig* José Giovanni/ *c* Marcel Combes/*m* Bernard Gérard/*lp* Lino Ventura, Paul Meurisse, Raymond Pellegrin, Christine Fabrega, Paul Frankeur.

O dia das profissionais/The Day of the Professionals

In this 'deadlier than the male' plot Scalizzi (Azevedo) is a diamond smuggler. He is robbed by Matar (Hungaro) and hires a hit man, Chileno (Portella), to kill the thief. Chileno executes the contract but keeps the loot and appropriates the smuggler's greedy wife in the bargain. Matar's daughter, the sexy Vicky (Moreira), hires someone to kill Chileno and his new mistress. She then kills her own companion and flees with the diamonds. In the end, an officially accredited macho man, Inspector Maidana (Rocha), restores law and order, giving Vicky her just deserts. Aragao had been a cartoonist, a journalist and a writer before turning director with this action thriller set in Sao Paulo. PW

1976/Brazil/100m/Cobras/*p* Flavio Santin/*d/co-s* Miguel Iglesias/*co-s* Raja de Aragao/*c* Pio Zamuner/*lp* Walter Portella, Arlette Moreira, Glaucia Maria, Dionisio Azevedo, Heitor Gaiotti.

Les Diaboliques/The Fiends

Clouzot's version of **Boileau and Narcejac**'s novel was filmed in utmost secrecy. Journalists were banned from the set, and on its release the doors were closed as soon as the film started, not allowing in any latecomers (a gimmick later adopted by **Hitchcock** for **Psycho**). Finally at the end of the film, a title card requested viewers not to spoil others' pleasure by divulging the outcome of the story. The plot tells of an odious tyrant, Michel Delasalle (Meurisse), in charge of a boarding school. His mistress Nicole (Signoret) and his wife Christina (Clouzot) decide to put an end to their suffering by drugging and drowning the tyrant in a bathtub, then throwing his corpse into a pool. Soon after, strange things start to happen. The pool is emptied and there is no corpse (causing the wife to suffer a heart attack) and a terrified Christina later finds the corpse, well and truly alive, in a bathtub, whence it rises. Inspector Fichet (Vanel) solves the mystery. Michel and Nicole

ABOVE Lino Ventura, *Le Deuxième Souffle*

arranged the whole charade to make Christina die of a heart attack. Clouzot manages to imbue the film with all the emotional intensity of a horror-thriller, providing a picture of small-town life in France which is as bleak as his *Le Corbeau* (1943). There was a lacklustre remake in Hollywood in 1996, titled *Diabolique*, with Sharon Stone and Isabelle Adjani. PW

1954/France/116m/Filmsonor/*p* Louis de Masure/*d/co-s* Henri-Georges Clouzot/*co-s* Jérôme Geronimi, René Masson, Frédéric Grendel/*orig* Boileau and Narcejac *Celle qui n'était plus/c* Armand Thirard/*m* Georges Van Parys/*lp* Paul Meurisse, Simone Signoret, Véra Clouzot, Charles Vanel, Pierre Larquey.

Dick Tracy

Unlike earlier screen versions of Chester Gould's strip, *Dick Tracy* accepts wholesale Tracy's peculiar universe and large supporting cast, with Headly as a steadfast Tess, Korsmo as Junior, Cassel as Sam Catchem and Durning as Chief Patton, plus a host of mainly disguised stars (James Caan, Dustin Hoffman, Mandy Patinkin) as Gould's freakish villains, with especially grotesque turns from Al Pacino as Big Boy Caprice, William Forsythe as Flattop and R. G. Armstrong as Pruneface. Patterned on the successfully stylised **Batman**, the film endeavours to create its own primary-coloured fantasy world . However, though it achieves this both visually, through lashings of latex and imagina-

tive art direction and aurally, with period songs from Stephen Sondheim, it is let down by a storyline that plods from incident to incident. The film unfortunately concentrates on by far the least interesting side of the Tracy story, his relationship with putative son Junior, a runaway delinquent he puts on the straight and narrow by setting a good example. With a deadening dose of family values, only slightly mitigated by Headly's surprisingly subtle performance, the film's procession of shootouts and escapes never manages to work up any verve, and the arch art direction further alienates any

ABOVE Al Pacino, *Dick Tracy*

possible involvement. Beatty makes of the square-chinned hero a middle-aged dullard who sits unemotionally behind a desk wrapped in his bright yellow trench-coat while Madonna writhes provocatively on his blotter. His empty central performance, more than anything else, renders the film an elaborate void. KN

1990/103m/Silver Screen Partners/
p/d Warren Beatty/s Jim Cash, Jack Epps/
c Vittorio Storaro/m Danny Elfman/
lp Warren Beatty, Charlie Korsmo, Glenne Headly, Madonna, Paul Sorvino, Charles Durning, Seymour Cassel.

Die Hard

This is a high-tech, high-voltage thriller which vastly improves Thorp's functional book, a direct sequel to the novel filmed as **The Detective**, by turning its hackneyed terrorist theme into a clever pseudo-terrorist plot. Knowing the authorities will follow the FBI rule-book for such situations, Rickman takes over an office tower during a Christmas party and poses as a terrorist, cutting off the power, which will open up the well-stocked vault. With its machine-like setting and almost robotic villains, the film upholds the ability of the fallible individual to stay alive in a destructive system by throwing a human spanner in the works. The spanner is vacationing cop Willis, who

ABOVE Bruce Willis, *Die Hard*

happens to be in the building to visit his ex-wife and manages, despite his crippling lack of shoes, to fight back, turning the tables on the villains in a series of ingenious stunt sequences that afford McTiernan the chance

to stage incredible set-pieces. With its dark, hard-edged action leavened by Willis's anarchic humour and some dryly scripted wit, this was a popular hit, adapting the scale of the disaster movie, specifically *The Towering Inferno* (1974), to the he-man adventure thriller. An even bigger-scaled sequel, *Die Hard 2* (1990), was directed by Renny Harlin from *58 Minutes*, a novel by Walter Wager, and takes *its* disaster cue from *Airport* (1970) as Willis stands against a group of paramilitary maniacs in a snowbound airport. In addition, *Die Hard* became one of the most imitated formulae of the 90s, hence *Under Siege* (1992), *Passenger 57* (1992), *Cliffhanger* (1993) and, of course, *Die Hard with a Vengeance* (1995) for which McTiernan returned to the directorial chair and Jeremy Irons provided yet another Euro villain. KN

1988/131m/FOX/p Lawrence Gordon, Joel Silver/d John McTiernan/s Jeb Stuart, Steven E. de Souza/orig Roderick Thorp *Nothing Lasts Forever*/c Jan De Bont/m Michael Kamen/lp Bruce Willis, Alan Rickman, Bonnie Bedelia, Alexander Godunov, Reginald Veljohnson, William Atherton.

Dillinger, John (1903–34)

A highly-successful bank robber and a criminal of undoubted flair and restraint – he hardly ever shot anyone – Dillinger is best

ABOVE Warren Beatty, *Dick Tracy*

remembered as being Public Enemy Number One. He was so nominated by J. Edgar Hoover, partly because the **FBI** (then the BI) had a policy of demonising outlaw loners whose careers could be ended by death or jail, rather than tackling the organised crime problem Hoover refused to admit existed until the 60s. In an action supervised by famed G-Man Melvin Purvis, that more resembled an assassination than an attempted arrest, Dillinger was allegedly shot dead outside the Biograph Theatre in Chicago, where a man who called himself James Lawrence had just watched Clark Gable go to the chair in *Manhattan Melodrama* (1934). At the last, Dillinger was still capable of inspiring legends, such as those surrounding the 'lady in red' who accompanied him to the Biograph (Romanian brothel-keeper Anna Sage, who betrayed him in return for leniency in an upcoming hearing and was deported anyway), and more extravagant rumours about the unnatural size of his penis (the position of his hands under the sheet in mortuary photographs makes the body seem to have a foot-long erection), and the hotly-debated possibility that a lookalike was killed in Dillinger's place, allowing him to escape along with Billy the Kid and Elvis Presley into an ahistorical happy ending. While Dillinger was barred by censorship as a screen subject during his career and for ten years after his death, many elements of his story filtered into other movies, with **The Petrified Forest** and **High Sierra** providing Humphrey Bogart with roles very much in the popular image of Dillinger, and many films borrowing bits and pieces from his biography: the theatre shoot-out in *Public*

Hero No. 1 (1935), the plastic surgery in *Undercover Doctor* (1939), the soap gun (a clever scheme undone by a sudden shower) in *Take the Money and Run* (1968), the parental visit in **Bonnie and Clyde**. Actual portrayals of the outlaw include Lawrence Tierney in the brisk B-film *Dillinger* (1945), Leo Gordon in Don Siegel's **Baby Face Nelson**, Myron Healey in *Guns Don't Argue* (1957), Scott Peters in **The FBI Story**, Eric Sinclair in *Ma Barker's Killer Brood* (1960), Nick Adams in *Young Dillinger* (1964), Warren Oates in John Milius's **Dillinger**, William Jordan in *Kansas City Massacre* (1975), Robert Conrad in the cunning John Sayles-scripted fantasy *The Lady in Red* (1979), Jon Martin making use of the penis legend in the porno *Bonnie & Clyde* (1988) and Mark Harmon in the bland made-for-TV *Dillinger* (1991). Dillinger is an oft-mentioned presence in *Melvin Purvis, G-Man* (1974) and in **The Private Files of J. Edgar Hoover**, which touch on the figure of Purvis. Several novels, including Robert Shea and Robert Anton Wilson's *The Illuminatus Trilogy* (1975), Harry Patterson/ Jack Higgins's *Dillinger* (1983) and Max Allan Collins' *True Crime* (1984), have featured Dillinger, usually elaborating the story of his reputed survival after his reported death. The name, pronounced to rhyme with 'finger' has enough connotations to serve an iconic use in Marco Ferreri's *Dillinger e morto/Dillinger is Dead* (1969). KN

Dillinger

After Roger Corman imitated Arthur Penn by developing the ideas of **Bonnie and Clyde** in **Bloody Mama**, a sub-genre of

hard-edged nostalgic Depression-era gangster movies developed (with rinky-dink music, rattling machine-guns and period cars), boosting the careers of talents as diverse as Martin Scorsese (**Boxcar Bertha**), Jonathan Demme (*Crazy Mama*, 1975) and Lewis Teague and John Sayles (*The Lady in Red*, 1979). Milius, making his directorial debut, hews closely to the famous facts of Dillinger's life: his escape from prison with a carved gun, his impulsive trip to a Chicago dance-hall with his girl-friend (Phillips) when he was at his most wanted, his betrayal by Romanian madame Anna Sage (Leachman), his partnership with other hoods like Baby Face Nelson (Dreyfuss) and Pretty Boy Floyd (Kanaly) and his death outside the Biograph Cinema in Chicago emerging from a performance of *Manhattan Melodrama* (1934). Oates, with a moustache that makes him look like a seedy Douglas Fairbanks, perfectly catches the mix of violence, charm and redneck conservatism that characterised the real Dillinger. However, Milius pits Dillinger against a heavily fictionalised and mythologised version of Melvin Purvis (Johnson), the dapper, neurotic young FBI agent who brought down Dillinger and earned the hatred of J. Edgar Hoover. Purvis is depicted as a fatherly, philosophical avenger pursuing Dillinger as much to destroy the man's myth as to end his crime spree. KN

1973/107m/AIP/*p* Buzz Feitshans/*d/s* John Milius/*c* Jules Brenner/*m* Barry Devorzon/ *lp* Warren Oates, Ben Johnson, Michelle Phillips, Cloris Leachman, Harry Dean Stanton.

Dirty Harry

A key film. Opening with Lieutenant Harry Callahan (Eastwood) of the San Francisco Police examining a sniper's spent cartridge as if he were John Wayne examining an Apache arrow, and closing with him throwing away his badge in explicit homage to Gary Cooper in *High Noon* (1950), the film updates the Western myth of the lone tracker. It also crystallises the figure of the rogue cop, embittered guardian of a law which at once confines and excludes him, that had been evolving in the cinema since **The Big Heat** and which in the late 60s and early 70s had thrown up such proto-Harrys as Dan Madigan, Frank Bullitt, Walt Coogan and

LEFT John Dillinger: Robert Conrad, *The Lady In Red*

Popeye Doyle. Harry is called 'Dirty' Harry because he 'gets every dirty job'. In this case, as in the sequels, the dirty job requires he perform a service to society by ridding it of an unredeemable element, using methods the law, represented by a horde of tired officials in shiny suits, cannot possibly sanction. Despite the 'Peace' buckle on his belt, Scorpio's psycho hippie (Robinson) rapes and buries alive a teenager, shoots innocent people at random, tries to blackmail the whole city and finally terrorises a busload of children. Eastwood considerably extends his range as the emotionally dead Harry (of his wife's death in a car accident, he calmly says 'there was no reason') who makes chilling speeches to people whom he is about to kill ('do you feel lucky?'), wields an ostentatiously phallic Magnum .44, and subtly undermines his own heroic stance as his kinship with Scorpio gradually comes out in an almost sadomasochist strain. Finally, Harry is a true movie hero stranded in a compromised real world that cannot bear his violent purity. At once an espousal and a critique of Harry's Old Testament philosophy, it is a deeper film than its thick-ear reputation suggests, but it was doubtless its overwhelming box office showing that made it so influential. Eastwood returned to the role, with diminishing returns, in Ted Post's *Magnum Force* (1973), Jim Fargo's *The Enforcer* (1976), his own *Sudden Impact* (1983) and Buddy Van Horn's *The Dead Pool* (1988). *Magnum Force*, written by John Milius and Michael Cimino, is the most intriguing follow-up, pitting Harry against an organised group of fascist vigilante cops, though it is *Sudden Impact*, a revenge-for-rape drama with roots in *I Spit on Your Grave* (1980), that introduced Harry's catchphrase 'make my day'. The sequels also influenced the evolution of TV cop shows, introducing in *Magnum Force* David Soul of *Starsky and Hutch* (1975–9) as an androgynous uniformed killer who could be the template of the monster cop from *Terminator 2: Judgment Day* (1991), and in *The Enforcer* Tyne Daly of *Cagney and Lacey* (1982–8) as the latest of Harry's unwanted partners. In addition, the Fred Williamson vehicle *The Big Score* (1983) and the Chuck Norris movie *Code of Silence* (1985) were made from Dirty Harry scripts commissioned but never used by Eastwood, who developed his cop image in his own excellent *The Gauntlet* (1977), Richard Tuggle's intriguing but flawed **Tightrope**, and his own dreary *The Rookie* (1990). Meanwhile, Harry Callahan changed forever the image of the American cop, his influence even extending to the careers of almost-Harrys, Wayne and Sinatra, who took the Callahan-style leads in *McQ* (1974) and *The First Deadly Sin* (1980). KN

1971/102m/WB-Malpaso/*p/d* Don Siegel/ *s* Harry Julian Fink, R.M. Fink, Dean Riesner/*c* Bruce Surtees/*m* Lalo Schifrin/ *lp* Clint Eastwood, Reni Santoni, Harry Guardino, Andy Robinson, John Mitchum, John Larch, John Vernon.

Distrito Quinto

This is regarded as one of Spanish cinema's most ambitious and formally interesting juvenile delinquent movies. The plot concerns a group of four juvenile thieves who meet with their boss and spend the night telling each other their life story, showing how each came to be a delinquent. In the end, their nerves on edge, the group's camaraderie begins to disintegrate and the night ends in violence. Based on a play by Espinás and adapted to the screen in a rather over-literary and over-written manner, the film's innovative use of temporal structures resulted in an unusual narrative pattern and constituted an effective (within the limits allowed by the censor) plea for an understanding rather than a demonisation of juvenile criminals. PW

1957/Spain/95m/Juro/*d/co-s* Julio Coll/ *co-s* German Huici, Luis José Comeron, Jorge Illa/*orig* Josep María Espinás *Es peligroso hacer esperar*/*c* Salvador Torres Garriga/*m* Xavier Montsalvaje/*lp* Alberto Closas, Montserrat Salvador, Arturo Fernández, Jesús Colomer, Carlos Mendy.

ABOVE Clint Eastwood, *Dirty Harry*

Diva

The success of this, Beineix's first feature, is largely due to Hilton McConnico's art direction and Rousselot's glossy colour-supplement images. The plot provides an excuse to play with the conventions of the gangster movie as well as those of silent serials and music videos. A postman, Jules (Andrei), adores the opera singer Cynthia Hawkins (Fernandez) and makes a pirate recording of her concert. The tape is then coveted by a recording company but inadvertently switched for a recording betraying the operations of a drug and prostitution ring led by the police inspector Saporta (Fabbri). Saporta's two picturesque hoods (Damon and the punkish Pinon) chase Jules to recover the tape. The film's prince charming is an over-aged hippie (Bohringer) sitting in a vast empty flat accompanied by a Vietnamese girl (Thuy An Luu). Jules eventually wins the affections of the maternal looking diva, having eliminated the baddies along the way. The death of Saporta, tricked into falling into a lift shaft, shows that Beineix has a grasp of narrative economy. The film offers a routine oedipal fantasy cloaked in up-market, fetishistic life-style iconography. Although by no means as innovative as it was made out to be (see e.g. *La Nuit de Saint Germain-des-Prés*, 1977), the film's slick look spawned a series of imitations such as *Subway* (1985). PW

1981/France/117m/Galaxie-Greenwich-Antenne 2/*p* Irène Silberman/*d/co-s* Jean-Jacques Beineix/*co-s* Jean Van Hamme/*orig* Delacorta/*c* Philippe Rousselot/*m* Vladimir Cosma/*lp* Frédéric Andrei, Richard Bohringer, Jacques Fabbri, Wilhelmina Wiggins Fernandez, Thuy An Luu.

Diyi Leixing Weixian/Dangerous Encounters of the First Kind/Don't Play with Fire

This is the third feature by the brilliant Tsui Hark [Xu Ke in Mandarin; real name: Tsui Man-kwong] and is one of the few genuine *films maudits*. His more poetically surreal features having flopped, he decided to provide what the industry urged him to make: a fast and violent action picture. The industry got more than it bargained for, as did the Hong Kong censor, who banned its first version and forced a drastic restructuring, especially of the first half hour and of the film's coda. The story follows three irresponsibly violent and cynical teenagers who are drawn into further crimes by a bright but even more cynical and cruel young woman. The group gets hold of a drugs consignment which is the bone of contention between local gangsters and a group of vicious American Vietnam veterans whose brutality exceeds all bounds, terrifying even the youngsters. The climactic scenes of the confrontation between the kids and the Americans are set in a cemetery high on a mountain side with crosses and tombs filling the scope screen. The finale sees the sole survivor of the hellish experience, a wounded youth, go insane and in a Langian gesture in the manner of *Der Tiger von Eschnapur* (1958) he empties his machine-gun at the sun. Originally, the teenagers were introduced as youngsters who made bombs 'for fun' and left them in public places, referring to the 1967 rebellion in Hong Kong. In the revised version, they have become mere hit-and-run drivers; a subplot with special-branch agents (played mostly by Hong Kong film-makers including the director himself) was introduced and the coda, originally a quick montage of newspaper photographs of the 1967 mayhem, was deleted in favour of youths throwing a bag of red paint onto a pedestrian. However, some of the cold fury animating the film remains visible in the released version, although shorn of its more pointed references to events in contemporary Hong Kong. The movie is so violent that at times it is painful to watch: the triad boss, mouth sewn tight with metal wire, being dunked in a vat of water: shot from below the water, with red billowing onto the screen as he struggles for breath; the young woman being thrown out of an apartment window, her head spiked onto railings below, just like her cat in a previous scene – which was accompanied by a TV set showing a Tom and Jerry cartoon. PW

1980/Hong Kong/100m/Yingyi [Fotocine]/*p* Ricky Chan/*d* Tsui Hark/*s* Szeto Cheuk-hon, Chan Fong, Fong Ling-ching/*c* Chung Chi-man/*m* Tang Siu-lam/*lp* Lo Lieh, Lin Chen-chi, Albert Au [Ou Ruiqiang or Au Shui Keung], Paul Che [Che Baoluo], Lung Tin-sang.

D.O.A.

Taking its title from forensic shorthand for 'dead on arrival', *D.O.A.* famously begins with Edmond O'Brien entering a police station and declaring that he wants to report a murder. Asked whose death, he replies 'Mine'. The subsequent action comprises a flashback account of how O'Brien, a small-town accountant, falls ill during a trip to San Francisco and learns from a doctor that he is suffering from terminal poisoning. Victim turns avenger and detective work enables him not only to elucidate the conspiracy, involving a criminal operation about which he unwittingly possessed documentary evidence, but to confront and dispose of his assassin. The paradox of the film is that while the plot posits a situation of nightmarish bleakness, the handling has a vitality and rococo elaboration that makes it frequently exhilarating to watch. These attributes coincide in the figure of Neville Brand's psychotic killer, levelling his pistol at an intended victim with a sneer of 'And baby makes three'. A remake under the same title in 1988 quite ingeniously transposes the basic plot premise to the groves of academe. TP

1949/83m/UA/*p* Leo C. Popkin/*d* Rudolph Maté/*s* Russell Rouse, Clarence Greene/*c* Ernest Laszlo/*m* Dimitri Tiomkin/*lp* Edmond O'Brien, Pamela Britton, Luther Adler, William Ching, Neville Brand.

Docks of New York

This better than average East Side Kids entry ties up Gorcey, Hall, and others of the dopey group in a murder mystery, foreign agents, and a stolen necklace. This film comes in during the 'better' years of the early Bowery Boys series of programmers, which generally featured Leo Gorcey (as Muggs, later as Spit) and Huntz Hall (as Sach, Glimpy, later Dippy), and which had its origins in *Dead End* (1937), where a slightly different group appeared as The Dead End Kids; this then evolved into Little Tough Guys with *Little Tough Guy* (1938) for a few films before they were reintroduced as *The East Side Kids* (1940). Finally as the Bowery Boys, Gorcey and Hall (and various other members) began a long series of low-budget double-billers with *Live Wires* in 1946 which lasted until *In the Money* (1958), by which time Hall led the Boys (Gorcey having left the group in 1956). The films were produced by Monogram during the 1940s and early 1950s, then by Allied Artists from the mid-1950s. TV

1945/63m/Monogram/*p* Sam Katzman, Jack Dietz/*d* Wallace Fox/*s* Harvey Gates/*c* Ira Morgan/*m* Edward Kay/*lp* Leo Gorcey, Huntz Hall, Billy Benedict.

The Docks of New York

Bancroft, a ship's stoker, rescues Compson when she attempts to drown herself, and a few hours later, more as a joke than any-

LEFT Al Pacino, *Dog Day Afternoon*

Considering it is scripted by Vance, who honed his skills in British exploitation films of the 50s, the film holds close to the established facts of the case. Pleasence plays the doctor who poisons, dismembers and buries his wife and, after a preliminary investigation into the wife's disappearance gets underway, flees to Canada with Le Neve (Eggar). He is caught after the ship's captain telegraphs his suspicions about the affections the pair display to each other to London – the first time wireless telegraphy had been used for this purpose. The only other version of the story is *Dr. Crippen an Bord* (1942) – in which Rudolf Fernau took the title role – but several films have borrowed details of the case, notably *The Suspect* (1942). PH

1962/GB/98m/Associated British/*p* John Clein/ *d* Robert Lynn/*s* Leigh Vance/*c* Nicolas Roeg/*m* Kenneth Jones/*lp* Donald Pleasence, Samantha Eggar, Coral Browne, Donald Wolfit.

Dr Mabuse

The Luxembourg writer Norbert Jacques devised the figure of Mabuse, using the name of a 16th-century Flemish painter, as a modernised version of **Conan Doyle**'s Moriarty. Mabuse is just as protean a figure as both Holmes and his antagonist, but Mabuse fuses within himself the megalomania of a feudal lord and the threat incarnated by the lower-class, upstart entrepreneur: Mabuse is a gambler (like the aristocrats) and a pseudo-scientific entertainer (Mesmer and Rasputin rolled into one). When Fritz Lang and his wife and scenarist Thea von Harbou first mobilised the figure in their two-part film *Dr. Mabuse, der Spieler* (*Part I Der grosse Spieler*; *Part II Inferno*; 1922), they apparently introduced the social conditions which generated Mabuse by means of a prologue-montage showing Germany's defeat in World War I and the beginning of the Weimar Republic, although current versions of the film do not include such a sequence. Nevertheless, Lang insisted on the contemporary relevance of his 'hero', admirably incarnated by Rudolf Klein-Rogge (von Harbou's companion after Lang). Lang retained the gambling aspects of the character but added to them the threat represented by unlimited industrial and financial power. While for Moriarty (or Holmes) the accumulation of wealth, or simply making a living, were rather distasteful activities, for Mabuse

thing, marries her. Next morning he goes back to his ship, sees a crowd gather, and finds that Compson has been arrested for shooting Lewis, an engineer on Bancroft's ship. Baclanova, Lewis' wife, confesses. Again Bancroft goes, again returns, on a whim, to find Compson in fresh trouble over stolen clothing. Bancroft admits his guilt, gets sixty days, and Compson waits for him. A trite story, redeemed by Sternberg's pictorial sense and by his feeling for his unhappy characters. Sternberg revels in the contrasts of the milieu, from the drab waterfront to the garish saloons to the austere courtroom, and however varied his characters, he views them with equal sympathy – gentle, hurt Compson, well-meaning, foolish Bancroft, even Baclanova's darkly spirited murderess, all are people who matter, and all are supremely well played. JL

1928/7202ft/PAR/*p* J.G.Bachmann/*d* Josef von Sternberg/*s* Jules Furthman/*orig* John Monk Saunders *The Dock Walloper*/*c* Harold Rosson/*lp* George Bancroft, Betty Compson, Olga Baclanova, Clyde Cook, Gustav von Seyffertitz, Mitchell Lewis.

Docteur Petiot

A disturbingly filmed account of a disturbing event which happened in Paris during the last half of World War II. During the Nazi occupation, Dr Petiot (Serrault), both a friend of the Resistance and a collaborator as well as a tireless family doctor, lured Jews to his apartment with a promise to help them escape, only to give them a lethal injection, after which he watched them die and stole their belongings. He was guillotined in 1946. The film blends horror-fantasy elements derived from German expressionist cinema with a nightmarish representation of the city, all darkness and jagged shadows, until the light breaks through with the Liberation, which ended Petiot's spate of serial murder. Through its form as much as through its acting, lighting and art direction, the film suggests that at a time when serial killing was the norm, psychopaths felt at home, raising troubling questions about the outbreaks of serial killing in more recent times. PW

1990/France/102m/MS-Sara-Cine5-Canal+-Sofica Investimage/*p* Alain Sarde, Philippe Chapelier-Dehesdin/*d*/*co-s* Christian de Chalonge/*co-s* Dominique Garnier/*c* Patrick Blossier/*m* Michel Portal/*lp* Michel Serrault, Berangère Bonvoisin, Pierre Romans, Zbigniew Horoks, Aurore Prieto.

Dr. Crippen

This rather anodyne film takes the view that Crippen was a mild-mannered doctor driven to murder by the love of Ethel Le Neve.

the accumulation of financial power is the key to everything else, making him into a thoroughly modern figure. Lang, however, went a step further and transformed Mabuse into a metaphor for the power of cinema, of industrial-visual entertainment itself. In this way, Mabuse is not only a figure emerging from the period of the industrialisation of culture, he represents the tensions at work in that process as perceived in the first half of the century. Lang's Mabuse not only controls the way he appears, he controls how people perceive the world by means of the superior scientific-technological media at his disposal. For Lang, the dangers inherent in the manipulation of audio-visual spectacle – dangers commensurate with the audience's desire for visual-emotional gratification – become the *leitmotiv* of all his Mabuse films, including his last version of the story, *Die tausend Augen des Dr. Mabuse* (1960), where the villain controls what looks like a television studio and a bank of surveillance cameras. Lang's second outing with Mabuse was in 1933, with *Das Testament des Dr. Mabuse*, where the villain is an imprisoned madman who still governs and pulls the strings from his cell by controlling bureaucrats and other intermediaries. The antagonist of Mabuse

was the same man, Inspector Lohmann, who had captured the child sex-killer in **M.** The story was seen as a barely veiled critique of the rising Nazi Party's organised terror and totalitarian aspirations, and Goebbels forbade the film, although it was shown in Austria. Lang immediately fled the country. Lang's 1960 update of the Mabuse story, *Die tausend Augen des Dr. Mabuse*, sparked a new series of Mabuse films by minor German directors featuring Wolfgang Preiss as the eponymous villain. The series included *Im Stahlnetz des Dr. Mabuse*, *Die unsichtbaren Krallen des Dr. Mabuse* (both 1961), *Das Testament des Dr. Mabuse* (1962), *Scotland Yard jagt Dr. Mabuse* (1963) and *Die Todesstrahlen des Dr. Mabuse* (1964). The villain was next resurrected in Spain by Jesus Franco in *La venganza del Dr. Mabuse* (1970) with Jack Taylor in the role, although this is more a remake of Franco's *Gritos en la noche* (1961), including identical footage. PW

Dog Day Afternoon

This black comedy has unnervingly cynical undertones. The nervy Sonny (Pacino) and gloomy Sal (Cazale) hold-up a minor Brooklyn bank one sweltering afternoon, then suffer through a siege that gets out of control as

crowds of interested parties gather to heckle the police and the hoods. When it emerges that Sonny is a bisexual who has staged the raid in order to finance a sex-change operation for his boyfriend (Sarandon), gay groups take up the cause and rally round, but the protagonist is unpolitical, never even considering the immediate consequences of his actions let alone the inevitably tragic outcome. When Sarandon learns Sonny's sidekick is Sal (who, when asked which country he wants to escape to, says 'Wyoming') he advises they give up immediately, a creepily touching scene in which the would-be transsexual, in conventional film terms a complete weirdo, abandons Sonny's crazily noble endeavours to align with the straightest-imaginable policemen. A deft mix of escalating comic tension and genuinely moving performances (the touching solidarity between losers Pacino and Cazale is a gem of understated shared misery) this demonstrates based-on-fact crime dramas need not turn out like the dullest TV docudramas. KN

1975/130m/WB/*p* Martin Bregman, Martin Elfand/*d* Sidney Lumet/*s* Frank R. Pierson/ *c* Victor J. Kemper/*m* none/*lp* Al Pacino, John Cazale, Sully Boyar, Penelope Allen, Charles Durning, Chris Sarandon.

Double Indemnity

Phyllis Dietrichson (Stanwyck) takes out a life insurance policy on her husband (Powers), then seduces Walter Neff (MacMurray), the insurance salesman, into helping her murder him, staging an accident in order to qualify for the double indemnity clause. The only obstacle in their way is a suspicious colleague of Neff's, claims adjuster Barton Keyes (Robinson). **Raymond Chandler**'s script based on a story by **James M. Cain** typically invents an equivalent for the novelist's voice, as Neff recounts his story into a dictaphone, and the film sums up the characteristic features of *noir*. Stanwyck's temptress oozes a deadly sexuality. MacMurray convinces as the Average Joe goaded into a fatal lapse. Robinson brings the authority of his gang boss persona to his role as the instrument of their destiny. Wilder directs with a cynical, pessimistic attention to nuances of character, exploiting shadows, acute camera angles and ruled patterns of light to create a parallel visual drama. The result is perfection. MP

1944/106m/PAR/*p* Joseph Sistrom/*d* Billy Wilder/*s* Raymond Chandler, Billy Wilder/ *c* John Seitz /*m* Miklos Rozsa/*lp* Fred

ABOVE Fred MacMurray, Edward G. Robinson, *Double Indemnity* (in a sequence cut from the final print)

Le Doulos

RIGHT Jean-Paul Belmondo, *Le Doulos*

MacMurray, Barbara Stanwyck, Edward G Robinson, Porter Hall, Tom Powers.

Le Doulos

Pierre Lesou, the author of the novel published in 1957, is said to have preferred Melville's film to his own book. Except for the title, a reference to a type of hat allegedly worn by stool pigeons, the book's extensive use of slang has been eliminated in favour of a sparse dialogue punctuating an enchantingly *noir* movie's engulfing visual rhythms, including a virtuoso sequence lasting nine and a half minutes in a cop's office. The plot has the ex-con Faugel (Reggiani) being caught red-handed during a robbery

by the police, tipped off by his accomplice, Silien (Belmondo), who has a special relationship with Inspector Clain (Desailly). While Faugel is questioned, Silien sets him up for two killings as well, blaming Faugel's girl-friend (Hennessy) for informing on her lover. The confusions generated by the complex double games played by nearly all the characters point to the film's central motif, Céline's famous dictum that one must choose between lies or death. But whereas Céline went on to say: 'Me, I'm alive', Melville shows his characters dying as well as lying. Silien is shot by a killer (Studer) and manages to return the compliment before seeing himself die in a mirror that at last shows him as he is. Many of the settings were copied from Hollywood movies: the cop's office was modelled after the one in Mamoulian's *City Streets* (1931); a US telephone booth and bar are used and the windows have slatted blinds instead of French shutters; there is a fleeting tribute to Huston's **The Asphalt Jungle** as Belmondo caresses a horse. The contrasted black and white imagery and the sinuous camera movements, the fascination with male bodies wearing heavy coats and hats moving through city spaces and alien-feeling interiors, all combine to make this a captivating piece of cinema. PW

1962/France, Italy/108m/Rome-Paris Films-CCC Champion/*p* Georges de Beauregard, Carlo Ponti/*d/s* Jean-Pierre Melville/*c* Nicolas Hayer/*m* Paul Misraki/*lp* Jean-Paul

LEFT Dan Aykroyd, *Dragnet*

minimalist production values on the original *Dragnet*. TP

1987/106m/U/*p* David Permut, Robert K. Weiss/*d* Tom Mankiewicz/*s* Dan Aykroyd, Alan Zweibel, Tom Mankiewicz/*c* Matthew F. Leonetti/*m* Ira Newborn/*lp* Dan Aykroyd, Tom Hanks, Christopher Plummer, Elizabeth Ashley, Dabney Coleman.

The Draughtsman's Contract

This slips between being a country house murder of the sort beloved of so many detective fiction writers – indeed with its concern with property and inheritance it follows the contours of the genre far closer than it seems on the surface – and a costume drama, with a wit and elegance that is all the more beguiling for being so elliptical. The film marked a decisive shift in its director's career from experimental, wholly personal films, to narrative (if not quite story-driven) films with characters as well as ideas at the centre. In short *Contract* is a film which demonstrates the power of the mystery story to hold together a slim plot. The film is also noticeable for being structured, like **Rear**

Belmondo, Serge Reggiani, Jean Desailly, Fabienne Dali, Michel Piccoli.

Dragnet

The TV series *Dragnet*, which was produced from 1952 to 1959, with a brief reprise ten years later, was highly influential in its emphasis on police procedure and the deadpan quality of its dialogue and especially of its voice-over narration. Given how much it belonged to its time, and the degree to which it was lampooned in its own day, so that it even began to assume an air of unwitting self-**parody**, the notion of producing a spoof of it thirty-six years after its inception might seem a curious one. Aykroyd appears as a cop who is nephew and namesake of Joe Friday (played in the original by Jack Webb), but after some preliminary allusions to the TV show, the scenario largely shakes off any satirical frame of reference and turns into a complex but fairly laboured comedy-thriller about the machinations of a phoney religious crusader (Plummer). Like some other comedies of the time, such as *The Blues Brothers* (1980), the film boasts conspicuously expensive effects and resources, which in this instance offer a wry contrast with the

ABOVE AND RIGHT Anthony Higgins, *The Draughtsman's Contract*

113

Dressed to Kill

Window, around looking and the difference between 'knowing' and 'seeing'; significantly it ends with Higgins' draughtsman being blinded before he is murdered. Higgins is a draughtsman who agrees to make twelve drawings of Suzman's estate in return for her favours while her husband is away. At Compton Anstey he organises the household as if he were its head and commences an affair with Suzman's daughter (Lambert), all the while uncovering a mass of hidden hostility between the various members of the family who are vying with each other to inherit the property. Yet while his drawings capture Compton Anstey and its daily goings on, Higgins remains blind to their significance. The climax of this comes when Suzman's husband is found dead and the drawings are somehow implicated. 'Somehow' is a key description of the film. For though the characters are set forth as such, their very formal speech and the heightened (indeed fetishistic) realism of their costume and the decor they move through give them a muted, unreal quality. An equally important element is Michael Nyman's pseudo-Purcellian score. PH

1982/GB/108m/BFI-Channel 4/*p* David Payne/*d/s* Peter Greenaway/*c* Curtis Clark/*m* Michael Nyman/*lp* Anthony Higgins, Janet Suzman, Anne Louise Lambert, Neil Cunningham, Hugh Fraser, Dave Hill.

Dressed to Kill

The keynote of *Dressed To Kill*, as the title hints, is elegance. Lowe is the suave and beautifully mannered thief whose very crimes are, in the words of a critic of the time, 'symphonies of social grace'. Much of the action is set in a luxurious **night-club**. Lowe lives in an impressive mansion and when his gang go out on business, they invariably wear evening dress and top-hats on the way. The heroine is played by Astor, a girl trying to prove her imprisoned lover innocent. Lowe falls in love with her, and the climax has him killed by his own gang in order to save her life. None the less, the film was rich in comedy, with witty captions by Malcolm Stuart Boylan which used a deal of gangster jargon, but also put highly-flown language in the mouths of arrant toughs. One contrived scene has Lowe's gang, who have just eliminated a stool-pigeon, turning up at the man's funeral in elaborate mourning, with attendant police watching helplessly. The film also employed real-life underworld characters in small roles, one of them,

ABOVE Drugs: *Human Wreckage*

a notorious New York operator named Joe Brown, actually playing himself. JL

1928/6556ft/FOX/*d/co-s* Irving Cummings/*s* Howard Estabrook, William M. Conselman/*c* Conrad Wells/*lp* Edmund Lowe, Mary Astor, Ben Bard, Robert Perry, Tom Dugan, John Kelly.

Dressed to Kill

On its release this film was accused of exploiting women and of encouraging violence against them. Its director De Palma preferred the film to be seen as his deliberate homage to Alfred Hitchcock. It opens with Dickinson in the shower fantasising about being raped, and follows her to an art museum, where she is picked up by a stranger and has sex with him in a taxi. Later, as is the way in De Palma, she pays a heavy price for such a blatant assertion of her sexuality. Caine is the villain, a schizoid psychoanalyst who's also a transsexual and second cousin to Norman Bates. Allen is memorable as a gutsy hooker, a role which goes some way to defending De Palma from the more simplistic charges of misogyny. The production has a high gloss, some ingenious plot twists, elaborate camerawork and a shocking murder in a lift. But De Palma is unable to do more than imitate the trappings of a Hitchcock film. Never does he manage the truly disturbing insights of the master. EB

1980/105m/Filmways/*p* George Litto/
d/s Brian De Palma/*c* Ralf D. Bode/*m* Pino
Donaggio/*lp* Michael Caine, Angie
Dickinson, Nancy Allen, Keith Gordon,
Dennis Franz.

Drew, Nancy (Detective)

Created by Carolyn Keene (1862–1930, real
name Edward L. Stratemeyer) in *The Secret of
The Old Clock* (1930) Drew was a girl detective. Other youthful detectives include the
Hardy Boys (also created by Stratemeyer as
Franklin W. Dixon) and Enid Blyton's The
Famous Five. In the main they were
involved in adventure stories rather than
detective tales, their milieu being old dark
houses with secret passages in foreign climes
rather than the mean streets of the urban
jungle. The energetic and resourceful Drew,
whose books have sold in excess of 60 million copies, was the most successful adolescent detective of all time. After the first three
volumes Stratemeyer's daughter Harriet S.
Adams (1897–1982) took over the authorship of the series. She also updated the early
novels. In 1938 Warners cast Bonita
Granville in a four-strong series, all directed
by William Clemens. Frankie Thomas, Jr.
played her crime-solving cohort, and John
Litel her attorney father. The first outing was
Nancy Drew, Detective (1938). Only one script,
the last, was actually adapted from a novel,
Nancy Drew and the Hidden Staircase (1939). In
1977 Pamela Sue Martin played Nancy Drew
in the teleseries, *The Nancy Drew Mysteries*. PH

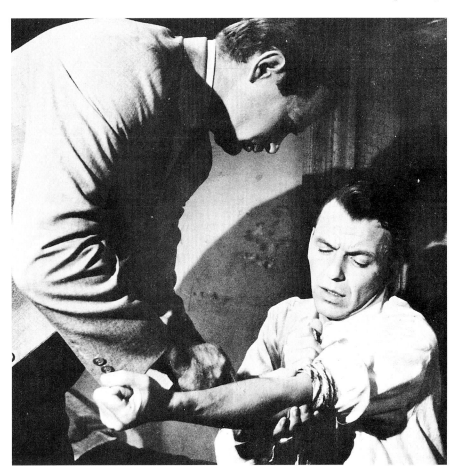

Drugs: Darren McGavin, Frank Sinatra,
The Man With the Golden Arm (above),
David Caruso, Christopher Walken, *King
of New York* (below)

Drugs

Given that the illegal drug of choice during
the period when the crime film was establishing itself as a genre was alcohol, under-
standably little attention, let alone understanding and accuracy, was given to other
stimulants. Certain silent films – *Slaves of
Morphine* (1911), *The Cocaine Traffic/The Drug
Terror* (1914), *The Secret Sin* (1915), *The
Devil's Needle* (1915), *The Greatest Menace*
(1923), *Human Wreckage* (1923), *The Pace
That Kills* (1928) touch upon addictive drugs
in much the same terms used by temperance
propagandists in depicting the evils of drink.
Especially·intriguing is D.W. Griffith's *For His
Son* (1912), based on the early history of the
Coca-Cola company, in which a physician
gets rich by creating Dopokoke, a soft drink
laced with cocaine, to which his son
becomes addicted. Aside from the cliché of
the oriental opium den and supporting players like the morphine addict who suffers cold
turkey under the third degree in *Mystery of
the Wax Museum* (1932), the crime film was
too wrapped up with bootleg booze and the
natural highs of Cagney-style psychosis to
bother much with real drugs. After the

Drugs

ABOVE Drugs: Dennis Hopper, Peter Fonda, *Easy Rider*

Woods and Sean Young in *The Boost* (1990), Matt Dillon in *Drugstore Cowboy* (1991) and Harvey Keitel in *Bad Lieutenant* (1992), plus such celebrity junkies as Sal Mineo in *The Gene Krupa Story/Drum Crazy* (1959), Dustin Hoffman as Lenny Bruce in *Lenny* (1974), Gary Oldman as Sid Vicious in *Sid and Nancy* (1986), Forest Whitaker as Charlie Parker in *Bird* (1988), Michael Chiklis as John Belushi in *Wired* (1988) and Meryl Streep as a substitute Carrie Fisher in *Postcards From the Edge* (1991).

High School Confidential (1958) unusually concentrates less on marijuana use, which it views in the same lurid and fantastic light as *Reefer Madness*, than on the organised crime network whereby the weed is distributed in the playground, paving the way for a few pictures which use drugs as a MacGuffin (**The Lineup**, *Wait Until Dark*, 1967) and then such inside dope movies, whether from the point of view of the dealers or the narcotics agents, as *The Connection* (1961), *The Poppy is Also a Flower* (1966), **The French Connection**, **Superfly**, **Scarface**, *Mixed Blood* (1985), *Less Than Zero* (1989), *Tequila Sunrise* (1989), *New Jack City* (1990), *King of New York* (1990), *London Kills Me* (1991) and *Rush* (1992).

The first person to use LSD in a movie, albeit under laboratory conditions, was Vincent Price in *The Tingler* (1958), though it

Production Code prevented further embarrassments like 'Reefer Man', Cab Calloway's hymn to marijuana in *International House* (1933), the subject was relegated to roadshow exploitationers like the unjustly well-remembered *Reefer Madness* (1936) and the deservedly-forgotten *Marijuana: Assassin of Youth* (1935), *Marihuana* (1936) and *Cocaine Fiends* (1936).

Film noir is full of delirious, hallucinogenic sequences like Elisha Cook's jazz drum orgy in **Phantom Lady** and Dick Powell's bad trip in **Murder My Sweet**, but censorship restrictions prevented actual mention of drug addiction until the 50s, when Frank Sinatra in *The Man With the Golden Arm* (1955) and Cameron Mitchell in *Monkey on My Back* (1957) did for heroin and morphine what Ray Milland had done for liquor in *The Lost Weekend* (1945). These dramas of cold turkey, bent needles and desperate addicts were followed by jittery performances from Al Pacino in *Panic in Needle Park* (1971), Nadja Brunkhorst in *Christiane F* (1981), Michael Keaton in *Clean and Sober* (1988), Jeremy Irons in *Dead Ringers* (1989), James

ABOVE Ronald Colman, Joan Bennett, *Bulldog Drummond*

was *Easy Rider* (1968), with its trippy visuals and cocaine-smuggling subplot, that most emblemised the acid craze, which was reflected in Roger Corman's surprisingly balanced *The Trip* (1967), Richard Rush's enjoyable demented *Psych-Out* (1968) and oddities like *Wild in the Streets* (1968), *Skidoo* (1968), *Is This Trip Really Necessary?* (1970) and *The People Next Door* (1970). Despite the reputation of the 60s for free-thinking on drugs, most of these films show hallucinogens in a negative light, as represented by a tripping Henry Jaglom buzz-sawing off his hand in *Psych-Out*. Hippie tracts like *Work is a Four Letter Word* (1968) and *Woodstock* (1970) are far outweighed by ridiculous anti-drug thrillers like *Riot on Sunset Strip* (1967), *The Depraved* (1967), *Blow the Man Down* (1968), *Jigsaw* (1968), *The Big Cube* (1969) and *I Drink Your Blood* (1971), in which victims dosed, usually surreptitiously, with LSD are raped, murdered, commit suicide, suffer amnesia and generally wreck their lives. The ultimate development of this thinking, perhaps triggered by the many versions of *Dr Jekyll and Mr Hyde*, are the idea of drugs that literally turn addicts into monsters, as seen in *Blue Sunshine* (1977), *Altered States* (1980), *Scanners* (1981), *Underworld/Transmutations* (1985), *Class of Nuke 'Em High* (1986) and *Alien Nation* (1990).

With the post-60s backlash against drugs, involvement in the heroin, cocaine or crack business has come to mark out screen characters as utterly despicable, whether they be crack-distributing urban gangsters or cocaine-cultivating Colombian cartel commanders. In such thrillers as *Lethal Weapon* (1986), *Death Wish 4: The Crackdown* (1987), *Fatal Beauty* (1987), *Crack House* (1989), *License to Kill* (1989), *Delta Force 2* (1990), *Wings of the Apache/Firebirds* (1990), *Robocop 2* (1990), *Predator 2* (1991) and *Rapid Fire* (1992), the mere involvement of a villain in drugs is enough to justify a hero in summarily executing him with a flip wisecrack, just as it was once sufficient to brand a baddie as an Apache, a Nazi, a commie or an alien. KN

Drummond, Bulldog

Captain Hugh 'Bulldog' Drummond made his debut in *Bulldog Drummond* (1920), in which the hulking and none-too-genteel Drummond tangles with a conspiracy of international trouble-makers (Bolsheviks to a man, and mostly Jewish) to rescue Phyllis Clavering, a damsel in distress whom he later marries. The novel disposes of its main villain, the vile Dr Lakington, but leaves at

ABOVE Claude Allister, Ronald Colman, *Bulldog Drummond* (1929)

liberty the all-powerful mastermind Carl Peterson for future instalments, along with Peterson's seductive mistress Irma, whose attentions he manfully resists throughout. Cruder than the contemporary adventure fiction of **John Buchan** and Dornford Yates, Sapper (the pen-name of Herman Cyril McNeile 1888–1936) is in the tradition of Sax Rohmer's **Fu Manchu**, with a super-patriotic hero who constantly upbraids degenerate villains for their stereotypical foreign shiftiness and unsavoury personal appearance. It takes Drummond and his band of uppercrust vigilante pals three further novels – *The Black Gang* (1922), *The Third Round* (1924) and *The Final Count*

(1926) – to dispose of Peterson, and a further three for Irma to attempt to avenge her lover – *The Female of the Species* (1928), *Temple Tower* (1929) and *Bulldog Drummond Returns* (1932). Sapper continued the series, less effectively, with *Knock-Out* (1933), *Bulldog Drummond at Bay* (1935) and *Challenge* (1937). Upon McNeile's death, Gerald Fairlie, who had collaborated with Sapper on a play *Bulldog Drummond Hits Out* (1936), took over the series and produced *Bulldog Drummond on Dartmoor* (1938), *Bulldog Drummond at War* (1940), *Captain Bulldog Drummond* (1945), *Bulldog Drummond Stands Fast* (1947), *Hands Off Bulldog Drummond* (1951) and *The Return of the Black Gang*

(1954). Subsequently, Drummond has appeared (along with John Buchan's Richard Hannay and Dornford Yates's Jonah Mansell) in Jack Smithers' novel *Combined Forces* (1985) and Jack Yeovil's 'Pitbull Brittan' (1990).

Bulldog Drummond was a 1921 London stage success, with Sir Gerald du Maurier biffing the Bolshies. A British silent *Bulldog Drummond* (1922) has Carlyle Blackwell as the hero. Blackwell, a blocky bruiser, approximated Sapper's description of Drummond but the miscast Jack Buchanan, who played in *Bulldog Drummond's Third Round* (1925), changed the image of the character on screen, bringing to the part a dapper charm the novel's character would have thought suspiciously effeminate and taking the nasty edge off the hero's xenophobia by flashing a jaunty smile whenever he disposed of a villain. All subsequent screen Drummonds would follow this pattern, suggesting a thoroughly decent chap rather than a proto-Mosleyite. The perfect incarnation of this Drummond was Ronald Colman, who appeared in Sam Goldwyn's early talkie production *Bulldog Drummond* (1929), with Joan Bennett as Phyllis and Claude Allister as Drummond's silly-ass friend Algy Longworth. Directed by F. Richard Jones, the film was a cracking success, but Sapper had split up the film rights to his novels, so the rival Fox was able to film the then-latest book, *Temple Tower* (1930) with Kenneth MacKenna a disastrous Drummond. Colman returned for Roy Del Ruth's *Bulldog Drummond Strikes Back* (1934), with C. Aubrey Smith as Inspector Neilsen of the Yard and Charles Butterworth as Algy. In Britain, Ralph Richardson was oddly inspired casting in *The Return of Bulldog Drummond* (1934), from *The Black Gang*, with Ann Todd as Phyllis, and also appeared, as an aptly fiendish villain, in Walter Forde's spoof *Bulldog Jack* (1935), in which Atholl Fleming's Drummond is laid up with a broken leg and has to turn over the heroic duties to comedian Jack Hulbert. With Fay Wray as the menaced heroine, *Bulldog Jack* is a surprisingly strong entry – probably the best film associated with the character – with an especially tense final struggle between Hulbert and Richardson over the live rail of the London Underground. John Lodge made a vain attempt at returning to Sapper's two-fisted character for Norman Lee's quota quickie *Bulldog Drummond at Bay* (1937), but the Colman image was too well established to be dented.

A Bulldog Drummond screen series did not start until 1937, when Paramount cast Ray Milland in James Hogan's *Bulldog Drummond Escapes*. John Howard was a fairly bland Drummond in seven outings starting with *Bulldog Drummond Comes Back* (1937) and ending with *Arrest Bulldog Drummond* (1939). Directed by Hogan or Louis King, these are variable Bs, distinguished at first by Barrymore's subversive craziness and thereafter by notable villains (Eduardo Ciannelli, J. Carrol Naish, Porter Hall, George Zucco) and the occasional eerie sequence, like the prowling-about in a supposedly haunted cavern where mild-mannered psycho Leo G. Carroll is at loose in *Bulldog Drummond's Secret Police* (1939). There have been several subsequent attempts to resurrect the character: Ron Randell appeared for Columbia in *Bulldog Drummond at Bay* (1947) and *Bulldog Drummond Strikes Back* (1947), while Tom Conway did his best in *The Challenge* (1948) and *13 Lead Soldiers* (1948) for 20th Century-Fox. Walter Pidgeon, somewhat elderly, turned up in Victor Saville's British *Calling Bulldog Drummond* (1951), co-authored by Gerald Fairlie, with David Tomlinson as idiot Algy. Robert Beatty played a Canadian Drummond in an unmemorable 1950s British TV series. Richard Johnson, under the obvious influence of James Bond, gave Drummond a license to kill for Ralph Thomas's glossy adventures, *Deadlier Than the Male* (1967) and *Some Girls Do* (1969). These at least afford Nigel Green and James Villiers the chance to make something of the usually-written-out role of Carl Peterson. Dick Clement's *Bullshot* (1983), with Alan Shearman as Captain Hugh 'Bullshot' Crummond, is a ghastly parody. It is enlivened only by Frances Tomelty's spoof of Irma Peterson, and typified by the observation, when faced with an evil German airman spared by the hero during a dog fight, that Crummond 'should have finished the Fokker off in the first place'. KN

Du Maurier, Daphne (1907–89)

The grand-daughter of George du Maurier (author of *Trilby*, 1894) and the daughter of Gerald du Maurier, a leading actor on the London stage before World War I, Daphne du Maurier had two of her novels and a story filmed by Alfred Hitchcock. These were **Rebecca** (novel 1938), *Jamaica Inn* (1939, novel 1936) and *The Birds* (1963, story 1952). Nicolas Roeg filmed her short story *Don't Look Now* (1971). *Rebecca* is her quintessential novel. The story of a beleaguered young innocent confronting a mysterious past in strange surroundings and finding her friends not to quite be what they seem can be traced back to *Jane Eyre* (1847), but the twist du Maurier gives to it is entirely new; and modern rather than gothic. From the very beginning – 'Last night I dreamt I went to Manderlay again' – du Maurier achieves a dreamlike quality that perfectly matches the slow unfolding of the plot and forces the reader to consider a non-naturalistic response to the novel. What makes the novel particularly fascinating is its double structure. Like so many films and novels of the period it features a hero unmanned by an evil woman, but whereas generally the woman who comes to his rescue merely does that and is not herself questioned by the narrative, the un-named heroine of *Rebecca* has to, as it were, confront a figure (figures actually, if you include Mrs Danvers and Mrs Van Hopper) who is her mother and her rival. In short she has to find herself before she can revive Max de Winter from his guilt-induced passivity. Other films drawn from du Maurier's novels include *Frenchman's Creek* (1944, novel 1941), *Hungry Hill* (1946, novel 1943, the only one of her novels which she scripted, with Terence Young), *My Cousin Rachel* (1952, novel 1951), and *The Scapegoat* (1957, film 1958). PH

Du Rififi chez les hommes/Rififi

The eccentric, gun-toting crime writer Le Breton claimed to have invented the word 'rififi' and proceeded to make it his trademark with the novel, published in 1953, underpinning American expatriate Dassin's first French film. The plot concerns an elaborately staged jewellery heist in Paris by a mortally ill Tony le Stéphanois (Servais) and his mates, Jo (Mohner) and Mario (Manuel), as well as an imported safe-cracker, Cesar (Dassin himself under the pseudonym Perlo Vita). Then a rival gang led by night-club owner Grutter (Lupovici) moves in on them and kidnaps Jo's little son. Tony eventually kills Grutter and saves the kid before collapsing dead himself. Shot in the same year as Becker's **Touchez pas au grisbi** but released in 1955, the two films triggered a wave of stylish French crime films in which the audience was invited to root for the criminals before they met their nemesis. The high point of the movie was a virtuoso sequence lasting twenty-five minutes showing the robbery without a word of dialogue. The immense success of the film spawned a series of further 'rififi' films based on Le Breton stories: *Du rififi chez les femmes* (1959), *Du rififi à Tokyo* (1961) and *Du rififi à Paname* (1965). Dassin tried to repeat his success with another caper movie, **Topkapi**, but by that time James Bond-type spectaculars had changed the cinematic landscape and the film, though successful, didn't have a renovatory impact. PW

1955/France/116m/Miracle-Indus-Pathé-Prima/*d*/*co-s* Jules Dassin/*co-s* René Wheeler, Auguste Le Breton/*orig* Auguste Le Breton/ *c* Philippe Agostini/*m* Georges Auric/*lp* Jean Servais, Carl Mohner, Robert Manuel, Perlo Vita [Jules Dassin], Janine Darcey.

E

8 Million Ways to Die

This thriller stars Bridges as an alcoholic LA sheriff who stumbles through various near-death encounters with the South American drug organisation that he is trying to destroy while at the same time harbouring a tender spot for the girl, played by a largely incoherent Arquette, of the drug kingpin (Garcia). The film is better remembered for its production history. The $18 million outing helped bring down the company (PSO), director Ashby was fired from the picture before it was finished, as was producer Roth. Both Ashby and Roth later sued PSO. TV

1986/115m/PSO-Tri-Star/*p* Steve Roth, Charles Mulvehill/*d* Hal Ashby/*s* Oliver Stone, David Lee Henry/*c* Stephen H. Burum/*m* James Newton Howard/*lp* Jeff Bridges, Rosanna Arquette, Alexandra Paul, Andy Garcia.

Electra Glide in Blue

The only film by the one-time producer of rock group Chicago, this is an astonishing movie, seamlessly incorporating echoes of bygone cinema into a melancholy, absurdist meditation on the nature of American heroism in the period of post-Vietnam malaise. Blake, a motorcycle cop whose beat runs through Monument Valley, justifies his short stature by claiming to be exactly the height Alan Ladd was. He seizes on a murder investigation as a way to move up to the elite position of detective, exchanging his leathers and crash-helmet for a string tie and a cowboy hat, but is unwilling to go along with his new colleagues in pinning the rap on a convenient fall-guy. The final irony is that, for the first time since *The Falcon's Alibi* (1946), the guilty party turns out to be perennial fall-guy Cook, a throwback mountain man who has killed a friend to avenge a defection to a new outlaw breed of drop-outs and drug pushers. The nice touch of cops using stills from *Easy Rider* for target practice is capped by a punch-line which can be seen as an answer to Dennis Hopper's film, as Blake pursues a hippie in a car simply to return his license and is pointlessly gunned down, his gut-shot corpse left stranded in the middle of the road with the Fordian splendours of the West as the background. KN

1973/106m/UA/*p*/*d* James William Guercio/ *s* Robert Boris/*c* Conrad Hall/*m* James William Guercio/*lp* Robert Blake, Billy 'Green' Bush, Mitchell Ryan, Jeannine Riley, Elisha Cook, Royal Dano.

Ellin, Stanley [Bernard] (1916–)

Best known for his short stories, notably the classic *The Speciality of the House* (1946), about a gourmet restaurant, filmed as part of the teleseries *Alfred Hitchcock Presents*. Ellin's novels have also formed the basis of several crime films. These include Joseph Losey's rite of passage film, *The Big Night* (1951, from *Dreadful Summit*, 1948), Claude Chabrol's formal tale of domestic infidelity (*A Double Tour*, 1959 from *The Key To Nicholas Street*, 1952) the classic account of upward mobility

ABOVE Daphne du Maurier

ABOVE Espionage: *Pickup on South Street*

in 60s Britain, Clive Donner's **Nothing But The Best** (from *The Best Of Everything*, 1952) and the lesser *House Of Cards* (1968, novel 1967). Though Ellin's plots and starting points are very diversified a common theme in the novels is of an outsider being offered a place by the fireside for an unspecified price. His only screenplay (co-authored with Losey) is *The Big Night*. PH

Ellroy, James (1948–)

Born in LA, and rendered motherless at an early age (due to her still unsolved murder), novelist James Ellroy was a petty thief and substance abuser until he began to write whilst working as a golf caddy. Since the publication of his first semi-autobiographical novel *Brown's Requiem* in 1981 Ellroy has produced a further ten novels, a collection of short stories and a non-fictional account of his mother's killing called *My Dark Places* (1996). Ellroy's distinctive, stylistically daring work, with its extensive vocabulary of vernacular expressions, slang, profanities and bravura description, is also characterised by its narrative complexity (often interweaving real historical events and characters).

Ellroy's books are also invariably but not gratuitously violent, sexually explicit and politically and racially ambiguous. Perhaps his most impressive work to date is contained in the LA Quartet series, which commenced with *The Black Dahlia* in 1986 and concluded with *White Jazz* in 1992. Set in the 1940s and 50s, with deliciously satirical references to Hollywood, the Quartet paints a savage and funny portrait of the vice and corruption of Los Angeles. **Cop** was the first adaptation of an Ellroy novel (taken from an early trio of police thrillers). Aside from this there has been a TV adaptation of Ellroy's short story 'Since I Don't Have You' made in 1995 by Jonathan Kaplan for the American *Fallen Angels* series. Currently nearing completion is *LA Confidential* (taken from the LA Quartet novel of the same name) directed by Curtis Hanson. AW

Engel aus Eisen/Iron Angel

This stylised and overtly symbolic crime drama is set during the blockade of Berlin and the airlift from May 1948 to May 1949, at the height of the Cold War. A former executioner in both East and West Germany,

Völpel (Thate), now a police informer, manipulates the teenage thug Werner Gladow (Wesselmann) into a gang-leader, organising robberies, black marketeering and so on. Werner's girl-friend Lisa (Thalbach) dreams of becoming a torch singer. Werner eventually organises a big hold-up and a man gets killed. Lisa tries to blame Völpel but the police track Werner down at his mother's house while Lisa escapes with the loot. In the end, Werner is caught in East Berlin, where he will be executed, while Völpel is imprisoned in West Berlin, where capital punishment has been abolished. The extremely stylised black-and-white imagery, including freeze-frame techniques to underline particularly meaningful points, and the elliptical editing concentrate on recreating the chaotic, paranoid atmosphere of the time, while sounds of America concretise the inauguration of the New Germany as well as the aspirations of the new generation. Thate's restrained performance and Thalbach's ability to suggest an extreme hunger for life give the film an emotional intensity which the image track often fails to sustain. PW

1980/Germany/105m/Vietinghoff Produktion-Independent Filmproduktion/ *p* Joachim von Vietinghoff/*d/s* Thomas Brasch/*c* Walter Lassall/*m* Christian Kunert/*lp* Hilmar Thate, Katharina Thalbach, Ulrich Wesselmann, Karin Baal, Ilse Page.

ABOVE Espionage: Ingrid Bergman, *Notorious*

Espionage

Strictly speaking, espionage falls outside the scope of this book. However, given that the rules of war tend to align spies with criminals rather than military personnel, there is a considerable overlap between the crime movie and the spy picture. Samuel Fuller's **Pickup on South Street** demonstrates the interface; an espionage picture about petty crooks mixed up in a Russian spy ring, it was dubbed for export to less Red-fearing countries with drugs in place of microfilm and the evil communists turned into evil gangsters. Espionage is a crime when *their* sneaky, shifty, frequently grotesque and sexually perverse agents are spying on *us* (cf.: *Confessions of a Nazi Spy*, 1939, *British Intelligence*, 1940, *Sherlock Holmes in Washington*, 1943, *The Ministry of Fear*, 1944, *Walk East on Beacon*, 1952), but an instrument of justice when *our* upright, decent, frequently attractive and sexually irresistible agents are spying on *them* (*Odette*, 1950, *I Was a Communist for the FBI*, 1951, *The Counterfeit Traitor*, 1962, *Torn Curtain*, 1966, *Shining Through*, 1992). The only setting which allows the movies to sympathise with enemy agents is World War I, perhaps due to the enduring glamour of the legend of Mata Hari: German agents of the period are surprisingly romantic and dashing in *Dishonored* (1931), *Mata Hari* (1932) and *The Spy in Black* (1939), though these films tend to confuse the Kaiser's Germany with the Ruritania of Anthony Hope.

The pattern for most spy films, whether the hero is a spy or a counterspy, is to pit a baffled innocent against a vast conspiracy, either by setting the story in a hostile country where the government itself is a criminal organisation or by suggesting our complacent democracy has been thoroughly infiltrated by fifth columnists who have achieved positions of power and are able to operate without fear of the legal authorities. *Cloak and Dagger* (1946) and *Man Hunt* (1941), both directed by Fritz Lang, who established the screen character of **Dr Mabuse**, illustrate the underlying assumptions of these approaches, telling stories of lone heroes beset by Nazi villains: Gary Cooper in *Cloak and Dagger* is trying to ferret out Nazi A-bomb secrets in Germany, while Walter Pidgeon in *Man Hunt* (1941) is being tracked by vengeful Nazi agents in London and the English countryside. Similar in approach are the films of Alfred Hitchcock, from *The 39 Steps* (1935) and *The Lady Vanishes* (1938) through both versions of *The Man Who Knew*

ABOVE Espionage: Cary Grant, *North By Northwest*

Too Much (1934, 1956) to **Notorious** and *North By Northwest* (1958). Both Lang and Hitchcock come out of a tradition established around World War I by E. Phillips Oppenheim and Erskine Childers, whereby no narrative weight at all is given to the (possible patriotic) motives of their side. Hitchcock's Nazis and Communists are no more than suave melodrama villains accompanied by eccentric thugs.

The House on 92nd Street, a sober account of the FBI's foiling of a Nazi spy ring, ushered in a 50s vogue for documentary spy movies, doubtless inspired by McCarthyite fears of Red agitators and leaked Bomb secrets, which in turn, coupled with a reaction against the fabulations of the James Bond cycle of superspy pictures, led to the grimmer, no-less-romanticised cycles of spy movies adapted from le Carré (*The Deadly Affair*, 1967, *The Looking-Glass War*, 1970) and Len Deighton (*The Ipcress File*, 1965, *Funeral in Berlin*, 1966). These are ever more cynical in their depiction of weary spies who realise their masters are as depraved and corrupt as their opponents, the most often-used cliché (cf. *The Ipcress File* or *Blue Ice*, 1992) being the hero's discovery that his own boss

Evil Angels

Evil Angels

RIGHT Espionage: Warren Beatty, *The Parallax View*

is in the pay of the enemy. Cynicism about the espionage community, raised to rococo heights by BBC adaptations of le Carré's *Tinker, Tailor, Soldier, Spy* (1979) and *Smiley's People* (1982) and enshrined by sombre farces like *The Innocent* (1994), was so prevalent that it triggered a backlash. Author Tom Clancy created Jack Ryan, a CIA hero as purposeful and integrity-driven as any World War II strategist, vigilantly eroding any Soviet military advantage just as a 1940s spy would always go after the plans that could 'shorten the war by months'. Ryan has been played in movies by Alec Baldwin in *The Hunt for Red October* (1990) and Harrison Ford in *Patriot Games* (1992) and *Clear and Present Danger* (1994).

The Bond films, commencing with *Dr. No* (1962), spun off an entire sub-genre whose antecedents are less the spy films of World War II or the Cold War – to which the cycle comes closest in *From Russia With Love* (1963) – than the adventures of Bulldog Drummond, Spy Smasher or Fu Manchu. Though Bond is a British secret agent, it is notable that, as the Cold War thawed and the Ian Fleming originals became dated, SMERSH was replaced by SPECTRE, a terrorist criminal organisation, and Bond's political enemies by megalomaniac billionaires with genocidal schemes or even, in *License to Kill* (1989), a comparatively mundane drugs baron. Spinoffs from Bond include *The Man From UNCLE* (1964–8) and the adventures of Derek Flint (James Coburn) in *Our Man Flint* (1966) and *In Like Flint* (1967) and Matt Helm (Dean Martin) in *The Silencers* (1966) and *The Wrecking Crew* (1968). John Frankenheimer's *The Manchurian Candidate* (1962) led to a run of paranoid conspiracy movies in which the espionage apparatuses of East and West are often interlinked with large-scale crime, political corruption and totalitarian tactics to create a vision of a nightmarish society bound together by compromise and cruelty. In this genre, satirical science-fiction movies like *Seven Days in May* (1964), *The President's Analyst* (1967), *The Parallax View* (1974) and *Rollover* (1979) disturbingly cede ground to the likes of *All the President's Men* (1976), *Missing* (1982), *Salvador* (1986) and *JFK* (1991), which all purport to be true. KN

Evil Angels/A Cry in the Dark

Schepisi's self-righteous version of the famous 'dingo baby' murder case pulls out all the emotional stops to convince viewers of the innocence of the religious maniac parents, the Chamberlains, accused of murdering their baby near Ayers Rock and blaming it on a dingo. The case was a sensation in Australia, not least because by the time

ABOVE Espionage: Michael Caine, *The Ipcress File*

Lindy Chamberlain was brought to trial, she was pregnant again. Convicted on circumstantial evidence, the Chamberlains were later acquitted for lack of evidence after major campaigns by the fundamentalist Christian sect they belong to. Schepisi accuses the media of behaving hysterically and causing a miscarriage of justice in a movie devoted mostly to courtroom dramatics designed to make the most of Streep's star appeal. However, Schepisi shamelessly stacks the decks in favour of the accused from the beginning, showing Lindy and her daughter gambolling happily amongst the rocks bathed in an idyllic sunset-glow, repudiating even the thought that she might have connived at infanticide. PW

1988/Australia/121m/Cannon-Cinema Verity/*p* Verity Lambert/*d/co-s* Fred Schepisi/ *co-s* Robert Caswell/*orig* John Bryson *Evil Angels/c* Ian Baker/*m* Bruce Smeaton/ *lp* Meryl Streep, Sam Neill, Maurice Fields, Charles Tingwell, Peter Hosking, Peter Aanensen.

Experiment in Terror/ The Grip of Fear

In this dark and heavily atmospheric suspense thriller Remick is the bank teller who is terrorised by psychopath Martin into embezzling $100,000 at the threat of her sister's (Powers) life and her own. FBI agent Ford comes in as her protector, although for the most part he is outfoxed by Martin (who remains unseen for most of the story except for his dark, menacing outline in the shadows and, in a clever touch, his asthmatic condition; the extortionist's raspy voice scenes are enhanced by Mancini's creepy score). The screenplay was based on the Gordons' original novel *Operation Terror*. TV

1962/123m/COL/*p/d* Blake Edwards/ *s* Mildred and Gordon Gordon/*c* Philip Lathrop/*m* Henry Mancini/*lp* Glenn Ford, Lee Remick, Stefanie Powers, Ross Martin.

F

The Falcon

When **Leslie Charteris** recovered the **Saint** movie rights back from RKO in 1941, the studio and star George Sanders were obliged to find a way of continuing, without the Simon Templar name, the profitable series they had been turning out for two years. The solution was to buy Michael Arlen's 'Gay Falcon', a forgotten mystery featuring suave

ABOVE Tom Conway, *The Falcon and the Co-Eds*

sleuth Gay Stanhope Falcon. The Falcon operated on a basis of friendly rivalry with the police rather than as an outlaw vigilante, but in the process of adaptation to the screen the character (renamed Gay Laurence, *aka* the Falcon) came to resemble exactly Sanders's interpretation of the Saint. Director Irving Reis rapidly turned out three 63-minute adventures, *The Gay Falcon* (1941), *A Date With the Falcon* (1941) and *The Falcon Takes Over* (1942). The first two are Saints in all but name, bland society murder mysteries with Sanders partnered by Wendy Barrie (a Saint fixture) as a fiancée who, in imitation of the ongoing Perry Mason-Della Street romance, never quite manages to get her man to the altar, and by Allen Jenkins as

Goldy Locke, a comic ex-crook chauffeur not dissimilar to the Saint's screen sidekick, Pearly Gates. A series signature is a resolution of the case at hand with the Falcon swearing to abandon his interest in crime and settle down, only to be approached by a beautiful girl in trouble who would drag him into his next adventure.

The third entry changes in tone, with Barrie dropped and a plot not from urbane Arlen but hard-boiled **Raymond Chandler**. RKO bought **Farewell, My Lovely** before Chandler's reputation as a writer was assured and used the plot and supporting characters for their own sleuth. The challenge of compressing into little more than an hour a plot even two official versions have

Fallen Angel

ABOVE Tom Conway, Cecilia Callejo, *The Falcon In Mexico*

been unable completely to encompass onto the screen means it moves faster than the average B, cutting down the intrusive comic relief that usually pads series mysteries. Ward Bond (as Moose Malloy), Anne Revere, Hans Conried and Turhan Bey suit Chandler's characters and, though Sanders is his usual bland self, this is definitely his best Falcon.

Stanley Logan's *The Falcon's Brother* (1942) is intriguing for the ingenious way it keeps the series going when faced with setbacks that would kill off any other detective. After five Saints and four Falcons, Sanders, who had graduated to leads and important supporting roles in major films, was fed up with the programmer treadmill and wanted out, so writers Stuart Palmer and Craig Rice called in Sanders's real-life brother Tom Conway to play Gay Laurence's less-embarrassingly-named brother Tom, another woman-chasing gadabout and adventurer. The Laurence brothers solve the case but in the finale Gay is shot dead and Tom swears to take on the mantle of the Falcon. Conway continued the fight against crime in nine further films, *The Falcon Strikes Back* (1943), *The Falcon and the Co-Eds* (1943), *The Falcon in Danger* (1943), *The Falcon in Hollywood* (1944), *The Falcon in Mexico* (1944), *The Falcon Out West* (1944), *The Falcon in San Francisco* (1945), *The Falcon's Alibi* (1946) and *The*

Falcon's Adventure (1946). The Conway Falcons are generally an improvement on the Sanders films: rather more at home in B-movies, Conway was less sullen when faced with material his brother clearly believed beneath him. The Conway Falcons, which take him to various corners of North America in imitation of Charlie Chan's globe-trotting, are more atmospheric than the Sanders episodes and, even if the plots are sometimes less than first-rate, there are always elements of chance felicitous writing and casting that turn up incidental pleasures, like the vicious satire on movie types in Gordon Douglas's *The Falcon in Hollywood* or Elisha Cook Jr's performance as a homicidal disc jockey in Ray McCarey's *The Falcon's Alibi*.

The best of Conway's Falcons is William Clemens's *The Falcon and the Co-Eds*, written by Ardel Wray and Gerald Geraghty with overtones of *The Seventh Victim* (1943). Set in a doom-haunted girls' school perched atop a cliff from which people topple with alarming regularity, the film is a wild tangle involving a hysterical psychic (Rita Corday) given to predicting the deaths, and a gloomy drama teacher (Jean Brooks) who seems liable to be the next casualty. If none of the other films live up to the mix of moodiness and sassiness of *The Falcon and the Co-Eds*, there are at least touches of eeriness surrounding the nocturnal fishing parties of William Berke's

The Falcon in Mexico, allegedly local colour footage shot by Orson Welles for the unfinished *It's All True*, and the flashes of talent displayed by directors clearly on their way up in Edward Dmytryk's *The Falcon Strikes Back* and Joseph H. Lewis's *The Falcon in San Francisco*.

After the Conway series wound up in 1946, RKO sold the rights to the character to skid row independent Film Craft and magician John Calvert was cast in three extremely quick quickies, *The Devil's Cargo* (1948), *Appointment With Murder* (1948) and *Search for Danger* (1949). Very talky, these have Calvert relying on occasional feats of prestidigitation to compensate for a demonstrable lack of the requisite suavity. Charles McGraw took the Waring role in 39 half-hour television episodes for *The Adventures of the Falcon* (1954). Like **Boston Blackie**, the **Crime Doctor**, the *I Love a Mystery* team, the **Lone Wolf**, **Mr Moto** and **Philo Vance**, the Falcon has failed to pick up on the long-term cult success of the **Saint**, **Batman**, **Charlie Chan**, **Ellery Queen**, **Perry Mason** or The Thin Man, and is now remembered as just another well-spoken private detective. KN

Fallen Angel

Though clearly intended to exploit the success of **Laura** by utilising several of the same talents, *Fallen Angel* is set in a very different milieu. The setting is a small Californian town, where an opportunist drifter (Andrews) fetches up penniless. The quality of ambiguity which would be subsequently recognised as Preminger's stock-in-trade is harnessed to a neatly plotted and sardonic script, as Andrews sets his sights on marrying a rich woman (musical star Faye in an against-type dramatic role) in order to run off with her money with local waitress (Darnell). When the latter is murdered, Andrews becomes a suspect, and is hounded by the cop (Bickford) who is in fact Darnell's former suitor and her killer. Faye selflessly helps Andrews to clear his name and in the process they discover mutual dependence. The reformation of Andrews's character may be somewhat arbitrary, but fortunately the film is unencumbered in its *mise en scène* by any of the symbolic implications at which the title might hint. TP

1945/98m/FOX/*p*/*d* Otto Preminger/*s* Harry Kleiner/*c* Joseph La Shelle/*m* David Raksin/ *lp* Alice Faye, Dana Andrews, Linda Darnell, Charles Bickford, Anne Revere.

124

ABOVE AND BELOW *Fantômas*

Family Plot

Dern and Harris play a couple of confidence artists who specialise in a phoney spiritualist routine. They attempt to defraud an elderly lady of her fortune. She wants to give it to her long-lost nephew (Devane), but he together with Karen Black is a professional kidnapper who is holding to ransom a Greek shipping magnate. Ernest Lehman's script ingeniously works a series of twists and turns involving a secret room in the kidnapper's house and the graveyard that provides the double entendre for the title. Hitchcock's last film is a light-hearted and stylishly entertainment, as one would expect from Ernest Lehman, the writer of *North by Northwest* (1959). The set pieces are technically superb and Devane is a truly chilling villain in the manner of Barry Foster in **Frenzy**. EB

1976/120m/U/*p/d* Alfred Hitchcock/*s* Ernest Lehman/*c* Leonard J. South/*m* John Williams/*lp* Karen Black, Bruce Dern, Barbara Harris, William Devane, Ed Lauter.

Fantômas

The popular novelists Marcel Allain and Pierre Souvestre had published, starting in 1911, 32 monthly stories featuring the supercriminal Fantômas, with immense suc-

cess. Victorin Jasset, one of France's leading directors at the time, took inspiration from the series for his *Zigomar* films (1911). But it was Gaumont which bought the rights and charged one of its most prolific directors who was also in charge of the studio's entire output, Feuillade, to adapt the stories to the screen. Allain and Souvestre collaborated closely with Feuillade, often improvising

new material during shooting. The first one, simple called *Fantômas* (1913), was followed by four more titles, each released as a separate film over a period of a year (1913–14) rather than as a conventional serial: *Juve contre Fantômas, La Mort qui tue, Fantômas contre Fantômas, Le Faux magistrat*. Each of them ran for about 45 to 55 minutes. The story begins with Fantômas (Navarre) seducing Lady Beltham (Carl) and murdering her husband. In the end, he manages to escape from the guillotine by sending the actor who plays Fantômas on the stage in his place. The next episodes extend the chase between the ever-changing Fantômas and his implacable enemy, Inspector Juve (Bréon), each of the films containing some unforgettable scenes and images: a gun battle among barrels on a quay-side, a fight with a boa constrictor, a glove made from the skin of a dead man's hand, blood and pearls raining down from a church tower, and so on. Feuillade went on to make further extraordinary crime serials, the best of which were **Les Vampires**, **Judex**, *La Nouvelle Mission de Judex* (1917), *Tih Minh* (1918) and *Barrabas* (1919).

The Hungarian expatriate Paul Féjos made a version of *Fantômas* in 1932, starring Tania Fédor (Lady Beltham), Jean Galland (Fantômas) and Thomy Bourdelle (Juve); Jean Sacha returned to the subject in 1946, starring Marcel Herrand in the title role and Alexandre Rignault as Juve; Robert Vernay directed *Fantômas contre Fantômas* in 1948, with Maurice Teynac as Fantômas and Rignault again as Juve. In 1964, a new *Fantômas* series was launched by André

The Far Paradise—Fatal Attraction

Hunebelle, starring Jean Marais in the title role and the comic Louis de Funès as Juve. This was followed by *Fantômas se déchaîne* (1965) and *Fantômas contre Scotland Yard* (1967), both with the same lead actors. PW

1913–14/France/45m/Gaumont/*d/co-s* Louis Feuillade/*co-s* Marcel Allain, Pierre Souvestre/*c* Guerin/*lp* René Navarre, Bréon, Renée Carl, Jane Faber, Georges Melchior.

The Far Paradise

The McDonagh sisters were the most accomplished Australian film-makers at the end of the 20s. Paulette directed, Phyllis was pro-ducer and art director while Isabel starred using the stage name Marie Lorraine. This, their last silent film, tells the story of Cherry Carson (Lorraine) whose father is a swindler and whose boyfriend's father is a public prosecutor. Cherry and her father go on the run but the hero finds his beloved again in a tourist resort where Cherry, still devoted to her degenerate father, has become an alcoholic. He saves her from himself and the crime melodrama ends happily for the lovers. The film's main qualities reside in the sophisticated *mise en scène* and pictorialism. The sisters' next movie, **The Cheaters** was conceived as a silent film but efforts to transform it into a sound feature ruined its rhythm. PW

1928/Australia/78m/MCD/*p* Phyllis McDonagh/*d/s* Paulette McDonagh/*c* Jack Fletcher/*lp* Marie Lorraine, Gaston Mervale, Arthur McLaglen, John Faulkner.

Fargo

The Coen brothers' most satisfactory film, *Fargo* on first sight seems to be a virtual remake of their debut feature **Blood Simple**, with the simple difference that this botched crime takes place in the freezing mid-West rather than a sweltering Texas. Actually, *Fargo* is the inverse of the Coens' debut feature. In the manner of **Raising Arizona**, *Fargo* is concerned not with the past but with the future, in this case the child which McDormand's chief of police is carrying, and the design for a US stamp her husband is competing for. Fittingly the film ends with the competition won (albeit for the 3 cent rather than the 29 cent stamp) and McDormand once again comfortable in bed after solving the case. Buscemi and Stormare are the kidnappers hired by over-extended car salesman Macy to kidnap his wife, and McDormand the chief of police called in when the pair kill a highway patrol-man and an innocent couple who stumble across them. If McDormand's comments about money being overvalued on a fine day such as this, which to the audience as well as Stormare's killer seems hardly different from any other snow-swept day, seem bland, almost comic, the film endorses her choice. McDormand is the film's still centre. Where others try to adjust to ever-changing circumstances she simply follows her training – as in the sequence where she quietly corrects the assumptions of a fellow officer at the scene of the crime – or her instincts, as in her concern with food and her considerate handling of the university friend she meets again in Minneapolis. PH

1996/77m/Gramercy-Working Title/*p/co-s* Joel Coen/*d/co-s* Ethan Coen/*c* Roger Deakins/*m* Carter Burwell/*lp* Frances McDormand, Steve Buscemi, William H. Macy, Peter Stormare, Harve Presnell, John Carroll Lynch, Kristin Rudred.

Fatal Attraction

A huge box-office hit which clearly struck a nerve with the public, *Fatal Attraction* is in fact quite a traditional movie in which, not for the first time in the crime movie, the

Fargo, Frances McDormand (above), William H. Macy (below)

ABOVE Michael Douglas, Glenn Close, *Fatal Attraction*

woman who willingly has sex outside the family pays with her life. Douglas is a successful lawyer, happily married to Archer, who meets Close and has sex with her. It's exciting, and so he does it again. But he makes it clear to her that there's to be no long-term involvement. Infuriated by his rejection, Close changes from a object of desire to avenging angel. She calls him constantly, damages his car, and finally invades his home. Audiences loved the ending, where Close becomes a homicidal maniac and in a final, blatantly manipulative twist rises from the bath after Douglas thinks he has drowned her. Critics turned up their noses at the metamorphosis of the film from melodrama to slasher movie, and feminists also attacked it for demonising the independently sexual woman and idolising the stay-at-home little wife. EB

1987/119m/PAR/*p* Stanley R. Jaffe, Sherry Lansing/*d* Adrian Lyne/*s* James Dearden/ *c* Howard Atherton/*m* Maurice Jarre/*lp* Michael Douglas, Glenn Close, Anne Archer, Ellen Hamilton Latzen, Stuart Pankin.

Faulkner, William [Harrison]
(1897–1962)
A Nobel prize winner, who after the success of *Sanctuary* (1931) regularly commuted between Oxford, Mississippi and Hollywood from 1932 to 1955, Faulkner was probably

the only major US novelist to survive Hollywood. He did this by continuing to write novels, returning to Mississippi whenever possible and using film work as a means to earn money. In this he was greatly helped by his friendship with director Howard Hawks, several of whose films he contributed to. Many of his own novels were filmed, generally with scripts by others. *Sanctuary* (filmed as **The Story of Temple Drake**, and as *Sanctuary*, 1961), the inspiration behind **James Hadley Chase**'s *No Orchids For Miss Blandish* (1948), and *Intruder In The Dust* (1949) were crime novels. Faulkner's contributions to many of the films he worked on are hard to identify. Often he provided treatments (e.g. *Drums Along the Mohawk*, 1939) or minor revisions (**Mildred Pierce**), often not used (*Slave Ship*, 1937). More is known about his work with Hawks but it remains difficult to pinpoint his contributions, particularly as all his work for Hawks was as a co-writer. Three elements have been identified: a sense of narrative clarity (seen at its best in his work on **The Big Sleep**), an ability to set up key moments, as in the 'just whistle'sequence of *To Have and Have Not* (1945) which Hawks credits Faulkner for, and a fidelity to sources wherever possible. Other scripts for Hawks include *Road To Glory* (1936) and *Land Of The Pharaohs* (1955). Films from Faulkner's novels include *Tarnished Angels* (1958, from *Pylon* 1935), *The Long Hot Summer* (1958, from *The Hamlet*, 1940), *The Sound and The Fury* (1959, novel 1929) and *The Reivers* (1972, novel 1962). PH

The FBI
In 1908, Attorney General Charles Bonaparte, faced with new regulations that prevented him borrowing investigators from the Secret Service, established the Bureau of Investigation as a sub-division of the Justice Department, appointing Stanley W. Finch as its first Director. In the first fifteen years of its existence, the BI went through a succession of Directors and became known as 'the Department of Easy Virtue', prompting Attorney General Harlan Fiske Stone in 1924 to clean house and appoint 29-year-old John Edgar Hoover, then Assistant Director under William J. Burns, to the Directorship, a post he would hold, despite innumerable challenges, until his death in 1972. The organisation, which incorporated the General Intelligence Division of the Department of Justice after 1929, was named the Federal Bureau of Investigation in 1935,.

Hoover, who ensured that the words

ABOVE The FBI: Jack Warner with J. Edgar Hoover

<small>ABOVE</small> The FBI: James Cagney, 'G' Men

'Federal Bureau of Investigation' were in larger print on official stationery than 'United States Department of Justice', identified himself so closely with the Bureau during his reign that the two became indistinguishable. The Director shouldered all the credit for the Bureau's successes in tracking down such hoodlums as **John Dillinger**, **Charles 'Pretty Boy' Floyd**, **Arizona Clark 'Ma' Barker** and George 'Machine Gun' Kelly, even to the extent of driving Melvin Purvis, the Chicago Special Agent responsible for many of these manhunts, from the Bureau and writing him out of official history. In the 30s, the BI became known for its direct methods, preferring to ambush and gun down public enemies rather than bring them in for trial, though George Kelly proved unusually timid (as depicted in Roger Corman's **Machine Gun Kelly**) and surrendered meekly, in the process hanging a nick-name on the federal agents with his cry of 'don't shoot, G-Men.' Having made his name as a participant in the Palmer anti-Red raids of 1919, personally supervising the deportation of anarchist Emma Goldman, Hoover's obsession through-

out his tenure was communism. He could far more legitimately than Joseph McCarthy be seen as the guiding force of the 'McCarthy Era', taking a vigorous part in the persecution of suspected fellow travellers, the surveillance of the Communist Party of America and the prosecutions of alleged 'atom spies' Alger Hiss and Julius and Ethel Rosenberg.

Until the early 60s, Hoover refused to believe organised crime existed in the USA, but probes, including those of his hated rival Attorney General Robert Kennedy, forced him to accept the existence of the **mafia**. Throughout his career Hoover, a lifelong bachelor allegedly linked romantically with Assistant Director Clyde Tolson, carried out personal feuds with the CIA and various incumbents of the offices of President and Attorney General, using the flimsiest legal grounds for resorting to telephone-tapping, bugging, break-ins, black propaganda, blackmail and the manufacture of evidence. Upon Hoover's death, a concerted attempt was made to break the power of the Bureau and to ensure no other demagogue could replace the late Director, whereupon a succession of officials have come and gone as director,

starting with Nixon appointee L. Patrick Gray, who opened the FBI to female agents and allowed the wearing of coloured shirts, and including Clarence M. Kelley, William Hedgcock Webster and William Steele Sessions.

Hoover enjoyed a reputation as America's 'Top Cop', and enthusiastically signed his name to ghosted accounts of the Bureau's greatest cases, encouraging positive images of the FBI in films such as *Let 'Em Have It* (1935), **'G' Men** and **The FBI Story** and TV shows like *The FBI* (1965–74). He also did his best to force his agents (overwhelmingly middle-class WASPs) to abide by a system even more rigid than the Hays Code, prohibiting sideburns and enforcing height-to-weight ratio restrictions he would have himself failed if he did not persistently falsify his height, even suggesting that agents model their appearance on Efrem Zimbalist Jr as the hero of *The FBI*. In addition to *'G' Men* and *The FBI Story*, A-feature epics combining several cases, with James Cagney and James Stewart respectively as super-agents on good terms with the sainted J. Edgar, Hoover sanctioned lesser films, including a loose Paramount B series initiated by *Persons in Hiding* (1939), based on a ghosted-for-Hoover book, including *Undercover Doctor* (1939), *Parole Fixer* (1940) and *Queen of the Mob* (1940), all co-written by novelist Horace McCoy.

The combination of clean-living and fast-shooting made the G-Man a popular hero in the 30s, 40s and 50s, whether pitted against mobsters, Nazis or communists. The FBI hagiographies of the Hoover period include *Daughter of Shanghai* (1937), an illegal alien drama unusual for casting Philip Ahn as a Chinese G-Man in a period when ethnic minorities were notoriously under-represented in the FBI, **The House on 92nd Street**, concentrating on the breaking of a German spy ring, *Walk East on Beacon* (1952), an apparent remake of with the Reds replacing the Nazis, and such serials as *G-Men Vs the Black Dragon/Black Dragon of Manzanar* (1943), *Federal Operator 99/FBI 99* (1945) and *G-Men Never Forget/Code 645* (1948), not to mention such quickies as *Trapped by G-Men* (1937), *Federal Bullets* (1937), *Border G-Men* (1938), *When G-Men Step In* (1938), *Federal Manhunt* (1939), *Federal Fugitives* (1941), *Parole, Inc* (1949), *Federal Man* (1950), *Federal Agents at Large* (1950), *I Was a Communist for the FBI* (1951), *FBI Girl* (1951) and *FBI Code 98* (1964).

It was not until after Hoover's death that

<small>ABOVE</small> The FBI: Jodie Foster, *The Silence of the Lambs*

the Bureau was shown in a negative light in the cinema, most devastatingly in Larry Cohen's **The Private Files of J. Edgar Hoover**, which covers much of the ground later probed in depth by Curt Gentry's definitive biography *J. Edgar Hoover: The Man and His Secrets* (1991), and has Broderick Crawford and James Wainwright as the old and young demagogue, and equally apt performances from Dan Dailey and Michael Sacks as Tolson and Purvis. The FBI's historical involvement in famous cases and issues was then reassessed in films like **Lepke**, with Tony Curtis surrendering to Erwin Fuller's Hoover, **The Brink's Job**, with Sheldon Leonard as a Red-hating Hoover, *The House on Carroll Street* (1988), about the HUAC period with Jeff Daniels as a conscience-stricken fed, **Prince of the City**, about an FBI investigation of the NYPD (the sort of case Hoover always avoided for fear of alienating local police), **Mississippi Burning**, about the civil rights movement of the 60s with G-Men Gene Hackman and Willem Dafoe going against the Klan, *Thunderheart* (1992), with part-Sioux G-Man Val Kilmer delving into a murder on an Indian Reservation and clashing with his corrupt superior Sam Shepard, and *Chaplin* (1992), with Kevin Dunn's Hoover maniacally persecuting Robert Downey Jr's allegedly red-tinged Charlie Chaplin.

The Bureau's long-standing feud with the counter-culture, the stuff of comedy in *Rude Awakening* (1989) and *Flashback* (1990), is taken seriously in *Running on Empty* (1988), all of which show federal agents patiently dogging fugitive 60s radicals. Even the most exposé-driven of these films can't bring themselves to be as blistering about the FBI as comparable pictures (*Three Days of the Condor*, 1975, *Missing*, 1982, *Blow Out*, 1982, *Company Business*, 1991) are about the CIA. Meanwhile, a run of TV movies delve into the files, yielding *The FBI Story: The FBI Versus Alvin Karpis, Public Enemy Number One* (1974), with Harris Yulin as Hoover, *Melvin Purvis, G-Man* (1974) and *Kansas City Massacre* (1975), both with Dale Robertson as Purvis, *Attack on Terror: The FBI Versus the Ku Klux Klan* (1975), *The Lindbergh Kidnapping Case* (1976), *J. Edgar Hoover* (1987), with Treat Williams, *Citizen Cohn* (1992), with Pat Hingle as Hoover, *Betrayed by Love* (1993), with Steven Weber as the first FBI agent convicted of murder, and *Marilyn & Bobby: Her Final Affair* (1993), with Richard Dysart as the first explicitly gay Hoover. Hoover's alleged transvestism is first alluded to in Woody Allen's *Bananas* (1972), where the Director is played by a black woman, and is the subject of throwaway gags in *Naked Gun 33⅓: The Final Insult* (1994) and *The Hudsucker Proxy* (1994).

In the late 80s and early 90s, the image of the Bureau finally separated from that of Hoover, initially through relegation to the role of comic stooges, whether unsympathetically (Robert Davi in **Die Hard**, Samuel L. Jackson in *White Sands*, 1992) or sympathetically (Matthew Modine in **Married to the Mob**). **The Silence of the Lambs**, with Jodie Foster as a trainee agent assigned to the case of a serial killer, is the culmination of two separate trends, the most obvious represented by **Manhunter**, also from a Thomas Harris novel, in which the Bureau is pitted against the supposed modern curse of the apparently random mass murderer. Equally important perhaps is the strand inaugurated by Lynn Whitfield in *Johnnie Gibson, FBI* (1987), Rebecca De Mornay in *Feds* (1988) and Debra Winger in *Betrayed* (1988), in which the traditionally macho FBI image is subtly transformed by the casting of an ambiguously womanly woman as the federal investigator. The contrast between James Stewart and Jodie Foster's Clarice Starling is as pointed as that between Efrem Zimbalist and Kyle MacLachlan's Dale Cooper. MacLachlan's impersonation of an FBI agent who is actually an alien in *The Hidden* (1988) develops to a bizarre turn in David Lynch's TV series *Twin Peaks* (1989–91) and its film spin-off *Twin Peaks: Fire Walk with Me* (1992). KN

The FBI Story

A postwar rewrite of **'G' Men** or *Persons in Hiding* (1939), this uses the story of a twenty-five-year FBI man (Stewart) to celebrate the methods and morals of J. Edgar Hoover's Federal Bureau of Investigation. The result is the 'straight' template for the grotesque, but more honest and convincing, vision of Larry Cohen's **The Private Files of J. Edgar Hoover**. The script is a succession of trite incidents, the most familiar of which (seen also in *'G' Men*) is the death in the line of the duty of the happy-go-lucky younger agent (Hamilton) that spurs Stewart on to greater zeal. Like the best-selling history upon which it is based, the film omits mention of such major figures as agent Melvin Purvis and gangster Roger Touhy and of the rise of the national crime syndicate, because Hoover, whose personal involvement in the film extended to ordering extensive reshoots because he did not like the politics of a couple of extras, wished them written out of the official record. KN

1959/149m/WB/*p*/*d* Mervyn LeRoy/ *s* Richard L. Breen, Jon Twist/*orig* Don Whitehead/*c* Joseph Biroc/*m* Max Steiner/

Femmes Fatales

lp James Stewart, Vera Miles, Murray Hamilton, Larry Pennell, Nick Adams, Diane Jergens.

Femmes Fatales

Lady Macbeth and Hedda Gabler are among the antecedents of the modern *femme fatale*, who uses sex, guile and sometimes intimidation to lure a weak man into committing a crime that ultimately destroys them both. In recent years the term has been used to describe any vindictive or psychopathic woman. In this century the earliest form of *femme fatale* is the vamp, originally derived from Rudyard Kipling's poem 'The Vampire', which inspired the play *A Fool There Was*, filmed in 1914 with Theda Bara in the lead. Bara established the vamp as a seductive creature in heavy eye-liner and outré clothes who exploits a man's weakness and breaks up his marriage. Other early leading exponents include Pola Negri, Valeska Suratt, Virginia Pearson and Louise Glaum. Within a few years the vamp had become a figure of fun, and Bara ended her screen career in 1926 parodying herself. In *Der blaue Engel/ The Blue Angel* (Germany 1930) Marlene Dietrich plays a modified vamp, the nightclub singer Lola-Lola who wrecks the life of her infatuated admirer, Professor Unrath. An overnight sensation in the film, Dietrich was taken immediately to the US, where she was cast in similar roles, notably in *The Devil Is a*

Woman (1935). Other man-eaters of the early talkies include Tallulah Bankhead in *Devil and the Deep* (1932), Jean Harlow in *Red-Headed Woman* (1932) and Bette Davis in *Of Human Bondage* (1934), as well as any number of chorus girls who tantalise and humiliate their sugar-daddies. In the 'hard-boiled' detective fiction of **Raymond Chandler**, **Dashiell Hammett** and others, female characters were often upgraded from mere molls and girl-friends to 'tough broads'. Such novels provided much of the source material or inspiration for the crime dramas of the 40s later categorised as *film noir*. These films popularised the modern *femme fatale*, immoral and unscrupulous in keeping with the degeneracy of the films themselves, yet not ludicrously malevolent like the primitive vamp, nor motivated solely by one deadly sin (usually jealousy or greed) like the home-wreckers and gold-diggers of the 30s. Far more complex a character, she often appears feminine and vulnerable but is in fact a match for the man prepared to use anyone in order to get what he wants. The great *femmes fatales* in *noir* of this period include Veronica Lake in **This Gun for Hire**, Barbara Stanwyck in **Double Indemnity** and **The File on Thelma Jordan**, Joan Bennett in **The Woman in the Window**, Ann Blyth in **Mildred Pierce**, Janis Carter in *Night Editor* (1946), Jean Gillie in *Decoy* (1946), Ava Gardner in **The**

ABOVE Femmes Fatales: Veronica Lake, Alan Ladd, *This Gun for Hire*

Killers, Lana Turner in **The Postman Always Rings Twice**, Rita Hayworth in **Gilda** and **The Lady from Shanghai**, Jane Greer in **Out of the Past/Build My Gallows High**, Gail Russell in *Calcutta* (1947), Helen Walker in *Impact* (1949), and Peggy Cummins in **Gun Crazy**. Simultaneously Hedy Lamarr played scheming temptresses in the melodramas *White Cargo* (1942) and *The Strange Woman* (1946). Murderesses were in vogue, often poisoners in period pictures, e.g. *Pink String and Sealing Wax, Ivy* (1947). **Sunset Blvd.**, with Gloria Swanson as the ageing vamp Norma Desmond, was the superior forerunner of a cycle of films beginning in the 60s in which veteran actresses played psychopaths in Gothic-style horror. In the 50s, when most women had reverted to work as housewives, women's screen roles were again chiefly limited to wives and girl-friends. Occasional bad girls included Sandra Dorne in *Roadhouse Girl* (1953), Gloria Grahame in **The Big Heat** and *Human Desire* (1954), Kim Novak in *Pushover* (1954), Barbara Payton in **Murder Is My Beat**, and Barbara Stanwyck in **Crime of Passion**. In the latter Stanwyck is willing to prostitute herself, but only in order to advance her husband's career. Angie Dickinson played the Ava Gardner role in the re-make of *The Killers* (1964). Inspired by the renewed popularity in the late 60s of the private-eye thriller, awareness of *film noir* grew throughout the 70s and cul-

ABOVE James Stewart, Murray Hamilton, *The FBI Story*

minated in the creation of *nouvelles femmes fatales*, notably Kathleen Turner in **Body Heat**, Kim Basinger in *Final Analysis* (1992), Lena Olin in *Romeo Is Bleeding* (1992), and Linda Fiorentino in *The Last Seduction* (1993). There is considerable cross-over between neo-*noir* and the erotic thriller genre, which often features a disturbed or vengeful woman, who is sometimes a killer. The earliest modern example is probably *Play Misty for Me* (1971); others include **Ms .45/Angel of Vengeance**, *Double Jeopardy* (1981), *Black Widow* (1987), **Fatal Attraction**, *The Hand That Rocks the Cradle* (1992), *Single White Female* (1992), **Basic Instinct**, *The Temp* (1993), *Malice* (1993), *The Crush* (1993), and *Elles n'oublient pas/Love in the Strangest Way* (France 1994). Curiously, the women in *Une femme fatale* (France 1975) and *Femme Fatale* (1991) are not *femmes fatales*. DM

La Femme infidèle/The Unfaithful Wife

After the transitional bisexual love story, *Les Biches* (1968), the former critic and co-inaugurator of the New Wave, Chabrol, embarked on an unrivalled series of brilliantly filmed thrillers chronicling the ambiguities of good and evil in a manner recalling Fritz Lang's work as much as Hitchcock's narrative techniques. This is the first of the series, introducing Bouquet, whom Chabrol had recruited from performance in a Pinter play.

A well-to-do lawyer, Charles (Bouquet), finds that his wife Héléne (Audran) is having an affair with Victor (Ronet). Unsettled, he goes to see the man and in a fit of uncontrollable anger bludgeons him to death. He laboriously but successfully dumps the corpse in a ditch, returns to his domestic life and observes, with some glee, his wife's suppressed grief. As she begins to realise he is the killer, she also begins to realise the depth of his feelings for her and responds to his emotions. When he is eventually arrested and driven away by the police, an extraordinary shot combining a track out with a zoom in sums up contradictory feelings that bind the couple together. The entire film is meticulously orchestrated, each camera movement being followed by its inverse movement, paralleling the doubling of contradictory emotions: the contented housewife having a passionate affair; the staid lawyer with the potential for sadism and violence; grief and hatred turning into love. Chabrol followed this classic with the equally complex **Que la bête meure** and **Le Boucher**, embarking on a series of both artistic and financial successes which came to an end with *Juste avant la nuit* and *La Décade prodigieuse* (both 1971). PW

1968/France, Italy, 98m/Films La Boétie-Cinegai/*p* André Genovès/*d/s* Claude Chabrol/*c* Jean Rabier/*m* Pierre Jansen/*lp* Stéphane Audran, Michel Bouquet,

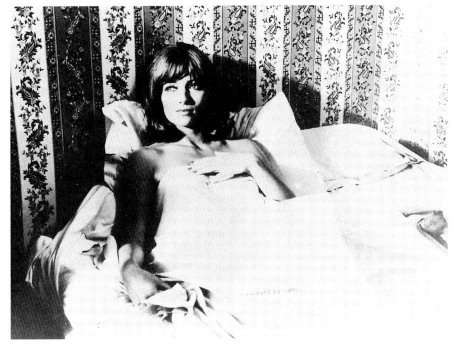

ABOVE Stéphane Audran, *La Femme infidèle*

Maurice Ronet, Serge Bento, Michel Duchaussoy.

The File on Thelma Jordan

The themes of the double, in the sense of a dual personality, and of the double cross recur in the films of Robert Siodmak. Here the theme is worked out through the duplicitous heroine at the film's centre. The ingenious story, which combines the *noir* thriller with elements of the 'woman's picture', centres upon an assistant D.A. (Corey) who has married for self-advancement and is dominated by his wife and her father. He embarks on an affair with the enigmatic Thelma (Stanwyck) only to discover too late that he is a pawn in a dangerous game. She is married to a shady character (Rober) and her rich aunt is found dead in suspicious circumstances. The ensuing murder trial is a pointed addition to the genre's satiric commentary on the workings of justice, with the prosecutor, in the manner of *Sleepers* (1996), sabotaging his own case in order to bring about the defendant's acquittal. The film ends with a sustained double-take. Stanwyck leaves town with Rober after rejecting Corey but undergoes a change of heart and causes their car to crash. TP

1949/100m/PAR/*p* Hal B. Wallis/*d* Robert Siodmak/*s* Ketti Frings/*c* George Barnes/*m* Victor Young/*lp* Barbara Stanwyck, Wendell Corey, Paul Kelly, Richard Rober, Joan Tetzel.

Film Noir

In the 40s and early 50s many contemporary American crime dramas were bleak, pessimistic tales featuring characters on either side of the law who were by turns ruthless, desperate, sexually obsessed and doomed. The hero was introverted and cynical, and often weak, the heroine manipulative and cruel, and often strong, a **femme fatale**. The oppressive mood was accentuated by monochrome low-key lighting and seemingly endless flashbacks which imprisoned the characters in a perpetual present.

The term *film noir* originated in France at the end of World War II. When **The Maltese Falcon**, **Laura**, *Murder My Sweet*, **Double Indemnity** and **The Woman in the Window** were shown within a week of each other in Paris, where very few American films had been released during the period of German occupation, they were labelled *films noirs* by French critic Nino Frank, who perceived thematic similarities

Film Noir

between the films and the pulp fiction previously published in France in the *Série Noire*. Many of its American authors, including **James M. Cain**, **Raymond Chandler**, **Dashiell Hammett**, Horace McCoy and **Cornell Woolrich**, had provided source material for the films. The first book to evaluate the new genre was *Panorama du film noir américain* (1955). Two decades after the war the term came into general use in England and America, but a decade before that a new generation of directors turned to making thrillers, often based on the books which had inspired the first *films noirs*, and usually in a style that drew on the earlier films. As a result today *film noir* is both an easily understood reference point and a confusing one. Often applied to any film featuring a rain-washed street or shadows cast by a venetian blind, in this book the term is (generally) restricted to films of the 40s and the 50s. For although *film noir* was clearly a style it was one which had its roots in a particular time. Subsequent homages and references back to this, the neo-*noir* films of the 1980s for example, generally pay tribute to *noir* as a style but pay less attention to the collection of forces that shaped the classic *films noirs* of the period. In particular, America's entry into the war in 1941 resulted in significant changes in the position of women, which made their portrayal as mere girl-friends or molls problematic. Traditional models for representing sex and gender relations increasingly came into conflict with the realities of a world where women were taking over men's jobs while their husbands were away fighting. In short, women became more active. The classic example of this is **Mildred Pierce**. A simple role reversal that follows from this change is that of seducer and seduced, as in **The Postman Always Rings Twice**, where it is the woman who takes the initiative. Another feature of the crime films of the 1940s is that women are not only **femmes fatales**, preying on confused males, but often the active party seeking to clear their partner's name, as in **Phantom Lady**. Masculine energy is not a common feature of *film noir*, and the rise-and-fall narrative typical of the gangster film, a plot in which energy was essential, is little found in *film noir* (and when it is, it is ironically book-ended by flashbacks, as in *Mildred Pierce*). The rise-and-fall structure is replaced by that of the investigation, often in a present that is seemingly stretched to fill the running time of a film, leaving the central character, as it were, trapped in a ceaseless present in which time is forever running out, as in **The Big Clock**.

The roots of *film noir*'s fatalism and visual intensity are traceable back to Josef von Sternberg, particularly his gangster film **Underworld**. Like Sternberg, many *noir* directors – Curtis Bernhardt, Fritz Lang, Max Ophuls, Robert Siodmak – came to Hollywood from Europe, where German expres-

ABOVE Film Noir: Humphrey Bogart, *The Maltese Falcon*

sionism and French poetic realism had permeated popular cinema. The latter movement produced the crime films *La Chienne* (1931), **La Bête humaine**, **Le jour se lève** and *Le Dernier Tournant* (1939). All these were re-made in Hollywood, the latter as *The Postman Always Rings Twice* (1946, 1981). Often identified as the first true film noir, the B-feature *Stranger on the Third Floor* (1940) clearly differed both dramatically and stylistically from the conventional melodramas and murder mysteries that had gone before. Apart from those already noted, key *noir* films that came after include **The Glass Key**, **The Killers**, **The Blue Dahlia**, **The Big Sleep**, *Crack-Up* (1946), **Out of the Past**, *The Naked City*, *The Accused* (1949), **The Asphalt Jungle**, *Caged* (1949), and **Gun Crazy**, which closed the most productive and daring period of *film noir*. This was the era of the 'hard-boiled' private eye film, usually adapted from a crime novel, as well as the voice-over, the flashback and the montage. During the period the hard-edged chiaroscuro of the films, so much admired today, was developed by such cameramen as John Alton, Burnett Guffey, Nicholas Musuraca and John F. Seitz. In the 50s, expressionistic lighting and camera angles gave way, following the example set by *The Naked City*, to documentary-style shooting on real locations. The caper film and juvenile

ABOVE Film Noir: Robert Mitchum, *Out of the Past*

delinquency replaced *film noir*, as public concerns (the fate of America) replaced the more private doubts and agonies of *film noir*. Directors such as Robert Aldrich, Samuel Fuller, Phil Karlson and Joseph H. Lewis made increasingly brutal films. Notable films from this period are **His Kind of Woman**, *Ace in the Hole* (1951), **The Big Heat**, *The Hitch-Hiker* (1953) – the only *film noir* directed by a woman (Ida Lupino) – **The Big Combo**, **Kiss Me Deadly**, **The Killing**, **Beyond a Reasonable Doubt** and **Touch of Evil**. *Film noir* became obsolete at the end of the 50s, when post-war malaise was superseded by the optimism of the new decade (and black-and-white photography was phased out). Its spirit was revived in 1966, when Paul Newman played a hard-boiled private eye of the old school in **Harper**.

Published in 1968, *Hollywood in the Forties* by Charles Higham and Joel Greenberg was the first book in English to acknowledge *film noir* as a genre, although it was anglicised as 'black film', confusing at the time of the emergence of the new black cinema. By the 70s, when reviewing the detective movies that came in the wake of *Harper*, critics had reverted to the French term. In recent years films inspired by vintage *film noir* have been dubbed neo-*noir*. Only a few are period pieces – **Chinatown**, *Farewell, My Lovely* (1975), *Under Suspicion* (1991). **Blade Runner** and *Trouble in Mind* (1985) are set in the future. The majority of films have used the best-known elements of classic *noir* and updated the visual style. The most interesting of these include *The Driver* (1978), **Body Heat**, *Breathless* (1983), *Against All Odds* (1984) – a re-make of *Out of the Past* – **Blood Simple** (and most of director Joel Coen's subsequent work), **Blue Velvet**, *Impulse* (1990), *Singapore Sling* (1990), **The Grifters**, *After Dark, My Sweet* (1990), *True Romance* (1993), and *The Innocent Sleep* (1995). DM

The Finger Points

John Monk Saunders and **W.R. Burnett**'s gangster-newspaper story was based on the previous year's Jake Lingle killing in Chicago. Lingle was an over-confident *Chicago Tribune* reporter on Capone's payroll. Here, Barthelmess is an innocent reporter new to the big city who is soon corrupted by gangster Gable's big-money offers to suppress any news involving the latter's gang. When a 'hot' story does accidentally get past Barthelmess, and the police move in on Gable, the mobster 'fingers' the reporter who

is then machine-gunned down by the mob. An early Gable is suitably sinister as an **Al Capone** figure. TV

1931/90m/First National-WB/*d* John Francis Dillon/*s* Robert Lord/*c* Ernest Haller/*lp* Richard Barthelmess, Fay Wray, Regis Toomey, Clark Gable.

A Fish Called Wanda

Wanda looks back to Ealing studio successes (particularly Crichton's own **The Lavender Hill Mob**) for its initial premises and forward to America in its casting (bringing in Curtis and Kline to give transatlantic appeal to the 'wacky' English humour on display from Cleese and Palin). That such a calculated mix should be so successful is only surprising if one associates Cleese (as writer and performer) only with the anarchy of *Monty Python* and forgets the discipline of his UK teleseries *Fawlty Towers*. Cleese as barrister Archie Leach (the real name of Cary Grant) raises embarrassment to new heights as he is pursued by Curtis (who seeks to seduce him) and Kline (who seeks to both scare Cleese into submission and is deeply jealous of what might happen between Cleese and Curtis). The pair are seeking the whereabouts of the jewels stolen by them and the imprisoned Georgeson (whom Cleese represents). The result, which was the most successful UK film (prior to *Four Weddings and a Funeral*, 1995), briefly made Cleese a sex star. The same team re-assembled for the less successful *Fierce Creatures* (1997). PH

1988/108m/U/*p* Michael Shamberg/*d* Charles Crichton/*s* John Cleese/*c* Alan Hume/*m* John Du Prez/*lp* John Cleese, Kevin Kline, Jamie Lee Curtis, Michael Palin, Maria Aitkin. Tom Georgeson.

Fisher, Steve [Gould] (1912–80)

Best known for the highly melodramatic **I Wake Up Screaming** (1941, filmed 1942 and 1953 as *Vicki*), Fisher after turning to screenwriting remained a prolific novel writer. Although most of these were in the crime mould Fisher's forty-plus scripts were far more varied. They included several crime classics (**Lady in the Lake** and *Dead Reckoning*, 1947) some Westerns (*Law Of The Lawless*, 1964, the first of 11 he would write for producer A.C. Lyles), some series outings (*Song Of The Thin Man*, 1947), war films and general melodramas. In the 70s he wrote extensively for television. He was also responsible for the light-hearted play *Susan Slept Here* (1951), which he wrote with Alex

Gottlieb, who did the film script (1954). Like *Screaming*, *Susan* was set in Hollywood. In the course of his career Fisher collaborated with several important screenwriters. These include his friend **Frank Gruber** (*Johnny Angel*, 1945), whose *The Pulp Jungle* (1967) details their days as pulp writers, Lamar Trotti (*To The Shores Of Tripoli*, 1942), and **W.R. Burnett** (*September Storm*, 1961). Fisher, who began writing in the 20s while in the navy, spent much of the 30s writing for pulp magazines, graduating finally to *Black Mask* in the early 40s. In his script for *Lady In the Lake* Fisher had Marlowe submit a story to *Lurid Detective* magazine. Though he subsequently wrote for the 'slicks' (*Colliers*, *Cosmopolitan*, etc.), his simple style and his unsubtle plots contained large doses of sentimentality. This carried on into his novels, which were robust rather than sophisticated. His scripts, however, were far more complex. He was responsible for the subjective point-of-view narrative of *Lady in the Lake*, the pervasive sense of malaise of *Roadblock* (1951), the compressed storyline (and sentimental ending) of **City that Never Sleeps** and the brevity of *I Mobster* (1958). PH

ABOVE Film Noir: Dana Andrews, Gene Tierney, *Laura*

RIGHT *Un Flic*

Un Flic/Dirty Money

Melville's last film rehearses the motifs he deployed in **Le Deuxième Souffle** and **Le Cercle rouge**: the affinities between a cop, Coleman (Delon), and a criminal, Simon (Crenna); betrayal, an impossible but ardently desired male friendship, the regrettable loss of the underworld's alleged code of honour. The anecdotal plot begins with a bank robbery in a small seaside town, continues with the hijack of a drugs shipment from a train and ends with Coleman and Simon facing each other in a desolate landscape one cold, grey morning, while their shared girl-friend Cathy (Deneuve) watches the two men do their virile thing. Simon pretends to reach for a gun he isn't carrying and Coleman shoots him dead, after which, feeling morose, Coleman turns his back on his girl-friend and drives off by himself. The film lacks the obsessive intensity of Melville's best work as his style deteriorated into mere repetition of his trademarks (silent men, elegant camera movements), leaving his central theme nakedly exposed: homosexuality repressed and transformed into the violent interpenetration of male bodies. The director's former mastery of the medium is here reduced to empty ritual celebrating the image as a fetish. PW

1972/France, Italy/98m/ Corona-Oceania-Euro Film/Robert Dorfmann/*d/s* Jean-Pierre Melville/*c* Walter Wottitz/*m* Michel Colombier/*lp* Alain Delon, Richard Crenna, Catherine Deneuve, Ricardo Cucciolla, Michael Conrad.

Flic Story/Cop Story/Police Story

Delon bought the rights to the retired Borniche's autobiography and cast himself as the inspector in a story set in the late 1940s, chronicling Borniche's first major case. Shown as a cop who bucks red tape and embraces the softly softly approach contrary to his brutal sidekick Barros (Manuel), Borniche is set on the trail of the escaped Emile Buisson (Trintignant), a petty gangster riddled with nervous ticks and prone to psychotic homicidal violence during hold-ups. When Buisson keeps escaping Borniche's traps, the inspector is reassigned to another case: the killing of Mario Poncini alias 'le Rital' (Salvatori). That too is Buisson's work and the cop eventually arrests his man in a provincial inn. Borniche's memoirs also pro-

vided plots for Francis Girod's *René-la-Canne* and Deray's **Le Gang** (both 1977). Borniche also wrote crime novels, including **L'Indic** filmed by Serge Leroy in 1982. PW

1975/France, Italy/112m/Adel-Lira-Mondial-TI-FI/*p* Alain Delon/*d/co-s* Jacques Deray/*co-s* Alphonse Boudard/*orig* Roger Borniche/*c* Jean-Jacques Tarbes/*m* Claude Bolling/*lp* Alain Delon, Jean-Louis Trintignant, Renato Salvatori, Claudine Auger, Marco Perrin.

Floyd, Charles Arthur 'Pretty Boy' (1901–34)

Charles Arthur Floyd, who no more liked being called 'Pretty Boy' than Lester Gillis cared to be referred to as 'Baby Face Nelson', was a fairly minor hoodlum, remembered now only for his brief association with **John Dillinger** and Woody Guthrie's Robin Hood-inspired ballad. A bank robber, he was quite probably not involved in the only famous crime (the so-called Kansas City Massacre of 1933) of which he was accused. Shot while fleeing an FBI trap organised by Melvin Purvis, who had already supervised the shooting of Dillinger, he died insisting he be addressed by his full name. Floyd has been often featured in films: played by Doug Wilson in *Guns Don't Argue* (1957), John Ericson in **Pretty Boy Floyd**, Robert Conrad in *Young Dillinger* (1964), Fabian Forte in *A Bullet for a Pretty Boy* (1970), Steve Kanaly in **Dillinger**, Martin Sheen in *The Story of Pretty Boy Floyd* (1974), Bo Hopkins in *Kansas City Massacre* (1975) and Don Fernando in the porno *Bonnie & Clyde* (1988). KN

Forbrydelsens element/ The Element of Crime

This movie, filmed in English, concerns a police detective, Fisher (Elphick), who has a mental breakdown while investigating the Lotto Murders, a series of killings of kids who sell lottery tickets. After some therapy in Cairo, he seeks the advice of his mentor, the retired policeman Osborne (Knight), author of *The Element of Crime* which advises investigators to identify with the criminal's mind. Fisher continues investigating the Lotto murders, guided by an Asian prostitute, Kim (Lai), in a bleak, seedy and terminally corrupt underworld. However, his investigation generates further Lotto murders and he discovers that his mentor had identified so thoroughly with the criminal that he continued the killings. When this father figure is revealed to be a murderer before he commits suicide, Fisher finds to his horror that he too has followed in the man's footsteps. Replete with references to other films, this European *film noir* is let down by its garish, ill-judged colours and contrived imagery masking the tired clichés (Oriental *femme fatale*, moody cop, intellectuals who are too clever for their own good, macho strutting, etc.) made to pass for a 'psychologically complex' narrative. A bald-headed von Trier himself plays a small role mockingly called 'the Schmuck of Ages'. PW

1984/Denmark/104m/Per Holst Filmproduktion-Danish Film Institute/*p* Per Holst/*d/co-s* Lars von Trier/*co-s* Niels Vorsel/ *c* Tom Elling/*m* Bo Holten/*lp* Michael Elphick, Esmond Knight, Me Lai, Jerold

Wells, Ahmed El Shenawi, Astrid Henning-Jensen.

Force of Evil

Reviving the previous association between Garfield and Polonsky that had made a success of **Body and Soul**, this is perhaps the most overtly political of all the crime films of the 1940s. Joe Morse (Garfield) is a lawyer who has sold out his expertise to Tucker (Roy Roberts), a gangster who runs an illegal lottery known as the 'numbers racket'. Joe's brother Leo has his own lottery in a small-time way, and the big syndicate want to buy him out, along with all its other competitors. Windsor is the moll whose role is to soften up Joe and prevent him thinking about the consequences of his actions. Only when his brother is killed does Joe recognise the extent to which he has become an instrument of corruption. He vows to assist the authorities, knowing that it will end in his own death. The analogy between the numbers racket and capitalism itself, with the reduction of human life to money and numbers, and the irresistible urge to monopoly, are there for all to see, reinforced by several location sequences in which the skyscrapers and steel bridges of New York dwarf the human dramas enacted below. Garfield, Polonsky and Roberts were all blacklisted, and Polonsky did not direct again for twenty years. EB

1948/88m/MGM/*p* Bob Roberts/*d* Abraham Polonsky/*s* Abraham Polonsky, Ira Wolfert/*c* George Barnes/*m* David Raksin/*lp* John Garfield, Beatrice Pearson, Thomas Gomez, Roy Roberts, Marie Windsor.

Fort Apache, the Bronx

A big-screen *Hill Street Blues*, dripping with public liberalism and overdone Western overtones. A beat cop iconically named Murphy (Newman) is the sole man of inviolable integrity amid a collection of eccentrics and deadbeats, while the station captain (Asner) is a rulebook-happy martinet, the equivalent of Henry Fonda in *Fort Apache* (1948), using methods that encourage random violence and urban discontent. Newman, in a star turn, gets to disarm a psycho, deliver a baby and solve several big cases, all the while conducting an affair with a junkie nurse and becoming disillusioned enough to quit the force. The film opens as if it were an exploitation picture like *Vice Squad* (1982), with Grier as a cop-killing hooker murdering a series of victims, but she is killed off by some less characterised thugs who then become the main villains while the hero deals with a hospital dope ring and

the agony of knowing that a fellow cop (Aiello) is a murderer. KN

1981/123m/FOX/*p* Martin Richards/*d* Daniel Petrie, Tom Fiorello/*s* Heywood Gould/*c* John Alcott/*m* Jonathan Tunick/*lp* Paul Newman, Edward Asner, Danny Aiello, Rachel Ticotin, Ken Wahl, Pam Grier.

48Hrs.

Nolte is a hard-bitten detective on the track of a cop-killer and Murphy is a crook who may know something in this variant on the ill-matched-buddy movie. Nolte gets Murphy released into his custody for 48 hours to help solve the crime. In appearance they couldn't be more different: the big, shambling white man whose response to any situation is to charge ahead; the small, neat-moving and quick-thinking black man, always looking to play the percentages. Nolte, who is averagely chauvinist, racist, nihilist, has the washed-up private life that was de rigeur for screen cops in the 1980s. Gradually, the initial hostility of the two towards each other is supplemented by a grudging respect, as together they cut a swathe through the San Francisco under-world. As usual with Walter Hill, the action scenes are directed with conviction and panache, and the dialogue rattles along. But the film lacks any of the metaphysical dimensions of Hill's Westerns. A sequel,

Another 48Hrs., reunited Nolte and Murphy in 1990. EB

1982/96m/PAR/*p* Lawrence Gordon, Joel Silver/*d* Walter Hill/*s* Roger Spottiswoode, Walter Hill, Larry Gross, Steven E. deSouza/*c* Ric Waite/*m* James Horner/*lp* Nick Nolte, Eddie Murphy, Annette O'Toole, Frank McRae.

Foul Play

This amusing Hitchcockian suspense drama (à la *The Man Who Knew Too Much*, 1956) teams librarian Hawn with detective Chase. The two make a romantic yet slightly offbeat pair who try to prevent an assassination plot (of a visiting Pope, no less) by a peculiar out-fit who want to end the tax-exemption sta-tus of religious properties (the MacGuffin element). While the comedy points are sometimes silly, the pairing of Hawn and Chase (downplaying their usual wacky char-acters) works well. In addition, a colourful roster of back-up players includes a pre-*10* (1979) Dudley Moore, as well as Chuck McCann and Billy Barty. TV

1978/116m/PAR/*p* Thomas L. Miller, Edward K. Milkis/*d/s* Colin Higgins/*c* David M. Walsh/*m* Charles Fox/*lp* Goldie Hawn, Chevy Chase, Burgess Meredith.

The French Connection

In 1961, after a two-and-a-half-year investi-gation, NYPD narcotics officers Eddie Egan

LEFT AND ABOVE Gene Hackman, *The French Connection*

and Sonny Grosso made an unprecedented $32 million heroin bust. Their story became the basis for *The French Connection*, with Egan and Grosso in bit parts. The critical and commercial success of the film did much to revive the cop genre for the 70s, emphasising grittily realistic settings, spectacularly destructive car chases and an underlying cynicism about law enforcement agencies later amplified in movies as diverse as **Dirty Harry**, *Cops and Robbers* (1973), **Serpico**, **Prince of the City**, **The Big Easy** and *Q&A* (1990). As he would with *The Exorcist* (1973), *Cruising* (1980) and *To Live and Die in L.A.* (1985), Friedkin turns his back on the seamless narratives of classical Hollywood genre, relying on frequent spurts of violent action to bind a confused plot. Gene Hackman's Popeye Doyle is superficially convincing (bigoted, unkempt, determined, trigger-happy) but his performance fizzles in Friedkin's dramatic vacuum. The elusive figure of Charnier (Rey), the French mastermind who cheekily waves to the pursuer he has coolly escaped on the New York subway, gives the film a much-needed core, but the dramatically necessary confrontation between Popeye and his nemesis never actually takes place. The film's mix of grimy realism with flashy action (a car chase under New York's elevated railway) paid off, and it was awarded Oscars for Best Picture, Best Screenplay, Best Actor (Hackman), Best Direction and

(deservedly) Best Editing. Surprisingly, Frankenheimer's *French Connection II*, which has no factual basis, is a far more interesting movie, loosely following the pattern of **Coogan's Bluff** as it sets the boorish cop adrift in an unfamiliar environment and has him clash with the local law as Popeye tries to track down Charnier on his home turf, Marseille. Hackman's performance is as powerful as ever, but in the sequel he is given a milieu to react to, and becomes a pathetic figure more in line with the tarnished knights of traditional *film noir*. In a genuinely disturbing sequence, he is captured and turned over to a harridan (Nesbitt) who shoots him full of heroin until he is addicted, cooing and cackling over him as if she were nursing a greedy baby. Thus given an all-consuming need to wipe out Charnier at the same time as he has to fight his craving for the villain's product, Popeye finally gains heroic status by overcoming his weaknesses during a protracted, brilliantly staged chase scene through the Marseille docks, shooting down Charnier just as it seems the drugs baron will escape yet again. The TV movie *Popeye Doyle* (1986), intended as a series pilot, has Ed O'Neill in the title role. KN

1971/104m/FOX/*p* Philip D'Antoni/ *d* William Friedkin/*s* Ernest Tidyman/ *orig* Robin Moore/*c* Owen Roizman/*m* Don

Ellis/*lp* Gene Hackman, Roy Scheider, Fernando Rey, Tony LoBianco, Marcel Bozzuffi.

French Connection II/1975/119m/FOX/*p* Robert L. Rosen/*d* John Frankenheimer/ *s* Robert Dillon, Laurie Dillon, Alexander Jacobs/*c* Claude Renoir/*m* Don Ellis/*lp* Gene Hackman, Fernando Rey, Bernard Fresson, Jean-Pierre Castaldi, Charles Millot, Cathleen Nesbitt.

Frenzy

The opening credits – a picture-postcard view of London – suggest that in the course of his twenty-year absence, Hitchcock lost touch with London as a real place. The ensuing film confirms this. Full of marvellous set pieces – the lengthy murder of Leigh-Hunt – and elaborately sustained metaphors – even more than **Blackmail**, it is Chabrolian in its use of the act of eating, food itself (it is set around Covent Garden) and hunger – it is populated by characters who are all nuance and individual tics but nonetheless remain marionettes whose strings are pulled by Shaffer's well-plotted screenplay and Hitchcock's impassive camera. They lack real substance (or the alternative charisma of a Cary Grant). Even sadder, (considering he is clearly more interested in the villain than hero) Hitchcock felt it necessary to change the ending of Bern's 1966 novel in which the hero is found guilty of the various murders he didn't commit; in the film he is saved. Accordingly, the film is better seen as a meditation upon past successes (notably **Strangers on a Train**) than a development of them. Down on his luck, Finch is suspected of being London's rapist-murderer when his estranged wife is murdered. While Finch is shown to be clearly capable of murder, he remains the film's nominal hero. For the first time in a Hitchcock the central character is explicitly the villain, Foster, who has befriended Finch. It is he who is privileged with the key subjective shots, notably during the initial murder and during the lengthy sequence of his disposal of Massey's body. Significantly during these and other moments, the audience is asked by Hitchcock to identify with Foster. In this way, the 'exchange of guilt' theme of *Strangers* is extended to the audience. Similarly, whereas Foster is visually associated with satisfying his hunger (for both food and sex) Finch and policeman McCowen are paralleled by being continually hungry, Finch because he has no money and McCowen because his wife specialises in inedible cordon bleu extravaganzas. How-

ABOVE Barbara Leigh-Hunt, *Frenzy*

ABOVE Barry Foster, *Frenzy*

ever, while all this makes the film theoretically fascinating, in contrast to the more repressed earlier films, the drives that animate *Frenzy* are visible rather than articulated in the film. The result is a film that tells us more about Hitchcock the man than Hitchcock the artist. PH

1972/GB/116m/U/*p*/*d* Alfred Hitchcock/ *s* Anthony Shaffer/*orig* Arthur La Bern *Goodbye Piccadilly, Farewell Leicester Square*/ *c* Gil Taylor/*m* Ron Goodwin/*lp* Barry Foster, Jon Finch, Barbara Leigh-Hunt, Anna Massey, Alec McCowen, Vivien Merchant.

The Friends of Eddie Coyle

This is a post-*noir* equivalent of **You Only Live Once** or **The Asphalt Jungle**, presenting crime both as a realistic, unsensationalised business and as an existential trap which sucks its three-time loser hero towards an inevitable doom. Eddie (Mitchum) is the ageing criminal out on bail before a trial which could send him to jail for the rest of his active life. He tries to plea-bargain by becoming a small-time informant, but carries on his everyday business of supplying untraceable guns to a gang of currently active heist men. Finally, Eddie's best friend (Boyle), a major informant, contributes to the arrest of the bank robbers but lets Eddie

take the blame with the mob, and even accepts the commission to murder him, taking him out for one last binge at a hockey game and introducing him to the young hit man who finishes him off, leaving the body in an abandoned car. Peter Yates does his best-ever job of direction, shooting the film as a series of edgy, open-air conversations between two or more characters as betrayals, crimes or compromises are arranged. Mitchum, sagging and melancholy, is effective as the doomed crook, a small-timer well past his sell-by date. KN

1973/102m/PAR/*p*/*s* Paul Monash/*d* Peter Yates/*orig* George V. Higgins/*c* Victor J. Kemper/*m* Dave Grusin/*lp* Robert Mitchum, Peter Boyle, Richard Jordan, Steven Keats, Alex Rocco, Joe Santos.

Fu Manchu

Dr Fu Manchu, the insidious criminal mastermind created by Sax Rohmer [Arthur Sarsfield Ward] (1883–1959), with his endless dreams of world domination (and hatred of communism) and his arch-enemy Sir Dennis Nayland Smith of Scotland Yard, first appeared in a series of short adventures published in *The Storyteller* magazine in 1912 and collected a year later as *The Mystery of Dr Fu-Manchu*. After two more collections of sto-

ries, *The Devil Doctor* (1916) and *The Si-Fan Mysteries* (1917) and a break of some 15 years Rohmer made Fu Manchu, minus his hyphen, the subject of a series of novels, *Daughter of Fu Manchu* (1931), *The Mask of Fu Manchu* (1932), *The Bride of Fu Manchu* (1933), *The Trail of Fu Manchu* (1934), *President Fu Manchu* (1935), *The Drums of Fu Manchu* (1939), *Shadow of Fu Manchu* (1948), *Re-Enter Fu Manchu* (1957) and *Emperor Fu Manchu* (1959). The character also appeared in radio serials, a Marvel comic (*The Hands of Shang-Chi*) and further novels (*Ten Years Beyond Baker Street*, 1984, *The Fires of Fu Manchu*, 1987) by Rohmer's biographer, Cay Van Ash.

The character's first screen outing was for the British Stoll company, which produced a series of fifteen shorts adapted from the first Fu Manchu stories and released them under the collective title T*he Mystery of Dr Fu-Manchu* (1923). Harry Agar Lyons was the Devil Doctor, and his Holmes-and-Watson team of opponents, Nayland Smith and the intrepid Dr Petrie, were Fred Paul and Humbertson Wright. Paul and Wright returned, with Paul replacing A. E. Colby as director, for eight instalments of *The Further Mysteries of Dr Fu-Manchu* (1924).

Warner Oland (already known for oriental characterisations but not yet cast as **Charlie Chan**) was Fu Manchu in Rowland V. Lee's *The Mysterious Dr Fu Manchu* (1929), a creaky melodrama shot in both silent and sound versions, with a spirited heroine in Jean Arthur. Oland and Arthur were also in

ABOVE Christopher Lee, *The Face of Fu Manchu*

ABOVE Myrna Loy, Charles Starrett, Boris Karloff, *The Mask of Fu Manchu*

Lee's *The Return of Dr Fu Manchu* (1930), but Arthur is absent from Lloyd Corrigan's *Daughter of the Dragon* (1931), in which *femme* interest is provided, and Oland's villainy outshadowed, by Anna May Wong as the slinky and ambiguous Fah Lo Suee. Oland's one other appearance as the devil doctor is in *Paramount on Parade* (1930), an all-star comedy/musical melange in which he shares a sketch with Clive Brook's **Sherlock Holmes** and William Powell's **Philo Vance**, both of whom he murders in the course of a silly joke in which the diabolical villain tries to convince the two great detectives that he is indeed a murderer. This marks the only screen meeting of Holmes and Fu Manchu, later the subject of *Ten Years Beyond Baker Street*, and the only time that Holmes died in a film.

The Mask of Fu Manchu (1932), from Rohmer's novel, remains the most elaborate film featuring the character, in great part because of the excellent casting of Boris Karloff as Fu Manchu and Myrna Loy as Fah Lo Suee. Karloff is outrageously evil, leering as he tries to acquire the mask and scimitar of Genghis Khan, which will cause the superstitious hordes of the East to rally round him as he exterminates the civilised

West. Lewis Stone is a properly xenophobic Nayland Smith, treating all heathens as beneath contempt, and the movie gets the most out of a bizarre series of torture devices: a giant bell that never stops ringing, driving mad the tethered victim beneath it; a see-saw positioned over an alligator pit; and a pair of spiked walls that close on a trapped subject. There are plenty of sparks from Fu Manchu's electrical devices, and Loy enjoys herself slobbering over the nearly-nude hero, but the plot is disjointed even by penny-dreadful standards. *Mask of Fu Manchu* is not the definitive, nor even the best, Fu Manchu film, but it is the most delirious.

Fu Manchu returns, in the shape of bald Henry Brandon, still searching for the long-lost tomb of Genghis Khan, in *Drums of Fu Manchu* (1940), a fifteen-chapter Republic serial directed by William Witney and John English, with William Royle as Nayland Smith, Olaf Hytten as Dr Petrie and Gloria Franklin as Fah Lo Suee. Given the rigid Saturday morning format, *Drums of Fu Manchu* uses a surprising amount of Rohmer, including the Si-Fan and an army of fanged, lobotomised Dacoit slaves. Aside from a Mexican outing called *El otro Fu Manchu* (1945), little was heard of the character for

ten years. In 1952, John Carradine and Sir Cedric Hardwicke played Fu Manchu and Nayland Smith in a television pilot directed by William Cameron Menzies. This was followed by a lacklustre and low-budget series of half-hour episodes, *The Adventures of Fu Manchu* (1955–9), with a miscast Glenn Gordon in the lead, supported by Lester Matthews and Clark Howat as Nayland Smith and Petrie, with Laurette Luez as Karamanêh, a former Fu Manchu slave who becomes Petrie's love interest in the novels.

The most substantial Fu Manchu film series began with *The Face of Fu Manchu* (1965), directed by Don Sharp and scripted by producer Harry Alan Towers under the pseudonym Peter Welbeck. Though inspired by the success of the Bond films (themselves derivative of Rohmer's originals, with Dr No obviously a cousin to Fu Manchu), Towers opts for a careful, picturesque period approach to the character. With Nigel Green and Howard Marion Crawford as Nayland Smith and Petrie and Tsai Chin as Lin Tang, the renamed daughter of Fu Manchu, the script is in good, melodramatic hands, even if Christopher Lee in the title role is a little colourless, lacking the gloating monstrosity Karloff brings to the role. The plot concerns a deadly poison distilled from Tibetan poppy seeds, a kidnapped scientist forced to work for Fu Manchu, secret papers that have been stolen from a London museum, and (most effectively) a seaside village silently wiped out by Fu Manchu's killer gas. In the finale, Fu Manchu is caught in a massive explosion, but his voice is heard on the soundtrack, declaring 'the world shall hear from me again'. This ending is repeated for all four follow-ups, each of which shows a decline in quality. Lee, Crawford and Chin stayed with the series, but Green was replaced by Douglas Wilmer for Sharp's *Brides of Fu Manchu* (1966) and Jeremy Summers' *The Vengeance of Fu Manchu* (1967) and by Richard Greene for a pair of multinational fiascos shot by Jesus Franco in 1968, the Spanish-Italian-German-Turkish *Castle of Fu Manchu* and the Spanish-British-German-American-Brazilian *Blood of Fu Manchu*. In the final entry, Lee's Fu Manchu is joined in evil by Shirley Eaton as the Black Widow, a character clearly based on Rohmer's female archvillain Sumuru, whom she played in Towers' production of *The Million Eyes of Sumuru* (1967) and Franco's *Rio '70* (1969). Subsequently, Fu Manchu has only appeared in *The Fiendish Plot of Dr Fu Manchu* (1980), a British atrocity directed by Piers Haggard in

ABOVE Bruce Cabot (in bow-tie), *Fury*

which Peter Sellers, in his last film, plays Fu Manchu and Nayland Smith. Sad to report, the Lord of Strange Deaths was last seen in white fringed buckskins impersonating Elvis Presley. KN

Fukushu Suruwa Wareni Ari/ Vengeance Is Mine

Imamura's detached but captivating study of a cold-blooded multiple murderer, Enokizu (Ogata), was based on a novelised account of a real murderer, Nishiguchi, who committed five murders and became the object of a sensational 78-day chase throughout Japan. The story is told in four intricately interwoven sets of flashbacks relating to different periods in the killer's life, beginning with his capture in January 1964 after killing two employees of the Japan Tobacco Monopoly Co. and ending with the most revealing one: his life

as a boy in a fishing village where he saw his father (Mikuni) failing to stand up to the Imperial Navy when they confiscated his boat. Although Imamura doesn't provide any psychological motivation, chronicling the murderer's life like an ethnographer with a grim sense of humour, the suggestion remains that Enokizu's actions are rooted in his fraught relationship with his father, whom he perceives to be weak and cowardly. All his callously brutal murders seem as if they don't matter because they do not touch the real target of his unresolved desire to settle accounts with his father. PW

1979/Japan/128m/Imamura/*p* Kazuo Inoue/ *d* Shohei Imamura/*s* Masaru Baba/*orig* Ryuzo Saki/*c* Masahisa Himeda/*m* Shinichiro Ikebe/*lp* Ken Ogata, Rentaro Mikuni, Chocho Mikayo, Mitsuko Baisho, Mayumi Ogawa.

Fury

Happy-go-lucky Joe Wilson (Tracy), travelling across country, passes a bill that was part of a ransom and is arrested on suspicion of kidnap. Entirely innocent, he is confident he will be acquitted but gradually the small town in which he is being held turns mean and a lynch mob forms. In the melee, the jail is burned down but Joe escapes. Embittered, he goes into hiding and gloats as the crusading D.A. (Abel) brings twenty mob leaders to trial, confronting them in court with filmed evidence of their bestial behaviour. Lang's first American movie, this is a 'social protest' film – comparable to the much more inclusively cynical *They Won't Forget* (1937) – overlaid with gloomy fatalism, expressed in an Expressionism that provides the missing link between German silent cinema and 40s Hollywood *noir*. A typically cartoonish indictment of American injustice, *Fury* pits the elaborately innocent and unrealistically decent Joe (one shred of circumstantial evidence against him is his homespun food preference for peanuts) against a collection of deliciously rotten mob members, all of whom are made to seem especially depraved when the D.A. freeze-frames newsreel footage of housewives and garage mechanics hurling firebrands and pouring kerosene while grinning maniacally. An impressive collective achievement, this is personalised in terms of Lang's career by the transformation, seen also in *The Return of Frank James* (1940), *Rancho Notorious* (1952) and **The Big Heat**, of genial hero into merciless avenger, nurturing his original hurt to the point when his drive to get even is as psychopathic as the actions of those who did him wrong. KN

1936/90m/MGM/*p* Joseph L. Mankiewicz/*d*/*cos* Fritz Lang/*co-s* Bartlett Cormack/*orig* 'Mob Rule' Norman Krasna/*c* Joseph Ruttenberg/*m* Franz Waxman/*lp* Spencer Tracy, Sylvia Sidney, Walter Abel, Edward Ellis, Walter Brennan, Bruce Cabot.

Futekino Otoko/The Lowest Man

In the wake of the success of Shintari Ishihara's delinquent novel *Taiyo No Kisetsu* (1955), Masumura contributed this item to the ensuing 'taiyozoku' genre, developing it into an ode to anti-social loners driven by all-consuming passions. Re-using the lead couple from his critically acclaimed but commercially unsuccessful *Kyojin To Gangu* (1958), this is a tale about a young criminal (Kawaguchi), a good father in the guise of a detective and a bad father in the shape of a gang boss. The latter kills the former and the youth eventually shoots the boss before being shot in his turn by the police as he goes to ascertain whether the picture's *femme fatale* (Nozoe) really loves him. The direction is characteristically energetic, adopting a garish, even a hysterical style that was the complete opposite of the trend towards atmospheric lyricism Masumura castigated at the time. He continued in this vein, at times going over the top (*Moju* 1969). He also initiated an odd series called *Heitai Yakuza* (1965) about hoodlums in the army during the war. His other contributions to the gangster genre include **Daiakuto** and *Shibire Kurage* (1970) as well as the script for Issei Mori's extraordinary **Aru Koroshiya**. PW

1958/Japan/84m/Daiei/*d* Yasuzo Masumura/*s* Kaneto Shindo/*c* Hiroshi Murai/*m* Tetsuo Tsukahara/*lp* Hiroshi Kawaguchi, Hitomi Nozoe, Eiji Funakoshi, Tomoe Nagai, Yasuko Kawakami, Kazuko Ichikawa.

ABOVE James Cagney, *'G' Men*

G

'G' Men

The first major film in the second great gangster film cycle in which the stars no longer played the heroic/tragic gangster roles but were instead lawmen who cleaned up the gangsters. In this glorification of FBI gangbusters, Cagney's struggling attorney joins the G-Men when his buddy is killed by gangsters and his following government assignments take him through just about every dramatic situation from the Depression Era-Dillinger days. As a Warner Bros. gangster picture it is one of the best of its type, with almost constant gunfire and action as well as featuring a knockout performance from Cagney. The film was produced with the approval of J. Edgar Hoover and when it was re-issued in 1949 to commemorate the 25th anniversary of the FBI, Warners added a prologue with David Brian as an FBI chief who proudly shows the film to his class of G-Men recruits. TV

1935/85m/WB/*p* Lou Edelman/*d* William Keighley/*s* Seton I. Miller/*c* Sol Polito/*m* Leo F. Forbstein/*lp* James Cagney, Ann Dvorak, Margaret Lindsay, Robert Armstrong, Barton MacLane.

Gabriel over the White House

This is the most disturbing of the early 30s vigilante law-and-order movies (which include *This Day and Age*, 1933, *Show Them No Mercy*, 1935, *Let 'Em Have It*, 1935); not for its comparatively conventional depiction of the evil of gangsterism but for its extraordinary, unironic suggested solutions.

ABOVE Spencer Tracy, *Fury*

141

ABOVE Gambling: Glenn Ford, *Gilda*

President-Elect Huston, a Harding-ish blowhard who has made so many promises he hopes the people won't remember he hasn't kept any of them, is killed in a car crash and returns to life inspired by a divine light. With the implied approval of God Almighty, Huston suspends the democratic process to wage all-out war on crime, giving his secretary (Tone) J. Edgar Hoover-ish authority as head of an army of the unemployed. This force crushes Capone-style mob boss Nick Diamond (Gordon), representative of the forces of Evil, with a frontal assault using tanks, winding up with summary executions by firing squad. Having cleaned up America, Huston calls in all European loans and decrees the rest of the world should abandon war or face destruction by the US fleet. Despite the fantasy element the film is too humourless to be considered a satire, and so gleeful in its know-nothing trigger-happiness that it remains deeply distasteful, particularly as La Cava haphazardly assembles the astonishing material into a collection of novelettish sub-plots and digressions. KN

1933/87m/MGM/*p* Walter Wanger/ *d* Gregory La Cava/*s* Carey Wilson/ *orig* Thomas Frederic Tweed/*c* Bert Glennon/*m* William Axt/*lp* Walter Huston, Karen Morley, Franchot Tone, Dickie Moore, C. Henry Gordon, Samuel Hinds.

Gaki Teikoku/Empire of Punks

This impossibly complicated plot about gangland vendettas and power struggles is an hysterically over-the-top parody of 60s yakuza movies. Former porn director Izutsu stages an orgy of violence in which three toughs band together to oppose the mob's control of Osaka's red light district. In the gangs, everyone seems to have divided loyalties and is betraying everyone else. Even the language spoken in the movie adds to the confusion as Korean is mixed in with gangland jargon and Osaka dialect. PW

1981/Japan/115m/Art Theatre Guild/ *p* Nobuo Hayashi/*d* Kazuyuki Izutsu, Shiro Sasaki/*s* Takuya Nishioka/*c* Itsuro Maki/ *lp* Shinsuke Shimada, Ryusuke Matsumoto, Bancho Cho, Takeshi Masu, Mayu Ito.

Gambling

Gambling is both an incidental activity indulged in by criminal types, as epitomised by the colourfully harmless Damon Runyon characters, and simultaneously a major source of income for organised crime. Typical of the professional profiteers are the numbers racketeers of **Force of Evil**, which concerns a scam to rig the results in a form of gambling which is itself illegal, and **The Phenix City Story**, which demonstrates how every dollar bet fuels a murderous crime empire. Common also are the under-hand manipulators of more-or-less aboveboard betting on sporting events practised by the fight-fixers of almost any film about boxing, the corrupted ball-players of *Eight Men Out* (1988) and Anjelica Huston at the racetrack in **The Grifters**. Those who profit from gambling, legitimately or otherwise, are almost invariably depicted in a bad light in the cinema, as is shown by the monstrous casino proprietors played by Ona Munson in *The Shanghai Gesture* (1941) and George Macready in **Gilda**; Rick (Humphrey Bogart) in *Casablanca* (1943) is a rare sympathetic gambling entrepreneur. Even more or less legitimate casino owners are depicted as crooked, like Alex Rocco in **The Godfather** or Warren Beatty in **Bugsy**, both gangsters who try to expand the mob's interests in areas where gambling is fortuitously legal. Accordingly heist men seem more sympathetic in *5 Against the House* (1955), **Bob le Flambeur**, **Ocean's Eleven**, *Seven Thieves* (1960), **Las Vegas 500 milliones/They Came to Rob Las Vegas** and *Las Vegas Lady* (1976) than they would be if they were out to rob a bank rather than a casino.

Films about games of skill and chance – *The Hustler* (1961, pool), *The Cincinnati Kid* (1965, poker), *Banning* (1967, golf), *Cockfighter/Born to Kill* (1974, cock-fighting) and *The Big Town* (1985, crap-shooting) – all involved gambling. Betting as a compulsion

ABOVE Gambling: Dean Martin, *Ocean's Eleven*

is examined in Robert Altman's *California Split* (1974), in which George Segal and Elliott Gould will even bet on whether they can remember the names of the Seven Dwarves, and Karel Reisz's *The Gambler* (1974), with James Caan as a literary professor whose idolisation of Dostoyevsky extends to an aping of the genius's vices. Similar frenzies grip Gregory Peck in *The Great Sinner* (1949), Marlene Dietrich in *The Monte Carlo Story* (1957), Ryan O'Neal in *Fever Pitch* (1985), Richard Dreyfuss in *Let It Ride* (1989) and Spike Lee in *Mo' Better Blues* (1990).

Casinos serve as colourful backdrops to earthquake, murder, espionage, romance, card sharpery and gangsterism in *Gambling Ship* (1933), *San Francisco* (1936), *Gambling on the High Seas* (1940), *Mr Lucky* (1943), *Flame of the Barbary Coast* (1945), *The Las Vegas Story* (1952), *Las Vegas Shakedown* (1955), *Loser Take All* (1956), *Casino Royale* (1967), *The Gamblers* (1969), *Farewell My Lovely* (1975), *Casino* (1980), *Atlantic City, U.S.A.* (1980), *Pleasure Palace* (1980), *Lookin' to Get Out* (1982), *Jinxed!* (1982), *Stacy's Knights* (1983), *The Vegas Strip War* (1984), *Things Change* (1988), *Strike It Rich* (1990), *Havana* (1990) and of course **Casino**. The gambling business serves as a MacGuffin in *The Last Boy Scout* (1991), where the villains are conspiring to force through the legalisation of betting on football. KN

See also **Con Men**.

Le Gang

The retired policeman Borniche's autobiography had provided Delon with the hit **Flic Story** and for the follow-up Delon turned to the same author's often-filmed story about the 1940s gangster Pierrot le fou (although Godard's *Pierrot le fou*, 1965, actually derived from Lionel White's novel *Obsession*). Here, Pierrot has become Robert the Nutter (Delon) who with four accomplices organises a series of daring hold-ups in the French provinces and in Paris. In the end, Robert is shot robbing a jewellery store and his mates discreetly bury him. Told in flashback by the idealised hoodlum's mistress (Calfan), the film dwells nostalgically on late 1940s period reconstructions. In extended scenes of ensemble acting, the five gangsters meet in a small suburban cafe and are portrayed as warm-hearted friends. Even Delon, wearing a frizzy wig, is seen laughing a lot in this unsurprisingly directed movie by Deray in his seventh collaboration with the star.

ABOVE Gambling: Paul Newman, *The Hustler*

Borniche's novel also provided inspiration for Claude Lelouch's *Le Bon et les méchants* (1976) ánd Francis Girod's *René-la-Canne* (1977). PW

1976/France, Italy/104m/Adel-Mondial-TE-FI/*p* Alain Delon/*d*/*co-s* Jacques Deray/*co-s* Alphonse Boudard, Jean-Claude Carrière/*orig* Roger Borniche/*c* Silvano Ippoliti/*m* Claude Bolling, Carlo Rustichelli/*lp* Alain Delon, Nicole Calfan, Roland Bertin, Xavier Depraz, Maurice Barrier.

Ganga bruta/Brutal Gang

Humberto Mauro's most famous film tells of a rich engineer who, on discovering that his bride is not a virgin, murders her. Acquitted by a sympathetic jury, he leaves for a village in the country where a factory is under construction. There, he meets a sensual young woman, falls in love and has to obtain her by fighting her fiancé. This is Mauro's most complex treatment of the tensions between the country and the city in Brazil and the disruptions caused by the pressures of modernisation. He relies on dramatic, expressionist lighting combined with a sophisticated, Soviet-style editing technique to enhance the drama's emotional impact. PW

1933/Brazil/85m/Cinedia/*p* Adhemar Gonzaga/*d*/*co-s*/*co-m* Humberto Mauro/*co-s* Otavio Gabus Mendes/*c* Afrodisio de Castro, Paulo Morano, Edgar Brasil/*co-m* Radames Gnatalli/*lp* Durval Belini, Dea Selva, Lu Marival, Decio Murilo, Andrea Duarte.

El Gangster

Conducted at a frenetic pace, this film proposes that it takes an American gangster to

ABOVE *Ganga bruta*

143

restore much-needed discipline to Mexico's modern youth and dizzy women. Ironically the film was scripted by the veteran director's wife and produced by a woman. De Cordova is the gangster who returns home to Mexico from Chicago. While his underlings settle down to watch Hollywood gangster films on TV, he finds that his family give him more trouble than his 'profession' ever did. In the end, he reasserts his authority wielding a strap, beating his unruly teenage nephew and dragging his girl-friend (Peluffo) by her hair. After this display of macho charm, all ends happily. PW

1964/Mexico/90m/Tecnicos y Manuales del STPC/*p* Angelica Ortiz/*d* Luis Alcoriza/*s* Janet Alcoriza/*c* Jose Ortiz Ramos/*lp* Arturo de Cordova, Ana Luisa Peluffo, Angelica Maria, Sofia Alvarez, Fernando Lujan.

The Gangster

An adaptation by Daniel Fuchs of his novel *Low Company*, *The Gangster* is self-consciously a mood piece, whose static quality and somewhat contrived poeticism might suggest that its origins might have been a play rather than a novel. Sullivan's protagonist is a man alienated by his own dubious success, and

ABOVE Diana Wynyard, Anton Walbrook, *Gaslight* (1940)

possessed by jealousy towards his mistress (Belita). He embodies the world-weariness of hard-earned experience, played off against the neurotic immaturity of the gambler (Ireland) who seeks to sponge off him and who eventually betrays him to the rival bent on seizing control of his operations. The end is traditional, with Sullivan gunned down by the rival's henchmen on a rainswept street. Critic Andrew Sarris sees the film as a hymn to Sullivan: 'Barry Sullivan was a born B-picture actor and a damned good one. *The Gangster* is his greatest vehicle, and worth watching for the pleasure of his understated authority setting up the histrionics of Akim Tamiroff and Joan Lorring. . . . In B-pictures Barry Sullivan could be a tragic hero.' TP

1947/84m/AA/*p* Frank and Maurice King/*d* Gordon Wiles/*s* Daniel Fuchs/*c* Paul Ivano/*m* Louis Gruenberg/*lp* Barry Sullivan, Akim Tamiroff, Belita, Joan Lorring, John Ireland.

Gangsterens laerling/The Gangster's Apprentice

Carlsen had made a well-crafted detective movie, *19 Red Roses* (1974) before he took over the direction of this film from its writer Leergard. The plot is set in Copenhagen's drug-ridden slums and charts the mental disintegration of a social worker (Kaysoe). He

leaves his wife for a teenage girl (Petersen), tries to make a living as a criminal but winds up in jail. Having escaped, he tries to become a more competent criminal. Carlsen criticised Danish cinema for its pretentious introspection, but this murkily shot quickie is also steeped in moralism. Only the vivacious performance of the teenage siren saves it from guilt-ridden sensationalism. PW

1976/Denmark/106m/LEA/*p* Anne Philipsen/ *d* Esben Høilund Carlsen/*s* Lars Leergard/*c* Dan Holmberg/*lp* Dick Kaysoe, Nina Louise Petersen, Peter Steen.

The Gangsters and the Girl

Shot in ten days, this is an action-packed two-reeler. Ray is the undercover detective posing as a member of a gang. There is a car chase and a gunfight, the action moves to the rooftops of New York, with some superb exteriors, and to the gang's underground hideout. There are split-screen effects, and a great deal of the rapid cutting associated with Ince's films of the period. Ince himself appears as one of the detectives from whom the girl is snatched away by a gangster. JL

1914/2 reels/Kay-Bee/*d* Scott Sidney/*s* J.G.Hawks, Richard V. Spencer/*lp* Charles Ray, Alma Ruben, Elizabeth Burbridge, Arthur Jarret, Margaret Thompson.

ABOVE Gia Scala, Robert Loggia, Kerwin Mathews, *The Garment Jungle*

The Gangsters of New York/The Gangsters

Crime is resolutely unglamorous in this characteristic melodrama of the period. Set among the tenements, sweatshops and saloons of New York's East Side, the film tells the story of two brothers and their sister. Dillon is a gang-leader, Walthall (cast much against type) his younger brother following along, Horine the sister dying of consumption. Bailey is the country girl who loves Walthall and contrives his arrest on minor charges to save him from worse. Finally Dillon's death in the electric chair, framed for a rival's killing, and a spell in prison put Walthall on the path of reform. At the end, he and Bailey are settling down happily in the countryside. Briskly directed by Kirkwood, who used close-ups more freely than was usual at the time, the film closely associated crime with political corruption and drinking saloons which, as a critic of the movie put it, 'catered to all that is low in man's nature, blunting his moral sense and perpetuating organised crime'. JL

1914/4 reels/Reliance/*d/co-s*/James Kirkwood/*co-s* Anita Loos/*lp* Henry B. Walthall, Consuelo Bailey, Jack Dillon, Ralph Lewis, Alice Horine, Jack Pickford.

Gangsterzy i filantropi/Gangsters and Philanthropists

A comedy consisting of two loosely connected stories. A criminal 'professor' (Holoubek) leads a meticulously planned hold-up which goes wrong because of the glorious unpredictability of the Poles: a road repair team unexpectedly starts working, a policeman is seized by a fit of jealousy, a farmer neglects to attach a red tail-light to his cart, etc. In jail Holoubek and his gang meet the hero of the second story, Kowalski (Michnikowski). When he impulsively tested the alcohol content of his drink in a restaurant, he was mistaken for a food inspector, bribed and flattered and finds the restaurant standards in the town start rising. Then the real inspector turns up. The restaurant owners accuse Kowalski of fraud but they find themselves in the dock for bribery instead. The two directors had collaborated on many documentaries before venturing into fiction and Hoffman went on to make the acclaimed nationalist epic *Pan Wolodyowski* (1969). PW

1962/Poland/90m/Kamera Unit-Film Polski/

RIGHT Charles Boyer, Ingrid Bergman, *Gaslight* (1944)

d/s Jerzy Hoffman, Edward Skorzewski/*c* Jerzy Lipman/*lp* Gustav Holoubek, Wieslaw Michnikowski, Gustaw Lutkiewicz, Hanna Bielicka, Magda Celowna.

The Garment Jungle

This is a tough, realistic exposé of the struggle of the International Ladies Garment Workers to do away with the sweat shops on New York's Seventh Avenue. Based on investigative journalist Lester Velie's series of articles for *Readers Digest*, this is one of the better dramas during the 1950s phase of gangsters and union corruption films that started with **On the Waterfront** and went on to include such B-thrillers as *New Orleans Uncensored* (1955), *The Big Operator*, (1959) and *Inside Detroit* (1955). Cobb is suitably defiant as the self-made dress plant owner who resists the union, while his son (Mathews) sees the dangers in hiring 'protection'. Director Robert Aldrich was replaced by Sherman some five days before completion. TV

1957/88m/COL/*p* Harry Kleiner/*d* Vincent Sherman/*s* Harry Kleiner/*c* Joseph Biroc/*m* Leith Stevens/*lp* Lee J. Cobb, Kerwin Mathews, Gia Scala, Richard Boone.

Gaslight

The hugely influential story of a coolly sadistic husband who methodically tries to drive his wife mad, *Gaslight* had far greater success than Hamilton's modern-set psychological horror stories on similar themes, like

ABOVE Michael Caine, Ian Hendry, *Get Carter*

Gaslight/Angel Street/1940/GB/80m/
British National/*p* John Corfield/*d* Thorold
Dickinson/*s* A.R. Rawlinson, Bridget Boland/
orig Patrick Hamilton/*c* Bernard Knowles/*m*
Richard Addinsell/*lp* Anton Walbrook, Diana
Wynyard, Cathleen Cordell, Robert Newton,
Frank Pettingell, Jimmy Hanley.

Gaslight/Murder in Thornton Square/
1944/114m/MGM/*p* Arthur Hornblow Jr./
d George Cukor/*s* John Van Druten, Walter
Reisch, John L. Balderston/*orig* Patrick
Hamilton/*c* Joseph Ruttenberg/*m* Bronislau
Kaper/*lp* Charles Boyer, Ingrid Bergman,
Joseph Cotten, Dame May Whitty, Angela
Lansbury.

Get Carter

One of the few effective 70s British gangster
movies, and clearly influenced by the brutal-
ism of **Point Blank**, the film has Caine as
the hard-man hero who travels through a
world populated entirely by criminals, pitting factions against each other as he grimly
seeks revenge. Returning from London,
where he is a strong-arm man, to his home
town of Newcastle, Jack Carter (Caine)
investigates the death of his estranged brother. He cuts a deadly swath through the
provincial underworld, disposing of two rival
crime-lords and bludgeoning the sadist
(Hendry) who committed the murder before
he is casually executed by a sniper in the
employ of gang boss Osborne. Often startling
in its callousness (a naked Carter forces a
pair of thugs out of his bed-and-breakfast
hotel with a shotgun, a girl locked in the
boot of a car is forgotten when the car is
pushed into the river, Carter impassively
watches the MacGuffin 8 mm porn movie
that stars the niece who might be his own
daughter), this presents a hero who is violent and professional without ever seeming
sympathetic. Especially praiseworthy is
Hodges' use of unfamiliar North-east locations and an unusual 70s milieu of sideburns, leather coats, flares and urban redevelopment, populated by well-cast character
actors familiar from British TV, capturing
with cruel brilliance a world denuded of any
morality or meaning beyond violence. Ice-
man Carter's one moment of emotional
involvement, as he loses his temper with
Hendry, comes just before his own death. KN

1971/111m/MGM/*p* Michael Klinger/
d/s Mike Hodges/*orig* Ted Lewis *Jack's Return
Home/c* Wolfgang Suschitzky/*m* Roy Budd/
lp Michael Caine, Ian Hendry, John Osborne,
Britt Ekland, Tony Beckley, George Sewell.

Hangover Square (1938), perhaps because the
mid-Victorian trappings of the story render it
acceptably thrilling rather than genuinely
disturbing. A major stage success on both
sides of the Atlantic, the play was filmed
twice. Though both versions have much to
recommend them, the British film, smaller-
scaled and less showily acted, is superior.
Walbrook's villain, outwardly suave but eyes
shining with cruelty, is a triumph of under-
statement in an exaggerated genre, snorting
lasciviously as he flirts with the disloyal
maidservant (Cordell) in front of his cowed,
terrified wife. Wynter is equally fine, far sub-
tler than the Oscar-winning Bergman in her
evocation of a forced madness which may

have become real. Dickinson makes the
stuffy and over-crowded Victorian home a
nightmarish private trap, while Cukor is
mainly concerned with creating an exotic,
gothic environment, making *grand guignol*
horror out of a situation Hamilton and
Dickinson play for more than melodrama.
Boyer is a more romantic figure as the villain, but there is nothing in his performance
to match the moment at the finale of the
1940 film when Walbrook, utterly defeated,
cradles the rubies for which he has been
searching as if he were a child threatened
with the loss of a favourite toy, and the
fatherly ex-detective who has finally caught
his man lets him be for the moment. KN

The Getaway

A forceful adaptation of **Jim Thompson**'s hard-boiled novel, this nevertheless displays a sentimental streak in its understated but affecting depiction of the relationship between the bank robber hero (McQueen) and his devoted wife (McGraw), which captures the uneasiness of a life outside the law but also conveys the couple's commitment to each other in such powerful terms that screenwriter Hill had to omit the novel's cynical last chapter, in which the characters are trapped in a Mexican hell-hole which swallows their personalities. The stripped down chase story has McQueen sprung from prison by folksy mastermind Johnson to carry out a robbery and then turning the tables on his corrupt manipulator by making a dash for the border. Contrasted to McQueen's criminal of integrity is Lettieri's brutal thug, who kidnaps a married couple on the road and incidentally ruins husband and wife as he pursues McQueen and McGraw. Less violent than other Peckinpah movies, this more subtly integrates Western themes into a modern setting than his other contemporary thrillers (**Straw Dogs**, *The Killer Elite*, 1975, *The Osterman Weekend*, 1983). Roger Donaldson's competent 1994 remake, with Alec Baldwin and Kim Basinger, closely follows the film, with Walter Hill collaborating with Amy Jones to update his script, rather than return to the novel. KN

1972/122m/First Artists/*p* David Foster, Mitchell Brower/*d* Sam Peckinpah/*s* Walter Hill/*orig* Jim Thompson/*c* Lucien Ballard/*m* Quincy Jones/*lp* Steve McQueen, Ali McGraw, Ben Johnson, Al Lettieri, Sally Struthers, Slim Pickens.

Gilda

Drifting through Buenos Aires, Johnny Farrell (Ford) is rescued from a hold-up and hired by German casino owner Ballin Mundson (Macready). He also has to mind Mundson's slippery girl-friend Gilda (Hayworth). Meanwhile Mundson has a power struggle with the members of the international tungsten cartel which he now controls. He fakes suicide, not only to escape his competitors, but also because he believes that Gilda and Johnny are having an affair. Gilda escapes to Montevideo. Obregon (Calleia) informs Johnny that her promiscuity was only a tease, and that she's actually a good girl. Johnny joins her and they're reconciled, until Mundson returns to take revenge. The heart of the film is Hayworth's provocative sexuality. She sings, she smoulders, she torments both men. The sex goddess of a postwar generation, she plays the archetypal bad woman provoking hatred as well as fascination. Ford plays an exhausted and repressed rage like no one else, and he wears the finest male fashion ensemble of any movie in the period. MP

1946/110m/COL/*p* Virginia Van Upp/*d* Charles Vidor/*s* Marion Parsonnet/*c* Rudolph Maté/*m* Hugo Friedhofer/*lp* Rita Hayworth, Glenn Ford, George Macready, Joseph Calleia, Steven Geray.

The Glass Key

Originally made in 1935 by Paramount, this version of the **Dashiell Hammett** novel was refurbished by Latimer to overcome what were considered faults in the earlier version. This is a distinctly tough murder mystery set in the world of politics and the gambling rackets. Donlevy's political boss is not unlike his earlier role in *The Great McGinty* (1940), while the laconic Ladd and silky Lake move through the solid paces that **This Gun for Hire** (released some five months later) would celebrate. However, it is Bendix's quite terrifying sadistic henchman

ABOVE Rita Hayworth, *Gilda*

The Godfather

with a determined passion for inflicting pain (his gleeful beating of Ladd is almost stomach-churning) that remains long after in the memory. TV

1942/85m/PAR/*p* Fred Kohlmar/*d* Stuart Heisler/*s* Jonathan Latimer/*c* Theodore Sparkuhl/*m* Victor Young/*lp* Brian Donlevy, Veronica Lake, Alan Ladd, William Bendix.

The Godfather

The cinema's most expansive gangster saga and also the most complicated, not simply in its multi-generational plot (which takes the Corleone family from suffering in Sicily at the turn of the century to intrigue in the Vatican in 1979) but in its production history and the multitude of versions in which it exists. Originally, Coppola filmed *The Godfather*, Puzo's best-selling account of the transfer of power from a mafia don to his son, and wrought a self-contained masterpiece, distinguished by the infinitely subtle performances of Brando as the dignified but dangerous Don Vito Corleone and Pacino as his son Don Michael, who changes from naive idealist into an experienced and corrupt patriarch. A picture about family values, the film contrasts Michael, who demonstrates both the spirit and the hollowness needed to succeed, with his actual and figurative brothers, the volatile, aggressive and doomed Sonny (Caan), the weak-willed and unstable Fredo (Cazale) and the intent, placid, born second-in-command Tom Hagen (Duvall).

The Godfather won the Best Picture Academy Award and, with its languid style and explosions of operatic violence, daringly redefined the manners and morals of the gangster movie, replacing the rat-tat-tat pacing and moralist endings of everything from **The Public Enemy** to **Bonnie and Clyde** with a measured, almost funereal procession of corruption and death, winding up with a moral and spiritual ruin rather than the customary death in the gutter. Surprisingly, *The Godfather Part II* also took the Best Picture Award and, adapting a flashback section from Puzo's novel omitted from the first film, found an effective way of extending the Corleone story into the past, with De Niro as the young Vito coming from Sicily to America and rising in the neighbourhood protection scheme that turns into a racket, while following Michael into the 50s as he gets mixed up with the downfall of Batista's Cuba, big-time corrupt politics, and internecine wars which finally reduce him to murdering his own brother. The two films were combined and re-edited in chronological order as a four-part television miniseries, *The Godfather A Novel for Television* (1978), which was patched up, with language and violence unacceptable on TV restored, as the home video release *The Godfather: The Complete Epic, 1902–58* (1981). Meanwhile, Puzo provided a glimpse of Michael Corleone in his novel *The Sicilian* (1985), omitted from Michael Cimino's 1987 film, and film critic David Thomson wove several Corleone strands into his novel *Suspects* (1985). The saga was not truly revisited until *The Godfather Part III*, which did not find the critical or commercial favour of the first two pictures. Set in 1979, the film is distinguished by the culmination of Pacino's masterly performance as the now-aged don. In transferring the sphere of Corleone activities from America to Italy, the film misses out on the earlier movies' immigrant vision of America as a tarnished land of opportunities. Taken as a whole, the *Godfather* saga has added much to the cinematic and pop cultural vocabulary ('make him an offer he can't refuse', the horse's head in the film producer's bed, Michael emerging from a restaurant toilet with gun blazing, the Nino

ABOVE Al Pacino, Marlon Brando, *The Godfather*

ABOVE James Caan, *The Godfather*

Rota theme music, the structural audacity of *Part II*) and has even yielded a parody, *The Freshman* (1990), with Marlon Brando spoofing Don Vito, and any number of imitations or variations, both expensive and important (**Scarface**, **Once Upon a Time in America**, **GoodFellas**) and cheap and disposable (*The Don is Dead*, 1973, *Mob Boss*, 1990, *Mobsters*, 1991). Lastly, in Pacino, Brando and De Niro, the films have created gangster icons worthy of comparison with Bogart, Cagney and Robinson. KN

The Godfather/1972/175m/PAR/*p* Albert S. Ruddy/*d/co-s* Francis Ford Coppola/*co-s/orig* Mario Puzo/*c* Gordon Willis/*m* Nino Rota/*lp* Al Pacino, Marlon Brando, James Caan, Robert Duvall, Diane Keaton, Talia Shire, Richard Conte, John Cazale, Sterling Hayden.

The Godfather Part II/1974/200m/PAR/*p/d/co-s* Francis Ford Coppola/*co-s/orig* Mario Puzo/*c* Gordon Willis/*m* Nino Rota/*lp* Al Pacino, Robert Duvall, John Cazale, Robert De Niro, Lee Strasberg, Diane Keaton, Talia Shire, Roger Corman.

The Godfather Part III/1990/161m/Zoetrope-PAR/*p/d/co-s* Francis Ford Coppola/*co-s/orig* Mario Puzo/*c* Gordon Willis/*m* Carmine Coppola, Nino Rota/*lp* Al Pacino, Andy Garcia, Eli Wallach, Diane Keaton, Talia Shire, Joe Mantegna, Sofia Coppola, Bridget Fonda.

Goodbye Paradise

This is an affectionate and stylish pastiche of Raymond Chandler's world set in the beach resort of Surfer's Paradise in Queensland, Australia's most corrupt state at the time. Stacey (Barrett) is the burnt-out journalist with the low-down on political corruption who gets embroiled with a senator's perverse and wayward daughter. Using a Robert Mitchum-type voice over and relying on the grotesquely artificial environment of the resort for his eccentric atmospheres, Schultz succeeds in making a thriller which pushes the conventions of the genre to their surreal limits while playing them off against characteristically Australian modes of speech and gesture. The result is an inventive and seductive film from the Hungarian-born former television director. PW

1982/Australia/119m/Petersham-NSW Film Corp/*p* Jane Scott/*d* Carl Schultz/*s* Bob Ellis, Denny Lawrence/*c* John Seale/*lp* Ray Barrett, Robyn Nevin, Janet Scrivener, Kate Fitzpatrick.

GoodFellas

With this Scorsese returns on an epic scale to the tough-talking New York Italian-American hoods ('wiseguys' or 'goodfellas') of **Mean Streets**, following a group of neighbourhood crooks through thirty years of organised crime. Punk kid Henry Hill (Liotta) progresses to hi-jacking, airport rob-

beries, extortion, grievous bodily harm, drug dealing and, finally, informing. Along the way, he gets a Jewish wife (Bracco). More important, of course, are Henry's close male relationships: with Jimmy (De Niro), a coolly violent heist-man, and Tommy (Pesci), an unstable psychopath with hopes of getting 'made' (inducted into the mafia hierarchy). Hill is turned by the FBI and informs on his friends, winding up condemned to a Federal Witness Protection limbo where 'if you ask for *spaghetti bolognese* they give you noodles with meatballs', so he can live the rest of his life as 'an ordinary schmuck'. A lengthy, based-on-fact tale of family life, more matter-of-fact in its insider's chattiness than **The Godfather**, this is a more serious **Married to the Mob**. Underlaid by a constant barrage of cunningly selected songs, from the likes of Tony Bennett through Phil Spector to Sid Vicious, this panorama of illegal America stays with a group of wholly repulsive, increasingly corrupt people for nearly two and a half hours but never bores. De Niro, underplaying in a secondary role, is quietly chilling as the repressed but unpredictable robber, while Pesci plays the maniacal Tommy as a homicidal Lou Costello, seguing instantly from foul-mouthed wisecrack routines into mortifying threats or slap-in-the-face atrocities. Without moralising, the film manages to convey the dead-end horrors of a life not just outside the law but outside all possible law. KN

ABOVE Robert De Niro, *The Godfather Part II*

1990/146m/WB/*p* Irvin Winkler/
d/*co-s* Martin Scorsese/*co-s*/*orig* Nicholas
Pileggi *Wiseguy*/*c* Michael Ballhaus/*lp* Robert
De Niro, Ray Liotta, Joe Pesci, Lorraine
Bracco, Paul Sorvino.

Goodis, David (1917–67)

Acclaimed in Europe, particularly France, for
his grim tales of desperation, Goodis until
very recently was largely ignored in the US –
he wasn't even given an entry in Chris
Steinbrunner and Otto Penzler's seminal
Encyclopedia of Mystery & Detection (1976). His
novels, the best of which are **Dark Passage**
(1946), **Nightfall** (1947) and *Down There*
(1956, filmed as **Tirez sur le pianiste**),
unusually for the period all featured strong
heroes determined to pull themselves from
the gutter but only sinking further; the title
of one of his novels, *The Wounded and The
Slain* (1955) neatly catches this. Though they
don't know it Goodis's characters are trapped.
The European and American films made
from his novels are markedly different in
tone. The European films, which include
Tirez sur le pianiste, *La Lune dans le caniveau*
(1983, from *The Moon In The Gutter*, 1953),
Descente aux Enfers (1986, from *The Wounded
and the Slain*, 1955) and *Street Of No Return*
(1989, novel 1954) are highly romantic with
their doomed central characters expressing
passions few of those around feel. The
Hollywood films are equally bleak but their
characters are the victims of circumstances
which they can never overcome. This fits
more closely with the novels themselves,
which though often told from one person's
(sometimes several people's) viewpoint are
full of third-person narratives in which even
individual parts of the body act on their own
– in *Dark Passage* even the dead speak – and
inanimate objects are given active feelings.
Though written in a spare style the novels
are sophisticated in their handling of plot
and narrative. Like so many crime writers
Goodis began his career in the pulps, reportedly writing five million words in five years
for magazines and radio series before joining
Warners as a screenwriter after they bought
Dark Passage. Amongst the films he worked
on were *The Unfaithful* (1947), *Up To Now*
(1948) and *Of Missing Persons* (1948). The
best is **The Burglar** from his own novel
(1953). PH

Grabenplatz 17/17 Canal Square

A mixture of melodrama, thriller, exploitation film and musical by a distributor-
turned-scenarist and director (not to be con-

ABOVE Paul Sorvino, Joe Pesci, Robert De Niro, Ray Liotta, *GoodFellas*

fused with Erich Engel, a theatre director
who worked with Brecht and made films in
East Germany). A boy suffering from
leukaemia witnesses the murder of his
mother and is kidnapped by the assassins led
by Flint (Lange) and headquartered in the
Black Spider night-club, a front for a huge
swindling operation: special radio equipment
allows the gang to defraud horse-racing
bookmakers. The stripper Isabella (Fischer),
although associated with the gang, takes pity
on the boy. Inspector Jaeger (Preiss) tracks
the villains with a Geiger counter, having
put a radioactive substance on the boy's
shoes. The final confrontation destroys the
night-club and Flint is shot just before he
can kill the boy. In addition to some singing
and dancing as well as striptease numbers,
the film has a female wrestling scene,
although it ostentatiously, and naively,
deploys technological gadgetry bordering on
science fiction. PW

1958/Germany/92m/Deutsche Film-Hansa/
d/*co-s* Erich Engels/*co-s* Wolf Neumeister/
c Georg Brückbauer/*m* Heino Gaze/
lp Wolfgang Preiss, Kai Fischer, Wolfgang
Wahl, Carl Lange, Gert Fröbe, Maria Sebald.

The Great Muppet Caper

The comedy-thriller form has often been
used to accommodate the talents of personalities from vaudeville, radio and television.
In this case the form is crossed with the

'tourist' movie, in a picture whose backgrounds draw on an heraldic evocation of
English life which considerably pre-dates the
period of its own production. Muppets
Kermit and Fozzie Bear are investigative
reporters, hitting London on the trail of a
story about jewel robberies, and Miss Piggy is
an aspiring model who along with sundry
other Muppets attempts to aid their quest.
The man behind the robberies eventually
proves to be Grodin, playboy brother of fash-
ion-house supremo Rigg. The humour's success may essentially depend on a predilection for the Muppets, but the musical numbers are well done, and there is a choice
moment when Miss Piggy, who has earlier
been serenaded by Grodin in the course of
his dissembling advances towards her, rejects
him with the declaration, 'You can't even
sing – your voice was dubbed!' TP

1981/97m/ITC/*p* David Lazer, Frank Oz/
d Jim Henson/*s* Tom Patchett, Jay Tarses,
Jerry Juhl, Jack Rose/*c* Oswald Morris/*m* Joe
Raposo/*lp* The Muppets, Diana Rigg, Charles
Grodin, John Cleese, Jack Warden.

Green for Danger

A sprightly comedy-thriller. Unlike Launder
& Gilliat's earlier scripts (e.g. *The Lady
Vanishes*, 1938) which blend spying and
melodrama in a heady but fantastical man-
ner in which the British are as exotic as their
Ruritanian enemies, *Danger* is firmly ground

in reality. Set in a country hospital under constant threat from doodlebugs, the film both closely follows and parodies the clichés of classic detective fiction in which Sim's animated Inspector Cockrill stumbles on, rather than deduces, the truth about a patient's mysterious death on the operating table in full view of assembled doctors and nurses. Launder & Gilliat wisely keep the comedy on a firm rein, indeed they remain remarkably faithful to Brand's carefully articulated wartime atmosphere to enliven their tricksy narrative. Particularly fine is the lengthy dance sequence in which the various suspects are momentarily brought together by the dance and taunt each other about the recent murder and their emotional entanglements. Similarly the few comic moments – Sim thinking he spotted the guilty party of the detective novel he's reading only to find he's wrong when he turns to the last page – are all the more effective for being used as punctuation rather than transformed into set pieces. Howard and Genn are well cast as the lovers competing for the affections of Gray's charming nurse. PH

1946/GB/91m/Individual Pictures/ *co-p/d/co-s* Sidney Gilliat/*co-p* Frank Launder/ *co-s* Claud Gurney/*orig* Christianna Brand/ *c* Wilkie Cooper/*m* William Alwyn/*lp* Alastair Sim, Sally Gray, Rosamund John, Trevor Howard, Leo Genn, Meg Jenkins.

Greene, Graham (1904–91)

A sometime journalist, film critic, occasional screenwriter, relentless traveller and possible spy (for the Foreign Office in World War II), Greene led a fascinating, restless life. He was also the author of some twenty-five novels that guarantee his position in the pantheon of great English writers of the twentieth century. The unique power of his imaginative world (christened Greeneland) created monumental works of art such as *The Power and the Glory* (1940) and *The End of the Affair* (1951). Nevertheless it is those five books subtitled 'Entertainments' (distinguishing them from the non-generic serious fiction) - *Stamboul Train* (1933, filmed as *Orient Express*, 1934), *A Gun for Sale* (1936, filmed as **This Gun for Hire**), *The Confidential Agent* (1939, filmed 1945), *The Ministry of Fear* (1943, filmed 1944) and *Our Man in Havana* (1958, filmed 1959) - that are directly relevant to the crime genre. In these novels Greene brings to bear all his customary brilliance with language and characterisation but restricts his focus to the more rigid demands of the sus-

ABOVE Graham Greene

pense thriller. A common theme is international espionage (either political or industrial) and the plight of ordinary men embroiled in unpredictable circumstances. All such categorisation omits **Brighton Rock** (1938, filmed 1947), a non-'Entertainment' masterpiece which is also a fabulous crime thriller set amongst race track gangsters. Most of Greene's work has been filmed. Of the 'Entertainments', the best include Fritz Lang's 1943 version of *The Ministry of Fear*.

Aside from the marvellous John Boulting film of *Brighton Rock* (co-scripted by Greene and Terence Rattigan), Greene's most notable scriptwriting contribution to the crime film genre came through his collaboration with film director Carol Reed on arguably the greatest British thriller of all time, **The Third Man**. They re-united on the enjoyable adaptation of *Our Man in Havana*. AW

The Grifters

This is the real stuff. Westlake's script does full justice to Jim Thompson's original novel, updating the story of three con artists (the 'grifters' of the title) from the 1950s to the 1990s without losing any of the atmosphere created by a world of seedy motels and dingy diners. Huston gives a towering performance as Lily, a tough and experienced professional who helps the mob fix odds at the racetrack. Her boss (Hingle) suspects she is cheating him and the scene in which he tortures her is truly terrifying. Her son (Cusack) has never risen above small-time scams with loaded dice, but his girl-friend (Bening) has a classy act, squeezing her body into a series of tight-fitting outfits in order to distract businessmen from noticing the crooked deals being put over on them. Another factor that gives the film its edge is the competition between Huston and Bening over the loyalty and love of the weak and unsuccessful Cusack as he recovers from a beating by a bartender he has cheated. The mechanics of

ABOVE Anjelica Huston, *The Grifters*

the grifter's trade are fascinating; but it's the intensity of the acting that grips right to the end of the painful climax. EB

1990/113m/Cineplex-Odeon/*p* Martin Scorsese, Robert Harris, James Painten/ *d* Stephen Frears/*s* Donald E. Westlake/ *c* Oliver Stapleton/*m* Elmer Bernstein/ *lp* Anjelica Huston, John Cusack, Annette Bening, Pat Hingle, Henry Jones.

Grisham, John (1955–)

Best-selling novelist Grisham was born in Jonesboro, Arkansas and studied law at Mississippi State University. He practised as a lawyer from 1981 to 1990 and was a member of the Mississippi House of Representatives from 1984 to 1990. His first novel was *A Time To Kill* (1989, filmed 1996), but it was his second novel, *The Firm* (1990, filmed 1993), that established him. The film departs from the novel for its climax (which subsequently led to Grisham demanding, and getting, a far greater degree of artistic control over films drawn from his novels than most authors generally obtain) but was faithful to the novel's detailed account of the practices of law firms, which Grisham contrasts with the requirements of the legal system. The novel (and film, its added high-speed chase notwithstanding) introduced the key Grisham theme of the vulnerable innocent who discovers he is heir to a wealth of corruption unless he resists. In *The Firm* the corruption is less that the legal firm in question represents the mafia, rather that it over-bills its clients. Directed by Sydney Pollack, *The Firm* established Grisham as a major film source. *The Pelican Brief* (1992, filmed 1993), directed by Alan J. Pakula, director also of **Presumed Innocent** (adapted from another book by a lawyer turned novelist, Scott Turrow). *The Pelican Brief* starred Julia Roberts and Denzel Washington as the ill-matched Nick and Nora Charles investigating the mysterious murders of two Supreme Court Justices, was almost as successful commercially as *The Firm*. However, the film that raised Grisham as a franchise to the level of Tom Clancy and Ian Fleming was *The Client* (novel 1993, film 1994), which was already in pre-production six weeks before the novel was published. Again the film set in motion two potential failures against an all-powerful organisation, only for the individuals (a lawyer with a drink problem and a wayward child) to succeed. The least successful Grisham adaptation was *A Time To Kill*. The story of a black man charged with killing the

ABOVE Irene Dailey, Don Keefer, Ralph Waite, Tony Musante, Joey Faye, *The Grissom Gang*

two men who raped his daughter, the novel, with its echoes of **To Kill a Mockingbird**, was highly personal. However, if Grisham's role as a co-producer meant that the young lawyer at the film's centre (Matthew McConaughey) was too close to an idealised version of the author's younger self, Joel Schumacher's direction was too pedestrian to bring the keenly created tensions to life. As a result simple melodrama supplanted the obvious liberal concerns of the novel. Grisham's 1994 novel *The Chamber* was filmed by James Foley in 1996, but flopped. PH

The Grissom Gang

The toughest of the so-called 'nostalgia' cycle of 70s-styled 30s gangster films, this depicts the **Depression** as a Darwinist hellhole where the brutal but organised Grissom gang snatch heiress Barbara Blandish (Darby) from a lesser group of sweaty kidnappers, and the case attracts a vulture gathering of pressmen, profiteers, hoods and hangers-on. Considerably deepening **Chase**'s once-notorious thriller, Aldrich elaborates on the strange dependence-dominance relationship that grows between Miss Blandish and her slow-witted but psychopathic protector Slim Grissom (Wilson). Surrounded by characters on both sides of the law so degraded that money and power come before everything, the strange love between the leads is daringly treated, with both characters slowly demonstrating odd strengths as they commit to each other. Miss Blandish subsides into drunken resignation while Slim ridiculously dudes himself up, to the amusement of his more callous and sophisticated comrades, and installs the girl in a luxurious cell complete with a 'gold-leaf flush toilet'. In the devastating finale, the heroine's disgusted father ignores the hillbillies who are claiming the reward for tipping off the police, while his 'rescued' daughter is cast off to be looked after by the only compassionate character in the film, cynical private eye Dave Fenner (Lansing). In Ma Grissom (Dailey), the film conjures a matriarchal harridan whose horrifying cruelty is even in excess of Shelley Winters in **Bloody Mama**. *No Orchids for Miss Blandish* (1939), a British writer's attempt to compete with the American crime fiction of James M. Cain, is essentially a conflation of the plot of William Faulkner's *Sanctuary* (1931) – filmed as **The Story of Temple Drake**, with Miriam Hopkins, and as *Sanctuary* (1961), with Lee Remick – with the real-life exploits of the Ma Barker gang. A *succès de scandale* which provoked the puritanical essay 'Raffles and Miss Blandish' (1944) by George Orwell, the novel was a best-seller, and Miss Blandish joined Lady Chatterley, Fanny Hill and Amber St Clair of *Forever Amber* (1944) as an icon of 40s 'steaminess'. It enjoyed equal fame as a long-running West End play and a 1948 British film, with Linden Travers as Miss Blandish and Jack La Rue (the film's sole American) as Slim Grisson (as he was called in the novel). Chase wrote a sequel, *Flesh of the Orchid* (1948), in which the daughter of Barbara and Slim grows up to be an unbalanced *femme fatale*; this less-successful book was filmed in France by Patrice Chéreau as *La Chair de l'orchidée* (1975), with Charlotte Rampling in the lead. Dave Fenner returned in Chase's *Twelve Chinks and a Woman* (1940). KN

1971/128m/Associates and Aldrich-Palomar/ *p*/*d* Robert Aldrich/*s* Leon Griffiths/ *orig* James Hadley Chase *No Orchids for Miss Blandish*/*c* Joseph Biroc/*m* Gerald Fried/ *lp* Kim Darby, Scott Wilson, Tony Musante, Robert Lansing, Connie Stevens, Irene Dailey.

Gruber, Frank (1904–69)

Gruber was a prolific crime and Western novelist and screenwriter. His best script was for **Eric Ambler**'s **Mask of Dimitrios**. *Pulp Jungle* (1967) documents his (and **Steve Fisher**'s) days as pulp writers in New York in the 30s and includes his 10-point formula for a successful crime novel. The one unusual point he makes is that the villain should be more powerful than the hero, who should only triumph through his possession of something little valued until it is used. In Gruber's 300 or so stories the unusual element is generally luck or coincidence. Gruber's experiences in the 30s, when several times he was locked out of his room by hoteliers keen to separate him from his belongings until he had paid the bill, provided the impetus for his first success *The French Key* (1940, filmed from his own script 1946) which featured his most regular series character Johnny Fletcher. The French key was a wax key which prevented a occupant gaining access to his room, which in the novel/film was occupied by a dead body. Though he wrote over 50 film scripts only two other novels were filmed, *Accomplice* (1946, from *Simon Lash, Private Detective*, 1941, the central character of which, like Gruber, collected first editions) and *Twenty Plus Two* (1961, novel 1961). Gruber's film scripts included *Johnny Angel* (1945) and numerous Westerns. From the 60s onwards he wrote almost exclusively for television, creating *Tales of Wells Fargo* and *The Texan* amongst others. PH

Gumshoe

A beautifully observed film. Finney is the bingo-caller at a Liverpool working man's club who dreams of writing (and starring in) **The Maltese Falcon** and recording 'Blue Suede Shoes'. He is plunged into a real (if bizarre) murder mystery when he tries to bring these dreams to life. However, unlike, say *Play It Again Sam* (1972), script and direction carefully tread the line between pastiche and homage and the narrative isn't bogged down by constant references to byways of the genre. In particular Smith is careful to emphasise (and the actor to articulate) that the Finney character is a self-conscious dreamer. Indeed, part of the charm of the film is that so successful is Finney in his role-playing that within his small world people accept his self-appointed role at face value. Similarly Frears, making his directorial debut, is careful to anchor the film in the gritty world of petty Liverpool crime before animating Finney's all-encompassing dreams. The complex plot, featuring political shenanigans of a South African nature and gun-running, is held together by delightful acting from Whitelaw, Rule, Finlay and Mackay as the hit-man who finally turns out to be yet another wannabe, hoping to make his way in crime through 'violence of the tongue'. PH

1971/GB/94m/Memorial/*p* MichaelMedwin/ *d* Stephen Frears/*s* Neville Smith/*c* Chris Menges/*m* Andrew Lloyd Webber/*lp* Albert Finney, Billie Whitelaw, Frank Finlay, Janice Rule, Fulton Mackay, Carolyn Seymour.

Gun Crazy

One of the great B-pictures, this is genre film-making at its best. Cummins and Dall are the two doomed lovers who embark on a crime spree across the mid-West and are finally run to ground in a swamp, but not before they have tasted the thrills of robbery, murder and high-speed car chases. The plot owes much to the real-life exploits of **Bonnie and Clyde**. Despite its limited means, dictated by the King Brothers fearsomely Poverty-Row economies, the film achieves genuine poetry. The intense desire of its protagonists to escape the humdrum of small-town life provides a parable evoking the flip side of the dream of success, and the hero's fascination with guns provides not only the title but a potent meditation on the role of firearms in American popular culture. Along with **The Big Combo**, this is one of two *noir* masterpieces by Lewis. Scriptwriter Dalton Trumbo was blacklisted at the time and had to work through a front. EB

1949/87m/UA/*p* Maurice and Frank King/ *d* Joseph H. Lewis/*s* MacKinlay Kantor, Millard Kaufman (as front for Dalton Trumbo)/*c* Russell Harlan/*m* Victor Young/ *lp* Peggy Cummins, John Dall, Berry Kroeger, Morris Carnovsky, Anabel Shaw.

ABOVE Peggy Cummins, John Dall, *Gun Crazy*

ABOVE B. S. Pully, Sheldon Leonard, Stubby Kaye, Marlon Brando, *Guys and Dolls*

Guys and Dolls

Damon Runyon's amusing ,if idealised, stories of New York gangsters and other denizens of the underworld, first collected in 1932, were turned into a successful Broadway musical, with book by Abe Burrows and Jo Swerling, and music and lyrics by Frank Loesser. Nathan Detroit (Sinatra) needs a location for his floating crap game – the cops are on his tail. In order to get the money to rent somewhere he bets that Sky Masterson (Brando) can seduce Salvation Army worker Jean Simmons into an assignation in Havana. Sky gets her to Cuba by promising to rustle up sinners for salvation. Eventually, of course, Sky falls for the pure but beautiful bible-puncher and the film ends with a lavish wedding scene. While the lines remain true to Runyon ('This is no way for a gentleman to act and could lead to irritation on the part of Harry the Horse.') the film remains static, almost set-led rather than script-led. EB

1955/150m/MGM/*p* Samuel Goldwyn/
d/s Joseph L. Mankiewicz/*c* Harry Stradling/
m Cyril J. Mockridge, Jay Blackton/
lp Marlon Brando, Jean Simmons, Frank
Sinatra, Vivian Blaine, Robert Keith.

H

Haevnens nat/Blind Justice/ Night of Revenge

After the spy drama, *Det hemmelighedsfulde X* (1913), Christensen, at the time probably the most technically accomplished film-maker in the world, made this stylish crime melodrama about a circus artist, Strong John (played by Christensen himself), falsely accused of murder and imprisoned. Released, he falls in with a bunch of burglars and dog thieves. He wants to take revenge on the well-off family of Dr West who betrayed and helped capture him. The extraordinary film constitutes the prototype of the 'woman in peril' thriller as Strong John stalks the heroine in a deserted mansion in the dead of night. While Griffith and Feuillade were still experimenting with short exercises, Christensen had already developed sophisticated narrative techniques like cross-cutting between two simultaneous actions, and deployed a complex lighting style not only modelling individual figures to great effect but also varying lights within a single shot. The most telling innovation, though, was Christensen's shooting style, starting shots on details and then pulling back to reveal the overall situation or, when the heroine has locked the door of the house to keep John out, Christensen's camera pulls back through the window, generating suspense while using the camera to tell the story instead of simply recording it. In addition, tinting is used to differentiate locations as well as day from night. The credits of the US-released version list the director's name as Benjamin Christie and Sandberg, whose real name was Karen Caspersen, is billed as Katherine Sanders. PW

1915/Denmark/1956metres/Dansk Biografkompagni/*d/s* Benjamin Christensen/ *c* Johan Ankerstjerne/*lp* Benjamin Christensen, Karen Sandberg, Peter Fjelstrup, Fritz Lamprecht, Jon Iversen.

Hamilton, Patrick (1904–62)

The author of the stage plays **Rope** (1929) and *Gaslight* (1938) and the novel *Hangover Square* (1939, filmed 1944), Hamilton was a master of suspense. His great achievement, seen at its best in the novel *Hangover Square* (but not the film which fudged the plot), was the ability to create disturbed, malevolent characters who prey on others. The novel's full title catches its subject matter perfectly: *Hangover Square: or, The Man with Two Minds: A Story of Darkest Earl's Court in the Year 1939*. The Gorse trilogy, a series of novels about a financial predator, was less successful. Born in Sussex in genteel poverty Hamilton worked as an actor briefly before turning to writing in 1925 (*Monday Morning*). A technical *tour de force*, *Rope*, loosely based on the Leopold-Loeb murder case, was hugely successful. Although Hamilton worked on the screenplay little of his work survived the translation from stage to screen. *Gaslight*, with its grim cast of Victorian characters, was an even better play. PH

Hammer, Mike

In the climax of Mickey Spillane's first Mike Hammer novel *I, the Jury* (1947), the private eye faces a problem his notable predecessors **Sam Spade** and **Philip Marlowe** were wont to suffer, having fallen in love only to discover that the object of his affections is an unredeemable murderess. While Spade chokes back emotion and lets Brigid O'Shaugnessy be taken off to Tehachapi and Marlowe walks away from Eileen Wade with a shrug and another layer of bruising, Hammer watches the seductive Charlotte strip naked in an attempt to dissuade him from bringing her to justice, then pumps a shot into her belly. 'How could you?' she asks, dying; 'It was easy,' he replies. Spillane

ABOVE Benjamin Christensen, *Haevnens nat*

writing style, he seems to suggest his narrator-hero's attitudes and activities are motivated by a deep neurosis he himself rigidly refuses to acknowledge. However, with the liberal Ross MacDonald, the conservative Spillane reshaped the private eye genre created by Chandler and Hammett to his own ends, importing a New York bustle and thick-ear vigilante attitude that cuts through the distance and distaste of Chandler's 'literary' world by self-consciously getting down in the gutter. Hammer (who would feel more at home with Carroll John Daly's Race Williams than Marlowe) is an important progenitor of the Judge-Jury-and-Executioner heroes of 1960s paperbacks (the Destroyer or Executioner series) and 1970s movies (**Dirty Harry**, **Death Wish**) though Spillane's testosterone-driven typewriter conjures up a world of concupiscent hulks and pin-up nymphomaniacs that suggests the crazier films of Russ Meyer – *Faster, Pussycat! Kill! Kill!* (1964), *SuperVixens* (1975) – rather than anything approaching a serious worldview.

Harry Essex's *I, the Jury* (1953), with the

well-named but otherwise inadequate Biff Elliott as Hammer, retained some of Spillane's brutality in the opening sequence (the sadistic murder of a cripple) in order to justify the hero's casual shooting of (clothed) villainess Peggie Castle in the finish. Otherwise, the 3-D production, the first of four United Artists Hammer movies, played down the book's sex and violence, which served to render the film identical with any other private eye programmer. Robert Aldrich's **Kiss Me Deadly**, which takes the novel on its own terms and then goes even further, is at once the best imaginable adaptation of Spillane's style and a potent critique of Hammer's neo-fascist qualities: note the slight smile on Ralph Meeker's face as his Hammer breaks a witness's irreplaceable opera records to force him to talk or slams a drawer on an old morgue attendant's hand. Ditching Spillane's drugs MacGuffin in favour of a thermonuclear box that provides a spectacularly destructive finish that might even consume Hammer and Velda (Maxine Cooper), Aldrich and screenwriter A. I. Bezzerides create a nightmarish world where

(born 1918) had been a writer for comics, and carried over his brutal, clipped, action-oriented style from the rougher medium. While Hammer only kills or assaults people who really deserve it, it is hard not to feel Spillane enjoys marginalising certain categories of people ('uppity' blacks, homosexuals, women, intellectuals, communists) by depicting them as thoroughly despicable killers, thus excusing lovingly-described punishments. Hammer, who beds a succession of dangerous blondes but always returns to his faithful and celibate secretary-companion Velda and enjoys a friendly rivalry with the marginally more sensitive policeman Captain Pat Chambers, was an instant success. Spillane brought him back in *Vengeance Is Mine* (1950), *My Gun is Quick* (1950), *The Big Kill* (1951), *One Lonely Night* (1951), *Kiss Me Deadly* (1952), *The Girl Hunters* (1962), *The Snake* (1964), *The Twisted Thing* (1966), *The Body Lovers* (1967) and *Survival . . . Zero!* (1970). While Spillane might be accused of cynicism, especially in coining his slightly camp titles, Hammer himself is humourless and entirely confident in his own righteousness. The author clearly admires Hammer's caveman qualities (unlike Doyle or Chandler, Spillane has gone out of his way to identify with his hero, even to the extent of playing Hammer in a movie) but, through his impossibly virile and violent

ABOVE Benjamin Christensen, *Haevnens nat*

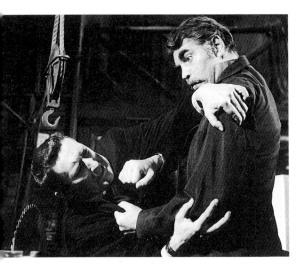

LEFT Mike Hammer: Mickey Spillane, Larry Taylor, *The Girl Hunters*

RIGHT Mike Hammer: Ralph Meeker, Maxine Cooper, *Kiss Me Deadly*

high culture – poetry, classical music and ancient mythology (the villain, Albert Dekker, refers to the much-sought Great Whatsit as both Pandora's Box and the Head of Medusa) – are juxtaposed with Hammer's world of mobsters, boxers, back-alley sleazes and trampy dames. Wesley Addy is a serious Pat Chambers, invoking the dread name of the Manhattan Project to rein in the vigilante, while the indispensable innocent victims, whose horrible deaths motivate Hammer's revenge crusade, are Cloris Leachman, found naked under a trench-coat on the road in the opening and quoting Christina Rossetti until tortured to death with a pair of pliers, and Nick Dennis as a Greek car mechanic, blown up in Hammer's sports model, who sums up Spillane's comic strip excitement with his repeated catchphrase 'va-va-voooom!' Subsequent Hammers have not equalled Ralph Meeker's neanderthal reading of the role, and none of the later movies have come near Aldrich's achievement. *My Gun is Quick* (1957), directed by George White and Phil Victor, has Robert Bray as Hammer, but is a thoroughly routine, anonymous picture. Roy Rowland's *The Girl Hunters* (1963), shot in England doubling for New York, is the movie with Spillane – who had played himself in the mystery *Ring of Fear* (1954), with Jack Stang as a guest-starring Hammer – in the lead, Shirley Eaton as Velda and Scott Peters as Chambers. *I, the Jury* (1981), directed by Richard Heffron after the departure of screenwriter Larry Cohen from the project, is an interesting but botched attempt, pitting Armand Assante's loose-cannon Hammer against a faceless government plot. Cohen re-used some scenes from his original script in *Deadly Illusion* (1987), from which he was

also fired and replaced as a director (by William Tannen), a disguised adaptation of *Vengeance Is Mine*, with Billy Dee Williams as a black Hammer renamed Hamburger and Vanity as the equivalent of Velda. Various television Hammers – Darren McGavin in a 1957–9 series with Bart Burns as Chambers, Kevin Dobson in the unsold pilot Mickey Spillane's *Margin For Murder* (1981), and Stacy Keach in the TV movies *Murder Me, Murder You* (1983), *More Than Murder* (1984) and *Murder Takes All* (1989) and two series, *Mickey Spillane's Mike Hammer* (1984–6) and *The New Mike Hammer* (1986–7) separated by Keach's un-Hammerlike jail term on a drugs charge – have not been able to come close to the sex and violence mark, with each Hammer mellower than his predecessors, Keach's sad-eyed softie approach to the role, accompanied by Tanya Roberts and Lindsay Bloom as Velda and Don Stroud as an exasperated Pat Chambers, suggests even Biblical psychopaths have to mellow sometime, though he had a few Meeker-like moments: in one episode, a villain clinging from a ledge begs Hammer to give him a hand, only to have Keach clap slowly as the miscreant falls to his death. KN

Hammett, [Samuel] Dashiell
(1891–1961)

Born Samuel Dashiell Hammett in Maryland, Hammett turned to writing while living in San Francisco in 1922, after ill health forced him to abandon working for the Pinkerton Detective Agency. An early contributor to *Black Mask*, he is widely regarded as, if not the originator, then the perfector of the so-called hard-boiled detective story. He

ABOVE Mike Hammer: Mickey Spillane, Pat O'Brien, Jack Stang, Pedro Gonzales-Gonzales, *Ring of Fear*

quickly became known for a series of stories about the Continental Op, a nameless private detective who works for the Pinkerton-like Continental Detective Agency. The Op first appeared in 1923 in 'Arson Plus' and 'Slippery Fingers'. Subsequent Op stories include 'The House in Turk Street' (1924), 'The Girl With the Silver Eyes' (1924), 'Fly Paper' (1924), 'Who Killed Bob Teal?' (1924), 'Dead Yellow Women' (1925), 'The Gutting of Couffignal' (1925), 'The Creeping Siamese' (1926), 'This King Business' (1928) and 'Death and Company' (1930). Hammett's novels *Red Harvest* (1929) and *The Dain Curse* (1929), which feature the Op, and *The Maltese Falcon* (1930) and *The Glass Key* (1931), which introduce new lead characters, are rewrites of Black Mask serials, as is the short novel *$106,000 Blood Money/Blood Money/The Big Knockover* (1943), which combines two 1927 Op novelettes, 'The Big Knock-Over' and '$106,000 Blood Money'.

After abandoning the Op for the more compromised heroes of *The Maltese Falcon* and *The Glass Key*, which feature 'blond Satan' P.I. **Sam Spade** and political strong-arm man Ned Beaumont, Hammett took another direction with *The Thin Man* (1934), a smart, slightly risqué society mystery with **Nick and Nora Charles**, a bantering married couple, as a sleuthing team. He made periodic attempts for the rest of his life to start new novels outside the mystery field but did not make much progress: 17,000 words of *Tulip*, an autobiographical novel,

ABOVE Dashiell Hammett's Nick and Nora Charles: William Powell and Myrna Loy, with Thomas Jackson, *The Thin Man*

exist, dating from 1955. His name was kept before the public by film and radio adaptations, including radio series continuing the adventures of Sam Spade and Nick and Nora, and by Ellery Queen's reissues of his *Black Mask* stories in eight volumes from *The Continental Op* (1945) to *A Man Named Thin and Other Stories* (1962). In addition, Ham-

mett scripted for the *Secret Agent X-9* newspaper strip (illustrated by Alex Raymond) from 1934 to 1935, provided original screen stories for a clutch of films (including *City Streets*, 1931, and *Mr Dynamite*, 1935), did much uncredited script-polishing (including *Ladies Man*, 1931, and *Blonde Venus*, 1931), and worked on a few adapted screenplays. He turned his lover Lillian Hellman's play *Watch on the Rhine* (1941) into a 1943 script but was unsuccessful enough in his last film assignment, **Detective Story**, to return his fee and demand no credit. In later life, he wrote by proxy, advising Hellman on her plays, and spent World War II producing a soldiers' newspaper in the Aleutians. He served six months in prison in 1951 on a charge of contempt of Congress for refusing to co-operate with an investigation into the Civil Rights Congress, a supposed Communist front organisation. A perennial invalid, from complications of influenza contracted during service as an army ambulance driver in Maryland during World War I, Hammett died of lung cancer.

All Hammett's novels have been filmed: *Red Harvest* unrecognisably as *Roadhouse Nights* (1930), with Jimmy Durante, also

LEFT Dashiell Hammett's Sam Spade (Humphrey Bogart) with Lee Patrick, *The Maltese Falcon*

ABOVE George Maharis, Robert Walker, Michael Parks, Faye Dunaway, *The Happening*

served as the loose inspiration for Akira Kurosawa's samurai drama *Yojimbo* (1961), which was remade as Sergio Leone's *Per un pugno di dollari/A Fistful of Dollars* (1964) – ironically in that Hammett's Op story 'Corkscrew' (1924) is a dry run for *Red Harvest* with a Western setting – and the sword and sorcery movie *The Warrior and the Sorceress* (1984); *The Dain Curse* as a 1978 TV miniseries, later edited into a feature version, with James Coburn as a Hammett-lookalike Op, directed by E.W. Swackhamer; *The Maltese Falcon* as *Dangerous Female* (1931) with Ricardo Cortez, *Satan Met a Lady* (1935), with Warren William, and, famously, as **The Maltese Falcon**, with Humphrey Bogart, inspiring many pastiches and parodies including a sequel *The Black Bird* (1975), with George Segal as Sam Spade Jr; *The Glass Key* by Frank Tuttle in 1935 with George Raft, Claire Dodd and Edward Arnold and by Stuart Heisler, in an improved version scripted by **Jonathan Latimer**, with Alan Ladd, Veronica Lake and Brian Donlevy in 1942; and *The Thin Man* in 1934, with William Powell and Myrna Loy as Nick and Nora Charles, kicking off a series that includes *After the Thin Man* (1936) and *Another Thin Man* (1939), from original stories by Hammett, and *Shadow of the Thin Man*

(1941), *The Thin Man Goes Home* (1944) and *Song of the Thin Man* (1947), followed by a 1957–9 TV series with Peter Lawford and Phyllis Kirk and a 1975 TV movie remake, *Nick and Nora*, with Craig Stevens and JoAnn Pflug.

Secret Agent X-9 became serials in 1937, with Scott Kolk, and 1945, with Lloyd Bridges, and *The Fat Man*, a 1946 radio series with J. Scott Smart as overweight sleuth Brad Runyon, nominally created by Hammett, was filmed by William Castle with Smart in 1950. Hammett is played by Jason Robards in *Julia* (1977), based on Lillian Hellman's memoir *Pentimento* (1973), and appears as a character in Joe Gores's private eye novel **Hammett** (1975, filmed by Wim Wenders in 1983) with Frederic Forrest (who also plays Hammett in *Citizen Cohn*, 1992), and in William Denbow's less successful *Chandler* (1977). Among many biographies and critical studies are Richard Layman's *Shadow Man: The Life of Dashiell Hammett* (1980), William F. Nolan's *Hammett: A Life at the Edge* (1983) and Diane Johnson's *Dashiell Hammett: A Life* (1983). KN

Hammett

While Gores's effective novel pitches Samuel Dashiell Hammett, Pinkerton detective turned

hard-boiled author, into a new-minted mystery involving real-life San Francisco figures of the 20s, this adaptation (a troubled production from Francis Ford Coppola's Zoetrope, with director Wenders staying at the helm despite numerous changes of script and personnel) opts instead to pastiche **The Maltese Falcon** as Hammett (Forrest) meets sinister characters we are supposed to take for the originals of the villains of the novel. The film suffers because its plot turns, dialogue exchanges and reliance on betrayal as a motif are transparent. A scheming Chinese prostitute (Lei) stands in for Brigid O'Shaughnessy, while the other main villain turns out to be Hammett's ex-partner (Boyle), supposedly the inspiration for his Continental Op, allowing for a rehearsal of the kind of broken friendship Hammett and Chandler after him would assign to a detective hero. Beautifully art-directed and shot entirely on studio sets, this is glossy and entertaining but ultimately hollow. It is far more stylish than *The Black Bird* (1975), the other major Maltese Falcon **parody**, but hardly more pointed. KN

1982/92m/Zoetrope/*p* Fred Roos, Ronald Colby, Don Guest/*d* Wim Wenders/*s* Ross Thomas, Dennis O'Flaherty/*orig* Joe Gores /*c* Philip Lathrop, Joseph Biroc/*m* John Barry/*lp* Frederic Forrest, Peter Boyle, Marilu Henner, Roy Kinnear, Elisha Cook, Lydia Lei.

Han matado a un cadaver/A Corpse Has Been Killed

The Barcelona-born Salvador has made some respectable thrillers, notably *Apartado de Correos 1001* (1950) and *Duda* (1951). Here he attempted a new gimmick: twin sisters played by the same actress, Ripert, and achieved some well-composed images as well as fine camera movements. A woman is found poisoned in Barcelona, her death is kept secret and her twin arrives to take her place, announcing plot aspects of Antonioni's *Professione: Reporter* (1975). However, the substitution doesn't lead to her death but to the rounding up of a counterfeiting gang and the heroine's marriage to the investigating cop (Campos). On its release in France, a Harry MacGraugh was credited with the original script. PW

1961/Spain/96m/Urania/*d*/*co-s* Julio Salvador/*co-s* E. del Rio/*c* Ricardo Albinana/ *m* J. Duran Alemanny/*lp* Jose Campos, Colette Ripert, Angel Picazo, Maria Mayer, Lina Legros, Marcel Portier, Howard Vernon.

Hangover Square

This was Cregar's last film and perhaps offered him his finest role as the madman-murderer. The first-rate thriller, set in gas-light era London, features a Jekyll-Hyde style drama. Director Brahm and cinematographer La Shelle, with embellishments from composer Herrmann, create a top-notch melodramatic nightmare world of fog and shadow for Cregar's sinister character to stalk around. Co-stars Darnell and Sanders, though splendid, remain merely bystanders to Cregar's powerful impact. The film, which was based on the 1941 novel by **Patrick Hamilton**, is an unofficial companion to the same team's earlier *The Lodger* (1944). TV

1945/77m/FOX/*p* Robert Bassler/*d* John Brahm/*s* Barré Lyndon/*c* Joseph La Shelle/*m* Bernard Herrmann/*lp* Laird Cregar, Linda Darnell, George Sanders.

The Happening

Mixing a modish late-1960s cocktail of broad satire and outlandish behaviour, *The Happening* musters enough energy and wit to avoid the facetiousness of some comparable undertakings. A quartet of middle-class drop-outs get involved for kicks in the kidnapping of a businessman (Quinn) who proves to be an ex-mobster. Farcically, neither his faithless wife (Hyer) nor his chief business associates are prepared to stump up. Quinn's response

ABOVE George Maharis, Anthony Quinn, *The Happening*

is to take over the operation with a scheme to fake his own death and extort huge sums from those supposedly implicated, with the hipsters as increasingly hapless pawns in the game. The twist ending, with Quinn torching the cash on the grounds that the notes will be marked, then strolling off alone, suggests that he may be more attuned to the drop-out ethos than his youthful confederates. TP

1966/101m/Horizon-Dover/*p* Jud Kinberg/*d* Elliot Silverstein/*s* Frank R. Pierson, James D. Buchanan, Ronald Austin/*c* Philip Lathrop/*m* Frank DeVol/*lp* Anthony Quinn, Faye Dunaway, George Maharis, Michael Parks, Martha Hyer.

The Harder They Fall

Eddie Willis (Bogart) was once a respectable sportswriter, now he's a PR fixer for Nick Benko (Steiger), a sleazy, crooked promoter. Benko has a great new prospect, a giant Argentinian Toro Moreno (Lane) who actually has a glass jaw and no punch. But the fights are fixed, and Toro goes from strength to strength, until he meets Gus Dundee (Pat Comiskey). But Dundee hasn't recovered from a bruising encounter with champ Buddy Brannen (Baer). He's so battered that Toro kills him. Eddie knows the cause is Nick's manipulation of the fighters and his conscience won't let him rest. From the novel by Budd Schulberg, this is an angry campaigning film which was so close to the bone that real life heavyweight Primo Carnera sued Columbia. The direction speeds the camera at a relentless pace through the stark black and white corridors of the boxing world, and maintains the tension, in spite of the distracting domestic drama between Eddie and his wife (Sterling). MP

1956/109m/COL/*p* Philip Yordan/*d* Mark Robson/*s* Philip Yordan/*c* Burnett Guffey/*m* Hugo Friedhofer/*lp* Humphrey Bogart, Rod Steiger, Jan Sterling, Mike Lane, Max Baer.

Harlem Nights

All too evidently conceived as a showcase for Murphy, *Harlem Nights* may have aspirations to a 'hip' recreation of the classic gangster movie – the film begins with a childhood prologue and then moves forward some twenty years to the Harlem club scene of the 1930s – but it emerges, lavish production values notwithstanding, as a dispiritingly reductive outing. The plot, concerning the efforts of Murphy and his partner-cum-mentor Pryor to gain the upper hand over the

ABOVE Paul Newman, *Harper*

mobster who seeks to take over their business, is complicated enough but lacks any tension. Murphy's own persona is remorselessly narcissistic, the misogynist violence is offensive and the dialogue is numbingly repetitive, leaving the impression that if the epithet 'motherfucker' were to be excised from the soundtrack, the running time would be reduced by half. TP

1989/116m/PAR/*p* Robert D. Wachs, Mark Lipsky/*d*/*s* Eddie Murphy/*c* Woody Omens/*m* Herbie Hancock/*lp* Eddie Murphy, Richard Pryor, Michael Lerner, Danny Aiello, Della Reese.

Harper/The Moving Target

Though Ross MacDonald's conscience-laden gumshoe Lew Archer became Lew *Harper* simply so star Newman could continue his run of H-for-hit movies (*The Hustler*, 1961, *Hud*, 1963, *Hombre*, 1967), this is a successful filming of MacDonald's first Archer novel (1949), discreetly updated from the late 40s to the mid-60s. Harper is sent out by rich bitch Bacall to find a missing husband on a recommendation from a mutual friend (Hill) and comes across a collection of unsavoury, neurotic, and/or unsympathetic characters: Wagner as a pretty boy pilot-cum-thrill-killer; Harris as a dope addict jazz pianist; Winters as a starlet running to fat; Webber as a Southern sadist; Martin as a wetback-smuggling phoney guru. Everyone turns out to be morally guilty except Harper and Hill, but Hill is revealed in the understated, daring finale to be the actual murderer and, it is suggested, is allowed to go free. A vulnerable man, first seen under the credits in an effective bit of character-setting re-using last night's coffee grounds for breakfast, Newman's Harper ends the movie with a resigned shrug. Newman, ideally suited to the role of MacDonald's liberal, paternal, soft-boiled sleuth, returned to the role in *The Drowning Pool* (1975), from the 1950 novel. KN

1966/121m/WB/*p* Jerry Gershwin, Elliott Kastner/*d* Jack Smight/*s* William Goldman/*orig* Ross MacDonald *The Moving Target*/*c* Conrad Hall/*m* Johnny Mandel/

ABOVE Al Pacino, *Heat*

lp Paul Newman, Lauren Bacall, Arthur Hill, Janet Leigh, Robert Wagner, Strother Martin, Shelley Winters, Robert Webber.

He Walked by Night

This is one of a group of films made by Eagle-Lion in the wake of **T-Men.** That broadly speaking the same technicians worked on the group of films is further highlighted by the fact that Anthony Mann, the earlier movie's director, worked uncredited on several sequences of this one. *He Walked By Night* offers a fairly threadbare assembly of the components of the semi-documentary thriller – the strident narrating voice of Reed Hadley, extensive use of exteriors, chiaroscuro camerawork by John Alton (though the last only really comes into his own in the climactic pursuit through the storm drains). The perfunctory air of the scenario may be

accounted for by its purporting to reconstruct not a composite case history but a single one, that of a former police department technician who turns his skills to burglary, and kills a patrolman whose suspicion he has aroused. The detectives (Brady and Roberts) leading the manhunt are colourless figures, though Basehart creates an incisive portrait of the cool-brained lawbreaker, whose 'underground man' solitude is rendered literal in his recourse to the drainage system for his getaways. TP

1948/79m/Eagle-Lion/*p* Robert T. Kane/*d* Alfred Werker/*s* John C. Higgins, Crane Wilbur/*c* John Alton/*m* Leonid Raab/*lp* Richard Basehart, Scott Brady, Roy Roberts, Jack Webb, Whit Bissell.

Heat

Michael Mann is a specialist in high tech, high voltage, beautifully made, visceral crime thrillers such as *Thief* (1982) and **Manhunter**. *Heat* is the culmination of his work to date and had its genesis in an old script of Mann's that he first directed as the television movie *L.A. Takedown* in 1989. The latter was made on a small budget, with a largely unknown cast and a much simpler narrative containing only the bare bones of what *Heat* would eventually become. Mann used *L.A. Takedown* to develop some scenes and sequences which he then incorporated into the considerably expanded and re-worked final script that would be filmed as *Heat*. The result is a classic heist movie that pits a crack team of professional thieves against LA's finest robbery detectives. Mann's storyline deliberately plots the adversaries on parallel tracks, with fascinating comparisons to each of their home lives, until he explosively converges them at the climax of the movie. Finely tuned, with painstakingly staged action sequences, pumped up star performances and a characteristically eclectic soundtrack of rock, soul and ambient music. AW

1995/172m/WB/*p*/*d*/*s* Michael Mann/*c* Dante Spinotti/*m* Elliot Goldenthal/*lp* Al Pacino, Robert De Niro, Val Kilmer/Diane Venora.

Heavenly Creatures

This film is based on a notorious 50s crime in Christchurch, New Zealand, a case of what Jacques Lacan called *folie-à-deux*, shared madness. The two in question are the school-friends Pauline (Lynskey) and Juliet (Winslet), whose fantasy lives, a mixture of

ABOVE Robert De Niro, *Heat*

ABOVE Ben Hecht

Hecht can claim to be the creator of the gangster film. His play *The Front Page* (1928), co-written with Charles MacArthur, another playwright turned screenwriter, is a good portrait of what was later called 'the Chicago school of journalism' at work. As a journalist Hecht knew the gangsters he wrote about, but even though he saw their actions in part as heroic response to corrupt officialdom, it was Josef von Sternberg who elevated Bull Weed in *Underworld* to mythic proportions. Hecht's collaboration with Hawks on *Scarface* was more equal. Others revised the script and added dialogue, but it was Hecht and Hawks who were responsible for the thrust of the film and of the paralleling of the Capones and the Borgias. A further indication of Hecht's powerful influence on the film is the unusually expressionistic style Hawks, normally a very unobtrusive director, used. Similarly the impact of Hawks on Hecht can be seen in his subsequent film work where Hecht forswore the florid 'Chicago' style that characterises his earlier films and so much of his non-film writing. Once established in Hollywood as a writer, Hecht eschewed crime subjects in the 30s. In the 40s he returned to crime-writing; he wrote **Spellbound** and **Notorious** for Alfred Hitchcock, and **Kiss of Death**, **Ride the Pink Horse** and **Where the Sidewalk Ends**. PH

Hell Drivers

This lorry-driving drama is unusually dynamic and proletarian for a British crime movie. An ex-convict (Baker) signs on with

teenage dime-novel clichés and megalomania, merge with reality, making them live in a world of their own (symbolised by their attempt to write a feudal romance together). Juliet's parents when they become aware of the intensity of the relationship between the girls try to separate them, triggering hysterical reactions and in the end the girls gruesomely murder Pauline's mother (Pierse). The film is told in flashback, starting with the blood-spattered girls running into a suburban garden crying 'Mother's terribly hurt', and has extensive voice-over readings from Pauline's diary as she describes her experiences with Juliet, referring to themselves in the third person. Jackson manages to maintain an uncomprehending distance from the girls by, paradoxically, strictly adhering to their point of view (often using claustrophobically near close-ups) so that their world is never quite available for critical scrutiny. PW

1994/New Zealand, Germany/Wingnut-Fontana-New Zealand Film Commission/ *co-p* Hanno Huth/*co-p/d/co-s* Peter Jackson/ *co-s* Frances Walsh/*c* Alun Bollinger/*m* Peter Dasent/*lp* Melanie Lynskey, Kate Winslet, Sarah Pierse, Diana Kent, Clive Merrison.

Hecht, Ben (1883–1964)
Author of the original story that **Underworld** was based on and writer of **Scarface**,

RIGHT Paul Muni, C. Henry Gordon, *Scarface*, made from Ben Hecht's script

ABOVE Humphrey Bogart, James Cagney, *The Roaring Twenties* produced by Mark Hellinger

a dodgy firm, joining a motley crew of lorry-drivers whose job is to break the speed limit by delivering loads of gravel through narrow rural roads. McGoohan, a brutal Irishman, and Hartnell, the crooked manager, turn out to be running a scam whereby they pocket five extra salaries by forcing the truckers to work at a dangerous pace, with inevitable injuries and deaths. Aside from the effective on-the-road action scenes, the film is notable for its use of British-flavoured wise-cracking dialogue, its non-caricature use of varied working-class characters, and its attention to a specific milieu of boarding houses, pull-in cafés, village dances, works huts and back-street newsagents. The movie, along with **The Criminal**, **Hell Is a City** and *A Prize of Arms* (1961), served to establish Baker as the closest thing to a British crime movie icon on the level of a Cagney or a Garfield. KN

1958/GB/108m/Rank-Aqua/*p* S. Benjamin Fisz/*d*/*co-s* Cyril Endfield/*co-s*/*orig* John Kruse/*c* Geoffrey Unsworth/*m* Hubert Clifford/*lp* Stanley Baker, Herbert Lom, Peggy Cummins, Patrick McGoohan, William Hartnell.

Hell Is a City

This Manchester-set *policier* was made in the first flush of Hammer's success with their gothic horrors. Just as Terence Fisher's horror films add sex and violence to a richly imagined and colourful mittel Europe, *Hell Is a City* adds sex (brief nudity involving Billie Whitelaw) and violence (after shooting the hero in the lung, the villain further takes the trouble to kick him in the side) to a grittily-realistic and wide-screen monochrome North of England. Baker is the hard-boiled copper on the trail of a jail-breaking jewel thief (Crawford) who masterminds a smash and grab robbery during which a girl courier is killed. Using Manchester locations as well as he used London for *The Quatermass Experiment* (1956), Guest stages robberies and chases against unfamiliar backdrops, and also offers intriguing insights into a specific criminal sub-culture in a Sunday morning shove ha'penny gathering on chilly moors just out of town. The large supporting cast perfectly incarnate distinctly British versions of traditional *noir* figures: Pleasence as a crookedly jovial bookie, Godsell as an ageing barmaid, Cooper as a publican-turned-squealer and Whitelaw as Manchester's answer to the Marilyn Monroe character in **The Asphalt Jungle**. KN

1960/GB/98m/*p* Michael Carreras/*d*/*s* Val Guest/*orig* Maurice Procter/*c* Arthur Grant/*m* Stanley Black/*lp* Stanley Baker, John Crawford, Donald Pleasence, Maxine Audley, Billie Whitelaw, Vanda Godsell, George A. Cooper.

Hellinger, Mark (1903–47)

A journalist turned producer Hellinger was

ABOVE Cornel Wilde, Arthur Kennedy, Humphrey Bogart, Alan Curtis, Ida Lupino, *High Sierra*, produced by Mark Hellinger

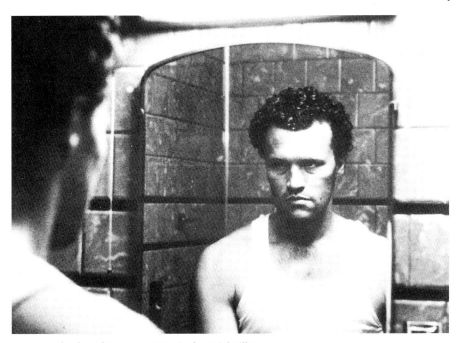

ABOVE Michael Rooker, *Henry Portrait of a Serial Killer*

responsible for several important gangster films, including **The Roaring Twenties**, from his own story, and **The Naked City**. Although he was a columnist and contributor to Broadway revues rather than a reporter, his films often had the feel of being ripped from newspaper headlines. His subtitle for the original treatment of *The Roaring Twenties* was 'the story of an era'. Hellinger originally went to Hollywood to work for Warners as a writer (*Broadway Bill*, 1934, *Comet Over Broadway*, 1938) but it was only when he moved into production that he achieved real success. His films at Warners include *Manpower* (1941), *They Drive By Night* (1940) and **High Sierra**, all strong masculine stories given a disturbing edge by their director Raoul Walsh. Generally billed as an associate producer, after a disagreement with Hal Wallis over billing Hellinger set up his own production company. Initially these films, which included **The Killers** and **Brute Force**, were similar in style, albeit more violent than his films at Warners, but **The Naked City**, written by Albert Maltz and Malvin Wald and directed by Jules Dassin, was a seminal film that mixed increased realism with social criticism. PH

Henry Portrait of a Serial Killer

Made in Chicago on a shoestring budget said to be only $120,000, *Henry* has a scenario partly based on the confessions (subsequently retracted) of a convicted serial murderer,

Henry Lee Lucas. But while the film deploys an ostensibly ciné-vérité style, its tenor is far removed from that of a documentary reconstruction. Rather, the spectator is thrust into reluctant intimacy with Henry, the random killer who as an adolescent murdered his abusive prostitute mother; Otis, a criminal associate whom he inducts into his 'leisure' killings and who comes to outdo him in depravity; and the latter's sister, to whom Henry forms an attachment of sorts. By the end, Henry has killed both the other two, as well as a variety of strangers. Combined with a rigorous construction, the ambiguity of the film's status as an exploitation picture only serves to strengthen its clammy grip. In the most indelible sequence, matter-of-factness is turned inside out, by showing a multiple murder through the lens of a camcorder Henry and Otis have discarded: the 'accidental' images, from a fixed tilted angle, create an aura of expressionist horror. In a microcosm of the film as a whole, resort to a distancing device only serves to make reality more appalling and more difficult to come to terms with. TP

1986/83m/Maljack Prods/*p* John McNaughton, Lisa Dedmond, Steven A. Jones/*d* John McNaughton/*s* Richard Fire, John McNaughton/*c* Charlie Lieberman/*m* John McNaughton, Ken Hale, Steven A. Jones/*lp* Michael Rooker, Tracy Arnold, Tom Towles.

Hickey & Boggs

The former TV *I Spy* series duo, Cosby and Culp, are a pair of low-life private eyes who get themselves involved in a missing-girl case which leads them onto the trail of a stolen $400,000 bank haul and, when Cosby's wife is murdered, a violent vendetta. Cosby and Culp share the slick patter and easy-going camaraderie that enhanced their TV series. This film also marks Culp's feature directorial debut (likewise for producer Said, who had been the TV series' cinematographer). Hill's screenplay fulfils the promise of explosive action at the climax. TV

1972/111m/UA/*p* Fouad Said/*d* Robert Culp/*s* Walter Hill/*c* Wilmer Butler/*m* Ted Ashford/*lp* Bill Cosby, Robert Culp, Rosalind Cash.

High Anxiety

Dedicated to Hitchcock, and apparently appreciated by him, *High Anxiety* is rather more judicious as a mock tribute than some of Brooks's other works, such as *Young Frankenstein*, might lead one to expect. While the film essentially revolves itself into a series of skits, there is some semblance of a governing plot drawing on **Spellbound** for its conceit of having Brooks arrive to take up a post at an unusual sort of psychiatric clinic. Subsequently the action shifts to the quintessentially Hitchcockian locale of San Francisco, where the hero is waylaid by *femme fatale* Kahn, sporting a blonde fright wig. Some of the comic business along the way is on the crude side (the nod to *The Birds* involves pigeons relieving themselves on Brooks's head) but there is some compensatory visual sophistication, as in the elaborately lighted shot depicting Brooks symbolically entrapped in a spider's web of shadows. TP

1977/94m/FOX/*p*/*d* Mel Brooks/*s* Mel Brooks, Ron Clark, Rudy DeLuca, Barry Levinson/*c* Paul Lohmann/*m* John Morris/*lp* Mel Brooks, Madeline Kahn, Cloris Leachman, Harvey Korman, Howard Morris.

High Sierra

Roy Earle (Bogart) is released from jail and plans one last job before retiring. But he's been inside too long. The real professionals have all gone. 'All that's left are soda-jerks and jitterbugs.' So the robbery goes wrong. Earle is chased by cops up into the remote fastness of Mount Whitney, where his position is revealed by a stray dog he's adopted. His death is mourned only by Marie (Lupino), who recognises a kindred doomed spirit. A crippled girl (Leslie) whom Roy falls for ditches him for a younger man once Roy has paid for an operation to cure her. It sounds a sentimental comment on the heartlessness of others. But the real point of the film is in Bogart's tough-minded response. He never expected anything better anyway. The film was a turning point in Bogart's career, the first in which the trademark world-weary integrity shines through the hard-bitten exterior. In 1949 Walsh remade the film as a Western, *Colorado Territory*, starring Joel McCrea. EB

1941/110m/WB/*p* Hal B. Wallis, Mark Hellinger/*d* Raoul Walsh/*s* John Huston, W. R. Burnett/*c* Tony Gaudio/*m* Adolph Deutsch/*lp* Humphrey Bogart, Ida Lupino, Joan Leslie, Alan Curtis, Arthur Kennedy.

Highsmith, [Mary] Patricia
(1921–93)
Highsmith was the creator of Tom Ripley whose exploits have been filmed by René Clément (**Plein soleil**, from *The Talented Mr. Ripley*, 1955) and Wim Wenders (*Der amerikanische Freund* (1977), from *Ripley's Game*, 1974) and author of the groundbreaking **Strangers on a Train** (novel 1950). She forms the link between writers who were interested in character and atmosphere at the expense of plot (e.g. **Cornell Woolrich**)

ABOVE Ida Lupino, Humphrey Bogart, *High Sierra*

and those interested in disturbed characters and criminals (e.g. Margaret Millar). In Julian Symons's phrase she 'fused character and plot most successfully'. In this way she

ABOVE Farley Granger, *Strangers on a Train*, from the book by Patricia Highsmith

gives life to fantastical ideas – two people swapping murders – and makes believable the idea that a possible victim would attach himself to his potential murderer rather than run a mile. Her cool detachment gives great impact to the ill-matching partnerships, generally between men, she returns to again and again, most notably in *The Two Faces Of January* (1964). Just as her novels were better received in Europe, so there are more European film adaptations of her novels. Although Alfred Hitchcock intensified the doubleness of *Strangers* to great effect, Claude Autant-Lara's version of *The Blunderer* (1954) as *Le Meurtrier*, in which an amateur copies the murder methods of a professional killer only to find the killer on his trail, is less successful. Even worse is *Once You Kiss a Stranger* (1969), a changed gender reworking of *Strangers*. PH

Himes, Chester [Bomar] (1909–84)
How Chester Himes became a crime writer is in itself a testament to the creative element in the relationship between French commentators (and consumers) and American art forms, with the former more often than not giving name (*film noir*), substance and interpretation to the latter, particularly at times when they were little considered in their home country. A former criminal, after

a stint on the WPA programme in the late 30s Himes became a writer of 'slice-of-life' black novels (e.g. *If He Hollers Let Him Go*, 1945) who settled in France in the 50s. Then in 1957 Marcel Duhamel, editor of the prestigious Série Noire, the French series devoted to, mostly, American crime writers, asked Himes to write him a black-centred crime novel. The result was *La Reine des Pommes* (1958), the first of a series of novels featuring black Harlem detectives Coffin Ed Johnson and Grave Digger Jones, who like their names were larger than life characters caught between corrupt officialdom and black criminals seeking to make the most of their blackness. This feature was further highlighted in the films drawn from the novels. All but the last of the novels were first published in French. In the course of the blaxploitation era of the 70s two of Himes's novels were filmed, **Cotton Comes to Harlem** (novel 1965) and *Come Back Charleston Blue* (1972, novel *The Heat's On*, 1966). *A Rage in Harlem* (1991), which was loosely based on *For Love of Imabelle* (1957), was significantly different from the earlier films. At its centre was not Himes's detective heroes but co-producer Forest Whitaker as the naive undertaker full of innocent love for a Memphis temptress determined to pro-tect her ill-gotten gains. Conceived of as a piece of nostalgia, the film depicted Harlem as a near-Eden about to burst apart under the pressure of black nationalism. PH

His Kind of Woman

The longer-than-average running time probably reflects the interventions of executive producer Howard Hughes, which extended to commissioning extensive reshooting under Richard Fleischer (whose autobiography offers a humorous account of his travails). These vicissitudes may also account for the film's somewhat divided tone. There is a nightmarish quality to the early sequences, in which Mitchum's out-of-luck gambler is set up by Burr's exiled crime czar in a scheme for the latter to dispose of him and purloin his identity, but the film subsequently segues into eccentric comedy with the arrival of Price as a Hollywood ham actor who rallies to Mitchum's defence. As a result, the return to a dark register for the climactic confrontation aboard Burr's yacht comes across as rather strained. Nonetheless, the movie is mounted with characteristic RKO crispness and the cast, incorporating Russell as the well-nigh statutory saloon singer, rises reliably to the occasion. There is also a pleasing vignette of Mitchum ironing

ABOVE Godfrey Cambridge, *Cotton Comes to Harlem*, from a novel by Chester Himes

banknotes and philosophising, 'When I need to think I iron my money, and when I'm broke I press my pants.' TP

1951/117m/RKO/*p* Robert Sparks/*d* John Farrow/*s* Frank Fenton, Jack Leonard/ *c* Harry J. Wild/*m* Leigh Harline/*lp* Robert Mitchum, Jane Russell, Vincent Price, Raymond Burr, Charles McGraw.

L'Histoire d'un crime

A leading director at Pathé from 1900, and later to become head of production, Ferdinand Zecca was the man who first brought crime into the cinema. Fantasy had been the dominating force in early movies, Zecca, who also in 1901 created the first recorded use of split screen in *A la conquête de l'air*, offered in its place brutal realism. The film is simply, yet ingeniously, staged. A condemned man sleeps, and dreams, in his cell. Above his head, seen in double exposure on a screen, six scenes play out the story. An apache stalks his victim (a bank clerk); he is arrested; is confronted by the investigating magistrates; goes on trial; is held in prison; faces his last day. Then he wakes, and in a seventh and final scene is

ABOVE Robert Mitchum, Jane Russell, *His Kind of Woman*

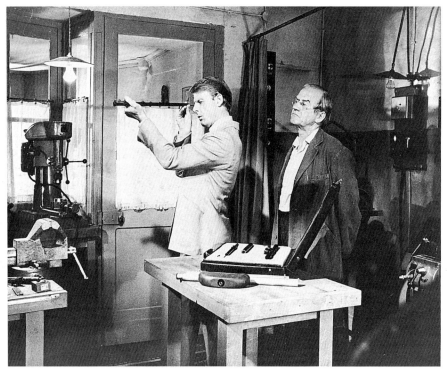

ABOVE Hit-Men: Edward Fox, Cyril Cusack , *The Day of the Jackal*

led out to execution. Zecca used six actors, including himself, made his film for 3,000 francs, and sold over 200 prints at 200 francs each. At 110 metres, the film ran a bare seven or eight minutes. The films owed much, perhaps, to two popular sources from which it derived, the waxworks of the Musée Grévin, which were said to have been Zecca's inspiration, and the realistic melodrama then in vogue in Parisian theatres. For a decade and more, the world of lower-class criminals would be the staple of the crime film. JL

1901/France/110m/Pathé/*d* Ferdinand Zecca/*lp* Ferdinand Zecca, Jean Liézer.

Hit-Men

When characters were 'taken for a ride' in early gangster movies, their murderers were usually the gangster protagonists themselves, often with the aid of the all-purpose hoodlums, ranging in stature and viciousness from George Raft to Vince Edwards, who constitute his entourage. The character of the professional assassin, a specialist in murder who could be called in when anyone needed elimination, did not become prominent until the 40s and 50s, when the extent of Murder Incorporated, the enforcement arm of the national crime syndicate run by

such notables as Bugsy Siegel and Lepke Buchalter, was revealed. As examined in films like *The Enforcer/Murder Inc.* (1950), *Murder, Incorporated* (1960) and **Lepke**, Murder Inc. was the instrument of wholesale murder most favoured by the crime bosses of the post-Prohibition era. The expressions 'hit-man' and 'torpedo' entered the language and the movies responded with coolheaded, menacing, incipiently insane characters: Jack Moss in *Journey Into Fear* (1943), William Conrad and Charles Bickford in **The Killers**, Frank Sinatra in *Suddenly* (1954) and Eli Wallach and Robert Keith in **The Lineup**. A touch of Murder Inc. professionalism even extends beyond strict genre confines to characters like gunslinger Jack Palance in *Shane* (1953) and the murderers employed by *Richard III* (1955).

One of the earliest films to concentrate on a hit-man is **This Gun for Hire**, with Alan Ladd as a trench-coated assassin who upstages the nominal leads to emerge as not only an ambiguous hero but an epitome of alienated *noir* cool. In the 60s and 70s, Ladd's image predominated, and emotionless (or pseudo-emotionless) murderers were made (via such accessories as the easy-assemble assassination rifle in a dustproof attaché case) to seem attractive if anti-heroic protagonists. Representing this trend are

Vince Edwards in **Murder by Contract**, Henry Silva in *Johnny Cool* (1963), Lee Marvin and Clu Gulager in *The Killers* (1964), Alain Delon in **Le Samouraï**, Oliver Reed in *The Assassination Bureau Limited* (1969), Alex Cord in *Stiletto* (1969), Edward Fox in *The Day of the Jackal* (1973), James Coburn in *Hard Contract* (1969), Charles Bronson and Jan Michael Vincent in *The Mechanic* (1972), Yvette Mimieux in *Hit Lady* (1973), Stuart Whitman in *Shatter/Call Him Mr Shatter* (1975), Donald Sutherland in *The Disappearance* (1977), the Japanese cartoon character *Golgo 13* (1983), John Hurt and Tim Roth in *The Hit* (1984), Kathleen Turner in **Prizzi's Honor**, James Woods in *Best Seller* (1987), Chow Yun-Fat in *Diexue Shuang Xiong/The Killer* (1989), Dennis Hopper in *Catchfire* (1989), Anne Parillaud in *Nikita/La Femme Nikita* (1990), Michael Nouri in *DaVinci's War* (1992), Jeff Fahey in *The Hit List* (1993) and Bridget Fonda in *Point of No Return/The Assassin* (1993). Most of these pay for their come-uppance. Their victims are almost invariably under-characterised stick figures: politicos or rival gangsters seen only in long-shot, often through the cross-hairs of a high-powered rifle. Variations on this theme are the 'good ole boy' contractors played by M. Emmet Walsh in **Blood Simple** and Dennis Hopper in *Red Rock West* (1992), grungy cowboys with slick grins and murderous hearts.

The idea of a good-hearted, sentimental hit-man surfaces in the morally dubious and otherwise dire *Grace Quigley* (1985), with Nick Nolte, and *Blame It on the Bellboy* (1991), with Bryan Brown, but some grim humour is gained from the old chestnut of a would-be suicide commissioning his own murder (cf.: *The Whistler*, 1944, *Five Days/Paid to Kill*, 1954) in *I Hired a Contract Killer* (1990), with Kenneth Colley as a dying assassin. More credible if scarcely more convincing are the psychotic and near-unstoppable hit-men (sometimes brainwashed) of a line of fantasy-touched thrillers: *The President's Analyst* (1967), *The Parallax View* (1974), *The Killer Elite* (1975), *Looker* (1981), *Dreamscape* (1984), *F/X* (1986), *Assassination* (1987), *Black Rainbow* (1989), *Hit List* (1989), *The Bodyguard* (1992), *In the Line of Fire* (1993). The most striking of the breed are the mind-wiped Laurence Harvey in *The Manchurian Candidate* (1962), borderline psychotic Robert Shaw in *From Russia with Love* (1963) and, most unstoppable of all, cyborg Arnold Schwarzenegger in *The Terminator* (1986). KN

The Hitcher

The perils of giving a lift to a hitchhiker were explored to tense effect in *The Hitch-hiker*, directed by Ida Lupino in 1953, but that film's realism of treatment gives way here to the stylisation of nightmare, albeit in natural surroundings made all the more immediate by Seale's immaculate Panavision cinematography. A teenager (Howell) is delivering a car from Chicago to San Diego and impulsively picks up a hitchhiker (Hauer). When the latter identifies himself as a murderer, the boy manages to push him out of the vehicle, but this proves to be only the start of a spiral of ever more violent episodes by means of which the satanic older man paints his victim into a corner of apparent guilt for his own crimes; the last of these entails the gruesome death of the young woman (Leigh) who has become Howell's helpmate. Even Hauer's eventual arrest provides a false resolution, and in the concluding sequence, resemblances to the horror movie become more overt, as the seemingly invincible maniac escapes from a police van for a final face-to-face encounter with his adversary. TP

1986/97m/HBO-Silver Screen Partners-Tri-Star/*p* David Bombyk, Kip Ohman/*d* Robert Harmon/*s* Eric Red/*c* John Seale/*m* Mark

Isham/*lp* Rutger Hauer, Thomas C. Howell, Jennifer Jason Leigh, Jeffrey DeMunn, Billy 'Green' Bush.

Holmes, Sherlock

Sherlock Holmes, the most instantly identifiable detective in fiction, has featured in every imaginable medium, gaining wider fame than comparables like James Bond, Dracula or Tarzan. Sir Arthur Conan Doyle (1859–1930) introduced the tenant of 221b Baker Street (along with faithful sidekick Dr John H. Watson, long-suffering landlady Mrs Hudson and unperspicacious Inspector Lestrade of Scotland Yard) in *A Study in Scarlet* (1888), first published in *Beeton's Christmas Annual*. Holmes returned in finer form for *The Sign of the Four* (1890), the first really great Sherlock Holmes story, with eccentric suspects, a missing Agra treasure, a chase along the Thames, a one-legged avenger, a locked-room murder, a faithful bloodhound, a sinister pygmy and more effective use of Doyle's favourite plot device, probably derived from **Wilkie Collins'** *The Moonstone*, the back-story of wrong done in a far-flung corner of the globe playing itself out in violent retribution in England, the hub of the Empire and heart of the world. At the end of the novel, Watson marries heroine Mary Morstan. However, the character really captured the public imagination in 56 short stories, from 'A Scandal in Bohemia' (1891), featuring the nearest thing to love interest for Holmes in 'adventuress' Irene Adler, to 'The Adventure of Shoscombe Old Place' (1927). The stories appeared first in *The Strand Magazine* and were collected in *The Adventures of Sherlock Holmes* (1892), *The Memoirs of Sherlock Holmes* (1894), *The Return of Sherlock Holmes* (1905), *His Last Bow* (1917) and *The Case Book of Sherlock Holmes* (1927). Doyle wrote two further novels, both serialised in *The Strand*, *The Hound of the Baskervilles* (1902) and *The Valley of Fear* (1915). Mycroft Holmes, Sherlock's even more insightful but infinitely lazier brother, makes his debut in 'The Greek Interpreter', while Professor Moriarty, possibly the only villain capable of giving Holmes a real battle, arrives in 'The Final Problem' only to be promptly killed off. Doyle half-heartedly revived Moriarty off-stage in *Fear* but subsequent hands have found him too useful to be dispensed with, making the Napoleon of Crime, after Dr Watson, the character most associated with Holmes.

In Doyle's own estimation, the outstanding stories, in order of merit, are 'The

ABOVE Sir Arthur Conan Doyle, creator of Sherlock Holmes

ABOVE Sherlock Holmes and Dr Watson illustrated in *The Strand Magazine*, 1892

Adventure of the Speckled Band', 'The Red-Headed League', 'The Adventure of the Dancing Men', 'The Final Problem', 'A Scandal in Bohemia', 'The Adventure of the Empty House', 'The Five Orange Pips', 'The Adventure of the Second Stain', 'The Adventure of the Priory School', 'The Adventure of the Devil's Foot', 'The Musgrave Ritual' and 'The Reigate Squires'. Doyle was deeply ambiguous about Holmes' success, resenting the way the detective's fame eclipsed that of historical novels (*Micah Clarke*, 1889, *The White Company*, 1891, etc.) he himself felt were major works. However, it is notable that Doyle's other most successful creations (lost-world-discovering Professor Challenger and Napoleonic adventurer Brigadier Gerard) are also series heroes operating within Holmes's modestly effective and resonant populist frame. In 1893, Doyle undertook to kill Holmes in 'The Final Problem' (he plunges over the Reichenbach Falls in a death struggle with Moriarty) and was not persuaded to revive him properly until 'The Adventure of the Empty House' in 1903, though in the interim he could not resist presenting *Baskervilles* as a posthumous reminiscence.

Holmes made his stage debut in 1894, when John Webb appeared in Glasgow in *Sherlock Holmes, Private Detective* by Charles Rogers, but did not find an official theatrical face until 1899, when William Gillette first appeared (in Buffalo, New York) in *Sherlock Holmes*, loosely adapted from 'A Scandal in Bohemia', 'The Final Problem' and *Scarlet*. *Sherlock Holmes* was a hit, Gillette continued in it off and on until his death in 1937 (also playing the role on film and radio), and it is still revived. Doyle himself adapted 'The Speckled Band' into a play in 1910, and H. A. Saintsbury and Lyn Harding were notable in the roles of Holmes and the dastardly Dr Grimesby Rylott (Roylott in the story). Doyle wrote the less successful *The Crown Diamond: An Evening With Sherlock Holmes* (1921), a one-acter he immediately recycled as a short story, 'The Adventure of the Mazarin Stone'. Subsequent theatrical Holmes adventures have included Max Goldberg's *The Bank of England: An Adventure in the Life of Sherlock Holmes* (1900), J. E. Harold Terry's *The Return of Sherlock Holmes* (1923), *The Holmeses of Baker Street* (1932), Margaret Dale's ballet *The Great Detective* (1953), Ouida Rathbone's disastrous *Sherlock Holmes* (1953), the musicals *Baker Street* (1965) by Jerome Coopersmith, Marian Grudeff and Raymond Jessell and *Sherlock Holmes – the Musical* (1989) by Leslie Bricusse, Charles Marowitz's *Sherlock's Last Case* (1974), John Southworth's *Sherlock Holmes of Baker Street* (1974), Paul Giovanni's *The Crucifer of Blood* (1979), Martyn Reed's *221b Baker Street* (1983), Hugh Leonard's *The Mask of Moriarty* (1985), Jeremy Paul's *The Secret of Sherlock Holmes* (1989) and F. G. Callan's *Partners in Crime* (1990). Stage Holmeses have included Fritz Weaver, Keith Michell, Paxton White-head, Hamilton Deane, Alfred Burke, John Wood, Leonard Nimoy, Tod Slaughter, Tim Preece, Julian Glover, Frank Langella, Charlton Heston and Ron Moody.

More than any other fictional character, Holmes has attracted authors intent on adding to the canon left by the originator of the property. H. F. Heard's *A Taste for Honey* (1941) has Holmes as 'Mr Mycroft', a retired bee-keeping detective who also appears in *Reply Paid* (1942) and *The Notched Hairpin* (1949). Adrian Doyle, Sir Arthur's son, and John Dickson Carr wrote a series of short stories collected as *The Exploits of Sherlock Holmes* (1954), in Sir Arthur's style and concentrating on the various intriguing cases mentioned in passing in the original tales. William S. Baring-Gould's *Sherlock Holmes: A Biography of the World's First Consulting Detective* (1962), endeavours to resolve Doyle's loose ends and continuity gaps by sorting the information given in the stories to arrive at a 'real' biography of Holmes. Baring-Gould also edited *The Annotated Sherlock Holmes* (1968), a definitive concordance to the original stories. The only author to attempt as much has been Michael

Harrison, who produced Holmes's autobiography *I, Sherlock Holmes* (1977), several pastiche novels (*The Prisoner of the Devil*, 1979, *Sherlock Holmes: My Life and Crimes*, 1984, *The Revenge of the Hound*, 1987), some non-fiction (*In the Footsteps of Sherlock Holmes*, 1958) and, with Mollie Hardwick, a tactful novelisation of Billy Wilder's *The Private Life of Sherlock Holmes* (1970).

Subsequently, with the lapse of copyright in 1974, there has been a flood of Holmes material led by Nicholas Meyer's *The Seven-per-Cent Solution* (1975), *The West End Horror* (1976) and *The Canary Trainer* (1993). *The Seven-per-Cent Solution* is the best of many books in which Holmes meets historical characters like Freud, Bram Stoker, Teddy Roosevelt, Houdini, Alfred Dreyfuss, H. P. Lovecraft or Wilde. Holmes has repeatedly exposed Jack the Ripper, most intriguingly in a cunning novelisation-expansion by Paul Fairman under the Ellery Queen byline of the film *A Study in Terror* (1966). Also popular are pairings with fictional contemporaries: Tarzan (Philip José Farmer's *The Adventure of the Peerless Peer*, 1974, republished for copyright reasons with Tarzan replaced by Mowgli), Dracula (Fred Saberhagen's *The Holmes-Dracula File*, 1978, Loren D. Estleman's *Sherlock Holmes vs. Dracula, or The Adventure of the Sanguinary Count*, 1978), Fu Manchu (Cay van Ash's *Ten Years Beyond Baker Street*, 1984), the Martians *and* Professor Challenger (Manly Wade and Wade Wellman's *Sherlock Holmes's War of the Worlds*, 1975), Dr Jekyll (Estleman's *Dr Jekyll and Mr Holmes*, 1979) and the Phantom of the Opera (*The Canary Trainer*). Supporting characters come into their own with star turns for Moriarty (John Gardner's *The Return of Moriarty*, 1974, and *The Revenge of Moriarty*, 1975, Michael Kurland's *The Infernal Device*, 1978), Lestrade (M. J. Trow's series), Irene Adler (Carole Nelson Douglas's *Good Night, Mr Holmes*, 1990, and *Good Night, Irene*, 1991) or Mycroft (Michael Hodel and Sean Young's *Enter the Lion*, 1979, Glen Petrie's *The Dorking Gap Mystery*, 1989, and *The Monstrous Regiment*, 1990). The suggestion advanced by Baring-Gould that Rex Stout's Nero Wolfe is Holmes's illegitimate son by Irene has yielded John Lescroart's *Son of Holmes* (1986) and *Rasputin's Revenge* (1987), in which the young Wolfe goes by the name of Auguste Lupa. Among many shocking revelations: Michael Dibdin's *The Last Sherlock Holmes Story* (1978: multiple personality Holmes is both Moriarty and the Ripper), Robert Lee Hall's *Exit Sherlock*

Holmes (1977: Holmes and Moriarty are time-travelling clones from the future), Ray Walsh's *The Mycroft Memoranda* (1984: Watson's brother is the Ripper) and Rohase Piercey's *My Dearest Holmes* (1988: Watson is gay). There are even a few straightforward Holmes stories, as in Martin Greenberg and Carol-Lynn Rossel-Waugh's collection *The New Adventures of Sherlock Holmes* (1987), which contains Stephen King's excellent 'The Doctor's Case', Richard Boyer's *The Giant Rat of Sumatra* (1977), Lloyd Biggle's *The Glendower Conspiracy* (1990), John North's *Sherlock Holmes and the German Nanny* (1990) and Edward B. Hanna's *The Whitechapel Horrors* (1992).

Sherlock Holmes Baffled, a one-minute trick film made between 1900 and 1903, finds the Great Detective outwitted by a Wellsian Invisible Man. The name of the first screen Holmes is lost to history, as are those of the stars of *Sherlock Holmes in the Great Murder Mystery* (1908, an adaptation of Poe's 'Murders in the Rue Morgue'), and some Italian comedies including *Sherlock Holmes* (1909), *Bloomer Tricks Sherlock Holmes* (1915) and *The Flea of the Baskervilles* (1915). The first identifiable film Holmes is Maurice Costello in *The Adventures of Sherlock Holmes* (1905), rapidly followed by Viggo Larsen in a lengthy Danish series starting with *Sherlock Holmes i livsfare/Sherlock Holmes in Deathly Danger* (1908) that often finds Holmes pursuing his literary cousins Raffles and Arsène Lupin, and which includes the first adaptation of *Baskervilles, Den graa dame/The Gray Dame* (1909), in which the ghost is not a hound but a veiled lady; Otto Lagoni, Holger Rasmussen, Alwin Neuss and Forrest Holger-Madsen in competing Danish films between 1908 and 1911; Alwin Neuss, Larsen's Watson, in a series of German films based on *Baskervilles* from 1914 to 1920, with Hugo Flink and Ferdinand Bonn taking the role in rival German productions; Georges Treville in a Franco-British series based closely on the Doyle stories, opening with *The Speckled Band* (1912); Harry Benham in *Sherlock Holmes Solves the Sign of the Four* (1914); James Bragington in *A Study in Scarlet* (1914); Harry Arthur Saintsbury, a stage Holmes, in *The Valley of Fear* (1917); Francis Ford in *A Study in Scarlet* (1914); and, of course, William Gillette, in his own *Sherlock Holmes* (1916), the most elaborate of the early movies, with Edward Fielding as Watson and Ernest Maupin as Moriarty.

From 1921 to 1923, the official screen Holmes was Eille Norwood, in two British

LEFT Sherlock Holmes filmed by Stoll at Cricklewood

(1908), *Hemlock Hoax, the Detective* (1910), *Sherlock Holmes, Junior* (1911), *Sherlock Bonehead* (1914), *A Study in Skarlit* (1915, with Fred and Will Evans as Sherlokz Homz and Professor Moratorium), *A Villainous Villain* (1916, featuring Hughie Mack as 'Sherlock Ooomph'), *Sherlock Brown* (1921) and a slapstick series featuring deerstalker bunglers Fred Mace and Mack Sennett as 'Two Sleuths' (1911–13) which was rivalled by the more obscure 'Sherlocko and Watso' series (1912), the French 'Charlie Colms' (1912) and 'Burstap Homes, Detective' (1913). In the sound era, such travesties abated to a trickle – the two-reel *Sherlock's Home* (1932) was a throwback – but porno movies like *The Adventures of Surelick Holmes* (1975), with David Chandler and Frank Massey as a gay detective team, or *Jack the Stripper # 1* (1992), with Mike Horner as Holmes, are identifiably in this tradition. All comedians from the Three Stooges to Daffy Duck have at some point assumed a 'detective' disguise of a deerstalker and a

magnifying glass, indicating how completely the Holmesian image, derived by Gillette from Doyle by way of Sidney Paget's *Strand* illustrations, has come to sum up the sleuth.

Basil Dean's *The Return of Sherlock Holmes* (1929) features the dryly British Clive Brook as the first screen Holmes to use the catch-phrase 'elementary, my dear Watson'. Brook resumed the deerstalker in *Paramount on Parade* (1930), where he meets William Powell's **Philo Vance** and Warner Oland's **Fu Manchu**. Brook progressed to William K. Howard's *Sherlock Holmes* (1932), a static version of the Gillette property with a marvellous Moriarty from Ernest Torrence. Brook never became as identified with the role as Norwood, Wontner, Rathbone or Brett, and there were several competing efforts during his tenancy of 221b Baker Street. Raymond Massey is a fine, younger-than-usual Holmes in Jack Raymond's *The Speckled Band* (1931), with Athole Stewart as Watson and Lyn Harding as the definitively dastardly Dr Grimesby Rylott, while the stocky, balding Robert Rendel is not up to much (despite dialogue from Edgar Wallace) in the first sound *Hound of the Baskervilles*

features directed by Maurice Elvey, *The Hound of the Baskervilles* (1921) and *The Sign of the Four* (1923) and three batches of Doyle-derived shorts, *The Adventures of Sherlock Holmes* (1921), *The Further Adventures of Sherlock Holmes* (1922) and *The Last Adventures of Sherlock Holmes* (1923). Norwood's Watson is Hubert Willis (except in *Four*, when the more romantic Arthur Cullin is called in to woo the heroine), Madame d'Esterre is Mrs Hudson, Arthur Bell is Lestrade, and Percy Standing is Moriarty in *The Final Problem* (1923). Doyle was reportedly far happier with Norwood's Holmes than that of John Barrymore in Albert Parker's *Sherlock Holmes* (1922). A free version of Gillette's already free play, with Roland Young as Watson and the unforgettably hideous Gustav von Seyffertitz as the Napoleon of Crime, this finds the Great Profile's Great Detective more interested in sighing over the heroine than capturing the villain. The last silent Holmes is Carlyle Blackwell, a dapper Englishman partnered by Georges Seroff's Watson in Richard Oswald's *Der Hund von Baskerville* (1929).

There were many silent American parodies of Holmes, notably Buster Keaton's *Sherlock Jr.* (1924) and Douglas Fairbanks' *The Mystery of the Leaping Fish* (1915), in which Fairbanks plays drug-crazed sleuth Coke Ennyday, but also *Miss Sherlock Holmes*

ABOVE Albert Parker filming John Barrymore in *Sherlock Holmes*, 1922

ABOVE Buster Keaton, *Sherlock Jr.*

(1931). Reginald Owen, Brook's rather subdued Watson in *Sherlock Holmes*, stepped up to the lead for Edward L. Marin's *A Study in Scarlet* (1933), with Warburton Gamble as the Good Doctor and Anna May Wong as an ambiguously sinister oriental.

Arthur Wontner was cast as Holmes in *The Sleeping Cardinal/Sherlock Holmes' Fatal Hour* (1931), with Ian Fleming (not the author) as Watson and Norman McKinnel as a fiendish Moriarty, then appeared in *The Missing Rembrandt* (1932, from 'Charles Augustus Milverton'), *The Sign of Four* (1932), *The Triumph of Sherlock Holmes* (1935) and *Silver Blaze/Murder at the Baskervilles* (1937). Wontner was the first Holmes to divest the character of the baggage loaded onto him by Gillette and get back to the original stories' conception of the unemotional, morally unwavering, wittily ingenious master sleuth. Fleming continued as Watson, though again the older man was dropped for *Four* (and replaced by Ian Hunter) to beef up the love interest. Lyn Harding is Moriarty in *The Triumph . . .* , adapted from *The Valley of Fear* (the least filmed of the novels), and returned for *Silver Blaze*, which finds it necessary to bring on a heavier heavy than the original story and relocate it to Baskerville Hall. Meanwhile on the continent, Martin Fric was in the Czech *Lelicek ve sluzbach Sherlocka Holmese/Lelicek in the Service of Sherlock Holmes* (1932), Bruno Guttner and

Fritz Odemar were Holmes and Watson in another *Hund von Baskerville* (1937), Hermann Speelmans investigated in the Danish *Sherlock Holmes, oder graue dame* (1937), and Hanns Albers and Heinz Ruhmann are comedy private eyes who impersonate Holmes and Watson in *Der Mann, der Sherlock Holmes war/The Man Who Was Sherlock Holmes* (1937).

In Hollywood, 20th Century-Fox cast Basil Rathbone and Nigel Bruce as Holmes and Watson in Sidney Lanfield's *The Hound of the Baskervilles* (1939), a top-drawer production with a stalwart supporting cast (Richard Greene, Wendy Barrie, Lionel Atwill, John Carradine, Morton Lowry). The story even then suffered from over-familiarity but Rathbone and Bruce were obviously born to the roles. They return in Arthur Werker's far more spirited and satisfying *The Adventures of Sherlock Holmes* (1939). George Zucco's magnetically oily Moriarty plots to steal the Crown Jewels but sets up an intricate case involving a limping assassin, imperilled heroine Ida Lupino, a chinchilla foot and South American *bolas* to distract Holmes. The best of Rathbone's Holmes-in-disguise sequences has the Great Detective

impersonating a music hall entertainer and performing 'I Do Like to Be Beside the Seaside'.

Fox, already sponsoring the detection of **Charlie Chan** and **Mr Moto** and soon to add **Mike Shayne** to the payroll, dropped their option to continue the costly period series. Rathbone and Bruce, along with Mary Gordon's Mrs Hudson, found new employment at Universal, where they were put into *Sherlock Holmes and the Voice of Terror* (1942), directed by John Rawlins who immediately handed over to producer-director Roy William Neill, who handled the eleven follow-up films. Dennis Hoey blustered as Inspector Lestrade throughout, and there were splendid one-shot Moriartys from Lionel Atwill and Henry Daniell in *Sherlock Holmes and the Secret Weapon* (1942) and *The Woman in Green* (1945), not to mention Alan Mowbray as Colonel Sebastian Moran in *Terror By Night* (1946). The initial entries find Holmes in a World War II setting, patriotically battling the Axis (as did series heroes like Charlie Chan, Tarzan, the Dead End Kids and the Invisible Man) and unmasking deep-cover Nazi spies, recovering stolen secret weapons and making Churchillian pronouncements

ABOVE Basil Rathbone, Nigel Bruce, *The Adventures of Sherlock Holmes*

on the course of the War. As Neill took over the series, things got more interesting, with bizarre villains, series of grotesque slayings ('the pyjama suicides', 'the finger murders', 'the creeper crushings') and genuinely twisted little plots.

Highlights are *Sherlock Holmes Faces Death* (1943), from 'The Musgrave Ritual', which inventively uses the War as a backdrop with its setting of a crumbling manor serving as a sanatorium for shell-shocked officers; *The Spider Woman* (1944), with Gale Sondergaard as a female Moriarty; *The Scarlet Claw* (1944), a fog-drenched creepy set in a Canadian village terrorised by a glowing werewolf finally unmasked as crazed actor Gerald Hamer, probably the best of the batch; *The Pearl of Death* (1944), from 'The Six Napoleons', with Miles Mander, Evelyn Ankers and the misshapen Rondo Hatton as a trio of strong villains; and *The House of Fear* (1945), notionally from 'The Five Orange Pips', a gloomy old house mystery in which the Good Comrades' Club are murdered and mutilated one by one and Holmes finally deduces a particularly ingenious solution. Even comparatively pedestrian entries like *Sherlock Holmes in Washington* (1943), *Pursuit to Algiers* (1945) and *Dressed to Kill/Sherlock Holmes and the Secret Code* (1946) offer brisk stories and comic by-play between Bruce (whose bumbling increasingly takes centre stage) and Rathbone. Rathbone and Bruce played the roles in a long-running radio series of the time, and make a cameo appearance as Holmes and Watson in the Olsen and Johnson vehicle *Crazy House* (1943).

Rathbone left such an impression on Holmes that it was twelve years before anyone had the nerve to take the role on the big screen, though the Great Detective's career in other media bustled along. The first television Holmes and Watson were Louis Hector and William Podmore in a pioneering NBC production, *The Three Garridebs* (1937). They were followed by Alan Napier/Melville Cooper (*The Adventure of the Speckled Band*, 1949), Milton Berle/Victor Moore with guest star Basil Rathbone as a Scotland Yard man (*Sherlock Holmes and the Mystery of the Sen Sen Murder*, 1949), John Longdon/Campbell Singer (*The Man with the Twisted Lip*, 1951), Alan Wheatley/Raymond Francis (*Sherlock Holmes*, 1951, series), Andrew Osborne/Philip King (*The Adventure of the Mazarin Stone*), Basil Rathbone/Martyn Green (*The Black Baronet*, 1953), Ronald Howard/Howard Marion Crawford (*Sherlock Holmes*, 1954, series), Boris Karloff in an adaptation

ABOVE Basil Rathbone, Evelyn Ankers, *Sherlock Holmes and the Voice of Terror*

of Heard's *A Taste for Honey/The Sting of Death* (1955), the voices of Paul Frees/Jim Backus (*Mr Magoo Storybook*, 1964), Douglas Wilmer/Nigel Stock (*Sherlock Holmes*, 1964–5, series), Peter Cushing/ Stock (*The Cases of Sherlock Holmes*, 1968, series), Czechs Radovan Lukavsky/Vaclav Voska (*The Longing of Sherlock Holmes*, 1972), Keith McConnell/Anthony Seerl (*Murder in Northumberland*, 1974), John Cleese/Willie Rushton (*Elementary, My Dear Watson*, 1975), Edward Fox solo as Watson (Kingsley Amis's *Dr Watson and the Darkwater Hall Mystery*, 1974), Leonard Nimoy/Burt Blackwell (*The Interior Motive*, 1975), Cleese/Arthur Lowe (*The Strange Case of the End of Civilisation as We Know It*, 1977), Christopher Plummer/Thorley Walters (*Silver Blaze*, 1977), Geoffrey Whitehead/Donald Pickering (*Sherlock Holmes and Dr Watson*, 1980, series), Keith Michell (*The Clue According to Sherlock Holmes*, 1980), Russians Vassily Livanov/Vitaly Solomin (*Sherlock Holmes and Dr Watson*, 1982 series), Frank Langella/Richard Woods, with George Morfogen as Moriarty, in *Sherlock Holmes* (1980), Peter Lawford/Donald O'Connor, with Mel Ferrer as Moriarty, in *Fantasy Island* ('Save Sherlock Holmes', 1982), Tom Baker/Terence Rigby (*The Hound of the Baskervilles*, 1982, serial), Guy Henry (*Young Sherlock: The Mystery of the Manor House*, 1982, serial), Peter Evans/William Griffis, actors working on a

Mystery Tour, on *Remington Steele* ('Elementary Steele', 1984), Roger Ostime/Hubert Rees, with Colin Jeavons as Moriarty, taking a back seat to a gang of urchin sleuths (*The Baker Street Boys*, 1984, series), Peter O'Toole/Ron Haddrick (four animated adaptations, *Sherlock Holmes and the Baskerville Curse*, *Sherlock Holmes and the Sign of Four*, *Sherlock Holmes and A Study in Scarlet*, *Sherlock Holmes and the Valley of Fear*, 1985), Brian Bedford/Patrick Monckton, with Graeme Campbell as Mycroft and John Colicos as Lestrade *and* Moriarty, in *Alfred Hitchcock Presents* ('My Dear Watson', 1988), Roland Rat (*Tales of the Rodent Sherlock Holmes*, 1989), Hugh Fraser/Ronald Fraser in *QED* ('Murder on the Bluebell Line', 1992), and Richard E. Grant, with Frank Finlay as Sir Arthur Conan Doyle, in *Encounters* ('The Other Side', 1992).

On radio in the UK and US, Holmes has been played by (among many) Carleton Hobbs, Basil Rathbone, William Gillette, Tom Conway, Richard Gordon, Clive Brook, John Stanley, Robert Powell, Dinsdale Landen, Arthur Wontner, Sir Cedric Hardwicke, Alan Wheatley, John Gielgud (with Ralph Richardson as Watson and Orson Welles as Moriarty), Hugh Manning, John Moffatt and Simon Callow.

In 1958, Hammer Films produced Terence Fisher's *The Hound of the Baskervilles*. Peter

Cushing and André Morell are an excellent Holmes and Watson, breaking the slightly camp and dithery Rathbone-Bruce mould with direct and sensible playing, depicting the heroes morally and physically as men of action who relish their peppery dialogue exchanges. Typically Hammer in its corrupt aristocracy (Christopher Lee's Sir Henry is cowardly and supercilious) and dangerous sensuality (Ewen Solon's web-handed Stapleton is a lesser villain than Marla Landi's barefoot peasant temptress), the film was less commercially successful than the studio's revivals of Dracula, Frankenstein and the Mummy, and plans for sequels were abandoned. Cushing's Holmes went to television, while Fisher decamped for Germany with Lee promoted to Holmes and Thorley

Walters as Watson for a bizarre, sub-Edgar Wallace adventure, *Sherlock Holmes und das Halsband des Todes/Sherlock Holmes and the Deadly Necklace* (1962), with Hans Sohnker as Moriarty. James Hill's *A Study in Terror* (1965) sets Holmes (Donald Houston) after Jack the Ripper in a further development of Fisher's *grand guignol* approach.

A gentle seam of pastiche/parody is opened up by Billy Wilder's *The Private Life of Sherlock Holmes* (1970), with Robert Stephens and Colin Blakely as Holmes and Watson and Christopher Lee demoted again to the role of Mycroft. Though it does some mildly scandalous delving into Holmes' love life, drug habits, psychological quirks and blatant exploitation of poor old Watson, the film is far from the cruel debunking one might

have expected from the acerbic Austrian. The ingenious plot involves a midget submarine, a dead canary, the Loch Ness Monster, Queen Victoria, a scheming spy (Genevieve Page), sinister Trappist monks, a mad Russian ballerina, and a gang of schoolboys 'with the faces of old men'. This was followed by broader spoofs. In *They Might Be Giants* (1971), a comedy with some fragile charm, George C. Scott is a judge who *thinks* he is Sherlock Holmes and is partnered by Joanne Woodward as a female Dr Watson, an idea reused for a TV movie, *The Return of the World's Greatest Detective* (1976), with Larry Hagman and Jenny O'Hara. Douglas Wilmer and Thorley Walters pop up briefly as Holmes and Watson in *The Adventure of Sherlock Holmes' Smarter Brother* (1975), with director-writer Gene Wilder doing his best as Sigerson, Holmes's insanely jealous and frankly inept sibling, to foil Leo McKern's amusing Moriarty. The worst Holmes and Watson are Peter Cook and Dudley Moore in Paul Morrissey's misguided tribute to the *Carry On* films, *The Hound of the Baskervilles* (1977). Michael Caine and Ben Kingsley in Thom Eberhardt's *Without a Clue* (1988) similarly flounder with the idea that Watson was the genius and Holmes merely a hired buffoon. Far better is the Venezuelan *Sherlock Holmes in Caracas* (1992), a loose adaptation of 'The Adventure of the Sussex Vampire', with Jean Manuel Montesinos and Gilbert Dacournan as a deconstructed Holmes and Watson tangling with a vampire beauty queen in South America amid anachronistic gags and Holmes's complaints that his character is unbelievable.

Nicholas Meyer's pastiche *The Seven-per-Cent Solution* was lavishly filmed by Herbert Ross in 1979, with Nicol Williamson and Robert Duvall as Holmes and Watson. In this revisionist adventure, Holmes suffers the delusion that his old mathematics tutor is an evil mastermind and the detective is treated for his cocaine addiction and personality problems by the eminent Dr Freud. Equally as radical in its own way is Bob Clark's *Murder By Decree* (1979), an apparent reworking of *A Study in Terror*. Christopher Plummer and James Mason are interesting, unstereotyped leads, again on the trail of the Ripper, but this time digging more into the background, and levelling indictments at the government of the day, the Royal Family and general social callousness. Holmes, the voice of pure reason, becomes an impassioned critic of injustice, playing the most effective emotional scene the unemotional

ABOVE André Morell, Peter Cushing, *The Hound of the Baskervilles* (1958)

character has ever been called upon to attempt, as he interviews cast-off Royal mistress Geneviève Bujold in the dustbin asylum to which she has been consigned. Barry Levinson's zestful *Young Sherlock Holmes/ Young Sherlock Holmes and the Pyramid of Fear* (1985), produced by Steven Spielberg, has Nicholas Rowe and Alan Cox as a teenage Holmes and Watson caught up in a plot that requires little deduction but does feature a hooded killer, a cult of Egyptian madmen with a pyramid concealed under London, a Jules Verne-esque flying machine, some startling hallucinations and a sneering Anthony Higgins as the young Professor Moriarty. Also aimed at younger audiences is the enchanting Disney cartoon *Basil of Baker Street/The Great Mouse Detective* (1986), with Rathbone returning briefly in voice and silhouette as Holmes. Basil is the fearless mouse who lives in the walls of 221b, Dr David Q. Dawson, his moustachioed sidekick, and Professor Ratigan, his rodent-like worst enemy.

The first Holmes movie made specifically for television was *The Hound of the Baskervilles* (1972) with Stewart Granger and Bernard Fox tracking down the perfidious William Shatner among notably seedy production values. Subsequently, Holmes has appeared in *Sherlock Holmes in New York* (1976), with Roger Moore and Patrick MacNee outclassed by an excellent Irene Adler from Charlotte

ABOVE Robert Stephens, Geneviève Page, Colin Blakely, *The Private Life of Sherlock Holmes*

Rampling and an outstanding Professor Moriarty from John Huston. Other telefilms include *The Masks of Death* (1984), with an aged Peter Cushing and John Mills facing perfidy during World War I, *The Return of Sherlock Holmes* (1986), with Michael Pennington as a defrosted Holmes partnered with Margaret Colin as a Watson descendant in a modern-day mystery patterned on the series *Adam Adamant Lives!* (1966–7), *Hands of a Murderer* (1989), with Edward Woodward and John Hillerman as Holmes and Watson, rescuing Mycroft (Peter Jeffrey) from Moriarty (Anthony Andrews) and clodhopping dialogue and performances all round; and *The Crucifer of Blood* (1991), with Charlton Heston and Richard Johnson. Ian Richardson is an impressive, slightly quixotic Holmes, in a pair of close adaptations, Douglas Hickox's *The Hound of the Baskervilles* (1983) and Desmond Davis's *The Sign of Four* (1983), with Donald Churchill and David Healy respectively as respectful Watsons and Cheri Lunghi as a winsome Mary Morstan. Christopher Lee and Patrick MacNee, returning to the roles after undistinguished initial attempts, are an ageing duo in the conceptually endearing but actually plodding multinational miniseries *Sherlock Holmes: The Golden Years* (1991), also released as two features, *Sherlock Holmes and the Leading Lady*, with Morgan Fairchild as Irene Adler, John Bennett as Sigmund Freud, Tom Lahm as Eliot Ness (!) and Cyril Shaps as Emperor Franz Joseph, and *Incident at Victoria Falls*, with Jenny Seagrove as Lillie Langtry, Claude Akins as Teddy Roosevelt and Alan Coates as A. J. Raffles, and flagging support throughout from Margaret John as Mrs Hudson, Kenway Baker as Lestrade and Jerome Willis as Mycroft.

These international co-productions were overshadowed by the success of Jeremy Brett's Holmes, who began in *The Adventures of Sherlock Holmes* (1984–5), with David Burke as Watson, and continued with *The Return of Sherlock Holmes* (1986), with Edward Hardwicke taking over as Watson, *The Casebook of Sherlock Holmes* (1991) and *The Memoirs of Sherlock Holmes* (1994), plus the feature-length *The Sign of Four* (1987), *The Hound of the Baskervilles* (1989), *The Master Blackmailer* (1992, from 'Charles Augustus Milverton'), *The Last Vampyre* (1993, from 'The Sussex Vampire'), and *The Eligible Bachelor* (1993, from 'The Noble Bachelor'). Brett absorbed the lessons of *The Seven-per-Cent Solution* and *Murder By Decree*, and used revisionist insights to illuminate

ABOVE Homosexuality: Donald Churchill, Dirk Bogarde, *Victim*

the darker corners of Doyle's originals, though his performance and the tone became erratic in later, murkier efforts. At once traditional in the return to the period minutiae of the Doyle stories and modernist in Brett's psychologically intense performance, the Granada adaptations currently stand as the definitive Sherlock Holmes, making the character accessible and widely popular over a century after his first appearance. KN

Homosexuality

While censorship was at its most severe, prior to 1960, homosexual characters had to be smuggled into crime drama as villains, whose theatricality masked their sexual preference. Such portrayals date back to Edward G. Robinson's unrequited love for Douglas Fairbanks Jr. in **Little Caesar**. Peter Lorre is a homosexual terrorist in *The Man Who Knew Too Much* (1934) and Gloria Holden a Lesbian vampire in *Dracula's Daughter* (1936). As played by Judith Anderson, there is little doubt about Mrs Danvers's inclinations in **Rebecca**. The stylistic excess of *film noir*, now regarded as camp, accommodated several homosexual villains. It is clear that casino boss George Macready once had a relationship with lackey Glenn Ford in **Gilda**. There are three homosexuals, played by Sydney Greenstreet, Elisha Cook Jr. and Peter Lorre, in **The Maltese Falcon**. Laird Cregar is a repressed homosexual cop in **Hot Spot/I Wake Up Screaming**. William Bendix gets significant pleasure from touching and beating Alan Ladd in **The Glass Key**. Hope Emerson is a lesbian masseuse in **Cry of the City**, and a sadistic prison governess in *Caged* (1950). Critic Keith Howes calls the murderer (Robert Walker) in **Strangers on a Train** 'one of the post-war screen's first queers.' Tokyo-based gangster Robert Ryan desires undercover agent Robert Stack and kills lover Cameron Mitchell in **House of Bamboo**. Hit men Earl Holliman and Lee Van Cleef are a couple in **The Big Combo**. Famously, the murder victim, homosexual in Richard Brooks's novel *The Brick Foxhole*, became a Jew in the film adaptation **Crossfire**. The first two films about the Leopold/Loeb murder case, **Rope** and **Compulsion**, made no mention of the killers' sexuality. Homosexuality was still being removed from literature as late as *Midnight Express* (1978) – in drug-smuggler Billy Hayes's autobiography, he accepts his Swedish cell-mate's advances. The gang boss's homosexuality in *The Great St. Louis Bank Robbery* (1958) almost vanished with the 19 minutes cut from the film by British censors. Up until the turn of the 60s no homosexuality could be inferred in British crime drama unless one counts the ambiguous leers perennial villain Harold Lang made at anything in trousers in many B-pictures. It was all the more surprising, therefore, that the ground-breaking film about a sympathetic, respectable homosexual came from Britain. In **Victim** Dirk Bogarde is the barrister who hunts down the blackmailers who caused his boyfriend's suicide. In introducing the concept of 'ordinary' homosexuals, the film is said to have been instrumental in the decriminalisation of male homosexuality in Britain in 1967.

Subsequent films were more open about homosexuality, but gay characters tended to remain villains or become tormented loners. The word 'gay', first used on screen in its modern sense by Cary Grant in *Bringing Up Baby* in 1938, was in use in Europe by the late 60s, but Gay Liberation, and latterly Awareness, has been largely unacknowledged in mainstream cinema. In the James Bond series, stereotyped gay villains – butch lesbian Rosa Klebb (Lotte Lenya) in *From Russia with Love* (1963), camp male couple Wint and Kidd (Bruce Glover, Putter Smith) in *Diamonds Are Forever* (1971) – could be said to complement the stereotyped heterosexual characters. But in other films of the period homosexuals inhabited an exclusively sleazy milieu. In **The Detective** the killer confesses, 'I felt more guilty about being a homosexual than a murderer.' *The Kremlin Letter* (1969), an espionage thriller obsessed with sexual 'perversion', includes two gay

ABOVE Homosexuality: William Windom, *The Detective*

men (George Sanders, Micheál MacLiammóir) and a lesbian (Vonetta McGee) seduction. In **Hickey & Boggs** a gay private eye (Robert Culp) is seen guiltily creeping out of a rent boy's apartment. In *Freebie and the Bean* (1974) rogue cop James Caan kills a psychotic transvestite in a public lavatory. Based on a true story, **Dog Day Afternoon** is about a bank robber (Al Pacino) who wanted to finance his boyfriend's sex-change operation. Even the gay crime farce *The Ritz* (1976) is set in a bath-house.

The 80s began with militant gay protests against *Cruising* (1980), about an undercover cop (Al Pacino) prowling the gay SM demimonde. To some critics the film appeared to suggest that all gay men are leather-clad degenerates and that homosexuality is contagious. The film was successful enough to encourage a wave of films in which cops or private eyes were confronted by gay life. These include *Partners* (1982), *La Triche* (1983), *El crack II, Delitto al blue* (1984). General acceptance of political correctness put paid to gay villains during the second half of the 80s. The homosexuality of 'Buffalo Bill', the serial killer in *The Silence of the Lambs* (1990), is integral to the plot, though there were protests by some gays.

'Queer' cinema (films with gay themes made by gay people) became well established in art houses during the 90s. Isaac

Julien, Britain's first black gay director, tried one commercial film, the murder mystery *Young Soul Rebels* (1991). Two HIV+ men go on a crime spree in *The Living End* (1992). A gay man kills his lover in *Being at Home with Claude* (1992). The third film about Leopold and Loeb, *Swoon* (1992), is specifically about homophobia. Hollywood answered back with *Bound* (1996), a gay-friendly suspense thriller in which the women who plot to cheat the mob happen to be lesbian. DM

L'Horloger de Saint-Paul/ The Watchmaker of St Paul

For his debut as a feature director, the former critic and publicist Tavernier changed Simenon's American location to Lyon for his tale of generational (mis)understandings. Michel Descombes (Noiret) is an ordinary watchmaker, abandoned by his wife, visiting the local café for chats with friends. His quiet life is disturbed by the police searching for his son (Rougerie). The boy has killed a night-guard at a factory and is on the run with his girl-friend. Gradually, a friendship develops between Michel and the investigating officer, Guibout (Rochefort), both being lonely men having trouble with their children. Michel also begins to realise that his son had become a stranger and he tries to get closer to his stubborn son's point of view. Only when the boy is in prison will father and son succeed in genuinely talking to each other. Tavernier's classic directorial style leaves centre stage to Noiret's contained yet intense performance, perfectly balanced by Rochefort's edgier, more cunning persona. PW

1973/France/105m/Lira/*p* Raymond Danon/ *d*/*co-s* Bertrand Tavernier/*co-s* Jean Aurenche, Pierre Bost/*orig* Georges Simenon *L'Horloger d'Éverton* (1954)/*c* Pierre-William Glenn/*m* Philippe Sarde/*lp* Philippe Noiret, Jean Rochefort, Jacques Denis, Julien Bertheau, Yves Afonso.

The Hot Rock/How to Steal a Diamond in Four Uneasy Lessons

An amusing if rather wayward caper comedy based on a novel by Donald Westlake, this features a quartet of professional crooks who are hired to steal a famous diamond only to lose it and then spend the rest of the picture creating elaborate capers to retrieve it. Moments of genuine suspense (via director Yates) mesh perfectly with wacky comedy scenes and characterisations (especially when Mostel's shyster lawyer steps into

frame). A later film, *The Bank Shot* (1974), was based on the same novel. TV

1972/105m/FOX/*p* Hal Landers, Bobby Roberts/*d* Peter Yates/*s* William Goldman/ *c* Ed Brown/*m* Quincy Jones/*lp* Robert Redford, George Segal, Ron Leibman, Paul Sand, Zero Mostel.

Hot Spot/I Wake Up Screaming

High-key lighting and a tight screenplay lend an edge to this example of the 'man in the frame' plot. Mature is a press agent arrested for the murder of a client (Landis) by a police detective bent on securing his conviction because Landis has spurned his own advances. Mature breaks jail and with the victim's sister (Grable in a rare non-musical role) succeeds in identifying the killer as a sexually inadequate neighbour of the dead woman. The proceedings are dominated by the obsessive, vengeful policeman, and the casting in this role of the bulky Cregar provides, as does the presence of Elisha Cook as the pathetic murderer, an extra layer of iconic resonance in what is in some respects a routine undertaking. Oddly, in Steve Fisher's source novel, laid in Hollywood rather than in the New York of the movie, the detective is characterised not as fat but as conspicuously thin. The property was remade by the same studio as *Vicki* (directed by Harry Horner, 1953). TP

1941/82m/FOX/*p* Milton Sperling/*d* H. Bruce Humberstone/*s* Dwight Taylor/ *c* Edward Cronjager/*m* Cyril J. Mockridge/ *lp* Betty Grable, Victor Mature, Laird Cregar, Carole Landis, Elisha Cook Jr.

House of Bamboo

In post-war Japan Ryan has gathered about him a group of ex-US Army personnel and formed them into a criminal gang. In a pre-credit sequence they rob an Army munitions train. Stack is sent by the Army to infiltrate the gang. He manages to gain Ryan's confidence and becomes his deputy, to the extent that Ryan disposes of his previous second-in-command by shooting him as he lies in a bath. Stack is aided by Mariko, a Japanese woman who is the widow of one of Ryan's men. While their relationship, played out through the clash of cultures, clearly fascinates Fuller, there is also a barely concealed sexual element in Ryan's feelings for Stack, which makes him a vulnerable figure despite his brutality and evident mental instability. At the end there is a shoot-out in a children's playground; Stack walks away leaving

Ryan's body spinning on a round-about. Fuller makes full use of CinemaScope and colour to contrast the visual icons of Japanese society (cherry blossom, Kabuki theatre) with the American military presence. EB

1955/105m/FOX/*p* Buddy Adler/*d* Samuel Fuller/*s* Harry Kleiner/*c* Joe MacDonald/ *m* Leigh Harline/*lp* Robert Ryan, Robert Stack, Shirley Yamaguchi, Cameron Mitchell, Brad Dexter.

The House on 92nd Street

Almost any issue that Hollywood wanted to make a film about could be refracted through the generic conventions of the crime film. This tells a story, based on FBI files, of the war-time penetration of a Nazi spy ring by American agents, done in the format of a police procedural, as reported in newsreel style. Producer de Rochemont had been the creator of the *March of Time* series (whose overly sonorous narration and sledgehammer editing were satirised in *Citizen Kane*, 1941). The film was partly shot on the actual locations where the events reported had happened, and many of the actors used were non-professionals. But the Nazis were portrayed in best Hollywood style, straight from the murky world of *film noir*. The central character, Dietrich (Eythe), is recruited by the Nazis before the war, but agrees to become a double agent. Once war breaks out he provides valuable information on German attempts to discover the secrets of the American atomic programme. Eventually the Nazis learn of his FBI connections, but not before he has uncovered the identity of their mole in the US government. The documentary style of the film spawned a number of imitations such as **Call Northside 777** and **The Naked City**. EB

1945/89m/FOX/*p* Louis de Rochemont/ *d* Henry Hathaway/*s* Barré Lyndon, Charles G. Booth, John Monks Jr/*c* Norbert Brodine/ *m* David Buttolph/*lp* William Eythe, Lloyd Nolan, Signe Hasso, Gene Lockhart, Leo G. Carroll.

Household, Geoffrey (Edward West) (1900–88)

Household was a British thriller novelist who specialised in the hunt or chase narrative usually focusing on gentleman-adventurers with a flair for blood sports and a deep-rooted sense of public school chivalry. Household's classic novel was *Rogue Male* (published in 1939) which was filmed as an

ABOVE Joan Dowling, Harry Fowler, *Hue and Cry*

exciting, atmospheric chase thriller by Fritz Lang in 1941 as *Man Hunt* (1941); and in which Walter Pidgeon's big-game hunter hero himself becomes the hunted animal. An enjoyable 1976 TV version was produced by BBC TV in collaboration with the original film's producer 20th Century-Fox under director Clive Donner. *Rough Shoot* (1952) features a similar Richard Hannay-type hero with Joel McCrea as a US Army officer who accidentally shoots a poacher, panics, and hides the body (it was not he who fired the fatal shot). Eric Ambler wrote the screenplay from Household's 1951 novel. Following on, the comedy *Brandy for the Parson* (1952) sees young couple James Donald and Jean Lodge becoming involved with Kenneth More's brandy smuggler while on a yachting holiday and ending up being pursued cross-country by customs men. Modern politics are at the centre of *Deadly Harvest* (1972), based on Household's 1960 novel *Watcher in the Shadows*, in which defected Russian army officer Richard Boone, living incognito in the US, is stalked by a mysterious figure from his past. TV

Hue and Cry

Explicitly a fantasy – 'Don't dream in my time' the school boy hero is instructed by his boss, only for those dreams to come true – *Hue and Cry* achieves a genuine sense of community in its depiction of gangs of boys making London's bomb-sites their private kingdom. This gives great force to the climax in which, in the manner of **The Blue Lamp**, crowds of youngsters, working together in unison, trap the criminals. The appeal of the film lies in Crichton's ability to animate this sense of community and so transform London's bomb-sites from sad to happy images. The result is a film remarkably similar to John Boorman's *Hope and Glory* (1987), but from the point of the working-class children, rather than the film it might have been expected to be like, *Emil and the Detectives*. Fowler is the youth who can't settle in a job who discovers that his favourite penny dreadful, *The Trump*, is being used by a criminal mastermind to tell his gang when and where to commit a series of robberies. When the police won't believe him, Fowler rounds together his own gang and with the reluctant help of eccentric seri-

al writer Sim they defeat the gang. The mix of location shooting and shadowy studio sets – notably Sim's echoey stairwell – works well, while the restless, continual movement of the boys give the narrative an energy it might not have had otherwise. A mark of the film's cheery innocence – a feature which won it instant approval on its release - is that, having failed to get White, the duplicitous secretary at *The Trump*, to tell who the criminal mastermind is by tickling her with a feather, the kids then think of the worst torture possible. They settle for frightening her with a white mouse – and succeed. Warner, soon to become Britain's favourite police constable, plays the villain with suitable oiliness. PH

1946/GB/82m/Ealing/*p* Michael Balcon/ *d* Charles Crichton/*s* T.E.B. Clarke/*c* Douglas Slocombe/*m* Georges Auric/*lp* Alastair Sim, Jack Warner, Harry Fowler, Valerie White, Frederick Piper.

Hughes, Dorothy B[elle] (1904–93)

Dorothy B. Hughes was one of a small number of seminal women American crimewriters who rose to prominence in the first half of the century. Born and brought up in Kansas City, she lived and worked for the majority of her life in New Mexico. Dorothy B. Hughes began her career as a journalist and published poetry before starting to write novels. The majority of her fourteen crime and mystery novels appeared during the 1940s and early 1950s. From her debut novel *The So Blue Marble* (1940) through *Ride the Pink Horse* (1946) to *The Davidian Report* (1952), Hughes's memorable writing, brought unusually complex, psychological suspense to the genre, foreshadowing the work of **Patricia Highsmith**. This formula found critical and popular acclaim and a number of her novels were optioned for the screen. This led to two interesting genre movies, *The Fallen Sparrow* (1943, Richard Wallace), a vehicle for John Garfield, and **Ride the Pink Horse**. The latter was made into a TV movie by Don Siegel in 1964 under the title *The Hanged Man*. Her main cinematic claim to fame, however, came in 1950 when Hollywood maverick Nicholas Ray adapted **In a Lonely Place** and created one of the masterpieces of the *film noir* cycle. Dorothy B. Hughes wrote her last novel, *The Expendable Man* (which exemplifies the leftward-leaning liberal strain of her work), in 1963. Dorothy B. Hughes was also a highly respected critic in the crime genre, publishing articles and reviews for various magazines and newspapers. AW

Den hvide slavehandels sidste offer/ The White Slave Trade's Last Victim

The first Scandinavian white slavery film was probably Viggo Larsen's 155 metre long *Den hvide slavinde* (1906) for Nordisk. Then Fotorama released Alfred Lind's *Den hvide slavehandel* (1910) which ran for almost an hour and proved so successful that Nordisk followed suit and asked August Blom to make *Den hvide slavehandel I* , promoting it as the first feature film in film history, although its running time was slightly shorter than Lind's film. In Britain and in Germany, this film established the feasibility of screening 'long films' in cinema halls. A sequel was quickly made, *Den hvide slavehandel II/Slavehandlerens flugt* (1910) by Fotorama, but Nordisk replied with their own sequel, *Den hvide slavehandel II/Den hvide slavehandels sidste offer*, again directed by Blom and released in January 1911. The plot tells of an orphan, Edith von Felsen (Wieth) who, on a journey to London, is befriended by a woman involved in a white slavery gang. In London, Edith is abducted and immediately delivered to her first client. A young engineer (Olsen) who met her during the journey and fails to find her at the London address he had been given, eventually tracks her down and rescues her after a spectacular rooftop chase. Although primarily shot with single-camera set-ups, Blom infused a sense of excitement into the film with his location shots on the train and on the boat, using natural light to expressive effect. A third instalment, *Den hvide slavehandel III*, directed by Urban Gad for Nordisk, followed in 1912 while Blom went on to make his best known spectacular, *Atlantis* (1913). PW

1910/Denmark/50metres/Nordisk/*p* Ole Olsen/*d* August Blom/*s* Peter Christensen/ *c* Axel Graatkjaer/*lp* Clara Wieth, Lauritz Olsen, Thora Meincke, Ingeborg Rasmussen, Ella la Cour, Aage Brandt.

I

I Am a Fugitive from a Chain Gang

One of a cycle of Warner Bros. melodramas (**The Public Enemy**, *Wild Boys of the Road*, 1933, *Black Legion*, 1936, **Angels with Dirty Faces**) which focus on the social causes of crime rather than follow **Little Caesar** and **Scarface** by demonising gangsters as inherently evil or perverted freaks. Based on

the autobiography of Robert E. Burns, the film follows James Allen (Muni), an innocent ex-doughboy who falls semi-accidentally into crime and then suffers the torments of the damned in a *grand guignol* labour camp in the Deep South. He escapes and through hard work rises from section-hand to architect in Horatio Alger style, only to be sucked back into the nightmare when his true identity is made known. While the sequences of suffering and servitude in the fields and swamps remain horrific, the most unsettling scenes in the film show the gradual dismantling of the success Allen has made of his life, as his wife (Farrell) and friends turn against him, and the inferno waits below. Finally, the girl (Vinson) who truly loves Allen meets him in the street, and finds him still a fugitive; she asks him how he lives, and he simply, bitterly explains 'I steal' as the film fades out. Influential enough in its time to prompt official enquiries into the practices of the chain gang (abolished in 1937) and imitative movies like *Hell's Highway* (1932), *Road Gang* (1933) and *Boy Slaves* (1936), this remains notable for its semi-documentary horrors and Muni's unforced, affecting performance. KN

1932/93m/WB/*p* Hal B. Wallis/*d* Mervyn LeRoy/*s* Brown Holmes, Howard J. Green *orig* Robert E. Burns/*c* Sol Polito/*m* Bernhard Kaun/*lp* Paul Muni, Glenda Farrell, Helen Vinson, Preston Foster, Edward J. McNamara, Hale Hamilton

I Confess

Set and filmed largely in Quebec, and exploiting the city's architectural atmosphere, rich in the traditions of French Catholicism, *I Confess* is the Hitchcock film which treats most fully the religious theme of the universality and transference of guilt which some commentators see as central to his work. The plot turns on what might be called a diabolic situation: a murderer (Hasse) admits his crime to a priest in the confessional; the latter (Clift) is bound by his vow of silence, and circumstantial evidence increasingly places him under suspicion for the murder, since the victim was blackmailing him over an affair, prior to his entering the priesthood, with a woman (Baxter) now married to a prominent citizen. The priest enters upon a form of Calvary, by being put on trial for the murder; his acquittal leaves the crowd hostile, and it is by a succession of events culminating in what might be construed as divine intervention that his name is ultimately cleared. Despite the sensuous quality of the flashback to the love affair, *I Confess* has an austerity which prefigures that of **The Wrong Man**. At an intra-mural level, it is interesting to speculate on the degree to which the protagonist's outcast status mirrors Hitchcock's attested unhappiness with Clift's adherence to 'method acting' in his performance. TP

1953/95m/WB/*p*/*d* Alfred Hitchcock/ *s* George Tabori, William Archibald/*c* Robert

ABOVE Paul Muni, Lew Kelly, Preston Foster, *I Am a Fugitive from a Chain Gang*

ABOVE Montgomery Clift, *I Confess*

Burks/*m* Dimitri Tiomkin/*lp* Montgomery Clift, Anne Baxter, Karl Malden, Brian Aherne, O.E. Hasse.

I Saw What You Did

Part suspense drama, part horror yarn, this curious second-feature tells of two teenage girls who make prank phone calls to complete strangers (they always announce 'I saw what you did; I know who you are') who unfortunately hit upon Ireland just after he has killed his wife. Believing them, he begins tracking them down. Crawford's only purpose in this film, outside of the drawing power of her name, is to appear as Ireland's predatory lover and the girls' eventual protector. McGivern's screenplay was based on the novel *Out of the Dark* by Ursula Curtiss. A Curtiss novel was also the basis for the Robert Aldrich-produced *What Ever Happened to Aunt Alice* in 1969. TV

1965/82m/U/*p/d* William Castle/*s* William P. McGivern/*c* Joseph Biroc/*m* Van Alexander/ *lp* Joan Crawford, John Ireland, Leif Erickson.

In a Lonely Place

Rebellious screen writer with a nasty temper (Bogart) hooks up with a smart B-movie actress (Grahame) and romance blossoms. Their happiness is, however, short-lived and the relationship begins to crack apart when

he becomes the prime suspect in a murder case. An almost unrecognisable adaptation of **Dorothy B. Hughes** novel (which was written as a first-person narrative from a killer's point of view), *In a Lonely Place* is nonetheless a classic psychological suspense thriller.

Moreover, it has at its heart the intelligent and sensuous depiction of an adult romance, undermined by violence and the betrayal of trust. Ray, after his astonishing debut feature **They Live by Night**, was hired by Bogart to direct the film for the star's own company, Santana Productions, and rewarded the choice by skilfully drawing out intense drama and dramatic depth in the characterisations. Embellished by edgy performances, particularly from Bogart in, arguably, his most challenging role ever, an articulate, sharp script, ever stylish direction and a smart use of Hollywood as an ironic backdrop to the story. AW

1950/94m/COL/*p* Robert Lord/*d* Nicholas Ray/*s* Andrew Solt/*c* Burnett Guffey/*m* George Antheil/*lp* Humphrey Bogart, Gloria Grahame, Frank Lovejoy, Carl Benton Reid.

In Cold Blood

In Kansas in 1959 two released convicts murder a farmer and his family, believing their house contains a safe full of cash. In fact they get away with a mere $43. They escape to Mexico, but eventually return to Kansas, where they are arrested, convicted and executed. Truman Capote's documentary novel sought to understand this banal yet shocking crime by the accretion of a mountain of detail concerning the criminals' background and the community they so bru-

ABOVE Frank Lovejoy, Jeff Donnell, Humphrey Bogart, Gloria Grahame, *In a Lonely Place*

tally disrupt. Brooks's film faced acute problems in following the same strategy, since the limitations of screen time require him to be selective with detail. Moreover, the tendency of audiences to identify with the protagonists (intensified by the emotive acting of Blake and Wilson) inevitably leads the two killers to be treated with a sympathy Capote had largely avoided. As a result the scene of the killers' execution at the end has been seen as making anti-capital punishment points in a way that are irrelevant to Capote's intentions. Far more successful is Hall's cinematography, which achieves a bleak but memorable poetry in its evocation of a desolate Kansas, a fitting locale for the grim events related. The end result is rather like Bruce Springsteen's *Nebraska* album, bleak in parts but a little too calculated to convince. EB

1967/134m/COL/*p*/*d*/*s* Richard Brooks/*c* Conrad Hall/*m* Quincy Jones/*lp* Robert Blake, Scott Wilson, John Forsythe, Paul Stewart, Jeff Corey.

In the Heat of the Night

When a rich white man is murdered in the Mississippi town of Sparta, Virgil Tibbs (Poitier), a black man waiting at the train station, is arrested. His wallet is full of money, but the sheriff, Gillespie (Steiger), is deflated by discovering that Tibbs is a Philadelphia detective. Tibbs is ordered by his boss to help, and Gillespie is forced to accept his assistance by the local hierarchy. In the process Tibbs exposes Sparta's underlying racism. Gillespie protects him, grudgingly, from the rednecks, and they begin to respect each other. Hailed as a liberal landmark, the film is a slick thriller. Steiger demonstrates his technical brilliance, adds a rocklike charisma reminiscent of Spencer Tracy and won an Oscar and Poitier shines in his finely crafted persona of an intelligent, sensitive, morally superior black man. MP

1967/109m/Mirisch/*p* Walter Mirisch/ *d* Norman Jewison/*s* Stirling Silliphant/ *c* Haskell Wexler/*m* Quincy Jones/*lp* Sidney Poitier, Rod Steiger, Warren Oates, Quentin Dean, James Patterson.

Indian Crime Films

Indian cinema cannot easily be divided into the same genres as Euro-American films because the narrative structures and the notions of character deployed in them vary considerably from those in the West. The narrative structures take a meandering route encompassing a large number of 'generic strands', ranging from the musical to comedy via adventure stories and thrillers, courtroom dramas or even ghost stories and horror or religious iconography. A linear plot development is a rare item in India's sound cinema prior to the mid-50s 'art cinema'. The idea of a drama as the interaction between psychologically complex individuals is also a fairly recent and by no means widespread phenomenon in Indian cinema. Instead, protagonists tend to be presented as carriers of specific social values and positions, and it is the historical conflict between incompatible values and aspirations which constitutes the drama, not the conflict between individuals or within individuals as conceptualised in Western notions of 'psychological realism'. Consequently, a western perspective would regard such protagonists as stereotypes or one-dimensional cardboard figures.

From a western perspective, there are few 'thrillers' or 'detective' movies in India but a great many melodramas revolving around or driven by criminal activities. For instance, wife-beating is often not presented as a crime but as a legitimate expression of loving though perhaps frustrated concern. Similarly, rape, though officially a crime, may be presented as a legitimate expression of irresistible desire to which the rape-victim is supposed to respond by falling in love with or at least settling down with the rapist. In Chandulal Shah's modernisation melodrama *Miss 1933* (1933), the heroine successfully resists a rape-attempt by a wealthy boy and she is put on trial for attempting to murder her attacker. Under the cloak of the custom of child marriage, the sale and rape of children was often not presented as a crime. Sisir Bhaduri and Naresh Mitra's *Andhare Alo (The Influence of Love*, 1922), based on a story by the Bengali 'reform novelist' Saratchandra Chatterjee, sympathises with the hero as he is torn between desire for his eleven-year-old bride and a courtesan. He is not presented as a rapist of children. The kind of banditry which in Hollywood films would be part of the Western genre (gangs hired by landowners to enforce their domination; attacks on small peasant communities; kidnapping and sexual assaults of various kinds; gangs robbing and killing travellers) is still a contemporary phenomenon in India where the rural gangster may be referred to as a dacoit, an outlaw (the iconography of the dacoit is close to that of the Mexican bandido in Westerns).

ABOVE Sidney Poitier, Rod Steiger, *In the Heat of the Night*

Initially, crime was represented primarily as a moral, rather than as a psychological or a legal, issue in a society in the throes of modernisation, that is to say, as a conflict between tradition (governed by strict caste codes the infringement of which, although strictly speaking not illegal, would trigger profoundly tragic and often lethal effects) and the modern, represented as 'alien' (imposed or introduced by the colonial power). The issue of, for instance, women's human rights does not figure very largely in such a conflict because women tend to be embodiments of what happens to 'the nation' or to 'traditional values' when urbanisation and individualism rear their heads. The conflict between an implied religious order (presented as traditional and indigenous) and a civil society based on the rights of the individual (presented as modern and Western-derived) is precisely what is dramatised in many of the 'socials' (a general term for dramas set in the twentieth century chronicling changes in the status of the family, problems of lineage and affiliation through marriage, conventions of caste and conflicts between a collective and an individual). In other words, the definition of what is legitimate social behaviour is often the central problem posed by the film and praised or condemned depending on whether one regrets or advocates social reform and change.

In the film generally accepted as the inauguration of melodrama, *Bismi Sadi* (*20th Century*, 1924), Homi Master tells of a street hawker who becomes a cotton mill owner ruthlessly exploiting his workforce and denying them even the most basic rights as workers; yet, retribution comes in moral terms rather than in legal intervention: it is the moral suffering of his wife and the 'dishonouring' of his daughter which signal that his behaviour is inhuman and he is redeemed as he apologises to his family on his deathbed. The perils of modernity are presented in the form of a crime-melodrama in Ardeshir Irani and Naval Gandhi's *Paap No Fej* (*The Debt of Sin*, 1924). The film consciously adopts Hollywood-derived strategies such as parallel cutting as a *femme fatale* and her jailbird cousin blackmail and swindle her aged husband and ruin her lover. The setting is 'the city' with its bars and racetracks symbolising the generalisation of corruption and moral turpitude; and, like the films of Cecil B. DeMille in Hollywood, *Paap No Fej* derives its energy from the depiction of what it purports to condemn. In *Sadguni Sushila* (*Sushila the Virtuous*, 1924), Kanjibhai Rathod embarked on the police-crime-melodrama, except that the police chief is the leader of a gang of thieves and murderers who frame a tradition-minded innocent man. The first recorded example of a crime film based on a contemporary event, known as the

Champsi-Haridas murder case in Bombay, was Kanjibhai Rathod's *Kala Naag* (*Triumph of Justice*, 1924). Homi Master followed this with a film based on the Bawla murder case, *Kulin Kanta* (1925): the maharaja of Holkar desired to possess a dancing girl who wished to remain faithful to her lover; the maharaja had the man abducted in full public view and murdered.

Corruption, theft, embezzlement, blackmail and pimping are the order of the day in two films set among Bombay's colonial bourgeoisie, Manilal Joshi's *Mojili Mumbai* (*Slaves of Luxury*, 1925) and Nanubhai Desai's *Mumbai ni Mohini* (*Social Pirates/Night Side of Bombay*, 1925). The moral-social changes at issue often become the focus, after numerous killings or other criminal acts, of a courtroom drama which closes the film, as in Homi Master's widow-remarriage drama *Samaj Ki Bhool* (1934), Mehboob Khan's *Andaz* (1949) and, in the South, Krishnan-Panju's *Parasakthi* (*The Goddess*, 1952). In the pre-Independence era, the main crime thriller, in Western terms, was the German émigré (and later Nazi) Franz Osten's *Jawani ki Hawa* (1935), starring Devika Rani. When a body is thrown off a moving train, a number of people accuse themselves of the murder for a variety of reasons. Their respective motivations are the focus of the movie which is actually about the right of a woman to choose her own husband. The Marathi-Hindi melodrama *Chhaya* (1936), by Master Vinayak, contains a catalogue of crimes ranging from prostitution and perjury (by the heroine) to extortion (by a doctor), robbery, infanticide, false accusations of rape and so on, all in the service of proving that a man's reputation is his greatest asset. Other films that could be described as crime thrillers include Moti B. Gidwani's *Zamindar* (1942), Roop K. Shorey's *Ek Thi Ladki* (1949), Kamal Amrohi's strange *Mahal* (1949) which does approximate closely to a psychological thriller, K. Ramnoth's updated version of Victor Hugo's *Les Misérables*, the Tamil/Telugu bilingual *Ezhai Padum Padu/ Beedala Patlu* (1950) and a number of others. However, excluding the adventure serials such as those starring the Australian circus performer Fearless Nadia in the 30s and 40s, the consensus is that the crime melodrama reached a new stage with Gyan Mukherjee's *Kismet* (1943) starring Ashok Kumar as a pickpocket, and especially Raj Kapoor's *Awara* (*The Tramp*, 1951), in which Raju, played by Kapoor as a Chaplinesque figure, has two father-figures: a dacoit (outlaw) and

a judge, and he is ultimately defended in court by his lover (in the film as well as in real life), Nargis.

The actor who came to embody the crime thriller genre in the 50s was Dev Anand. Guru Dutt contributed to the genre with *Jaal* (*The Net*, 1952), starring Dev Anand as a gold smuggler in Goa. Dutt's film contains some classic thriller scenes, particularly the opening sequences, and an extraordinary song-sequence in which the smuggler seduces the heroine (Geeta Bali) into becoming his accomplice. The main directors of the genre at the time were Raj Khosla whose *CID* (1956) starred Dev Anand as a police inspector investigating the death of a newspaper editor, and Shakti Samanta with *Howrah Bridge*, *Detective* (both 1958) and *China Town* (1962), until he abruptly switched to romances in colour in the mid-60s. Raj Khosla was also responsible for the classic *Woh Kaun Thi* (*Who Was She?*, 1964), reminiscent of both **Vertigo** and **Laura**. Vijay Anand's *Jewel Thief* (1967) starring Dev Anand deploys aspects of the *Fantômas*-type serial with concealed bars, moving walls and hidden safes as well as the scenery of international tourism (snow-lifts, aeroplanes), setting the tone for much of the late-60s Hindi cinema. The great Satyajit Ray also filmed two of his Sherlock Holmes pastiches written for children, featuring the detective Feluda: *Sonar Kella* (*The Golden Fortress*, 1974) and *Joi Baba Felunath* (*The Elephant God*, 1978).

The most recent redirection of the crime movie was inaugurated by Amitab Bachchan in Yash Copra's **Deewar/I'll Die for Mama**. Whereas, in Western terms, Dev Anand belongs to the era of Cary Grant, Bachchan belongs to the era of Clint Eastwood and his *Dirty Harry*-type heroes. Bachchan tends to play a vigilante, a martyr driven to take the law into his own hands, violently. From the films that followed in the wake of **The Godfather**, the most interesting is Mani Rathnam's *Nayakan* (1987) starring Kamalahasan in a fictional version of the Bombay gangster Varadarajan Mudaliar's life.

Finally, given the tendency in Indian cinema to remake successful Hollywood films, it is worth signalling Balu Mahendra's remake of **Psycho** in Tamil, *Moodupani* (1980). The latest crime film to gain national as well as international notoriety is Shekar Kapur's *Bandit Queen* (1994) recounting the harrowing life of the female dacoit Phoolan Devi. Although Phoolan Devi's real-life career had

ABOVE Indian Crime Films: Seema Biswas as Phoolan Devi, *Bandit Queen*

sparked a number of female dacoit movies, including a musical version of her own exploits, Kapur's film ran into serious censorship problems in India for its explicit denunciation of the ghastly crimes committed by the local elite Thakur caste, the crimes committed by the police who routinely rape their female prisoners, and especially for conveying to the audience the ways in which men use rape as a way of asserting power over women. PW

L'Indic

Leroy followed up his routine thriller *Légitime défense* (1981) with *L'Indic*, a story taken from the ex-cop Roger Borniche's novel. Auteuil as inspector Bertrand gets Sylvia (Rocard) to inform on the gang of her lover (Lhermitte) against a background of Parisian mob wars between the Corsicans, led by Malaggione (Donnadieu) and their rivals. Leroy's often poorly scripted films usually contained some captivatingly filmed sequences, like Malaggione's escape from a police dragnet. He went on to make an exposé of the world of journalism scripted by Françoise Giroud, *Le 4e Pouvoir* (1985). PW

1982/France/95m/TF1/*p/co-s* Jean

ABOVE Informants: Robert De Niro, Ray Liotta, *GoodFellas*

Kerchner/*d/co-s* Serge Leroy/*co-s* Didier Decoin/*orig* Roger Borniche/*c* André Domage/*m* Michel Magne/*lp* Daniel Auteuil, Thierry Lhermitte, Pascale Rocard, Bernard-Pierre Donnadieu, Michel Beaune.

Informants

Schoolboy prejudice against tale-tellers influences most movie depictions of informants, who tend to be squirming, treacherous rats in prison movies like **Brute Force** just as they are, more legitimately, in prisoner-of-war movies like *Stalag 17* (1953) or *Danger Within* (1959). From the dope addict (Arthur Edmund Carewe) suffering under the Third Degree in *Mystery of a Wax Museum* (1932) through the pathetic loser (Elisha Cook Jr) of **The Big Sleep** and the mendacious harridan (Betty Garde) who puts an innocent man in jail in **Call Northside 777** to the more-or-less comic use of characters like Antonio Fargas as Huggy Bear on *Starsky and Hutch* (1975–9), Peter Jurasik as Sid the Snitch on *Hill Street Blues* (1981–7) and Joe Pesci in the *Lethal Weapon* sequels, there is a feeling that informants, whether on a one-off basis or habitual snitches, squealers or stoolies, are pathetic and parasitic individuals, held in as much contempt by police contacts as they are by criminal associates. The bullying tactics used by the police to make crooks turn informant are examined in **La Balance**, one of the few films to touch on the symbiosis between cop and snitch. A rare exception to the snivelling rule is the eponymous 'squeaker' of Edgar Wallace's oft-filmed novel (1930, 1937, 1965), a master criminal fence who sends informing notes to Scotland Yard to discipline the underworld he rules.

The archetypal movie squealer is the self-

ABOVE Informants: Marlon Brando, *On the Waterfront*

ABOVE Roger Livesey, Mary Murphy, *The Intimate Stranger*

about a divorcé (James Caan) searching for his children when his wife's new husband, a mafia turncoat, enters the Federal Witness Protection Program. The scheme is used to comic effect in *My Blue Heaven* (1990) in which Steve Martin is sent to a suburban community which turns out to consist entirely of ex-mob informers. KN

An Inspector Calls

This interesting film uses the process of investigation of a death to lay moral not legal blame on a collection of characters. Sim is the mysterious inspector of the title. He interrupts a family gathering hosted by Young's gruff paterfamilias to celebrate the engagement of his daughter (Moore) to the son of a titled local landowner, bearing news of the suicide of an innocent young girl (Wenham). It transpires that all gathered there are responsible in some part for her downfall: the father unfairly sacked her, the fiancée briefly befriended her, the son also, and finally when she was in desperate need of help the mother saw to it she received none. Talky and stagy – notwithstanding the flashbacks to the events under discussion – the film nonetheless has a sombre charm and, in its way, is compelling. Sim in particular is fine as the unwelcome guest at the feast who brings the younger members of the family into a sense of their responsibili-

hating Victor McLaglen in *The Informer* (1935), cringing in the shadows and selling out an IRA hero to the British during the Irish Rebellion. However, there have been attempts, doubtless inspired by a dose of social responsibility, to depict informers as heroes, as witness the agonised soul-searching of stool pigeons Victor Mature and Marlon Brando in **Kiss of Death** and **On the Waterfront**. **Marked Woman** and *The Enforcer/Murder Inc.* (1950) both deal with crusading District Attorneys and show how difficult it is to get minor crime figures to testify against the syndicate tyrants who can wipe them out from a distance. The theme is amplified by **The Narrow Margin**, *Dangerous Mission* (1954), *Tight Spot* (1955), **Murder by Contract**, **Bullitt**, *The Hit* (1984), **Witness**, *The Supergrass* (1985), *Narrow Margin* (1990) and *Another Stakeout* (1993), which feature lawmen trying to protect vital informants from underworld reprisals. Real-life mafia informers are played by Charles Bronson in **The Valachi Papers** and Ray Liotta in **GoodFellas**, while *Hide in Plain Sight* (1980) retells a true story

ABOVE *The Italian Job*

ties while their betters attempt to fob matters off. The climax has Sim found to be a bogus inspector, only for the family's relief to collapse after a call from the police to the effect that Wenham has died and they would like to talk to them. PH

1954/GB/79m/Watergate/*p* A.D. Peters/ *d* Guy Hamilton/*s* Desmond Davis/*orig* J. B. Priestley/*c* Ted Scaife/*m* Francis Chagrin/ *lp* Alastair Sim, Arthur Young, Olga Lindo, Eileen Moore, Bryan Forbes, Jane Wenham.

The Intimate Stranger/ Finger of Guilt

This is one of two films directed pseudonymously (in this case as Joseph Walton) by Losey in the UK after being blacklisted in Hollywood. Its writer Koch was also a blacklist victim and used the name Peter Howard. Basehart is the American director who has made a success of his exile in Britain. As he begins work on his next lavish production, he is pursued by blackmailing letters from a mysterious girl (Murphy) claiming once to have been his mistress. His problems are complicated by the fact that his wife (Brook) is the daughter of his boss (Livesey) and the star of his new film is a one-time lover (Cummings). Told in flashback, this wonderfully slow thriller neatly contrasts the problems of the film-makers – how to end the film – with Basehart's own, and ends with a fitting conflation of the private and the public when the all-revealing conversation between Murphy and Johns, Basehart's supposed best friend and the real blackmailer, is overheard by all because the sound equipment in the dubbing theatre is turned on. A minor masterpiece. PH

1956/GB/95m/Anglo-Guild/*p* Alec Snowden/*d* Joseph Losey/*s* Howard Koch/ *c* Gerald Gibbs/*m* Trevor Duncan/*lp* Richard Basehart, Mary Murphy, Constance Cummings, Roger Livesey, Mervyn Johns, Faith Brook.

The Italian Job

A caper film in the mould of **Topkapi** in which a number of eccentric characters come together to pull off an amazing heist, *The Italian Job* is remembered for the stunning sequence featuring a trio of Minis making a getaway with their gold ingots in the middle of a Turin traffic jam over rooftops, down steps, through sewers and finally across a weir. The sequence, like the car chase in **Bullitt**, gave birth to many a TV commercial. The actual coming together of

the assorted criminals – Caine's minor crook who inherits the plan, Coward's autocratic mastermind and Hill's computer expert (and luster after fat women) – is more conventionally handled and suffers as a result. PH

1969/GB/100m/Oakhurst-PAR/*p* Michael Deeley/*d* Peter Collinson/*s* Troy Kennedy Martin/*c* Douglas Slocombe/*m* Quincy Jones/*lp* Michael Caine, Noel Coward, Benny Hill, Raf Vallone, Tony Beckley, Irene Handl.

J

Jack the Ripper

Between 31 August and 9 November 1888, five prostitutes were murdered in Whitechapel, then a semi-slum in the East End of London. Earlier slayings have also been attributed to the killer, who favoured cutting his victims' throats and then mutilating the corpses. Known at first as 'Leather Apron' or 'The Whitechapel Murderer', the killer was given a lasting nickname by anonymous letters sent to a news agency, signed 'yours truly, Jack the Ripper'. The Ripper murders remain the most famous unsolved criminal mystery of all. The prevailing contemporary idea was that the murderer must be a filthy foreigner. More recently suspicion has fallen on a Jekyll-and-Hyde aristocrat, perhaps a surgeon or a connection of the Royal family, protected by a conspiracy of privilege. The case at once embodies a melodramatic vision of the Victorian era (gaslight, fog, **Sherlock Holmes**, gin-swilling drabs) and sets the agenda (forensic medicine, gutter journalism, criminal psychology) for the supposedly twentieth-century phenomenon of the **serial killer**.

The first nonfiction about the killings were the anonymous *The Whitechapel Murders: or The Mysteries of the East End* and Richard Kyle Fox's *The History of the Whitechapel Murders: A Full and Authentic Narrative of the Above Murders with Sketches*, which appeared in late 1888. The many other studies include William Stewart's *Jack the Ripper: A New Theory* (1939), Donald McCormick's *The Identity of Jack the Ripper* (1959), Daniel Farson's *Jack the Ripper* (1973), Donald Rumbelow's *The Complete Jack the Ripper* (1975), Stephen Knight's *Jack the Ripper: The Final Solution* (1976), Martin Fido's *The Crimes, Detection and Death of Jack the Ripper* (1987), Melvin Harris's *Jack the Ripper: The Bloody Truth* (1987), Colin Wilson and Robin

ABOVE Jack the Ripper, *Illustrated Police News*, 1889

Odell's *Jack the Ripper: Summing Up and Verdict* (1987) and Paul Begg, Martin Fido and Keith Skinner's *The Jack the Ripper A to Z* (1991). Among the people most commonly put forward as being Jack the Ripper are Montague John Druitt, a barrister, Aron Kosminski, a Polish hairdresser, Sir William Withey Gull, the Queen's physician (acting in concert with John Netley, a coachman), Robert D'Onston Stephenson, a journalist, Dr Alexander Pedachenko, rumoured to have been a Russian spy, Dr Neill Cream, a poisoner, the Duke of Clarence, heir to the throne, James Kenneth Stephen, allegedly Clarence's homosexual lover, and James Maybrick, a Liverpool poison victim.

Almost immediately, Jack featured in fiction, often with supernatural themes stirred in, as in J.F. Brewer's *The Curse Upon Mitre Square* (1889). Frank Wedekind put the Ripper in his plays *Erdgeist* (1895) and *Die Büchse der Pandora* (1902), and Alban Berg later turned them into an opera, *Lulu* (1937), with the killer emerging from the London fogs to put an end to the seductive but self-destructive heroine, Lulu. Wedekind used the Ripper to symbolise certain male characteristics but Marie Belloc-Lowndes' enormously popular *The Lodger* (1911) set the seal on the sinister aristocratic image, with a lower middle-class family gradually convinced that Mr Sleuth, their gentlemanly boarder, is the killer terrorising the city. **Robert Bloch**'s much-anthologised 'Yours Truly, Jack the Ripper' (1943) takes up a throwaway notion of Aleister Crowley's that the killer was trying to achieve immortality through a magical ritual and has lived on.

Bloch was also the author of *The Night of the Ripper* (1984), one of several historical novels on the subject: Patrice Chaplin's *By Flower and Dean Street, and the Love Apple* (1976), Richard Gordon's *The Private Life of Jack the Ripper* (1980), Pamela West's *Yours Truly, Jack the Ripper* (1987), Alan Moore and Eddie Campbell's comic *From Hell* (1991–), Paul West's *The Women of Whitechapel/The Women of Whitechapel and Jack the Ripper* (1991) and Hilary Bayley's *The Cry From Street to Street* (1992). Various attempts combine the Ripper with the Sherlock Holmes canon: Paul W. Fairman's *Sherlock Holmes vs Jack the Ripper/A Study in Terror/Ellery Queen vs Jack the Ripper* (1966, written as Ellery Queen), Michael Dibdin's *The Last Sherlock Holmes Story* (1978), Arthur Byron Cover's *An East Wind Coming* (1979), Ray Walsh's *The Mycroft Memoranda* (1984), M.J. Trow's *Lestrade and the Ripper* (1988) and Edward B. Hanna's *The Whitechapel Horrors* (1992). There also have been a slew of increasingly bizarre novels that have taken science fiction, fantasy, horror, thriller or literary approaches: Philip José Farmer's *A Feast Unknown* (1969), in which Tarzan's father is Jack the Ripper (!), Karl Alexander's *Time After Time* (1979), Michael Corby and Michael Geare's *Dracula's Diary* (1982), Farmer's *The Gods of Riverworld* (1984), Frederick Lindsay's *Jill Rips* (1987), Terence Lore Smith's *Yours Truly, From Hell* (1987), Ian Sinclair's *White Chappell, Scarlet Tracings* (1988), Brian Augustyn's Batman comic *Gotham by Gaslight* (1988), Kim Newman's *Anno Dracula* (1992), Richard Laymon's splatter Western *Savage* (1993) and Roger Zelazny's *A Night in the Lonesome October* (1993). At least three anthologies are devoted entirely to Ripper stories: Michel Parry's *Jack the Knife: Tales of Jack the Ripper*, 1975), Martin H. Greenberg, Charles Waugh and Frank McSherry's *Red Jack* (1988) and Susan Casper and Gardner Dozois' *Jack the Ripper* (1988). Ron Pember and Denis de Marne turned out a musical history, *Jack the Ripper* (1974), while Screaming Lord Sutch and Link Wray cut 60s singles. *The Diary of Jack the Ripper* (1993), which purports to be the work of the killer and fingers James Maybrick as the culprit, is very probably a cunning, anonymous fiction.

Jack the Ripper made a quiet screen debut in the last reel of *Erdgeist/Earth Spirit* (1923), murdering Asta Nielsen's Lulu. That film was eclipsed by G.W. Pabst's superior handling of the same material, *Die Büchse der Pandora/Pandora's Box* (1928). Pabst's Ripper (Gustav Diessl) is a tragic figure in an anonymous trench-coat and slouch hat, excluded from the Christmas celebrations around him, desperately trying to resist the impulse to kill Louise Brooks. The property has been often remade: *Lulu/No Orchids for Lulu* (1962), with Nadja Tiller as Lulu and Charles Regnier as the Ripper; *Lulu* (1978), a minimalist production shot entirely in abandoned zoo cages; *Lulu* (1978), a three-part French TV version of the Wedekind plays; *Lulu* (1979), a televised version of the Berg opera, completed by Friedrich Cerha, with Teresa Stratas; and Walerian Borowczyk's *Lulu* (1980), with Ann Bennent as Lulu and Udo Kier killing her. The notion of a timeless, Ripper-and-fog-blighted London was perpetuated by German films of the 60s, specifically Terence Fisher's *Sherlock Holmes und das Halsband des Todes/Sherlock Holmes and the Deadly Necklace* (1962), which sets up an unmade Holmes-vs-Jack sequel, and *Das Ungeheuer von London City/The Monster of London City* (1964), in which the killer stalks the cast of a play based on his murders, but also including a run of Ripper-influenced items like *Das Phantom von Soho/The Phantom of Soho* (1963), which has a skullmasked Ripper stand-in doing the bloody work.

ABOVE Jack the Ripper: *Dr Jekyll and Sister Hyde*

Marie Belloc Lowndes's novel was first filmed, by Alfred Hitchcock, as *The Lodger* (1926), with Ivor Novello as the sinister boarder, a role he reprised in Maurice Elvey's 1932 sound remake, also known as *The Phantom Fiend*. *The Lodger* was remade again in 1943, directed in Hollywood by John Brahm, the first major Jack the Ripper film to be set in 1888. Moving into the cosy, bric-à-brac-cluttered house of Sir Cedric Hardwicke and family, Mr Slade (Laird Cregar), a mysterious religious fanatic, is eventually unmasked as the Ripper. Brahm's film is definitive, but there have been remakes and variations. These include *Room to Let* (1949), from a radio play by Margery Allingham, with Valentine Dyall as Dr Fell, a gaunt boarder ultimately revealed as Jack the Ripper; and *Man in the Attic* (1953), Hugo Fregonese's exact remake of the Brahm film.

After the success of *The Lodger*, there was a vogue for period-set melodramas of sadism and psychosis, as witness *The Suspect* (1944), **Gaslight**, *Bluebeard* (1944), **The Spiral Staircase**, *Ivy* (1947), *Moss Rose* (1947), and **Hangover Square**, from the outstanding 1938 novel by **Patrick Hamilton**, author of *Gaslight*. It could be argued that *all* the cinema's mad killers in cod-Victorian or Edwardian settings are Ripper-inspired: the copperkiller of *The Mystery of Mr X* (1934) and its remake *The Hour of 13* (1952), Jean-Louis Barrault in *Drôle de Drame/Bizarre, Bizarre* (1937, France), the back-scratcher murderess of *She-Wolf of London* (1946), Robert Strauss as Jack the Slasher in *Here Come the Girls* (1953), Vincent Price in *House of Wax* (1954), Boris Karloff as the Haymarket Strangler in *Grip of the Strangler* (1958), Tutte Lemkow as the Brighton Strangler in *The Wrong Box* (1966, UK), Patrick O'Neal as the Baltimore Strangler in *Chamber of Horrors* (1966) and even Rondo Hatton as the Oxton Creeper in *Pearl of Death* (1944). In *Curse of the Wraydons* (1946), barnstorming Tod Slaughter plays Spring-Heel'd Jack, a penny dreadful character identified with the Ripper by the Victorian popular press but who actually pre-existed the Whitechapel Murderer.

Jack the Ripper (1959), directed by Robert S. Baker and Monty Berman, confirmed the Ripper's place in the horror movie canon. A threadbare B, mixing history, horror and mild carousing, it presents a sadistic surgeon (Ewen Solon) as the killer, finally crushed to death under a lift, whereupon the black and white film turns to colour to show off dripping blood. It was followed by Roy Ward

Baker's *Dr Jekyll and Sister Hyde* (1971), a Hammer film with Dr Jekyll (Ralph Bates) transforming into Mrs Hyde (Martine Beswick), a predatory sex kitten who takes to the streets as Jack the Ripper; Peter Sasdy's *Hands of the Ripper* (1971), another Hammer film, with proto-psychiatrist Eric Porter taking in Angharad Rees, daughter of Jack the Ripper, and trying to fathom the psychological triggers which cause the placid girl to drive pokers through a corrupt medium or shove a fistful of hat-pins into a prostitute's eye; *Jack, el Destripador de Londres/Jack the Ripper* (1971), with Paul Naschy, Madrid's Lon Chaney, cutting loose; Jesus Franco's *Der Dirnenmörderer von London/Jack the Ripper* (1976), with a mad-eyed Klaus Kinski wandering around Zurich (with one insert shot of Big Ben to establish the London setting) dismembering tailor's dummy prostitutes; Nicholas Meyer's spirited *Time After Time* (1979), with H.G. Wells (Malcolm McDowell) pursuing a time-travelling Jack (David Warner) to modern San Francisco; *The Ripper* (1985), a direct-to-video dodo with cackling Tom Savini in scleral lenses manifesting in the present day; Gerard Kikoine's lurid but stupid *Edge of Sanity* (1988), with Anthony Perkins as a cocaine-snorting Dr Jekyll turning into Jack Hyde and slicing tarts; and Peter B. Good's shot-on-video dud *Fatal Exposure* (1989), with Blake Bahner as the killer's slicealike descendant Jack T. Rippington.

James Hill's *A Study in Terror* (1965) is very much in the horror mould, despite a distinguished cast and a literate script, as Sherlock Holmes (John Neville) demonstrates that vindictive aristocrat John Fraser is the murderer. Its strategy of pitting fictional detectives against the real killer is echoed by *Jack the Ripper* (1974), a drama-documentary series in which Chief-Superintendent Charley Barlow (Stratford Johns) and Detective-Superintendent John Watt (Frank Windsor), tough cops from the UK teleseries *Z Cars* (1962–78), sift through the evidence and assess the likely guilt of several suspects. Far better is Bob Clark's *Murder By Decree* (1979), which borrows several tricks and actors from *A Study in Terror* as Holmes (Christopher Plummer) exposes a Masonic conspiracy and a Royal scandal surrounding the Whitechapel murders. In *Jack the Ripper* (1988), a two-part miniseries timed for the centenary of the murders, Michael Caine and Lewis Collins play real-life Victorian policemen who conclude that Gull (Ray McAnally), with no help from the freema-

sons, was the guilty party. A later 'final solution' was examined on the direct-to-video 'documentary' *The Diary of Jack the Ripper* (1993).

Of the many modern-set slasher films that make use of the Ripper, poaching plot twists or motivations from either history or earlier Ripper fictions, the most nauseating is Lucio Fulci's *Lo Squartatore di New York/The New York Ripper* (1982). Rowdy Herrington's *Jack's Back* (1988) is a fairly canny mystery with a series of murders of LA hookers taking place on the same dates as the original Ripper murders, but one hundred years later. Other modernised Jacks include Niall MacGuinness in *East of Piccadilly* (1946), Victor Buono in *The Strangler* (1964), Nicholas Worth in *Don't Answer the Phone* (1979), Cameron Mitchell in *The Toolbox Murders* (1979), John Diehl in *Angel* (1984) and the surprise mystery villains of several Italian *gialli*, including *Sei donne per l'assasino* (1964) and *L'uccello dalle piume di cristallo* (1968).

Ripper-related oddments include *Dr. Strangelove, or: How I Learned to Stop Worrying and Love the Bomb* (1964), with Sterling Hayden as General Jack D. Ripper; *Primitive London* (1965), a *Mondo Cane*-style documentary that explores the wild side of the city; Peter Medak's *The Ruling Class* (1972), from Peter Barnes's play, with mad peer Peter O'Toole cured of his belief that he is Jesus Christ when convinced that he is Jack the Ripper; *From Beyond the Grave* (1973), an anthology that opens with an adaptation of R. Chetwynd-Hayes' 'The Gatecrasher', in which David Warner is influenced by the spirit of Jack the Ripper (Marcel Steiner), who has been lurking in a haunted mirror for a century; *The Groove Room/What the Swedish Butler Saw* (1974), a 3-D sex film set in a Victorian London brothel, with Jack the Ripper (Martin Ljung) leering and slobbering at chubbily nude continental sex kittens; *A Knife for the Ladies* (1975), a Western originally entitled *Jack the Ripper Goes West*, which actually features a purely local murderer; *Amazon Women on the Moon* (1986), which features a brief parody of *In Search of Bigfoot*-style documentaries, as Henry Silva poses the question 'Was the Loch Ness Monster Jack the Ripper?'; and Mandie Fletcher's *Deadly Advice* (1994), with Sir John Mills's avuncular Ripper joining Hywel Bennett's Crippen and other famous Chamber of Horrors refugees in persuading the disturbed Jane Horrocks to murder her mother. KN

Jagged Edge

This highly efficient courtroom drama is another 'adjective + noun' two-word title in the manner of *Sudden Impact* (1983), **Fatal Attraction** and **Basic Instinct**. Bridges is a newspaper publisher whose wife is the victim of a particularly vicious killer. Since he will inherit her considerable fortune, he becomes a suspect and is arrested. Close is his defence lawyer. Over the course of the case, she also becomes his lover. We don't know if Bridges is guilty; maybe she is defending a man wrongly accused, but maybe she will eventually become his victim. Bridges gives the publisher just enough edge to make you think he is capable of the murder, but there again the prosecution lawyer (Coyote) has a reputation for sharp practice and may be stitching him up. If in the end the film depends too much on suspense, the finale remains effective if slightly too predictable. EB

1985/108m/COL/*p* Martin Ransohoff/ *d* Richard Marquand/*s* Joe Eszterhas/ *c* Matthew F. Leonetti/*m* John Barry/ *lp* Glenn Close, Jeff Bridges, Maria Mayenzet, Peter Coyote, Robert Loggia.

Jaguar

Brocka became internationally known for *Maynila sagma kuko ng liwanag* (1975) and *Insiang* (1976), two stylish but bleak exposé films about the brutalising effects of Marcos's regime on the Filipino underclasses. After making a dozen or so more commercially oriented films, *Jaguar* continues the earlier vein. The film is a chronicle of a young slum-dweller, Poldo (Salvador), who rescues his rich playboy boss, Sonny (Cobarrubias) from an assault by the gang of Direk (Delgado). Sonny uses Poldo as his 'jaguar', i.e. bodyguard, and proceeds to seduce the gangster's girl-friend, Cristy (Austria) with promises of movie roles. Trapped in Direk's night-club, Poldo kills Direk and has to go on the run. Brocka portrays Poldo and Cristy with considerable tenderness: both have to sell their bodies, except that Cristy is cannier than the naive Poldo, who simply takes orders and only slowly begins to realise that servitude is no solution. In the end, Poldo rebels and tries to kill Sonny who ruthlessly used him, but the police intervene and save the wealthy wastrel. The Filipino version was scored by Vanishing Tube, the international one by Jocson. Brocka was awarded a prize for the film in Manila but publicly refused to accept Marcos-sponsored honours. PW

1979/Philippines/120m/Ancom Audiovision/ *p* Rolando S. Atienza/*d* Lino Brocka/*s* Jose L. Lacaba, Ricardo Lee/*c* Conrado Balthazar/ *m* Max Jocson, Vanishing Tube/*lp* Philip Salvador, Amy Austria, Menggie Cobarrubias, Anita Linda, Johnny Delgado.

El jefe/The Boss

A moral tale about a teenage delinquent portrayed as a suburban bully who becomes the leader of a gang of aimless youths. As he expands his criminal activities, an ambitious young woman attaches herself to him, egging him on until he stupidly commits a murder. After trying to pin the blame on one of his followers, he is finally discovered to be a wimpish coward. Instead of a teenage delinquency movie, Ayala's film, scripted by a socialist writer, was read as an exposé of the populist dictator Perón and his associate, Eva. It also contains an amusing performance by Alfaro as a fan of the tango star Carlos Gardel. PW

1958/Argentina/85m/Aries/*co-p* Hector Olivera/*d*/*co-s*/*co-p* Fernando Ayala/*co-s* David Vinas/*c* Ricardo Younis/*m* Lalo Schifrin/ *lp* Alberto de Mendoza, Duilio Marzio, Graciela Borges, Leonardo Favio, Ignacio Quiros.

Jiafa/Law Don

Abandoning his career as a romantic lead in Hong Kong and Taiwanese movies, Tang set up his own production house, Wing Scope, and made *The Discharged* (1977) followed by a series of gangster pictures of which *Law Don* is the best. Taking his cue from **The Godfather**, Tang's film treats the gangster organisation as a family business, playing the lead role of the newly installed boss himself. When two weaker brothers threaten the business's smooth operations, he eliminates the obstacles to the family's continued prosperity and re-establishes a tightly knit and controlled family group. The direction is basic, even raw, giving the picture a roughness that sets it apart from Hong Kong's glossier products. The numerous fight sequences for this Cantonese-language film were choreographed and supervised by the leading martial arts instructor Ba Shan. PW

1979/Hong Kong/91m/Wing Scope/*p* He Yuntai/*co-d*/*co-s* Alan Tang [Deng Guangrong]/*co-d* Xiao Rong/*co-s* Liu Rongju/ *c* Wu Fayuan/*m* Chen Xunqi/*lp* Alan Tang, Ren Dahua, Gao Xiong, Lin Jiao.

Jingi Naki Tatakai/The Yakuza Papers/War without Honour/ Uncivil War/Battle without Honour and Morality/Dishonourable Combat

This was the first of a series of gangster movies by Fukasaku which marked the end of the genre's heyday in Japan. The films chronicled the gang wars that ravaged Hiroshima from 1945 to the mid-60s as narrated in Koichi Iiboshi's book based on the prison diaries of Kozo Mino, a yakuza who had participated in the events. He was transformed into the fictional character Shozo Hirono (Sugawara), a callously brutal gangster who comes to the attention of the godfather Yamamori (Kaneko). Shozo also strikes up a friendship with a thug (Umemiya) from a rival gang. However, both men are killed in a gruesomely physical gang battle. These killing scenes and Fukasaku's fast-paced, abrupt editing gained him the reputation of Japan's most violent director. His critique of yakuza is tinged by a strong nostalgia for the feudal days, bemoaning that the erstwhile samurai have now become stunted and brutish killers who exercise their profession because they can no longer think of another way of living, having been disoriented by Japan's defeat and industrialisation. This ideology seems to have struck a chord amongst its viewers: the film not only spawned many sequels over the next three years but it was also voted best film of the year by the readers of Japan's most influential film journal. Fukasaku's final two yakuza films, *Jingi No Hakaba* and its 1976 sequel, are equally violent. PW

1973/Japan/105m/Toei/*p* Koji Sundo, Goro Hikabe/*d* Kinji Fukasaku/*s* Kazuo Kasahara/ *orig* Koichi Iiboshi/*c* Sadaji Yoshida/ *m* Toshiaki Tsushima/*lp* Bunta Sugawara, Tatsuo Umemiya, Nobuo Kaneko, Hiroshi Nawa, Hiroki Matsukata.

Joe Macbeth

In attempting to modernise *Macbeth*, writer Yordan and director Hughes created a curious modern gangster story with an American setting but produced in England with a mainly British cast portraying (rather ridiculously at times) US underworld types. However, the characterisations of gangster Douglas, as he changes from henchman to frightened bully, and Roman, as his pushy wife, as well as the gangster-themed updating of the Shakespearean character, remain strangely compelling. TV

1955/90m/COL/*p* Mike Frankovich/*d* Ken Hughes/*s* Philip Yordan/*c* Basil Emmott/ *m* Trevor Duncan/*lp* Paul Douglas, Ruth Roman, Bonar Colleano.

Johnny O'Clock

The directorial debut of Rossen, whose earlier screen-writing credits included **Marked Woman** and **The Roaring Twenties**, this possesses the rather superficial air of an exercise in genre. The eponymous hero (Powell) is a shady gambler, caught up in the empire-building of a criminal associate (Gomez) and in the amorous schemes of the latter's wife (Drew). He emerges from his travails as an ostensibly regenerated character, thanks in part to the affections of the showgirl (Keyes) with whom he has become romantically entangled. The laconic atmosphere is effectively created, aided by the playing of Powell, and of Cobb as the jaundiced detective on his trail, but the machinations of the gangster and his dissembling wife fail to assume the symbolic resonance, in terms of their corrupt social values, for which Rossen would appear to be striving. TP

1946/95m/COL/*p* Edward G. Nealis/ *d/s* Robert Rossen/*c* Burnett Guffey/ *m* George Duning/*lp* Dick Powell, Ellen Drew, Lee J. Cobb, Evelyn Keyes, Thomas Gomez.

Le jour se lève

This is a superior essay in poetic realism by Carné and Prévert. Its mood of bleak yet romantic pessimism was hugely influential in France even though it was banned under the Nazi occupation. Gabin plays a working man whose tedious life of toil has been lightened by a love affair with a music-hall performer (Arletty). He is driven to murder her sadistic partner (Jules Berry) and retreats to his attic bedroom, where he barricades himself in. Though making token efforts at resistance, he is resigned to his fate. Waiting for the police to arrive, he reviews his life, which is revealed in a series of dove-tailing flashbacks. At dawn, despairing of his future, he shoots himself. EB

1939/France/95m/Sigma/*d* Marcel Carné/ *s* Jacques Viot, Jacques Prévert/*c* Curt Courant/*m* Maurice Jaubert/*lp* Jean Gabin, Jules Berry, Arletty, Jacqueline Laurent.

Jowobachi No Ikari/Queen Bee

Ishii's tale of two rival gangs, one led by a woman (Bubo), trying to take control of a port, stars Amish as Reckless Mass, a government agent masquerading as a tough lone wanderer. He gets close to the female gang boss as well as to the daughter of the rival male godfather before interrupting the final shoot-out in the docks with a fleet of police cars. He repeated his role in the sequel, *Jowobachi No Gyakushu* (1959) in which Yoko Mihara plays the female gang boss. In *Jowobachi To Daigaku No Ryu* (1960), Ishii tells of a young woman (Mihara again) who succeeds her gangster father. In Ishii's *Jotai Uzumaki-to* (1960), Mihara stars as a gang-

ABOVE Jean Gabin, *Le jour se lève*

ster's moll. There were several more movies featuring female gangsters in the 70s, including *Mesubachi Ni Gyakushu* (1971), *Mesubachi No Chosen* (1972), and *Zankoku Onna Rinchi* (1969). PW

1958/Japan/75m/Shintoho/*d* Teruo Ishii/ *s* Kozo Uchida/*c* Shigenari Yoshida/*lp* Shigeru Amish, Naoko Bubo, Ken Utsui, Miyuki Takakura, Terumi Hoshi, Yoko Mihara.

Judex

Having been accused of glorifying crime with his **Fantômas** films as well as with **Les Vampires**, his next serial featuring a female criminal played by Musidora, Feuillade devised this even more outlandish 12-part series around a vigilante super-hero called Judex, describing the films as 'a spectacle for all the family, exalting the most noble sentiments.' Using the name Judex and disguised by a black cape, usually thrown back over one shoulder, and a broad-rimmed felt hat, the young Corsican Count de Trémeuse (Cresté), whose father, a banker, was ruined by an old friend and who committed suicide,

ABOVE Jacqueline Laurent, Jean Gabin, *Le jour se lève*

Juvenile Delinquency

ABOVE *Judex*

sets out to avenge his father. He finds the villain, Favraux (Leubas), gains his confidence, shoots him during a social gathering in a castle and abducts the wounded Favraux to throw him into a dungeon. However, Judex, who has fallen in love with his enemy's daughter, Jacqueline (Andreyor), relents and imprisons the villain, generally assumed to be dead, in the ruins of a castle where he has his secret laboratory. He then sends a cage with pigeons to Jacqueline who is threatened by Favraux's mistress, the evil Marie Verdier (Musidora), so that she may be able to summon his help. The rest of the serial recounts the endless alternation of threats and rescues in the most varied circumstances. Whereas the surreal aspects of *Fantômas* came about largely through the way the films were made (constant improvisation and the need to have spectacular scenes that would sustain the viewers' curiosity), *Judex* consciously strives for a delirious, dark romanticism combined with an equally extravagant utopianism concerning the gadgetry generated by 'modern' science, such as electricity, the car, typewriters and so forth. In addition, Feuillade succeeded in filming ordinary landscapes and locations as if they contained unspeakable threats and corruption. The serial was extremely successful. It was serialised as a feuilleton in *Le Petit Parisien* (where the *Fantômas* feuilleton had appeared) and Feuillade went on to make a sequel called *La nouvelle mission de Judex* (1917). The actress who played the villainess in *Judex*, Musidora, who had been

the focus of *Les Vampires*, received her own serial a year later, *Tih Minh* (1918). *Judex* was remade as a feature by Feuillade's son-in-law, Maurice Champreux, in 1933, entitled *Judex 34*, starring René Ferté (Judex), Louise Lagrange (Jacqueline) and Mihalesco (Favraux). In 1963, Feuillade's grandson, Jacques Champreux, helped to write Georges Franju's brilliantly surreal version of *Judex*, starring Channing Pollock (Judex), Edith Scob (Jacqueline) and Michel Vitold (Favraux), with Francine Bergé playing Musidora's part. PW

1916/France/Gaumont/450metres/*d*/*co-s* Louis Feuillade/*co-s* Arthur Bernède/*c* Klausse, A. Glattli/*lp* René Cresté, Musidora, Yvette Andreyor, Marcel Levesque, Bout-de-Zan, Louis Leubas.

Juvenile Delinquency

Teenage criminality of various stripes was a staple of nineteenth-century fiction from *Oliver Twist* to *Huckleberry Finn*, but in the first flourishing of the crime film juvenile delinquency is simply a stage in the maturation of the adult gangster, as witness the segment of **The Public Enemy** in which Frankie Darro plays the James Cagney character as a tearaway kid, or the later presentation of the Dead End Kids in *Dead End* (1937) and **Angels with Dirty Faces** as basically good-hearted roughs who are dissuaded from growing up like the do-badders played by Humphrey Bogart. While *Wild Boys of the Road* (1933) and *Boy Slaves* (1938) give lip-service to the social problems that cause various brands of juvenile unrest, the basic tenet is that kids will be kids and need to have their energies channelled by decent adult influences, like Spencer Tracy in *Boys' Town* (1938), if they aren't to turn out as bad as the grown-up hoods whose manner they ape. The recurrence of James Cagney, who generally played gangsters as mother-domi-

ABOVE René Cresté, *Judex*

ABOVE Juvenile Delinquency: Mary Murphy, Gene Peterson, Alvy Moore, Marlon Brando, *The Wild One*

nated, overgrown children (most disturbingly when middle-aged himself in **White Heat**) as a negative role model is extremely apt, for the Dead End Kids tend, like many real kids of the era, to model their tough-talking and jaunty mannerisms on Cagney. The Dead End Kids' reformation was signalled when they progressed from relatively straight social dramas like *They Made Me a Criminal* (1939), *Hells' Kitchen* (1939) and *Angels Wash Their Faces* (1939) to such empty-headed knockabout as *Bowery Blitzkrieg* (1941), *Spooks Run Wild* (1941) and *Dig That Uranium* (1956).

The jazz age turned out a few awful warnings about wild youth but in the early talkie era examination of the specifics of juvenile delinquency tended to crop up only in road-show exploitation films like *Reefer Madness* (1936). Worries about home-front morale during the war threw up a couple of cheapies like *Youth Runs Wild* (1944) and *I Accuse My Parents* (1944). In the immediate post-war era, there was a flurry of traditional gangster films that happen to feature teenage protagonists, like Richard Attenborough in **Brighton Rock** and Farley Granger in **They Live by Night**, but it was not until the turn of the decade that 'juvenile delinquency' became a buzz-word and was tackled in a run of high-profile movies

which combine moralising with sensationalism. *City Across the River* (1949) is the first picture to deal with youth gangs, while *Knock on Any Door* (1949) offers John Derek as a

sneering hood whose motto was 'live fast, die young, leave a goodlooking corpse'. The film also signalled a new predominantly teenage audience which in *Blackboard Jungle* (1955) responded less to Glenn Ford's sincere attempts to reform troubled Sidney Poitier than to the rock 'n' roll of Bill Haley and the switch-blade cool of Vic Morrow. Other teenage style statements of the 50s were Marlon Brando's biker in **The Wild One**, responding to 'what are you rebelling *against*?' with 'what have you got?', and James Dean, about to live up to John Derek's credo, as the chicken-racing high school hero in *Rebel Without a Cause* (1955).

High-profile 'serious' films on the subject of juvenile delinquency like *Crime in the Streets* (1956), *The Young Stranger* (1957) and *The Young Savages* (1961) continued to be made, along with oddities like the comedy *The Delicate Delinquent* (1957) and even the Academy Award-winning musical **West Side Story**, but gradually the genre was swamped with lurid, variously effective exploitation pictures: *Rumble on the Docks* (1956), *Teenage Doll* (1957), *Teenage Wolfpack* (1957), *Untamed Youth* (1957), *The Flaming Teen-Age* (1957), *The Delinquents* (1957), *High School Confidential* (1958), *Juvenile Jungle* (1958), *High School Hellcats* (1958), *Hot Car Girl* (1958), *Dragstrip Riot* (1958), *The Cool and the Crazy* (1958) and *Cry Baby Killer*

ABOVE Juvenile Delinquency: *West Side Story*

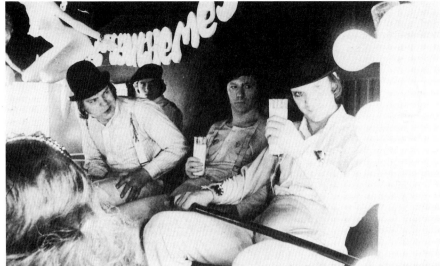

Juvenile Delinquency: Malcolm McDowell, *A Clockwork Orange* (above); Ricki Lake, Johnny Depp, Traci Lords, *Cry-Baby* (left)

(1958). The best-remembered title of the period, *I Was a Teenage Werewolf* (1957) is remarkably apt as a metaphor for the general feeling that teenagers were liable to turn into monsters in an instant. Teenage fashions have changed, yielding a run of j.d. movies keyed in to specific youth movements: **Beat Girl** (beatniks), *Beach Party* (1963, surfies), *Crazy Baby/Battle of the Mods* (1967, mods), *The Wild Angels* (1967, bikers), *Free Grass* (1969, hippies), *The Strawberry Statement* (1970, campus activists), *Saturday Night Fever* (1977, disco dancers), *Over the Edge* (1978, bored suburban youth), *Suburbia* (1980, punks), *River's Edge* (1986, Reaganite lost generationers), *Heathers* (1987, high school princesses), *Less Than Zero* (1987, yuppie puppies), *Boyz N the Hood* (1991, ghetto gangs). Throughout, movie conventions have remained in place, always leavening the moralising about trouble-making tearaways with celebrations of their music, fashions, hairstyles and slang, even throwing up such sub-genres as the nostalgia-fuelled retro-j.d. movie (*American Graffiti* 1973, *Quadrophenia*, 1978, *The Wanderers*, 1979, *Porky's*, 1982, *The Outsiders*, 1983), the Western j.d. movie (*Dirty Little Billy*, 1971, *Bad Company*, 1972, *Young Guns*, 1988), the bizarre futuristic j.d. movie (**A Clockwork Orange**, *Class of 1999*, 1988, *Prayer of the*

Rollerboys, 1990) and even the parodic musical retro-j.d. movie (*Grease*, 1978, *Hairspray*, 1988, *Cry-Baby*, 1990). KN

See also **The Musical**.

K

Kansas City Confidential/The Secret Four

Buoyed by hard-boiled dialogue and boasting an impressive triumvirate of subsidiary hoodlums in Brand, Elam and Van Cleef, this is an ingenious variation on the 'rogue cop' premise. A retired Kansas City police captain (Foster) with a grudge against the force blackmails three criminals into becoming his confederates in an armoured car robbery, intending eventually to turn them in and collect the insurance reward, and to embarrass his old employers into the bargain. When circumstantial evidence implicates an ex-con (Payne), the police arrest him and in an uncompromising sequence seek to get a confession by means of the 'third degree'. Released, he goes in pursuit of the real perpetrators, and via an affair with Foster's daughter (Gray) and a culminating gun battle, contrives to clear his name. Payne's embittered ex-con is a characteristic Karlson protagonist (compare *99 River Street*, 1953) and the film provides a suitable showcase for the director's acerbic, muscular style. TP

1952/98m/UA/*p* Edward Small/*d* Phil Karlson/*s* George Bruce, Harry Essex/

c George E. Diskant/*m* Paul Sawtell/ *lp* John Payne, Preston Foster, Coleen Gray, Jack Elam, Neville Brand, Lee Van Cleef.

Kawaita Hana/Pale Flower

Best known for his *Shinjo Tenno Amijima* (1969), Shinoda made this film set in the yakuza milieu a memorable contribution to genre in the same year as Suzuki's **Yaju No Seishun**. Based on a best-selling novel, it tells of a professional killer, Muraki (Ikebe), who enjoys his job. Released from jail, he finds that power relations have shifted in the underworld. This, a standard opening for a yakuza tale, enlivened by scenes such as the godfather urging his soldier to get his teeth fixed, develops into a coolly sensual yet satirical piece about Muraki's fascination with Saeko (Kaga), a beautiful woman gambler. A silent but dangerous opponent emerges, a drug-addicted Chinese half-caste and a ruthless killer (Fujiki). On his next killing assignment, Muraki takes Saeko along to watch him in action. Intent on showing off, he becomes careless and lands back in jail. Besides its sophisticated pictorial style and Takemitsu's outstanding score, the film's originality resides in its attempt to convey the aesthetics of the *hanafuda* flower card game, a favourite of the yakuza movies (*Hibotan Bakuto*, 1971, and its many sequels). Partly to underscore the parodic aspect of the yakuza rituals, Shinoda filmed the amputation of a finger joint so vividly that he was asked to remove the scene from the release print. PW

1963/Japan/98m/Ninjin Club-Shochiku/
p Masao Shirai, Shigeru Wakatsuki/*d*/*co-s*
Masahiro Shinoda/*co-s* Ataru Baba/
orig Shintari Ishihara/*c* Masao Kosugi/*m* Toru
Takemitsu/*lp* Ryo Ikebe, Mariko Kaga,
Takashi Fujiki, Chisako Hara, Shinichiro
Mikami.

Key Largo

The origin of *Key Largo* is a 'poetic' play by
Maxwell Anderson, in which the effects of a
criminal's incursion into an isolated community is detailed, in the manner of an earlier
stage success in similar vein, Robert
Sherwood's **The Petrified Forest**. The role
of the fleeing gunman in the Broadway production and in the 1936 film version of the
latter established the reputation of Humphrey
Bogart, who appears in *Key Largo* on the
opposite side of the fence. The action is set in
an hotel on the Florida coast where deported
mobster Rocco, who has returned to the US
to carry on business as usual and is now
bound for Cuba, arrives with his entourage
and takes over the place until his boat
arrives. A storm blows up and a war of
nerves ensues between the gangster and the
world-weary war veteran (Bogart) who is
caught up in events along with the hotel's
crippled owner (Barrymore) and his daughter-in-law (Bacall). The writing retains a theatrical tenor, but the elaborate direction
imbues the situation with considerable tension, and there are virtuoso performances by
Robinson as the reptilian gang lord and by
Trevor as his ill-used, alcoholic mistress. The
climax, opening out the stage original to take
place at sea, is the film's least successful passage. The re-motivated Bogart character's
ability to put paid to Rocco and his coevals
registers as not simply glib but as physically
less than convincing. TP

1948/100m/WB/*p* Jerry Wald/*d* John
Huston/*s* John Huston, Richard Brooks/
c Karl Freund/*m* Max Steiner/*lp* Humphrey
Bogart, Edward G. Robinson, Lauren Bacall,
Claire Trevor, Lionel Barrymore.

The Killer Inside Me

Astonishingly well-cast with cannily selected
veterans and interesting younger players,
Kennedy's adaptation of **Jim Thompson**'s
1952 novel suffers because Kennedy's direction isn't quite up to the texture of the original. Outwardly amiable Montana deputy
sheriff Lou Ford (Keach) does not carry a
gun, manages to be everybody's friend and
conceals his razor-sharp intellect behind
crackerbarrel banalities. He's also a mentally

ill and bungling schemer who plays various
local political factions off each other in an
attempt to murder and extort his way to a
comfortable life. Finally, in a brilliantly-acted
encounter with a psychiatrist (Carradine)
posing as a buyer for his house, he diagnoses
himself as 'a schizophrenic, paranoid type.
When things get a little rough, I just go out
and kill a few people – that's all.' Keach is
compelling as Thompson's villain, a man
unhinged enough to function perfectly in a
festering small town society. Although the
movie has a made-for-TV visual blandness, it
is given spark by a collection of supporting
performances (especially Tyrrell as another
one of her abused sluts and Stroud as a born
good ole boy fall guy) perfectly in tune with
the rural *noir* grit of the novel. KN

1976/99m/Devi-Leighton/*p* Michael W.
Leighton/*d* Burt Kennedy/*s* Edward Mann,
Robert Chamblee/*orig* Jim Thompson/
c William A. Fraker/*m* Tim McIntire, John
Rubinstein/*lp* Stacy Keach, Susan Tyrrell,
Tisha Sterling, Charles McGraw, John
Dehner, John Carradine, Don Stroud.

The Killer Is Loose

Boetticher's reputation rests upon his
Westerns, though he also directed a notable
gangster movie, **The Rise and Fall of Legs
Diamond**. He has described *The Killer Is
Loose* as 'not my kind of film', suggesting in
rather literal-minded spirit that Cotten and
Fleming were 'too elegant' to play a modestly paid policeman and his wife. In fact, this
tense narrative, in which a crook (Corey),
whose wife was accidentally killed during his
arrest by Cotten, subsequently breaks jail to
pursue a vendetta against the cop by seeking
to kill his wife, has much of the economy
and compression of the director's best
Westerns. The difference is that here the
melodrama is played off against nondescript
suburban surroundings, and it is even possible to see Corey's driven villain, a short-
sighted bank teller who has acted as inside
man in a robbery, as a reductive parody of
the questing avenger figure heroically incarnated by Randolph Scott in Boetticher's
Westerns. The wife-in-jeopardy device was
subsequently deployed more elaborately in
Cape Fear. TP

ABOVE Edward G. Robinson, Claire Trevor, Lionel Barrymore, Thomas Gomez, Humphrey
Bogart, Lauren Bacall, Harry Lewis, *Key Largo*

The Killers—The Killing of Angel Street

1956/73m/UA/*p* Robert L. Jacks/*d* Budd Boetticher/*s* Harold Medford/*c* Lucien Ballard/*m* Lionel Newman/*lp* Joseph Cotten, Wendell Corey, Rhonda Fleming, Michael Pate, Virginia Christine.

The Killers

Al and Mak (Charles McGraw and William Conrad) enter a diner searching for the Swede (Lancaster). The Swede is warned of their approach but refuses to escape, and instead, lies on his bed waiting. After the murder, an insurance investigator Jim Reardon (O'Brien) begins interviewing the Swede's friends in order to reconstruct his past and the events which led to his death. In flashback it emerges that the Swede was a young boxer manipulated by crime boss Big Jim Colfax (Dekker). He is seduced by Kitty Collins (Gardner), Big Jim's girl-friend, into participating in an armoured car robbery in order to double-cross Big Jim and run off with the loot and the girl. From the Hemingway short story, this is a classic thriller. The alternation between light and shadow, violent transitions from long shots to close-up gives a air of tragic inevitability and the sadness of wasted potential. The film featured Lancaster's first screen role and Gardner's drama debut. It was remade in 1964 by Don Siegel, starring John Cassavetes, Lee Marvin, Clu Gulager and Angie Dickinson. MP

1946/102m/U/*p* Mark Hellinger/*d* Robert Siodmak/*s* Anthony Veiller/*c* Woody Bredell/*m* Miklos Rozsa/*lp* Edmond O'Brien, Ava Gardner, Burt Lancaster, Albert Dekker, Sam Levene.

The Killing

This early Kubrick picture shows all of his characteristic precision and care in the construction of the narrative, pieced together through flashback and voice-over narration. Johnny Clay (Hayden) is a petty crook who plans the robbery of a race-track. The film details the assembly of the gang who will carry out the heist: a corrupt policeman, various personnel working at the track, and a marksman whose job is to shoot one of the horses as a diversion. The robbery goes wrong when the marksman is killed. The wife of one of the gang has told her boyfriend about the plan, and he attempts to steal the money off the gang before they make good their escape. In the ensuing mayhem most of the gang are shot. Clay appears just in time to take the money, but as it is being loaded on to a plane the bag falls off on to the tarmac and bursts open. The wind, in literally a cruel twist of fate, disperses the money. EB

1956/84m/UA/*p* James B. Harris/*d*/*s* Stanley Kubrick/*c* Lucien Ballard/*m* Gerald Fried/*lp* Sterling Hayden, Coleen Gray, Vince Edwards, Jay C. Flippen, Marie Windsor.

ABOVE Timothy Carey, Sterling Hayden, *The Killing*

The Killing of a Chinese Bookie

In *Gloria* (1980), Cassavetes subscribes more or less to the requirements of the thriller-suspense genre as a framework for his usual concerns, but this earlier venture into organised crime is far closer in structure to his other films, a semi-improvised, self-confessedly rambling character study that happens to play out inside a very basic gangster story-line. Cosmo Vittelli (Gazzara), struggling manager of a sparkly but seedy Los Angeles **night-club**, is duped by a mobster (Cassel) into running up a gambling debt he can only pay off by carrying out the assassination of Ling (Hugh), who turns out not to be a humble bookie but a well-guarded mastermind. Escaping with a stomach wound from the site of the crime, Vittelli is pursued by an eccentric killer (Carey) whom he convinces not to rub him out, but the emotional climax is neither of these gangland confrontations but Vittelli's return to the club, where he delivers a pep talk to the exotic dancers and the neurotic comedian (Roberts) who serves as compere. Like Vittelli, the film is surprisingly able to work up desperate enthusiasm for the third-rate Crazy Horse West Club, investing the speciality turns with a compelling erotic sadness and turning Roberts' renditions of 'I Can't Give You Anything But Love, Baby' and 'Imagination' into affectingly pathetic emblems of the lowlife scene. Gazzara continues his association with the director, gives a marvellously unshowy performance, inhabiting his role with a host of tiny, telling gestures. KN

1976/135m/*p* Al Ruban/*d*/*s* John Cassavetes/*c* Mitchell Breit/*lp* Ben Gazzara, Timothy Agoglia Carey, Azizi Johari, Seymour Cassel, Meade Roberts, Soto Joe Hugh.

The Killing of Angel Street

This political thriller was based on the case of Juanita Nielsen, who opposed the schemes of property developers in Sydney and disappeared in 1975, probably murdered. Jessica Simmons (Alexander) resists the redevelopment of her street. Her father is killed and she becomes the target of intimidation and violence from gangsters who, almost literally, own city hall, the police and even the union machinery. Shot like an urban thriller in which every car or shadow contains a possible threat, Crombie's film effectively creates a sense of all pervasive menace leading inexorably to the fatal ending. PW

1981/Australia/96m/Forest Home/
p Anthony Buckley/*d* Donald Crombie/

LEFT Meade Roberts, *The Killing of a Chinese Bookie*

hanged for the one death he was not responsible for, all the more ironic since he both represents the new blood essential to the continuation of the d'Ascoynes and, because of his energetically pursued activities, is the last of that line. Guinness's delicate performances (which made his international reputation) were often commented upon, but equally fine is that of Greenwood as the woman Price loves. She brings to her verbal exchanges with Price an eroticism rarely seen in British cinema and does much to give warmth to the film. PH

1949/GB/106m/Ealing/*p* Michael Balcon/*d*/*co-s* Robert Hamer/*co-s* John Dighton/*orig* Roy Horniman *Israel Rank*/ *c* Douglas Slocombe/*m* Ernest Irving/ *lp* Dennis Price, Alec Guinness, Joan Greenwood, Valerie Hobson, Miles Malleson, Arthur Lowe.

Kindergarten Cop

With Schwarzenegger's screen image in mid-metamorphosis as he segues from 'Violent' to 'Cute', this weird crossbreed shows how malformed the cop genre had become by the 90s. John Kimble (Schwarzenegger), an Austrian somehow working for the LAPD, transfers from his macho man action film

s Michael Craig, Cecil Holmes, Evan Jones/ *c* Peter James/*m* Brian May/*lp* Liz Alexander, John Hargreaves, Reg Lye, Alexander Archdale, David Downer, Norman Kaye.

Kind Hearts and Coronets

Despite its frothy surface, the bleakest of films, *Coronets* features Price as the shop assistant who murders his way to a title (The Duke of Chalfont) and the family fortune. The film is told in flashback from the condemned man's cell and narrated by Price with a cool, ironic detachment that does much to set the tone. Like *The Life and Times*

Of Colonel Blimp (1943), it attacks the ossified class system that has led the d'Ascoynes to cut off Price's mother who married beneath her, but Hamer is far more rigorous than Michael Powell (who also celebrates what he attacks). Thus Price's proletarian Louis Mazzini is positively contrasted with the eight, mostly effete, members of the family (all played by Guinness) he murders. This makes the ending, in which he is to be

Kind Hearts and Coronets: Alec Guinness (right), Valerie Hobson (below)

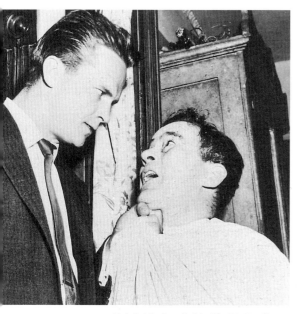

ABOVE Ralph Meeker (left), *Kiss Me Deadly*

streets into a kiddie movie suburbia when he has to go undercover as a kindergarten teacher. The plot device is that the drug scumlord villain's wife, who can testify against him, has fled to Oregon and the only clue Kimble has to her whereabouts is the fact that her son is in the class he is teaching. Though the first and last thirds are a densely plotted, satisfying blend of humour and thrills, *Kindergarten Cop* sags desperately in the middle. The initial joke of facing the man-mountain from *The Terminator* (1984) with the one obstacle he can't possibly overcome (a classroom full of six-year-olds) fades instantly as the Macaulay Culkin-wannabe tykes proudly trot out in succession their personalised cute mannerism, and Arnie miraculously but expectedly turns from gruff kid-hater to dewy-eyed superteacher in the space of an aerobics montage. KN

1990/110m/U/c-op Brian Grazer/co-p/d/ Ivan Reitman/s Murray Salem, Herschel Weingrod, Timothy Harris/c Michael Chapman/m Randy Edelman/lp Arnold Schwarzenegger, Penelope Ann Miller, Pamela Reed, Linda Hunt, Richard Tyson, Carroll Baker.

A Kiss before Dying

This clever thriller stars an offbeat Wagner, at the height of his teen-throb career, murdering his pregnant girl-friend and then romancing her sister in order to continue pursuing the girls' family's wealth. A slick and at times grim novel by **Ira Levin** was

the basis for the screenplay. Oswald's direction, as always when dealing with abhorrent personalities, scores with depicting Wagner in his killer role alongside creating suspense as the deviations develop. A bland remake was produced in 1991, with Matt Dillon taking on the Wagner part and Sean Young portraying both sisters. TV

1956/94m/UA/p Robert L. Jacks/d Gerd Oswald/s Lawrence Roman/c Lucien Ballard/m Lionel Newman/lp Robert Wagner, Jeffrey Hunter, Virginia Leith, Joanne Woodward.

Kiss Me Deadly

Private eye **Mike Hammer** (Meeker) swerves to avoid running down Christina (Leachman). He picks her up, but is later forced off the highway and knocked unconscious. Disturbed by Christina's disappearance, Hammer and his faithful sex kitten secretary Velda (Cooper) investigate, although his policeman buddy Pat (Addy) warns him to lay off. Velda is kidnapped, Hammer's mechanic Nick is crushed to death, and Christina is tortured and killed. Hammer retaliates, leaving a trail of damaged villains and eventually claiming the mysterious package everyone is after.

Director Aldrich converts Mickey Spillane's right-wing paranoia into a terrifying polemic about government secrecy and the threat of the atomic bomb. Hammer is a brutal automaton confronting totalitarian ruthlessness. The opening sequence, where Hammer drives through an unwinding spool of pulp fiction titles, is masterly, and Leachman's desperate panting and screaming punctuate the sound-track with horror. MP

1955/105m/Parklane/p/d Robert Aldrich/s A.I. Bezzerides/c Ernest Laszlo/m Frank DeVol/lp Ralph Meeker, Albert Dekker, Paul Stewart, Maxine Cooper, Cloris Leachman, Wesley Addy.

Kiss of Death

The story, subsequently a novel, upon which *Kiss of Death* is based is by Eleazar Lipsky, who had been an assistant district attorney in New York County, and the film contains a good deal of inside detail on the workings of the judicial system. But despite this and quite extensive recourse to location shooting, including scenes filmed at Sing Sing penitentiary, the movie's dominant mode is that of melodrama rather than social realism. Mature plays a convicted criminal who obtains parole in exchange for turning

ABOVE Brian Donlevy, Richard Widmark, Victor Mature, *Kiss of Death*

informer. Matters go wrong when a sadistic killer against whom he is also obliged to give evidence is freed as a result of legal chicanery. The latter becomes his tormentor and at the climax Mature is driven to goad him into a showdown which ends with his adversary being shot by the police. The giggling murderer, addressing Mature as 'big man', and in one sequence disposing of a wheelchair-bound old woman by pushing her downstairs, marked Widmark's screen debut and accorded him instant stardom. The surrounding film has the narrative assurance characteristic of Hathaway's best work. TP

1947/98m/FOX/*p* Fred Kohlmar/*d* Henry Hathaway/*s* Ben Hecht, Charles Lederer/*c* Norbert Brodine/*m* David Buttolph/*lp* Victor Mature, Richard Widmark, Coleen Gray, Brian Donlevy, Taylor Holmes.

Kiss Tomorrow Goodbye

'At last I was safe and secure in the blackness of the womb from which I had never emerged' are the closing words of Horace McCoy's novel, but the subjectivity which underpins his psychotic criminal is missing from its screen adaptation. Perhaps more importantly, the film, a 'run for cover' undertaking by the struggling independent company operated by James Cagney and his brother William, betrays in its impoverished production values the signs of cut-price manufacture. The story, with Cagney breaking jail and successfully expanding his criminal activities in a corrupt small town, only to be gunned down by his discarded mistress, is not without similarities to the earlier **White Heat**, but the film lacks its predecessor's drive and conviction, and Cagney's playing is less persuasive. The picture's chief redeeming virtue lies in the hard-bitten performances of Bond and MacLane as the dishonest policemen whom Cagney utilises in his schemes. TP

1950/102m/WB/*p* William Cagney/*d* Gordon Douglas/*s* Harry Brown/*c* J. Peverell Marley/*m* Carmen Dragon/*lp* James Cagney, Barbara Payton, Steve Brodie, Ward Bond, Barton MacLane.

Klute

Structured as a mystery (with a brooding third-billed respectable suspect and a last-minute psycho confrontation which ends with the villain falling to his death), *Klute* is more concerned with being a study of different kinds of alienation: the coldness of the

ABOVE Donald Sutherland, Jane Fonda, *Klute*

detective, the disappointment of the hooker, the fanatical dementia of the killer. John Klute (Sutherland), an emotionally deep-frozen small-town cop, takes leave and travels to New York to investigate the disappearance of a family friend, acting literally as a private detective. The only lead is the vanished man's relationship with Bree Daniel (Fonda), a struggling actress who moonlights as a call girl. Pakula directs with an appropriately chilly tone, favouring blue steel and grey walls, while Sutherland's melancholy title character is constantly challenged and prodded into the background by Fonda's Oscar-winning performance, which takes centre stage to such a degree that the film becomes far more obsessed with probing the unfathomable riddles of Bree's personality

than getting to the bottom of the fairly transparent murder mystery. Like many of Pakula's subsequent films (*The Parallax View*, 1974, *All the President's Men*, 1976, *Rollover*, 1981, **Presumed Innocent**, *The Pelican Brief*, 1993), *Klute* is about investigators trapped in a society ruled by conspiracy and surveillance, trying to find answers of doubtful use, invariably overseen by silently nodding psychiatrists, gently-revolving tape recorders or coolly observant remote cameras. As an *oeuvre*, Pakula's works present a remarkably cerebral, persuasive and distinctive vision, but as individual films, they often err on the side of the ambiguously monolithic, sometimes resulting in thrillers where thrills are the ingredient left off the menu. KN

Koroshi No Rakuin—The Krays

1971/114m/WB/*p*/*d*/ Alan J. Pakula/*s* Andy K. Lewis, Dave Lewis/*c* Gordon Willis/ *m* Michael Small/*lp* Jane Fonda, Donald Sutherland, Charles Cioffi, Roy Scheider, Dorothy Tristan.

Koroshi No Rakuin/Branded to Kill

With **Tokyo Nagaremono**, this is Suzuki's most deliriously stylish and fascinating film. Its main character is Hanada Goro (Shishido), ranked No. 3 Killer amongst the yakuza. He works for the boss Yabuhara (Tamagawa) and has to pick up a mysterious man (actually Killer No. 1) from a boat and escort him to a villa in the mountains. While he does this the boss seduces his wife. He acquires a girl-friend, Misako (Mari), who also works for the same boss. Next, Hanada has to kill a customs officer, an optician, a diamond merchant and a foreigner. He misses the target when a butterfly settles on his telescopic sight and has to pay the price for failure: he becomes a target himself for No. 1 Killer. The movie hurtles from one stylised set piece to another, each enlivened by a myriad of inventive and often humorous touches, exploding all the conventions of the genre, achieving something close to Godard's most iconoclastic films of the period. The president of Nikkatsu was so outraged by the film's style that Suzuki was sacked, triggering major student protests in Tokyo. PW

1967/Japan/91m/Nikkatsu/*p* Iwai Kaneo/ *d* Seijun Suzuki/*s* Hachiro Guryu/*c* Kazue Nagatsuka/*m* Naozumi Yamamoto/*lp* Jo Shishido, Mariko Ogawa, Ann Mari, Koji Nanbara, Isao Tamagawa, Hiroshi Minami.

The Krays

'Mummy loves you, you little monsters,' Violet Kray (Whitelaw) tells her twin sons as children. The film then shows how mother love turns them into actual monsters. Playing off an expected screen image (Berkoff's doomed George Cornell calls the twins 'movie gangsters'), *The Krays* invokes the family of **The Godfather**, but depicts a different, matriarchal underworld. Michael Corleone shuts out his wife and uses his sister as a pawn, but the Krays hold business meetings in their mum's cosy terraced house with Violet forever bringing in tea and biscuits. Neither Kay Corleone nor Ma Barker, Violet is the centre of a film which is pointedly not called *The Kray Brothers*. Whitelaw remains sympathetic but resists the temptation to turn Violet into a Julie Walters character: for all her tea-making and manners-

ABOVE Jo Shishido, *Koroshi No Rakuin*

minding, she is as responsible for the brief, horrifying explosions of violence as her sons. The brothers are either trying semi-erotically to brutalise each other, as in a funfair boxing sequence that turns into a blood-soaked free-for-all, or urging each other on to excesses neither would be capable of on his own. Seeing Ronnie with a boyfriend, Reggie draws attention to his brother's unnatural sexuality with 'your tie's crooked,' only to have Ronnie retort, aptly, 'so's yours.' A confident and gripping glide through the crimes of the recent past, with direction that does not flinch, as other British crime-class-nostalgia movies do, from graphic violence. KN

1990/GB/119m/Parkfield-Fugitive/

p Dominic Anciano, Ray Burdis/*d* Peter Medak/*s* Philip Ridley/*c* Alex Thomson/ *m* Michael Kamen/*lp* Billie Whitelaw, Gary Kemp, Martin Kemp, Susan Fleetwood, Steven Berkoff, Tom Bell.

Krotki film o zabijaniu/A Short Film about Killing

The best of Kieslowski's ten films illustrating the Ten Commandments, in this case 'thou shalt not kill'. An unremittingly bleak, grainy film shot in sickening greens and yellows, it shows the young, brutalised and intellectually challenged Jacek (Baka) murdering a misanthropic cab driver (Tesarz) in graphic detail. This harrowingly difficult killing is later followed by an equally botched judicial murder as Jacek is hanged for his crime. The liberal core of the film is represented by the defence lawyer and priest, Piotr (Globisz), who learns, when it is too late, something of Jacek's miserable background that might have allowed him to plead extenuating circumstances. Kieslowski's film is an effective tract against capital punishment. It was released as a feature in 1988 a few months before the only other episode of the teleseries to have received a cinema release, *Krotki film o milosci/A Short Film about Loving*. PW

1988/Poland/84m/PRF Zespoly Filmowe-Tor/*d*/*co-s* Krzystof Kieslowski/*co-s* Krzysztof Piesiewicz/*c* Slawomir Idziak/*m* Zbigniew Preisner/*lp* Miroslaw Baka, Krzysztof Globisz, Jan Tesarz, Zbigniew Zapasiewicz, Barbara Dziekan-Vajda.

L

The Lady from Shanghai

In the best *noir* tradition, this has a near-incomprehensible plot. In its place is a murky world of intrigue, a fitting subject for Welles's love of baroque camerawork and lighting effects. Michael O'Hara (Welles) saves a beautiful young woman from assault. Later he finds work on a yacht owned by a rich lawyer, who turns out to be the woman's husband. O'Hara is sucked into a maelstrom of confusing and threatening events, culminating in the murder of the lawyer's business partner, of which crime he is unjustly accused. In a bravura finale in an dilapidated amusement park, there is a shoot-out in a hall of mirrors, in which the lawyer and his wife are killed. Hayworth is more stunning than ever as a platinum blonde, as alluring as she is treacherous. A box-office flop, this led to Welles's exile from major Hollywood studios until his other great noir work, **Touch of Evil**. EB

1948/86m/COL/*p*/*d*/*s* Orson Welles/*c* Charles Lawton Jr/*m* Heinz Roemheld/*lp* Rita Hayworth, Orson Welles, Everett Sloane, Glenn Anders, Ted De Corsia.

Lady in the Lake

Like *The Thief*, the silent (rather, wordless) movie made in 1952 and *Scent of Mystery* (1960), the first (and only) feature in Smell-o-Vision, *Lady in the Lake* is best remembered as a monument to the inadvisability of creating an entire film around a technically interesting but fundamentally undramatic concept. Several Chandler adaptations (*Murder, My Sweet*, 1944, *Farewell, My Lovely*, 1975) evoke his distinctive first-person feel by incorporating voice-over narration and scrupulously ensuring the audience only sees scenes at which Marlowe is present. Montgomery, starring in his first feature as a director, unwisely shoots the entire film (one or two link scenes aside) through a subjective camera, effectively casting the audience in the lead role. Though a few moments (when Marlowe is punched in the face, or kissed by Totter) work in the 'lion in your lap' manner favoured by 50s 3-D movies, the trick soon loses credibility: people do not perceive the world in black and white, in elegant panning shots and with a music track. Sadly, the subjective camera cripples what might otherwise have been a fine adaptation of the 1943 novel: in ruthless shoulder-pads, Totter is perfectly cast as an ambiguously corrupt Chandler heroine, and Nolan is excellent as the desperate, crooked cop mixed up in the case. It was the only Chandler adaptation upon which Chandler actually worked (though he did not finally take screen credit), and to him the film owes such details as Marlowe's sideline as a pulp writer, turning out a story called 'I Wake Up Bleeding'. Montgomery's direction is far better on **Ride the Pink Horse**. The subjective camera was semi-retired until the 70s when, thanks to *Halloween* (1977), it made a comeback in stalk-and-slash movies. KN

1946/103m/MGM/*p* George Haight/*d* Robert Montgomery/*s* Steve Fisher/*orig* Raymond Chandler/*c* Paul C. Vogel/*m* David Snell/

ABOVE Orson Welles, Rita Hayworth, *The Lady from Shanghai*

ABOVE Robert Montgomery, Audrey Totter, *Lady in the Lake*

lp Robert Montgomery, Audrey Totter, Lloyd Nolan, Tom Tully, Leon Ames, Jayne Meadows.

The Ladykillers
With **Kind Hearts and Coronets**, probably the best known Ealing film, *The Ladykillers* like that film is a decidedly black comedy. A mark of the length of the film's shadow is the variety of sympathetic explications it has evoked. Thus Ray Durgnat has identified the central opposition in the film as being Johnson's ignorant benevolence versus Guinness' seething, impotent malice, while Charles Barr, without deforming it, has persuasively suggested the gang can be read as the post-war Labour Government unable to triumph over Johnson's implacable quaint little England. What both these views highlight is the centrality of Johnson's role and the power of Edwardian visions of England to prevent modern Britain entering the twentieth century, a theme addressed with even greater sadness by Michael Powell. The simple plot has five members of a gang planning a complex wages robbery masquerade as a string quartet to rent a room in Johnson's ramshackle house as their HQ. A social mix, rather than a **League of Gentlemen**, ranging from academic (Guinness) via ex-officer (Parker) and thug (Lom) to Sellers's uneducated youth, the gang can deceive Johnson for long enough to pull off the robbery but no longer. Their downfall is the result of social embarrassment – it's as though they haven't learnt to say no to an invitation to tea – and thus, rather than bring themselves to deal with Johnson, they turn against each other. The finale, with the gang gone and the money now Johnson's, is deeply ironic: Johnson returns to the police station she first visited at the film's opening to talk about her 'dream', only this time she can afford to give the pavement artist a

The Ladykillers:
Alec Guinness, Herbert Lom, Danny Green, Katie Johnson (right)
Alec Guinness, Katie Johnson (below)

pound for his portrait of Churchill. A mark of how static an image of Britain the film evokes is that for all the talk the film never leaves the St. Pancras area. PH

1955/GB/97m/Ealing/*p* Seth Holt/ *d* Alexander Mackendrick/*s* William Rose/ *c* Otto Heller/*m* Tristram Cary//*lp* Katie Johnson, Alec Guinness, Cecil Parker, Herbert Lom, Peter Sellers, Danny Green, Jack Warner.

Landru/Bluebeard

In 1919, the 50-year old Desiré Landru was arrested and in 1922 executed for the murder of ten women and possibly one boy. When Chabrol took up the character (Chaplin had already done so in *Monsieur Verdoux*, 1947), the serial killer's girl-friend, Fernande Segret, sued and obtained 10,000 Fr damages. She committed suicide, aged 72, in 1968. Chabrol shows how Landru (Denner), an impecunious antique dealer, starts killing marriageable women for their savings to support his own family. Then he kills a maid for no apparent financial gain, which seems to trigger something in the murderer: he becomes indiscriminate, takes a lover and uses the money acquired to maintain his love nest, totally neglecting his family. When arrested, he defends himself so effectively that many doubt his guilt. Chabrol's film can be seen on different levels: as a chronicle of understated horror (merely showing props like a meat-grinder and an oven to suggest what happens to the victims), acknowledging that such a person defies human understanding; or as a black comedy about bourgeois morality after World War I, leading up to World War II and no doubt still relevant today. A further dimension seems to be the delight Chabrol took in killing off leading French stars of the 1940s and 1950s such as Morgan and Darrieux. The *mise en scène* is meticulous and Denner masterfully plays the killer like a charming chameleon adapting his roles and behaviour to the personalities of his intended victims. In that respect, Chabrol followed in the footsteps of Buñuel's unsettling version of everyday bourgeois hypocrisy, *Ensayo de un crimen* (1955). After some parodic secret agent movies, Chabrol turned to less extreme examples of the way charm, desire and even love can coexist with the most abject sadism and violence in the 'respectable' bourgeoisie of today: **La Femme infidele**, **Que la bête meure** and **Le Boucher.** PW

ABOVE Stéphane Audran, Charles Denner, *Landru*

1962/France, Italy/115m/Rome-Paris Films-Champion/*p* Georges de Beauregard, Carlo Ponti/*d* Claude Chabrol/*s* Françoise Sagan/ *c* Jean Rabier/*m* Pierre Jansen//*lp* Charles Denner, Michèle Morgan, Danielle Darrieux, Hildegarde Neff, Juliette Mayniel, Stéphane Audran.

Las Vegas 500 milliones/They Came to Rob Las Vegas

Isasi started his career with the thriller *Relato policiaco* (1954) and became Spain's best action director with *Estambul 65* (1965), often using an international cast, as in his biggest success, *El perro* (1977) and in this heist movie set in the Nevada desert. The plot revolves around the robbery of a cash-transporting van guarded by a blundering Palance and the crooked operator (Cobb) of the armoured truck. Isasi judiciously uses long shots and high angles to dwarf his main protagonists (Lockwood and Sommer) in Los Angeles cityscapes as well as in the desert. Cops and crooks are equally callous in a film dealing primarily with all the topics later treated in the more prestigious *Zabriskie Point* (1970): the disturbing effects of dependency on technology, the depersonalised city, the hostility of the vast landscapes, rebelliousness leading to outlaw status, etc. Isasi went on to make a 70mm attempt to emulate Sam Fuller's **Underworld U.S.A.** with *Un verano para matar* (1972), starring Karl Malden and with Chris Mitchum in the role of the boy who sees some hoods kill his father and spends his life trying to avenge the murder. Although not as accomplished as the robbery film, it has some excitingly cinematic sequences such as the sharply edited murders that open the story and three horsemen pursuing a motorbike rider through a forest at night. PW

1968/Spain, France, Germany, Italy/129m/Isasi-Capitole-Eichberg-Franca/ *p* Nat Wachsberger/*d*/*co-s* Antonio Isasi/ *co-s* Jo Eisinger, Luis Cameron, Jorge Illa/ *c* Juan Gelpi/*m* Georges Garvarent//*lp* Gary Lockwood, Elke Sommer, Lee J. Cobb, Jack Palance, Georges Geret.

The Late Show

A nostalgic-ironic private eye movie, this amiable diversion lacks the genre-dissecting rigorousness producer Altman brought to **The Long Goodbye.** Through the death of his ex-partner (Duff), aged ex-dick Ira Wells (Carney) gets involved in an apparently ridiculous case, the kidnapping of wealthy kook Tomlin's cat, and doggedly pursues leads which reveal a complex conspiracy of blackmail, fantastically valuable postage stamps and multiple murder. Carney is an amusing hero, hard-arteried rather than hard-boiled, even faking an ulcer attack to turn the tables on the villains in the climax. Like many a 70s retro-*noir*, the film suffers because, unlike Ross MacDonald or the writers of *The Rockford Files*, Benton is unable to come up with an *original* mystery in the Hammett-Chandler tradition and falls back on recycling elements of **The Maltese Falcon** and **The Big Sleep**. KN

1977/94m/WB/*p* Robert Altman/*d*/*s* Robert Benton/*c* Chuck Rosher/*m* Ken Wannberg/ *lp* Art Carney, Lily Tomlin, Bill Macy, Eugene Roche, Joanna Cassidy, John Considine, Howard Duff.

Latimer, Jonathan [Wyatt]
(1906–83)

A former crime reporter for the *Chicago Herald-Examiner* (1930–3), Latimer became a successful genre novelist with his series of (five) screwball mystery novels featuring boozy private detective **Bill Crane**, two of which were adapted by Universal as a part of their Crime Club programmer series, *The Westland Case* (1937; from his novel *Headed for a Hearse*) and *The Last Warning* (1938; from *The Dead Don't Care*). A third Universal Bill Crane mystery was *Lady in the Morgue* (1938). Latimer turned to screen-writing with *The Lone Wolf Spy Hunt* in 1939 and went on to write the screenplays (among numerous others) for **The Glass Key**, a fine adaptation of the **Dashiell Hammett** murder mystery, **The Big Clock**, based on Kenneth Fearing's paranoid melodrama about a reporter hired to solve a murder with all the clues pointing back at him, and George Hopley's **[Cornell Woolrich] Night Has a Thousand Eyes** (co-scripted with Barré Lyndon), with Edward G. Robinson's vaudeville magician trying to save his friends from the disaster which he foresees. Latimer wrote two more (unfilmed) novels in the mid 1950s before he became a regular writer on the *Perry Mason* (1957–66) series for television. TV

The Laughing Policeman/An Investigation of Murder

Starting off with a tersely handled set-piece in which all the passengers aboard a San

ABOVE Gene Tierney, Dana Andrews, *Laura*

Francisco bus are massacred by a killer wielding a sub-machine gun, this fails to sustain any comparable degree of effect. One of the victims is the partner of a dogged homicide cop (a dourly anti-typecast Matthau), and the narrative concerns the efforts of Matthau and his new partner (Dern) to unravel the mystery, a process which defies any brief synopsis. The ensuing crooks' tour takes in a variety of lurid low-life, which sits ill with its source, a novel in the police-procedural form by the Swedish writers Per Wahlöö and Maj Sjöwall, in which the slow process of police work, rather than exotica, was central. The film shares its Bay area locale with **Dirty Harry**, but any comparisons are to its disadvantage. TP

1973/112m/FOX/*p*/*d* Stuart Rosenberg/ *s* Thomas Rickman/*c* David Walsh/*m* Charles Fox/*lp* Walter Matthau, Bruce Dern, Lou Gossett, Anthony Zerbe, Val Avery.

Laura

This is a story full of spite, deceit, snobbery and heartlessness, told with great elegance, and one of the defining moments of *film noir*. Andrews, playing a rather stolid detective, is investigating the death of a young girl who has been swept up into the world of New York high society. He falls asleep in her apartment with a painting of the dead girl on the wall, only to wake and find her standing

over him as large as life. It's a delicious moment in an expertly made thriller, based on **Vera Caspary**'s novel, with Preminger in his element depicting with cool detachment a bright and brittle world. Webb gives a memorable performance as the acidic gossip-columnist Waldo Lydecker, while Tierney provides a dazzlingly beautiful surface for the shallow Laura. David Raksin's theme (with words by Johnny Mercer) was a big hit for Woody Herman, Frank Martin and Dick Haymes amongst others in 1945. EB

1944/88m/FOX/*p*/*d* Otto Preminger/*s* Jay Dratler, Samuel Hoffenstein, Betty Reinhardt/*c* Joseph La Shelle/*m* David Raksin/*lp* Dana Andrews, Clifton Webb, Gene Tierney, Judith Anderson, Vincent Price.

The Lavender Hill Mob

If ever the thesis that the meek will inherit the earth was put to the test, it is in this comic thriller in which Guinness and Holloway, as the worms, take so long to turn. Director Crichton was the most plot- (and joke-) oriented Ealing director. Accordingly, some forty years later he was able to neatly disentangle the plot of *Lavender Hill Mob* from its time and re-use much of it for **A Fish Called Wanda**. Guinness is the timid security guard, in sight of riches beyond belief for some twenty years, who finally turns his mind to acquiring rather than protecting wealth. In a justly celebrated sequence he seduces Holloway, the manufacturer of mini Eiffel Towers (an essential element of the plan), and subsequently the pair ensnare Bass and James, two overly Cockney petty thieves, to help put Guinness's plan into practice. The charm of the film is that this unlikely quartet of innocents are successful, so much so that at a time when crime explicitly couldn't pay the finale has Guinness recounting the story in a bar in South America. Subsequently it is revealed that he is handcuffed to his listener, but it is the story not the handcuffs that the film celebrates. Writer Clarke won an Oscar for his literate and witty script, which includes a delightful parody of the police car chase from his own **The Blue Lamp**. However, in contrast to the earlier **Hue and Cry** or *Passport to Pimlico* (1949), both of which had a social dimension (if only at the level of a collective fantasy), *Lavender Hill* signalled a retreat to individual fantasies. The result is a perfect example of a well-made film, if a lesser work than either **Kind Hearts and Coronets** or **The Ladykillers**. Clarke and Crichton collaborated on one more comedy thriller, *Law and Disorder* (1958), in which crooks rally round to prevent a son finding out his father is an amiable rogue. PH

1951/GB/78m/Ealing/*p* Michael Balcon/ *d* Charles Crichton/*s* T.E.B. Clarke/*c* Douglas Slocombe/*m* Georges Auric/*lp* Alec Guinness, Stanley Holloway, Sidney James, Alfie Bass, Edie Martin, Marjorie Fielding.

Lawyers

In the gangster film, lawyers come in two flavours: crusading district attorneys out to put hoods behind bars (Humphrey Bogart as characters based on racket buster Thomas E. Dewey in **Marked Woman** and *The Enforcer/Murder Inc.*, 1950); or sneaky shysters intent on helping hoods escape justice (Warren William, John Barrymore and Keenan Wynn as characters based on 'attorney of the damned' William J. Fallon in *The Mouthpiece*, 1932, *State's Attorney*, 1932, and *King of the Roaring 20s: The Story of Arnold Rothstein*, 1962), with the occasional crossover as bad lawyers turn good (Spencer Tracy in *The People Against O'Hara*, 1951, Robert Taylor in **Party Girl**). However, the genre has little truck with the mechanics of the law, preferring to see off villains in a cinematic gun battle rather than haul them into court for talky pettifoggery and an anticlimactic jail sentence. Not until **The Undercover Man** was the gangster film, its gothic excesses evolved into semi-documentary realism, ready for an accurate account of

ABOVE Lawyers: Raymond Burr as Perry Mason

the evidence-gathering and legal manoeuvring that actually ended Al Capone's crime empire as opposed to the fictionalised machine-gun holocaust that finished off Capone's incarnation in **Scarface**.

In the mystery novel, there is a tradition of lawyer-detectives, most famously represented by Erle Stanley Gardner's **Perry Mason** but also Melville Davisson Post's Randolph Mason, Harold Q. Masur's Scott Jordan, Arthur Train's Ephraim Tutt, Sara Wood's Anthony Maitland and Robert Van Gulik's Judge Dee. The typical Perry Mason case finds him defending an innocent whom unlikely circumstance makes seem incredibly guilty, a situation favoured by many heroic screen lawyers (Henry Fonda in *Young Mr Lincoln*, 1939, Robert Donat in *The Winslow Boy*, 1950, Gregory Peck in **To Kill a Mockingbird**, Dean Martin in *Mr Ricco*, 1975, Peter Weller in *Blue Jean Cop*, 1987, James Woods in *True Believer/Fighting Justice*, 1989, Tom Cruise in *A Few Good Men*, 1992). The purest example of this brand of drama, which closely approximates the classical detective story as the hero can only get his client off by deducing the truth behind the crime and hence intuiting the real solution to the mystery, finds Henry Fonda as the juror who does the defence attorney's job for him by exonerating the accused in *12 Angry Men* (1957).

Aside from Mason, few lawyer-detectives have made it to the screen. Movie mysteries with a legal setting tend to focus on defence attorneys with a borderline unethical involvement with their clients, the convention being that a supposedly disinterested

ABOVE Stanley Holloway, *The Lavender Hill Mob*

ABOVE Lawyers: Jessica Lange, *Music Box*

with a run of best-sellers turning on points of law and labyrinthine mysteries. These include *The Firm* (1993), in which Tom Cruise realises he works for a mafia front, *The Pelican Brief* (1993) in which trainee Julia Roberts uncovers a conspiracy against the government, *The Client* (1994) with Susan Sarandon as a lawyer in need of redemption, and *A Time To Kill* (1996), with Matthew McConaughey as the independently minded lawyer. Interestingly, none of Grisham's lawyers are D.A.s, rather they reflect a world in which the state is weakened by all-encompassing corruption, including that of the practice of law itself, and only independently minded lawyers can defend the very principles of law.

More credible, perhaps, are dramas which deal with the intricate tangles of a given case as complicated by the unwieldy machinery of the law itself, typified by the trials of flexible D.A. William Powell in *Lawyer Man* (1932), ambitious prosecutor Claude Rains in *They Won't Forget* (1937), ghosts Roger Livesey and Raymond Massey in *A Matter of Life and Death/Stairway to Heaven* (1946), naval attorney José Ferrer in *The Caine Mutiny* (1954), accused traitor Paul Newman in *The Rack* (1956), cracking-up barrister Nicol Williamson in *Inadmissible Evidence* (1968), public defender Judd Hirsch in *The

Law (1974), ambulance chaser Paul Newman in *The Verdict* (1982), lawyer Kelly McGillis and client Jodie Foster in **The Accused**, accused Tom Hanks in **The Bonfire of the Vanities** and D.A. Kevin Costner in *JFK* (1991). While many supposedly straight movie trials are played as farce (nightmare farce in the case of *The Trial*, 1963, 1992), actual comedy lawyers include Will Hay in *My Learned Friend* (1944), Spencer Tracy and Katharine Hepburn in *Adam's Rib* (1949), Ian Carmichael in *Brothers-in-Law* (1956), Peter Sellers in *The Dock Brief/Trial and Error* (1962), Walter Matthau in *The Fortune Cookie/Meet Whiplash Willie* (1966), Robert Redford and Debra Winger in *Legal Eagles* (1987) and Joe Pesci in *My Cousin Vinny* (1992).

The drama-documentary format, in which actual trials are recreated, was originally the province of such socially-crusading films as *The Life of Emile Zola* (1937), *The Court Martial of Billy Mitchell* (1955), *The Crucible/The Witches of Salem* (1958), *Inherit the Wind* (1960), **Compulsion**, *The Trials of Oscar Wilde* (1960), *Judgment at Nuremberg* (1961) and **Evil Angels/A Cry in the Dark**, but evolved into a common form of TV drama with *The Execution of Private Slovik* (1974), *QB VII* (1974), *The Trial of Chaplain Jensen* (1975), *Helter Skelter* (1976), *Judge Horton and

legal mind finds the realities of crime brought home when their personal life gets mixed up with the case. Lawyers in love with perhaps murderous clients include Gregory Peck in **The Paradine Case**, Glenn Close in **Jagged Edge** and, in a variation, Jessica Lange defending her father (Armin Mueller-Stahl), accused of being a war criminal, in *Music Box* (1989). Other ethics-torn attorneys include James Stephenson in *The Letter* (1940), Charles Laughton in *Witness for the Prosecution* (1957), Ellen Barkin (falling for the corrupt cop she is investigating) in **The Big Easy**, Cher (falling for juror Dennis Quaid) in *Suspect* (1987), Ed Harris in *The Last Innocent Man* (1987), Theresa Russell in *Physical Evidence* (1989), Harrison Ford (a lawyer accused of murder) and Raul Julia in **Presumed Innocent**, Gene Hackman and Mary Elizabeth Mastrantonio (father and daughter lawyers defending and prosecuting a case) in *Class Action* (1991) and Edward James Olmos in *The Burden of Proof* (1990)

John Grisham made significant contributions to the popularity of the legal thriller

ABOVE Lawyers: Jodie Foster, Kelly McGillis, *The Accused*

the *Scottsboro Boys* (1976), *Sergeant Matlovich vs the U.S. Air Force* (1978), *Fatal Vision* (1984), *Three Sovereigns for Sarah* (1985), *Roe Vs Wade* (1989), *The Court Martial of Jackie Robinson* (1990) and *Getting Gotti* (1994) and even spun off such courtroom fantasies as *The Trial of Lee Harvey Oswald* (1977) and *The Court Martial of George Armstrong Custer* (1977). Television has always had a fondness for courtroom shows, with single sets and dialogue transcript performances, a fascination that has even extended in America to televised trials that verge upon game-shows. Series lawyers include Jay Jostyn as a Dewey type in *Mr District Attorney* (1951–4), E.G. Marshall in *The Defenders* (1961–5), Peter Mark Richman in *Cain's Hundred* (1961–2), Edmund O'Brien as *Sam Benedict* (1962–3), Chuck Connors in *Arrest and Trial* (1963–4), Peter Falk in *The Trials of O'Brien* (1965–6), Carl Betz in *Judd for the Defence* (1967–9), Lee J. Cobb and counterculture crusaders in *The Young Lawyers* (1970–1), Barry Newman in *The Lawyer* (1970) and the series *Petrocelli* (1973–4), Arthur Hill as *Owen Marshall, Counselor at Law* (1971–4), procurator fiscal Iain Cuthbertson in *Sutherland's Law* (1972–6), exasperated Gretchen Corbett as James Garner's devoted lawyer in *The Rockford Files* (1974–80), jailhouse lawyer-turned-courtroom lawyer Ron Liebman in *Kaz* (1978–9), Leo McKern as *Rumpole of the Bailey* (1978–), Vincent Baggetta in T*he Eddie Capra Mysteries* (1979), public defender Veronica Hamel in *Hill Street Blues* (1981–7), the entire regular cast of *LA Law* (1984–), Andy Griffith as *Matlock* (1986–), Michael Moriarty in *Law and Order* (1990–) and Treat Williams (replacing James Woods in a spin-off from *True Believer*) in *Eddie Dodd* (1990).

Since James Stewart's cynical loophole-enlarging on the behalf of ambiguous murderer Ben Gazzara in Otto Preminger's **Anatomy of a Murder**, there has been a tendency to dwell on the problems of a lawyer whose client is most likely guilty, as with Al Pacino, Judd Nelson, Timothy Hutton and Gary Oldman, defending the indefensible John Forsythe, John Hurt, Nick Nolte and Kevin Bacon in *. . . And Justice for All* (1979), *From the Hip* (1987), *Q&A* (1990) and *Criminal Law* (1991). Reflecting this change is the significant alteration between the 1962 and 1991 versions of **Cape Fear**: in the original film, Robert Mitchum persecutes Gregory Peck because he was the prosecutor who put him in jail, while in the remake, Robert De Niro persecutes Nick Nolte because he was the defender who

deliberately failed to raise evidence that would have got the guilty man off. KN

See also **Perry Mason**.

The League of Gentlemen

Almost a realistic version of **The Lavender Hill Mob**, this is less interesting for its efficient-but-standardised they-don't-quite-get-away-with-it heist than as a cynical and darkly satirical re-reading of the stiff-upper-lip war films it takes its stars from and whose plot structure it imitates. Hawkins, booted out of the army after twenty-five years, assembles a squad of cashiered ex-officers unable to fit in to civilian society and trains them to commit a robbery with exactly the military efficiency he would expect if he were, as in earlier films, planning to retake Malta or blow up the bridge on the River Kwai. Forbes' witty script introduces a succession of familiar officer-material types, only to undermine their images with bizarre little vignettes: staunchly upright Patrick worrying about the overdraft, Alexander exchanging innuendo baby-talk with sex-kitten wife Newman in the bathroom, Attenborough fixing one-armed bandits, and, most radically, Livesey as a padre cashiered for 'gross indecency in a public place' slobbering over his collection of health magazines. A deliberate corruption of cherished national myths, this – along with that curious mirror image *The Dirty Dozen* (1968), in which criminals become soldiers – is an attempt to shrug off the image of World War II which hung over into the 50s. Gradually, the idea of ex-soldier hoods – also in Sam Fuller's **House of Bamboo** – melded with the new 'professional' image of crime: the next key transition is *A Prize of Arms* (1962), in which the object of the attack is an army payroll, making the military the victims rather than the instigators of the raid. KN

1960/GB/116m/Allied/*p* Michael Relph/
d Basil Dearden/*s* Bryan Forbes/*orig* John Boland/*c* Arthur Ibbetson/*m* Philip Green/
lp Jack Hawkins, Nigel Patrick, Roger Livesey, Richard Attenborough, Bryan Forbes, Terence Alexander, Norman Bird, Nanette Newman.

Leonard, Elmore (1925–)

The acclaimed American thriller writer Elmore Leonard began his working life in Detroit (his long-time home and the setting of many of his novels) as an advertising copy writer in the 1950s while producing Western short stories and novels on the side. In the

late 1960s, the successful adaptation of a number of these for the cinema, such as *Hombre* (1967), allowed Leonard to write full-time. Almost simultaneously, Leonard shifted from writing Westerns to crime thrillers. *Fifty Two Pick-up* (1974) was his first classic thriller, demonstrating his gift for gripping stories featuring delightfully laconic heroes, blackly comic yet violently disturbing villains, description littered with pop culture references, and his wonderful ear for brilliantly witty, naturalistic dialogue. This template was developed in a stream of novels like *Swag* (1976), *The Switch* (1979), *Stick* (1984), *LaBrava* (1984) and his first major best-seller *Glitz* (1985). Elmore Leonard has written numerous original screenplays and, largely unsuccessful, adaptations of his own work, the experience of which provided background material for his Hollywood-set comedy thriller *Get Shorty* (1990). Several other big and small screen adaptations of Leonard's work have been released, such as John Frankenheimer's underrated *52 Pick-up* (1986), but it was not until 1995 – with the release of Barry Sonnenfeld's film of *Get Shorty* – that any garnered critical or box office success. Since then various new productions have been announced, including Paul Schrader's version of *Touch,* due for release in 1997. AW

Lepke

One of several 'historical' gangster movies produced in the wake of **The Godfather,** this dramatised biography of Louis 'Lepke' Buchalter assumes a chronicle structure to the extent of including a sepia prologue depicting its protagonist's youthful experiences in a reformatory. The story goes on to detail his rise in the rackets and his uneasy alliance with **Lucky Luciano**, the encroachment of a 'corporate ethos' into criminal organisation, and Lepke's supposedly fatal mistake in ordering a killing in the presence of witnesses. A deal with the law falls through and in 1944 he goes to the electric chair, the only 'top' American criminal of the era to be legally executed. The presentation of his death is gruesomely detailed, and the film as a whole possesses a ritualistic quality, enhanced by use of (simulated) recordings of Walter Winchell as a continuity device. While the portrait of Lepke may lack any real depth, capable as Curtis's performance is, the film is put together with suitably old-fashioned drive and assurance, and its set-pieces include a dynamically contrived shooting affray in a movie theatre. TP

1974/110m/AmeriEuro Pictures Corp/
p/*d* Menahem Golan/*s* Wesley Lau, Tamar
Simon Hoffs/*c* Andrew Davis/*m* Ken
Wannberg/*lp* Tony Curtis, Michael Callan,
Anjanette Comer, Gianni Russo, Vic
Tayback.

Leroux, Gaston (1868–1927)

Born in Paris, Leroux was an adventurer, a
journalist, a war correspondent and a lawyer
as well as a well-known writer of popular
fiction, author of more than 30 novels. His
two most enduring creations are the energetic, playful and astute journalist Roulета-
bille (8 novels), a variation on **Edgar Allan
Poe**'s Dupin, and the gangster Chéri-Bibi (5
novels). His first fiction, generally regarded
as the masterpiece of French detective literature, was the classic locked-room plot *Le
Mystère de la chambre jaune* (1907), published
in the magazine *L'Illustration*. It revolved
around a family drama and made the police
detective into the villain. It featured Joseph
Josephson aka Rouletabille as a reporter
with a bullet-shaped head (hence his name)
who plays the Holmes role while his friend
Sainclair chronicles the reporter's adventures. This was followed by *Le Parfum de la
dame en noir* (1908), the sensationalist *Le fantôme de l'opéra* (1911) and many others.
Leroux's first adaptations to the screen date
back to 1913, with the theatre actor Marcel
Simon as Rouletabille in **Le Mystère de la
chambre jaune**, followed by Emile
Chautard's *Le Parfum de la dame en noir*
(1914) with Maurice de Féraudy. Chautard
went on to direct a **Mystery of the Yellow
Room/The Yellow Room Mystery** in the
US in 1919 starring William S. Walcott. The
best of the silent films based on Leroux's
work was an original contribution written
especially for the screen: Henri Fescourt's
10-episode serial, in true Feuillade style,
Rouletabille chez les bohémiens (1921) starring
Gabriel de Gavrone. Marcel L'Herbier made
the first sound versions of the diptych **Le
Mystère de la chambre jaune** and *Le
Parfum de la dame en noir* in 1930 starring
Roland Toutain. Henri Aisner made the next
version of **Le Mystère de la chambre
jaune** (1948) and Louis Daquin followed
this with *Le Parfum de la dame en noir* (1949),
both starring Serge Reggiani. Istvan (*aka*
Steve) Szekely made *Rouletabille aviateur*
(1932) again with Toutain, while Christian
Chamborant starred Jean Piat in loose adaptations of Leroux's work, *Rouletabille joue et
gagne* (1946) and *Rouletabille contre la dame de
pique* (1947). In the 1960s, Rouletabille was

ABOVE Gaston Leroux

resurrected for a television series in France,
one episode being directed by Yves Boisset
prior to making his name with controversial
thrillers about corrupt cops and politicians.
Claude Brasseur also incarnated Rouletabille
on television under the direction of Jean
Kerchbron.

Chéri Bibi also made it to the screen,
although less auspiciously. After a 1913 version of the story, directed by Gérard
Bourgeois and starring René Navarre, simply
called *Chéri Bibi*, Charles Krauss directed *Les
premieres aventures de Chéri Bibi* (1914) starring Emile Keppens in the title role. This was
followed by Edouard-Emile Violet's *Nouvelle
Aurore/Nouvelles aventures de Chéri Bibi* (1919)
starring José Davert. John S. Robertson used
the character, played by John Gilbert, for his
The Phantom of Paris (1931). Léon Mathot
cast Pierre Fresnay in his *Chéri Bibi* (1937)
and the Italian Marcello *aka* Marcel Pagliero
made a Franco-Italian co-production, *Chéri
Bibi/Il forzato della Guiana* (1955) starring
Jean Richard.

The film versions of *The Phantom of the
Opera* are many: Rupert Julian's version
starred Lon Chaney in 1925; Claude Rains
was the Phantom in Arthur Lubin's film
(1943), Herbert Lom in Terence Fisher's
(1962, the best version to date); Robert
Markowitz directed a version for US television in 1983, followed by Dwight H. Little in
1989; the latest version was Tony
Richardson's, made for US television in
1990. Victorin Jasset filmed a serial with a
Frankenstein-theme based on Leroux's
work, *Balaoo* (1913). *L'Homme qui revient de
loin* was filmed by René Navarre (who also
starred in it) in 1916 and by Jean Castanier
in 1949. Other Leroux adaptations include:
Henri Pouctal's *Alsace* (1915), René Navarre's
Tue-la-Mort (1920) and René Navarre and M.
Manzoni's *La sept de trefle* (1921), M.
Manzoni's *Il était deux petits enfants* (1922),
Richard Rosson's *The Wizard* (1927) and
Robert Siodmak's *Mister Flow* (1936). PW

Levin, Ira (1929–)

New Yorker Ira Levin cut his teeth in the
movies writing training films for the US
Army during the early 50s. His first notable
thriller was **A Kiss before Dying**, and in
1956 it gave Robert Wagner his first starring
role as the sinister Bud who kills off his girl-
friend to conceal her pregnancy. At the same
time Levin was developing as a playwright.
The Broadway comedy *No Time for Sergeants*,
reflecting his experience in the services, was
a vehicle for Andy Griffith, who also starred
in the subsequent film (1958). Half a dozen
stage comedies and formula mysteries followed, but *A Kiss before Dying* was more obviously representative of Levin's most successful themes, focusing on an unwary individual stumbling into a hidden world, normal
on the surface, but evil underneath. In
Rosemary's Baby (1967) a Satanist group
mounts a secret conspiracy to help the Devil
impregnate a young woman. Directed by
Roman Polanski, the film (1968) was a runaway success, which had an enduring influence on horror fiction. Similarly, *The Stepford
Wives*, published in 1972 and filmed in 1975,
entered the language as a metaphor for the
repression of women. *The Boys from Brazil*
was published in 1976 and filmed in 1978,
but *Deathtrap* (1982), a successful Broadway
play in 1978, with its plot about an exhausted playwright using murder as an instrument of plagiarism, seemed prophetic, and
Sliver (novel 1991, film 1994) failed to reach
Levin's own high standards of creepiness and
originality. In 1991 there was a lacklustre
remake of *A Kiss before Dying*. MP

The Lineup

The Lineup/San Francisco Beat (1954–60) was
the CBS answer to NBC's *Dragnet* (1952–9),
with Anderson and Reed as Inspectors
Guthrie and Asher, dedicated but colourless
San Francisco cops, investigating based-on-
fact cases. This spin-off minimises the roles
of regular cast-members, adding a grouchier
cop (Meyer) to bulk out the team, and is

interesting not for its buttoned-down police procedural but for the offbeat treatment it accords criminals. On the trail of three packages of heroin smuggled into the country are a pair of eccentric professionals, icy killer Dancer (Wallach) and his mentor-manager Julian (Keith). Taylor is the wheelchair-bound executive who listens in impassive silence to Dancer's lengthy excuse about the missing third package (a child has used the heroin to powder her doll's face) and then calmly informs him 'you're dead'. Siegel and Silliphant underline the functioning strangeness of the criminal team, allowing them tight-lipped banter about points of grammar and giving Keith a fetish for collecting the last words of the people Dancer kills. The film makes clever use of the San Francisco setting, prefiguring **Bullitt** and Siegel's **Dirty Harry** in a last-reel car chase that takes place on half-built freeway flyovers and winds up memorably with the criminals simply running out of road. Unfussy and direct, this is one of Siegel's best 50s films. KN

1958/85m/COL/*p* Jaime del Valle/*d* Don Siegel/*s* Stirling Silliphant/*orig* TV series creator Lawrence L. Klee/*c* Hal Mohr/ *m* Mischa Bakaleinikoff/*lp* Eli Wallach, Robert Keith, Warner Anderson, Richard Jaeckel, Mary LaRoche, Emile Meyer, Marshall Reed.

ABOVE Kirk Douglas, George C. Scott, *The List of Adrian Messenger*

The List of Adrian Messenger

What gives this film its special interest is the parade of major stars in cameo roles; at strategic moments Tony Curtis, Kirk Douglas, Burt Lancaster, Robert Mitchum and Frank Sinatra each appear heavily disguised, to throw the audience off the scent. The list in question is held by Scott. It contains the names of eleven people, all of whom he discovers have been murdered by a mysterious killer. Eventually Scott discovers what the names have in common: that they were all prisoners of the Japanese, and that amongst them had been an informer who betrayed each in turn to their captors. The killer, as well as neutralising those seeking vengeance, is also on the track of an inheritance, which requires that he remove a child who stands before him in the family tree. Thanks to Scott, who clearly delights in the 'Britishness' of his character and essays tight-lipped rather than full-bodied heroics, the villain meets a satisfying end, impaled on a giant rake. EB

1963/98m/U/*p* Edward Lewis/*d* John Huston/*s* Anthony Veiller/*c* Joe MacDonald/ *m* Jerry Goldsmith/*lp* George C. Scott, Dana Wynter, Clive Brook, Gladys Cooper, Herbert Marshall.

Little Caesar

Though not quite the first of the gangster cycle – it was preceded notably by *Doorway to Hell* (1930) – this established the rise-and-fall plot that has been a staple of the genre from immediate follow-ups like **The Public Enemy** and **Scarface** to 90s equivalents like

ABOVE George C. Scott, *The List of Adrian Messenger*

King of New York (1990) and *New Jack City* (1990). The film follows the career of Cesare Enrico Bandello (Robinson), known as Rico, a brutish hoodlum from the sticks who rises in the rackets purely through the unhealthy diversion of all his sexual energies into *Macbeth*-like ambition – his only attachment is a peculiar quasi-homosexual fondness for Dancer (Fairbanks) – and, after a period of flamboyant success, winds up down and out, finally shot to death in the traditional gutter, croaking 'mother of mercy, is this the end of Rico?' Despite good dialogue and performances, the film is flawed by its strangely naïve vision of what gangsters actually do – Rico's crime empire seems founded on society jewel robberies, for all the world like the fantasy Sheik-figure of Sternberg's **Underworld** – and by LeRoy's merely competent direction. KN

1930/77m/First National/*d* Mervyn LeRoy/ *s* Francis Edwards Faragoh, Robert N. Lee/*orig* W.R. Burnett/*c* Tony Gaudio/*m* Erno Rapee/*lp* Edward G. Robinson, Douglas Fairbanks Jr, Glenda Farrell, Sidney Blackmer, Thomas Jackson, Ralph Ince.

ABOVE Edward G. Robinson, *Little Caesar*

Lone Star

A companion piece to Sayles's earlier *City of Hope* (1991), which was about urban corruption in New Jersey, *Lone Star* is set in rural south-west Texas. It begins with the revelation of a murder which occurred many years ago. In tracing back the events which led to the killing and its aftermath the film uncovers institutionalised racism and civic corruption embedded in a complex pattern of ethnic and sexual interrelations. Sayles's method is strongly didactic, insisting that we are all products not just of our individual pasts but of a collective and social history. But the film also has all the merits of classic *film noir*; as we flash forward and back in time, the mystery of who killed Sheriff Charlie Wade (Kristofferson) deepens with each successive revelation, until the final stunning dénouement. A film of genuine intelligence, as well as considerable style. EB

1995/135m/Castle Rock/*p* John Sloss/ *d/s* John Sayles/*c* Stuart Dryburgh/*m* Mason Daring/*lp* Chris Cooper, Elizabeth Peña, Joe Morton, Matthew McConaughey, Kris Kristofferson.

The Lone Wolf

A heroic thief, The Lone Wolf was created by novelist Louis Joseph Vance (1879–1933) in *The Lone Wolf* (1914). All heroic thieves reform eventually (in films, if not the original stories) but Michael Lanyard went straight in his first outing, changing for the love of a good woman and turning vigilante to destroy the Pack, an international crime ring who turn out to be puppets of Imperial Germany. In the sequel, *The False Faces* (1918), the Germans have killed Lanyard's girl and he joins the Secret Service to use his outlaw skills against the foes of democracy. Subsequent novels find Lanyard struggling with jewel thieves in *Alias the Lone Wolf* (1921) and godless communists in *Red Masquerade* (1921), then settling down somewhat as a family man in *The Lone Wolf Returns* (1923), *The Lone Wolf's Son* (1931) and *The Lone Wolf's Last Prowl* (1934). In the movies, Lanyard was first played by Bert Lytell (who was also the screen's first **Boston Blackie** in *Boston Blackie's Little Pal* (1918) and its second Jimmy Valentine in *Alias Jimmy Valentine* (1920)), in *The Lone Wolf* (1917), *The Lone Wolf Returns* (1926), *Alias the Lone Wolf* (1927) and the talkies *The Lone Wolf's Daughter* (1929) and the optimistically-titled *Last of the Lone Wolf* (1930). Henry B. Walthall played Lanyard in *The*

ABOVE Melvyn Douglas as The Lone Wolf

False Faces (1919) and a first version of *The Lone Wolf's Daughter* (1919), with which Vance was evidently so taken that he incorporated the Lone Wolf's daughter, invented by Paramount, into subsequent novels. Jack Holt starred in *The Lone Wolf* (1924), a remake of the first story, while Thomas Meighan appeared as Lanyard in *Cheaters at Play* (1932), a sentimental melodrama which omitted to mention the retired thief's Lone Wolf sobriquet.

The best-remembered Lone Wolf was featured in a long-running series from Columbia, who had made all but the first Lytell film. The new series started with a remake of *The Lone Wolf Returns* (1936) starring Melvyn Douglas, later **Arsène Lupin** in *Arsène Lupin Returns* (1938), under the direction of Roy William Neill, who would make the bulk of the Basil Rathbone **Sherlock Holmes** entries. Thurston Hall plays Inspector Crane, a detective who refuses to believe the Lone Wolf is retired as he claims to be and, like the **Saint**'s Inspector Teal, constantly fails to catch him in any misdemeanour. Another continuing character is Lanyard's valet, here called Jenkins and played by Raymond Walburn and by Eric Blore, who misses the old days and is always trying to manipulate his employer, like an inept and crooked Jeeves, into returning to crime. Francis Lederer, a future Dracula, took over, as 'Michel' Lanyard, for Albert S. Rogell's *The Lone Wolf in Paris* (1938), but was quickly replaced by Warren William – a sometime **Perry Mason**, **Philo Vance** and d'Artagnan who had failed to pin anything on Douglas as the detective in *Arsène Lupin Returns* – for Peter Godfrey's *The Lone Wolf Spy Hunt* (1939) and eight follow-ups, Sidney Salkow's *The Lone Wolf Strikes* (1940), *The Lone Wolf Meets a Lady* (1940), *The Lone Wolf Takes a Chance* (1941) and *The Lone Wolf Keeps a Date* (1941), Edward Dmytryk's *Secrets of the Lone Wolf* (1941), and *Counter-Espionage* (1942), Michael Gordon's *One Dangerous Night* (1943) and André de Toth's *Passport to Suez* (1943).

Despite the efforts of three notable Hollywood blacklistees (Dmytryk, Gordon and Dalton Trumbo, who wrote *The Lone Wolf Strikes*) and, for *The Lone Wolf Spy Hunt*, the writing talents of **Jonathan Latimer**, the series is light and undistinguished, with the ever-suave William solving murders of society blackmailers or catching Nazi spies with ease. While the Salkow entries tend to be plodding mysteries, the last four films benefit from improved direction, with exotic locales for *Counter-Espionage* (the London Blitz) and *Passport to Suez* (Constantinople). As usual in series entries, the films as a group cast a pleasing mix of up-and-coming faces (Ida Lupino, Rita Hayworth, Forrest Tucker, Lloyd Bridges) with reliable B characters (Ann Savage, Marc Lawrence, Victor Jory, Sheldon Leonard).

Gerald Mohr, a blackmailing scoundrel in *One Dangerous Night* and **Philip Marlowe** on radio, appeared some time after Williams's departure in three unsuccessful quickies, Ross Lederman's *The Notorious Lone Wolf* (1946) and *The Lone Wolf in Mexico* (1947) and Leslie Goodwin's *The Lone Wolf in London* (1947). William Davidson was Crane in the first film. Ron Randell, a one-time **Bulldog Drummond**, was given a shot in *The Lone Wolf and His Lady* (1949), an obvious attempt to relaunch the series, with Alan Mowbray as Jamison and William Frawley as Crane. On radio the Lone Wolf was played by Mohr and Walter Coy, and on television by Louis Hayward, a one-time Simon Templar, Count of Monte Cristo, d'Artagnan and Son of Dr Jekyll. Though Vance's books were popular enough in their day to add the expression 'lone wolf' to the language – as used to describe the heroes of Chuck Norris's *Lone Wolf MacQuade* (1983), Barry Malzberg's series of 70s paperback action novels and a

ABOVE Bob Hoskins, *The Long Good Friday*

popular Japanese samurai saga of film, television and *manga* – they are practically forgotten now, and the film Lone Wolf (best seen, perhaps, in *The Lone Wolf Returns* and *The Lone Wolf Spy Hunt*) does not have the lasting cult appeal of **Charlie Chan** or **Sherlock Holmes**. KN

The Long Good Friday

Developing the central idea of **The Godfather Part II**, the desire of those in organised crime to become legitimate, *Friday* sees Hoskins attempting to translate his London gangland earnings into a multi-million pound Docklands development in association with the American **mafia** only for the deal to run aground on the rocky shores of the IRA. The film leans heavily on clichés – Hoskins's overblown Cockney with the upper-class girl-friend (Mirren) and the homosexual best friend, the weasely crooked councillor. But Keeffe's dense plotting (particularly of the opening third when Hoskins's empire is under siege – but from whom?) and MacKenzie's staging of the set-pieces – the bombing of the restaurant, the shoot-out at the dog track – give it a real edge.

Similarly the structure of a series of short, highly theatrical sequences in which Hoskins's dreams of empire are shattered give the film a decidedly modern feel. It is only when the script leaves the public arena for the private that drama quickly gives way to melodrama. The film's political dimension (which delayed its distribution in the UK by a year) is well handled. The implication is that if Hoskins's soldiers cannot defeat the IRA – who have turned on him because one of his underlings took some of the money intended as a pay off to the IRA – in London, what hope does the British government have in Northern Ireland? PH

1979/GB/114m/Calendar-Black Lion/*p* Barry Hanson/*d* John MacKenzie/*s* Barrie Keeffe/ *c* Phil Meheux/*m* Francis Monkman/*lp* Bob Hoskins, Dave King, Helen Mirren, Bryan Marshall, Derek Thompson, Eddie Constantine.

The Long Goodbye

This unconventional adaptation of Chandler's late masterpiece casts a slobbish Gould as **Philip Marlowe**, a man out of time in a

ABOVE Elliott Gould, Mark Rydell, *The Long Goodbye*

casually corrupt and sun-struck early 70s. Opening with a brilliantly sour comedy sequence as Marlowe tries to dupe his cat into eating an inferior brand of pet food, the main strand is the hurt done to the hero by his only friend (Bouton), who uses him to escape the country when he seems likely to take the rap for the brutal murder of his wife, a crime of which, diverging from the novel, he turns out actually to be guilty of. Among the well-cast supporting characters are Roger Wade (Hayden), a drunken Hemingwayesque writer who holds forth in several brilliantly argumentative scenes written by Hayden himself, and Marty Augustine (Rydell), a mod mobster with Schwarzenegger as an imposing bodyguard who unforgettably smashes a Coke bottle into his teenage mistress's face and then tells Marlowe 'that was someone I love, you I don't even like'. The film ends with a cunningly amoral moment of glory for Marlowe as he discovers that Bouton has faked his own suicide to escape justice and perfectly legally kills his officially deceased former friend. John Williams' score cleverly trots out an infinite number of variations on a single title song, heard as a jazz improvisation, a torch song, musak and a Mexican funeral march. KN

1973/112m/UA/*p* Jerry Bick/*d* Robert Altman/*s* Leigh Brackett/*orig* Raymond Chandler/*c* Vilmos Zsigmond/*m* John T. Williams/*lp* Elliott Gould, Nina Van Pallandt, Sterling Hayden, Henry Gibson, Mark Rydell, Jim Bouton, Arnold Schwarzenegger.

Looking for Mr. Goodbar

Keaton stepped out from the Woody Allen social-comedy school and made a strong impression with her role of a lonely schoolteacher who indulges in a dark double life by seeking her Mr Right in nocturnal singles bars. The downbeat story sees Keaton's degeneration through easy pick-ups and one-night stands until she becomes victim to the habitués of this seamy side of life. Brooks's rather moralising screenplay was based on the novel by Judith Rossner. TV

1977/135m/PAR/*p* Freddie Fields/. *d/s* Richard Brooks/*c* William A. Fraker/ *m* Artie Kane/*lp* Diane Keaton, Tuesday Weld, William Atherton.

Love Me or Leave Me

A musical biography of Prohibition era singer Ruth Etting and her mentor (actually her husband) and Chicago underworld figure 'The Gimp' Snyder. Despite its 1920s Chicago background, the gangland element is for the most part supplied by Cagney's cruel, obsessed hoodlum. Saturated with popular standards of the time, which Day performs excellently, the dramatic impact, however, is shared by Day and Cagney in their uneasy love-hate relationship. The use of CinemaScope and Eastmancolor actually pays off in recreating the mood and flavour of the Roaring 20s. TV

1955/122m/MGM/*p* Joe Pasternak/*d* Charles Vidor/*s* Daniel Fuchs, Isobel Lennart/ *c* Arthur E. Arling/*m* George Stoll/*lp* Doris Day, James Cagney, Cameron Mitchell.

Luciano, Charles 'Lucky'
(1897–1962)

Born Salvatore Luciana in Sicily, the New York-based organised crime figure rose to prominence in the 20s. In 1931, he seized control of the New York underworld from feuding gangsters Joe Masseria and Salvatore Maranzano, arranging the murder of his long-time boss Masseria before defecting to Maranzano's mob and then having him killed too. With Vito Genovese, Meyer Lansky, Frank Costello, Lepke Buchalter, Dutch Schultz and Bugsy Siegel, Luciano survived the repeal of Prohibition and set a tone of cold efficiency that stood in direct contrast to the flamboyance of **Al Capone** and Legs Diamond. His main contribution to the structure of crime in America was the transformation of a confederation of the nine top **mafia** families into a national crime syndicate. Luciano was almost certainly instrumental in setting up the murders of Diamond and Schultz. In a 1927 incident, he became notable as a rare hoodlum who survived being 'taken for a ride', recovering after

ABOVE 'Lucky' Luciano

being left for dead by unknown assailants probably connected with Diamond.

In 1937, Special Prosecutor Thomas E. Dewey secured a conviction against Luciano on sixty-one specific charges of compulsory prostitution and the gangster was sentenced to thirty-five years. During World War II, Luciano turned his energies to patriotic ends, directing his organisation from his cell in Dannemora penitentiary, working against dock-front sabotage in New York and, through his extensive overseas contacts, assisting the allies in the Sicilian campaign. Released on a pardon granted by now-Governor Dewey in 1946, Luciano was deported to Italy and spent the rest of his life allegedly involved in the international drugs trade, frequently coming as close to the US as Cuba. He died of a heart attack just as he was about to meet movie producer Martin Gosch to discuss a film of his life.

Luciano has often featured as a major or supporting character in gangster movies, whether under his own name or in thin aliases. The segments of his career are covered, in variously unsatisfactory manner, by Michael Karbelnikoff's *Mobsters* (1991), Lloyd Bacon's **Marked Woman** and Francesco Rosi's **Lucky Luciano**. In *Mobsters*, Christian Slater leads a brat pack of fellow gangsters – Meyer Lansky (Patrick Dempsey), Frank Costello (Costas Mandylor) and Bugsy Siegel (Richard Grieco) – against crabby old-timers Masseria (Anthony Quinn) and 'Faranzano' (Michael Gambon), avenging the death of Arnold Rothstein (F. Murray Abraham) by taking over the New York gangs. In *Marked Woman*, Luciano is represented under the non-ethnic name Johnny Vanning by the highly-ethnic Eduardo Ciannelli, with Humphrey Bogart as the equivalent of Dewey and Bette Davis as a euphemised prostitute, based on a real-life informant known to history as 'Cokey Flo', whose testimony puts the mob leader away. *Lucky Luciano* opens with the solemn Luciano (Gian Maria Volonté) emerging from prison en route to Sicily, where he passes the rest of his life being harried by narcotics agents as Rosi carefully refuses to make up his mind as to how sincere the gangster's apparent rehabilitation is.

Other screen Lucianos are Angela Infanti in **The Valachi Papers**, Vic Tayback in **Lepke**, Michael Nouri (also Tony Raymond and Paul Regina as younger versions) in The *Gangster Chronicles/Gangster Wars* (1981), Joe Dallessandro in **The Cotton Club**, Stanley Tucci in *Billy Bathgate* (1991), Bill Graham in

ABOVE *Lucky Luciano*

Bugsy, Robert Davi in *White Hot: The Mysterious Murder of Thelma Todd* (1991), Leonard Donato in *Hit the Dutchman* (1992) and Billy Drago in *The Outfit* (1992). Luciano equivalents are played by Frank DeKova in **The Rise and Fall of Legs Diamond**, Henry Silva in *Sharky's Machine* (1981) and Marc Lawrence in *Ruby* (1992). The aspect of Luciano's career that has most caught the Hollywood imagination is his deportation, as referred to in the first film to mention him by name, **The Big Heat**, where the villain complains 'I don't want to land in the same ditch with the Lucky Lucianos', while Edward G. Robinson in **Key Largo** and Raymond Burr in **His Kind of Woman** play deported hoods trying to sneak back into the USA. KN

Lucky Luciano

Described by critic Tom Milne as the perfect example of Catch 22, the defining feature of Rosi's enquiry into the development of the **mafia** in Italy and the US is its circularity. As US Narcotics commissioner Anslinger (O'Brien) wearily puts it: 'We chase Luciano, Dewey chases us, Kefauver chases Dewey and everybody finds himself back where he started'. Thus, it is entirely fitting that Volonté's Luciano dies in the arms of a Hollywood scriptwriter. The film opens with the release from prison of Luciano in 1946 and deportation to Italy. He has been pardoned in recognition of his help in facilitat-

ing co-operation between the **mafia** and the American occupying forces during the Sicilian campaign in World War II. Once in Italy the corruption of the US occupying forces by the Italians they profess to control is made clear as in the set piece fraternisation dance. Luciano is kept under investigation by narcotics agent Siragusa (playing himself). Rosi comes to no conclusions about Luciano's later involvement in the drugs trade. His interest is more in the wider network of crime and corruption, especially the links between the US government and the mafia, which he records in semi-documentary style. The one bravura moment in the film is the depiction of the Night of the Sicilian Vespers, a purge which brought Luciano to the head of the New York criminal world in 1931. EB

1973/Italy, France/115m (English version 94m)/Vides-Les Films de la Boétie/p Franco Cristaldi/d Francesco Rosi/s Francesco Rosi, Lino Jannuzzi, Tonino Guerra/c Pasqualino De Santis/m Piero Piccioni/lp Gian Maria Volonté, Rod Steiger, Charles Siragusa, Edmond O'Brien, Vincent Gardenia.

Lupin, Arsène

Gentleman burglar Arsène Lupin was created by Maurice Leblanc (1864–1941) in 1905. The first collection of stories published in book form was *Arsène Lupin Gentleman Cambrioleur* (1907). Born in Rouen, Leblanc was saved from a burning house when he was only four. When the war of 1870 broke out, the 6-year-old was sent to Scotland for a year. Back in France, the young Leblanc listened avidly to Gustave Flaubert's stories, later frequenting another fellow Normandian, Guy de Maupassant, before becoming a blue-collar employee in a factory and subsequently a hack journalist, crime reporter in Paris and dramatist described by his wife as a dandy who, in 1900, invented the fashions of 1835. He published a few novels and stories in the styles of Flaubert and de Maupassant. In 1905, the publisher Pierre Laffitte commissioned Leblanc to write a story with a Holmes or Raffles type hero for the monthly journal *Je sais tout*. Instead, Leblanc followed the model of Ponson de Terrail's *Rocambole* (1866), a lovable rogue adventurer. Leblanc called his hero Arsène Lopin, after a Parisian councillor. When the real Lopin protested, Leblanc changed his character's name to Lupin. Immediately successful, the Lupin stories featured a hero who was constructed as the opposite of both **Raffles** and **Sherlock Holmes**. They feature no feats of deductive reasoning, no menacing conspiracies and world-threatening criminals, merely the raffish charm of their hero. From the outset of the stories, it is known that the light-hearted, philandering Lupin did it. Rather than restoring the rule of law, Lupin amuses himself making fools of the police and living the life of a cultured rentier while occasionally helping damsels in distress, relying on a quaintly idiosyncratic code of honour sustained by robbery and dedicated to self-indulgence. *Arsène Lupin Gentleman Cambrioleur* included a parody of Holmes (*Holmlock Shears Arrives Too Late*) and the title of Leblanc's second collection took the confrontation even further, *Arsène Lupin contre Herlock Sholomes* (1908). Further collections and novels followed, including *813* (1910, filmed 1920), *The Golden Triangle* (1917) and *The Memoirs of Arsène Lupin* (1925). Towards the end of his career, in line with the growing pressures of censorship and political radicalism, Lupin becomes increasingly more conservative and ends up collaborating with the police.

The first film often identified as a Lupin adaptation is Edwin S. Porter's *The Gentleman Burglar* (1908), shown in France as *Une aventure d'Arsène Lupin*. However, the eponymous gentleman bears no resemblance to Lupin's character. In Porter's film, he abandons his thieving, marries and settles down before succumbing to blackmail from an old

ABOVE Jean-Claude Brialy, Jean-Pierre Cassel, *Arsène Lupin contre Arsène Lupin*

accomplice, landing in prison for murder and losing his family. The story has a 'crime does not pay' moral, wholly unlike Leblanc's work. Porter later remade the film as *Fate* (1911). Ironically, it was this theatrical version, rather than the stories, of Lupin which inspired most US film adaptations. Prior to this Paul Otto starred as Lupin in five German one and two reel films made under the generic title of *Arsène Lupin contra Sherlock Holmes* (1910–1911) These were directed by Viggo Larsen, who also played Holmes, on the trail of Lupin until the last episode. The first feature-length film to include Lupin (Gerald Ames) was the UK outing *Arsène Lupin* (1916). Two further US silent films were *Arsène Lupin* (1917) with Earle Williams and *The Teeth of the Tiger* (1919) with Wedgewood Nowell. A superior European silent offering was Paul Fejos' *Arsène Lupin's Utolso Kalandja* (1921).

In the sound era John Barrymore played Lupin in *Arsène Lupin* (1932), Melvyn Douglas in *Arsène Lupin Returns* (1938), Charles Korvin in *Enter Arsène Lupin* (1944) and Ramon Perado in the Mexican *Arsenio Lupin* (1945), which was also produced and directed by its star. Lupin featured in several French offerings, including Jacques Becker's *Les Aventures d'Arsène Lupin* (1956), in which he was impersonated by Robert Lamoureux, and *Arsène Lupin contre Arsène Lupin* (1962, with Jean-Claude Brialy). In 1970–1 there was also a French-Swedish television series,

Arsène Lupin in which, as ever, Holmes was the gentleman thief's nemesis. PW

M

M

This, Lang's first sound film, was based on the case of serial murderer Peter Kurten, known as the Vampire of Dusseldorf. Its original title was *Mörder unter Uns (The Murderer Is Among Us)*. Lorre is the killer who compulsively preys on children. The police, following ponderous bureaucratic procedures, fail to catch him, and it is left to the underworld, whose forces are marshalled by the master criminal Schrenke, to trap him. He is then put on trial by a kangaroo court and condemned to death, but the police finally arrive and take him into custody. Lang's masterly use of shadowy lighting and menacing off-screen sound create a memorable atmosphere of fear and loathing. Lorre is compelling as the disturbed and pathetic child-killer, in a performance which provided the model for many of his subsequent roles. Lang's depiction of the blood lust of the criminal mob has often been described as a non-too-veiled comment on the rise of the Nazis. Lang left Germany soon after, as did Lorre. EB

1931/Germany/118m/Nero Film/*p* Seymour Nebenzahl/*d* Fritz Lang/*s* Thea von Harbou, Fritz Lang/*c* Fritz Arno Wagner/*m* Adolf

Jansen/*lp* Peter Lorre, Ellen Widmann, Inge Landgut, Otto Wernicke, Gustaf Gründgens.

M: The kangaroo court (above), Peter Lorre (below)

Macao

In this deceptively fast-moving film in lustrous black-and-white, Mitchum is a world-weary drifter ('I've been lonely in Times Square on New Year's Eve') who gets a new direction in life when due to the amorous attentions of a down-on-her-luck chanteuse (Russell) and the moral example of an undercover cop (Bendix), he intervenes to help in bringing to book an American murderer (Brad Dexter) now running a gambling club in Macao, the Portuguese colony introduced by a voice-over as 'where international law ends'. The film was the last American undertaking of Sternberg, who was presumably hired on the expectation that he would supply an overlay of exoticism. In the event, the studio deemed the film unsatisfactory, and in the interests of narrative momentum it was substantially reshot by Nicholas Ray. However, the latter took pains to duplicate Sternberg's style, and the result is seamless –

ABOVE Charles Bronson, *Machine Gun Kelly*

a deluxe piece of thick-ear fiction which happily transcends the considerations of auteur theory. TP

1952/81m/RKO/*p* Alex Gottlieb/*d* Josef von Sternberg/*s* Bernard C. Schoenfeld, Stanley Rubin/*c* Harry J. Wild/*m* Anthony Collins/ *lp* Robert Mitchum, Jane Russell, William Bendix, Gloria Grahame, Brad Dexter.

McBain, Ed (1926–)

Real name Salvatore A. Lombino, pseudonyms Evan Hunter, Ed McBain, Curt Cannon, Hunt Collins, Ezra Hannon, Richard Marsten. McBain is best known as the prolific author of the 87th Precinct stories, perhaps the longest and most popular of all literary police procedural series. The 87th Precinct and its diverse characters were introduced with the publication of *Cop Hater* in 1956. The late 1950s saw the United Artists release of three 87th Precinct B-movies, *Cop Hater* (1957), *The Mugger* (1958) and, in 1960, *The Pusher*, before his stories were taken up by the Japanese in 1963 (*Tengoku To Jigoku*, novel basis *King's Ransom*) and later in 1981 (*Kofuku*, novel basis *Lady, Lady, I Did It!*); and by the French in 1963 with *Soupe aux poulets* (novel basis *Killer's Wedge*) and in 1971, *Sans mobile apparent* (novel basis *Ten Plus One*). *Fuzz* (1972), with Hunter scripting from the McBain novel, ended up being an unfortu-

nate episodic film featuring a string of Hollywood actors attempting comedy. However, on a more positive note, Claude Chabrol's 1977 French-Canadian production of McBain's *Blood Relatives* presented a suitably grim-looking Donald Sutherland as Carella. TV

MacDonald, John D[ann] (1916–86)

Popular mystery writer and creator of the long-running Travis McGee series of detective stories, MacDonald will also be known as the author of the original suspense-laden novel, *The Executioners*, that J. Lee Thompson's spooky **Cape Fear** and its 1991 remake were based on. Given MacDonald's narrative mastery as well as his descriptive evocation of 1950s crime movies it's surprising that more films have not been derived from his generous body of work. The few that were produced are merely moderate. *Man-Trap* (1961), a heist drama featuring a Korean war hero who is tricked by an army buddy into a bloody $3 million robbery, directed by actor Edmond O'Brien, was based on a 1958 MacDonald novelette. A fishing-boat skipper finds his daughter dead under the influence of drugs in the routine *Kona Coast* (1968), taken from a MacDonald short story, which used the Honolulu fishing-boat milieu as a background. His famous private detective Travis McGee appeared for the first and only film time in the brutal

Darker Than Amber (1970), featuring Rod Taylor as McGee in a series of killings and revenge plots set among the Florida Keys. *Travis McGee* (1983), a leisurely two-hour pilot film for TV adapted by Stirling Silliphant and starring Sam Elliott as McGee, was produced to inspire a possible series. Apparently, MacDonald was pleased with writer-director Victor Nuñez's adaptation of his 1962 novel *A Flash of Green* (1984) which observed a small Florida town and the corruption that enshrouded it. TV

McGivern, William P[eter]
(1922–82)

A fascination with the crooked and rogue cop was McGivern's forte. He is perhaps best known for his powerful gangsters-and-corruption novel which became Fritz Lang's classic **The Big Heat**. This brutal story of the determined Sergeant Bannion (Glenn Ford in the film) as he experiences and at the same time applies the pressure of the big heat on the big city crime ring is one of social frustration as well as personal revenge. The 'tempting indulgence' (as McGivern called it) in crossing the line between law and lawlessness is represented in a trio of films based on his novels. Crooked police detective Robert Taylor tracks down his brother's killer in *Rogue Cop* (1954) by turning against the Syndicate that pays him. Detective Edmond O'Brien murders a bookmaker for twenty-five grand and tries to hold on to the loot while avoiding capture in *Shield for Murder* (1954). While in *Hell on Frisco Bay* (1956), based on the novel *The Darkest Hour*, ex-waterfront cop Alan Ladd out of prison goes after the gangland Mr Big who was responsible for framing him. On a different level, distrust and fear is the focus of *Odds Against Tomorrow* (1959) as the racial tension between a former cop, an ex-con and a black jazzman threatens their joint bank caper. Since turning to Hollywood in the early 1960s, McGivern's screenplays for *The Wrecking Crew* (1968), based on one of Donald Hamilton's Matt Helm novels, **Brannigan** and McGivern's own *Night of the Juggler* (1980) remain his most interesting. TV

Machine Gun Kelly

One of a cycle of biographies of noted hoodlums appearing in the wake of Don Siegel's **Baby Face Nelson**, this was produced and directed by Corman who from the early 1950s started to systematically work his way through the major genres. On the surface it's a period reconstruction of the 1930s era, with the FBI in pursuit of Machine Gun Kelly. In fact, like Siegel's prototype Corman's interest is scarcely at all in the sociological aspects of 30s crime and almost exclusively in the neurotic personality of the central character. Bronson as Kelly is morbid, childish and totally dominated by his girl-friend (Cabot). She persuades him to forsake bank-robbery for kidnapping, hoping that one big job will set them up for life. But jealous of fellow gang member Amsterdam's interest in Cabot, Bronson kicks him out. Amsterdam then squeals to the police and Bronson is captured. This was Bronson's first starring role, and in it he perfected the stone-faced hard-man persona he rarely deviated from, no matter which side of the law was on. However, in this offering the hysteria behind the stone-cold face gave the performance an added edge. EB

1958/84m/AIP/p/d Roger Corman/s R. Wright Campbell/c Floyd Crosby/m Gerald Fried/lp Charles Bronson, Susan Cabot, Morey Amsterdam, Jack Lambert, Wally Campo.

Das Mädchen Rosemarie/The Girl Rosemarie

Thiele, later famous for stylised sexploitation films and baroque thrillers (such as *Der Tod eines Doppelgängers*, 1966) established himself with this controversial movie based on the murder of Rosie Nittribitt, a Frankfurt call-girl who counted prominent industrialists and politicians among her clients. When she threatened to expose some of her clients, she was strangled with her own nylons and the murder remained 'unsolved'. The case hit the tabloid press and many of the German viewers would have been able to decode the thinly veiled references to the directors of the munitions cartel involved (the politicians have been left out of the picture). Thiele adopts an ironic, at times even a farcical tone to chronicle the mores of Germany's captains of industry during the Economic Miracle. The film opens with a neat row of nine black Mercedes cars pulling up at a hotel and nine millionaires wearing Homburg hats file into the place. Two of them, Bruster (Fröbe) and Hartzog (Raddatz) pick up a prostitute, Rosemarie (Tiller), and she soon becomes a high-class call-girl with a white Mercedes. When she gives information about the German munitions business, called the Insulating Materials Cartel in the film, to a French competitor, Fribert (Van Eyck), and seems to know more than the

industrialists can feel comfortable with, nine black Mercedes cars draw up at her flat, shortly afterwards a scream resounds, and then the nine cars depart. The film was one of the biggest German hits of the year. The next year, Rudolf Jugert made a melodramatic film warning against the evils of prostitution, *Die Wahrheit über Rosemarie* (1959). Rolf Thiele returned to the subject with his last film *Rosemaries Tochter* (1976), in which the prostitute's daughter searches for her mother's murderer. PW

1958/Germany/97m/Roxy/p Luggi Waldleitner/d/co-s Rolf Thiele/co-s Erich Kuby, Jo Herbst, Rolf Ulrich/c Klaus von Rutenfeld/m Norbert Schultze/lp Nadia Tiller, Peter Van Eyck, Gert Fröbe, Carl Raddatz, Werner Peters, Horst Frank.

Madigan

The first of a trio of films, followed by **Coogan's Bluff** and **Dirty Harry**, in which Siegel changed the face of the cop movie, This is the most obviously transitional. It uses a 40s face in the lead and has cops in hats and suits, but then sets them loose in a complicated, morally uneven world. The commissioner (Fonda) is an unbending hypocrite who has an affair with a hippie (Clark), while Dan Madigan (Widmark), struggling with a shaky marriage, is out on the streets on the trail of a hoodlum (Ihnat)

he must bring in within 72 hours, under pressure because Ihnat has stolen his gun and used it to commit murder. The changing times seep in along with a collection of modern eccentrics like Stroud's bohemian thug ('the kid needs a haircut,' snaps Madigan), and Ihnat's alarmingly sadist, subtly suggesting that whatever the outcome of this pursuit, the cops are losing the war. Getting out on location, Siegel allows the grimy details of his cops' lives to accumulate, packing more of a wallop with the simple weariness of Madigan on the case than in the overstated soap of his arguments with an unsympathetic wife (Stevens). Though Madigan, like George Dixon before him, is shot dead in the finale, he returned from the grave for six TV movies, top-lining Widmark, in the 1972–3 season. KN

1968/101m/U/p Frank P. Rosenberg/d Don Siegel/s Henri Simoun, Abraham Polonsky/orig Richard Dougherty *The Commissioner*/c Russell Metty/m Don Costa/lp Richard Widmark, Henry Fonda, Inger Stevens, Steve Ihnat, James Whitmore, Don Stroud.

The Mafia

The word *mafia*, still so resented by Italian-Americans that it was cut from the script of **The Godfather**, is either derived from the same root as the French *maquis* or is an

ABOVE Henry Fonda, Richard Widmark, Harry Guardino, *Madigan*

213

ABOVE The Mafia: *Salvatore Giuliano*

Kennedy prompted the use of mafia backgrounds for American quickies like *Johnny Cool* (1963) and *Stiletto* (1969) and old-world items like *Je vous salue Mafia* (1966) and **Le Clan des Siciliens/The Sicilian Clan**. However, it was the publication of a trio of best-selling books, Peter Maas's *The Valachi Papers* (1968), about the testimony of mafia informant Joe Valachi, and Gay Talese's *Honor Thy Father* (1969), an inside account of life in the Bonanno family, and Mario Puzo's novel *The Godfather* (1969) that brought the subject to the attention of America.

The shift was radical. Martin Ritt's **The Brotherhood**, with Kirk Douglas as a don, lacked any defining sense of the mafia as a group (and was a box-office disaster). Just a few years later Francis Ford Coppola's Corleone family chronicles **The Godfather**, which spawned the sequels **The Godfather Part II** and **The Godfather Part III**, established the compelling ground-rules of the mafia movie. Henceforth the patriarch in a darkened room spouting assassination orders, family-first philosophy and pasta recipes; the scheming underlings, relatives and hangers-on trying to get ahead in the family; soap opera unhappy marriages punctuated by the occasional burst of machine-gun fire; lyrical music and sharp suits; the

acronym for the Italian phrase that means 'All Italy Cries Death to France'. It dates back to a French occupation of Sicily that prompted traditional bandits to become a secret society of resistance fighters. Strictly speaking, most movie mobsters, even if they are Bandellos or Camontes, are not *mafiosi*, because – as is shown in **The St. Valentine's Day Massacre**, in which Al Capone (Jason Robards) has to humble himself because he isn't eligible to become a don – the organisation is exclusive to those of pure Sicilian descent. Also known, at various times, as the Black Hand, the *unione Siciliana* and *cosa nostra* ('our thing'), the mafia was imported to America before the turn of the century. The early days are dealt with in *The Black Hand* (1950), *Pay or Die* (1960) and *La Mano Nera/The Black Hand* (1973), which cover, as does the flashback section of *The Godfather Part II* (1975), the transplanting of the Sicilian secret society to melting pot New York, with honest Italians tangling with the conspirators who come across less like gangsters than a political-religious faction. That the mafia continued to remain powerful in the old country is dealt with in a series of Italian films including *Mafia* (1949),

Salvatore Giuliano, *Mafioso* (1962), *Cadaveri eccellenti/Illustrious Corpses* (1976), **The Sicilian** and *La scorta* (1993) which veer between political conspiracy theories and Western-style horseback banditry.

Although the word mafia is dropped casually in a few films (*Tight Spot*, 1955), the organisation was not much dealt with before the 60s, not only because of the Production Code's well-known touchiness about depicting real-life criminals but also because J. Edgar Hoover was on record as repeatedly denying the existence of the mafia or the nation-wide crime syndicate which evolved out of it. The accidental 1957 exposure of a major mafia meet in Apalachin forced Hoover to concede that organised crime was at least as much a threat to the American way of life as communism. The Apalachin incident along with the 1957 murder of Don Albert Anastasia inspired the quickie *Inside the Mafia* (1959), and 50s and 60s probes of mafia activities orchestrated by figures like Federal Bureau of Narcotics Director Harry Anslinger and Attorney General Robert

RIGHT Francesca DeSapio, Robert De Niro
The Godfather Part II

intersection of showbiz gossip (Frank Sinatra anecdotes) and political history (mafia involvement in anti-Communist intrigues, especially around the time of the Cuban revolution); and a nostalgic feeling that murder and extortion were more dignified and bearable when carried out by wise, folksy Italians than by a newer breed of dope-crazed, kill-happy psychopaths, were all to become the conventions and clichés of the mafia movie.

After inevitable dramatisations of **The Valachi Papers**, with Charles Bronson as the informant, and *Honor Thy Father* (1971), with Joseph Bologna as Bill Bonanno, 'true life' mafia stories have been common: *Crazy Joe* (1975), with Peter Boyle as 70s Don Joseph Gallo; *Mafia Princess* (1986), with Tony Curtis as Don Sam Giancana and Susan Lucci as his daughter Antoinette; **GoodFellas**, with Ray Liotta as witness protection scheme squealer Henry Hill; and *Getting Gotti* (1994), with Anthony John Denison as reputed Gambione family boss John Gotti and Lorraine Bracco not as the lawyer who put actually him away but as Diane Giacalone, a prosecutor whose investigation was less successful than her ability to land a TV movie deal; with flash-backs in **Lucky Luciano**, *The Gangster Chronicles* (1981) and *Mobsters* (1991) to the 20s and 30s when Charles Luciano introduced a multi-ethnic crime syndicate in opposition to the Black Handers from the Old Country.

The Corleone influence can be determined in such violence-punctuated, pasta-heavy productions as *The Family Rico* (1972), **Across 110th Street**, *The Italian Connection* (1973), *The Don is Dead* (1973), *Our Family Business* (1981), *Fear City* (1984), *The Sicilian Connection* (1985), *Blood Ties* (1986), *Blood Vows: The Story of a Mafia Wife* (1987), *Crime Story* (1987) and the TV series *Wiseguy* (1987–90), and there have been comic takes on the *cosa nostra* in **Prizzi's Honor**, *Wise Guys* (1986), **Married to the Mob**, *Things Change* (1988), *The Freshman* (1990) and *My Blue Heaven* (1990). The mafia have become so domesticated as screen characters that they can appear in supporting roles as the out-moded hoods seen off by newer ethnic or social groups in *Black Caesar* (1972), **Scarface**, *The Punisher* (1989), *King of New York* (1990) and *New Jack City* (1990), or as a background menace faced off by movie heroes like Walter Matthau in **Charley Varrick**, which casts Joe Don Baker and Benson Fong as part of the Sicilian mob, Charles Bronson in *Mr. Majestyk* (1974), Chuck Norris in *Code of Silence* (1985) and

Patrick Swayze in *Next of Kin* (1989). KN

See also **The Mob**, **The Godfather**, **GoodFellas**, **Lucky Luciano**.

La maffia/Mafia

After the classic *Fin de fiesta* (1960), a tale of political gangsterism involving hired assassins, Torre Nilsson returned to the 30s with this more oblique genre movie. After a mafia boss, Francesco (Slavin), is decorated by the government, his lieutenant, Luciano (Alcon) seduces his daughter Ada (Biral) and embarks on a campaign to displace the old man. He does so in a wonderfully hysterical scene where the lovers smash Francesco's furniture and rip each other's clothes off to the accompaniment of grand opera music. Eventually, the family's lawyer (Alterio) becomes top dog and Luciano is killed in a bank robbery intended to finance the couple's getaway. The film adheres closely to the Hollywood *film noir* conventions, with dramatic lighting and camera angles, while Torre Nilsson has an eye for grotesque details which enlivens his sense of perverse melodrama. PW

1972/Argentina/120m/Litoral/*p/d/co-s* Leopoldo Torre Nilsson/*co-s* Beatriz Guido, Luis Pico Estrada, Rodolfo Mortola, Javier Torre/*orig* Jose Dominiani, Osvaldo Bayer/ *c* Anibal Di Salvo/*m* Gustavo Beytelman/ *lp* Alfredo Alcon, Thelma Biral, Jose Slavin, Chia Zorilla, Hector Alterio, Jose Maria Gutierrez.

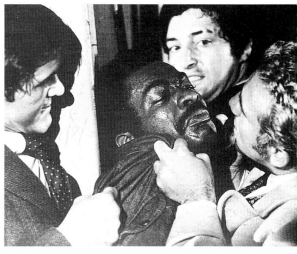

ABOVE *Across 110th Street*

Mahiru No Ankoku/Darkness at Noon

Imai's film constituted a major intervention in an ongoing legal case. In a village in the Yamaguchi region, two old people were murdered on 24 January 1951. Five people were arrested and confessions were obtained leading to one death sentence and long-term imprisonment for the others. Imai's film was made and released prior to the appeal court's verdict, arguing that the police had tortured the suspects to obtain the confessions and that the court had ignored important evidence. In 1957 the appeal court set aside the original verdict and ordered a retrial. The

ABOVE *Lucky Luciano*

film's narrative style is disconcertingly innovative, as the French critic Marcel Martin noted: '[it] is edited so freely, with abrupt cuts [that give] the impression of a universe broken into pieces.' As the defence counsel describes the murder, it is presented on the screen in accelerated or retarded motion, even in stop-motion, undercutting the arguments of the prosecution. PW

1956/Japan/125m/Gendai/*p* Tengo Yamada/ *d* Tadashi Imai/*s* Shinobu Hashimoto/ *orig* Hiroshi Masaki *Saibankan* [*The Judge*]/ *c* Shunichiro Nakao/*m* Akira Ifukube/ *lp* Kojiro Kusanagi, Teruo Matsuyama, Noboru Yano, Matsugu Makita, Hiroshi Kobayashi.

Maigret

A character invented by the Belgian novelist Georges Simenon (1903–89) in 1929 for a series published by Fayard. Apparently modelled on the author's great-grandfather, the perennially 45-year-old (with but a few exceptions) inspector came to represent the solid, lower-middle-class decency attributed to 'ordinary' Frenchman enhanced by the residues of a pre-modern sense of honour. The inspector is not particularly clever nor does he rely on vast amounts of police work. Instead, being an integral part of the social and geographical milieu on which he exercises his profession, he operates more on the

basis of an intuition nurtured by the complete absorption in the minutiae of everyday life: the 'feel' of a place and its inhabitants, in the manner of **Miss Marple**. As such, Maigret represents not so much a standard of moral integrity imposed by the state through its police upon the people, but a deep-rooted, popular sense of justice and fairness allegedly inherent in the lower-middle class during the Third and Fourth Republics, whose avuncular emblem Maigret thus becomes. The first series of Maigret novels (1929–33) was followed by a second (1938–41, published by Gallimard) and a third (1945–72, published by Presses de la Cité).

The first adaptation was also one of the best. Jean Renoir's **La Nuit du carrefour** starred the director's brother Pierre, who remained Simenon's favourite Maigret. That same year, Jean Tarride made *Le Chien jaune* starring his father Abel Tarride. Julien Duvivier followed with *La Tête d'un homme* (starring a rather overweight and overage Harry Baur, 1933), while the next three Maigret films starred a too young Albert Préjean (Richard Pottier's *Picpus*, 1943; Maurice Tourneur's *Cécile est morte*, 1943; Richard Pottier's *Les Caves du Majestic*, 1945). The first English-language Maigret was Charles Laughton in *The Man on the Eiffel Tower* (1949; another version of *La Tête d'un homme*). This was followed by some US tele-

vision adaptations in 1950 (with Herbert Berghof) and 1952 (with Eli Wallach). *Le témoignage de l'enfant de choeur*, an episode in Henri Verneuil's *Brelan d'as* (1952) featured Michel Simon as one of the best Maigrets ever. Stany Cordier's *Maigret dirige l'enquête/Maigret mène l'enquête* (1955) had Maurice Manson. Then Jean Gabin finally gave the character a more enduring image in Jean Delannoy's **Maigret tend un piège**, followed by Gilles Grangier's **Maigret voit rouge**.

However, it was on television that Maigret received most exposure of all, starting with Basil Sydney's performance in *Maigret and the Lost Life* for the BBC in 1959. Rupert Davies continued the role in a BBC series with 51 episodes (1960–3) and in the BBC's *Play of the Month: Maigret At Bay* (1969), directed by William Slater. Gino Cervi played the part on Italian television (1962–73) as well as in the film *Maigret à Pigalle* (1966), Heinz Rühmann on German television (1965–8) as well as in Alfred Weidenmann's Austrian production *Maigret und sein grösster Fall* (1966). Weidenmann also made a German film *Maigret spielt falsch* (1966) starring Rupert Davies. Jan Teuling was Maigret on Dutch television (1965), Jean Richard was the most popular but also the least intriguing Maigret on French television from 1965 onwards. The French feature-length episodes included Maurice Cravenne's *L'Amie de Madame Maigret*; Jean Kerchbron's *Maigret a peur*, Denys de la Patellière's *Maigret et les témoins recalcitrants* and Yves Allégret's *Maigret et l'indicateur*. Boris Tenine was Maigret on Soviet Union television (1969), Kinya Aikawa on Japanese television (the Japanese Mrs Maigret was Simenon's favourite embodiment of the inspector's constant companion. She is rather sexier than Simenon's own Mrs Maigret, who maintains a chaste relationship with her husband, substituting gastronomy for sex). Richard Harris was Maigret in Paul Lynch's HTV 2-hour drama simply called *Maigret* (1988). Bruno Cremer (1991) was also a televisual Maigret but Michael Gambon provisionally closed the list with twelve hour-long episodes on Granada television in Britain (1992–3), some being directed by Stuart Burge. PW

Maigret tend un piège/Maigret Sets a Trap

Gabin's first of three performances as Maigret (the others are Delannoy's *Maigret et l'affaire Saint-Fiacre* (1959); Grangier's **Maigret voit rouge**). On the trail of a killer of women in

the area of the Place des Voges in Paris, one of Maigret's assistants (Hussenot) notices the suspect behaviour of Yvonne Maurin (Girardot). Maigret goes to see her, which leads to the arrest of her architect husband, Marcel (Desailly). While Marcel is in custody, another woman is murdered, but this turns out to have been committed by Marcel's mother (Bogaert) in order to divert suspicion from her son. The film is notable mainly for the way Gabin sets the tone for most subsequent Maigret performances and for the loving depiction of a specific Parisian quarter. Lino Ventura, already on his 12th film and having made an impact in Jacques Becker's **Touchez pas au grisbi**, is here given the minor role of a secondary police inspector. PW

1957/France, Italy/116m/Intermondia-Jolly/*d/co-s* Jean Delannoy/*co-s* R.M. Arlaud, Michel Audiard/*orig* Georges Simenon/ *c* Louis Page/*m* Paul Misraki/*lp* Jean Gabin, Annie Girardot, Jean Desailly, Olivier Hussenot, Alfred Adam.

Maigret voit rouge/Maigret Sees Red

This, Gabin's third appearance as Maigret, pits him against three US contract killers (Cooper, Harris and Constantin) sent to France to eliminate a gangster who could endanger a New York mobster. The villain is kept under wraps by MacDonald (Carpenter), an FBI agent masquerading as a diplomat. Maigret loses his cool when the Yanks kill a French cop and he puts on the pressure. In the end, the Americans allow him to keep the two remaining hit-men in compensation for the dead French cop. Professionally shot by a competent director, the opening sequence sets the tone: one night in Pigalle, a patrolling cop sees a man being shot from a passing car; as he telephones to the station, a white Citroën pulls up, snatches the victim and drives off. Maigret then has to start by finding out who the victim was before he can proceed with his investigations. Gabin's mythical star image blended well with the persona of Simenon's pipe-smoking inspector, giving him the right kind of middle-class respectability tinged with a sardonic world-weariness. However, the most effective film derived from Simenon's work remains Renoir's **La nuit du carrefour**. PW

1963/France, Italy/90m/Copernic-Titanus/ *p* Georges Charlot, Raymond Danon / *d/co-s* Gilles Grangier/*co-s* Jacques Robert/

ABOVE Peter Lorre, Humphrey Bogart, *The Maltese Falcon*

orig Georges Simenon *Maigret: Lognon et les gangsters*/*c* Louis Page/*m* Francis Lemarque/ *lp* Jean Gabin, Françoise Fabian, Paul Carpenter, Michel Constantin, Brad Harris.

Mainwaring, Daniel (1902–77)

Veteran journalist turned novelist-screenwriter who, under the pseudonym of Geoffrey Homes, had a couple of his early mystery novels filmed as *No Hands on the Clock* (1941) and *Crime By Night* (1944; from the novel *Forty Whacks*) before his 1946 novel *Build My Gallows High* was made into the powerful *film noir* **Out of the Past** (in Britain the film retained the title of the original novel). Directed by Jacques Tourneur, and starring Robert Mitchum and Kirk Douglas, this masterpiece of murder, double-dealing, and the recurrence of events from a haunted past became a classic example of the 1940s thriller. It was rather feebly remade by Taylor Hackford as *Against All Odds* (1984), based on the screenplay of the 1947 film. In 1946 Mainwaring abandoned novels to become a full-time screenwriter, writing or contributing to various Westerns and action B-movies including such outstanding genre entries as the US-to-Mexico chase thriller *The Big Steal* (1949), the gritty and disturbing exposé **The Phenix City Story**, the Depression Era gangster **Baby Face Nelson**, as well as the third filmed ver-

sion of Hemingway's *To Have And To Have Not*, *The Gun Runners* (1958), starring Audie Murphy. TV

Maliutka Ellie/Little Ellie/Bezdna Zhizni/The Abyss of Life

Protazanov followed Ermoleev's company into exile after the revolution, first to Yalta and then to France, before returning to become one of the USSR's most distinguished directors best known for his classic science fiction story, *Aelita* (1924). This doom-laden crime film tells of a perverted town mayor (superbly played by Moshukhin) who murders a little girl and, overcome by guilt, commits suicide. Only four reels of the film appear to have survived but these suffice to demonstrate the remarkably modern tone and style of the film, avoiding the kind of emotive histrionics expected and demanded by the contemporary critics. PW

1918/Russia/6 reels/Ermoleev/*p* Iosif N. Ermoleev/*d/s* Yakov Protazanov/*orig* 'La petite Rocque' Guy de Maupassant/*c* Fedor Burgasov/*lp* Ivan Moshukhin, Natalia Lissenko, Kudrina, Nikolai Panov, Polykarp Pavlov, Ilona Talanov.

The Maltese Falcon

Miles Archer is killed on a job involving the beautiful and mysterious Brigid O'Shaughnessy (Astor). His partner Sam Spade (Bogart)

investigates and finds himself struggling over the Maltese Falcon, a priceless statue. He's threatened and opposed by 'the fat man', Kaspar Gutman (Greenstreet), Gutman's psychotic gunsel, Wilmer (Cook), and an effeminate neurotic, Joel Cairo (Lorre). Huston's screenplay is faithful to the devious plotting of **Dashiell Hammett**'s book, but the eccentricity which the direction imposes on the minor characters means that the film lacks Hammett's moral passion, and a feeling of tragic inevitability. Nevertheless, this is a seminal creative moment in the development of the genre. Spade's dalliance with his partner's wife establishes a moral ambiguity which is picked up and elaborated by the treachery of the sexy and devious Astor. The falcon is an appropriate metaphor for the world of double-crossing greed around whose shadows the camera relentlessly probes. MP

1941/100m/WB/*p* Henry Blanke/*d/s* John Huston/*c* Arthur Edeson/*m* Adolph Deutsch/*lp* Humphrey Bogart, Mary Astor, Gladys George, Peter Lorre, Sydney Greenstreet, Elisha Cook Jr.

ABOVE Humphrey Bogart, Elisha Cook Jr, *The Maltese Falcon*

The Man from Hong Kong

This was made by stunt man turned director Trenchard-Smith and Chinese action star and director Wang Yu (credited with co-direction in Chinese sources), famed for his

ABOVE William Petersen, *Manhunter*

brutal martial arts movies. The plot is patterned on Don Siegel's **Coogan's Bluff**. Inspector Fang Sing-ling (Wang) goes to Sydney to extradite a Chinese drug smuggler. When his prisoner is murdered, he takes on the Australian syndicate headed by Wilton (Lazenby). Siegel's opening scenes are mimicked by a kung fu fight on top of Ayers Rock which is intercut with a helicopter chase in the desert before the action moves to the city. Wang's trademark and the film's delight in brutality are evidenced in the panoply of weapons deployed, including meat hooks and javelins. Wilton is finally disposed of by the hero shoving a grenade into his mouth. PW

1975/Australia, Hong Kong/103m/The Movie Company-Golden Harvest/ *p* Raymond Chow, John Fraser/*co-d/s* Brian Trenchard-Smith/*co-d* Jimmy Wang Yu/ *c* Russell Boyd/*lp* Jimmy Wang Yu, George Lazenby, Ros Spiers, Hugh Keays-Byrne, Roger Ward.

Manhunter

Several years before **The Silence of the Lambs**, the malign figure of Hannibal Lecktor was introduced to the screen in this adaptation of an earlier Thomas Harris novel, *Red Dragon* (1981). Lecktor was played, as later, by a British actor, Cox, who offers a study in sardonic condescension quite equal to Anthony Hopkins's more celebrated performance in the role. The plot of *Manhunter* concerns a retired federal agent (Petersen), once responsible for Lecktor's conviction, who is cajoled back into action to track down a sadistic serial killer known as the Tooth Fairy (Noonan). He warily consults Lecktor for advice, only for Lecktor to attempt, in suitably devious fashion, to contact the murderer and direct him towards Petersen's own family. Mann had achieved success with the TV series *Miami Vice*, the influence of which can be detected in both the inventive music score and the colour styling. The use of pastel shades and (especially in the meeting between Petersen and Cox in the high-security hospital) of clinical white, creates a creepy counterpoint to the gruesomeness of the subject matter. The environment which this hi-tech forensic drama creates has been aptly described by Leighton Grist as 'obverse noir'. TP

1986/120m/De Laurentiis Entertainment Group/*p* Richard Roth/*d/s* Michael Mann/ *c* Dante Spinotti/*m* Michael Rubini, The Reds/*lp* William L. Petersen, Kim Greist, Brian Cox, Dennis Farina, Tom Noonan.

Le mani sulla città

Nottola (Steiger) is a property developer in Naples who is adept at using the mechanisms of town planning and local government to his own ends. His associates on the city council channel civic development towards the part of town where he has already bought up all the land. Meanwhile, the collapse of a building in an area where Nottola's company is doing construction work leads to a public enquiry. When his supporters on the right-wing party are unwilling to guarantee his immunity Nottola switches sides and the centre party is elected and Nottola is made a Building Commissioner. Such is the intelligence of the script and the clarity of Rosi's direction that the film develops into a lesson on corruption and political skulduggery which is as fascinating as any of Hollywood's dissections of the mob. EB

1963/105m/Galatea/*p* Lionello Santi/ *d* Francesco Rosi/*s* Francesco Rosi, Raffaele La Capria, Enzo Provenzale, Enzo Forcella/ *c* Gianni Di Venanzo/*m* Piero Piccioni/*lp* Rod Steiger, Guido Alberti, Carlo Fermariello, Salvo Randone, Dany Paris.

La Mariée était en noir/The Bride Wore Black

Shortly after his classic interview book with Hitchcock, Truffaut made this tribute to the master enhanced by humanising touches borrowed from his second mentor, Jean Renoir. Julie Kohler (Moreau) sees her husband killed on the steps of the church as they emerge from their wedding service. Pretending to leave town, she then systematically sets out to kill the five men, each representing a standard attitude towards women. Truffaut's great achievement, learned from Hitchcock, is to establish and maintain the audience's identification with the ruthless killer, even after we learn that her victims' guilt is not at all certain, generating suspense by making us wish for the success of the cold-blooded murderer (as in **Psycho** when the car containing Marion's body threatens to refuse to sink in the pool). This could be the counter-part to Truffaut's most misogynist film, *L'Homme qui aimait les femmes* (1977), as Julie manages to kill her victims by turning their fantasies of women against them, were it not for the way Moreau is filmed: emphasising the way she crosses her legs, lovingly fetishising her every appearance. The narrative rhythm of each sequence is timed to perfection, playing with the audience's foreknowledge of what is to happen, and diversions such as the revelation of the killer's motives are dealt with by means of short flashbacks punctuating

the flow. As in his **Tirez sur le pianiste**, Truffaut manages to keep up the suspense by stripping all the police-procedural stuff from Cornell Woolrich's mediocre novel and by revealing all the relevant motivations half way through the film so that he and the viewer may concentrate on the purely cinematic dimensions of storytelling and suspense. PW

1968/France, Italy/107m/Les Films du Carrosse-Artistes Associés-Dino De Laurentiis/*p* Marcel Berbert/*d*/*co-s* François Truffaut/*co-s* Jean-Louis Richard/*orig* William Irish [Cornell Woolrich]/*c* Raoul Coutard/*m* Bernard Herrmann/*lp* Jeanne Moreau, Claude Rich, Jean-Claude Brialy, Michel Bouquet, Michel Lonsdale, Charles Denner.

Marked Woman

Based distantly on revelations about a brothel owned by gangster Lucky Luciano, this was one of Warners' hardest-hitting crime melodramas of the 1930s. Davis plays Mary, who works in the Club Intime (bowdlerised from a brothel into a clip joint) and is using her wages to put her little sister through college. All the girls have a cynical attitude to their work and no illusions about the men who are their customers, or about those who employ them. When the sister finds out it's tainted money she rejects Mary, only to lose her life when she falls into the clutches of Vanning's mobster. Mary vows revenge and although beaten up by Vanning she eventually persuades the other girls to join her in providing evidence for the crusading D.A. (Bogart). The criminals are convicted, but there is little sense of justice triumphant at the end. The girls walk off separately into the fog, their future uncertain. Society may have scored a few points in the battle against crime, but it's a bleak world all the same. EB

1937/95m/WB/*p* Lou Edelman/*d* Lloyd Bacon/*s* Robert Rossen, Abem Finkel/ *c* George Barnes/*m* Bernhard Kaun, Heinz Roemheld/*lp* Bette Davis, Humphrey Bogart, Lola Lane, Isabel Jewell, Eduardo Ciannelli.

Marlowe, Philip

The first private eye stories of **Raymond Chandler** feature a first-person nameless detective along the lines of **Dashiell Hammett**'s Continental Op ('Finger Man', 1934), third-person gumshoes Mallory ('Blackmailers Don't Shoot', 1933) and Ted Carmady ('Guns at Cyrano's', 1936) or first-person sleuth John Dalmas ('Bay City Blues', 1938). It seems likely Carmady became

Dalmas simply because Chandler switched allegiance from *Black Mask* after the departure of editor Captain Joseph T. Shaw, and moved to *Dime Detective Magazine*. When he graduated from stories to novels, Chandler chose to cannibalise his earlier works, turning 'Killer in the Rain' (1935) and 'The Curtain' (1936) into *The Big Sleep* (1939) and 'Try the Girl' (1937), 'The Man Who Liked Dogs' (1936) and 'Mandarin's Jade' (1937) into *Farewell, My Lovely* (1940). Thus, Mallory, Carmady and Dalmas coalesced into Philip Marlowe, the protagonist of these and all of Chandler's subsequent novels, *The High Window* (1942), *The Lady in the Lake* (1943), *The Little Sister* (1949), *The Long Goodbye* (1953) and *Playback* (1959).

Byron Preiss edited *Raymond Chandler's Philip Marlowe* (1988), in which 23 mystery authors provided additions to the Chandler cannon. In Richard Maher and Roger Mitchell's play *Private Dick* (1982), Marlowe is hired by Raymond Chandler to locate a missing manuscript. Chandler had, late in life, abandoned *The Poodle Springs Mystery*, a final novel which would have found Marlowe married to heiress Linda Loring, whom he had met in *The Long Goodbye*, and Robert B. Parker was contracted to complete the piece, with mildly effective results, in *Poodle Springs* (1990). Parker subsequently wrote the far better *Perchance to Dream* (1991), a direct sequel to *The Big Sleep*, in which he is able to go back to Marlowe in his prime, rather than being stuck with the mistakenly-married and unhappily-moneyed detective of the Chandler remnant.

A heavy-drinking romantic with a rigid code of integrity, a knack for befriending the wrong people and a flair for elaborate metaphors, Marlowe is the epitome of the private eye. Although Marlowe is a shadowy figure, with many details about his background and appearance being left in the dark, he is among the most memorable, convincing and influential in detective fiction, at least as important a figure as **Sherlock Holmes**. All subsequent dicks and private eyes owe much to him, whether (like Ross MacDonald's Lew Archer, Mickey Spillane's **Mike Hammer** or James Garner's Jim Rockford) they are conceived in terms of their differences from the mock-cynical loner, or (like Robert B. Parker's Spenser and Timothy Harris's Thomas Kyd) they are so close in character as to suggest an illegitimate family relationship. One odd consistency (perhaps unconscious?) of Chandler's works is that the author's misogyny tends to

ABOVE Philip Marlowe: Humphrey Bogart, *The Big Sleep*

fee, and make a more faithful version. **Murder My Sweet**, an adaptation of *Farewell, My Lovely* directed by Edward Dmytryk, is the first real Marlowe movie and in many ways the best. Howard Hawks' **The Big Sleep**, in every way a bigger production than *Murder My Sweet*, stands as a classic in its own right but is perhaps less satisfactory an adaptation. After establishing his Chandler-ish character in the opening sequence, Humphrey Bogart's Marlowe turns into a development of his already-established screen image. Bogart's Marlowe reappears, in clips from *The Big Sleep*, as a supporting character in Carl Reiner's ingenious **Dead Men Don't Wear Plaid**, providing inspiration and a few tips for Steve Martin's private eye hero.

After Powell and Bogart, Marlowe's screen career faltered. Robert Montgomery's **The Lady in the Lake**, almost entirely shot with a first-person camera and Montgomery thus barely glimpsed as 'Phillip' Marlowe, is a misguided experiment and all but un-watchable. John Brahm's *The Brasher Doubloon* (1947) is a 72-minute quickie, geared to cash in on the success of *The Big Sleep* and the publicity attendant upon *The Lady in the Lake*, with second-string players and minimal pro-duction values. A moustached George Montgomery is Marlowe, perhaps because the coincidence of his name would create confusion with the more prestigious Robert Montgomery film. Despite its drawbacks, the film does have an authentic *noir* feel (Brahm was a horror specialist) and is a rare Chand-ler film that plays up his misogynous streak.

On the radio Marlowe was played by Van Heflin and Gerald Mohr (and, much later, for the BBC, Ed Bishop), and made the transfer to television, with live TV versions in the 50s of *The Little Sister* and *The Long Goodbye* (with Dick Powell returning to the role). By the time of the *Philip Marlowe* TV series (1959–60), with Philip Carey in the lead, there was little to distinguish the hero from any other nice guy private eye.

When the cinema returned to Marlowe, twenty years after *The Brasher Doubloon*, times had changed and each successive adaptation has to deal with the way Chandler's books have become period pieces. Paul Bogart's **Marlowe**, from *The Little Sister*, Robert Altman's **The Long Goodbye** and Michael Winner's *The Big Sleep* (1978) all variously update their stories to contempo-rary settings, while Dick Richards' *Farewell, My Lovely* (1975) and the television series *Marlowe: Private Eye* (1985) attempt to recre-

negate their status as mysteries, with the killer almost always turning out to be the most powerful female character in the plot, from the nymphet of *The Big Sleep* to the bitch matriarch of *The High Window*, though the betrayal that most shakes Marlowe is not that of any of the tricky dames he encoun-ters but of Terry Lennox, the mercurial best friend who dupes him in *The Long Goodbye*, prompting some to suggest, supported by his overemphatic homophobia, that Marlowe is a latent homosexual. The best, most richly-characterised and most ambitious of the books is *The Long Goodbye*; but *The Big Sleep* and *Farewell, My Lovely* are the most vital and entertaining, *The Lady in the Lake* is the best

mystery, and *The Little Sister*, very acidic about Hollywood, is the most embittered and cynical. Only *Playback*, adapted from an un-produced screenplay and ironically the only novel never to be filmed, fails to come up to the mark.

The first film adaptations of Chandler's novels omit Marlowe, with George Sanders' Gay **Falcon** and Lloyd Nolan's **Mike Shayne** appropriating the plots of *Farewell, My Lovely* and *The High Window* for *The Falcon Takes Over* (1942) and *Time to Kill* (1942). The stu-dios purchased the books for their plots. In both cases, the studios were able to dust off the properties after Chandler had become a major writer, without paying an additional ate the feel of the 40s, adding a nostalgic sheen to the grit. In *Marlowe*, James Garner is a charmer with a suntan, a warm-up for Rockford, while Elliott Gould in *The Long Goodbye* is a crumpled clown, a surprisingly successful rethinking of Chandler's original in 70s terms. Robert Mitchum, who would have been ideally cast in the role in 1948, is a bulky Marlowe in *Farewell, My Lovely*, but manages to approximate some of the late Chandler world-weariness albeit in a sentimental context the author would have despised. Winner's *The Big Sleep* has the sex and drug sub-plots and the ending the censors stopped Hawks from using, but weirdly relocates the whole story to a flavourless Home Counties setting, wasting a distinguished cast (James Stewart, John Mills, Edward Fox, Sarah Miles, Oliver Reed, Richard Boone, Candy Clark, Joan Collins, Richard Todd) and a returning Mitchum. *Marlowe: Private Eye*, an Anglo-American series, converts stories like 'The King in Yellow' (1938) and 'Smart Aleck Kill' (1934) that originally featured other protagonists into Marlowe adventures, but also adapts Chandler's late Marlowe story 'The Pencil' (1959, aka 'Marlowe Takes on the Syndicate', 'Wrong Pidgeon'). With an effective Powers Boothe in the lead, the somewhat sun-struck series brought in Kathryn Leigh Scott as Annie Riordan, Marlowe's love

ABOVE Philip Marlowe: Robert Montgomery, *The Lady in the Lake*

interest in *Farewell, My Lovely* and 'The Pencil', as a continuing character. A second, less lavish, series was made in Canada with Boothe, under the slightly altered title *Philip Marlowe: Private Eye* (1986). David Garrison plays a character impersonating Marlowe on a Mystery Tour in 'Elementary Steele', an episode of *Remington Steele* (1984). KN

Marlowe/The Little Sister

As with Sherlock Holmes stories until *The Adventures of Sherlock Holmes* (1939), it was until recently thought unnecessary to set adaptations of Raymond Chandler's novels in the period they were written, though it has long been accepted that Chandler's evocation (like Doyle's before him) of a precise milieu of time and place is one of his great appeals. The lacklustre *Farewell, My Lovely* (1975) is the sole Chandler movie to date with a period setting. However, it was not until this version of *The Little Sister* (1949) that the discrepancy began to show. The updating of Chandler's Hollywood film setting to television works well, and O'Connor's tired cop and Daniels' nervy TV exec (he has to explain to the PI what a 'sitcom' is) are perfectly Chandleresque figures within the updated frame. Moreover, Garner is an acceptable private eye, but his particular qualities as an ironic hero are far better used in *The Rockford Files* (1974–80), which successfully transposes the Chandler ethos into a contemporary setting but also takes pains to play off the Marlowe myth by presenting

ABOVE Philip Marlowe: Elliott Gould, *The Long Goodbye*

an investigator who is anything but a loner and whose cases are not crusades but reluctantly-accepted chores. Nevertheless, two sequences in *Marlowe* showcase cult performers playing off Garner with insouciant ease: as Lee's well-spoken Chinese thug demolishes Marlowe's office with a few kung fu moves, and *fatale* tramp Moreno is exposed as the killer during a marvellously raucous jazz strip routine. KN

1969/95m/MGM/*p* Gabriel Katzka, Sidney Beckerman/*d* Paul Bogart/*s* Stirling Silliphant/*orig* Raymond Chandler *The Little Sister*/*c* William H. Daniels/*m* Peter Matz/*lp* James Garner, Gayle Hunnicutt, Carroll O'Connor, Rita Moreno, William Daniels, Sharon Farrell, Bruce Lee.

Marnie

Hedren is Marnie, a kleptomaniac who keeps one jump ahead of the police by constantly changing her identity and appearance. Connery is a wealthy businessman who guesses Marnie's secret, but is too attracted to her to turn her over to the law. Instead, he forces her into marriage, only to discover that she is frigid. He also discovers Marnie's mother (Latham) is a former prostitute and that Marnie had killed one of her clients in defence of her mother. While Marnie's kleptomania and frigidity are 'explained' by her suppression of the memory of this incident, which allows for a 'happy ending', Hitchcock is clearly more concerned with detailing the links between sexual excitement and criminal acts than explaining them. It is this that gives added tension to the celebrated sequence of Marnie robbing the safe in imminent danger of discovery by an office cleaner. EB

1964/130m/U/*p/d* Alfred Hitchcock/*s* Jay Presson Allen/*c* Robert Burks/*m* Bernard Herrmann/*lp* Tippi Hedren, Sean Connery, Diana Baker, Martin Gabel, Louise Latham.

Marple, Miss

The most famous spinster in the history of detective fiction, Miss Marple was created by Agatha Christie in *Murder at the Vicarage* (1932). Reportedly based on Christie's own grandmother, Miss Marple was born and lived in the village of St. Mary Mead. Observers see it as a sleepy English village, but Miss Marple knows it is a modern equivalent to Sodom and Gomorra. She draws from the (seemly innocent) actions of under-maids and butcher's boys a schema of human activity (and depravity) that serves

ABOVE Margaret Rutherford as Miss Marple, *Murder She Said*

her well as examples of, and parallels to, the crimes she is faced with. Essentially an observer and commentator after the fact, she is luckier than Christie's **Hercule Poirot** in that unlike him she sees, and accommodates herself to, change in St. Mary Mead. Accordingly as a character she is easier to use as a map of the developments that took place in England between some mythical Golden Age (the 1920s) and a present (that is in effect the 1940s). The BBC TV series starring Joan Hickson as Miss Marple, which ran 1984–7, best captured this. Miss Marple was also played on television by legendary British singer and actress Gracie Fields in a 1956 adaptation of *A Murder Is Announced* (1950). Miss Marple made her first screen appearance impersonated by Margaret Rutherford in **Murder She Said**. That led to three more (lesser) films featuring Rutherford and a brief appearance of the character in *The Alphabet Murders* (1965), in which Tony Randall played Poirot. PH

Married to the Mob

A suburban gangster comedy, this stars Pfeiffer as the recently-widowed housewife of a gangster who attempts to set up a new life for herself and her young son away from the social restrictions of the mob world. Into her 'new life' (which is one of demeaning jobs and a cheap tenement apartment) comes eager FBI man Modine, operating undercov-er, and mob chief Stockwell, the latter led by his continuing infatuation for the attractive widòw. The result is a wild and funny angle on the **GoodFellas** type of New York gang-sters, their lives and their wives, with Pfeiffer giving a wonderful deadpan comic perfor-mance. TV

1988/103m/Orion/*p* Kenneth Utt, Edward Saxon/*d* Jonathan Demme/*s* Barry Strugatz, Mark R. Burns/*c* Tak Fujimoto/*m* David Byrne/*lp* Michelle Pfeiffer, Matthew Modine, Dean Stockwell.

Marusa No Onna/A Taxing Woman

The essayist, actor, playwright and TV News-caster Itami, who had become an interna-tionally known director with the delicious *Tampopo* (1986), continued his examination of Japanese social strata with this story of a woman 'of Marusa' (in Japanese, Marusa is a jargon term for the tax office's investiga-tion bureau). Based on an actual case of the investigation of a pachinko-parlour propri-etor, Itami's film chronicles, with consider-able humour as well as drama, the way Ryoko Itakura (Miyamoto, Itami's wife) goes after the gangland boss Gondo (Yamazaki) for tax evasion. In the process, the film shows the various, often bizarre ways in which the powerful hang on to their ill-gotten gains. In the end, the gang-boss is caught, but his personal charm together with his grudging admiration for the doggedly tenacious and fearless Ryoko seduce the intrepid investigator, making for a rather ambiguous ending. Itami followed up this major hit with *Marusa No Onna 2* (1988), in which Ryoko investigates the real estate business and the way religious organisations manipulate land sales to launder money as well as to defraud the nation. The film focus-es on the dealings of the feared Onizawa

ABOVE Dean Stockwell, Michelle Pfeiffer, *Married to the Mob*

(played by Rentaro Mikuni) who turns out to be a pawn in the dirty games of political power-brokers. PW

1987/Japan/127m/Itami-New Century/ p Yasushi Tamaoki, Seigo Hosogoe/d/s Juzo Itami/c Yonezo Maeda/m Toshiyuki Honda/ lp Nobuko Miyamoto, Tsutomu Yamazaki, Masahiko Tsugawa, Hideo Murota, Shuji Otaki.

The Mask of Dimitrios

Leyden (Lorre) is a Dutch mystery writer on holiday in Istanbul. He meets a fan, Colonel Haki (Katch), who is head of the secret police and who tells him that the body of a master criminal, Dimitrios Makropoulos (Scott) has been picked up on a beach stabbed to death. Leyden goes to see the body and decides to trace the footsteps of this man whose career was 'murder, treason, and betrayal.' He encounters a farrago of blackmail, espionage and assassination. Frank Gruber's script is from the novel by **Eric Ambler**, one of the greatest works of English crime fiction, and based on the intrigues of a real life arms dealer, Basil Zaharoff. The roles played by Lorre and Greenstreet as the writer and the blackmailer who befriends him reverse the personas they established in **The Maltese Falcon**. The murky lighting, the angular Bauhaus sets and the repeated railway sounds echo

The Mask of Dimitrios: Sydney Greenstreet, Peter Lorre (above), Eduardo Cianelli, Faye Emerson, Peter Lorre (below)

the desperate intrigue and mournful memories of pre-war Europe. MP

1944/95m/WB/p Henry Blanke/d Jean Negulesco/s Frank Gruber/c Arthur Edeson/m Adolph Deutsch/lp Sydney Greenstreet, Zachary Scott, Faye Emerson, Peter Lorre, George Tobias, Kurt Katch.

Mason, Perry

Perry Mason, attorney for the defence, first appears in Erle Stanley Gardner's *The Case of the Velvet Claws* (1933), already accompanied by his faithful secretary Della Street and already assigning most of his leg-work to private eye Paul Drake. A further 88 titles followed. Warner Bros. purchased rights to the Mason character and cast Warren William, a former **Philo Vance** and future **Lone Wolf**, as Perry in Alan Crosland's *The Case of the Howling Dog* (1935), Michael Curtiz's *The Case of the Curious Bride* (1935), Archie Mayo's *The Case of the Lucky Legs* (1935) and William Clemens's *The Case of the Velvet Claws* (1936). William plays Mason as a Nick Charles-style alcoholic-cum-hypochondriac who enjoys banter with his Della of the moment ('Did you hear that, Miss Street,' he says, referring to a doctor's diagnosis, 'no excitements, no stimulants. I'll have to get rid of you'), but is

Perry Mason: Raymond Burr, William Hopper (above left); Raymond Burr, Barbara Hale (above right)

always prepared with the right question for a witness on the stand ('Is it not a fact, Lucy Benson, that you are *ambidextrous*?'). Breezily unfaithful to the novels, these are smart little programmers, distinguished by rapid pace, cynical dialogue and quality in the supporting performers (in *The Case of the Curious Bride*, the corpse is Errol Flynn) of Warners' stock company. When William departed, the less-effective Ricardo Cortez (like William, a former **Sam Spade**) stepped in for William McGann's *The Case of the Black Cat* (1936), based on *The Case of the Caretaker's Cat*, and Donald Woods took up the brief for William Clemens's *The Case of the Stuttering Bishop* (1937). Neither replacement satisfied, and Warners used up its remaining screen rights by adapting *The Case of the Dangerous Dowager* into a non-Mason *Granny Get Your Gun* (1940). Though Claire Dodd was an excellent Della in two entries, other actresses (Helen Trenholme, June Travis, Ann Dvorak) came and went, while Paul Drake turned sometimes into a comic foil named Spudsy (Allen Jenkins, Eddie Acuff) and was sometimes played by Joseph Crehan. This Mason spent very little time in court, tending to act as any other gentleman sleuth and unravel mysteries at cocktail parties or other informal suspect get-togethers.

From 1943 to 1955, Perry Mason was a fixture on radio, first played by Bartlett Robinson, then many others, including Santos Ortega, Donald Briggs and John Larkin. A daily program, radio's *Perry Mason* was half-detective show and half soap opera; when, in 1956, it transferred to television, the crime elements were dropped and the characters renamed, transforming into the daytime soap *The Edge of Night*. It was the more familiar *Perry Mason* (1957–66) TV show that made the character a household name. Raymond Burr, a plump and glowering presence then associated with villain roles, was approached to play Mason's perennial opponent, District Attorney Hamilton Burger, but made a successful bid for the lead and remade the suave, sometimes amoral advocate of the novels as a grey-suited, implacably honourable, hard-working champion of the innocent. A major aspect of the series was its emphasis on the courtroom, with Burr's Mason always springing a last-minute surprise witness or making a sudden disclosure that would reverse the course of the case. Often, Paul Drake (William Hopper) would have to barge into the court and give his boss the final piece of evidence just as the lawyers were about to deliver their summing-up, and invariably a tolerant judge would admit into evidence something Burger was never given the opportunity to look at or allow onto the witness stand someone the D.A. never got to cross-examine. Barbara Hale was Della, William Talman Ham Burger and Ray Collins police Lt Arthur Tragg. Of 271 cases, Mason lost three (and then only as plot gimmicks – he always triumphed at the end of the show), and was unable to appear several times, prompting Bette Davis, Michael Rennie, Hugh O'Brian, Walter Pidgeon, Mike Connors and Barry Sullivan to step in as associates more than willing to take up the slack. Erle Stanley Gardner himself played a judge in the last episode 'The Case of the Final Fadeout'.

A bland revival – *The New Adventures of Perry Mason* (1973–4), with Monte Markham, Sharon Acker, Albert Stratton, Harry Guardino and Dane Clark as Mason, Della, Drake, Burger and Tragg – was short-lived, but a bulkier, greyer, bearded Burr was lured back for a TV movie *Perry Mason Returns* (1986), with Hale as Della, accused of murder so Mason could be lured from his new position as a judge to take her case, and William Katt, Hale's son, as Paul Drake Jr. A subsequent series of TV specials with Burr and Hale (and sometimes Katt), almost all directed by Ron Satlof or Christian I. Nyby II, followed (1991).

Matador

This corrosive comedy thriller and love story is Almodóvar's most accomplished but underrated film to date. The opening sequence sets the tone: a naked woman, Maria (Serna), 'rides' a man and celebrates her climax by stabbing a long hairpin in his neck, killing the stud while enjoying his last twitches. She turns out to be a lawyer in love with the bullfighter Diego (Martinez), who is also a serial killer. A guilt-ridden youth, Angel (Banderas), is a disciple of Diego and has medium-like trances in which he sees all murders committed in the city, according to his psychiatrist (Maura). In the end, Maria and Diego love each other to death in a scene of operatic grandeur. Told with a perfectly straight face, the film fatally exposes the hilariously neurotic aspects of the bullfighting cult and of Spanish machismo in general while its exuberant style and glorification of mad sexual passion (quoting the end of *Duel In The Sun*, 1946) imbue the film with a sense of joy rarely matched in contemporary cinema. PW

1986/Spain/96m/Ibero-Americana de TV-Television Española/*p* Andres Vicente Gomez/*d/s* Pedro Almodóvar/*co-s* Jesus Ferrero/*c* Angel Luis Fernandez/*m* Bernardo Bonezzi/*lp* Assumpta Serna, Antonio Banderas, Nacho Martinez, Eva Cobo, Julieta Serrano, Chus Lampreave, Carmen Maura.

Matou a familia e foi ao cinema/Killed the Family and Went to the Movies

Inspired by Albert Camus's classic novel *L'Etranger* (1942), Bressane's film pushes the

ABOVE Robert De Niro (right), *Mean Streets*

outrage of **O anjo nasceu** yet further. The result is virtually a catalogue of violence. In the opening sequence shot, a middle-class young man murders his parents with a razor and goes to see a film called *Perdidas de amor*. There a series of murderous episodes explode onto the screen: a rich young woman is tired of her gun-loving husband

and goes on holiday in Petropolis with a girl-friend; in a hovel, a man kills a woman for love; a man is tortured; two young suburban lesbians love each other and one of them kills her mother, who criticised the relationship; a husband kills his wife who complained too much about their financial plight; the Petropolis girl-friends reminisce about their schooldays, love each other and then kill each other. The different story fragments, roughly shot and nervously edited, resonate with each other to build up a picture of a society prey to unconscionable violence which devours love. PW

1970/Brazil/80m/*p/d/s* Julio Bressane/*c* Thiago Veloso/*lp* Antero de Oliveira, Maria Rodrigues, Renata Sorrah, Vanda Lacerda, Paulo Padilha.

Mean Streets

The crucial moment in *Mean Streets* comes when Charlie (Keitel), a sharply-dressed Italian-American hustler who claims 'you pay for your sins on the street not in church', has lectured his epileptic girl-friend (Robinson) on the almost saintly rights and responsibilities which rule his life only for her to exclaim 'but St Francis didn't run numbers'. With its strong streak of autobiography, especially in the religious elements and the casual love for cinema (Charlie and

ABOVE Harvey Keitel, *Mean Streets*

his gang watch John Ford's *The Searchers*, 1956, and Roger Corman's *Tomb of Ligea*, 1964), and lively ethnic double-talk that derives as much from Hope and Crosby as the tough guy school of escalated insult, *Mean Streets* is an affecting chronicle of a specific neighbourhood lifestyle, as personal and universal as *American Graffiti* (1973), *Diner* (1982) or *Boyz N the Hood* (1991). It deals with the lower edges of life in organised crime, as Charlie tries to persuade his *mafioso* uncle (Danova) to let him advance in the rackets, but is held back and ultimately involved in a blood-bath shoot-out by his commitment to Johnny Boy (De Niro), an unreliable cousin whose mounting debts and refusal to respect traditional obligations marks him as a dangerous man to know. An effective counterpart to **The Godfather**, this examines the lives of the foot-soldiers in the Corleone army, a connection made explicit in Scorsese's more elaborate return to the turf in **GoodFellas**. It is less concerned with the business of crime (Charlie angrily denies that he runs numbers and the only crooked acts we see him commit involve bilking college kids out of cinema money on a fake drug deal and other petty scams) than with the day-to-day lives of fringe criminals, strutting their stuff in music bars, letting off steam in fights and random foolishness, and trying to avoid serious violence (a barroom shooting) when it comes up. However, the finale, which prefigures later Scorsese holocausts and winds up with Charlie forced by his shattered legs to adopt a position of prayerful supplication, is a reminder that the axe is always ready to fall. KN

1973/110/Taplin-Perry-Scorsese/*p* Jonathan T. Taplin/*d*/co-*s* Martin Scorsese/co-*s* Mardik Martin/*c* Kent Wakeford/*lp* Harvey Keitel, Robert De Niro, David Proval, Amy Robinson, Richard Romanus, Robert Carradine, David Carradine.

Mildred Pierce

Mildred (Crawford) is having trouble with her husband Bert (Bennett). Mildred leaves Bert and starts work as a waitress. She spends her income on indulging her vain, snobbish daughter Veda (Blyth), but works hard enough to establish a chain of restaurants, and now rich, gets engaged to playboy Monte Beragon (Scott). He marries her, then spends all her money, and winds up having an affair with Veda. From the novel by **James M. Cain**, his bleak view of human nature and society is counteracted by Crawford's heroic performance. The *noir* elements of the movie – the murder, and the infiltration of evil into Mildred's painfully constructed and respectable domesticity, are seen eventually as a setting for the real drama in which determined female virtue triumphs over malevolent greed and duplicity. This is the template for a long line of soap operas. Blyth is, unexpectedly, magnificent as the corrupted daughter, both temptress and victim, riding for a fall. MP

1945/111m/WB/*p* Jerry Wald/*d* Michael Curtiz/*s* Ranald MacDougall/*c* Ernest Haller/*m* Max Steiner/*lp* Joan Crawford, Jack Carson, Zachary Scott, Eve Arden, Ann Blyth, Bruce Bennett.

Miller's Crossing

From the makers of **Blood Simple**, the Coen brothers, this is a story of love and loyalty, intrigue and betrayal set in an unnamed American city during the gang warfare era of the late 20s. Byrne is Tom, the lieutenant of Leo (Finney), the Irish head of the local mob. Turturro is a cheap bookie who's threatening his territory. Leo ought to have him taken out, but he's in love with the bookie's sister. His unwillingness to act renders him vulnerable to the rival mob. Tom has to sort things out, which eventually he does after some switches in loyalties and some bloody murders. Unusually the Coens dwell too long on the fastidiousness of the decor, or the carefully chiaroscuro of the lighting. There is some powerful acting, and any film with Albert Finney is a rare treat. But its creators seem a little too in love with their art. Only later, in **Fargo**, did they perfectly integrate their feeling for time, place, narrative and character into the tradition of the American crime film. EB

1990/115m/FOX/*p* Ethan Coen/*d* Joel Coen/*s* Joel and Ethan Coen/*c* Barry Sonnenfeld/*m* Carter Burwell/*lp* Gabriel Byrne, Marcia Gay Harden, John Turturro, Jon Polito, Albert Finney.

Minbo No Onna Minbo/The Gentle Art of Japanese Extortion

After the internationally successful **Marusa No Onna** and its sequel, Itami took a cynical look at the world of the yakuza, intending to debunk the romantic myths that became central to the image of Japanese gangsters (particularly when viewed from the West, for example, Ridley Scott's **Black Rain**). The management of a top-class hotel decides to rid the establishment of gangsters and corruption, but things only get worse until Mahiru (Miyamoto, the star of *Marusa No Onna*) is hired. A lawyer specialising in anti-gang actions, she is assisted by two minor hotel employees. She evades the fiendish traps laid for her and cleans up the place. Like *Marusa No Onna*, this film mixes aspects

ABOVE Joan Crawford, James Flavin, *Mildred Pierce*

ABOVE Gene Hackman, Willem Dafoe, *Mississippi Burning*

of thrillers and action films with comedy, deploying sight-gags as well as situation comedy devices. Shortly after the film, which ridicules the gangsters and shows them being bested by a woman (which is intended as the ultimate deflation of yakuza pretensions), opened in Tokyo, Itami was attacked and stabbed by three young gangsters. PW

1992/Japan/123m/Itami/*p* Yukio Takenaka/ *d*/*s* Juzo Itami/*c* Yonezo Maeda/*m* Toshiyuki Honda/*lp* Nobuko Miyamoto, Akira Takarada, Hideji Otaki, Noboru Mitani, Shiro Ito.

Mississippi Burning

This is a dramatised account of the disappearance of three civil rights workers in Mississippi in 1964 and the subsequent investigation by federal agents which revealed that they had been murdered by members of the Ku Klux Klan, the local deputy sheriff among them. The film was criticised when it appeared on the grounds of distorting the contemporary context, in terms both of minimising the role of black people within the Civil Rights movement and of depicting Hoover's FBI as more liberally slanted that was actually the case. Moreover, as a detective story, the script is somewhat awkwardly and repetitively structured, concluding with a flurry of stratagems in the last

half-hour, and the device of antagonism between pragmatic old-timer (Hackman) and youthful hothead (Dafoe) risks seeming platitudinous. Where the film scores heavily, however, is in its detailed recreation of a climate of bigotry; the opening sequence of the murders carries a real charge of dread, and the atmosphere of the oppression-ridden little town is pungently conveyed, utilising a strong line-up of character actors, notably Ermey as the reptilian mayor. TP

1988/127m/Orion/*p* Frederick Zollo, Robert F. Colesberry/*d* Alan Parker/*s* Chris Gerolmo/*c* Peter Biziou/*m* Trevor Jones/ *lp* Gene Hackman, Willem Dafoe, Frances McDormand, Brad Dourif, R. Lee Ermey.

The Mob

Towards the end of **The Rise and Fall of Legs Diamond** Diamond (Ray Danton), who represents the flamboyant but small-thinking hoodlums of the 20s, returns from a European trip to discover his outfit has been taken over by a group of unemotional executives who sit in a boardroom planning to establish a nationwide crime syndicate. This incident is typical of similar moments in many gangster movies (**Al Capone**, **Point Blank**, **The Godfather**, **The Cotton Club**, **Once Upon a Time in America**, *Mobsters*, 1991, **Bugsy**) that establish the old days are

over and the individual must now yield ground to politicians and corporations. Reflecting the actual situation, early gangster movies tend to focus on Diamond-style petty bosses or outlaws (John Dillinger, Hymie Weiss, Dion O'Banion) whose careers end in a hail of bullets rather than on the cannier types (Charles Luciano, Frank Costello, Meyer Lansky) who saw Prohibition as a chance to establish a national infrastructure for organised crime that would concentrate on such cinematically unexciting matters as book-keeping and profit-sharing rather than the spectacular gang warfare that actually served as a hindrance to the continuing business of crime. Al Capone, usually and incorrectly aligned with the old-style thugs in the movies, was actually, despite his well-known outbursts of blood frenzy, more akin to Luciano, the model for the Chairman in *Legs Diamond*, in his ambitions and achievements. Before the 20s, gangsterism in America was essentially a question of street-corner factions, but when Prohibition was repealed, ethnic and family squabbles had been subsumed by business practices and demarcation lines.

In the 1950s, which significantly also saw

ABOVE The Mob: Ray Danton, *The Rise and Fall of Legs Diamond*

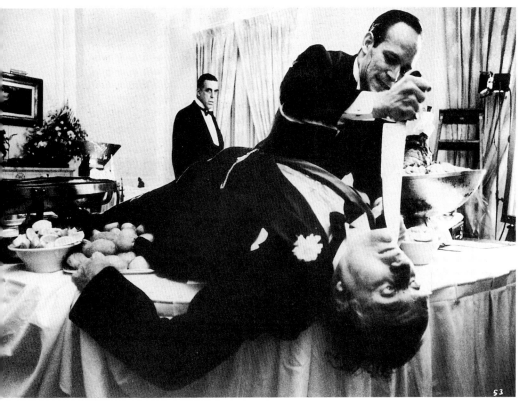

ABOVE The Mob: Fred Gwynne, James Remar, John P. Ryan, *The Cotton Club*

a run of bloodthirsty boardroom sagas about legitimate businesses (*Executive Suite*, 1954, *The Man in the Gray Flannel Suit*, 1956, *Patterns*, 1956), the mob (represented by terms like 'organised crime', 'the outfit', 'the Syndicate' and 'Murder, Incorporated') became the bugbear of the gangster movie, thanks to fact-based exposés like *The Enforcer/Murder Inc.* (1950), *The Captive City* (1952), **The Phenix City Story**, *The Case Against Brooklyn* (1958) and *Murder, Inc.* (1960), and paranoid visions like *The Mob* (1951), **The Narrow Margin**, **The Big Heat**, **On the Waterfront**, **The Big Combo**, *Tight Spot* (1955), **Kiss Me Deadly**, **The Garment Jungle** and **Underworld U.S.A.** Whereas the old-style gangster films tend to concentrate on rampaging monsters who have to be as definitively machine-gunned as King Kong, these mob movies align themselves with the paranoia of *Invasion of the Body Snatchers* (1956) by presenting a deeply corrupted world where the grey-suited crime executives hold sway over entire towns, cities and countries, and petrified witnesses are likely to be casually executed by faceless assassins. Honest cops, like Glenn Ford in *The Big Heat* and Cornel Wilde in *The Big Combo*, are driven outside the law and

turned into the moral equivalent of criminal vigilante Cliff Robertson in *Underworld U.S.A.*, able to bring down smart-suited and untouchable crime czars only because obsession fuels their campaign. Those movies which deal with legitimate attempts to crack the power of the mob (*The Enforcer, The Narrow Margin, On the Waterfront, The Phenix City Story, Tight Spot*) tend to be more convincing when they depict the frustrations of assembling solid evidence and relying on panicky witnesses who refuse to testify than they are when it comes to turning up the one plot twist which enables the heroes to prevail.

After the 50s, the existence of a national crime syndicate was so well-accepted that films could be made like *Point Blank, The Outfit* (1973), **Charley Varrick**, **Prime Cut**, *99 & 44/100% Dead/Call Harry Crown* (1974) and *A Better Tomorrow* (1987) in which almost all the characters are criminals, with civilians or even the police barely impinging on the plots. The various mafia movies, from *The Godfather* (1971) through to **Good-Fellas**, made familiar the internal affairs of the most prominent ethnic brand of organised crime, though there is a tendency, in films from *Black Caesar* (1973) through to

King of New York (1990), to see the Sicilian Mob as the flabby old-timers replaced by multi-ethnic, younger, more ambitious factions. KN

Molls

In the world of the gangster movie, the function of the mistress is related to that of the sharp suit and the ritzy apartment for which the hood exchanges his street clothes and slum home as he rises. Typically, a moll counterpoints the mobster's broken-hearted old immigrant mother, illustrating the flashy but ephemeral lifestyle he desires. Whether trampy like Mae Clarke or classy like Jean Harlow, the moll is less love interest than a visible trapping of short-lived success. In the first flurry of gangster movies – **Little Caesar**, **The Public Enemy** and **Scarface** – molls are incidental, but it is noticeable that none of the criminal protagonists of these films have 'normal' relationships with women. By **The Roaring Twenties**, the genre was ready to present a moll (Gladys George) with sincere feelings for James Cagney, the hood who spends all his time pursuing dull good girl Priscilla Lane before realising the boot-legging good-time gal is not only better for him but his only chance for romantic fulfilment.

During the heyday of *film noir*, the moll was somewhat eclipsed by the character of the *femme fatale* who would attempt to lure the corruptible hero into some crime or other. If the hero was worthy – like Humphrey Bogart in **The Maltese Falcon** or Dick Powell in **Murder My Sweet** the dame would be defeated, but more often she would completely entrap a weak man, and lead him along a road to inevitable death and degradation. While Barbara Stanwyck in **Double Indemnity** and Joan Bennett in **Scarlet Street** are not strictly molls – in the sense that a moll is a gangster's girl-friend – Yvonne De Carlo in **Criss Cross**, Ava Gardner in **The Killers**. Jane Greer in **Out of the Past** and Virginia Mayo in **White Heat**, all of whom dominate and manipulate their men, do turn the moll position to their advantage.

Less fortunate are the molls whose plot function is to demonstrate just how brutal the gangster villains are, and suffer even more indignities than the grapefruit in the face Mae Clarke receives from Cagney in *The Public Enemy*. From Claire Trevor's drunken tramp in **Key Largo** to Gloria Grahame's scarred stoolie in **The Big Heat**, molls in late *noir* begin to bridle under the ill-treatment, turning on their men (Edward G. Robinson, Lee Marvin) in the climax and helping the hero break the power of the mob, a theme developed by several 50s films (**The Narrow Margin**, *Tight Spot*, 1955) that hinge on molls testifying against former lovers. In a rare triangle plot, **The Big Combo** presents a desirable moll (Jean Wallace) who is the property of mobster Richard Conte, with Cornel Wilde as a cop whose obsessive need to bring Conte down is fuelled not by righteousness but a mad lust for the girl. Amid this seriousness, the stereotype of the gangster's dumb blonde girl-friend also became a comic regular, usually in a plot-line which has the girl transferring her allegiance to an upright john: Barbara Stanwyck in *Ball of Fire* (1941), Judy Holliday in *Born Yesterday* (1950), Jayne Mansfield in *The Girl Can't Help It* (1956).

While the rural crime cycle initiated by **Bonnie and Clyde** rethinks the moll stereotype and tends to present women who are at least equal partners with their criminal boyfriends, the gangster epics of the last twenty-five years return molls almost to the status of their 30s counterparts, literally so in Michelle Pfeiffer's reincarnation of the Harlow stereotype as a coke-sniffing designer beanpole in **Scarface** or Lara Flynn Boyle as the dancer who gets it on with Lucky Luciano (Christian Slater) in *Mobsters* (1991). In **The Godfather** and sequels, the Corleone women lurk dutifully in the background (with even Diane Keaton hardly denting her husband's complacency by turn-

ABOVE Molls: Michelle Pfeiffer, Al Pacino, *Scarface*

ing against him) while **Married to the Mob** and **GoodFellas** present remarkably similar portraits of vulgar, marginalised and dispensable mafia wives. Greater license has allowed the molls of **Get Carter**, **Charley Varrick**, **Raw Deal**, *Mobsters* (1991), *Showdown in Little Tokyo* (1991) and numberless others to be frequently-naked bimbos provided by the Mob for the entertainment of their soldiers as a relief from the usual round of killing and extortion, but only *Prime Cut* (1972) has given much thought to where these girls

come from and what happens to them. Light relief is provided by parodies of the old-time moll stereotype from Jodie Foster in **Bugsy Malone** and Lesley Ann Warren in *Victor/Victoria* (1982). The most elaborate portraits of the moll in the modern cinema come from Annette Bening as the scheming loser of **The Grifters** and as Virginia Hill, Benjamin Siegel's duplicitous girl-friend in **Bugsy**. KN

La Môme vert-de-gris/Poison Ivy

Peter Cheyney's novel had been the first title in Marcel Duhamel's celebrated *Série Noire* publishing venture and the film inaugurated the popular Lemmy Caution series starring the American crooner Constantine as the G-Man in France. Caution is sent by the FBI to investigate the rumour that a bullion shipment from the US to Italy is to be attacked by the mob. In a club run by Joe Madrigal (the singer Moreno) he finds his contact man murdered. Through a drunken journalist (Tennberg), Caution is led to the performer Carlotta de la Rue (Wilms), nicknamed 'la môme vert-de-gris' because of the colour of her eyes. Carlotta's lover, Rudy Saltierra (Vernon) is the mob boss who, warned by the journalist, captures Caution, but the G-Man escapes from the yacht where he is held and finally rounds up the gang. This first instalment establishes Caution and his charming, gravely-voiced way of speaking French with a heavy American accent. Although a laconic action man,

ABOVE Molls: Annette Bening, *The Grifters*

Caution is still presented as a serious investigator rather than a nonchalant philanderer casually beating up an entire gallery of assorted villains. Vernon is a credibly menacing opponent and we can glimpse a young Hanin among Vernon's hoods. Later instalments of the Caution series included Jean Sacha's *Cet homme est dangereux* (1953), Bernard Borderie's *Les Femmes s'en balancent* (1954), Pierre Chevalier's *Vous pigez?* (1956), Bernard Borderie's *Comment qu'elle est?* (1961), *Lemmy pour les dames* (1961) and *A Toi de faire, mignonne* (1963). PW

1953/France/97m/CICC-Pathé/*d*/*co-s* Bernard Borderie/*co-s* Jacques Berland/ *orig* Peter Cheyney *Poison Ivy*/*c* Jacques Lemare/*m* Guy Lafarge/*lp* Eddie Constantine, Howard Vernon, Dominique Wilms, Jean-Marc Tennberg, Dario Moreno, Maurice Ronet.

Mona Lisa

One of the best British films of the 80s, *Mona Lisa* is also one of the simplest. Hoskins's portly minor league villain confronted with a society he cannot understand, after a lengthy time in prison, takes refuge in Nat King Cole and 'Mona Lisa'. Cole's warm romanticism washes him clean, but Hoskins doesn't listen to the words – 'many dreams have been brought to your doorstep, they just lie there and they die there . . . Mona Lisa are you warm, are you real, or just a cold and lonely, lovely work of art?' – and so he lets Tyson's

ABOVE Michael Caine, Cathy Tyson, *Mona Lisa*

'thin black tart' become his dream object. The result is one of the most rigorous analysis of male romanticism ever attempted: at one point Jordan even literally shows Hoskins with stars – sun glasses in the shape of stars – in his eyes. Hoskins gives a superior performance as the innocent adrift in a sea of sleaze, be it upmarket (the Ritz or a Hampstead mansion) or downmarket (the streets behind Kings Cross, which Jordan shoots as though they were Hell, and Soho's profoundly seedy sex emporiums). Equally fine is Tyson as the mysterious prostitute Hoskins is given the job of shepherding from assignation to assignation and with whom he falls in love. To show his love for her, he looks for, and finds, her friend (in actual fact her lover) the heroin-addicted Hardie. Whereupon Jordan and co-writer Leland beautifully change tack. Caine, whose place in jail Hoskins took, can only betray, as in the Brighton gunfight, but Tyson can finally educate, if only by releasing him from his adoration of her. A further mark of Jordan's confidence is the role played by Coltrane, the friend who fractures the realist skin of the film from the beginning with his addiction to thrillers and his careful sublimation

of a need for relationships into collecting oddities of all description. PH

1986/GB/104m/Palace/*p* Stephen Woolley/ *d*/*co-s* Neil Jordan/*co-s* David Leland/*c* Roger Pratt/*m* Michael Kamen/*lp* Bob Hoskins, Cathy Tyson, Robbie Coltrane, Michael Caine, Kate Hardie.

The Money Trap

Among the last major studio productions to be filmed in black and white, *The Money Trap* is self-consciously a throwback, to the extent that its featured performers might well have played corresponding roles fifteen years earlier. It even has erstwhile **Gilda** co-stars Ford and Hayworth as former lovers. Crafted with the formal precision which marks the director's Westerns, the picture (derived, like **The Killing**, from a novel by Lionel White) casts Ford as a police detective who strays into criminality when he discovers that a society doctor (Cotten) is using his practice as a front for drug dealing. He formulates a plan to double-cross the doctor. A twist to the expected plot pattern is that the colleague (Montalban) who becomes suspicious of Ford's activities tries not to keep his friend

ABOVE Cathy Tyson, Bob Hoskins, *Mona Lisa*

straight but instead to get himself cut in on the deal. Inevitably the scheme goes awry, and after several violent deaths the cop is left alone beside the floodlit swimming-pool of the luxury home which his rich wife (Sommer) has financed, and which symbolises his social ambitions, as police sirens wail ever nearer. 'It's never the money,' he opines by way of an epitaph to his schemes, 'it's people, and the things they want.' TP

1965/91m/MGM/*p* Max E. Youngstein, David Karr/*d* Burt Kennedy/*s* Walter Bernstein/*c* Paul C. Vogel/*m* Hal Schaefer/ *lp* Glenn Ford, Elke Sommer, Rita Hayworth, Joseph Cotten, Ricardo Montalban.

Moonrise

This sombre melodrama features a tormented Clark who kills a man who has been persecuting him about his past (his father had been hanged for murder) and attempts to escape life by starting a romance with a schoolteacher (Russell) in a small southern town. For the most part the dark, introspective plot moves at a leisurely pace but is quickened by an exciting manhunt through murky swampland (with some fine low-key work by cinematographer Russell). Based on the novel by Theodore Strauss, reportedly the production was originally planned to be directed by William Wellman, starring James Stewart or John Garfield. TV

1948/90m/REP/*p* Charles Haas/*d* Frank Borzage/*s* Charles Haas/*c* John L. Russell/ *m* William Lava/*lp* Dane Clark, Gail Russell, Ethel Barrymore.

Mord und Totschlag/A Degree of Murder

Hans (Enke) visits his ex-lover Marie (Pallenberg). As he tries to rape her, she shoots him dead and pays a stranger, Günther (Hallwachs), and his friend Fritz (Fischbeck) to bury the corpse. They do so in the country near some roadworks. After visiting Fritz's mother, the group return to Munich where Marie leaves both men, whose lover she has become, without a thought. Next morning, back in the café where she works, Marie is invited on holiday in Greece by a stranger as Hans's body is uncovered by a bulldozer and lifted out of the shallow grave by a crane. Schlöndorff's breakthrough film, draining all the successive *film noir* situations of their emotional content, is the stylistic opposite of his first, rather literary movie, *Der junge Törless* (1965). Here he tells the story in a disjointed manner, juxtaposing individual scenes as if giving a noncommittal report, one action simply following another without apparent forethought or concern, except in the overtones of the scenes' framing, bleak lighting and the settings: places of transition and waiting: the café where Marie works, the motorway, the builder's crane lifting the corpse. Similarly, the characters, although extremely physically intimate with each other, seem utterly disconnected from each other as well as from the rest of the world. The film's form, rather than its story or characters, raises questions about Germany and its culture: needing to be more commercial than expressive and closer to American models than to German actualities, the film's narrative style becomes a commentary on German cinema as well as on the sense of aimlessness pervading life in a provincial German city. PW

1966/Germany/87m/*p* Rob Houwer/*d*/*co-s* Volker Schlöndorff/*co-s* Gregor von Rezzori, Niklas Frank, Arne Boyer/*c* Franz Rath/ *m* Brian Jones/*lp* Anita Pallenberg, Hans P. Hallwachs, Manfred Fischbeck, Werner Enke, Angela Hillebrecht.

La mort d'un tueur/Death of a Killer

The haunted-looking Hossein had been a noted theatre actor when he was noticed on

ABOVE Anita Pallenberg, *Mord und Totschlag*

the screen in Dassin's **Du Rififi chez les hommes**. He turned director with Fréderic Dard's *grand guignol* play *Les Salauds vont en enfer* (1955), although he continued to act in, for instance Lampin's *Crime et châtiment* (as Raskolnikov, 1956) and as the sex-killer Peter Kürten in his own *Le Vampire de Düsseldorf* (1965). Here he plays Massa, an armed robber who is released from jail and returns to Nice, intending to get the man who betrayed him, Luciano (Andreu). He is doubly distraught to find that his sister (Pisier), whom he loves with incestuous intensity, is now living with the grass. The mob which controls Nice tries to mediate, ordering Massa and Luciano to play Russian roulette. Massa wins the game, but his sister then denounces him to the police for having cause the death of her lover, and the cops hunt down the demented Massa and kill him in the narrow streets of Nice's old quarter. Hossein's direction is uneven, lurching from sentimentality to overblown theatrics, but he at times creates remarkably effective sequences with lovingly gliding camera movements in atmospheric locations. PW

1963/France/79m/Copernic-Cinedial/*p* Guy Lacourt/*d*/*co-s*/*m* Robert Hossein, Raymond Danon/*co-s* Louis Martin, Claude Desailly, Georges Tabet, André Tabet/*c* Jean Boffety/*m* André Hossein/*lp* Robert Hossein, Marie-France Pisier, Simon Andreu, Robert Dalban, Jean Lefebvre.

A Mort l'arbitre/Kill the Referee/The Death Penalty

Outraged by a referee's decision to award a penalty kick to the opposing team, a group of football supporters led by the bully Rico (Serrault) hound the referee, Maurice (Mitchell), and his girl-friend Martine (Laure) throughout the city. Rico mistakenly kills one of his own yobs and blames the ref-

eree. Finally, Maurice and Martine are trapped in a flat, assaulted by the football hooligans. They escape, but Rico catches up with them before Inspector Granowski (Mocky himself) can arrive on the scene. The film, which begins as a rowdy comedy and ends in tragedy, recounts the night's events in real time. The brutishness of the football hooligans is set in the context of an alienating suburban environment full of desolate, dark alleyways and soulless blocks of flats. PW

1984/France/82m/Lira Elephant-TF1-RTZ/*p* Raymond Darmon/*d*/*co-s* Jean-Pierre Mocky/*co-s* Jacques Dreux/*orig* Alfred Draper *The Death Penalty*/*c* Edmond Richard/*m* Alain Chamfort, Rossini/*lp* Michel Serrault, Eddy Mitchell, Carole Laure, Laurent Malet, Claude Brosset, Jean-Pierre Mocky.

Motel

A cross between **Psycho** and **The Postman Always Rings Twice**, Mandoki's first feature is set mostly in and around a rundown motel in the mountains. The young couple Marta (Guerra) and Andres (Alonso) who run the place are getting on each other's nerves. When a garrulous old lady arrives one night with a bag full of money, they kill her, which results in a long, explicit sex scene between the couple. A friend of the

old woman alerts the police and the rest of the film concentrates on the way a cop harasses the couple he suspects until they crack under the strain. PW

1983/Mexico/110m/Cherem-Mandoki/*co-p*/*d*/ Luis Mandoki/*co-p*/*co-s* Abraham Cherem/*co-s* Jordi Arenas/*c* Miguel Garzon/*m* Eduardo Diazmunoz/*lp* Blanca Guerra, Jose Alonso, Salvador Sanchez, Carmelita Gonzalez, Ignacio Retes.

Los motivos de Luz/Luz's Reasons

Cazals's controversial film is based on a notorious crime of the early 80s involving the murder of four children, probably by their mother. The director uses the story to explore the living conditions of women in the slums and portrays a heroine crushed by poverty, abused by her common-law husband and the father of three of her four children, oppressed and brutalised by every aspect of her life. Told in flashbacks as the main protagonist is being interrogated, the film abounds with nasty, claustrophobic spaces imprisoning the characters, who turn all their frustration and violence upon each other, adding to the violence exerted by the society they live in. The controversial aspect of the movie is that Cazals brackets the question of guilt or innocence, implicitly supporting the real-life woman's statement that she couldn't remember what happened and that

ABOVE Peter Lorre, *Mr. Moto's Last Warning*

her husband or her mother-in-law must have killed the kids. PW

1986/Mexico/117m/Chimalistac/*p* Hugo Sherer/*d* Felipe Cazals/*s* Xavier Robles/ *c* Angel Goded/*lp* Patricia Reyes Espindola, Delia Casanova, Alonso Echanove, Ana Ofelia Murguia, Martha Aura.

Mr Moto

John P. Marquand introduced his Japanese master-of-disguise sleuth-cum-spy I. O. Moto in the *Saturday Evening Post* serial 'Mr Moto Takes a Hand' (1935), republished as *No Hero* or *Ming Yellow*. After three more pre-war outings he was a changed man in the wartime *Last Laugh, Mr Moto* (1942), in which he is outwitted by canny Americans. In the postwar *Stopover Tokyo* (1957) an older, embittered Moto remarks 'Americans are always so very sentimental when they are not using flame-throwers and napalm'.

Mr Moto, now Kentaru, came to the screen, courtesy of 20th Century-Fox, in *Think Fast, Mr. Moto* (1937), a 66-minute B picture. Director Norman Foster was then a mainstay of Fox's **Charlie Chan** series. By reusing stock players (J. Carrol Naish, Lotus Long, Virginia Field, Thomas Beck) and exotic third-world sets from the Chans, *Think Fast, Mr. Moto* seems like a spin-off from the series. However, the oriental sleuths are (their inscrutable good manners aside) completely different characters, and, despite carry-overs from series to series, the films are well differentiated, with the Chan the more philosophical and Mr Moto the more athletic. In his use of ju-jitsu, Mr Moto is an early Hollywood martial arts hero, though the need to double Peter Lorre in the title role means they are done mainly in Saturday morning serial-style long shots.

In the first movie, the hero seems for much of the time to be an unscrupulous adventurer on the trail of a gang of ruthless diamond smugglers purely for his own profit. By the fade-out, it is revealed that he is a government-authorised investigator rather than an outside-the-law adventurer like the **Saint** or the **Falcon**. *Think Fast, Mr. Moto*, well enough received to kick off a series, was rapidly followed by *Thank You, Mr. Moto* (1937), *Mr. Moto's Gamble* (1938, directed James Tinling), *Mr. Moto Takes a Chance* (1938), *The Mysterious Mr. Moto* (1938), *Mr. Moto's Last Warning* (1939), *Mr. Moto in Danger Island* (1939, directed by Herbert I. Leeds) and *Mr. Moto Takes a Vacation* (1939). Foster directed the remainder and in general

these are cracking programmers. The pick of the crop is *Mr. Moto's Last Warning*, a complex story of sabotage in the canal zone with excellent **Fu Manchu**-style death-traps, including an uncharacteristically heroic John Carradine being depressurised in a diving bell, and a tossed-overboard Lorre escaping Houdini-like from a sinking sack. The exotic locales are nicely recreated on the backlot (Peking in *Thank You, Mr. Moto*, Puerto Rico swamps in *Mr. Moto in Danger Island*, Ankor Wat in *Mr. Moto Takes a Chance*, Devil's Island in *The Mysterious Mr. Moto*, Port Said in *Mr. Moto's Last Warning*) and capers frequently revolve around interesting MacGuffins like the crown of the Queen of Sheba, the treasure of Genghis Khan or a League of Assassins. Lorre enjoys the opportunity to impersonate Cambodian high priests and Arab beggars.

The series ended in 1939, partially because current events made a Japanese hero (especially one who was, in *Mr. Moto Takes a Chance*, working for the imperial secret service in China) untenable, and partially because Lorre had grown tired of solving murders rather than committing them and wanted to move out of the B-hive into more important roles in major movies.

Though Mr Moto entered public consciousness to such a degree that Porky Pig plays a sleuth called Mr Motto in *Porky's*

Movie Mystery (1939) and he gets a name-check in the lyric of 'Java Jive', he has made only a single screen appearance since the termination of the Lorre series. In the film of Marquand's *Stopover Tokyo* (1957), Moto does not appear, ceding ground to Robert Wagner, Joan Collins and Edmond O'Brien as intrepid American agents fighting communists in the Far East. *The Return of Mr. Moto* (1965) has Henry Silva – like Lorre best known as a villain, and a proven martial artist in *The Manchurian Candidate* (1962) – cast as Moto, now a James Bondian Interpol agent who adopts the disguise of a Japanese businessman to foil a plot by ex-Nazis to gain control of the world's oil resources. It's a dull, standard little film. KN

Ms .45/Angel of Vengeance

In their first film, *The Driller Killer* (1979), Ferrara and St John side-stepped the sexism inherent in splatter movies by presenting a psycho whose preferred victims are not desirable young women but unappetising old men. Aided by the ethereal presence of Zoe Tamerlis, they here tackle the issue with a feminist reading of the problematic *I Spit on Your Grave* (1980) revenge-for-rape plot, producing a work that stands between **Repulsion** and **Death Wish**. Thana (Tamerlis), a mute teenager who works as a seamstress in Manhattan's Garment Centre,

ABOVE Zoe Tamerlis, *Ms .45*

is attacked twice in the first ten minutes, by a masked thug (Ferrara himself) who rapes her in an alley and by a housebreaker whom she kills with an iron. While she disposes of the burglar's corpse piece by piece, she withdraws further, only to blossom as an anti-sexist vigilante. Armed with the dead man's .45, she stalks the city at night, killing any man who harasses her: a street punk who propositions every girl who passes, a smooth-talking photographer who lures her to his studio with promises of a *Vogue* layout, a violent pimp, a kerb-crawling Arab, a gang of muggers. As her actions get more extreme, her appearance becomes more seductive. Rather than turning Thana into a gun-toting fetish like the heroines of New World's girl gangster movies, Ferrara makes her a neutral figure whose power over her victims is rooted in her ability to inspire and contradict fantasies of femininity. In an extraordinary finale, Thana takes a last stand at a Halloween party, dressed in suspenders and a nun's habit. She shoots all the men in the room but is stabbed in the back by her gay/feminist workmate. Unable to shoot a woman, she utters the single world 'sister' and dies. KN

1981/84m/Rochelle-Navaron/*p* Rochelle Weisberg/*d* Abel Ferrara/*s* Nicholas St John/*c* James Momel/*lp* Zoe Tamerlis, S. Edward Singer, Darlene Stuto, Jack Thibeau, Peter Yellen, Jimmy Laine (Abel Ferrara).

Muerte de un ciclista/Death of a Cyclist

Bardem and Luis Garcia Berlanga, his long-term collaborator, led the revival of Spanish cinema in the 50s. They achieved international success with this criminal melodrama highlighting the moral corruption of the Spanish bourgeoisie under Franco. After visiting his mistress, a university professor kills a cyclist with his car and drives off. Eventually, guilt overwhelms him, but as he goes to give himself up to the police, his mistress runs him over and then crashes her car as she tries to avoid another cyclist. The story is told in a simple, even schematic style, skilfully mixing psychological realism with political symbolism, extending the guilt of his protagonists to the rest of the Spanish middle class. PW

1955/Spain, Italy, France/91m/Suevil-Cesareo Gonzalez-Trionfalcine-Guion/*p* Manuel J. Goyanes/*d*/*co-s* Juan Antonio Bardem/*co-s* Luis F. De Igoa/*c* Alfredo Fraile/*m* Isidro B. Maiztegui/*lp* Lucia Bosé, Alberto

Closas, Bruna Corra, Otelo Toso, Carlos Casaravilla, Manuel Alexandre.

Murder!

Probably the most expressionistic of Hitchcock's films, *Murder!*, despite being both a relative commercial failure and subsequently critically neglected, is with **Blackmail** the most important of the director's early British films. The film follows the trajectory of a whodunit. Actor-manager Marshall is the juror convinced Baring is innocent of the murder she is found guilty of who sets out to prove it by repeating the police investigation. But where most mysteries are of necessity plot-driven, Hitchcock is far more interested in intensifying key moments in the story. Thus, the first meeting of Marshall and Baring is shot subjectively from both points of view. Even more extraordinary is the sequence where Marshall while shaving and listening to music – which at the time required a 30 piece orchestra to be hidden behind the wireless set – begins a long stream of conscious monologue about how he became involved with Baring. The film also includes an extended take with the camera following two women as they walk back and forth discussing the case. Interestingly, the handling of the declaration of the verdict, with the camera on a clerk tidying up the jury room while it is heard offscreen, is remarkably similar to that of **Frenzy**. The film also introduces Hitchcock's first extensive play with seeing and appearances. The finale, for example sees Baring and Marshall speaking love together only for the curtain to come down, revealing they were on stage. Sometimes, however, appearances are the truth. Thus Fane, who kills the woman because she knew he was a homosexual – this is thinly disguised in the film, where he is called a 'half-breed' – though he is engaged to Baring, wears women's clothes for much of the film and escapes from the scene of the crime by wearing first women's clothes and then a policeman's. Earlier, to trap Fane Marshall gets him to read a section of a play he has specially written in the character of a man who committed a similar murder. Also of interest is the finale in which, realising his guilt is known, Fane commits suicide during his trapeze performance at the circus. *Murder!* is not a fully achieved film, in the manner of **Blackmail**, but where that film first introduced Hitchcock's obsession with watching women suffer, *Murder!* sees the first mature example

of the game player, a major feature of his later films, be it the villainous Robert Walker in **Strangers on a Train** or the ambiguous Sean Connery in **Marnie**. Hitchcock shot a German language version of the film (*Mary*) with Alfred Abel in the Marshall role. PH

1930/GB/92m/British International/*p* John Maxwell/*d* Alfred Hitchcock/*s* Alma Reville/*orig* Clemence Dane, Helen Simpson *Enter Sir John*/*c* Jack Cox/*lp* Herbert Marshall, Norah Baring, Phyllis Konstam, Edward Chapman, Miles Mander, Esme Percy.

Murder by Contract

The originality of this B-picture, shot in only a few days, lies in its depiction of a hired killer as a technician, a man who is in a steady job but wants to 'better' himself and make big money, and who outwardly and officially is the essence of white-collar respectability. The film's distinctiveness stems from its coolness of tone, which is suitably complemented by Perry Botkin's guitar accompaniment. After some expository scenes of the blandly handsome Claude (Edwards) plying his trade, the action moves to Los Angeles, where he is to dispose of a closely guarded federal witness. Claude balks on learning that the mark is a woman, but despite his disclaimer ('It's not a matter of sex, it's a matter of money. Women are more unpredictable – I want double') it seems that the undertaking is obscurely jinxed, and the somewhat anti-climactic ending shows him unable to strangle his victim and then being shot down by police as he attempts a getaway. The film was made back-to-back with *City of Fear* (1958, also directed by Irving Lerner), which employed many of the same personnel. Similarly ironic in tone, it is an ingenious little thriller about a criminal (Edwards) who steals a canister which he believes contains heroin but which actually holds deadly radioactive material. TP

1958/80m/COL/*p* Leon Chooluck/*d* Irving Lerner/*s* Ben Simcoe/*c* Lucien Ballard/*m* Perry Botkin/*lp* Vince Edwards, Herschel Bernardi, Phillip Pine.

Murder Is My Beat

This second-feature mystery drama offers more than at first meets the eye. Payton, convicted of a murder she denies, en route to prison under homicide detective Langton's escort spots the man believed to have been murdered (the body was found with head and hands burned beyond recognition). The two then set out to solve the mystery. Ulmer removes the routine of the join-the-dots narrative by injecting an off-beat visual style that tends to make the viewer lose track of how little is actually happening in the plot. TV

1955/76m/AA/*p* Aubrey Wisberg, Ilse Lahn/*d* Edgar G. Ulmer/*s* Aubrey Wisberg/*c* Harold E. Wellman/*m* Al Glasser/*lp* Paul Langton, Barbara Payton, Robert Shayne.

Murder My Sweet/Farewell My Lovely

The first screen adaptation of **Raymond Chandler**'s 1940 novel *Farewell, My Lovely* was *The Falcon Takes Over* (1942), with George Sanders's already-established suave detective standing in for **Philip Marlowe**. Two years later RKO gave Marlowe his film debut in *Murder My Sweet* (the title was changed to prevent audiences thinking it a schmaltzy wartime romance, though the original was retained in England where Chandler was even then considered a writer of note). The result is the closest the cinema has come to the Chandler spirit. Powell is exactly right as Marlowe, convincingly tough and insolent but carrying echoes of his naive image as the hero of Busby Berkeley musicals which make him seem credibly purer than the surrounding *noir* world of shadows, rain, slimy master criminals, worthless *femmes fatales*, gorilla-brained thugs, quack doctors, random cruelty and occasional moments of pulp poetry. While Powell handles Chandler's wisecracks perfectly and throws in a few touches of his own like playing hopscotch on the marbled floor of millionaire Lewin Lockridge Grayle's mansion, Dmytryk and cameraman Wild make this among the darkest, most beautiful films of the 40s. There is a bravura hallucination with Marlowe under the influence of drugs shot into him on the orders of smartly unscrupulous 'psychic consultant' Kruger, but this expressionist horror hardly seems any different from the rest of the movie, which takes place almost exclusively at night in claustrophobically unlit rooms, and is populated by performers (Mazurki, Kruger, Trevor, Mander) who incarnate their characters exactly as written. The 1975 remake includes political sub-plots dealing with racketeering and police corruption that Dmytryk was unable to handle for censorship reasons, eliminates the conventional romance that provides a slight dead spot in the first film, and beefs up an already rough story with touches like replacing Kruger's

ABOVE Jean-Pierre Cassel, Anthony Perkins, Vanessa Redgrave, Sean Connery, Ingrid Bergman, George Coulouris, Albert Finney, John Gielgud, Rachel Roberts, Wendy Hiller, Denis Quilley, Michael York, Jacqueline Bisset, Lauren Bacall, Martin Balsam, *Murder on the Orient Express*

crooked medium with a butch lesbian brothel madame. Otherwise, this (the first Chandler movie to be made as a period piece) is carefully put together but rather redundant. Mitchum comes to the part twenty years too late but does what he can (and is better than in Michael Winner's disastrous *The Big Sleep*, 1978), lending an aptly world-weary presence though Goodman's script substitutes a softie sentimentality expressed through kindness to black orphans and crippled news-vendors for Chandler's tougher, nobler hero. The problem is that the period trappings (pastel colours, neon signs, careful set decoration, a sinuous jazz score) overlay Chandler's gritty, gutsy story with a veneer of nostalgia that makes this a far less effective version of the author's tone than the much more radical betrayals of Robert Altman's **The Long Goodbye**. KN

1945/92m/RKO/*p* Adrian Scott/*d* Edward Dmytryk/*s* John Paxton/*c* Harry J. Wild/*m* Roy Webb/*lp* Dick Powell, Claire Trevor, Anne Shirley, Otto Kruger, Mike Mazurki, Miles Mander.

Farewell, My Lovely/1975/97m/EKITC/*p* George Pappas, Jerry Bruckheimer/*d* Dick Richards/*s* David Zelag Goodman/*c* John

Alonzo/*m* David Shire/*lp* Robert Mitchum, Charlotte Rampling, John Ireland, Sylvia Miles, Jim Thompson, Harry Dean Stanton.

Murder on the Orient Express

This is the film that revived the **Hercule Poirot** industry, changing the emphasis from plot to decor, from character to 'acting'. Henceforth **Agatha Christie**'s great detective would become a mass of actorly tics awash in glittering 30s decor (and ironically find a natural home on television). The film follows Christie's novel closely, even down to the exposition of the whys and wherefores of the crime by Finney's Poirot, given a slightly more dramatic edge than such scenes usually have by staging it as a re-creation of the moment of the murder narrated by Finney. But where the novel was constructed by Christie as a clever inversion of the normal puzzle (which allowed for several murders but one murderer), though Dehn's script addresses the puzzle element, Lumet's camera celebrates the actors rather than interrogating the characters they play. Nowhere is this more in evidence than in the case of Finney. His Poirot is a marvellous creation, a testament to the make-up and wardrobe departments as much as to his act-

ABOVE Margaret Rutherford, *Murder She Said*

ing. Equally important is Lumet's and cinematographer Unsworth's celebration of the locale – the palatial Orient Express. As the film proceeds it becomes clear that the cutaways from the actorly confrontations are not punctuation but as substantial a part of the pleasures of the film as the plot. Bacall, Bergman, Perkins, Bisset, Gielgud, Connery, Hiller are among the suspects of the complicated twelve-stab murder of Widmark. Of these Bergman, who won herself an Oscar for her performance as the dowdy missionary, most successfully manages to show off and show off her character. Though subsequent outings, with Peter Ustinov in the Poirot role, took their direction from the Lumet film, none achieved the balance as well. PH

1974/GB/131m/GW-EMI/*p* John Brabourne, Richard Goodwin/*d* Sidney Lumet/*s* Paul Dehn/*orig* Agatha Christie/*c* Geoffrey Unsworth/*m* Richard Rodney Bennett/*lp* Albert Finney, Lauren Bacall, Anthony Perkins, Jacqueline Bisset, Ingrid Bergman, Martin Balsam, Wendy Hiller, John Gielgud, Sean Connery.

Murder She Said

This was the first of four enjoyable little whodunits starring Rutherford as **Agatha Christie**'s inquisitive **Miss Marple**. It was based on the novel *4:50 From Paddington* (1957) and featured the amateur criminolo-

gist hunting for a murderer in a country household full of red herrings and eccentric types. Three more amiable murder mysteries (filmed at Metro's British Studios in Borehamwood) followed: *Murder at the*

Gallop (1963), *Murder Ahoy* (1964), and *Murder Most Foul* (1964). All featured Rutherford as Miss Marple, usually assisted by (real-life husband) Stringer Davis, and were efficiently directed by Pollock. Goodwin's catchy title music (played on harpsichord) lingers in the memory long after the final fadeout. TV

1961/87m/MGM/*p* George H. Brown/ *d* George Pollock/*s* David Pursall, Jack Seddon, David Osborn/*c* Geoffrey Faithfull/ *m* Ron Goodwin/*lp* Margaret Rutherford, Arthur Kennedy, Muriel Pavlow.

The Musical

A surprising number of musicals have taken crime as their theme: witness, the crooked politicians of *The Phantom President* (1932), *Louisiana Purchase* (1942), *Up in Central Park* (1948) and *Never Steal Anything Small* (1959), the mystery killers and showgirls of *Murder at the Vanities* (1934), *Queen of Burlesque* (1946) and *Murder at the Windmill* (1948), the con men of *Yolanda and the Thief* (1948) and *The Music Man* (1962), the buccaneers of *The Pirate* (1948), the gambling Damon Runyon hoods of *It Ain't Hay* (1943), *Bloodhounds of Broadway* (1952) and **Guys and Dolls**, the juvenile delinquents of **West Side Story** and *Grease* (1978), the joke

The Musical: Marlon Brando, Jean Simmons, Frank Sinatra, Vivian Blaine, *Guys and Dolls*

ABOVE The Musical: George Chakiris (centre), *West Side Story*

girl-friend's showbiz career: a relationship played out by Paul Kelly and Constance Cummings in *Broadway Thru a Keyhole* (1933), Dana Andrews and Barbara Stanwyck in *Ball of Fire* (1941), Arturo De Cordova and Betty Hutton in *Incendiary Blonde* (1945), James Cagney and Doris Day in **Love Me or Leave Me**, Edmond O'Brien and Jayne Mansfield in *The Girl Can't Help It* (1956), Omar Sharif and Barbra Streisand in *Funny Girl* (1968) and *Funny Lady* (1975), Joe Viterelli and Jennifer Tilly in Woody Allen's *Bullets Over Broadway* (1994) and, outside the musical, Eric Roberts and Mariel Hemingway in *Star 80* (1983). Other entertainers who have found their careers mixed up with crookery include Frank Sinatra in *The Man With the Golden Arm* (1956) and, as Joe E. Lewis, in *The Joker is Wild* (1957), Elvis Presley in *Jailhouse Rock* (1957), *King Creole* (1958) and *Follow That Dream* (1962), the Platters in *Rock All Night* (1957), Bobby Darin in *Too Late Blues* (1961), Al Martino, as a character loosely based on Frank Sinatra, in **The Godfather** and John Belushi and Dan Aykroyd as *The Blues Brothers* (1980). Several other movies have capitalised on the fringe criminality of showbiz and cut between rubouts and torch songs, most notably Jack

ABOVE The Musical: Tony Curtis, Jack Lemmon, Marilyn Monroe, *Some Like It Hot*

gangsters of *Anything Goes* (1934), **Some Like It Hot**, *Robin and the 7 Hoods* (1964) and **Bugsy Malone** and the white slavers of *Thoroughly Modern Millie* (1967).

However, these are at best footnotes to the crime film proper, often taking a parodic approach to criminal elements, best demonstrated by the private-eye **parody** sequence of *The Band Wagon* (1953). Nevertheless, many musicals with showbiz settings, reflecting the real-life careers of the likes of Texas Guinan, George Raft, Ruth Etting and Benjamin 'Bugsy' Siegel, are tinged with racketeering. *Broadway* (1929), the story of a dancer who gets mixed up with a bootlegging murder, was remade in 1942 with

George Raft, purportedly playing himself, in the lead. This displays an overlap between the world of the gangster movie and the musical, suggested by the reincarnation of hoofers like Raft and Cagney as gangster stars, which also adds an undertone of tough-talking menace to such froth as *Roadhouse Nights* (1930), *Hold Everything* (1930), *Manhattan Merry-Go-Round* (1937), *I Can't Give You Anything But Love* (1940), and *Hold That Ghost* (1941), and the use of sparkly musical numbers in such *noirish* grit as **The Roaring Twenties**, *Road House* (1948), **Dark City** and **Party Girl**.

Especially common is the stock figure of the mobster who sponsors or discourages his

Webb's *Pete Kelly's Blues* (1955), with Webb's jazzman and Peggy Lee's singer menaced by hood Edmond O'Brien, and Francis Ford Coppola's **The Cotton Club**, which intercuts the stories of the various showfolk who worked the famous Cotton Club in Harlem with those of the famous gangsters who owned and patronised the place. KN

Musketeers of Pig Alley

Filmed on the lower East Side of New York in the summer of 1912, *Musketeers of Pig Alley* is one of the most vivid pictures of tenement life that the early American cinema produced. The first American gangster film, it introduced one of the basic conventions of the genre, a story about civic corruption ripped from the newspaper headlines of the day. It was also notable for, unlike earlier Griffith films, not including a temperance lecture. In its place is the compelling, matter-of-fact, final inter-title 'Links in the chain' as money is passed from crook to policeman. While Gish and Miller are Dickensian rather than modern characters, the melodramatics of the film are essentially modern (in part

because of the location shooting) rather than Victorian and stage-bound. Miller is the young musician robbed of his earnings while on his way home. He goes out on an optimistic quest to recover the money, while his young wife (a 16-year-old Lillian Gish) visits a dance hall with a girl friend. Each is involved with local gangsters and the two gangs, led by Booth and Paget, stalk one another down the dark alleys, with Griffith cross-cutting between Miller still hunting his assailants, the dance hall, and the girl's sick mother at home. Miller contrives to snatch his money back, a shoot-out ensues and Booth, apprehended by the police, is released when the forgiving Miller and Gish speak up for him. Bitzer's camerawork is remarkable, with one astonishing close-up as three gangsters sidle threateningly round the corner of a wall, and the acting impressive. Booth, in particular, in a jaunty hat with a cigarette hanging from his mouth, is outstanding, an descendent of Huck Finn rather than a hissable Victorian villain. JL

1912/1 reel/Biograph/*d/s* D.W. Griffith/*c* G.W.Bitzer/*lp* Elmer Booth, Lillian Gish,

Walter C. Miller, Alfred Paget, Harry Carey, Robert Harron.

My Name Is Julia Ross

A B-feature that enjoyed 'sleeper' success and was largely responsible for its director's promotion to relatively more prestigious pictures such as **Gun Crazy**, *Julia Ross* owes its inception to **Rebecca**. Like its predecessor it locates a 'frightened lady' narrative in a Hollywood impression of a mansion on the Cornish coast. In the story, derived from an English novel by Anthony Gilbert, the hard-up heroine (Foch) is hired as a secretary, only to be drugged and transported to Cornwall under a scheme by which a deranged rich man and his doting mother plan to fake her suicide as a cover for the former's murder of his wife. Macready is suitably sinister as the psychopath, with Whitty as the mother cast against her usual image. The director provides a number of stylistic flourishes, such as the circular pan which follows the heroine's strange awakening in her new surroundings. TP

1945/65m/COL/*p* Wallace MacDonald/*d* Joseph H. Lewis/*s* Muriel Roy Bolton/*c* Burnett Guffey/*m* Mischa Bakaleinikoff/*lp* Nina Foch, Dame May Whitty, George Macready, Leonard Mudie.

Le Mystère de la chambre jaune

This and *Le Parfum de la dame en noir* (1913) are based on the novels of **Gaston Leroux**, best known as the author of *Le Fantôme de l'Opéra*. There were four versions of *Le Mystère de la chambre jaune*, a classical sealed room mystery, and three of its sequel, *Le Parfum de la dame en noir*. The basic plot is much the same in all versions. A girl, Mathilde Stangerson, is working with her father, a scientist, in his laboratory. She leaves him at midnight, and goes to her room. Shots and screams are heard, the professor finds the door locked, breaks in, and finds Mathilde alive but injured, the room wrecked, and valuable papers missing. A famous detective, Frederic Larsan, investigates, as does cub reporter Rouletabille. Mathilde's fiancé, Robert Darsac, is the main suspect, but in a surprise twist the reporter proves that Larsan himself is guilty. Meanwhile, Mathilde has married Larsan, who then escapes. In *Le Parfum*, Mathilde, believing him dead, returns to Darsac, finds that Larsan is still alive, and lives in fear. Rouletabille comes to her rescue. The Eclair company made the first version of *Le Mystère*

ABOVE Lillian Gish, *Musketeers of Pig Alley*

ABOVE *Le Mystère de la chambre jaune* (1930)

in 1913, five years after publication of the novel. The director was Emile Chautard, but Maurice Tourneur worked on the production, and appears to have been virtually co-director. Like most Eclair films of those years, this one is lost, but it was successful enough for Eclair to proceed to a version of *Le Parfum*, with Tourneur as sole director, and the same cast, headed by Maurice de Féraudy of the Comédie Française. JL

1913/France/Eclair/*co-d*/*s* Emile Chautard/ *co-d* Maurice Tourneur/*orig* Gaston Leroux/ *lp* Maurice de Féraudy, Mme. van Doren, Jean Garat, André Liabel, Josette Andriot, Devalence (Note: a modern source gives Marcel Simon and Laurence Duluc as the leading actors).

Le Mystère de la chambre jaune

The third version of *Le Mystère* was made in France in 1930, and directed by Marcel L'Herbier, one of the most stylish and adventurous of silent directors. He produced a film as fantastic as it was entertaining, with imaginative sets, marvellous lighting effects (notably in the Stangerson laboratory, a fit home for any Dr. Frankenstein), inventive sound, and even, a decade before Orson Welles, spoken credits. With all this there was clear and vigorous story-telling, a lively

Rouletabille from Toutain in his first important part, and a daringly changed ending. In the novel, Rouletabille tells Larsan that he knows, and gives him time to escape, for it is not his job, he says, to play the policeman. L'Herbier substituted a public denunciation, which left Larsan no option but suicide. That could have been awkward, for the Osso company insisted that L'Herbier next make the sequel, *Le Parfum*, in 1931. This, an equally brilliant exercise in style, began with an exhumation of Larsan's grave. It was empty. JL

1930/France/109m/Films Osso/*d*/*s* Marcel L'Herbier/*orig* Gaston Leroux/*c* Georges Périnal/*lp* Huguette Duflos, Roland Toutain, Marcel Vibert, Edmond Van Daele, Leon Bélières, Vera Engels.

Le Mystère de la chambre jaune

This, the final version to date of Gaston Leroux's novel of the same title, was Henri Aisner's debut feature film in 1948. Reggiani was Rouletabille, Pierre Renoir was Stangerson, and Herrand, Larsan. Aisner was praised for the mysterious and intensely dramatic atmosphere, but the sequel was directed by the better-known Louis Daquin. He introduced an occasional touch of comedy, but gave the more macabre elements full

scope, with eerie scenes in the old family house, and a climax which saw Larsan at the head of a band of criminal lunatics. JL

1948/France/90m/Alcina/*d* Henri Aisner/ *s* Wladimir Pozner/*orig* Gaston Leroux/ *c* André Bac/*lp* Serge Reggiani, Hélène Perdrière, Marcel Herrand, Pierre Renoir, Lucien Nat, Janine Darcey.

The Mystery of the Yellow Room

Before making the 1913 version of **Le Mystère de la chambre jaune**, Chautard had worked in America, and he returned there in 1915. In 1919, for the Mayflower company, he made a second version as *The Mystery Of The Yellow Room*. This film also seems not to have survived, but contemporary critics praised the lavish production, convincing French atmosphere, and delicately shaded photography. Josef von Sternberg in his autobiography claims that he was Chautard's assistant. JL

1919/6 reels/Mayflower//*p*/*d*/*s* Emile Chautard/*orig* Gaston Leroux/*c* Jacques Bizeul/*lp* Lorin Raker, Ethel Grey Terry, George Cowl, William S. Walcott, Edmund Elton, Jean Gauthier.

N

The Naked City

A beautiful young woman has been murdered. An older, experienced policeman and a callow young one (Fitzgerald and Taylor respectively) are assigned to the case. The film is mainly concerned to present a quasi-documentary account of police procedure, and a down-beat perspective on its location, the streets of New York. But along the way director Dassin and writer Maltz offer a jaundiced view of the wealthy socialites who exist on the fringe of the story. Maltz later was one of the Hollywood Ten. The rich are mostly avaricious or degenerate, and the murdered girl's parents deliver an attack on the materialism of city life when they come to view the body. The film lacks the distinctive edge of hysteria or paranoia that marks Dassin's other crime films, but the ending is justly celebrated. De Corsia, one of the murderers, is chased along the subway track and up on to the steel girders of the Brooklyn Bridge, from where he falls to his death. EB

1948/96m/UI/*p* Mark Hellinger/*d* Jules Dassin/*s* Albert Maltz, Marvin Wald/ *c* William Daniels/*m* Miklos Rozsa, Frank

Skinner/*lp* Barry Fitzgerald, Howard Duff, Dorothy Hart, Don Taylor, Ted De Corsia.

The Naked Gun from the Files of Police Squad!

Based on the short-lived television series *Police Squad*, created by the Zucker brothers and Abrahams team responsible for *Airplane!* (1980), *The Naked Gun* is sustained by Nielsen's disaster-prone lieutenant of detectives, who grasps the wrong end of every possible stick on the way to foiling a dastardly plot to assassinate the Queen during a royal visit to Los Angeles. The picture is rather less successful than *Airplane!* in providing narrative accommodation for its succession of skits, puns and innuendo, and objection might be made that, as with the *Carry On* movies, it plays better in excerpts than as a continuous whole. However, the whole thing is so disarmingly foolish, and the performers so tireless, that such criticism can only seem churlish. Its success led to two sequels, *Naked Gun 2¹/₂ The Smell of Fear* (1991) and *Naked Gun 33¹/₃ The Final Insult* (1994). TP

ABOVE Don Taylor, *The Naked City*

1988/85m/PAR/*p* Robert K. Weiss/*d* David Zucker/*s* Jerry Zucker, Jim Abrahams, David Zucker, Pat Profit/*c* Robert Stevens/*m* Ira Newborn/*lp* Leslie Nielsen, Ricardo Montalban, Priscilla Presley, George Kennedy, O.J. Simpson.

The Naked Kiss

One of the bleakest of all Fuller's assaults on small-town smugness and corruption, *The Naked Kiss* also opens with one of his most striking scenes. Kelly (Towers), a prostitute, gets into a fight with her pimp. Suddenly he pulls off her wig to reveal her shaved head. The sequence ends with him scrabbling about on the floor for his money; some crumpled dollar bills are strewn over a calendar which reads '4ᵗʰ July'. Kelly decides to declare her own independence and to make a new life for herself. She goes to a small town but finds the local cop knows of her past. She can remain so long as he enjoys her favours. She finds satisfying work in a children's home and becomes involved with the town's leading citizen, a wealthy and cultured man, only to discover he is a child molester. He tries to persuade her that since she is a prostitute there is no essential difference between them. Horrified, Kelly kills him. The town refuses to believe her explanation, and though she is later exonerated she leaves in disgust that her reformation has had so little effect in changing her treatment by 'respectable' citizens. EB

1964/92m/Allied Artists/*p/d/s* Samuel Fuller/*c* Stanley Cortez/*m* Paul Dunlap/*lp* Constance Towers, Anthony Eisley, Michael Dante, Virginia Grey, Patsy Kelly.

The Narrow Margin

This inexpensive second-feature garnered critical recognition and box-office success. An exemplary thriller, it owes its distinctiveness to ingenuity of casting, staging and above all scripting. The action occurs almost

ABOVE Barry Fitzgerald, *The Naked City*

entirely aboard a train from Chicago to Los Angeles, on which a gangster's widow is being taken under police escort to testify before a federal grand jury – unless underworld functionaries can get to her first. The escorting cop (McGraw, more usually an aggressive heavy) has seen his partner killed in an initial affray in Chicago, and does not conceal his resentment towards the hardboiled widow ('the 60 cent special – strictly poison under the gravy'), and the latter role is played to the hilt by Windsor, one of the great screen floozies. The screenplay's trump card is that the witness proves to be a decoy, a policewoman who loses her life in the cause of protecting the real widow. This revelation occasions a narrative 'break' of a sort which perhaps prefigures **Psycho**, but the dramatic action has no trouble in shifting back into high gear for the dénouement. A 1990 remake by Peter Hyams amplifies and so dilutes the original movie's central situation. TP

1952/71m/RKO/*p* Stanley Rubin/*d* Richard Fleischer/*s* Earl Felton/*c* George E. Diskant/ *lp* Charles McGraw, Marie Windsor, Jacqueline White, Don Beddoe, Paul Maxey.

Ness, Eliot (1902–57)

A Chicago-based agent of the Department of Justice Prohibition Bureau, Eliot Ness was put in charge of the special squad known as 'the Untouchables' in 1929, entrusted with the breaking of **Al Capone**'s liquor-based empire. While Ness achieved great successes in cutting off Capone's supply of booze, the gangster was actually brought down by Treasury investigators who successfully assembled a case against him for tax evasion. In 1933, with the Capone case wrapped up, Ness transferred to Cincinnati, where he coordinated action against the moonshiners of Kentucky, Tennessee and Ohio. After the war he ran unsuccessfully for the post of Mayor of Cleveland, then went into business as president of the Guaranty Paper Corporation and Fidelity Check Corporation. He did not become widely-known for his part in the war against Capone until the publication of *The Untouchables* (1957), an autobiography written with Oscar Fraley which might well exaggerate his role in the case. After Ness's death, Fraley wrote *Four Against the Mob* (1961), covering his career in Cleveland.

In fiction, Ness appears as a minor character in Max Allan Collins's *True Detective* (1983) and assumes central status in Collins's follow-ups *The Dark City* (1987) and *Butcher's Dozen* (1988), John Payton Cooke's *Torso* (1992) and Kim Newman and Eugene Byrne's 'Tom Joad' (1992). *The Untouchables* was adapted as a two-part television film *The Scarface Mob* (1959), with stone-faced Robert Stack as Ness and Neville Brand as Capone, which led to a 1959–63 television series in which Stack led his squad in campaigns against sundry underworld figures. Narrated by Walter Winchell, *The Untouchables* was

ABOVE Richard Allan, Marilyn Monroe, *Niagara*

remarkably popular, triggering a cycle of bigscreen biopics of Legs Diamond, **Dutch Schultz**, Arnold Rothstein and others. **The Untouchables** was remade as a 1987 feature by Brian De Palma. Its success prompted Stack to re-appear in *The Return of Eliot Ness* (1991), set in Cleveland in the late 40s, and Tom Amandes to take the part in a new version of the TV series (1992–). Phillip R. Allen played Ness in *The Lady in Red* (1979), and Scott Paulin in *The Revenge of Al Capone* (1989). The character also appeared in *Frank Nitti: The Enforcer/Nitti* (1988) The oddest of the lawman's screen parts must be, as played by Tom Lahm, meeting with Christopher Lee's **Sherlock Holmes** and romancing Morgan Fairchild's Irene Adler while on his first case (in 1910, when the historical Ness was eight) in *Sherlock Holmes and the Leading Lady* (1991). Frederick Weller took the role in *Young Indiana Jones and the Mystery of the Blues* (1993), a feature-length episode of the *Young Indiana Jones Chronicles*. KN

Niagara

The celebrated falls are the backdrop to this tale of marital infidelity and murder, planned as one of Monroe's first starring vehicles. George (Cotten) is an army veteran

ABOVE Constance Towers (right), *The Naked Kiss*

ABOVE Richard Widmark, *Night and the City*. JL

married to a young wife Rose (Monroe). At a motel near the falls they encounter young honeymooners Polly and Ray. Rose is having an affair with another man (Patrick) and they plan to murder George. When Patrick is found dead Rose fears for her life; not without reason, for George, who we learn has been released from a mental hospital, is intent on killing her and eventually does. Attempting to escape across the river to Canada, he is carried towards the falls and plunges to his death below. As so often in the Hollywood crime film, an openly sexual woman (Monroe appears in a succession of revealing dresses) is seen as someone who has to be punished. Monroe doesn't really have the right look or personality for a hard-bitten *femme fatale*; she's more victim than perpetrator. But Cotten, in a role not unlike that in **Shadow of a Doubt**, is thoroughly plausible in suggesting the madness that lies below his unassuming exterior. EB

1953/92m/FOX/*p* Charles Brackett/*d* Henry Hathaway/*s* Charles Brackett, Walter Reisch, Richard Breen/*c* Joe MacDonald/*m* Sol Kaplan/*lp* Marilyn Monroe, Joseph Cotten, Jean Peters, Casey Adams, Dennis O'Dea.

Nick Carter le roi des détectives

Nick Carter, master detective, was created in American pulp magazines. He reached the cinema in 1908, in a series filmed by the Eclair company that derived from Jean Petithuguenin's French translations. The guiding spirit was Victorin Jasset, Eclair's leading director/producer, who was notable for the clarity of his narration and his skill with rapid action. The Nick Carter films were not true serials. They were a series of independent episodes. *Nick Carter, le roi des détectives* (1908), was made up of six separate films, with such titles as 'The Ambush', 'The Forgers', 'The Bank Robbers'. *Les Nouveaux exploits de Nick Carter* (1909) comprised nine films. *Nick Carter contre Paulin Broquet* (1911) maintained the pattern, and the series ended in 1912 when Jasset brought Carter face to face with another Eclair creation, the master criminal Zigomar. This last, a four-part film entitled *Zigomar contre Nick Carter*, was directed by Jasset in person. The earlier films he may well have co-directed, and certainly supervised. Through-out the series, Carter was played by Pierre Bressol; Zigomar, in the last film by a noted stage actor, Alexandre Arquillière. JL

1908/France/1 reel episodes/Eclair/
p/s Victorin Jasset/*d* Robert Saidreau (?)/
c Agnel/*lp* Pierre Bressol, Josette Andriot, André Liabel, Camille Bardou, Gilbert Dalleu.

Night and the City

Arguably the best *film noir* made outside the USA, albeit by a Hollywood exile, this follows the struggle of desperate night-club tout Harry Fabian (Widmark) to 'control wrestling in all London'. Fabian tries to play dangerous characters against each other. Thus he gets a hold over Greek Kristo (Lom) by convincing the hood's ex-champion father Gregorius (Zbyszko) that he intends to uphold the pure tradition of Graeco-Roman wrestling rather than the grunt-and-sweat style epitomised by Lom's goon, the Strangler (Mazurki). He coaxes money out of Helen (Withers), ex-hostess wife of bloated club owner Nosseross (Sullivan), supposedly to secure her a liquor licence so she can escape her husband but actually to sink into his own venture. When Fabian's schemes collapse, Kristo puts a price on his head and he is chased by the entire underworld across a bomb-blighted London dockland, finally caught, executed and tossed into the muddy Thames. With a setting that recalls both Charles Dickens and Dr Mabuse as much as the American *noir* model and an energetic but obviously doomed protagonist this is among the most horrific of its genre. The city's night is populated by monsters who

ABOVE Francis L. Sullivan, Googie Withers, *Night and the City*

ABOVE Robert Mitchum, Billy Chapin, Sally Ann Bruce, *The Night of the Hunter*

have strangely tender relationships (the sequences between Kristo and Gregorius and Nosseross and Helen are weirdly touching, with one partner tolerant of the foibles of the other). Widmark's nervous grin and Greene's dark cinematography often make Fabian seem like Lon Chaney's unmasked Phantom of the Opera, and the supposed hero loses all sympathy after his smooth talk has run out and he robs his girl-friend's flat to keep afloat, attempting to redeem himself at the last by ensuring the girl (Tierney) will collect the reward Kristo has posted on him as he accuses her of a betrayal she has not committed. Irwin Winkler's ill-advised 1992 remake, with Robert De Niro playing for sympathy as Fabian, weirdly betrays the title by relocating the story in New York and mainly in daylight. KN

1950/GB/96m/FOX/*p* Samuel G. Engel/ *d* Jules Dassin/*s* Jo Eisinger/*orig* Gerald Kersh/*c* Max Greene/*m* Benjamin Frankel/ *lp* Richard Widmark, Gene Tierney, Herbert Lom, Googie Withers, Francis L. Sullivan, Mike Mazurki, Stanislaus Zbyszko.

Night Has a Thousand Eyes

Much of Farrow's most interesting work was within the sphere of the dark melodrama. Several films, notably the Faustian *Alias Nick Beal* (1949), have shown, possibly because of Farrow's Catholicism, an engagement with

the nature of evil. The supernatural element of *Alias Nick Beal* is manifested more subliminally in **Night Has a Thousand Eyes**, whose central figure (Robinson) is a former professional mind-reader who has discovered with unnerving consequences that his clairvoyant powers are genuine. In contrast to the rambling source novel by **Cornell Woolrich**, the screenplay is conspicuous for its compactness, enhanced by the manner in which the action begins *in medias res*, with the exposition retailed via a subsequent flashback. The plot involves Robinson's rescuing the daughter (Russell) of a former associate (Cowan) from what proves to be a conspiracy against her life by a business rival, though he succeeds at the cost of his own death. In authentic *noir* fashion, the protagonist is entrapped by forces beyond himself. The premise of a theatrical mind-reader whose 'gift' proves to be real had earlier been used in the British film *The Clairvoyant*, directed by Maurice Elvey in 1935. TP

1948/80m/PAR/*p* Endre Boehm/*d* John Farrow/*s* Barré Lyndon, Jonathan Latimer/ *c* John F. Seitz/*m* Victor Young/*lp* Edward G. Robinson, Gail Russell, John Lund, Jerome Cowan, William Demarest.

Night Moves

Night Moves is a deconstruction of the private

eye movie that finds the ethics and attitudes of **Sam Spade**, **Philip Marlowe** and Lew Archer redundant in the post-Kennedy, post-Vietnam, post-Watergate 70s. Harry Moseby, superbly played by Hackman, is an ex-pro ball-player PI whose catch phrase is 'I want to know what it's all about', and whose investigative methods are a character flaw rather than a heroic tool. He jeopardises his marriage through obsessive curiosity, recounts that he tracked down the father who deserted him as a child only to avoid contacting the man, and learns through his current case that doing the job and loyalty to the client, precious tenets of the Chandler code, are meaningless unless the consequences are thought through. Hired by a drunken ex-actress to trace her runaway nymphet daughter (Griffith), Moseby finds himself caught in a plot so complex as to lose all meaning, revolving around blankly mysterious artefacts smuggled in from Mexico and involving practically the entire supporting cast in guilt. Though he acts in true private eye fashion throughout, Moseby is finally of no use to anybody. Because he does his job, Griffith is brought home to be a murder victim, and the finale finds all the guilty and the innocent dead while the wounded detective lies unconscious on a boat that proceeds aimlessly in circles on an empty sea. With a script rich in melancholy aphorism ('nobody's winning,' Moseby says of a football game, 'this side's just losing slower than the other') and bitter wisecracks from Sharp ('I took second prize in a fight,' explains a bruised Woods) and deceptively laid-back direction from Penn, *Night Moves* goes beyond even **The Long Goodbye** and **Chinatown** to emerge as the most thoroughgoing and intelligent critique of the private eye in the cinema. KN

1975/99m/WB/*p* Robert M. Sherman/ *d* Arthur Penn /*s* Alan Sharp/*c* Bruce Surtees/*m* Michael Small/*lp* Gene Hackman, Jennifer Warren, Edward Binns, Harris Yulin, James Woods, Melanie Griffith.

The Night of the Hunter

Harry Powell (Mitchum) is a sex killer in jail on a minor charge, with LOVE and HATE tattooed on his knuckles. He shares a cell with Ben Harper (Graves), a bank robber condemned to death. Powell guesses that Harper has hidden the loot from his robbery somewhere, but can't get him to talk. After the execution Powell is released and heads for the dead man's widow, Willa (Winters),

ABOVE Night-Clubs: Fred Gwynne, James Remar, Richard Gere, *The Cotton Club*

who marries him. Her son John (Billy Chapin) realizes that Powell is after his father's money, which is concealed in the doll that his sister Pearl (Sally Ann Bruce) drags around with her. Powell soon loses patience and kills Willa, but the children run away, and take to the nearby river in a boat, with Powell tracking them one step behind along the bank. From the novel by Davis Grubb, this was a box office failure and Laughton's only film as a director. It's a masterpiece whose style and performances continue to influence directors and actors as diverse as Martin Scorsese, Robert De Niro and Spike Lee. MP

1955/93m/UA/*p* Paul Gregory/*d* Charles Laughton/*s* James Agee/*c* Stanley Cortez/ *m* Walter Schumann/*lp* Robert Mitchum, Shelley Winters, Lillian Gish, Evelyn Varden, Peter Graves.

Night-Clubs

The traditional movie night-club, with its hat-check girl, cigarette girl, dreary cabaret and crooked owner checking the goings-on through the two-way mirror in his office, is long gone. But for forty years it was an internationally recognised hang-out for shady characters of every hue, a fair reflection of life at a time when mafia connections with gambling, striptease and other night life were widely reported. An often used plot has a reporter, sometimes assisted by a prostitute thinly disguised as a 'hostess', investigating

crimes occurring in, or leading inexorably to, the night-club. Almost invariably the owner is implicated, as in *Smart Blonde* (1936), *While New York Sleeps* (1938), *Murder in Soho* (1939), *The Girl from Rio* (1939), *Missing Daughters* (1939), *Late at Night* (1946), *Under the Gun* (1950) and *Million Dollar Pursuit* (1951). Rare exceptions to this rule are *King Solomon of Broadway* (1935) and *Man with a Gun* (1958). Hapless hostesses are also accomplices or victims in *The Woman Racket* (1930), *Missing Daughters* (1939) and *Alibi* (1942). Real-life prostitute 'Cokey Flo', who testified against her gangster boss, is represented in **Marked Woman**. Sometimes the web of crime extends to singers, dancers and songwriters, as in *Romance in Rhythm* (1934), *Charlie Chan on Broadway* (1937), *False Faces* (1943), *Why Girls Leave Home* (1945), *Scene of the Crime* (1949), *The Armchair Detective* (1951), *Affair in Trinidad* (1952), *The Green Buddha* (1954), *Bedevilled* (1955) and *Killer's Kiss* (1955). *Strangers Kiss* (1983) is a fictionalised account of the making of the latter film. *In Meet Danny Wilson* (1951) singer Frank Sinatra's career is manipulated by gangsters. At the turn of the 60s the new striptease and 'Continental revue' clubs began to appear in British films such as *Expresso Bongo* (1959), **Beat Girl** and *Striptease Murder* (1963). *The Sicilians* (1964) was one of the last contemporary British films to be set in an old-style night-club with gangland connections. Following the police crackdown on London crime syndicates, the

institution was seen only in period films such as **Dance with a Stranger**, **Scandal** and **The Krays**. In the USA, the traditional night-club appeared sporadically in films into the 70s, but usually with a wronged or impoverished owner tangling with hoodlums, as in *Black Gunn* (1972), *Framed* (1974), **The Killing of a Chinese Bookie**.

What now appears to be the ingenuous and happy-go-lucky disco boom of the 70s was reflected by the likes of *Saturday Night Fever* (1977) and *The Music Machine* (1979). The sleazier club culture of the 80s and 90s has often inspired a much tougher kind of film in which the dance club is a dark retreat in both senses of the phrase: *Body Double* (1984), *Empire State* (1987), *Less Than Zero* (1987), *Two Wrongs Make a Right* (1989), *Night Club* (1990), *The Crying Game* (1992), and *Carlito's Way* (1993). DM

Nightfall

Several of the more personal movies directed by Jacques Tourneur turn upon the unravelling of an enigma, a syndrome summed up within crime movie terms by the hero's remark in **Out of the Past**: 'I'm in a frame and I want to get a look at the picture.' *Nightfall*, derived from a novel by David Goodis, is a less achieved work than *Out of the Past*, but places its protagonist (Ray) in an extreme version of the same predicament, as a man caught up in a spiral of malign events. The early episodes of his pursuit and capture by two gunmen (Keith, Bond), their preparations for torturing him, and his subsequent escape, have Kafkaesque overtones of unexplained fear. The film's narrative weakness resides in the far-fetched flashback explanation of the hero's situation, arising from his fortuitous involvement, as a good Samaritan, with fleeing bank robbers whose car has crashed. Despite this shortcoming, the film is mounted with Tourneur's characteristic refinement of technique, and the deployment of machinery – an oil derrick in the early sequence where Ray is held captive, a motorised snowplough in the cathartic showdown – creates potent metaphors for the destructive power of fate. TP

1956/78/COL/*p* Ted Richmond/*d* Jacques Tourneur/*s* Stirling Silliphant/*c* Burnett Guffey/*m* George Duning/*lp* Aldo Ray, Anne Bancroft, Brian Keith, James Gregory, Rudy Bond.

No Way to Treat a Lady

The fact that Rod Steiger was a performer not readily associated with humorous roles lent an added effect to his casting as a sex strangler in a black comedy that could at the time, given the recent nature of relaxation in censorship, be promoted as somewhat outré. The film is essentially a vehicle for its star, and theatricality is the order of the day, not only in the killer's adoption of a variety of elaborate disguises – Irish priest, camp hairdresser, etc. – but in the cod psychology of his having a fixation upon his late mother, an eminent actress. Though overlong, the film is often amusingly observed, with a neat eye for detail, and there is self-effacing support from Segal as the cop on Steiger's trail and Remick as his girl-friend, who narrowly escapes becoming another victim. TP

1967/108m/PAR/p Sol C. Siegel/d Jack Smight/s John Gay/c Jack Priestley/ m Stanley Myers/lp Rod Steiger, Lee Remick, George Segal, Eileen Heckart, Murray Hamilton.

Nocaut/Knock Out

Garcia Agraz's first feature combines documentary techniques with a *film noir* style. Shot in 16mm blown up to 35mm, the story of a boxer is told in flashbacks modelled on **The Killers**. Rodrigo Saracho (Vega) becomes embroiled with gangsters and alienates his friends and family. When he kills a mobster (played by the popular wrestler star Ruvinskis) he becomes a target for the mob. In the end, past and present fuse as the hunters and the prey finally come together.

ABOVE Toshiro Mifune, Takashi Shimura, *Nora Inu*

Garcia Agraz imbues nocturnal Mexico City with a sense of brooding danger and festering corruption threatening to explode, cruelly and irrationally. PW

1983/Mexico/90m/Co-operativa Kinam/ p Jorge Diaz Moreno/d/s Jose Luis Garcia Agraz/c Angel Goded/m Gerardo Suarez/ lp Gonzalo Vega, Blanca Guerra, Guillermo Orea, Wolf Ruvinskis, Alejandro Parodi.

Nora Inu/Stray Dog

Having read in a newspaper about a detective who lost his pistol, Kurosawa used the incident to make one of his best films. Murakami (Mifune) must search throughout Tokyo for his stolen gun, since the loss of this precious object is as devastating for a young detective in famine-ridden Japan as was the theft of a bicycle in post-war Italy. Following up one clue after another, with the kind assistance of his section chief (Shimura in a wonderfully controlled, low key performance: 'Cops who are all nerves are no good', he warns), he eventually locates his pistol but not before it has been used for a robbery and a murder. In spite of some felicitous ideas, such as the suspense-inducing device of counting the number of bullets left in the gun, the narrative technique is sometimes awkward (a voice-over narration at the beginning which is abandoned shortly afterwards, flash-backs for explanatory purposes, etc.). However, the urban imagery and the atmosphere of swel-

tering heat imbue the film with a sense of menace and desolation as the young cop's moral fibre is tested. The resolution is announced by the killer's hard-boiled girl-friend (Awaji's first screen performance) when she starts to cry real tears, followed by an outburst of thunder and rain, breaking the heat-wave while revealing the murderer's whereabouts. PW

1949/Japan/122m/Shintoho/p Sojiro Motoki/d/co-s Akira Kurosawa/co-s Ryuzo Kikushima/c Asakazu Nakai/m Fumio Hayasaka/lp Toshiro Mifune, Takashi Shimura, Ko Kimura, Keiko Awaji, Reisaburo Yamamoto.

Nothing but the Best

The high-point of this engaging black comedy is Elliott's definitive performance as an aristo on the skids. Bates is the ambitious clerk who clambers, marries and kills his way to the top, Andrews the business magnate and Martin the daughter in question. Similar in attitude to Billy Wilder's better known comedies of social advancement (e.g. *The Apartment*, 1960), it is more incisive and less sentimental than them. Where Wilder too often draws back from the brink, Donner and Raphael are more thoroughgoing in their cynicism, delighting in what in *Room At The Top* (1958) had been handled with dour solemnity, as Bates lies his way through Hunt balls, Ascot, smart restaurants and the world of huntin', shootin' and fishin'. When Bates's clerk starts thinking of bigger things and realises his social background is a disadvantage, Elliott first pours scorn on his social pretensions, then educates him before finally becoming as much of an embarrassment as Bates's actual parents. Bates and Elliott spark off each other, like Jack Lemmon and Walter Matthau. Equally fine is Roeg's chocolate-box cinematography. PH

1964/GB/99m/Domino-Anglo-Amalgamated/ p David Deutsch/d Clive Donner/s Frederic Raphael/c Nicolas Roeg/m Ron Grainer/ lp Alan Bates, Denholm Elliott, Harry Andrews, Millicent Martin, Pauline Delaney.

Notorious

This is one of Hitchcock's best films, one in which the rival claims of love and duty are tested almost to breaking point. Grant is a US agent sent to South America to investigate Nazi activity just after the war. Bergman, whose father has been imprisoned by the Americans for being a Nazi agent, accompanies him and they fall in love, but

ABOVE Ingrid Bergman, Cary Grant, *Notorious*

Grant forces her to marry Rains, so that she can spy on his Nazi activities. She is discovered, and Rains and his sinister mother begin to murder her with arsenic. The film contains one of Hitchcock's least convincing MacGuffins, uranium dust hidden in wine bottles in Rains's cellar. But the anguish of Grant's position is wonderfully expressed. Duty forces him to order Bergman into Rains's bed. She agrees, for duty and love of him. He is then tormented by his doubts about her. How can she do such a thing if she truly loves him? How can he make her do it, she asks herself, if he really loves her? EB

1946/102m/RKO/*p*/*d* Alfred Hitchcock/*s* Ben Hecht/*c* Ted Tetzlaff/*m* Roy Webb/*lp* Ingrid Bergman, Cary Grant, Claude Rains, Louis Calhern, Leopoldine Konstantin.

La Nuit du carrefour/Night at the Crossroads

This, the first film based on a Simenon novel, was also, according to the author, the best of the many subsequent Maigret films. Renoir also retained happy memories of the film, made with his brother Pierre in the lead, his nephew Claude debuting as a cameraman, his friend and disciple Becker taking charge of the production and many other long-term friends being part of the crew and the cast, including the celebrated film critic and historian Jean Mitry. The plot, which merely provided an excuse for the creation of dream-like, atmospheric imagery full of fog, rain and car-lights piercing the darkness, concerns the murder of a Dutch diamond dealer and later of his wife (Pierson) at a

lonely crossroads just north of Paris. The corpse of the dealer is found in a car belonging to a mysterious couple living nearby, Carl Andersen (Koudria) and his sister Else (Winfried). Maigret (Renoir) has a gallery of suspects but eventually uncovers that Else is the boss of a drug-smuggling gang. The film remains a little mysterious because Renoir shot two extra reels which, through a mix-up with Jean Mitry who was using some of Renoir's stock for a movie he was making at the time, could not be used or reshot, leaving some gaps in the plot. But although this may account for the film's lack of success at the box office, the film is one of Renoir's most poetic and fascinating works. PW

1932/France/75m/Europa/*p* Jacques Becker/*d*/*s* Jean Renoir/*orig* Georges Simenon/*c* Marcel Lucien, Georges Asselin/*lp* Pierre Renoir, Winna Winfried, Georges Térof, Georges Koudria, Jean Gehret, Jean Mitry, Jane Pierson.

Nuvem/Clouds

Derived (uncredited) from **Graham Greene**'s *Brighton Rock*, Guimaraes's debut feature, released in 1991, tells of a young waitress, Laura (Castro), who bumps into a man on the run. The man is killed shortly afterwards and the gang responsible delegates Tomas (de Melo) to silence the witness. He seduces her and when she begins to connect him

ABOVE Ingrid Bergman, Reinhold Schunzel, *Notorious*

ABOVE Frank Sinatra, *Ocean's Eleven*

with the murder, he marries her assuming a wife cannot testify against her husband. The representative of the law is Raul (Filipe), a suspended rogue cop. The film borrows various plot elements from Greene's novel, including the criminal recording an ambiguous love message to his girl-friend: here a video tape rather than a record. PW

1989/Portugal/99m/Tropico/*co-p*/*d*/*co-s* Ana Luisa Guimaraes/*co-p*/*co-s* Victor Goncalves/ *co-p* Jose Bogatheiro/*co-s* Joao Maria Mendes/*c* Octavio Espirito Santo/*m* Andrew Poppy/*lp* Alfonso de Melo, Rosa Castro Andre, Guilherme Filipe, Sao Jose Lapa, Filipe Cochofel.

O

Obsession

This psychological suspense drama draws heavily on Alfred Hitchcock's **Vertigo** with its story-line about the reincarnation of a beloved late wife and De Palma's visual assault of Hitchcockiana (even to the extent of incorporating an appropriate Herrmann score). The one major difference between the two films is the time of their making. Thus the blackness of Hitchcock's film is restricted to the central bleakness at the heart of James Stewart's character. However, Robertson and Bujold as the husband and

wife – and father and daughter – indicate more pointedly the hidden desires that Hitchcock's film merely suggested. John Lithgow is the greedy villain of the piece, all good ole boy charm. Schrader's screenplay was developed from a story by De Palma. TV

1976/98m/COL/*p* George Litto/*d* Brian De Palma/*s* Paul Schrader/*c* Vilmos Zsigmond/ *m* Bernard Herrmann/*lp* Cliff Robertson, Genevieve Bujold, John Lithgow.

Ocean's Eleven

A glossy, chic heist movie, close in tone to *Seven Thieves* (1960), *5 Against the House* (1955) and *Assault on a Queen* (1966), this is not quite the outright spoof fantasy of later genre variants like **The Thomas Crown Affair** or *Dead Heat on the Merry-Go-Round* (1968), but is still vastly removed from the gritty, realistic likes of **The Asphalt Jungle** or **Rififi**. The leads, mostly members of the Sinatra 'rat pack', never remotely pretend to be doing anything but riffs on their showbiz personae, giving the whole thing the self-indulgent feel of a million-dollar home movie, down to chummy guest appearances from hangers-on Red Skelton, Shirley MacLaine and George Raft. After a muddled build-up, the heist, the military-style simultaneous robbery of five Las Vegas hotels, is filmed with machine-like efficiency, but there is the inevitable ironic punch-line, as

the money, concealed in a coffin, is cremated. KN

1960/127m/WB/*p*/*d* Lewis Milestone/*s* Harry Brown, Charles Lederer/*orig* George Clayton Johnson, Jack Golden Russell/*c* William H. Daniels/*m* Nelson Riddle/*lp* Frank Sinatra, Dean Martin, Sammy Davis Jr, Peter Lawford, Angie Dickinson, Richard Conte.

The October Man

Ambler's production debut, *October Man* centres not on his interest in exotica (as in **The Mask of Dimitrios** or in *The Light of Day*, the source novel for the caper film **Topkapi**) but on the writer's concern with the even more nightmarish pressures of everyday life (as in his script for *The Cruel Sea*, 1951). Mills is the hero, a suicide-prone industrial chemist convalescing from a traumatic accident in which a child was killed, suspected of the murder of Walsh's sad would-be playgirl. Script and cinematography amply capture the drabness and pettiness of small-town hotel life in post-war Britain, while Carey's spitefulness and Chapman's spidery suggestiveness provide the distaste for mental affliction that fuels the plot. In the end Chapman is found to be the guilty (and, ironically, needlessly jealous) party. But the film's topography which posits a (decidedly British) **Psycho**-like hotel at one end of the common and Greenwood's

ABOVE Richard Conte, *Ocean's Eleven*

house (in which also lives Mills' doubting chemical partner) at the other end, while it finally liberates Mills from its ominous darkness, is less forgiving of the film's other characters who remain trapped within its shadows. PH

1947/GB/98m/Two Cities-GFD/*p/s* Eric Ambler/*d* Roy Baker/*c* Erwin Hillier/*lp* John Mills, Joan Greenwood, Kay Walsh, Edward Chapman, Joyce Carey, Felix Aylmer.

El ojo de cristal

This thriller derived from a **Cornell Woolrich** short story clearly illustrates the novelist's main theme that reason can never eliminate the unreasonable. A murderer commits the perfect crime, having foreseen all eventualities. The inspector (the Mexican actor Moctezuma) sent to investigate receives the unexpected help of a group of children who like to play at being detectives. The criminal had not been able to foresee childish ways of reasoning and the kids discover the clue that leads to the criminal's undoing, a glass eye found in the turn-up of a pair of trousers. PW

1955/Spain/79m/IFI/*p* Ignacio F. Iquino/*d* Antonio Santillán/*s* José Antonio de la Loma, Joaquin Algars/*orig* William Irish [Cornell Woolrich] *Through a Dead Man's Eye/c* Ricardo Albiñana/*m* José Casas Augé/*lp* Carlós López Moctezuma, Manolito Fernández, Armando Moreno, Beatriz Aguirre, Francisco Alonso.

Olsen-banden/The Olsen Gang

The Olsen gang, three inept petty criminals perennially looking for a big score led by Egon Olsen (Sprogøe), hit the screens first in 1968 under Balling's direction. Their comic adventures continued at the rate of a film a year. Egon is the quick-witted professional, Benny (Grunwald) is the naive youngster and Kjeld (Bundgaard) is the cautiously reluctant one dominated by his loud and forceful wife. The law is represented by Inspector Mortensen (Steen), the implacable enemy of the gang. This cast of characters provides the framework for very popular series in Denmark. Others in the series include *Olsen-banden på spanden* (1970), *Olsen-banden i Jylland* (1971), *Olsen-bandens store kup* (1972), *Olsen-banden går amok* (1973), *Olsen-bandens sidste bedrifter* (1974), *Olsen-banden på sporet* (1975), *Olsen-banden ser rødt* (1976), *Olsen-banden går i krig* (1978), *Olsen-banden overgiver sig aldrig* (1979), *Olsen-bandens flugt over plankevaerket* (1980) and *Olsen-banden over alle bjerge* (1981). PW

ABOVE Karl Malden, Marlon Brando, Eva Marie Saint, *On the Waterfront*

1968/Denmark/80m/Nordisk/*d/co-s* Erik Balling/*co-s* Henning Bahs/*c* Claus Loof, Jeppe M. Jensen/*m* Bent Fabricius-Bjerre/*lp* Ove Sprogøe, Morten Grunwald, Poul Bundgaard, Peter Steen, Poul Reichhardt.

L'Ombre du doute/A Shadow of Doubt

One of the rare films to deal with a father's sexual abuse of his daughter; the central figure is the 12-year-old Alexandrine (Blancke), whose behaviour and schoolwork leads her teacher (Lavanant) to suspect that something is amiss. Alexandrine tells the police that her father, Jean (Bashung) molests her, but she is not believed as both her parents deny the suggestion. Only her younger brother Pierre (Issermann) supports her, and the two kids eventually run away from home. The mother, Marie (Perrier, giving the finest performance in the film), slowly comes to realise the truth of her daughter's allegations and Jean, it is later revealed, had been a sexually abused child himself. In the end, he confesses and asks for therapy. The film, the imagery of which is dominated by huge, lurking shadows and unsettling close-ups inviting the viewer to read the unspoken or denied truth on people's faces, ends on a happy note as Alexandrine plays by the sea-

side, cured of her fear of water. Issermann avoids any trace of sensationalism but her film, at times recalling the disturbing atmosphere of Fritz Lang's **M**, succeeds in conveying the horror at the heart of the story as the sickeningly corrosive effects of child abuse spread through a family and beyond. PW

1992/France/106m/CiBy 2000-TF1 Films-Cofimage 4-Investimage 4/*d/s* Aline Issermann/*c* Darius Khondji/*m* Reno Isaac/*lp* Sandrine Blancke, Mireille Perrier, Alain Bashung, Emmanuelle Riva, Michel Aumont.

On Dangerous Ground

'Make up your mind to be a cop, not a gangster with a badge,' detective Jim Wilson is told by a superior early in the film. Wilson (a powerfully felt performance by Ryan) is a man who has internalised the violence and corruption to which his work exposes him, and to whom brutality has become second nature. 'Why do you make me do it?' he almost beseechingly asks a low-lifer from whom he has beaten a confession. Having established this portrait of Wilson, the film switches to a rural locale, where Wilson has been sent to 'cool off' in investigating a child murder. Here he is drawn into a relationship with an enigmatic woman (Lupino), whose spirituality is symbolised by blindness, and whose disturbed younger brother is the wanted man. In this wintry landscape, Wilson is exposed both to love and to a more elemental form of violence, and the effect is ambiguously purgative. The bipartite story construction might seem awkward, but this is over-ridden by the intensity of realisation, and though the ending is more sentimental than had evidently been the original intention, it is carried off with genuine conviction. TP

1951/82m/RKO/*p* John Houseman/ *d* Nicholas Ray/*s* A.I. Bezzerides/*c* George E. Diskant/*m* Bernard Herrmann/*lp* Robert Ryan, Ida Lupino, Ward Bond, Ed Begley, Charles Kemper.

On ne meurt pas comme ça

One of the few crime thrillers set in a film studio. The famous director Eric von Berg (Stroheim's first post-war appearance in France) is finishing his film, knowing that his lover Lynn Laureno (Vernac in her French debut) is having an affair with the actor Pierre Vannier (Delbo), the husband of the nice Marianne (Blanc), the film's star. In the last scene, Vannier is supposed to die and he seems to fluff it, provoking the director into shouting: 'One doesn't die like that.' However, Vannier really does die, of poisoning. Two policemen (Temerson and Tabet) come to investigate. It turns out that the wardrobe mistress (Sylvie) is Marianne's natural mother and has released a poisonous snake to bite the star's selfish and philandering husband. The police are sympathetic and conclude that Vannier committed suicide. PW

1946/France/105m/Tracali-Neubach/*p*/*co-s* Ernest Neubach/*d* Jean Boyer /*co-s* André Tabet/*c* Charles Suin/*m* José Hajos/*lp* Eric von Stroheim, Anne-Marie Blanc, Denise Vernac, Jean-Jacques Delbo, Temerson, Georges Tabet, Sylvie.

On the Waterfront

Terry Malloy (Brando) is a punchy former boxer, whose brother Charley (Steiger) is a crooked lawyer employed by racketeer union boss Johnny Friendly (Cobb). Terry's career went down the tube taking dives for Johnny, and he now runs errands for the gangsters and keeps pigeons. In the opening sequence he sets up a worker who is out of line, and whom Johnny's hoods then push off a roof. Later on Terry meets the victim's sister Edie (Saint), falls in love, and falls prey

to guilt. Local priest (Malden) exploits Terry's confusion by urging him to inform on Johnny. Brando is more charismatic here than ever before or since. His speech in the taxi to Steiger must be one of the best known in the English language: 'I could have been a contender.' The vérité-style photography highlights the grim world of the dockside slums, commenting effectively on the conditions surrounding the hoods and their victims. MP

1954/108m/COL/*p* Sam Spiegel/*d* Elia Kazan/*s* Budd Schulberg/*c* Boris Kaufman/ *m* Leonard Bernstein/*lp* Marlon Brando, Karl Malden, Lee J Cobb, Rod Steiger, Eva Marie Saint.

ABOVE Marlon Brando, Eva Marie Saint, *On the Waterfront*

Once Upon a Time in America

The only film directed by Leone during the last fifteen years of his career, this takes the themes of his Westerns into the twentieth century, using the gangster movie as a vehicle to probe the dark heart of the American dream. While **The Godfather Part II**, with which it invites comparison through specific ethnicity and juggling of chronological order, presents gangsterism as a caricature of the American way of life, Leone locates crime as just another strand of social history, with Woods's segue from boot-legging to behind-the-scenes political power simply a logical progression. It moves from ghettos to Long Island mansions and traces the line of corruption from street-corner cops to bent congressmen, but its heart is the relationship between Noodles (De Niro) , the brutal fall guy, and Max (Woods), the psychopathic schemer. With first-rate work from De Niro and Woods, this is at once a panoramic recreation of a half-century of New York, an extraordinarily decadent romance of thwarted love and a daring, fantastical look into the American psyche. KN

ABOVE James Woods, Robert De Niro, William Forsythe, Burt Young, *Once Upon A Time in America*

1984/250m/Ladd/*p* Arnon Milchan/*d*/*co-s* Sergio Leone/*co-s* Leonardo Benvenuti, Piero De Bernardo, Enrico Medioli, Franco Arcalli, Franco Ferrini/*orig* Harry Grey *The Hoods*/ *c* Tonino Delli Colli/*m* Ennio Morricone/ *lp* Robert De Niro, James Woods, Elizabeth McGovern, Tuesday Weld, Larry Rapp.

Ossessione

Visconti's version of **James M. Cain**'s novel *The Postman Always Rings Twice* was made in Fascist Italy, though censorship problems before and after the fall of Mussolini meant that the film was not widely known for some time. Shot by Visconti in a naturalistic style amid Sicilian locations, the film has been seen as one of the harbingers of Italian neo-realism. In place of the sexual magnetism and naive economic opportunism that is central to both American versions (1946 and 1981), Visconti's film has a sense of fatality in which the characters become almost ciphers merely going through the motions. A drifter arrives at a small country inn and begins an affair with the inn-keeper's wife. They plan to go away together but she changes her mind. Later on, the drifter encounters the married couple again and the husband insists he stay with them. The two lovers murder the husband, making it appear an accident. The woman, to her surprise, inherits a large sum from her husband's life insurance. The police are suspicious. Driving away to escape them the two lovers crash and are killed. Visconti made some important modifications to the original plot. The main difference is that in Cain's novel the drifter is acquitted of the murder of the husband, but then convicted of the death of the wife, which is fact is an accident. EB

1942/135m/ICI Rome/*p* Libero Solaroli/ *d* Luchino Visconti/*s* Mario Alicata, Gianni Puccini, Giuseppe de Santis, Luchino Visconti/*c* Aldo Tonti, Domenico Scala/ *m* Giuseppe Rosati/*lp* Clara Calamai,

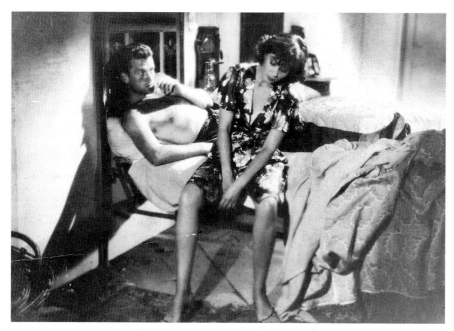

ABOVE Massimo Girotti, Clara Calamai, *Ossessione*

Massimo Girotti, Juan De Landa, Elio Marcuzzo, Dhia Cristiani.

Out of the Past/Build My Gallows High

A complex tale of love and betrayal, deceit, greed and murder, *Out of the Past* is one of the defining moments of *film noir*. Told largely in flashback by the doomed hero (Mitchum), the story tells how he is recruited by gangster Douglas to find his missing mistress (Greer), who, Douglas alleges, has stolen money from him. Mitchum tracks her down in Mexico. Her first appearance, coming out of the strong sunlight into the shadows of a little café where Mitchum is waiting, is a magical moment: she is so beautiful we know Mitchum must fall for her. He allows her to persuade him that she has not stolen the money. Together they escape from Douglas, but Mitchum comes to realise that Greer has lied, that she has stolen the money. He leaves her and builds a new life for himself in a small town in the mountains. But his past catches up with him. He cannot escape the clutches of Greer or Douglas, who has set the police on him. He and Greer die smashing through a roadblock. A doomed but stoical hero, a beautiful but treacherous woman, memories of the past, a world of flashy night-clubs, seedy hotels, fast cars, bright lights, deep shadows: it's all there. EB

ABOVE Paul Douglas, Richard Widmark, Alex Minotis, *Panic in the Streets*

1947/96m/RKO/*p* Warren Duff/*d* Jacques Tourneur/*s* Geoffrey Homes (Daniel Mainwaring)/*c* Nicholas Musuraca/*m* Roy Webb/*lp* Robert Mitchum, Jane Greer, Kirk Douglas, Rhonda Fleming, Richard Webb.

P

Panic in the Streets

This film can be bracketed in Kazan's filmography with *Boomerang!* (1947), which is scripted by the same writer, Murphy. Both are instances of the location-based crime movies which were prevalent at the time, particularly at Fox. But where the factually-based *Boomerang!* now appears somewhat stodgy in its delineation of a judicial imbroglio, *Panic* retains considerable dynamism. A

LEFT Virginia Huston, Robert Mitchum, *Out of the Past*

ABOVE Jack Palance, *Panic in the Streets*

fictional story, though it seeks to dramatise the work of the Public Health Service, it was filmed in New Orleans, and concerns the discovery that a murder victim, an illegal alien, is a carrier of bubonic plague, and follows subsequent endeavours to capture the murderers before an epidemic can start. The film is underpinned by the urgency of a 48-hour race against time, but its strongest suit is its deployment of locales in the city's dockside and low-life areas, creating a febrile, almost gothic, atmosphere. Palance, in his screen debut, and Mostel are ideally cast as the sleazy subjects of the manhunt, and Widmark is effectively used against his then prevailing villainous vein as the liberal-spirited doctor who leads the search. TP

1950/96m/FOX/*p* Sol C. Siegel/*d* Elia Kazan/*s* Richard Murphy/*c* Joe MacDonald/*m* Alfred Newman/*lp* Richard Widmark, Paul Douglas, Barbara Bel Geddes, Jack Palance, Zero Mostel.

Papa les petits bateaux . . .

La Fiancée du pirate (1969), Kaplan's deliciously subversive tale of a woman's revenge against the corruption and repression that passes for everyday normality, was followed by this crazy comedy starring White as the ebullient blonde Venus de Palma. She is kidnapped by gangsters who seek to extract a huge ransom from her father, who refuses to pay. However, she proves too much for the gangsters and neatly turns the table on them, getting them to exterminate each other while she pockets the money eventually paid over by her father. The liberating inversion of the standard woman-in-peril scenario is crammed with comic strip gags (including Popeye, spinach tin and all). In Kaplan's version of Laborde's novel *Bandes de raptes*, all the macho gangster clichés are lampooned, showing machismo to be nothing but the behaviour of adults whose emotional development got arrested some time during adolescence. Kaplan ridicules both the gangsters and the conventions of the male action movie which revels in machismo even when pretending to deflate it. PW

1971/France/100m/Cythère/*p*/*co-s* Claude Makovski/*d*/*co-s* Nelly Kaplan/*co-s* René Guyonnet/*orig* Jean Laborde *Bandes de raptes*/*c* Ricardo Aronovich/*lp* Sheila White, Michel Bouquet, Michael Lonsdale, Judith Magre, Pierre Mondy.

The Paradine Case

'I will tell you about Mrs Paradine – she's bad, bad to the bone.' So says the valet (Jourdan) with whom the lady has been dallying, according to rumours preceding her trial for the murder of her wealthy husband. Hitchcock's film, adapted from a 1933 novel by Robert Hichens, centres upon the trial and the manner in which the accused woman (Valli) manipulates the affections of her defence counsel (Peck) in an ultimately vain bid to secure her acquittal. The film, mounted with characteristic Selznick opulence, suffers from a somewhat dated view of English life, and Peck is less than ideally cast as a London barrister. The director's preoccupations come to the fore in the near-fetishistic treatment of Mrs Paradine's initial arrest and incarceration, and in a fascination with the rituals of the law. There is an elaborate Old Bailey mock-up, and visually the most striking moment occurs in the extreme high-angle shot of Peck leaving court after the case has collapsed, threatening to take his marriage and professional future with it. Charles Laughton serves up some thickly sliced ham as the lecherous presiding judge. TP

1947/110m/Selznick International/*p*/*s* David O. Selznick/*d* Alfred Hitchcock/*c* Lee Garmes/*m* Franz Waxman/*lp* Gregory Peck, Alida Valli, Louis Jourdan, Charles Laughton, Ann Todd.

Paris-Béguin

Immediately after playing Inspector Miral in the Osso-produced serial *Méphisto* (1930), Gabin went on to play the other role that would become part of his standard repertoire throughout the rest of his career, the sympathetic criminal who in the end has to pay with his life (a role which, with Duvivier's

ABOVE Michel Bouquet, Sheila White, *Papa les petits bateaux . . .*

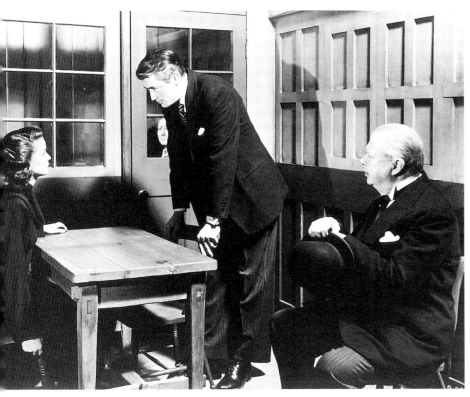

ABOVE Alida Valli, Gregory Peck, Charles Coburn, *The Paradine Case*

Pépé le Moko in 1936, made him a star). Here Gabin is Bob, a burglar who breaks into the apartment of the cabaret actress Jane Diamand (Marnac). When she unexpectedly returns and surprises him, the two end up spending the night together. The next day, Bob is arrested for a murder he did not commit, and Jane supplies him with an alibi, claiming he spent the night with her maid (Barry). Bob's steady girl-friend Gaby (Berendt), out of jealousy, sends the two actual murderers (Fernandel in an early role, and Max) after Bob. They kill him and he dies in Jane's arms, just before she has to go on stage. PW

1931/France/117m/Osso/*p* Adolphe Osso/ *d* Augusto Genina/*s* Francis Carco/*c* Friedl Behn-Grund, Louis Née, Paul Briquet/*m* Maurice Yvain/*lp* Jean Gabin, Jeanne Marnac, Rachel Bérendt, Jean Max, Violaine Barry.

Parker, Bonnie (1910–34) and Barrow, Clyde (1910–34)

Clyde Barrow was already established as a bank bandit and a killer, in partnership with his brother Marvin, when he teamed up with Kansas City waitress Bonnie Parker, previously girl-friend of another hold-up man, Roy Hamilton. They robbed a few banks in Texas together and combined with Marvin and his wife Blanche for further crimes. Marvin was fatally wounded in a shoot-out in Iowa in 1933, but Bonnie and Clyde, subjects of a massive federal manhunt, eluded the law until 23 May 1934, when they were ambushed in Shreveport, Louisiana, and filled full of holes. Linked in death, film title and Georgie Fame's hit 'The Ballad of Bonnie and Clyde', Barrow and Parker were only two members of a loose gang, and may never have been intimate, the probability being that Barrow was homosexual and Parker involved with Hamilton, whose rescue from jail she and Clyde arranged. If **Dillinger** had daring and **Ma Barker** a warped sense of family values, Bonnie and Clyde owe their myth status to each other, and to a conscious attempt to build a legend by sending poems and pictures to the newspapers. Most couple-on-the-run pictures derive from the legend of Bonnie and Clyde, including such romanticised visions as Fritz Lang's **You Only Live Once**, with Sylvia Sidney and Henry Fonda, Nicholas Ray's **They Live by Night**, with Cathy O'Donnell and Farley Granger, Joseph H. Lewis's **Gun Crazy**, with Peggy Cummins and John Dall, Luke Moberly and Bob

Woodburn's *Little Laura and Big John* (1973), with Karen Black and Fabian Forte, John Hough's *Dirty Mary, Crazy Larry* (1974), with Susan George and Peter Fonda, and Robert Altman's *Thieves Like Us* (1974) with Shelley Duvall and Keith Carradine. There have been fewer actual depictions of the pair. The most extensive and mythomaniacal biopic is Arthur Penn's **Bonnie and Clyde**. Others include Tamar Cooper and Baynes Baron in *Guns Don't Argue* (1957), Dorothy Provine and Jack Hogan (as 'Guy Darrow') in *The Bonnie Parker Story* (1958), Jo Enterentree and Lucky Mosley in *The Other Side of Bonnie and Clyde* (1968), Mary Woronov in *The Lady in Red* (1979), Gayle Sterling and Billy Dee in the porno *Bonnie & Clyde?* (1988), Tracy Needham and Dana Ashbrook in *Bonnie & Clyde: The True Story* (1992) and Maureen Flannigan (as 'Bonnie Baker') and Scott Wolf in *Teenage Bonnie and Klepto Clyde* (1993). KN

Parodies

By the turn of the century, the conventions of the crime melodrama, particularly the clues left by the criminal and the brilliant deductions of the detective, were so familiar from the stage, literature and comics that

ABOVE Parodies: Leslie Nielson, *The Naked Gun*

they were parodied during the infancy of the cinema, witness *The Would-Be Detective* (GB, 1913), featuring a character called Bexton Slake, and *Baffles, Gentleman Burglar* (1914). Douglas Fairbanks played Coke Ennyday, a Sherlock Holmes parody, in *The Mystery of the Leaping Fish* (1915). By the 1920s, however, parody (in the US, burlesque) was out of fashion, and subsequent attempts were uncommon and unsuccessful, e.g. *The Villain Still Pursued Her* (1940), a parody of silent melodrama, and John Huston's *Beat the Devil* (1953), which pokes fun at his own **The Maltese Falcon**. Hitchcock often parodied himself but his films could still be enjoyed as thrillers by those unaware of the self-mockery. The first successful modern film entirely conceived and executed as parody is *L'Homme de Rio* (1963), a James Bond spoof which began a trend. In the early 70s a pair of private-eye parodies – the superior **Gumshoe** and the lesser *The Black Bird* (1975) – were in the vanguard of an onslaught of wild lampoons. Writer Neil Simon parodied five private eyes in *Murder by Death* (1976), and *Casablanca* (1942) and other Humphrey Bogart movies in *The Cheap Detective* (1978). Mel Brooks parodied Hitchcock in **High Anxiety**. From his days in television in the 1950s, Brooks has made a career out of parody, as has his colleague Carl Reiner, who parodied *film noir* in **Dead Men Don't Wear Plaid**, the mad scientist genre in *The Man with Two Brains* (1983), and erotic thrillers in *Fatal Instinct* (1992). Heavily influenced by Brooks, Gene Wilder made *The Adventure of Sherlock Holmes' Smarter Brother* (1975). The early careers of the Zucker brothers consisted entirely of parody, including *Top Secret!* (GB 1984) and three films in **The Naked Gun** series, parodies of the TV series *Dragnet*, as indeed was **Dragnet** itself. Other private-detective parodies include the extraordinary Paul Morrissey version of *The Hound of the Baskervilles* (1977), *The Man with Bogart's Face* (1980), about a would-be private eye named Sam Marlow; and *Bullshot* (1983), a slapstick spoof of Bulldog Drummond. Gangster movies are parodied in *Johnny Dangerously* (1984); B-features of the 1940s in *Crimewave* (1985); splatter movies in many films, among them *Blood Diner* (1987) and *Bloodsucking Pharaohs from Pittsburgh* (1988); **The Godfather** in *The Freshman* (1989); and the serial killer vogue in *So I Married an Axe Murderer* (1993) and *Serial Mom* (1994). The phoney documentary, later dubbed 'mockumentary', was introduced in the early 80s. The style was used to record the killings of a mass murderer in the controversial **C'est arrivé près de chez vous/Man Bites Dog**. DM

ABOVE Cyd Charisse, Robert Taylor, *Party Girl*

La parte del leon

A thriller in the classic style, this is dedicated 'To Warner Bros. 1930–50' and a series of directors ranging from Michael Curtiz through Jacques Tourneur and Fritz Lang. Although no real crime seems to be committed (the script called for a killing but that was abandoned during shooting), the protagonist's world – Argentina under military dictatorship – drips with criminality and corruption, urging everyone to grab what they can and damn the rest. The central figure, Bruno di Toro (De Grazia), is an ordinary, rather weak lower middle-class man who finds a bag full of money dumped by bank robbers. He then tries to pursue his dreams of wealth and encounters the obligatory *femme fatale* while the bank robbers are on his trail. Underacting and dramatic *noir* lighting enhance the atmosphere in this fascinating film. Although Aristarain had worked on more than thirty films in Argentina and in Spain, this was his first feature. He went on to make some remarkably atmospheric thrillers about corrupt politicians and multinational businessmen, including *Tiempo de revancha* (1981) and *Ultimos dias de la victima* (1982). PW

1978/Argentina/85m/JNC/*p* Jorge N. Cuomo/*d*/*s* Adolfo Aristarain/*c* Horacio

ABOVE Parodies: *The Mystery of the Leaping Fish*

ABOVE John Ireland, Cyd Charisse, Irving Greenberg, *Party Girl*

Maira/*m* Anibal Gruart, Jorge Navarro/ *lp* Julio De Grazia, Luisina Brando, Fernanda Mistral, Julio Chavez, Ulises Dumont.

Party Girl

A smartly turned demonstration of genre cinema in the 'retro' gangster mode – the setting is Chicago in 1932 – *Party Girl* is buoyed up not just by the careful production associated with the veteran producer Pasternak but by an incisive if broadly conventional screenplay. This centres upon the regeneration of a cynical 'mouthpiece' (Taylor) through his relationship with a showgirl (Charisse) who is also in the entourage of the Capone-like chief mobster (Cobb). The courtroom episodes, with the lawyer shamelessly manipulating the jurors, have a sardonic edge, which is matched by the plot development whereby the ruthless district attorney (Smith) virtually blackmails Taylor into co-operation. Ray's biographer, Bernard Eisenschitz, observes: 'Party Girl owes its homogeneity less to the director than to studio know-how.' Nonetheless, the film intermittently bears the imprint of Ray's personality, in the concealed vulnerability of the lawyer, the baroque use of colour and CinemaScope, and the startling imagery, not least the shot of Charisse's room-mate (Kelly) dead in a bath overflowing with pink-hued water after slashing her wrists. TP

1958/99m/MGM/*p* Joe Pasternak/*d* Nicholas Ray/*s* George Wells/*c* Robert Bronner/*m* Jeff Alexander/*lp* Robert Taylor, Cyd Charisse, Lee J. Cobb, Kent Smith, John Ireland, Claire Kelly.

Pascual Duarte

Cinematographer Cuadrado gave Franco's debut feature about a serial killer (Gomez) in rural Spain at the time of the Civil War an unusual style. The characters speak Estramadurian dialect and the images alternate between a cool, distant narrative style taken over from Cela's 1942 novel and the gruesome brutality of the killings: Duarte shoots his dog with a shotgun, knifes his horse, shoots his mother and then blasts a number of other people until he is garrotted. The director said of the 'hero': 'he doesn't kill because he is a criminal, Pascual acquires the condition of a criminal because he kills'. The film refuses detailed psychological explanations and leaves the viewers to draw their conclusions about the generation of killers who went on to rule Spain for three decades. PW

1976/Spain/98m/Querejeta/*p*/*co-s* Elias Querejeta/*d*/*co-s* Ricardo Franco/*co-s* Emilio Martinez/*orig* Camilo Jose Cela/*c* Luis Cuadrado/*m* Luis de Pablo/*lp* Jose Luis Gomez, Paca Ojea, Hector Alterio, Diana Perez de Guzman, Eduardo Calvo.

Payroll

Starting off with a strong sense of place – a decade before **Get Carter**, most of the film was shot in and around a grimy Newcastle – *Payroll* in the second half becomes a pure melodrama with Whitelaw as an avenging angel out to revenge herself on the already disintegrating gang for the death of her husband in the course of the payroll robbery. The oddly assorted cast is lead by Craig as the gang boss, Lucas as the inside man, Prévost as his French wife and Bell as the muscle. The robbery itself is well staged, with cinematographer Steward taking advantage of his zoom lens for the sandwiching of the wages van between a lorry laden with concrete slabs and the gang's armoured vehicle. But once the robbers share out the money disintegration swiftly follows – Prévost hankers for Craig, Whitelaw breaks down Lucas who in remorse burns his share of the loot, only to perish in the conflagration, and a further gang member (Griffith) takes to drink and has to be disposed off (by a poison which doesn't work and has him coming to and rising zombie-like from a car boot only to perish in a handy swamp). Too complicated and densely plotted, these incidents obscure the possibly intriguing battle between the two

ABOVE Tom Bell, *Payroll*

ABOVE Tom Bell, Michael Craig, *Payroll*

women which never quite reaches boiling point in the film. PH

1961/GB/105m/Lynx/*p* Norman Priggen/ *d* Sidney Hayers/*s* George Baxt/*orig* Derek Bickerton/*c* Ernest Steward/*m* Reg Owen/ *lp* Michael Craig, Billie Whitelaw, Françoise Prévost, William Lucas, Tom Bell, Kenneth Griffith.

Peeping Tom

So reviled on its original release that it virtually ended Powell's career, this now looks like one of the greatest British movies. Mark Lewis (Boehm), a lonely young man victimised as a child by his psychologist father's voyeurist experiments, works by day as a focus-puller in a cosy film studio, in the evening as a pornographic photographer in a dingy room above a newsagent's, and by night as a psycho killer in a duffel coat, recording his victims' dying agonies with his 8mm camera. Not the least of Powell's 'crimes' in *Peeping Tom* was his turning his back on the lush, 'quality' tradition of his earlier works with Emeric Pressburger in favour of the lurid colours of the horror film. Made in wonderfully garish Eastmancolor (harsh oranges and deep blues) for a company that made Hammer seem respectable, it was slotted into Anglo-Amalgamated's release schedule between *Horrors of the Black Museum*

(1959) and *Circus of Horrors* (1960). In a deliberately provocative scene, Powell rewrites his own career by bringing in Moira Shearer of *The Red Shoes* (1948) and has her play a jazz-dancing tramp in slacks who becomes the killer's victim. Similarly sacrilegious in British cinema terms is Miles Malleson, typecast for years as a dotty old vicar, now as a leering pervert buying dirty postcards. A psychological study in the manner of **Psycho**, it's also a witty dissection of the process of film-making itself, full of wicked jokes about UK mainstream cinema magazine *Sight and Sound*, Field's shortcomings as an actress, home movies and the horror genre. Made before *Psycho*, it gives an insider's view of homicidal mania, and presents its madman as a completely sympathetic (if not admirable) character. KN

1960/GB/109m/Anglo-Amalgamated/ *p/d* Michael Powell/*s* Leo Marks/*c* Otto Heller/*m* Brian Easdale/*lp* Carl Boehm, Anna Massey, Maxine Audley, Moira Shearer, Esmond Knight, Shirley-Ann Field, Miles Malleson.

The People against O'Hara

In an unlikely role, Tracy stars in this downbeat melodrama as an alcoholic civil lawyer who will go to any lengths, even bribing a star witness, to win his defence case (of a

young James Arness on a murder charge). He fails and Arness is convicted but Tracy manages to convince the assistant D.A. to let him prove that a frame-up is involved. The finale sees a wired-up (with tiny lapel mike) Tracy getting caught in a crossfire when he tries to trap the actual killer. The film's overall mood is enhanced by John Alton's low-key photography. The screenplay was based on the novel by Eleazar Lipsky. TV

1951/101m/MGM/*p* William H. Wright/ *d* John Sturges/*s* John Monks Jr/*c* John Alton/*m* Carmen Dragon/*lp* Spencer Tracy, Pat O'Brien, Diana Lynn.

Pépé le Moko/Nuits blanches

Duvivier's best-known film, this launched Gabin on his superstar career. Pépé (Gabin), a Frenchman who has emigrated to Algeria, then under French colonial rule, is the head of a gang of thieves and uses the casbah of Algiers as his hiding place, perpetually eluding the police. On a tip-off from the informer Régis (Charpin), the police raid the house of the gang's fence (Fabre). The casbah's internal alarm system warning of intruders, together with Pépé's mistress, Inès (Noro), allow Pépé to escape, though wounded. He then seduces the wealthy Gaby (Balin), a French tourist, and kills Régis who was responsible for betraying a young gang member (Gil) who was shot by the police. Gaby's friend, the Algerian policeman

ABOVE Carl Boehm, *Peeping Tom*

Slimane (Gridoux), manages to lure Pépé out of the casbah and arrests him as he tries to join the departing Gaby on her ship. The story was based on the account by a French detective who had worked in Algiers, where he had known a criminal nicknamed 'le moko' who used the casbah as a hideout and was a notorious womaniser. The film downplays the thief's criminal activities in favour of a romanticised, glamorous view of a colonial stereotype: the lonely Frenchman who manages to make himself loved by the natives but keeps dreaming of returning to France. The part of Pépé had first been offered to Charles Boyer, who eventually did play it in the Hollywood remake of the film, John Cromwell's *Algiers* (1938), co-starring with Hedy Lamarr. John Berry made another American version of the story, *Casbah* (1948), starring the singer Tony Martin and Marta Toren. PW

1936/France/93m/Paris Films/*d* Julien Duvivier/*s* Julien Duvivier, Détective Ashelbé [Henri La Barthe]/*orig* Ashelbé/ *c* Jules Krüger, Marc Fossard/*m* Vincent Scotto, Mohammed Yguerbbuchen/*lp* Jean Gabin, Mireille Balin, Lucas Gridoux, Marcel Dalio, Fernand Charpin.

The Perils of Pauline

Pearl White's first, and most famous, serial, tells a simple enough story. If Pauline dies before she marries her Harry Marvin (Wilbur), Owen (Panzer) gets all the money left her. Hence Owen has two aims, to stop the marriage, and to kill her. On this thread, the twenty episodes, most of them self-contained stories, hang fights with Indians, pirates and gypsies, the destruction of a ship, the shearing of a wing from a plane, the sinking of a submarine, and the stalling of the heroine's boat beside a navy target vessel, with a gallant dog swimming to shore with a life-saving message. Amateurishly directed and technically crude, the film had enormous success in America and abroad; the non-stop action, together with White's attractive personality, saw to that. Some episodes survive, and the illiteracy of the titles has caused much mirth at the film-makers' expense – unfairly so, for these prints are reissues, hastily made from French 28mm copies, retranslated by Frenchmen at Pathé's American studio. In the original, it was Pauline's 'immortal', not her 'immoral', strength that the Indians wished to test. By reissue time, too, the war was on, and every villain had to be German; hence the evil

Owen became Teutonic Koerner. The camera operator, beginning a famous career, was the eighteen-year-old Arthur Miller. In the wake of its success *Pauline* was followed by numerous other similarly alliteratively titled serials, of the like of *The Exploits of Elaine*, *The Hazards of Helen*. JL

1914/20 episodes/Eclectic/*p* Leopold Wharton, Theodore Wharton/*d* Louis Gasnier, Donald MacKenzie/*s* George B. Seitz/*orig* Charles W. Goddard/*c* Arthur C. Miller/*lp* Pearl White, Crane Wilbur, Paul Panzer, Edward Jose, Eleanor Woodruff, Clifford Bruce.

The Perils of Pauline

The screenplay was based on a story (by Wolfson) suggested by incidents in the life of silent serial queen Pearl White as well as Charles W. Goddard's original 1914 serial. The beautiful-looking Technicolor musical-comedy biography, featuring the high-energy Hutton as Pearl White, recreates the life and frolics involved in early film-making. A later *Perils of Pauline* (1967), produced by Universal, attempted a return to the original cliff-hanger format as a part of the fleeting mid-1960s 'camp' phase. TV

1947/92m/PAR/*p* Sol C. Siegel/*d* George Marshall/*s* P.J. Wolfson, Frank Butler/*c* Ray Rennahan/*m* Robert Emmett Dolan/*lp* Betty Hutton, John Lund, Billy de Wolfe.

The Petrified Forest

A critical and commercial success on Broadway, Sherwood's philosophical play, which pits a suicidal intellectual against a brutal gangster during an Arizona gas station siege, has not worn well. This straight filming of the piece, which practically retains the act breaks and is stuck with pages of high-flown dialogue from the hero (Howard), similarly now looks much less effective than most of the movies (**Key Largo**, **The Desperate Hours**, *The Tall T*, 1957, *When You Comin' Back, Red Ryder*, 1979, *The Lightship*, 1985) that have copied its basic plot-line of grouping together a cross-section of representative types in an isolated locale where they can be menaced by an almost demonic gangster. While the romance between the world-weary failed poet and an unconvincing desert waif (Davis) is not strong enough to carry the symbolic weight Sherwood puts upon it, the rest of the action works much better, especially the interplay between the gangster's sidekicks and the hostages. Most significantly, the film was the

first major break for Bogart, repeating his stage role as Duke Mantee. KN

1936/83m/WB/*d* Archie Mayo/*s* Charles Kenyon, Delmer Daves/*orig* Robert E. Sherwood/*c* Sol Polito/*m* Leo F. Forbstein/ *lp* Leslie Howard, Bette Davis, Humphrey Bogart, Genevieve Tobin, Dick Foran, Porter Hall.

Phantom Lady

In the source novel by William Irish (**Cornell Woolrich**), literary sleight of hand is deployed to conceal the fact that the old friend rallying to the aid of a man falsely sentenced to death for the murder of his wife is himself the killer, and is using a reinvestigation of the case to destroy the condemned man's professed alibi by putting paid to any potential witnesses. Such a deception is scarcely available to a screen treatment, and the screenplay makes apparent from his first appearance the villainy of the supposed helpmate, whom the film turns into a demented sculptor. That said, Tone is miscast and his exaggerated performance verges on a parody of the 'homicidal aesthete' figure familiar in *film noir* (notably in **Laura**). This weakens the film's later episodes, but does not detract from the skill of Siodmak's handling, with its powerful compression and sense of malign fate (the trial is visually rendered by shots of the court stenographer's shorthand record). One sequence in particular, that in which Raines as the condemned man's devoted secretary visits the *jazz* club where Cook plays the drums, has a startling expressionistic intensity which would qualify it for a place in any anthology of *noir* stylistics. TP

1944/87m/U/*p* Joan Harrison/*d* Robert Siodmak/*s* Bernard C. Schoenfeld/*c* Woody Bredell/*m* Hans J. Salter/*lp* Ella Raines, Franchot Tone, Alan Curtis, Thomas Gomez, Elisha Cook Jr.

The Phenix City Story

In Phenix City, Alabama in the 1950s organised prostitution, drugs-dealing and gambling had taken over the town. The struggle to control these profitable activities had led to outbreaks of violence, culminating in the murder of the state prosecutor. When local citizens tried to form vigilante groups to fight back, the National Guard were sent in. The story was widely reported in the national press and Phil Karlson's picture was shot on location in the town soon after. It has a strongly documentary, or more precisely newsreel, feel about it, overlaid with a narrative structure that depends on a struggle between organised crime and a lonely but brave individual who will not, unlike the timid citizenry, be intimidated. The film is part of a group of films which in the wake of the Kefauver hearings of 1950–1 took organised crime as their subject. Others are *The Enforcer/Murder Inc.* (1950), *New York Confidential* (1955), **The Big Heat** and Karlson's own **The Brothers Rico**. EB

1955/100m/Allied Artists/*p* Samuel Bischoff, David Diamond/*d* Phil Karlson/*s* Crane Wilbur, Daniel Mainwaring/*c* Harry Neumann/*m* Harry Sukman/*lp* Richard Kiley, Edward Andrews, John McIntire, Kathryn Grant.

Pickpocket

Bresson followed his austere, obsessive **Un Condamné à mort s'est échappé** with this equally austere, meticulous depiction of another taciturn, withdrawn and isolated man whose hands are constantly busy, a professional pickpocket working the train stations, metro and racing courses of Paris. With grainy, quasi-newsreel imagery and a largely improvised script, Bresson shows how the Henry Fonda lookalike Michel (Lasalle) begins by stealing a wallet and then, seduced by the easy money as well as by the thrill, becomes a professional. The

ABOVE Marika Green, Martin Lasalle, *Pickpocket*

film lingers on the close-ups of faces and skilful hand-manoeuvres, drastically downplaying the possible element of suspense (Bresson attached a special warning to the opening of the film pointing out to his audiences that this is not a thriller). Michel is so self-absorbed that he neglects the woman who loves him (Green), who has a child by

his best friend (Leymarie). He is eventually caught and jailed by the police (Pelegri), where he is redeemed by his steadfast girlfriend. The comic Etaix appears as one of Michel's accomplices. PW

1959/France/75m/*p* Agnès Delahaie/*d/s* Robert Bresson/*c* Léonce-Henri Burel/*m* Jean-Baptiste Lully/*lp* Martin Lasalle, Pierre Leymarie, Jean Pelegri, Marika Green, Pierre Etaix, Kassagi.

Pickup on South Street

In the original story from which Fuller drew his script, the object of criminal activity is drugs. Fuller substituted a piece of microfilm and the villains became Communist spies. But in spirit and in iconography the film remains a crime picture. Skip (Widmark) is a small-time pickpocket who acquires the microfilm by chance. In the course of the picture the spy (Kiley) attempts to retrieve it from Candy (Peters), his former lover whom he savagely beats, and Moe (Ritter), an elderly female fence whom he murders. Skip ends up helping the authorities catch the spies, but not for reasons of patriotism (when asked what Communism stands for, he replies cynically, 'Who cares?'). Significantly, America is defended by thieves and other low-life characters; and for their own motives. Skip develops a relationship with Candy in one of the best 'meeting cute' scenes devised. In the opening scene we see him picking her handbag on the subway;

ABOVE *Phenix City Story*

later he will smack her in the mouth and she will knock him out as each tries to use the other to get the missing piece of film. Yet there is a compelling eroticism in their exchanges, and Fuller gives these bottom of the heap characters, who fight beneath posters proclaiming America's right and might, a powerful, albeit inarticulate sense of themselves as Americans. EB

1953/83m/FOX/*p* Jules Schermer/ *d/s* Samuel Fuller/*c* Joe MacDonald/*m* Leigh Harline/*lp* Richard Widmark, Jean Peters, Thelma Ritter, Murvyn Vye, Richard Kiley.

The Pink Panther

With a memorable Henry Mancini score, witty animated titles by Friz Freleng and array of beautiful people, *The Pink Panther* could have been a mod updating of the adventures of **Raffles** and **Arsène Lupin** were the film not stolen completely by Sellers as Inspector Jacques Clouseau of the Sûreté, a blithely self-confident bumbler as

maladroit with his own accent, a caricatured French which other supposedly French characters mainly played by British actors are unable to understand, as he is with any inanimate object that happens to get in his way. The finale finds Clouseau framed by the Phantom (Niven), who has turned out to be in league with the inspector's wife (Capucine), and sent off to jail. However, the character was so well-received that he returned immediately in a superior sequel, *A Shot in the Dark* (1964), adapted by Edwards and William Peter Blatty from a Marcel Achard French farce Americanised by Harry Kurnitz, with the original's magistrate hero replaced by Clouseau. Here, Clouseau is pitted against villain George Sanders and the innocent Elke Sommer in a trail of multiple murders that includes a wonderful side-trip to a nudist camp where Bryan Forbes appears (under the name Turk Thrust) as a guitar-strumming hippie. The sequel's best invention is Herbert Lom as Dreyfus, Clouseau's perpetually enraged superior, a

ABOVE Peter Sellers, Capucine, *The Pink Panther*

humourless bureaucrat driven to a homicidal frenzy by his doting subordinate's blundering, and finally revealed as the mysterious bomber who has been trying to murder the inspector. While the title sequences spun off a series of wry shorts, which were bracketed for television with a series of somewhat less likeable cartoons involving a Clouseau sound-alike called 'the Inspector', the series was not resumed until *Inspector Clouseau* (1968) with Alan Arkin in the title role. Edwards and Sellers, after separate set-backs, both revived flagging careers with *The Return of the Pink Panther* (1975), featuring Christopher Plummer as the Phantom and with the Pink Panther again the MacGuffin, and *The Pink Panther Strikes Again* (1976), allowing Lom centre-stage as the raving Dreyfus, now a Bond-style master villain out to destroy the world. The act was wearing decidedly thin by *Revenge of the Pink Panther* (1978), a witless procession of rehashed jokes, silly disguises and tired fart gags. Edwards ill-advisedly continued the series after Sellers's death with *Trail of the Pink Panther* (1982), which combines out-take footage of Sellers with reappearances from Niven, Capucine

ABOVE Jean Peters, *Pickup on South Street*

and Lom and a cameo from Richard Mulligan as Clouseau's fumble-alike father. *Curse of the Pink Panther* (1983) has Ted Wass as a pathetic American Clouseau imitation and adds Robert Wagner, from the original cast, to the other returning castmembers, finally calling in Roger Moore (billed as 'Turk Thrust II') to play a Clouseau transformed externally by plastic surgery but otherwise unchanged. *Son of the Pink Panther* (1992) has Italian comic Roberto Benigni as Clouseau's incompetent son, partnered by Cardinale and Lom (Capucine and Niven both having died since the last episode). Among the other series regulars are Burt Kwouk as Clouseau's devoted sidekick Cato, named after the Green Hornet's Kato, Peter Arne as the Prime Minister of Lugash, and Graham Stark in a variety of character parts, including theatrical costumier Auguste Bals. KN

1963/115m/UA-Mirisch/*p*/*d*/*co-s* Blake Edwards/*co-s* Maurice Richlin/*c* Philip Lathrop/*m* Henry Mancini/*lp* David Niven, Peter Sellers, Robert Wagner, Capucine, Claudia Cardinale, Brenda De Banzie.

Pink String and Sealing Wax

The directorial debut of Hamer, *Pink String* with, as the *Variety* reviewer noted, its careful contrasting of black high-necked bom-

LEFT David Niven, *The Pink Panther*

bazine and lacy, billowing cleavages, anticipates the elegant sense of period and eroticism of his better known **Kind Hearts and Coronets**. Jackson is the respectable chemist's son who escapes repressive family life in Victorian Brighton when he wanders into a public house and becomes infatuated with Withers, the landlady. The plot has her manipulating Jackson (to provide the poison to murder her loutish husband), but Hamer imbues her with warmth and sexuality (in contrast to the filming of the Jackson family) and presents her as a fitting transitional love object for a young man escaping home. Thus the end – Withers throws herself into the sea and Jackson marries his long-standing fiancée – is downbeat rather than the traditional happy ending. Similarly it is the pub's clientele, not the sober Jackson's household, that are memorable: Garry Marsh's thuggish Bill Sykes of a husband, Catherine Lacey's gin drinker and John Carol's sweet-talking jockey. PH

1945/GB/89m/Ealing/*p* Michael Balcon/*d*/*co-s* Robert Hamer/*co-s* Diana Morgan/*orig* Roland Pertwee/*c* Richard Pavey/*m* Norman Demuth/*lp* Googie Withers, Gordon Jackson, Sally Ann Howes, Mary Merrall, Jean Ireland, Colin Simpson.

Plein Soleil/Blazing Sun/Purple Noon

In his breakthrough film, Delon plays, for the first time, a role he would continue to play as a star for the rest of his career: a loner who is a charismatic hero and a criminal at the same time. As **Patricia Highsmith**'s Tom Ripley, he is hired by a rich American to bring the man's playboy son, Philip Greenleaf (Ronet) back to the US from Italy. The unbearably arrogant and spoiled Philip, accompanied by his lover, Marge (Laforêt), sadistically humiliates Ripley until the latter kills him, adopts his identity and acquires Philip's wealth as well as his girl-friend. As Philip's friend Freddy (Kearns) suspects that Ripley killed the playboy, Freddy too has to be eliminated, a crime Ripley manages to have attributed to Philip Greenleaf, so that all he has to do is to resume his real identity as Ripley to avoid suspicion and to enjoy his new life of leisure with Marge. However, when his yacht is put in dry-dock, Philip's corpse is found caught in the propellers. Gégauff, Chabrol's scenarist for *A Double Tour* (1959) and for most of

Chabrol's later thrillers, provided an excellent adaptation of Highsmith's cleverly plotted novel and the film was hugely successful. PW

1960/France, Italy/118m/Paris-Titanus/*p* Robert and Raymond Hakim/*d*/*co-s* René Clément/*co-s* Paul Gégauff/*orig* Patricia Highsmith *The Talented Mr. Ripley*/*c* Henri Decaë/*m* Nino Rota/*lp* Alain Delon, Maurice Ronet, Marie Laforêt, Elvire Popesco, Erno Crisma.

Poe, Edgar Allan (1809–49)

The American short-story writer, essayist, poet and journalist stands as a major influence in at least three fields of genre writing: horror, science fiction and the detective story. In 'The Murders in the Rue Morgue' (1841), he introduced the dilettante sleuth C. Auguste Dupin, unmistakably the forerunner of Sherlock Holmes and all other eccentric busy-bodies who side-step the official channels and show up the police by reaching bizarre conclusions that happen to be the truth. Having in this first outing deduced that an especially brutal locked room murder is the work of a runaway orang-utan, Dupin returned in 'The Mystery of Marie Roget' (1842–3), a pioneering drama documentary in which Poe used his creation to posit a possible solution to a real-life murder, and 'The Purloined Letter', which not only contains one of the great MacGuffins but also sets the pattern for the espionage genre with its tale of missing

ABOVE Edgar Allan Poe

papers and potential scandal averted at the last minute.

Screen Dupins include Leon Ames (as 'Pierre Dupin') in Robert Florey's *Murders in the Rue Morgue* (1932), Patric Knowles (as 'Dr Paul Dupin') in Phil Rosen's *The Mystery of Marie Roget* (1942), Steve Forrest (as 'Paul Dupin') in Roy Del Ruth's *Phantom of the Rue Morgue* (1954) and George C. Scott, making a lonely attempt to use Poe's full character name and traits, in Jeannot Szwarc's *Murders in the Rue Morgue* (1986). Gordon Hessler's *Murders in the Rue Morgue* (1972) entirely omits Dupin, and the rest of Poe except for the ape, while *Sherlock Holmes in the Great Murder Mystery* (1908), the first screen adaptation of the story, writes out Dupin and substitutes his most famous successor.

If Poe is on one hand responsible for originating the figure of the rigidly controlled and controlling sleuth in his tales of mystery, then in the mad and guilt-ridden protagonists of his tales of imagination he is also father of the school of psychological fiction that presents the distorted and disordered viewpoint of a compulsive crook as almost an objective world-view. Poe's body of horror fiction – with its premature burials, mad loves, frenzied torments, moral and physical decay, pervasive cruelty, dwelling on deformity and terror of disease – is rich and still vastly influential, and has perhaps made him the most often-adapted author in the history of the cinema, with 'The Black Cat' as the most often filmed single story. KN

Point Blank

Walker (Marvin) and his partner Mal Reese (Vernon) rob a mob shipment. Mal, who is having an affair with Walker's wife Lynne (Acker), shoots Walker and leaves him for dead in the deserted Alcatraz prison. Walker survives, and comes back to LA looking for revenge. Lynne has committed suicide, and aided by her sister Chris (Dickinson), Walker attacks the hierarchy of the organised crime syndicate, now doubling as a respectable business corporation, demanding his money. Director Boorman uses European art-house techniques to construct a new departure for the gangster movie, part film critique, part allegory, part dream journey. Marvin is a dogged individual confronted by a soulless corporation mirrored by the city's architecture of monumental concrete and opaque glass. Adapted from *The Hunter* by Richard Stark (Donald Westlake), the film throws up imagery of startling and enduring power, as when Reese falls off a balcony and the bed-

ABOVE Lee Marvin, *Point Blank*

sheet in which he's wrapped billows out like a sail, composing a moment of extraordinary flight. MP

1967/92m/Bernard-Winkler/*p* Judd Bernard, Robert Chartoff/*d* John Boorman/*s* Alexander Jacobs, David Newhouse, Rafe Newhouse/*c* Philip Lathrop/*m* Johnny Mandel/*lp* Lee Marvin, Angie Dickinson, Keenan Wynn, Carroll O'Connor, John Vernon, Sharon Acker.

Poirot, Hercule

Created by **Agatha Christie**, Poirot is one of the most celebrated detectives in crime fiction. A former policeman, Poirot was forced to flee his country after the German invasion of Belgium in 1914. In England he set up as a private enquiry agent with the assistance of his old friend Captain Hastings (who like **Sherlock Holmes**'s amanuensis and assistant Dr. Watson was slightly dim-witted). After Hastings's marriage in the early 1930s Poirot moved to London's Whitehaven Mansions. Short – he is only five feet four inches tall – with a waxed moustache and 'patent-leather hair' atop his egg-shaped head and patent leather shoes on his small feet, Poirot exercised his 'little grey cells' in some forty novels and numerous short stories before dying in the 1940s in *Curtain: Poirot's Last Case* (1975, but written much earlier), which returns Poirot to Styles, the scene of one of his most celebrated cases. Clearly a descendent of Holmes, Poirot's claim to fame is as the solver of the most ser-

ABOVE Hercule Poirot: Albert Finney, *Murder on the Orient Express*

pentine of puzzles. However, precisely because the majority of his cases were puzzles rather than stories that unfolded in a complex manner, Poirot never achieved the wide cinematic appeal of Holmes. Indeed his greatest successes as a character was as an opportunity for Albert Finney to indulge himself (in **Murder on the Orient Express**, from the 1934 novel) and then Peter Ustinov, in a lesser series of films that included *Death on the Nile* (1978, novel 1937), *Evil under the Sun* (1982, novel 1941) and *Appointment with Death* (1988, novel 1938), as well as several television movies. All these films were as much costume dramas as puzzles. David Suchet's impersonation of *Poirot* in the UK television series (1989–91) was similarly constructed. A more interesting television exercise was *Murder by the Book* (1986) in which Ian Holm's Poirot investigates his own murder (when he learns that his creator is about to publish a book in which he is killed off). Poirot first appeared in print in *The Mysterious Affair at Styles* (1920) and on screen in *Alibi* (1931 from the

novel *The Murder of Roger Ackroyd*, 1926). His best film prior to *Orient Express* was Frank Tashlin's *The Alphabet Murders* (1965, from *The ABC Murders*, 1936), in which Tashlin cleverly mixed slapstick and detection, although not to the taste of purists. Tony Randall played Poirot. Julian Symons's *The Great Detectives* (1981) includes a biography of Poirot. PH

Poison

Difficult or impossible to detect, poison was at one time a staple of melodrama, the whodunit and the serial. A classic image is the close-up of the ring with the secret compartment tipping poison into a victim's drink. A poison ring features in the famous melodrama *The Face at the Window*, filmed in 1920, 1932 and, with the redoubtable Tod Slaughter, in 1939. During the 40s, when the *femme fatale* was in great demand, poison was considered to be the most ladylike method of murder. Among female poisoners were Margaret Lockwood in *Bedelia* (1946), Merle Oberon in *Temptation* (1946), Joan Fontaine in *Ivy* (1947), and Ann Todd in *Madeleine* (1949). But the most celebrated murderesses of the period are the two old ladies in the black comedy *Arsenic and Old Lace* (1941). Subsequent comic poisonings occur in *How to Murder a Rich Uncle* (1957) and *A Jolly Bad Fellow* (1963). Joan Fontaine suspects Cary Grant of poisoning her milk in **Suspicion**. Gene Tierney is at first unaware that Vincent Price poisoned his first wife in *Dragonwyck* (1946). Charles Boyer is believed to have poisoned his wife in *A Woman's Vengeance* (1947), but even from the title it's obvious he didn't. Audie Murphy came to stardom as a troubled teenager suspected of poisoning his mother in *Bad Boy* (1949). Perhaps the most creative use of poison is in **D.O.A.** in which stricken Edmond O'Brien has only hours to find a poisoner. (This film was unsuccessfully re-made twice.) Other peculiar instances include poison sent down a telephone line in *The Invisible Killer* (1940), and stolen money accidentally contaminated by poison in *Touch of Death* (1962). Children are nearly poisoned in *70 Deadly Pills* (1963); animals are deliberately poisoned in *Malefices* (1961) and *Who Killed the Cat?* (1966).

In the 70s poison went the way of the old-fashioned murder mystery, and appeared to have little chance of revival while filmmakers remained obsessed with guns, knives and other weapons that inflict visible damage. Surprisingly, however, the poisoner made a modest comeback at the turn of the

1990s. Inspired by real-life incidents, *Deadly Obsession* (1989) is about a blackmailer who poisons supermarket food. Hospital patients are poisoned in *Exquisite Tenderness* (1994). *The Young Poisoner's Handbook* (1994) is based on the true story of a young man who poisoned his family, friends and work colleagues. DM

Police Academy

Modelled on the successful formula of *National Lampoon's Animal House* (1978), this appropriates the plot of *Carry On Sergeant* (1958) as a group of misfits and cut-ups go through police training amid much slapstick and humiliation of authority figures, ultimately graduating to a slew of sequels. Co-star Cattrall managed to get out of appearing in follow-ups, but Guttenberg, evidently stuck with a different contract and anyway the most workaholic actor in Hollywood, grimly went through the paces until Number Four. Weirdly, the high-point of the series is Jerry Paris's *Police Academy 2 Their First Assignment* (1985), which has an inspired performance from Bobcat Goldthwait as a strangle-voiced punk villain and a wonderful sick joke about the man who unwisely takes his pet goldfish to a sushi restaurant. Goldthwait repeated his characterisation to less effect in uniform in two further sequels, Paris's *Police Academy 3 Back in Training* (1986) and Jim Drake's *Police Academy 4 Citizens on Patrol* (1987), before he called it a day, leaving Alan Myerson's *Police Academy 5 Assignment: Miami Beach* (1988), Peter Bonerz's *Police Academy 6 City under Siege* (1989) and *Police Academy 7 Mission to Moscow* (1994) to those series regulars (hulking Smith, shrill-voiced Ramsey, mild-mannered lackwit Gaynes, human sound-effect Winslow, token sexist caricature Easterbrook) unable to secure employment elsewhere. KN

1984/95m/Ladd/*p* Paul Maslansky/ *d*/co-*s* Hugh Wilson/co-*s* Neal Israel, Pat Proft/*c* Michael D. Margulies/*lp* Steve Guttenberg, Kim Cattrall, G.W. Bailey, George Gaynes, Michael Winslow, Bubba Smith.

Policias de narcoticos/ Narcotics Police

A sequel of the same star and director team's self-explanatory *Un hombre violento* (1985) featuring Trujillo as the Ramboesque Carrera. This time he has joined the Mexican police to hunt down gangs of drugs traffickers. His partner is the other leading Mexican

ABOVE *Police Academy*

the Gentleman Burglar, is the prototype which led to Louis Feuillade's **Fantômas** and numerous other shadowy heroes, the echoes of whom can still be found in the professional killers or thieves at the centre of Jean-Pierre Melville's films. The other strand is that of **E. A. Poe**'s cerebral investigator, Dupin, introduced into France by Charles Baudelaire (although Poe allegedly based his character on the French criminal, police chief and spy Vidocq who published his ghost-written memoirs in 1828). This current was enhanced by the indigenous detection stories of Emile Gaboriau, whose Inspector Lecoq and Father Tabaret incarnated the hopes for a new, logical, rationalist and scientific era in the feuilleton *L'Affaire Lerouge* (1863), although these 'rationalist' stories are still heavily melodramatic, making them a truly transitional type of cultural production.

The hybrid genre of the *policier* spawned many serials and led to mystery novels such as the classic closed-room murder (committed by the detective, well before Agatha Christie adopted the device) of *Le Mystère de la chambre jaune* by Gaston Leroux (1907). At this stage, the *policier* genre already fulfilled a function that would remain its main motif throughout the century: it provided a way of dramatising the tensions inherent in the rapid industrialisation of culture. As such, it was the companion to the melodrama. But whereas the melodrama mapped the tensions of modernisation onto the realm of the domestic and the emotions, the detection novel, the crime novel and later the *policier* addressed these same tensions in terms of property relations and the utopian fantasies generated by rationalism (with the figure of Fantômas symbolising its dangers to the fabric of the old social relations).

The next major phase, in the 20s and 30s, was inaugurated by Stanislas-André Steeman (and his Inspector Wens, filmed a number of times in the 30s and 40s) and by Georges Simenon's **Maigret** (first filmed in 1932 by Jean Renoir, with **La Nuit du carrefour**), an avuncular figure who represents the everyday decency attributed to but manifestly lacking in the French lower-middle class. The pleasures of detection and rationalism's ability to restore order and to portray the world as fundamentally coherent and knowable were extended, via the figure of Maigret, into broader sections of society. The detective no longer needed to have aristocratic connections or pretensions, and the 'underworld' acquired new, less threatening

action star, Goyri. The producer plays the nasty narcotics boss assisted by his moll (Chain). Violence includes feeding human entrails to dogs, a beheading, the disembowelling of a child and other commercial attractions. The film is part of a flourishing action genre using drugs as a MacGuffin to spin violent tales. Others in the sub-genre include Alfonso de Alva's *El narco* (1986) and Ruben Galindo's *Narco terror* (1987). PW

1986/Mexico/87m/Sol/*p* Rodolfo de Anda/ *d* Gilberto de Anda/*s* X. Randa/*c* Antonio de Anda/*m* Gustavo Pimentel/*lp* Valentin Trujillo, Sergio Goyri, Rodolfo de Anda, Angelica Chain, Julio Aleman.

Policier
The French variety of crime fiction, simultaneously developed in literature and in cinema, is variously called the *policier* or the *polar* genre. It tends to use a narrower canvas than its American equivalent, concentrating on the violent interpenetration of two incompatible worlds, each working according to its own logic: the world of crime, and that of the professionals dedicated to the restoration of at least the semblance of normality. One strand that fed into the genre was the picaresque, somewhat dandified and surreal world of the uncatchable criminal familiar from early twentieth-century century popular novels. Leblanc's **Arsàne Lupin**,

Policier

ABOVE *Policier: La Nuit du carrefour*

dimensions as its depiction began to merge with echoes of late nineteenth-century naturalism.

During World War II, the irrationalist backlash represented by the triumph of fascism in Europe fundamentally affected the genre. The negotiation of the tensions of modernisation lost some of its utopian overtones, and with the banning of American films and stories from occupied France, home-grown talent had to fill the gap in subtly devious ways. Léo Malet's work (including his **Nestor Burma** stories, featuring France's first private eye, an indirect way of extending the American reference), Pierre Véry's novel **L'Assassinat du père Noël**, filmed by Christian-Jaque in 1941, Jacques Becker's **Dernier Atout**, Henri-Georges Clouzot's **L'Assassin habite. . . au 21** (both 1942) all kept the genre going.

In 1945, Marcel Duhamel created the *Série Noire* crime novels, introducing mostly American (and some British) hard-boiled novelists as well as, later, indigenous writers. The most notable early French *noir* novel was published in 1946: Boris Vian's *J'irai cracher sur vos tombes*, written under the pseudonym Vernon Sullivan and filmed later by Michel Gast (1959). However, the classic film of the immediate post-war *policier* genre was *Quai des orfèvres*, filmed in 1947 by Clouzot. Contrasting with the US-derived hard-boiled genre with its emphasis on phys-

ical action, **Boileau and Narcejac**, who wrote a number of Clouzot's films, helped to recodify the genre, emphasising French regional settings and stressing the mental-psychological dimension of coolly calculated and diabolically engineered crimes revolving around the greed, corruption and, above all, the hypocrisy of the indigenous bourgeoisie. Contrary also to Georges Simenon's Paris-based stories focusing on the restoration of law and order by patriarchal policemen, Boileau and Narcejac's work, set in macabre, small-town atmospheres, is deeply marked by the sense of moral and psychological disorientation characteristic of 1950s France and best exemplified in Sartre's existential philosophy. Boileau and Narcejac concentrated on what they called 'the dark side of reason' as their criminals found themselves trapped by circumstances and compulsions they could neither understand nor control, but which reflected deep-seated, culturally- and class-specific neuroses. In this way, they opened up a narrative space which, while addressing the traumatic disturbances of the recent past and its discomforting revelations about human nature, was able to combine the thriller with the older melodramatic tradition, locating the disturbances not in gaps in the surface fabric of the world which detection stories could restore to seamless completion, but within people themselves. Their narratives provided an alternative to the predominant way of dramatising the changes in the post-war world: instead of resorting to the deployment of an imaginary

ABOVE *Policier:* Louis Jouvet (left), Bernard Blier (second from right), *Quai des orfèvres*

America to dramatise tensions within French society, Boileau and Narcejac proposed a kind of narrative that could chart such tensions by showing that the older forms of human relations and values had lost their internal coherence and could no longer be restored. New kinds of nightmares were on the loose. Boileau and Narcejac thus provided an indigenous French equivalent to the American *film noir*, but without having to detour through a reference to the USA.

The lighter side of the *policier*, revealing the typical mixture of contempt and envy often felt in France towards the US, is incarnated by Eddie Constantine's G-Man **Lemmy Caution**, and by a series of cynically comic crime films in which murder is played for laughs. George Lautner's *Les Tontons flingueurs* of 1963 was a prototype, followed by crazy comedies about hired killers and various other eccentric, absurdist crime films which took their cue from Ionesco's grotesque plays (e.g. the films of Bertrand Blier). However, the *série noire*-type of novel made its main impact via Jacques Becker's film of the Albert Simonin novel **Touchez pas au grisbi** in 1954. The same year Auguste Le Breton's **Du Rififi chez les hommes** was filmed by Jules Dassin, and a new era was inaugurated for the French crime film, coinciding with the emergence of critical polemics about Hollywood authors in *Cahiers du cinéma* and, soon after, the films made by the *Cahiers* critics (Godard, Chabrol, Truffaut). At this stage, the negotiation of modernity in terms of a dramatisation of a reference to an American imaginary became dominant and displaced the Boileau-Narcejac type of thriller-melodrama. At the same time, the industrialisation of culture proceeded apace and the more commercially oriented crime films of the 50s generally introduced a greater sense of eroticism (as the novels did too), a trend further developed in the 60s, although the *policier* genre was then overtaken by spy stories.

The 1970s, in the wake of Jacques Deray's immensely successful **Borsalino** and Claude Chabrol's Hitchcockian thrillers, were dominated by *policier* movies (with stars such as Alain Delon, Jean-Paul Belmondo, Lino Ventura and others), often combined with adventure and action elements (as in José Giovanni and Robert Enrico's work). At the same time, the *policier* genre became politicised, with a spate of films (and novels) denouncing police corruption and brutality, the complicity between politicians, especially Gaullist ones, business-

ABOVE *Policier: Touchez pas au grisbi*

men, gangsters, thugs of all kinds and senior police officers. This signalled the end of the typical old-style criminal: a consummate professional (represented in Melville's films but also often by Jean Gabin) who was supposed to adhere to a feudal-aristocratic code of honour and to hold male friendship sacred. Instead, the criminals become irredeemably vile while the cops become their mirror-image: either criminals with a respectable facade or, from a right-wing point of view, vigilante figures trying to maintain law and order in the face of incipient anarchy symbolised by the spread of drugs, prostitution and general moral decline.

In keeping with prevailing cultural trends, the increasing impact of advertising imagery and styles together with the development of fashion trends based on advertising's interpretation of British and American popular culture iconographies yielded a new style of *policier* movies, exemplified by Jean-Jacques Beineix's **Diva** and Luc Besson's work. The films emphasise set decoration, slick and glossy imagery, with characters filmed in fetishistically fragmented shots detailing items of clothing or consumer goods as if they were fashion magazine models in Calvin Klein publicity spots, a trend that merged with the prevailing styles in music video promos. PW

Politicians

Institutionalised political corruption has been an American fact of life since the Declaration of Independence, with the roots of machine politics demonstrated on an urban scale by the likes of Vincent Price as New York's infamous Boss Tweed in *Up in Central Park* (1948) or Bob Hope as the same city's easy-going Mayor Jimmy Walker in *Beau James* (1957), and in the sticks by bullying Broderick Crawford as the Huey Long-style demagogue of *All the King's Men* (1950) and windy John Carradine as the blusterer in the pay of the cattle kings in *The Man Who Shot Liberty Valance* (1963). Many American sagas, from **The Godfather Part II** to *An American Tail* (1986), contrast idealist notions of the Land of the Free with realities of graft and crookedness.

During Prohibition, the crooked politician was seen as less a villain in himself than an adjunct to the activities of the gangster, doubtless a reference to such figures as Chicago's Mayor Big Bill Thompson, who is parodied as the feather-bedding buffoon of *The Front Page* (1931). Disillusionment with politics even goes so far, in the 1936 and 1942 versions of Dashiell Hammett's **The Glass Key**, as to allow a hero who is hired muscle working for a reasonably sympathetic ward-heeler. The ultimate expressions of this brand of vaguely loveable corruption are represented by Brian Donlevy, the politico from the second **Glass Key**, as *The Great McGinty* (1940), sluicing public money into pointless building programs. But Depression-era anger led Frank Capra to create villains like corrupt Senator Claude Rains in *Mr Smith Goes to Washington* (1939) and fascist behind-the-scenes manipulator Edward Arnold in *Meet John Doe* (1941). If the McGinty-style comic grafters persisted after the War in the person of tear-jerking Spencer Tracy in *The Last Hurrah* (1958) and Faustian loser Thomas Mitchell in *Alias Nick Beal* (1949), they were at least outweighed by genuinely nasty types like Sydney Greenstreet in *Flamingo Road* (1949) and Ed Begley in *Sweet Bird of Youth* (1962) and authentically dangerous loose cannons like James Cagney in *A Lion is in the Streets* (1953) and Andy Griffith in *A Face in the Crowd* (1957), whose ultimate incarnation must be yuppie folk singer Tim Robbins in *Bob Roberts* (1992).

The impact on the image of politics of a succession of real-life figures from Senator Joseph McCarthy to President Richard Nixon has given birth to a genre of political thriller in which corruption is less an adjunct to old-fashioned gangsterism and illicit profit than it is part of the process whereby vested interests perpetuate themselves in power. The paranoid speculations of *The Manchurian Candidate* (1962), *Seven Days in May* (1964), *The President's Analyst* (1967), *The Parallax View* (1974), *Winter Kills* (1979) and *Blow Out* (1981) and the cynical observations of *Advise and Consent* (1962), *The Best Man* (1964), *The Candidate* (1972), *Nashville* (1975) and *Power* (1986) perhaps find their logical apotheosis in based-on-fact movies like *All the President's Men* (1976), *Cadaveri eccellenti/Illustrious Corpses* (1976), *Blind Ambition* (1982), *Missing* (1982), *Silkwood* (1983), *Secret Honor* (1984), **Scandal**, *JFK* (1991), *Ruby* (1992) and *Nixon* (1995), all of which present an image of a monolithically criminal state willing to spy on or eliminate its own citizens or elected leaders to remain in control. Though these are more concerned with crimes that are apparently part of normal political life, their attitudes leak over into films in which self-serving or larcenous politicians are involved in personal rather than national misdeeds, as demonstrated by Satanic Ambassador Sam Neill in *The Final Conflict* (1981), mob-owned labour leader-congressman Treat Williams in **Once Upon a Time in America**, murdering Secretary of State Gene Hackman in *No Way Out* (1986), the serial-killing reform candidate of *Mirror Images* (1991), cocaine-

funded Senator Cliff DeYoung in *Nails* (1992) and Gotham City mayoral candidate Penguin (Danny DeVito) in *Batman Returns*.
KN

Pornography

Pornography is usually not taken into consideration when discussing genres in cinema, partly, no doubt, because the information about the films is not easily available. But the main reason is that as long as most countries ban explicit sex scenes from mainstream cinema, that is to say, as long as sexual activity cannot fully be integrated into the stories cinema tells us, pornography will remain a special 'reserve' where the scenes missing from 'acceptable' films are to be found. This does not make for coherent and nuanced plot structures, but rather for the isolation, the 'autonomisation' of the scenes that constitute the genre, loosely strung together rather like the pre-Gene Kelly and Stanley Donen musicals. In that sense, pornographic cinema is only a genre by default: when explicitly represented sexual activity can be represented within the public forms of cinematic storytelling, the current form of the genre will have lost its reason to exist. Since pornography contains the bits missing from other films, it follows that each genre will have its pornographic shadow, including crime films, gangster films, thrillers, Westerns and so on.

Crime plots often provide a framework for porn's concatenation of sex scenes, including the redeployment of well-known film plots (although the reference often remains at the level of a pun in the title). The figure of the detective or the blackmailer and occasionally the burglar provide the kind of social mobility enabling the film to string together a variety of sexual encounters. J. H. Lewis's *Triples pénétrations explosives* (1983) has a character called Arsène Lapin (Christophe Clark) seduce women in a hotel as he steals their jewellery, until the delectable Shirley Holmes (Patricia Violet), dressed in a black body stocking, gets the better of him. Clark played the role again in *Ecole pour salopes très spéciales* (1984). Lupin returned in *Entrecuisses en chaleur* (1984), again as a hotel jewel thief. All the familiar characters of detective and crime fiction are also to be found in porn.

Blackmail and entrapment are the excuse for sexual activities in *Adolescentes brulantes pour soirées très spéciales* (1981). One of the earliest US sex features, Richard Robinson's *Adultery for Fun and Profit* (1971) has a stud

who gathers information for a divorce lawyer. Traci Lords makes her services available to uncover the guilty party in *The Case of the Missing Stiff* (1985). Comic investigators are deployed in *Les aventures des queues nickelés* (1978) as three men look for stolen diamonds in women's vaginas. *Amanda By Night* (Harold Lime and Robert MacCallum, 1980) has a prostitute (Veronica Hart) helping the police as an undercover agent to solve the murder of some of her colleagues. More conventional police stories and television series are evoked as Erica Boyer and Stacey Donovan play *Cagney and Stacey* (1984) or when Ginger Lynn, in one of her best films, Paul Vatelli's *Beverly Hills Cox* (1986), plays Policewoman Cox.

White slavery and prostitution provide common plot structures (*Las alumnas de Madame Olga* by José Gil, 1981; *Brigade Call Girls*, 1977, a porn version of Just Jaeckin's *Madame Claude*, 1976; *Dirty Shary*, 1988; and so on). Somewhat less common are films featuring male brothels. Kidnap and rape films, partly because violence is still censored even in countries allowing the representation of explicit sex, are a minor sub-genre of the crime-porn film. Here, rape is often depicted as a way of revealing a woman's repressed sexuality to herself, and she ends up enjoying the experience (Richard Aldrich and Jeffrey Fairbanks's *American Pie*, 1980, probably the first porn feature in Dolby sound, operates with a plot reminiscent of Nelly Kaplan's **Papa les petits bateaux**). However, there are equally numerous examples of women kidnapping men in this particular genre (in *Chattes mouillées*, 1978, three women abduct men to their cabin in the forest).

Serial killers drive the film forwards in *Femmes entre hommes* (1982) and *Dick of Death* (directed by Sharon Mitchell, 1985, and featuring Jerry Butler as 'James Bonde'). Porn versions of gangster films include Michel Antony's *Pamela* (1980) and John Stagliano's *The Godmother I* and *II*, 1987 and 1988 respectively, starring Ebony Ayes, all derived from Coppola's series. Although almost all commercially successful films have their pornographic version, some of the most intriguing ones are the pastiches of famous classics: *Ces sacrées anglaises* (1977) offers a variation on Kurosawa's **Rashomon**. **The Maltese Falcon** has many porn versions, from *Godfinger ou Certaines chattes n'aiment pas le mou* (1974) to Richard Aldrich and Bob Chinn's *The Jade Pussycat* starring Georgina Spelvin, and the same duo's *The China Cat*

ABOVE John Garfield, Lana Turner, *The Postman Always Rings Twice*

(both 1977), the latter invoking the television series *Charley's Angels* as well. **Double Indemnity** became Stanley Kurlan's *Eruption* (1978); **Sunset Blvd.** turned into Jerome Tanner's film of the same title (1987) starring Rachel Ryan and Shanna McCullough; **Dressed to Kill** became Warren Evans's *Hot Dreams* (1983) starring Sharon Mitchell and Tiffany Clark; **Farewell, My Lovely** became Armand Weston's *Expose Me Lovely* (1976) starring Jennifer Welles. The most intriguing of these adaptations are the versions of Otto Preminger's classic **Laura**, Pamela Ben's *Good Girl Bad Guy* (1984) with Colleen Brennan as Laura, and the best of the bunch, Warren Evans's *Fiona on Fire* (1978) starring Amber Hunt as Laura and containing a pre-

credit sequence evoking **Psycho**'s shower murder. PW

Porto das caixas

Based on a notorious murder case in Rio de Janeiro in the 1950s, the plot of this understated and slow-moving film has much in common with **The Postman Always Rings Twice**. A young woman trapped in a miserable marriage seeks to escape by killing her husband and seeks a male accomplice to do the deed. She fails to convince a soldier but a bar-owner agrees, hoping his desire for the woman will generate the strength required. They buy an axe at a market stall and kill the husband but the heroine finds no release. Saraceni occasionally overdoes the symbolism: when the heroine has decided to kill

her husband, she starts coming across a narratively redundant woman dressed in black. The performance of Alvarez and the delicious cinematography make this a promising debut feature for the director who went on to make *O Desafio* (1965). PW

1963/Brazil/76m/Equipe/*p* Elisio de Sousa Freitas/*d*/*co-s* Paulo Cesar Saraceni/*co-s* Lucio Cardoso/*c* Mario Carneiro/*m* Antonio Carlos Jobim/*lp* Irma Alvarez, Reginaldo Faria, Paulo Padilha, Sergio Sanz, Josef Guerreiro, Margarida Rey.

The Postman Always Rings Twice

Frank Chambers (Garfield) drifts into a California gas station. The dim and hospitable owner Nick Smith (Kellaway) offers him a job which he is about to turn down when he spots Nick's provocative wife, Cora (Turner). The two soon become passionate lovers, and although Frank fights against temptation, running away before being lured back by Cora, it's obvious that her husband has to go. Turner personifies the ice and fire blonde sex goddess who emerged uniquely from California's boiling surf, and the plot derives from the first lingering survey of her body, a feast for the gods, staked out in a sleazy desert pit stop. Frank is a man who, from that moment, surrenders his will to the inevitable urgency of passion. The film, from **James M. Cain**'s novel, is a dark and claustrophobic memory of shadowed interiors and furtive night-time sins, contrasted with the harsh and pitiless light of the desert landscape; a classic and creative moment. The 1981 remake with Jack Nicholson and Jessica Lange in the leading roles is more explicit but no more compelling. MP

1946/113m/MGM/*p* Carey Wilson/*d* Tay Garnett/*s* Harry Ruskin, Niven Busch/ *c* Sidney Wagner/*m* George Bassman/*lp* Lana Turner, John Garfield, Cecil Kellaway, Hume Cronyn, Leon Ames.

Presumed Innocent

A riveting courtroom murder mystery based on Scott Turow's 1987 best-seller featuring Ford as a deputy prosecutor whose colleague, and secret lover (Greta Scacchi), is found brutally murdered. In trying to both find the murderer and cover his tracks Ford gets himself deeper into the situation and is eventually arrested and brought up before a grand jury investigation (part of a piece of political chicanery brought about by his re-electioneering boss, Dennehy, and the opposition for the chief prosecutor's office). In

ABOVE Raul Julia, Bonnie Bedelia, Harrison Ford, *Presumed Innocent*

Ford's defence, cunning lawyer Raul Julia is a delight to observe, making the proceedings hang by a tight thread until the bitter end. TV

1990/127m/WB/*p* Sydney Pollack/*d* Alan J. Pakula/*s* Frank Pierson, Pakula/*c* Gordon Willis/*m* John Williams/*lp* Harrison Ford, Brian Dennehy, Raul Julia, Bonnie Bedelia.

Pretty Boy Floyd

This is one of a cycle of films in the late 1950s and 1960s based on the biographies of noted Public Enemies of the 1930s. Released from prison where he has been doing time for a hold-up, **Charles 'Pretty Boy' Floyd** returns to his home in rural Oklahoma to find his father has been murdered in a feud. Floyd avenges him, then launches on a crime wave across the mid-West, acquiring a girl-friend (Harvey) and a gang to assist him in a series of bank robberies. After killing an **FBI** agent he is declared Public Enemy No. 1 and eventually he is cornered in Ohio and shot dead by federal agents. Floyd's belief that he is some kind of Robin Hood figure engaged in a struggle against the banks that oppress the poor connects him back to such films as *The Grapes of Wrath* (1940) and forwards to **Bonnie and Clyde**. In 1994 Larry McMurtry and Diana Ossana published a novel, *Pretty Boy Floyd*, that had begun life as a screenplay for Warner Bros. EB

1960/96m/Le-Sac/*p* Monroe Sachson/*d/s* Herbert J. Leder/*c* Chuck Austin/*m* Del Sirino/*lp* John Ericson, Barry Newman, Joan Harvey, Herbert Evers, Carl York.

Pretty Poison

Black's debut feature makes imaginative use of location shooting in the small town of Winslow, Mass., to provide an atmospheric context for a darkly humorous story which deals in the deceptiveness of appearances and presents a collision between differing brands of fantasy. As a young man newly released from custody after an act of arson which killed his aunt when he was a teenager, Anthony Perkins imports echoes of his role in **Psycho**. The twist is that the seemingly vivacious, all-American schoolgirl (Weld) whom he enlists in a charade that he is an undercover agent of the CIA, proves to be more psychotic by far. Play acting becomes violently real, and ultimately the girl shoots dead her much-resented mother and contrives to lay the blame on Perkins; in a coda, she is seen complaining to another young man about problems with her foster-parents. Black's subsequent career has been sporadic, and with the exception of *Jennifer on my Mind* (1971), also a youth movie with eccentric dark undercurrents, has not borne out his early promise. TP

1968/89m/FOX/*p* Marshal Backlar, Noel Black/*d* Noel Black/*s* Lorenzo Semple Jr/*c* David Quaid/*m* Johnny Mandel/*lp* Anthony Perkins, Tuesday Weld, Beverly Garland, John Randolph, Ken Kercheval.

Prime Cut

One of a wave of semi-abstract, pop art gangster films which also includes such cynical comic book pictures as *Hard Contract* (1969), *99 & 44/100% Dead!* (1974), **Charley Varrick** and *The Killer Elite* (1975). In *Prime Cut*, the urban cool of Marvin's Syndicate enforcer is set against the folksy rural viciousness of Mary Ann (Hackman), a meat-farmer who raises girls for whorehouses as if he were raising cattle, and his demented hillbilly brother (Walcott), first seen turning Marvin's predecessor into a string of pink sausages. Typical of the cartoon approach are the stereotyping of the respective factions, with Marvin's aides all besuited Irishmen with shotguns, and Hackman calling upon an army of dungaree-clad Waltons with pitchforks. Wittily directed by Ritchie the film as a whole remains deeply and consistently amoral until the finish. KN

1972/86m/Cinema Center/*p* Joe Wizan/ *d* Michael Ritchie/*s* Robert Dillon/*c* Gene Polito/*m* Lalo Schifrin/*lp* Lee Marvin, Gene Hackman, Angel Tompkins, Sissy Spacek, Gregory Walcott.

Prince of the City

A true story about a NYC cop (Williams) who decides to become an informer for the Justice Department about police corruption in his special investigations unit during the 1960s. The lengthy saga is powerfully told by Lumet, though it moves at too stately a pace. The final stages, as the Williams character himself is sucked into the uncontrollable rush for Federal indictments, is very effective. TV

1981/167m/Orion-WB/*p* Burtt Harris/ *d* Sidney Lumet/*s* Jay Presson Allen, Sidney Lumet/*c* Andrzej Bartkowiak/*m* Paul Chihara/*lp* Treat Williams, Jerry Orbach, Richard Foronjy.

The Prison Movie

Obviously a logical off-shoot of the crime film, the prison movie is less a discrete sub-genre than a sub-category of almost any other movie type. While certain films (*The Big House*, 1930, **Brute Force**, *Riot in Cell Block 11*, 1954, *Escape From Alcatraz*, 1979) suggest a self-contained prison movie cycle that serves as an off-shoot of the gangster film, there are prison movies in every recognisable genre: horror (*Prison*, 1987, *The Chair*, 1987), musical (*Jailhouse Rock*, 1957), science fiction (**A Clockwork Orange**, *Terminal Island*, 1973, *Escape From New York*, 1981, *Moon 44*, 1989, *Alien3*, 1992, *No Escape*, 1994), historical (*The Prisoner of Shark Island*, 1936, *It's Never Too Late to Mend*, 1937),

Western (*Escape from Fort Bravo*, 1953, *There Was a Crooked Man. . .* , 1970), comedy (*Pardon Us*, 1931, *Two Way Stretch*, 1960, *Stir Crazy*, 1980), romantic fantasy (*Peter Ibbetson*, 1935), swashbuckler (*The Count of Monte Cristo*, 1934, *The Man in the Iron Mask*, 1939), softcore sexploitation (*The Big Bird Cage*, 1972, *Chained Heat*, 1983), hardcore porn (*Play Pen*, 1986), war movie (*The Hill*, 1965), gay art movie (*Un chant d'amour*, 1950), gay porn movie (*Les Minets sauvage*, 197?), juvenile delinquent (*Boys Town*, 1938, *Untamed Youth*, 1958, *Scum*, 1979), he-man action (*Breakout*, 1975, *Lock Up*, 1989, *Death Warrant*, 1991), biopic (*The Birdman of Alcatraz*, 1962, *McVicar*, 1980, *Silent Scream*, 1991), social protest (**I Am a Fugitive from a Chain Gang**, *Jackson County Jail*, 1976), allegories (*Cool Hand Luke*, 1967), true-life drama of suffering and the human spirit (*Papillon*, 1973, *Midnight Express*, 1978), sports picture (*The Loneliness of the Long Distance Runner*, 1962, *The Longest Yard/The Mean Machine*, 1974, *The Jericho Mile*, 1979), political gay romantic fantasy (*Kiss of the Spider Woman*, 1985), historical social protest biopic (*The Life of Emile Zola*, 1937), science fiction comedy action sexploitation (*Prison Ship: Starslammer*, 1984), political science fiction horror social protest (*Ghosts . . . of the Civil Dead*, 1988). And so on.

Occasionally, films set in other institutions – a convent in *La Religieuse* (1965), a mental hospital in *One Flew Over the Cuckoo's*

ABOVE The Prison Movie: Howard Duff, Burt Lancaster, *Brute Force*

Nest (1975) – import the conventions of the prison movie (sadistic guards, defiant convicts, shifty squealers, escape attempts, riots) to make a point. The prisoner-of-war movie (*La Grande Illusion*, 1937, *The Wooden Horse*, 1950, *Stalag 17*, 1953, *The Bridge on the River*

Kwai, 1957) is a genre in its own right, separated from the prison film proper in that its heroes are not only sympathetic but also not criminals. It is very notable that, aside from a few films about crusading wardens (*Prison Warden*, 1949, *Brubaker*, 1980) and one lonely but bizarre film about a mildly corrupt guard (*Fast-Walking*, 1979), the prison movie invariably takes the side of the prisoner against the guards, which perhaps explains the species of self-righteous glee that informs the prisoner-of-war picture, which does not need to justify its sympathies. Typically, prison movies tell of the compromised innocent who has to get tough to survive (James Cagney in *Each Dawn I Die*, 1936, Tom Selleck in *An Innocent Man*, 1991), the determined break-out artist who finally makes his getaway (Clint Eastwood in *Escape from Alcatraz*, Jon Voight in *Runaway Train*, 1985) or the real-life doomed loser who pays the ultimate price (Susan Hayward as Barbara Graham in *I Want to Live!*, 1958, Alan Alda as Caryl Chessman in *Kill Me If You Can*, 1977, Tommy Lee Jones as Gary Gilmore in *The Executioner's Song*.) From the tough-talking era of the 1930s gangster movie (*Numbered Men*, 1930, **The Criminal Code**, *The Last Mile*, 1932, *20,000 Years in Sing Sing*, 1932, *San Quentin*, 1937, *You Can't Get away with Murder*, 1939) through the neurotic shadows

ABOVE The Prison Movie: Paul Muni, *I Am a Fugitive from a Chain Gang*

ABOVE Private Eyes: Gail Patrick, Melvyn Douglas, *The Lone Wolf Returns*

of the *noir* period (Jules Dassin's extraordinarily violent *Brute Force*) and the semi-documentary drama of the 50s and 60s (Don Siegel's remarkably balanced *Riot in Cell Block 11*, John Frankenheimer's intimate but epic *Birdman of Alcatraz*) to the brutalities of contemporary machismo (*Fortune and Men's Eyes*, 1971, *The Glasshouse*, 1972, *Short Eyes*, 1977, *Penitentiary*, 1979, *Bad Boys*, 1983) little has changed in the iconography (cell bars, clanking doors, lights dimming as 'the chair' is used), character types (evil guards, cell-block bullies, kindly doctors, ineffectual wardens, fatherly lifers, nervous youngsters) or the events (exercise yard scuffles, mess-hall message-passing, time in solitary) of the prison movie, though there has been an increasing concentration on homosexuality (rape in the showers).

Often films begin with heroes (Humphrey Bogart in **High Sierra**, Steve McQueen in **The Getaway**, Dustin Hoffman in *Straight Time*, 1978) or villains (Robert Mitchum and Robert De Niro in **Cape Fear**, David Carradine in *Bird on a Wire*, 1990, John Lithgow in *Ricochet*, 1991) being released or escaping from prison to return to a life of crime or revenge, or, less often, to clear their name (Bogart in **Dark Passage**) or, very infrequently indeed, to go straight (Emlyn Williams in **They Drive by Night**, Stanley Baker in **Hell Drivers**).

Though several prisons have attained iconic presence in period movies (the Chateau d'If, the Bastille, Devil's Island, Colditz, the Tower of London), they have tended to be in movies whose agenda is more political than criminal. The only prison to achieve universal recognition (beating off rivals like San Quentin and Sing Sing) is Alcatraz Island in San Francisco Bay, which is so famous that it even features in the title of *Birdman of Alcatraz* though for most of its length lifer Robert Stroud (Burt Lancaster) is actually doing his time in Leavenworth. 'The Rock' is also the location for *Alcatraz Island* (1937), *The Last Gangster* (1937, mainly before the prison opened in 1934), *Alcatraz: The Whole Shocking Story* (1980) and *Six Against the Rock* (1987) and *The Rock* (1996). The deserted island also features on a resonant and symbolic level, in the opening and closing sequences of John Boorman's **Point Blank**, where it serves to suggest that the enclosed city-world of the film is just a larger prison. KN

Private Eyes

The first non-constabulary detective was C. Auguste Dupin, introduced by Edgar Allan Poe in his story 'The Murders in the Rue Morgue' (1841), the source of several films. The vast majority of the screen's private detectives have literary origins. The first on

film was **Sherlock Holmes**, who appeared in a 1-minute trick film, *Sherlock Holmes Baffled*, made between 1900 and 1903. Comic book hero **Sexton Blake** made his screen debut in 1909. **Raffles**, first seen on screen in 1905, **Arsène Lupin** (1910) and **Boston Blackie** (1918) were reformed criminals. Most of these early sleuths were gentlemen and scholars, more at home in a country house than a dockside dive. The 20s and 30s saw the evolution of the debonair adventurer with criminal leanings such as the **Lone Wolf** and the **Saint**. What we now think of as the typical private eye, the world-weary, wise-cracking misanthrope, only arrived on screen in the 40s. What all these private detectives have in common is reckless independence, and more importantly the ability to outsmart the usually clueless police. The link between the polished and the rough diamond is **Philo Vance**, played by several actors in films between 1929 and 1947. Also part of the process were the amateur detectives, mostly female, popular in series of films beginning in the 30s. Schoolteacher Hildegarde Withers, first seen in 1932, was followed by reporter Torchy Blane (1937) and teenager **Nancy Drew** (1938). These mostly appeared in second features, but the **Thin Man** series (1934–47), featuring **Nick and Nora Charles**, were quality productions with big stars (William

ABOVE Private Eyes: Lauren Bacall, Humphrey Bogart, *The Big Sleep*

ABOVE Private Eyes: Richard Roundtree, *Shaft*

Powell, Myrna Loy.) During the 40s every studio had at least one series detective on the go. This was the era of **Nick Carter** (1939–40), **Michael Shayne** (1940–47), Boston Blackie (1941–9) and **The Falcon** (1941–9) as well as such definitive portrayals as Humphrey Bogart's Sam Spade in **The Maltese Falcon** and Philip Marlowe in **The Big Sleep**. Marlowe was also played by Dick Powell in **Murder My Sweet** and by Robert Montgomery in **The Lady in the Lake**. Interest in private detectives dwindled during the 50s. Tough guy **Mike Hammer** was introduced in *I, The Jury* (1953). **Lemmy Caution** featured in nine French films (1953–67), notably *Alphaville* (1965). Another two amateur sleuths made their screen debuts, *Father Brown* in the film of that name (GB, 1954), and **Miss Marple** in a short series of second-features (GB, 1962–4). Paul Newman's success in **Harper** paved the way for a run of films which tried for a blend of *film noir*, swinging pop culture, and sex and violence. Examples of this are *New Face in Hell* (1967); *Tony Rome* (1967) and its sequel *Lady in Cement* (1968). **Shaft** and two sequels adapted the formula for the blaxploitation era. Other similar films were *Shamus* (1972), **Night Moves**, *The Drowning Pool* (1975), in which Newman returned as Harper, and **The Late Show**. The adventures of Philip Marlowe were updated in

Marlowe, **The Long Goodbye** and *The Big Sleep* (GB, 1978). Two films in elegantly recreated period settings, **Chinatown** and *Farewell, My Lovely* (1975), are more satisfactory. By the 80s private eyes were rare in the cinema, but not uncommon on television. Private-eye movies have not fared well in the 90s. Among them are *Just Ask for Diamond* (GB, 1988), a children's film spoofing *The Maltese Falcon*; *The Two Jakes* (1991), a belated sequel to *Chinatown*; *Dead Again* (1991), a comedy-thriller about reincarnation; *V.I. Warshawski* (1991), with the female private eye of that name. Far better, but still insubstantial, was *Devil in a Blue Dress* (1995) with Denzel Washington as Easy Rawlins, a black investigator in 1948 Los Angeles. Despite appearances to the contrary, the following were not private eyes, but policemen: **Dick Tracy** (his first screen appearance in 1937 was as a **FBI** agent), Nero Wolfe, **Ellery Queen**, and **Charlie Chan**. DM

The Private Files of J. Edgar Hoover

'I'll bug and burglarise who I please,' declares Hoover when Nixon aides ask to get in on the act, 'but damned if I'll let anyone else do it.' This radical revision of **The FBI Story** comes complete with a dissection of the life of a sexually-stunted demagogue-cum-demigod whose career began with the birth of American Anti-Communism in the Palmer Raids of 1919 and extended to Prohibition, Dillinger, World War II, McCarthyism, bitter rivalry with Robert Kennedy, assassinations, the Civil Rights movement and Vietnam. The film reaches beyond Hoover's death with the speculation that Clyde Tolson (Dailey), his long-time friend and rumoured homosexual lover, was the 'Deep Throat' who brought down, using Hoover's files, the Nixon administration. Cohen, signalling his respect for the Warner Bros. tradition in his exceptional casting of old-time faces and use of a brassy Miklos Rozsa score, makes Hoover a semi-comic monster, particularly in old age as he drunkenly listens to the taped seduction of an opponent, unintentionally horrifies a favourite waiter by revealing the extent of his knowledge of the man's private life, or is found asleep in his office by the creeping Bobby Kennedy (Parks). A comic horror story of the corruption of American power, the film still, like the agent (Torn) who serves as narrator, has to admire the 'top cop' for his bull-headed refusal to bow to passing administrations of whatever political stripe, and consistently shows other political

figures, whether sainted – Roosevelt (Da Silva), Martin Luther King (St Jacques), the Kennedys – or demonised – McCarthy, Nixon as compromised in ideals and outwitted by Hoover. KN

1977/112m/Larco-AIP/*p*/*d*/*s* Larry Cohen/*c* Paul Glickman/*m* Miklos Rozsa/*lp* Broderick Crawford, James Wainwright, Rip Torn, Michael Parks, José Ferrer, Ronee Blakley, Howard Da Silva, Raymond St Jacques, Dan Dailey, Lloyd Nolan.

Prizzi's Honor

Nicholson is Charley Partanna, a hit-man for the mob in New York. It's a close-knit family affair; Charley is the grandson of the Godfather, and it is intended he marry his cousin (Huston). But he breaks it off, against the instructions of the family. Huston appears to have forgiven him, but hasn't. He meets the beautiful Turner and falls for her heavily. He discovers that she too is a professional killer. Despite this he establishes a romance with her and as she's based in California this involves much long-distance commuting, one of the film's running jokes. In a neat twist, each is hired to kill the other. The sexual chemistry between Nicholson and both Turner and Huston (her off-screen relationship with Nicholson adding an extra dimension) contributes hugely to the dynamism of the picture, which manages to be consistently funny about gangsters without ever descending into coarse knockabout. EB

1985/129m/ABC Motion Pictures/*p* John Foreman/*d* John Huston/*s* Richard Condon, Janet Roach/*c* Andrzej Bartkowiak/*m* Alex North/*lp* Jack Nicholson, Kathleen Turner, Robert Loggia, William Hickey, Anjelica Huston.

Prohibition

The 18th Amendment to the United States Constitution (which came into force on 17 January 1920) prohibited the manufacture, transport and sale of alcoholic beverages. The climax of over fifty years of lobbying and anti-drink propaganda, 'the noble experiment' ensured the growth of organised crime by providing gangsters like **Al Capone** not only with a multi-million dollar industry but also a great measure of public support. The widespread violation of the Volstead Act, from Warren G. Harding's White House down to the speakeasies of the cities and the backwoods stills of rural areas, made Prohibition effectively unenforceable, and the vast profits made from boot-legging encouraged the spread of corruption within law-enforcement agencies. Despite the image of Prohibition as a universally disliked law, it had been adopted in twenty-six states before the passage of the Volstead Act, and in 1928, a 'dry' Presidential candidate, Herbert Hoover, defeated the decidedly 'wet' Alfred Smith by a landslide. Towards the end of the 20s, public concern about gangsterism was raised not by boot-legging but by such incidentals as machine-gun massacres, prompting various city and state authorities to target the gangsters themselves. When the Amendment was repealed on 5 December 1933, the gangs were too powerful and entrenched to be completely demolished.

The chief legacy of Prohibition was undoubtedly the creation of an infrastructure for American organised crime which persists to the present day. Before it was actually put into practice, Prohibition was generally deemed to be the only solution to the problem of drink. Film-makers (many of whom, like D.W. Griffith, had personal experience of alcoholism) dutifully turned out melodramatic stories of good men ruined by the bottle, including *John Barleycorn* (1914), *The Outer Edge* (1915) and *The Girl Glory* (1917). A campaigning epic entitled *Prohibition* (1915), directed by James Halleck Reid, features contributions by such anti-drink campaigners as William Jennings Bryan. Rather more prescient was Griffith's *Intolerance* (1916), which has reformers shutting down saloons only to have gangsters move in to take over the drink industry. While Prohibition was in force, Hollywood movies generally took the attitude they would adopt in the 70s to the use of marijuana. In films like *It's the Old Army Game* (1926), W.C. Fields pre-empts Cheech and Chong by making comic capital of his illegal appetites. *Mystery of the Wax Museum* (1932) has an incidental plot about boot-legging, but makes it clear that the wisecracking heroine (Glenda Farrell) isn't averse to a shot or two, presenting a police force who are broadly tolerant of such lapses while getting on with real work, like entrapping the deformed abductor who has been terrorising the city. Subsequent to Prohibition, many films (*The Lost Weekend*, 1945, *Come Fill the Cup*, 1951, *Bottom of the Bottle*, 1956, *Days of Wine and Roses*, 1962) have tackled alcoholism in horrific terms, but all suggest solutions should be personal rather than legislative.

During Prohibition, an awareness grew

ABOVE Prohibition: Priscilla Lane, James Cagney, *The Roaring Twenties*

that the Amendment was the chief plank of the gangster's power, but a surprising number of gangster films (**Underworld**, **Little Caesar**) manage to get by with villains whose means of support seems to be comparatively trivial robberies. A few silent pictures – *Those Who Dance* (1924), with Warner Baxter as an Eliot Ness-type Prohibition Agent, and *Twelve Miles Out* (1927), with John Gilbert as a Larry Fay-like racketeer touch on the source of the gangster's quick money, but mainly as a minor theme in traditional melodramas. It was not until Prohibition was on the way out, with Franklin D. Roosevelt promising to end it if elected, that gangster movies began to offer anything like documentary detail of the way boot-legging worked. **The Public Enemy**, **Scarface**, *Song of the Eagle* (1933) and **The Roaring Twenties** made familiar the speakeasies, strong-arm sales methods, gang wars, hi-jackings and huge profits that became a cliché of the Prohibition movie. *The Roaring Twenties*, the first film to take a historical approach, set the tone for later retro items like *Pete Kelly's Blues* (1955), **Love Me or Leave Me**, **Party Girl**, *The Untouchables* TV series (1959–63, 1992–), **The Cotton Club**, **The Untouchables** and *Mobsters* (1991), all of which flavour the picturesque details of bygone crimes with flap-

per fashions and wild jazz to create what amounts to a nostalgia, if not for Prohibition then certainly for the Prohibition Era. *A Slight Case of Murder* (1938) opens hilariously on the night Prohibition is repealed, with beer baron Edward G. Robinson forced to taste his own product. This key moment is treated more seriously in **Once Upon a Time in America**, prompting a betrayal that sends bootlegger Robert De Niro into limbo and propels his more ambitious partner (James Woods) into big league power politics.

It is rarely noted that Prohibition is still in force in some areas of the United States (including the Tennessee county which contains the Jack Daniel's distillery) though a small sub-genre (*Thunder Road*, 1958, *The Last American Hero*, 1973, *White Lightning*, 1973, *Moonshine County Express*, 1977, *Thunder and Lightning*, 1977) concentrates on the activities of hard-driving moonshine runners and revenue men clashing over illegal stills and home-brewed whiskey. Currently, as in **Scarface**, *New Jack City* (1990), *King of New York* (1990) and many others, the plot structures and moral attitudes of the Prohibition-era gangster movie tend to be applied to the drug problem. For all the demonising of crack dealers and 'just say no' indictments, the suggestion is that current laws on drug abuse serve like Prohibition merely to ensure huge profits go to organised crime while doing little if anything to discourage the manufacture and use of illicit substances. KN

See also **Al Capone**.

Prostitution

For many years, the Hollywood Production Code expressly forbade mention of prostitution, forcing film-makers to all manner of euphemisms, the most familiar of which is the 'dance-hall girl' of many Westerns, epitomised by Claire Trevor in *Stagecoach* (1939). Whenever the gangster movie touched on the subject – as in **Party Girl**, a rackets exposé, and **Marked Woman**, the story of a group of call girls who testified against the mob – discreet scripting ensured the women in question could be deemed 'party girls' or '**night-club** hostesses'. Into the 40s and 50s, such subterfuges were in use, so that Laird Cregar's Jack the Ripper in *The Lodger* (1943) preys on 'actresses' while the sewing machine glimpsed in Joan Bennett's apartment in *Man Hunt* (1941) theoretically identifies her as a seamstress rather than a streetwalker. Otherwise, the nearest an actress could get to prostitution was loitering in bars in a trench-coat looking bedraggled but glamorous, preferably in tidied-up adaptations of works of unquestionable literary

ABOVE Prostitution: Joan Crawford, *Rain*

ABOVE Prostitution: Roy Scheider, Jane Fonda, *Klute*

merit: Louise Brooks in *Pandora's Box* (1928), Greta Garbo in *Anna Christie* (1930), Joan Crawford in *Rain* (1932), Miriam Hopkins in *Dr Jekyll and Mr Hyde* (1932), Bette Davis in *Of Human Bondage* (1934), Claire Trevor in *Dead End* (1937), Vivien Leigh in *Waterloo Bridge* (1940) and Simone Simon in *Mademoiselle Fifi* (1944). These women tend to pay for their sins by suffering, often being assaulted or murdered by maddened 'protectors'. Other dominant images of prostitution were represented by Marlene Dietrich's vampish courtesans in *Shanghai Express* (1932) and *The Devil is a Woman* (1935) and the cheerfully mercenary chorines of *The Gold Diggers of 1933* (1933), with Mae West's screen character poised somewhere in between.

During and after World War II (which, like World War I, ensured many male Americans had enough experience of prostitution to become impatient with euphemisms) the veil was lifted somewhat, so excuses became unnecessary for the hardbitten hookers and pathetic drudges of *film noir*: Ona Munson in *The Shanghai Gesture* (1941), Joan Bennett in **The Woman in the Window** and **Scarlet Street**, Gloria Grahame in **Crossfire**, Shelley Winters in *A Double Life* (1947), Mary Astor in *Act of Violence* (1949), Susan Hayward in *I Want to*

Live! (1958) and Constance Towers in **The Naked Kiss**. This frankness spread to other genres: the war film (Donna Reed in *From Here to Eternity*, 1954), the soap opera (Shirley MacLaine in *Some Came Running*, 1957) and the Western (Felicia Farr in *3:10 to Yuma*, 1957). European cinema familiarised such ethereal presences as Giulietta Masina in *Notte di Cabiria* (1957), Anna Karina in *Vivre sa vie* (1962), and Catherine Deneuve in *Belle de jour* (1967). The earthy Melina Mercouri in *Never on Sunday* (1960) set a trend for comic lustiness and scatterbrained romanticism echoed by Audrey Hepburn in *Breakfast at Tiffany's* (1961), Shirley MacLaine in *Irma la Douce* (1963) and *Sweet Charity* (1969), Barbra Streisand in *The Owl and the Pussycat* (1970), Claudia Jennings in *Truck Stop Women* (1974), Lynn Redgrave in *The Happy Hooker* (1975), Dolly Parton in *The Best Little Whorehouse in Texas* (1982), Jamie Lee Curtis in *Trading Places* (1983), Rebecca De Mornay in *Risky Business* (1983), Shelley Long in *Night Shift* (1987), Julie Walters in *Personal Services* (1987) and Julia Roberts in *Pretty Woman* (1990).

After it ceased to be shocking simply to preserve the prostitute status of characters from novels or plays – as with Shirley Jones in *Elmer Gantry* (1960), Elizabeth Taylor in *Butterfield 8* (1960), Nancy Kwan in *The*

ABOVE Anthony Perkins, *Psycho*

World of Suzie Wong (1960), Capucine in *Walk on the Wild Side* (1962) or Lee Grant in *The Balcony* (1963) – films began to delve deeper, presenting non-stereotypes like would-be actress Jane Fonda in **Klute**, unforgettably checking her watch while encouraging a client to orgasm, and French émigré Catherine Deneuve in *Hustle* (1976). A run of films examine prostitution as one strand of organised crime, with the girls themselves, Sissy Spacek in **Prime Cut** and Jodie Foster in **Taxi Driver**, hopeless victims caught in greater struggles between male outlaws. An extraordinary number of films still persist in presenting prostitution as glamorous (Brooke Shields in *Pretty Baby*, 1978 and

Julia Roberts in *Pretty Woman*, 1990) or funny (Georgina Spelvin in **Police Academy**), but there have been many grim, street-level victims (abused junkies, usually underage and invariably beaten up by violent pimps and johns) like Kitty Winn in *Panic in Needle Park* (1971), Isela Vega (and almost every other actress to appear for Sam Peckinpah) in *Bring Me the Head of Alfredo Garcia* (1974), Jill Clayburgh in *Hustling* (1975), Eve Plumb in *Dawn: Portrait of a Teenage Runaway* (1976), Nadja Brunkhorst in *Christiane F.* (1981), Season Hubley in *Vice Squad* (1982), Melissa Leo in *Streetwalkin'* (1984), Donna Wilkes in *Angel* (1983), Jennifer Mayo in *Scarred* (1983), Rosanna

Arquette in **8 Million Ways to Die**, Kathy Baker in *Street Smart* (1987) and Theresa Russell in *Impulse* (1990, a vice cop in disguise) and *Whore* (1991). Pam Grier's razor-slashing psycho hooker in **Fort Apache, the Bronx** is a rare instance of fighting back, though various forms of violence are done to unwary johns in *Vampire Hookers* (1978), *I, Desire* (1982), *Hollywood Chainsaw Hookers* (1987) and *Beverly Hills Vamp* (1989).

Male prostitutes are almost always exploited and ashamed: Jon Voight in *Midnight Cowboy* (1970), Leigh McCloskey in *Alexander: The Other Side of Dawn* (1977), Robert Downey Jr in *Less Than Zero* (1987), River Phoenix and Keanu Reeves in *My Own Private Idaho* (1991), Kevin Bacon in *JFK* (1991). Pimps, however, range from potent villains like Harvey Keitel in *Taxi Driver*, Wings Hauser in *Vice Squad* and Morgan Freeman in *Street Smart* and minor heavies like Dan Duryea in *Scarlet Street*, through jokes like Dan Aykroyd in *Dr Detroit* (1983) and Tom Cruise in *Risky Business* and desperate operators like Ben Gazzara in *Saint Jack* (1979) and John Hurt in **Scandal** to ethnic stereotypes like Max Julien in *The Mack* (1972), John Daniels in *The Candy Tangerine Man* (1974) and, in an amusing caricature of the breed, Antonio Fargas in *I'm Gonna Git You Sucka* (1988). Though hookers still most often appear as disposable victims – witness the parade of corpses left in such Jack the Ripper-inspired slashers as *Don't Answer the Phone* (1979), *Jack's Back* (1988) and *Streets* (1990) – there have also been glamorous yuppie call-girl heroines like Nancy Allen in **Dressed to Kill** and Sigourney Weaver in *Half Moon Street* (1986), whose sharp shoulder-pads and business portfolios mark them out as survivors of the Sex Wars. Kathleen Turner in *Crimes of Passion* (1984) and Cathy Tyson in **Mona Lisa**, which effectively deal with the problems faced in private life by women who professionally enact male fantasies, are genuine queens of erotic adventure, but the cinema's most convincing professional women are the credible, putting-out-to-get-by ensemble of Lizzie Borden's *Working Girls* (1986) and, inevitably, the real-life runaways and hustlers of the documentary *Street Life* (1984). KN

The Prowler

The plot dynamics recall those of **Double Indemnity**, but the tone is more external, and the difference in narrative terms is that the killing, disguised as an accident, of a wealthy older man by a younger one – here a policeman (Heflin) – who lusts after the other's wife (Keyes) is not plotted with her connivance. The couple subsequently marry, but her pregnancy introduces an ironic complication; her former husband was sterile, and Heflin paranoically fears that this will be construed as a motive for murder. When Keyes realises he intends to kill the doctor they have summoned to their ghost-town hide-out, she contrives the doctor's escape and calls the police. The fleeing Heflin is ultimately shot down in a barren desert landscape, somewhat akin to that in Losey's *The Lawless* (1950). This setting adds its own comment to the sardonic social critique, though the film provides an element of sympathy for its warped exponent of the go-getter ethos. TP

1950/92m/UA/*p* S.P. Eagle (Sam Spiegel)/ *d* Joseph Losey/*s* Hugo Butler/*c* Arthur Miller/ *m* Lyn Murray/*lp* Van Heflin, Evelyn Keyes, Emerson Tracy, John Maxwell, Robert Osterloh.

A proxima vitima/The Next Victim

During the 1982 election campaign, a serial killer of prostitutes is on the loose in the seedy Bras quarter of Sao Paulo. The television reporter David (Fagundes) covers the story and befriends Luna, the prostitute marked to be the killer's next victim (the murderer always writes the name of his next victim in blood on the walls of the scene of the crime). However, the plot is only marginally concerned with the identity of the Jack the Ripper-like criminal and doesn't bother much with his victims. Instead, it is

ABOVE Psychopaths: Jack Nicholson, *The Shining*

David's political and personal sense of disorientation which is the core of the movie. His tribulations include an ex-wife, a girl-friend, more politically involved colleagues, various low-life characters and the cynical police chief who manages to ensnare David into the investigation. PW

1983/Brazil/96m/Raiz/*d* Joao Batista de Andrade/*s* Lauro Cesar Muniz/*c* Antonio Meliande/*m* Marcus Vinicius/*lp* Antonio Fagundes, Louise Cardoso, Othon Bastos, Ester Goes, Gianfrancesco Guardini.

Psycho

Marion Crane (Leigh) runs away after stealing a large sum of money, hoping it will remove the obstacles to her romance with married boyfriend Sam (Gavin). In the middle of the night she stops at the sinister Bates Motel, where she's greeted by Norman Bates (Perkins). Norman is a boy/man dominated by his bullying mother, and while Marion is taking a shower Ma Bates appears to burst into the bathroom and stab her to death. Norman cleans up the mess, but subsequently Marion's sister, Lila (Miles), accompanied by a private detective Milton Arbogast (Balsam), appears and begins to ask awkward questions. Everything about this film has been parodied and imitated to the point where its imagery has an intense and instant familiarity. But this doesn't detract from the shock of its black humour and agonising suspense. A redefinition of horror which centred the genre in the weird alleyways of the human mind, its influence is incalculable. From the novel by **Robert Bloch**. MP

1960/109m/PAR/*p*/*d* Alfred Hitchcock/ *s* Joseph Stefano/*c* John L Russell/*m* Bernard Herrmann/*lp* Anthony Perkins, Janet Leigh, Vera Miles, John Gavin, Martin Balsam.

Psychopaths

Mad characters are quite common in early horror films: Conrad Veidt's catatonic somnambulist in *The Cabinet of Dr Caligari* (1919), Lon Chaney's disfigured megalomaniac in *The Phantom of the Opera* (1925), Dwight Frye's fly-eating lunatic in *Dracula* (1930), Irving Pichel's drooling retard in *Murder By the Clock* (1931), Brember Wills' pyromaniac in *The Old Dark House* (1932), Bill Woods's multi-afflicted head-case in *Maniac* (1934). Similarly, several crime films, for example, *The Cat and the Canary* (1927), use the convention of a sane criminal who poses as a madman for an easily understandable motive like avarice. However, the perfor-

ABOVE Psychopaths: Tony Curtis, *The Boston Strangler*

mances and romantic attachments of jittery misogynist James Cagney, latent homosexual Edward G. Robinson and incest-obsessed neanderthal Paul Muni in **The Public Enemy**, **Little Caesar** and **Scarface** suggest something far deeper. These are men who may have turned to crime through a combination of social conditions but they are also men who have severe mental problems. The neuroses, however, are mainly character frills that serve to make the protagonists more colourful rather than a coherent attempt to suggest they are actually insane. Chester Morris in **Blind Alley**, a dream-obsessed hoodlum analysed and defused by pipe-smoking Ralph Bellamy, is an early attempt at a psychologically damaged criminal. In the end, Morris is simply maladjusted rather than psychopathic, and additionally suffers when he is cured of his ability to kill because he is instantly shot dead by the policemen he can no longer mow down with mental impunity.

Before the spread of psychoanalysis to Hollywood in the 40s, there was a tendency to discriminate between normal criminals and psycho killers, demonstrated by the confrontation between the underworld kangaroo court and child-murderer Peter Lorre in

Psychopaths

M or the contrast between ex-con suspect Emlyn Williams, a down-to-earth hero, and actual murderer Ernest Thesiger, a prissily ranting weirdo, in **They Drive by Night**. During the heyday of *film noir*, the psycho became a more familiar screen character, either as a seemingly normal and respectable individual who turns into a ranting homicidal lunatic (Albert Dekker in *Among the Living*, 1941, Joseph Cotten in **Shadow of a Doubt**, Franchot Tone in **Phantom Lady**, George Brent in **The Spiral Staircase**, Olivia de Havilland in **The Dark Mirror**, Humphrey Bogart in *The Two Mrs. Carrolls*, 1947) or the amnesiac/shell-shocked/intoxicated hero who suspects he is a killer or can't quite remember other crucial information (Dan Duryea in *Black Angel*, 1946, John Hodiak in *Somewhere in the Night*, 1946, DeForrest Kelley in *Fear in the Night*, 1947, Robert Taylor in *The High Wall*, 1947, Gregory Peck in **Spellbound**).

A few 40s characters, usually of a suspiciously artistic bent, have relatively complex psychoses: George Sanders's masochist mastermind with an unnatural wish to get caught in **Quiet Please Murder**, Laird Cregar's schizophrenic composer/murderer in **Hangover Square**, Laraine Day's kleptomaniac in *The Locket* (1947), Humphrey Bogart's paranoid and violent screenwriter in **In a Lonely Place**. There was essentially still a belief, never quite expunged, that mental illness consists mainly of an uncontrollable urge to kill people, as demonstrated by Peter Lorre in *Stranger on the Third Floor* (1940), James Bell in *The Leopard Man* (1943), Richard Basehart in **He Walked by Night** and John Drew Barrymore in **While the City Sleeps**. The most typical use of the psycho in the crime film is as a lumbering henchman or giggling menace, as incarnated by Mike Mazurki in **Murder My Sweet**, William Bendix in **The Dark Corner**, Richard Widmark in **Kiss of Death**, Neville Brand ('I'm afraid he's a sadist.') in **D.O.A.**, Alan Arkin in *Wait Until Dark* (1967), Andrew Robinson in **Dirty Harry**, Gary Busey ('Where did you get him? Psychos R Us?') in *Lethal Weapon* (1986) and Joe Pesci in **GoodFellas.**

Some movie criminals, like Frank Sinatra's assassin in *Suddenly* (1954) and Robert Mitchum's rapist in **Cape Fear**, continued to display incidental symptoms of mental disorder, but the psychopath as a screen character really came into his own as a result of Anthony Perkins's Norman Bates in Alfred Hitchcock's **Psycho**. More than considered dramas like *The Three Faces of Eve* (1957) and *Lizzie* (1957), *Psycho* established an image of the psycho, though Perkins's carefully sympathetic performance and Hitchcock's manipulation of audience identification ultimately render Norman as understandable and even likeable a character as the disturbed heroes of earlier Hitchcock movies, the voyeur and agoraphobic played by James Stewart in **Rear Window** and **Vertigo**.

Subsequently the criminal psychopath, usually but not invariably homicidal, has become a standard screen character: scopophilic Carl Boehm in **Peeping Tom**, Jean Arliss in *Homicidal* (1961), Bobby Darin in *Pressure Point* (1962), Bette Davis *and* Joan Crawford in *What Ever Happened to Baby Jane?* (1962), Oliver Reed in *Paranoiac* (1963), fake erotomaniac-cum-real catatonic Peter Breck in *Shock Corridor* (1963), troubled Jean Seberg in *Lilith* (1964), frigid kleptomaniac Tippi Hedren in **Marnie**, Catherine Deneuve in **Repulsion**, Margaret Johnston as *The Psychopath* (1966), schizophrenic Tony Curtis as **The Boston Strangler**, Tuesday Weld as **Pretty Poison**, sniper Tim O'Kelly in **Targets**, Richard Attenborough in **10 Rillington Place**, Mimsy Farmer in *Quattro mosche di velluto grigio/Four Flies on Grey Velvet* (1971), Jessica Walter in *Play Misty for Me* (1971), the whole cast of *Asylum* (1972), Robert Hardy in *Demons of the Mind* (1972), Susannah York in *Images* (1972), Margot Kidder in *Sisters* (1973), David Hess in *Last House on the Left* (1973), Roberts Blossom in *Deranged* (1974), the family of *The Texas Chain Saw Massacre* (1975), Stacy Keach in **The Killer Inside Me**, John Amplas in *Martin* (1976), Lynne Frederick in *Schizo* (1976), Robert De Niro in **Taxi Driver**, Peter Firth in *Equus* (1977), Dennis Christopher in *Fade to Black* (1980), Klaus Kinski in *Schizoid* (1980), Jack Nicholson in *The Shining* (1980), Joe Spinell in *Maniac* (1980), Jimmy Laine/Abel Ferrara in *The Driller Killer* (1980), Robert De Niro in *The King of Comedy* (1983), Brian Cox and Tom Noonan in **Manhunter**, Alex McArthur in *Rampage* (1986), Michael Rooker in **Henry Portrait of a Serial Killer**, Anthony Hopkins and Ted Levine in **The Silence of the Lambs** and pyromaniac Donald Sutherland in *Backdraft* (1981). Alongside runs a tradition, popularised but not originated by *Halloween* (1978) and *Friday the 13th*

<small>ABOVE Edward Woods, James Cagney, Lee Phelps, *The Public Enemy*</small>

ABOVE James Cagney, *The Public Enemy*

blend of charisma and awkwardness as the upwardly mobile hood forces a cowering barman to take his brand of beer, is measured for his first tuxedo, fumbles through unsatisfactory relationships (famously shoving a grapefruit in moll Clarke's face), embarrasses his sternly moralising brother (Cook) and indulgent mother (Mercer), and impulsively gets gunned down trying to avenge the machine-gun murder of his best friend (Woods). Most impressive and influential of all is Tom's death, stumbling gut-shot in the gutter with an exclamation of 'I ain't so tough' and then left a mummified corpse on his mother's doorstep, tumbling out of the rain like a side of beef. KN

1931/84m/WB/*p* Darryl F. Zanuck/*d* William A. Wellman/*s* Kubec Glasmon, John Bright/ *c* Dev Jennings/*m* David Mendoza/*lp* James Cagney, Edward Woods, Donald Cook, Joan Blondell, Jean Harlow, Beryl Mercer, Mae Clarke.

Pulp Fiction

Tarantino's earlier **Reservoir Dogs** announced the arrival of a new talent. The gloriously titled *Pulp Fiction* is an even better film, one less confined by its influences. The film's central devices – the extended conversations, a belief in pop culture and an insistent use of music – can be traced back to Martin Scorsese's **Mean Streets**, a trail highlighted by the appearance of Keitel, but the film is

(1980), of using a masked or shadowy homicidal maniac as an unknowable monster, a strain which reaches its epitome in the dead child molester (Robert Englund) of *A Nightmare on Elm Street* (1985) and sequels. KN

The Public Enemy/Enemies of the Public

Following **Little Caesar**, this archetypal early 30s gangster film kicks off with a caption upholding its protagonist as a bad example and a social problem, then follows Tom Powers (Cagney) from Chicago slum childhood through juvenile delinquency to a brief life as a flashy leg-man in a beer gang who are wiped out by a more powerful mob. With incidents drawn from the lives of Hymie Weiss and Louis Altieri (both enemies of Al Capone) the movie is less grandiose than **Scarface** or **Little Caesar**, in that its protagonist, for all his moments of success, is a strong-arm soldier rather than a would-be gang boss. In a fashion still in vogue as late as **GoodFellas**, the film essentially shows the rackets as a combination of hard-nosed business and irresponsible lifestyle, best summed up by the moment, based on Altieri, when Powers combines honour and sadism by executing the horse responsible

for the death of his gangland mentor. Cagney, establishing his screen image, is constantly on the move, flashing his grin and peculiarly aggressive mock-thump gestures. The movie takes advantage of his natural

ABOVE Uma Thurman, *Pulp Fiction*

entirely Tarantino's. Whereas *Reservoir Dogs* was about group dynamics, *Pulp Fiction* is essentially about giving its individual characters the space to breath, and die. Other differences between the two films are the filming, which, with its wide wide-screen shots and looming close-ups, is far more mannered in *Pulp Fiction*, and the involvement Tarantino asks of the audience. Although Tarantino partially distances the characters from the audience, they are presented as would-be heroes, particularly Travolta's Vincent Vega and Jackson's Jules Winfield. Accordingly, Travolta's death halfway through the film (which in real time comes after the film's climax), is a real shock, and gives an added dimension to Jackson's decision to quit as a hit man. Roth and Plummer, acting like refugees from *Reservoir Dogs*, first discussing, then attempting, the hold-up of a diner, bookend the stories of hit-men Travolta and Jackson, their boss (Rhames), his wife (Thurman) and Willis, a boxer owned by Rhames. In the amoral world they inhabit, conversation is the touchstone to character. Thus we know Vincent Vega is likeable (and limited) not merely because he's played by Travolta but because he is more interested in the European names for hamburgers than in Europe itself, and that Jackson is a chilling character because he has ritualised his dispensing of death with a speech from Ezekiel, and that he can change his life when he disavows the speech as mere words. The film is uneven. The bizarre speech of Walken to the young Willis as he gives him the watch of his dead father, though compelling, seems out of place. Similarly, the episode in which Rhames and Willis are attacked by a pair of hillbilly racists feels as though it is included to legitimise the attitude to violence taken in the rest of the film. That said, some of the films tropes – the paralleling of the heart stimulation Travolta gives Thurman after she overdoses with his careful retreat from romance/sex with her, discussed in terms of foot massage – are beautifully worked out. Travolta and Jackson take the chances the script offers them perfectly. The film's lasting effect on Hollywood was that talk as much as action could be a mark of character. PH

1994/154m/A Band Apart-Jersey Films/ *p* Lawrence Bender/*d/co-s* Quentin Tarantino/*co-s* Roger Avary/*c* Andrzej Sekula/*lp* John Travolta, Samuel L. Jackson, Uma Thurman, Harvey Keitel, Tim Roth, Amanda Plummer, Ving Rhames,

ABOVE John Travolta, Samuel L. Jackson, *Pulp Fiction*

Christopher Walken, Bruce Willis, Quentin Tarantino.

Putapela/Money's Bitch

Barcelona's middle-class suburbs are the setting for a struggle between two gangs over control of the prostitution racket. The rival gang leaders, one of whom has a sidekick called Scarface, are manipulated by the beautiful Pilar (Ros) who is presented as the real villain of the piece rather than the pimps and the thugs. Bayona provided the story and co-wrote this virulently misogynist feature in which a scheming bitch introduces business efficiency into prostitution and manipulates the men into massacring each other. One reading of the film suggests that Spain under Franco may well have been a brothel but at least women were kept in their place. The lethal Pilar shows what happens when repressive machismo loses control over Pandora's box. PW

1981/Spain/94m/Teide-Llanterna/ *d/co-s* Jordi Bayona/*co-s* Andreu Martin/ *c* Carlos Gusi/*lp* Mireia Ros, Ovidi Montllor, Teresa Estrada, Walter Cots, Arnau Vilardebo.

Q

Quai des brumes

In Le Havre Gabin, a deserter from the French army, becomes involved with the underworld. He is trapped by the police and is eventually shot down when his love for a woman forces him to make a move. Gabin, as the deserter, is an icon of the stoical pessimism which became the mark of the French *film noir*. He had already perfected his persona in **Pépé le Moko**, which had a very similar plot. Working entirely within the studio, Carné creates an emotionally charged poetic realism. So powerful was the atmosphere of fatalism which the film conveyed that a Vichy spokesman later blamed it for France's defeat in the war. EB

1938/89m/Ciné-Alliance/*p* Gregor Rabinovitch/*d* Marcel Carné/*s* Jacques Prévert/*c* Eugen Schufftan/*m* Maurice Jaubert/*lp* Jean Gabin, Michèle Morgan, Michel Simon, Pierre Brasseur.

Que la bête meure/The Beast Must Die

Chabrol followed the captivating **La Femme infidèle** with this equally ambivalent thriller about a writer of children's stories, Charles (Duchaussoy) who sets out to kill the driver who killed his young son in a traffic accident. He finds the culprit in Paul (Yanne), a brutally tyrannical garage owner in La Rochelle, and cynically starts an affair with Hélène (Cellier) to worm his way into the family. The plot twists and turns as the two men stalk and seek to outmanoeuvre each other (including, literally, a spectacular cliff-hanger sequence) until the villain apparently by accident drinks a lethal potion from his medicine cabinet. But Paul was such a beast that when Charles is arrested for the killing (by a cop played by the director Pialat), the man's young son claims to have killed his own father. The ending sees the released Charles sailing away in a small boat never to return, having taken responsibility for the murder to save the boy who had become his surrogate son. As in *La Femme infidèle*, Chabrol's meticulous *mise en scène* and plotting tracks the emergence of contradictory emotions as good (love) comes from evil (murder and hatred), but neither impulse is able to overcome the rigours of fate however much the characters seek to control the course of events. In this respect, Chabrol's real master is Fritz Lang rather than the often cited Hitchcock. PW

1969/France, Italy/110m/Les Films de la Boétie-Rizzoli/*p* André Genovès/*d/s* Claude Chabrol/*orig* Nicholas Blake *The Beast Must Die/c* Jean Rabier/*m* Pierre Jansen, Brahms/*lp* Michel Duchaussoy, Jean Yanne, Caroline Cellier, Anouk Ferjac, Marc di Napoli, Maurice Pialat.

ABOVE AND LEFT Jean Gabin, *Quai des brumes*

Queen, Ellery

Ellery Queen was created by cousins Manfred B. Lee (1905–71) and Frederic Dannay (given name Daniel Nathan, 1905–82) as the hero of *The Roman Hat Mystery* in 1928 for a mystery novel competition sponsored by *McLure's* magazine. Unusually the authors took the name of their detective, who was to subsequently feature in 39 novels, as their pseudonym. Lee and Dannay later briefly adopted the pseudonym of Barnaby Ross for a four-strong series of novels featuring retired actor Drury Lane. Queen the writer later became equally well known as an anthologist (primarily through *Ellery Queen's Mystery Magazine*, founded in 1941) and commentator on detective fiction. The early novels drew on **Philo Vance** in the level of erudition they gave Ellery Queen. However, Queen was far more democratic in his dispersal of information. Moreover the novels were fairer with their readers. The first 11 even went so far as to offer a challenge to the reader, which was printed in the books at a stage when the reader was in possession of all the relevant information. While the early Queen novels highlighted the 'dying message' of the novel's victim, from *Calamity Town* (1942) onwards the novels became less puzzle-oriented and 'Golden Age' in their approach and more inclined to what critic Julian Symons has called 'the crime novel'. However, due to Queen's unwillingness as author to give up Queen the character the late novels were caught between two stools, in which realistic events are investigated by an unbelievable figure. It was primarily as publisher and commentator that Queen represented a bridge from the detective novel to the crime novel. *Queen's Quorum* (1951, revised 1969) is a widely respected annotated list of the 125 most important volumes of crime/detective short stories selected by Queen.

Queen the character fared less well on the screen. The central character of one the most successful series of detective novels ever written, he was the star of one of the least successful ever film series, the gap between the two reputations speaking volumes about the impetus and attraction of the detective in literary and cinematic fiction. Donald Cook was the first screen Queen in the minor *The Spanish Cape Mystery* (1935, novel 1935). He was followed by

ABOVE Bob Elliott, Bill Murray, *Quick Change*

comedian Eddie Quillan in the mediocre *The Mandarin Mystery* (1937, novel *The Chinese Orange Mystery*, 1934). More substantial was the Columbia series starring Ralph Bellamy as Ellery Queen, Charley Grapewin as his Inspector father, Margaret Lindsay as his Girl Friday Nikki, and James Burke as Inspector Queen's dim-witted aide. However, from the start the character, despite the film's title, *Ellery Queen, Master Detective* (1940, novel *The Door Between*, 1937), was a comic bumbler. William Gargan replaced Bellamy in 1942 for *A Close Call for Ellery Queen* (1942, novel *The Dragon's Teeth*, 1939). Gargan's three efforts as Queen were undistinguished, and his last outing, *Enemy Agents Meet Ellery Queen*, (1942), in which Queen battled Axis spies, was also the last in the short-lived series.

Queen, who had appeared on radio from 1939 onwards, transferred to television in 1949 where he was impersonated by Richard Hart (1949), Lee Bowman (1950–4), Hugh Marlow, who had previously played him on the radio (1954–8), George Nader (1958) and Lee Phillips (1959). In 1971 Peter Lawford played an Anglicised Queen to little effect in the telefilm *Don't Look Behind You*. In 1972 French director Claude Chabrol made the best film derived from a Queen novel, *La Décade prodigieuse* (novel, *Ten Day's Wonder*, 1948). In 1975 Richard Levinson and William Link co-wrote and produced a telefilm with Jim Hutton as Queen. Set in 1947 it revived the challenge to the reader of

the early novels and radio shows and led to the short-lived television series, *Ellery Queen*. PH

Quick Change

Enjoyable New York-set bank caper comedy which sees balloon-carrying clown Murray, his body rigged with dynamite, heist a bank of a million dollars and execute a clever getaway, to the confusion and annoyance of

grizzled cop Robards. The latter half of the plot follows Murray and his partners, girl-friend Davis and loveable buffoon Quaid, as they attempt to make their way to the airport through every characteristic NYC obstacle (scuzzy street types, mafia bag men, muggers, by-the-book bus drivers, etc.). En route, the trio engage in some amusing personal discussions and eventually make it to the airport only to be confronted with another set of bizarre complications and delays. It is easy to see that writer Franklin and co-producer Murray had fun in their co-directing work. TV

1990/88m/WB/*p* Robert Greenhut, Bill Murray/*d* Howard Franklin, Bill Murray/ *s* Howard Franklin/*c* Michael Chapman/*m* Randy Edelman/*lp* Bill Murray, Geena Davis, Randy Quaid, Jason Robards.

Quick Millions

A superior gangster drama from the genre's first cycle, this features a then relatively unknown Tracy as an ambitious truck driver who climbs to the top of the racketeering business by preying on organised business. Brown's tight direction makes the most out of a gangland rise-and-fall story typical of the era while Tracy's tough racketeer characterisation helped project him to stardom. This was Brown's first film as director; it also featured an early gangster appearance by a pre-**Scarface** Raft. TV

ABOVE George Walcott, Richard Denning, George Sanders, *Quiet Please Murder*

1931/69m/FOX/*d*/*co-s* Rowland Brown/*co-s* Courtenay Terrett, John Wray/*c* Joseph August/*lp* Spencer Tracy, Marguerite Churchill, Sally Eilers, George Raft.

Quiet Please Murder

This is a remarkably tight, non-formula B picture, affording George Sanders one of his definitive roles, as a mild-mannered bibliophile who is also a master forger and casual murderer. His colossal schemes are flawed by his self-aware masochism, a neurotic compulsion explained in deliriously cod-Freudian terms that drives him to flirt always with the possibility of capture and finally leads him, as he is arrested and faces the possibility of the rope, to murmur in ecstasy, 'oh, to die in terror!' After an introductory passage in which Sanders steals a volume of *Hamlet* annotated by Richard Burbage and sells forgeries to unscrupulous collectors, the film turns into a clever variation on the old dark house theme. All the characters – including a vest-pocket Sam Spade (Denning), who may not be as crooked as he seems – are trapped in a library during a bogus murder investigation carried out by Sanders and his gang in disguise as a homicide team. Foulger, in a rare sympathetic role, is fine as the meek librarian who swiftly turns from milquetoast into ARP martinet when the blackout is called for. Larkin, making his directorial debut, was a prolific screenwriter of Fox B pictures, working on some of the best Charlie Chans and other intriguingly off-beat items (*Bermuda Mystery*, 1944), but he followed up this striking start with only one further B picture, the minor *Circumstantial Evidence* (1945). KN

1942/70m/FOX/*p* Ralph Dietrich/*d*/*s* John Larkin/*c* Joseph MacDonald/*m* Arthur Lange/*lp* George Sanders, Gail Patrick, Richard Denning, Sidney Blackmer, Lynne Roberts.

R

The Racket

In *The Racket* Meighan is an honest police captain, Wolheim a bootlegger who has local politicians safely in his pocket, and Prévost a chorine who loathes Wolheim and pursues his young brother to annoy him. When Meighan arrests Wolheim, the politicians have him released, and Meighan is transferred to a quiet backwater before finally getting his man in the end. By the mid-1930s that would be a routine script, but in 1928, though the film betrayed its stage origins, it broke new ground. Indeed the original play by Bartlett Cormack was initially banned in Chicago so explicit was the attack on corrupt local government. In the New York run of the play (and briefly in Los Angeles) the part of the bootlegger was played by Edward G. Robinson. Both film and play placed its action firmly in Chicago, not, as **Underworld** had done, in an anonymous great city. Hence its attack on corrupt local government could clearly be read as aimed at the notorious mayor, 'Big Bill' Thompson. It was Thompson who protected the Capone mob, and Wolheim's character, Italianate, nattily dressed, woman-hating, is unmistakably meant to be **Capone**. Similarly the scene of the gangster funeral, where Wolheim in a memorable moment objects to a street organ which is disturbing the solemn occasion, would have taken audiences back to the lavish funeral of Capone's slaughtered rival, O'Bannion. There was a lacklustre remake in 1951. JL

1928/7646ft/Caddo/*d* Lewis Milestone/ *s* Harry Behn, Del Andrews, Bartlett Cormack/*c* Tony Gaudio/*lp* Thomas Meighan, Marie Prévost, Louis Wolheim, George Stone, John Darrow, Skeets Gallagher.

Racket Busters

The trucking business racket in New York City was the focus of this Warner Bros. gangster drama featuring Bogart as the head racketeer pursued by special prosecutor Abel. Bogart's gangster role was typical of the parts Warners handed him during the late 1930s, but Abel's New York prosecutor is of interest because his character is clearly (though for legal reasons not named) based on real-life, racket-busting New York District Attorney Thomas E. Dewey. Otherwise, plot and characters move along conventional paths. TV

1938/65m/WB/*p* Samuel Bischoff/*d* Lloyd Bacon/*s* Robert Rossen, Leonardo Bercovici/ *c* Arthur Edeson/*m* Adolph Deutsch/*lp* Humphrey Bogart, George Brent, Gloria Dickson, Walter Abel.

Rackets

The criminal connotations of the words 'racket' and 'racketeer' date back to the late nineteenth century, when New York gangs would hold dances called 'rackets' and sell wedges of tickets to merchants who weren't expected to attend but were afraid of the damage their businesses might sustain if they refused to make the purchase. This scam, a harmless variation of which was much employed by Phil Silvers' Sergeant Bilko (who once held a 'Forgive and Forget Dance'

ABOVE *Racket Busters*

in honour of Benedict Arnold's birthday), has come to stand for all the other money-making practices which make organised crime a vastly profitable business. The term is extremely common in connection with various forms of crime and crime prevention, as is suggested by such titles as **The Racket**, *Racketeers in Exile* (1937), **Racket Busters**, *Racketeers of the Range* (1939), *The Racket Man* (1944), the TV series *Racket Squad* (1950–3) and *The Racket* (1951).

The system of protection and patronage features in many mafia movies, and comes under especial examination in the flashback sections of **The Godfather Part II**, though comparatively few films (*The Frightened City*, 1962, is one) deal exclusively with 'protection', the archetypal racket, as opposed to the many screen depictions of such activities as prostitution, drug-dealing and boot-legging. These are not strictly rackets since they actually offer some service, no matter how degraded, in return for the mug's money, while the essence of a real racket is that it should extort money from its victims and give back nothing in return, which, by extension, explains the use of the term in connection with any crooked business venture, like the insider trading of *Wall Street* (1987). Aside from the protection racket, the criminal activity most associated with the term is gambling, as in the numbers racket, most effectively examined in **Force of Evil**,

and the sports racket, as exposed in *The Set-Up* (1949), **The Harder They Fall**, *Eight Men Out* (1988) and **The Grifters**. Most other rackets have rated at least one *Crime Does Not Pay* short subject apiece: slot machines (*Jack Pot*, 1940), loan-sharking (*Money to Loan*, 1939), illegal adoption (*Women in Hiding*, 1940). KN

See also **Boxing**; **Drugs**; **Gambling**; **Prohibition**; **Prostitution**.

Radio Detectives

The first detective series on American radio was probably *Detectives Black and Blue* in 1931. From that time until all drama on commercial network radio ceased in the mid-1960s, it was more common for films to be adapted for the wireless than *vice versa*. Almost without exception programmes created for radio transferred to the cinema as **serials** or B-features. The earliest featured **The Shadow**, first identified by that name in 1932 and later played by Orson Welles. It became a feature film in 1937 and a serial in 1940. Originally a newspaper cartoon strip, **Dick Tracy** debuted on radio in 1935. As portrayed by Ralph Byrd, Tracy was the most popular serial detective (1937–1941). The high-profile feature film, with Warren Beatty in the title role, came in 1990.

The Green Hornet (1936–52) was adapted as two movie serials (1939 and 1944), but

it is the 1966 television series, in which Bruce Lee played the crime-fighter's sidekick Kato, that is best known today. *Aviator Captain Midnight* (1938–49) came to the cinema in a 1942 serial. **The Crime Doctor**, which began on radio in 1940, begot a series of ten films (1943–9); Warner Baxter was the eponymous Dr Ordway in all. *The Whistler* (1942–52) was the basis of one of the most successful film series of the period (1944–8); Richard Dix was in all but one of the eight films, but as different characters. *I Love a Mystery* (1939–52), with its team of three detectives, inspired three films between 1945–6. **Dashiell Hammett**'s *The Fat Man* (1946–50) was turned into the 1950 film of that name. The last radio series to transfer to the cinema was *Dragnet* (1949–56), but it was the TV version (1952– 9) that immortalised Sgt Joe Friday (Jack Webb). Webb was also in the 1954 film and the 1969 TV movie. A parody film, with Dan Aykroyd as Friday's nephew, followed in 1987.

In Britain the first radio detective was probably Inspector Hornleigh, who had a regular slot in *Monday Night at Seven* (1937–40). He appeared in three films between 1939–41. Francis Durbridge's *Paul Temple* (1938–68) was more enduring, but his two films (1946 and 1948) were insignificant. The popular *P.C. 49* (1947–53) was also in two minor films (1949 and 1951). Ernest Dudley re-created his role as *The Armchair Detective* (1942–57) in the 1951 film of that name. Recently the BBC has adopted the American initiative of adapting films as radio plays. Kathleen Turner was brought to London for a radio version of her 1991 film *V.I. Warshawski*.

Television detectives have appeared in a handful of forgotten films. Dan Duryea played the title role in *China Smith* (1952–5) and re-created it in the 1954 film *World for Ransom*. The influential series *Peter Gunn* (1958–61) reached the screen in 1967 as *Gunn*. During the British mania for film spin-offs from TV series, *The Sweeney* (1974–8) was turned into two films (1976 and 1978). Today, although television detectives remain popular, particularly in Britain, the custom is to make feature-length episodes that are not released theatrically. DM

Raffles, A.J.

Created as a criminal inversion of Sherlock Holmes by Ernest William Hornung (1866–1921), Sir Arthur Conan Doyle's brother-in-law, A. J. Raffles is the epitome of the gen-

ABOVE Rackets: Howland Chamberlin (left), John Garfield (right), *Force of Evil*

ABOVE John Rogers, Ronald Colman, Alison Skipworth, *Raffles* (1930)

in *Baffles, Gentleman Burglar* (1914), and a run of British knockabout shorts, from *What Happened to Pimple, the Gentleman Burglar* (1914) through *Mrs Raffles, Nee Pimple* (1915) to *Saving Raffles* (1916), featured comics Fred and Joe Evans as bungling crooks named Pimple and Raffles. All subsequent American screen appearances of the character have been stagy adaptations of the Hornung and Presbury play. These include L. Lawrence Weber's *Raffles, the Amateur Cracksman* (1917), with John Barrymore, later a screen Holmes, in the lead, King Baggot's *Raffles, the Amateur Cracksman* (1925), with House Peters as Raffles and Freeman Wood as Bunny; Harry D'Abbadie D'Arrast and George Fitzmaurice's *Raffles* (1930), with Ronald Colman as Raffles, Bramwell Fletcher as Bunny and David Torrence as Mackenzie. A later version is Sam Wood's *Raffles* (1940), with David Niven as Raffles, Douglas Walton as Bunny and Dudley Digges as Mackenzie. Despite apt casting, none of these stage adaptations have achieved much status, strangled as they are by the drawing room-bound dramatics of a play which has very little of the dash and excitement of Hornung's best stories.

tleman crook, and forerunner of such adventurers as **Arsène Lupin**, **Boston Blackie**, the **Lone Wolf** and the **Saint**. A cricket-playing amateur thief and upper-class patriot who lives in London's exclusive Albany, his exploits are narrated by a Watson-style side-kick Bunny Manders, who used to be his public school fag. Raffles first appeared in a series of stories published in the *Strand* magazine in the 1890s, collected in *The Amateur Cracksman* (1899, *aka Raffles, The Amateur Cracksman*), constantly lifting jewels from the undeserving as he literally outclasses his less well-bred criminal rivals and his frustrated nemesis, the dour Inspector Mackenzie. Further stories appeared in Hornung's collections *The Black Mask* (1901) and *A Thief in the Night* (1905), which concludes with the hero redeeming his misdeeds by dying in the service of his country during the Boer War. Hornung also added to the slim canon a less-successful novel *Mr Justice Raffles* (1909) and two plays, *Raffles, The Amateur Cracksman* (1903), with Eugene W. Presbury, and *A Visit From Raffles* (1909), with Charles Sansom.

Raffles was revived in a long-running series by Barry Perowne (Philip Atkey), who presents a Raffles living on into the twentieth century, his larceny sometimes muted into Saint-style heroics, in five novels, including *Raffles vs. Sexton Blake* (1937) and *Raffles and the Key Man* (1940), and several short story collections including *Raffles Under Sentence* (1936) and three, *Raffles Revisited* (1974), *Raffles of the Albany* (1976) and *Raffles of the M. C. C.* (1979), which revert to the 1890s for their settings. Other footnotes to the Amateur Cracksman's career include Graham Greene's play *The Return of A. J. Raffles: An Edwardian Comedy Based Somewhat Loosely on E. W. Hornung's Characters in 'The Amateur Cracksman'* (1975), Peter Tremayne's novel *The Return of Raffles* (1981), Philip José Farmer's science fiction pastiche 'The Adventure of the Sore Bridge' (in *The Book of Philip José Farmer*, 1973), and Kim Newman's *Anno Dracula* (1992), which features Raffles but gives a larger role to Inspector Mackenzie.

Raffles was a familiar character in early silents, with J. Barney Sherry appearing in *The Adventures of Raffles, The Amateur Cracksman* (1905), an American short, Danish (1910) and Italian (1911) films simply called *Raffles*, and most notably, played by Forrest Holger-Madsen, opposing Sherlock Holmes (Viggo Larsen) in several episodes of a Danish Holmes. Mack Sennett spoofed the character

ABOVE David Niven, *Raffles* (1940)

Raising Arizona—Rashomon

Gerald Ames and Lionel Watts are Raffles and Bunny in *Mr Justice Raffles* (1921), a British silent directed by Ames and Gaston Quiribet, while the roles were taken by George Barraud and Claud Allister in *The Return of Raffles* (1932), a British quickie directed by Mansfield Markham. There have also been Italian (*Raffles, ladra gentiluomo*, 1920) and Mexican films (*Raffles/El Raffles Mexicano*, 1958), the latter with Rafael Bertrand as Raffles. Horace Braham, Frank Allenby and Jeremy Clyde have played the character on radio, and the major television adaptation has been in a TV pilot, *Raffles, the Amateur Cracksman* (1975), with Anthony Valentine as Raffles, Christopher Strauli as Bunny and James Maxwell as Mackenzie, followed by thirteen episodes of *Raffles* (1977), with Valentine and Strauli supported by Victor Carin as the Yard man. The most recent screen appearance of the Amateur Cracksman, like his first, involves him with his alter ego, in *Incident at Victoria Falls*, an episode of the television miniseries *Sherlock Holmes: The Golden Years* (1991), with Alan Coates as A. J. Raffles, hiding out in Africa after faking his death and involved with Lillie Langtry (Jenny Seagrove), uncharacteristically innocent of all wrong-doing for once and rescued by Holmes (Christopher Lee) from an unjust charge. KN

Raising Arizona

Forsaking the straightforward *noir* of **Blood Simple**, the Coen brothers opt for an offbeat, highly stylised approach in this kidnapping farce. Cage is a recidivist robber who is saved from prison by Hunter as the cop who falls in love with him. Their married idyll in a trailer park lacks only one thing: a baby. Since they can't have one of their own they resolve to redistribute wealth by lifting one of the quintuplets of a local furniture-store magnate. Goodman and Forsythe are a pair of escaped cons who become besotted with the baby, and there's a Hell's Angel biker who roars up and down the Arizona highways attempting to reclaim the child for its parents. The film proved too quirky and unexpected for critics, who wanted a repeat of **Blood Simple**, but Cage in particular gives a wonderfully demented performance. EB

1987/92m/FOX/*p* Ethan Coen, Mark Silverman/*d* Joel Coen/*s* Ethan and Joel Coen/*c* Barry Sonnenfeld/*m* Carter Burwell/*lp* Nicholas Cage, Holly Hunter, Trey Wilson, John Goodman, William Forsythe.

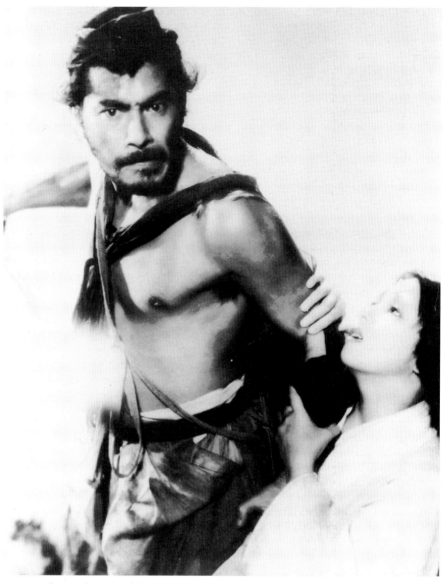

ABOVE Toshiro Mifune, Machiko Kyo, *Rashomon*

Rashomon

This anti-whodunit was the Japanese cinema's first world-wide success. Set in Kyoto in the twelfth century, it tells of a rape and a murder from four different perspectives. A priest (Chiaki) retells the story provided by the rapist, Tajomaru (Mifune), executed after a trial; he then tells the woman's (Kyo) version; through a female medium, he then provides the account given by the dead samurai husband (Mori). Finally, a woodcutter (Shimura), who claims to have witnessed the events in the woods, tells his story. All versions agree that the bandit raped the woman, that the husband died from a stabbing and that the wife disappeared, but the stories don't agree about who did the killing: all three participants in the events claim to have killed. The film is an extended reflection on the notion of narrative truth, playing with point of view, camera-style (courtesy of the extraordinary skills of the great Miyagawa) and narrative voice to undermine the status of each narrator. In the end, it is not the reconstruction of the crime nor the assignation of guilt which matters, but the fact that each narrator presents a version of events which, although acknowledging crime, nevertheless presents the teller in the best possible light. Received in Japan as a thoroughly westernised movie and in the West as an intellectual puzzle, the film's obsession with 'saving face' marks its cultural origins clearly, a dimension lacking in the

Hollywood remake, Martin Ritt's *Outrage* (1964), starring Paul Newman as the rapist, Claire Bloom as the raped woman, Laurence Harvey as the husband and Edward G. Robinson as the narrator. PW

1950/Japan/88m/Daiei/*p* Jingo Minoru/ *d*/*co-s* Akira Kurosawa/*co-s* Shinobu Hashimoto/*orig* 'Rashomon' and 'In A Grove' Ryonosuke Akutagawa/*c* Kazuo Miyagawa/ *m* Fumio Hayasaka/*lp* Toshiro Mifune, Masayuki Mori, Machiko Kyo, Takashi Shimura, Minoru Chiaki, Kichijiro Ueda.

Raw Deal

Made the same year as **T-Men**, and using the same principal talents, *Raw Deal* lacks the 'semi-documentary' apparatus of the other film. A tale of dishonour among thieves, it describes a downward spiral of violence and pessimism. O'Keefe, who breaks jail to pursue a vendetta against the confederates who framed him, has some ostensible resemblance to the 'three-time loser' of **You Only Live Once**, but there is no comparable sense of his being a victim of circumstances. His bringing about the demise of his adversaries, threateningly portrayed by Ireland and Burr, carries with it the corollary of his own impending death, and the blazing building in which the action climaxes carries symbolic overtones of the flames of hell. The fact that the narration is provided by O'Keefe's discarded mistress (Trevor) adds a further layer of disenchantment. Alton's camerawork provides near-expressionistic effects. TP

1948/79m/Eagle-Lion/*p* Edward Small/ *d* Anthony Mann/*s* Leopold Atlas, John C. Higgins/*c* John Alton/*m* Paul Sawtell/*lp* Dennis O'Keefe, Claire Trevor, Raymond Burr, Marsha Hunt, John Ireland.

Ray, Jean (1887–1964)

Born in Ghent, Belgium in 1887 as Raymond Jean-Marie De Kremer, Ray has become a legendary figure. Stories circulate around him, often encouraged or invented by the author, claiming he was a cut-throat pirate in the China Seas who retired to his native Ghent to write lugubrious yet exhilarating stories. Frequenting circus milieus while working for the municipal council in Ghent and writing both in Dutch (the Belgian variant) and French, his prolific journalistic and short-story output includes a spell as editor of a film magazine in 1919 and again in 1931. Briefly jailed for embezzlement (1927–9), he used the name John Flanders as well as Jean Ray from 1930 onwards. In the crime genre, his main contribution is the Harry Dickson series (1931–40), initially fortnightly, then monthly. The series consists of 99 short novels, 21 short stories and 19 brief tales, with 6 more novels of which authorship is uncertain. At the same time, he also wrote and published an entire weekly comic book, *Bravo*. The Harry Dickson stories, of which about half are horror and fantasy stories, the other half crime and detection tales, originated with a German publisher who wanted his apocryphal **Sherlock Holmes** dime novels to be

translated into French while avoiding copyright problems with the Conan Doyle estate. Ray simply wrote completely new stories, usually in one go without corrections, making sure that each one contained a reference (often a very cursory allusion) to the scene depicted on the cover of the dime novels. Ray's Harry Dickson, flanked by an amanuensis called Tom, also lives in Baker Street, but his character is miles removed from the puritanical, heroin-addicted Holmes. Dickson is more an intrepid *bon vivant* who moves through hallucinatory spaces in which the atmosphere can change within one sentence from detection story to horror story, creating a unique blend probably best described as gothic surrealism. All manner of terrifying experiences and outlandish crimes, mostly set in London's fog-bound or dank and rainy docklands, are combined with obsessive references to the earthy gastronomic delights enjoyed by his characters. At the same time, the tales exude a Victorian sense of sexuality (except in the horror stories which at times border on the orgiastic) and a disturbingly casual kind of racism. To date, only a few of Ray's horror stories have been filmed (the best being Harry Kümel's *Malpertuis*, 1972, a story about a strange house in which a taxidermist keeps the weakened Greek Gods sown into the bodies of Ghent burghers). For many years Alain Resnais cherished the idea of filming the adventures of Harry Dickson and, more recently, a television series featuring Dickson has been planned but not as yet brought to fruition. The Dickson stories remain one of the crime genre's most mysterious unused treasures. PW

Rear Window

Jeff Jeffries (Stewart), a magazine photographer with a broken leg, is confined to a wheelchair in his apartment. Looked after by his nurse Stella (Ritter) and his fashion model girl-friend Lisa Fremont (Kelly), all he can do for entertainment is to look out of the back window and, using his binoculars and a camera, watch the routine activities of his neighbours. He focuses on Lars Thorwald (Burr), who he begins to suspect of murdering his wife. Lisa agrees to take on the active part of the investigation and the plot starts to unwind. Based on the **Cornell Woolrich** story *It Had To Be Murder*, the film seduces its audiences into the guilty pleasures of voyeurism. Confined to a single set, the camera converts the view from the window into a teeming landscape of characters, a different story in every window, and Hitchcock

ABOVE Toshiro Mifune, Daisuke Kato, *Rashomon*

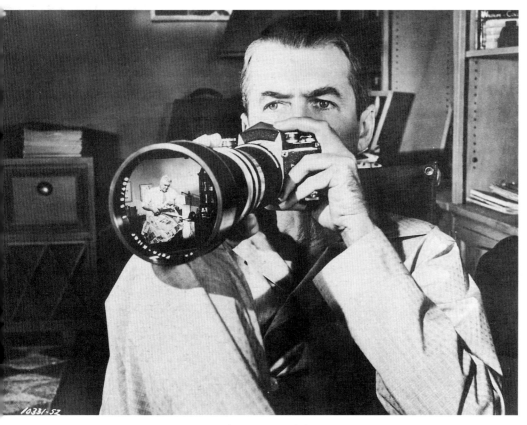

ABOVE James Stewart, Raymond Burr, *Rear Window*

sketches out each mini-drama with an economy which convinces, but doesn't interfere with the main narrative. MP

1954/112m/PAR/*p* Alfred Hitchcock/*d* Alfred Hitchcock/*s* John Michael Hayes/*c* Robert Burks/*m* Franz Waxman/*lp* James Stewart, Grace Kelly, Wendell Corey, Thelma Ritter, Raymond Burr.

Rebecca

Du Maurier's novel formed the basis for Hitchcock's first American picture. *Rebecca* owes more to the romantic tradition of *Jane Eyre* than to either the British or American crime novel. Hitchcock later regretted that he had been unable to incorporate much of his trademark humour, but the film is the better for that and more a melodrama about fearful women than a film about weak men fending off reality with wit. *Rebecca* is the story of Maxim De Winter (Olivier) and his two wives. The first is Rebecca herself, dead in mysterious circumstances; did De Winter murder her? The second – she is never given a name – is played by Fontaine as a fearful but trusting innocent, easy prey to the machinations of De Winter's scheming housekeeper Mrs Danvers, brilliantly played

by Anderson. While Manderley, the big old Cornish house in which the melodrama is played out, is in the tradition of old dark houses which Hitchcock was later to exploit to the full in **Psycho**, the centre of the film is the achieving not the losing of identity, which makes Fontaine's lack of a name all the more germane. EB

1940/130m/Selznick International/*p* David O. Selznick/*d* Alfred Hitchcock/*s* Robert E. Sherwood, Joan Harrison/*c* George Barnes/*m* Franz Waxman/*lp* Laurence Olivier, Joan Fontaine, George Sanders, Judith Anderson, Nigel Bruce.

The Reckless Moment

Based on a Elisabeth Sanxay Holding story *The Blank Wall*, Ophuls's tense melodrama sees concerned mother Bennett become involved in murder and blackmail in order to save daughter Brooks from the consequences of a romance with an unsavoury older man (Strudwick). However, it is Mason's underworld type, working for the blackmailer while feeling sympathy for Bennett, that remains the centre of interest for the latter half. TV

1949/81m/COL/*p* Walter Wanger/*d* Max Ophuls/*s* Henry Garson, Robert W. Soderberg, Mel Dinelli, Robert E. Kent/*c* Burnett Guffey/*m* Hans Salter/*lp* James Mason, Joan Bennett, Geraldine Brooks, Shepperd Strudwick.

Red Heat

A prime example of 'high concept' film-making, *Red Heat* is one of a cycle of late 1980s cop movies featuring an 'odd couple' duo of ill-assorted partners. Its gimmick is that the film was, in the glasnost era of the former Soviet Union, the first American production to be afforded location shooting facilities in Moscow. Some atmospheric early sequences are set there, involving the botched arrest of a drug dealer (O'Ross), during which a brother officer of Schwarzenegger's police captain is killed. The scene then shifts to Chicago, where O'Ross is sprung from custody, and in a rather mechanical succession of plot inventions Schwarzenegger and slobbish local detective Belushi join forces to bring him to book. Though the handling is not without force, the central implausibility of a Soviet cop on the rampage in America is never really assimilated. Instead the film appears to adopt the curious ideological position of implicitly endorsing the 'unfettered' police methods of the USSR. TP

1988/104m/Carolco/*p* Walter Hill, Gordon Carroll/*d* Walter Hill/*s* Walter Hill, Harry Kleiner, Troy Kennedy Martin/*c* Matthew F. Leonetti/*m* James Horner/*lp* Arnold Schwarzenegger, James Belushi, Peter Boyle, Ed O'Ross, Gina Gershon.

Regeneration

Owen Kildare published *My Mamie Rose: the Story of My Regeneration*, in New York in 1903. Kildare told of his wretched childhood in the East Side slums, of his involvement in the local gangs, and of his reformation and education at the hands of a schoolteacher named Marie Deering. A play followed, and then, in 1915, Walsh's film. Walsh and his co-writer, his half-brother Carl Harbaugh, took liberties with the material. Marie Deering became a bored socialite who visited the slums from idle curiosity, and found her life changed by the experience. The real Marie died of natural causes whereas Walsh's Marie died from a gangster's bullet. The result is one of the greatest gangster films, and perhaps the most convincing picture of the underside of a great city ever to reach the screen. Walsh made his film in the real locations of Kildare's story, enormously helped by Georges Benoit's remarkable camerawork, and used the local population, gang members included, as extras, which gave him an extraordinary array of memorable faces. The film is also notable for its modern tone, which celebrated success for its own sake. The film was reissued in 1919, then lost for 60 years, and rediscovered just in time to prevent its disintegration. JL

1915/5 reels/FOX/*d*/*co-s* Raoul Walsh/ *co-s* Carl Harbaugh/*orig* Owen Kildare/ *c* Georges Benoit/*lp* Rockcliffe Fellowes, Anna Q. Nilsson, William Sheer, Carl Harbaugh, James Marcus, Maggie Weston.

A reinha diaba/Devil Queen

Described by the director as a pop-gay-black-thriller, the plot of this unintentionally comic movie tells of a vicious gay mobster known as the Reinha Diaba (Gonçalves) who rules Rio de Janeiro's drugs and vice rackets. He spends most of his time dolling himself up and slashing faces with razors to enforce discipline. Deciding to trick the police, his gang groom the inoffensive Bereco (Nercessian) as a bogus crime king. But the stooge identifies with his role and a gang war develops between him and the gay mob, enlivened by some gratuitously sadistic scenes like the gay hoods torturing a woman. Medeiros's garish and fetishistic imagery received the best cinematography award in Brazil. PW

1973/Brazil/106m/Lanterna Magica-R.F. Farias-Ventania-Do Lirio-Ipanema/ *p* Mauricio Nabuco/*d*/*co-s* Antonio Carlos Fontoura/*co-s* Plinio Marcos/*c* Jose Medeiros/*m* Guilherme Vaz/*lp* Milton Gonçalves, Odette Lara, Stepan Nercessian, Nelson Xavier, Iara Cortes, Wilson Grey.

El reino de los gangsters

Orol was one of the artisanal prototypes of Sylvester Stallone's Rocky figure: an abjectly sentimental megalomaniac presented as the saviour of family and country underneath his brutalised appearance. Orol controlled all aspects of the production and marketing of this self-indulgent but successful feature. In keeping with the times, Orol pushed the melodramatic aspects of his scenes to their extremes. In order to free his gangster-ridden country, Johnny Carmenta (Orol) becomes a Zorro figure heading his own gang. Before triumphing, Carmenta has to kill his brother-in-law (Zambrano) for seducing his sister (Prado); a second sister, ignoring his identity, tries to poison him and Helen (Carmina), his lover, lures him into a trap where he has to confront his policeman-brother (Arvide) who, also ignoring Carmenta's real identity, shoots him. Carmenta dies, making all who wronged him very sorry for their behaviour. Affecting the mannerisms of an angelic **Al Capone** guarding the nation and the family's honour, Orol also peppered his films with sala-

ABOVE Catherine Deneuve, *Repulsion*

cious night-club scenes featuring his regular co-star, Carmina. Orol simultaneously shot a second Carmenta-feature with the same cast at the Azteca studios, *Gangsters contra Charros* (released in 1949). PW

1947/Mexico/122m/España Sono/*p*/*d*/*s* Juan Orol/*c* Domingo Carillo/*lp* Juan Orol, Rosa Carmina, Lilia Prado, Manuel Arvide, Enrique Zambrano.

Repulsion

Carol (Deneuve), a Belgian manicurist living in London, left alone when her flatmate and sister (Furneaux) goes off with a married lover (Hendry), spends a week slowly going mad. She wanders around an Earl's Court flat in her night-gown, imagining clutching hands coming out of the wall, while a rabbit gradually and disgustingly decays on the sideboard in the kitchen. When the lecherous landlord (Wymark) turns up for the rent, Carol knifes him. Finally, her madness is discovered and she is taken away while nosy neighbours wander through the flat. In an unforgettable final shot, the camera closes in on a family photograph to find Carol as a little girl, staring abstractedly out beyond the audience, already twisted out of true. At the time, *Repulsion* was seen as a follow-up to

ABOVE Joan Fontaine, Judith Anderson, *Rebecca*

287

Reservoir Dogs

Alfred Hitchcock's **Psycho** – with which it shares an odd triangle, as a pair of adulterous lovers are too wrapped up in their practical problems to notice that a seemingly normal third party has gone desperately, violently insane. But Polanski takes a different approach to the horror of madness. While Anthony Perkins' Norman Bates is only revealed at the finish to be the mad killer, we follow Carol through her insanity from the first, sharing her horrific hallucinations, even understanding her reactions to an ever-so-slightly caricatured London. We are told specifically why Norman Bates has gone mad but *Repulsion* never says what it is that has driven Carol out of her mind, suggesting that it takes a lifetime of quiet abuse to make a psychopath. With Catherine Deneuve's best-ever screen performance as the fragile, breathtakingly beautiful Carol, the film terrifies by giving an audience the experience of insanity. KN

1965/GB/104m/Compton/*p* Gene Gutowski/
d/*co-s* Roman Polanski/*co-s* Gérard Brach/
c Gilbert Taylor/*m* Chico Hamilton/
lp Catherine Deneuve, Ian Hendry, John Fraser, Patrick Wymark, Yvonne Furneaux.

Reservoir Dogs

A groundbreaking film, *Reservoir Dogs* established Tarantino as a writer/director of note.

The film, which is set mostly in an abandoned warehouse, follows the disintegration of a gang after a jewel robbery goes wrong. Despite its reputation as physically violent – notably the sequence in which Madsen tortures a policeman (Kirk Baltz), which we endure in real time but do not see – it is the emotional violence of *Reservoir Dogs* that is more disturbing. Similarly, although the characters are given would-be anonymous identities from a colour chart (Mr Blue, Mr White, Mr Orange, etc.), and Tierney's Joe Cabot endlessly insists they not reveal their true identities to each other, the drama of the film is the dynamics of a group. In the beginning, seated around a table discussing the meaning of Madonna's *Like A Virgin*, they seem like refugees from *Diner* (1982), but whereas in *Diner* banter is a substitute for confrontation, in *Reservoir Dogs* it is a preparation for violence. Thrown together in the manner of a Howard Hawks film, such as *Only Angels Have Wings* (1939) or *Rio Bravo* (1958), the characters of *Reservoir Dogs* must find their identities as members of the group. The one difference is that whereas Hawks's characters aspire to professionalism, Tarantino's, with the exception of Keitel's Mr White and Roth's Mr Orange who at least aim at competence, are merely claustrophobically locked together. Like characters from a film by Jean-Luc Godard but filmed in Hawks's unfussy style, they are denied the expression of their identities, for in place of

Reservoir Dogs:
ABOVE Steve Buscemi, Harvey Keitel;
LEFT Michael Madsen, Harvey Keitel, Tim Roth, Quentin Tarantino

the traditional unfolding of plot there is only a fractured narrative. Thus finally they are as anonymous as their given names. PH

1992/99m/Dog Eat Dog Productions/
p Lawrence Bender/*d/s* Quentin Tarantino/
c Andrzej Sekula/*m* Karyn Rachtman/
lp Harvey Keitel, Tim Roth, Michael Madsen, Christopher Penn, Steve Buscemi, Lawrence Tierney, Quentin Tarantino.

Reversal of Fortune

This tightly structured drama was based on the sensational Claus von Bülow case. Irons is excellent as the inscrutable Rhode Island society figure von Bülow on trial for the attempted murder of his wealthy wife with a near-fatal dose of insulin. Close, as the wife Sunny von Bülow, narrates as well as appears in flashback sequences. Taking the story of the trial, conviction and acquittal on appeal, and the questions arising from it, Schroeder and company use (alongside the flashbacks) various different observations of the events-leading-up-to; was von Bülow guilty of murder, was he framed, or was it a suicide attempt by the emotionally self-destructive woman? TV

1990/120m/WB/*p* Edward R. Pressman, Oliver Stone/*d* Barbet Schroeder/*s* Nicholas

Kazan/*c* Luciano Tovoli/*m* Mark Isham/
lp Glenn Close, Jeremy Irons, Ron Silver.

Ride the Pink Horse

Set against the fiesta background of a small New Mexico town, this suspense outing follows the mysterious Montgomery character as he arrives in the colourful town to track down a war profiteer who was responsible for a friend's killing. Montgomery, working in the dual function of star and director, gives a sturdy performance as the hard-nosed avenger making his way around the unconventional fiesta setting, stalking and being stalked by various henchmen. The screenplay was based on the 1946 novel by **Dorothy B. Hughes**. It was remade by Don Siegel as *The Hanged Man* (1964), an early made-for-TV movie. TV

1947/100m/U/*p* Joan Harrison/*d* Robert Montgomery/*s* Ben Hecht, Charles Lederer/
c Russell Metty/*m* Frank Skinner/*lp* Robert Montgomery, Thomas Gomez, Wanda Hendrix, Andrea King.

The Ringer

Though **Edgar Wallace** himself scripted a 1928 film, this is the best version of his oft-filmed play. Curwen has the title role as the master criminal and master of disguise deter-

mined to avenge himself on crooked lawyer Dyall (who was responsible for the death of the Ringer's sister) despite his being protected night and day by the police. The result is a variant on the haunted house film in which things rarely are what they seem. Directed by Forde with a slickness and pace unusual in British films of the period, especially considering the film's stage origins, the film has an engaging relentlessness that overcomes such implausibilities as the welcome presence of the Ringer's wife (Goodner) at Dyall's house. Hokum, but enjoyable. The other versions of the film are a silent one (1928, directed by Arthur Made), another by Forde (*The Gaunt Stranger*, 1938) and Guy Hamilton's 1952 offering. The novel, *The Gaunt Stranger* (1925) came first, but it was Wallace's transformation of that into the play *The Ringer* in 1926, which was his biggest theatrical success, that led to the material being filmed. PH

1931/GB/75m/Gainsborough-British Lion/
p Michael Balcon/*d* Walter Forde/*s* Angus McPhail, Robert Stevenson/*c* Leslie Rowson/
lp Gordon Harker, Franklyn Dyall, John Longden, Patric Curwen, Carol Goodner, Henry Hallat.

The Rise and Fall of Dr Oyenusi

Ugbomah's first feature, shot in English in 16mm under extremely difficult circumstances, recounts the story of a well-known thief and gang boss who operated in Lagos in the early 70s, calling himself Dr Oyenusi. He was eventually arrested and publicly executed, showing courage in the face of death. The BBC- and theatre-trained Ugbomah glorified the character, turning him into a romantic and tragic outlaw rather than self-centred bully, a strategy that raised some eyebrows in Lagos. As nobody agreed to play the role of this gangster, Ugbomah played it himself. A real doctor called Oyenusi tried to prevent the film being made. Ugbomah went on to make some eight features, mostly action adventure stories with contemporary political overtones, including *Death of a Black President* (1983). PW

1977/Nigeria/120m/Edifosa/*p/d/s* Eddie Ugbomah/*c* Bob Davies/*m* Segun and Shina Peters/*lp* Eddie Ugbomah, Enebeli Elebuwa, Moses Ajumbi.

The Rise and Fall of Legs Diamond

Given freedom to do what he wanted so long as he did *not* follow the actual story of the 20s New York racketeer, Boetticher

ABOVE *The Ringer* (1952): Campbell Singer (left), William Hartnell (right)

made this genre piece, which echoes innumerable gangster biopics by following a protagonist from petty crookery through flamboyant success to a sordid death, into his most substantial film outside the Western cycle for which he is best known. The film is less about the familiar business of taking over the rackets through violently eliminating the competition than it is a character study of the subtly mad Jack Diamond (Danton), a dapper mobster with pistols in his waistcoat pockets who moves through the film with fancy footwork, propelled by Leonard Rosenman's ominously jaunty theme, rising to a position from which he can demand tribute from all the other crooks of Prohibition-era New York. Legs gradually divests himself of all ties, allowing the death of his dead-weight brother (Oates) to prove he cannot be touched emotionally or physically. Finally, in a sequence reflecting the corporate crime pictures of the 50s rather than the realities of the early 30s, Diamond, charm turned to boorishness, is confronted by a room full of syndicate executives who have progressed beyond his strong-arm tactics and treat crime as simply a business rather than the psycho-sexual compensatory game Diamond has been playing. Danton plays the part with hawk-faced intensity very unlike the temperamental real-life Legs, returning to the role for a cameo in *Portrait*

ABOVE James Cagney, Priscilla Lane, Gladys George, *The Roaring Twenties*

of a Mobster (1961), a biopic of **Dutch Schultz** with Vic Morrow as the criminal lead. KN

1960/101m/WB/*p* Milton Sperling/*d* Budd Boetticher/*s* Joseph Landon/*c* Lucien Ballard/*m* Leonard Rosenman/*lp* Ray

Danton, Karen Steele, Elaine Stewart, Jesse White, Simon Oakland, Warren Oates.

Roadgames

Road movies became a staple narrative formula for Australian cinema in the 70s. The major films were Michael Thornhill's *The F.J. Holden* (1976), Phil Noyce's *Backroads* (1977) and above all George Miller's *Mad Max* (1978). This, Franklin's follow up to his supernatural thriller *Patrick* (1978), features Keach as a truck driver in the Nullarbor desert between Melbourne and Perth. To avoid being arrested himself, he has to find and unmask a psycho killer and rapist driving a green van and preying on hitch hikers. The landscape scenes are handled very effectively and the film opens well but the contrived plot involving Curtis as a runaway American heiress and inept performances spoil the movie. PW

1981/Australia/100m/Quest-Essaness/ *p/d* Richard Franklin/*co-p* Barbi Taylor/ *s* Everett de Roche/*c* Vincent Monton/ *m* Brian May/*lp* Stacy Keach, Jamie Lee Curtis, Marion Edward, Grant Page, Thaddeus Smith.

The Roaring Twenties

This Warners super-production returns to the concerns of their early 30s Prohibition-era gangster movies. The picture is framed

ABOVE Ray Danton, *The Rise and Fall of Legs Diamond*

ABOVE Humphrey Bogart, James Cagney, *The Roaring Twenties*

by a stentorian narrator and extraordinary symbolic montage newsreels (directed by Don Siegel), tagging the career of protagonist Eddie Bartlett (Cagney) as something that could only happen under the conditions that existed between World War I and the New Deal. The honest, naive doughboy progresses through post-war unemployment to a rise in the booze racket, partnered with the more psychotic George (Bogart), that stalls when he is wiped out by the stock-market crash and forced back into driving a cab. The singer (Lane) with whom Eddie is obsessed marries his other war buddy (Lynn), a lawyer who wants to wipe out the left-over mobsters. In a redemptive finish Eddie guns down the cowardly George to prevent him assassinating the lawyer, and is himself shot, finally expiring on the steps of a church, ministered to by Panama (George), the blowsy broad who has stuck with him and who delivers his epitaph, 'he used to be a big shot'. Walsh effortlessly weaves together social history, romantic comedy, gang warfare, nostalgia and a great Cagney performance into one of the first period-set gangster movies, using the fashions and music of an already-bygone era to illuminate a traditional rise-and-fall story-line. Newsman Hellinger loosely based Eddie and Panama on real-life bootlegger Larry Fay (also the model for Jay Gatsby) and hostess Texas Guinan. KN

1939/106m/WB/*p* Samuel Bischoff/*d* Raoul Walsh/*s* Jerry Wald, Richard Macaulay, Robert Rossen/*orig* Mark Hellinger/*c* Ernest Haller/*m* Heinz Roemheld/*lp* James Cagney, Gladys George, Humphrey Bogart, Jeffrey Lynn, Priscilla Lane.

Robocop

Idealistic cop Murphy (Weller) is shot in near-future downtown Detroit, but the corporation which has privatised the city's law enforcement has a use for the leftovers. His limbs replaced, his body armoured and his brain wiped and partially replaced with a computer, he is back on the streets as Robocop, an automated warrior who politely solves any and all crimes. Typical of his mechanical but humane approach is an incident in which he calmly disposes of a mugger who has been terrorising a woman, and picks up the damsel in distress, informing her 'you have been emotionally traumatised, I'll alert the nearest rape crisis centre'. Gradually Robocop comes to distrust the cynical corporation men (Cox, Ferrer) who have control of him (and who have programmed him not to intervene whenever an official of the corporation is breaking the law) and regains part of his lost humanity. As its melodramatic villains suggest, it is essentially a comic-strip movie; but it's a great comic-strip movie. Sequels (Irvin

Kershner's disastrous *Robocop 2*, 1990, and Fred Dekker's ordinary *Robocop 3*, 1992). A comic book and animated and live-action TV series inevitably followed. KN

1987/102m/Orion/*p* Arne Schmidt/*d* Paul Verhoeven/*s* Edward Neumeier, Michael Miner/*c* Jost Vacano/*m* Basil Poledouris/*lp* Peter Weller, Nancy Allen, Ronny Cox, Dan O'Herlihy, Kurtwood Smith, Miguel Ferrer.

Rope

Based on the play by **Patrick Hamilton**, which owes something to the Leopold–Loeb case of the 1920s (more faithfully dramatised in Richard Fleischer's **Compulsion**), this is the story of two arrogant young men who murder a friend for kicks. Guests then arrive for a party, unaware that the body is hidden in a chest in the same room. Stewart, the young men's former professor, begins to suspect as the culprits' compulsion to boast of their crime starts to get the better of them, and eventually he discovers the body. Another of Hitchcock's studies in the paranoid personality, the film is now chiefly

ABOVE Peter Weller, *Robocop*

ABOVE James Stewart, John Dall, Farley Granger, *Rope*

remembered for its remarkable technical experiment in preserving the real-time duration of the action and shooting the whole film in ten long takes. The interest of the action stands up well under this self-imposed limitation, though on the second or third viewing the urge to spot the joins becomes irresistible. EB

1948/81m/Transatlantic/*p* Sidney Bernstein, Alfred Hitchcock/*d* Alfred Hitchcock/*s* Arthur Laurents/*c* Joseph Valentine, William V. Skall/*m* Leo F. Forbstein/*lp* James Stewart, Farley Granger, John Dall, Joan Chandler, Sir Cedric Hardwicke.

Runyon, [Alfred] Damon
(1884–1946)
Runyon produced a flow of stories and novels based on his acquaintance with low life and gangsterism in New York, written in an individual idiom which gave the word Runyonesque to the English language. The most famous film drawn from his stories was **Guys and Dolls**, based on *The Idyll of Miss Sylvie Brown*. Under the flamboyant and picturesque language the stories were mordantly witty, stuffed full of black humour, and by parodying issues such as police corruption and organised crime, he escaped the criticism which might have stemmed from a more realistic treatment. Part of the public's affection for his stories was also due to their vein of rampant sentimentality, exemplified by a story like *Little Miss Marker*, which became a vehicle for Shirley Temple, and was remade in 1980. Runyon's language and his colourful portraits were hugely influential, not only in musicals between the 30s and 50s, but also in the gangster genre. Writers like Frank Capra and **Raymond Chandler** used variants of his idiom, and actors like William Bendix and Mike Mazurki drew on his types to build their characterisations. By the end of the 30s Runyon was a national institution, especially in New York. He held nightly meetings with friends and colleagues at Lindy's restaurant, and even when cancer forced the removal of his larynx, he continued meeting them, communicating by written notes. After his death in 1946, his ashes, by his own request, were scattered over Manhattan. MP

Ruthless People
Slickly paced black comedy, somewhat along the lines of O. Henry's *Ransom of Red Chief*, in which an impoverished couple (Reinhold and Slater) kidnap the frightful Midler, wife of the expertly crass DeVito, and hold her for ransom. The plot behind the ransom is that DeVito had made a fortune on an idea stolen from Slater. Some brilliant performances from all concerned embellish the story – particularly when it turns out that DeVito is quite happy to be rid of his horrendous wife so that he can continue an affair with his mistress. A splendid screenplay supports the director trio's more zany moments. As *Variety* put it, 'a 1980s equivalent of a Frank Tashlin picture'. TV

1986/93m/Buena Vista/*p* Michael Peyser/ *d* Jim Abrahams, David Zucker, Jerry Zucker/*s* Dale Launer/*c* Jan De Bont/*m* Michel Colombier/*lp* Danny DeVito, Bette Midler, Judge Reinhold, Helen Slater.

S

The Saint
The 'modern-day Robin Hood' Simon Templar, alias the Saint, was introduced by Leslie Charteris in the novel *Meet the Tiger* (1928) and became a fixture as a continuing character in *Thriller* magazine and then in *The Saint Magazine* (1953–67). A crook-turned-vigilante-do-gooder, Templar is far more urbane than such contemporaries as **Bulldog Drummond** and – perhaps because of his creator's Anglo-Chinese ancestry (his original name was Leslie Charles Bowyer Yin) – is unique among club-land heroes for his lack of racism. However, initially he was just as brutal when he had to be before, in the later stories, shrinking from the casual violence of the earlier entries.

The major supporting characters are Inspectors Claude Eustace Teal of Scotland Yard (who first appears in a non-Saint story, *The Story of a Dead Man*, 1929) and John Fernack of the NYPD, while first among Templar's many romantic attachments is the incredibly tolerant Patricia Holm. Like Doc Savage, the Saint is so efficient in disposing of his enemies that few wrong-doers last beyond their initial encounter, although the megalomaniac Crown Prince Rudolf and the spy-cum-war-monger Dr Rayt Marius prove slightly more troublesome than most. From the first, the Saint's trade-mark is a haloed stick man, and later a distinctive whistle (devised for the Saint films but also used on radio and television) becomes a signature of sorts.

Aside from his various comics appearances – he several times had his own comic – the Saint also appeared on radio, first played by Terence de Marney for Radio Eirrann in 1939, then by Edgar Barrier, Brian Aherne, Vincent Price, Tom Conway and Barry Sullivan in the US. RKO's *The Saint in New York* (1938) came well after the big-screen bows of Bulldog Drummond,

Boston Blackie and the Lone Wolf, and the ensuing series of American quickies did little to distinguish the hero from the heavy competition of these gentleman rogues. *The Saint in New York* features Louis Hayward, usually best as ineffectual or corrupt characters, as Simon Templar. He plays the role with a mix of slightly hollow suavity and genuine sadism. Hayward was replaced by George Sanders for John Farrow's *The Saint Strikes Back* (1939), a sequel-cum-rehash with the same plot but a less surprising final twist. Sanders stayed on for *The Saint in London* (1939), *The Saint's Double Trouble* (1940), *The Saint Takes Over* (1940) and *The Saint in Palm Springs* (1941), films so similar that Wendie Barrie is able to appear as a different heroine in three of them. Although the location-shot *The Saint in London* makes use of local talent John Paddy Carstairs, the bulk of the series was entrusted to Jack Hively, whose lack of effort is typified by *The Saint's Double Trouble*, which retreads the venerable mistaken identity theme as Sanders plays the Saint and a gangster twin and wastes Bela Lugosi as a characterless supporting hood. *The Saint in Palm Springs* is probably the best of Sanders's outings, with a neat MacGuffin in some valuable postage stamps constantly passed around the supporting cast, and a slightly drier than usual Sanders performance.

ABOVE *The Saint*: Roger Moore as Simon Templar

Though RKO released *The Saint's Vacation* (1941), it was not part of their series. Directed in London by Leslie Fenton from a screenplay part-authored by Charteris himself, this casts Hugh Sinclair as the Saint but retains Sally Gray from *The Saint in London* as yet another sub-Lois Lane leading lady. Sinclair is a little closer to the Templar of the novels, but he employs Sanders's favourite sleuthing device: perching on the rear bumper of the villains' car as they speed back to their secret hide-out. Gordon MacLeod, Inspector Teal in both *The Saint in London* and *The Saint's Vacation*, returned with Sinclair in Paul Stein's *The Saint Meets the Tiger* (1943), with Jean Gillie as Patricia, a creaky adaptation of the very first Saint novel. Seymour Friedman's *The Saint's Return/The Saint's Girl Friday* (1954) returned a now-ageing Hayward to the role, with Charles Victor as Teal, in a slight and particularly dull mystery. Felix Marten and Jean Marais play the Saint in a pair of obscure French films, Jacques Nahum's *Le Saint mène la danse/The Saint Leads the Dance* (1959) and Christian-Jaque's *Le Saint prend l'affût* (1966), which Charteris personally ensured would not be released in English-speaking territories.

Simon Templar found a near-definitive media image in 1962, when Monty Berman and Robert S. Baker began producing a British television series with Roger Moore raising a quizzical eyebrow to his halo as *The Saint*. John Paddy Carstairs, who facilitated the arrangement between the producers and Charteris, returned to direct several episodes. Although Patricia was written out, there was no shortage of 60s ladies (Shirley Eaton, Kate O'Mara, Julie Christie, Dawn Addams, Samantha Eggar, Nanette Newman, Annette Andre, Sue Lloyd, Sylvia Syms) for Moore to pursue. The series lasted until 1968, and has been followed by several attempted revivals: *The Return of the Saint* (1978–9), with Ian Ogilvy as an acceptable Templar in sub-par stories; *The Saint/The Saint in Manhattan* (1987), a TV movie with Andrew Clarke and Kevin Tighe as Templar and Fernack; and six TV movies, commencing with *The Brazilian Connection* (1989), starring Simon Dutton as the Saint. In 1996 Val Kilmer appeared in a flashy, big-budget film entitled simply *The Saint*, co-starring Elizabeth Shue and directed by Phillip Noyce. KN

The St. Valentine's Day Massacre

This takes a docu-drama approach to the struggle between **Al Capone** (Robards) and Bugs Moran (Meeker) in Chicago in the late 20s, documenting the events that culminated in the famous garage massacre which wiped out most of Moran's supporters but not Bugs himself. While Moran engineers a take-over of the mafia, which will rob Capone of his Sicilian backing, Capone counters by having Machine Gun Jack McGurn (Ritchie) set up a lure, which will supposedly bring Bugs and his lieutenants together so they can be wiped out by a hit team disguised as cops. Constructed as a series of vignettes, Corman allows his players (especially Robards as the unstable Capone and Segal as a Cagneyish thug) to enliven dry material with bizarrely humorous turns, including a classic minor exchange between the assassins as Miller asks raspy-voiced Nicholson what Bakalyan is rubbing on his bullets only to be told 'it's garlic, if the bullets don't kill ya, ya die of blood poisoning'. KN

1967/100m/FOX/*p/d* Roger Corman/ *s* Howard Browne/*c* Milton Krasner/*m* Fred Steiner/*lp* Jason Robards, George Segal, Ralph Meeker, Jean Hale, Clint Ritchie, Richard Bakalyan, Dick Miller, Jack Nicholson.

Salvatore Giuliano

Rosi filmed his account of the infamous *mafioso* Salvatore Giuliano as a kind of documentary reconstruction of his life and times. Beginning with the bandit's death in 1950, the film tracks back into his past, piecing together the story of his activities in a series of overlapping flashbacks. Rosi is not interested in the bandit as a personality (Giuliano only ever appears in long-shot, or dead). Rather, he seeks to investigate central questions about the relationship between the allies and the **mafia** during the post-war occupation of Sicily, connections between the mafia and the police, and between the mafia and politicians. The official version was that Giuliano was killed by the carabinieri. But his second-in-command, Pisciotta, later claimed to have done the deed. He was himself later murdered in prison, as was Minasola, the chief liaison between the police and the mafia. Sticking to the known facts, but probing beneath the surface, Rosi produces a fascinating and powerful dissection of a corrupt world in which Giuliano, far from being the chief instigator of events, becomes a pawn who is eliminated when he becomes a nuisance to the underworld and to the politicians who have made their accommodation with it. EB

ABOVE *Salvatore Giuliano*

1961/125m/Lux-Vides-Galatea/*p* Franco Cristaldi/*d* Francesco Rosi/*s* Francesco Rosi, Suso Cecchi D'Amico, Enzo Provenzale, Franco Solinas/*c* Gianni Di Venanzo/*m* Piero Piccioni/*lp* Frank Wolff, Salvo Randone, Federico Zardi.

Le Samouraï

Melville's most accomplished colour film is a portrait of a professional killer Jef Costello (Delon, in the most remarkable performance of his long career). After fulfilling a contract killing on a night-club proprietor, Jef is recognised by Valerie (Rosier) but she refuses to pick him out of a line-up organised by the police Inspector (Périer). After an attempt on his life by his unknown employer, Jef gets paid for the job and he is given a new contract: to kill Valerie. After finding and killing his employer (Posier), Jef goes to the night-club to fulfil the contract on Valerie. However, the police are waiting for him and he is shot while taking aim at his beloved. It is revealed that his gun was not loaded. Melville uses the minimal plot to create some of the most hypnotic sequences

ever achieved in the cinema. The long silences (as Delon escapes from his police tail in the Paris Métro, or as he discovers that someone has intruded upon his private space because his little caged bird seems disturbed) and the absorbing, almost musical rhythms of the protagonists' and the camera's movements, together with the stylised use of colour make this a piece of virtuoso cinema which is both intellectually and emotionally engulfing. PW

1967/France, Italy/105m/Filmel-CICC-Fida/*p* Raymond Borderie, Eugène Lépicier/*d/s* Jean-Pierre Melville/*orig* Joan McLeod *The Ronin*/*c* Henri Decaë/*m* François de Roubaix/*lp* Alain Delon, François Périer, Nathalie Delon, Caty Rosier, Jacques Leroy, Jean-Pierre Posier.

Sapphire

A standard British thriller notable for its racial angle and attempt at relevance to the time of the Notting Hill riots. Sapphire (Buckingham), a coloured girl passing for white, is murdered and the police, led in the usual raincoats by Patrick and Craig, politely enquire into her background, running across an assortment of dignified and decent black folks before pinning the crime on the hysterically prejudiced sister (Mitchell) of the dead girl's duffelcoated art student boyfriend (Massie). While sequences dealing with

black life are stereotypical (a girl passing for white is 'given away' when her feet respond unconsciously to a bongo beat) the situation of the murderess is far more interesting in terms of her social squalor, as she is left behind in the slum with her horribly bigoted Dad (Miles) and children while Massie escapes to an exotic coffee bar world which Sapphire (like most blacks in the film, seen to be better off than poor whites) represents. KN

1959/GB/92m/Rank/*p* Michael Relph/*d* Basil Dearden/*s* Janet Green/*c* Harry Waxman/*m* Philip Green/*lp* Nigel Patrick, Yvonne Mitchell, Michael Craig, Paul Massie, Bernard Miles, Earl Cameron, Yvonne Buckingham.

Scandal

The John Profumo-Christine Keeler affair holds a place in British popular and political history that cannot be underestimated. Hurt suffers as usual as Stephen Ward, a political hanger-on who commits suicide when accused of pimping for Christine (Whalley-Kilmer) and Mandy Rice-Davies (Fonda), free-spirit sex kittens at the disposal of stuffy, elderly dignitaries like Profumo (McKellen) and alleged Russian spy Ivanov (Krabbé). Superficial and surprisingly tasteful, this lacks the insight into class and cruelty that power comparable nostalgia-scandal

ABOVE Frank Wolff, *Salvatore Giuliano*

ABOVE Alain Delon, *Le Samouraï*

could be inserted, though Hawks cannily cast players usually seen as vile villains in these spokesman roles, thus undermining the message. Muni's performance doesn't work all the time, but there is genuinely strange comic by-play with his jester-like sidekick (Barnett), whom he leaves in the theatre to take notes on the ending of *Rain* when he is called away to a killing, coin-tossing right-hand man (Raft) and soon-to-be-replaced boss (Perkins). Determined to one-up the deaths of Robinson's Rico and Cagney's Tom Powers, Hawks has Muni go down like Richard III, escaping from his steel-lined hide-out to be riddled with machine-gun bullets under a Cook's Tours sign that reads 'the world is yours'. KN

1932/90m/UA/*p* Howard Hughes/*d* Howard Hawks/*s* Ben Hecht, W.R. Burnett, John Lee Mahin, Seton I. Miller/*orig* Armitage Trail/ *c* Lee Garmes, L. William O'Connell/ *m* Adolph Tandler, Gus Arnheim/*lp* Paul Muni, Ann Dvorak, Karen Morley, George Raft, Osgood Perkins, Boris Karloff, Vince Barnett, C. Henry Gordon, Tully Marshall.

Scarface

In remaking the 1932 *film à clef* about **Al Capone** and prohibition, De Palma and Stone change the ethnic milieu from Italian

items like **Dance with a Stranger** and *Prick Up Your Ears* (1987), and even misses the sleaze absurdism of the earlier, far more disreputable *The Christine Keeler Affair* (1963), an almost surreally cheap Danish-British sexploiter starring Yvonne Buckingham and John Drew Barrymore. KN

1989/GB/114m/Palace-Miramax/*p* Stephen Woolley/*d* Michael Caton-Jones/*s* Michael Thomas/*orig* Christine Keeler/*c* Mike Molloy/*m* Carl Davis/*lp* John Hurt, Joanne Whalley-Kilmer, Bridget Fonda, Ian McKellen, Jeroen Krabbé.

Scarface/Scarface, The Shame of a Nation

With the ground rules of the gangster genre established in **Little Caesar** and **The Public Enemy**, Hawks here offers an operatic variation on the theme. Using the now-familiar rise and fall of a hoodlum scenario and incidental detail drawn from the life of **Al Capone**, Hawks constructs an extraordinarily bizarre black horror comedy of monstrous individuals locked in a labyrinthine struggle patterned on the lives of the Borgias (one gangster is not unaptly played by Boris Karloff, while Muni's Tony Camonte comes across as a mix of Fredric March's Mr Hyde and the Jewish-Italian clowning of Chico Marx). Full of strange touches like the incestuous passion that erupts between Tony and his trampy sister (Dvorak) and the Xs that appear in the frame whenever anyone is

killed, and less a plot than a succession of sketches, the film was lurid and off-beat enough to excite even more censorious interest than Warners' gangster pictures. Its release was delayed until a few moralising sequences (with newspaperman Marshall and honest cop Gordon vilifying Camonte)

ABOVE Bridget Fonda, *Scandal*

to Cuban and the racket from booze to drugs, but otherwise cleave surprisingly close to the original story-line. Expelled by Castro, the near-illiterate Tony Montana (Pacino) arrives in Miami in 1980 and rises swiftly through the ranks of organised crime by virtue of his ruthlessness, establishing a useful international link with Bolivian cartel kingpin Shenar. He dissipates his new-found success through violent excess, murdering his best friend (Bauer) because he has dared to sleep with his sister (Mastrantonio), plunging his face into a Paramount mountain of cocaine on his desk, and finally wiped out in an extravagant hail of bullets under a sign that reads 'the world is yours'. While it lacks the compactness of Hawks's film, De Palma's habitual chain-saw overkill is not inappropriate for the subject matter, emphasising that the one thing Montana's huge fortune cannot buy him is good taste, and even making work such 30s plot devices as Montana's post-murder discovery that Bauer and Mastrantonio were secretly married. Pacino's neanderthal performance, shouting out Stone's profane dialogue at his cringing, spaced-out WASP mistress (Pfeiffer) or at alarmed fellow diners in a plush restaurant, is perfectly in tune with the grand gestures of the character, who finally goes down under the kind of firepower usually reserved for Godzilla. It's not a subtle movie, but its excesses, while occasionally tiresome, are often startling. KN

1983/170/U/*p* Martin Bregman, Peter

ABOVE Al Pacino, *Scarface*

Saphier/*d* Brian De Palma/*s* Oliver Stone/ *orig* Armitage Trail/*c* John A. Alonzo/ *m* Giorgio Moroder/*lp* Al Pacino, Michelle Pfeiffer, Steven Bauer, Mary Elizabeth Mastrantonio, Robert Loggia, F. Murray Abraham.

Scarlet Street

This is one of two Jean Renoir films from the 1930s which Lang remade in post-war America (the other is *Human Desire*, drawn originally from Zola's *La Bête humaine*). Based on *La Chienne*, a novel and play by Georges de la Fouchardière, this is the story of a mild-mannered man (Robinson) who escapes his humdrum existence through painting. He falls for a beautiful younger woman (Bennett) and steals money from his employer to set her up in an apartment so he can paint her. She and her unscrupulous lover (Duryea, at his leering, sneering best), take the old man for a ride. When he discovers how much the woman despises him he kills her, and subsequently Duryea is executed for the murder. Robinson's mind disintegrates under the pressure of guilt and fear. This is a companion piece to **The Woman in the Window**, filmed by Lang with the same cast a few months earlier. But whereas in the earlier picture Robinson's descent from respectability into the depths of crime and disgrace turns out to be merely a bad dream, this time there is no easy way out. Trapped between the misery of his dreary job and shrewish wife, and a fantasy that can only

end in disaster, Lang's protagonist is well and truly doomed. EB

1945/102m/U/*p/d* Fritz Lang/*s* Dudley Nichols/*c* Milton Krasner/*m* Hans J. Salter/ *lp* Edward G. Robinson, Joan Bennett, Dan Duryea, Jess Barker, Margaret Lindsay.

Schultz, Dutch (1902–35)

Born Arthur Flegenheimer in the Bronx, Dutch Schultz, who took his nickname from a New York hoodlum of the 1890s, was a successful boot-legger and extortionist noted for his unpredictable temperament. Instrumental in the murders of rivals and associates like Bo Weinberg, Jack 'Legs'' Diamond and Vincent 'Mad Dog' Coll, he was executed on the orders of the crime syndicate he had joined, when Lepke Buchalter and **Charles 'Lucky' Luciano** refused to go along with his proposal that Special Prosecutor Thomas E. Dewey be assassinated. Schultz was murdered along with associates Abe Landau, Lulu Rosencrantz and Otto Berman by Charlie Workman, presumably a Murder Incorporated hit-man acting under Albert Anastasia.

Schultz has inspired two major literary fictions, William S. Burroughs's *The Last Words of Dutch Schultz* (1970), based on the dying gangster's stenographically-recorded ravings, and E.L. Doctorow's *Billy Bathgate* (1989), a meticulous evocation of 30s gangland. On *The Untouchables* teleseries Lawrence Dobkin guest-starred in 'The Dutch Schultz Story' (1959). In films, Schultz has been played by Vic Morrow in *Portrait of a Mobster* (1961), Jonathan Banks in *The Gangster Chronicles/Gangster Wars* (1981), James Remar in **The Cotton Club**, Dustin Hoffman in *Billy Bathgate* (1991), Lance Henriksen in *The Outfit* (1992) and Bruce Nozick in *Mad Dog Coll* (1992) and *Hit the Dutchman* (1992). KN

Seance on a Wet Afternoon

Attenborough is undoubtedly one of the most intriguing talents to emerge in post-war Britain. What makes him particularly interesting is the different identities he has established in the course of his lengthy career. His public persona is that of the acceptable face of the Establishment, while as a director he has installed himself as the maker of 'big subjects' (*Young Winston*, 1972; *Cry Freedom*, 1987 and *Chaplin*, 1992). But as an actor, Attenborough has continually been attracted to, and shown a real ability to understand, seedy characters. Hence his

ABOVE Kim Stanley, Patrick Magee, Gerald Sim, Richard Attenborough, *Seance on a Wet Afternoon*

appearance in **Brighton Rock**, **10 Rillington Place** and this, *Seance On a Wet Afternoon*, which together comprise his three finest acting performances. Set in what Tom Milne has neatly identified as 'the dangerous area between private fantasy and public madness', *Seance* features Attenborough, borrowing equally from his performances in *Brighton Rock* and *The Dock Brief* (1962), as the reluctant guardian of Stanley's failed medium, whose guide to the nether world is her stillborn son, Arthur. Her plan in order to revive a flagging career is to kidnap a child and then 'find' it and Attenborough is to be her instrument. Forbes' direction, greatly aided by Turpin's probing camera (as in the opening sequence where the pair prepare a room for the child) neatly unpicks Stanley's growing madness while Attenborough powerlessly looks on, able to save the child but not his wife who, like Gloria Swanson in **Sunset Blvd.**, above all craves recognition. PH

1964/GB/116m/Allied-Beaver/*co-p/d/s* Bryan Forbes/*co-p* Richard Attenborough/*orig* Mark McShane/*c* Gerry Turpin/*m* John Barry/ *lp* Richard Attenborough, Kim Stanley, Nanette Newman, Mark Eden, Patrick Magee.

The Secret Six

A gutsy, violent gangster drama featuring Beery as a particularly nasty, back-shooting mob leader not too discreetly patterned after **Capone**. Even the story's location settings are clearly indicated (Chicago and its western suburb Cicero, the latter Capone's headquarters), as is a character linked with another Capone-connected Prohibition Chic-

ago gangster, Big Jim Colosimo. The vigilante committee against Beery, the Secret Six of the title, remain in the background. Rising starlet Harlow plays another moll, while Brown and newcomer Clark Gable are young reporters covering the gang wars. TV

1931/80m/MGM/*p* Irving Thalberg/*d* George Hill/*s* Frances Marion/*c* Harold Wenstrom/ *lp* Wallace Beery, Lewis Stone, John Mack Brown, Jean Harlow.

Serial Killers

Sexually motivated multiple killing appears not to have been recorded prior to the mid-19th century. The term was first coined in 1978 by **FBI** agent Robert Ressler to distinguish the growing number of sexually motivated 'repeat killers' from mass murderers who kill for profit. The definition therefore excludes such films as *Monsieur Verdoux* (1947), *Bluebeard's Ten Honeymoons* (1960), **Landru**, *The Honeymoon Killers* (1969), and *Barbe-Bleue* (1972), as well as those about secondarily sexual psychopaths – *The Sniper* (1952), **While the City Sleeps**, **The Bad Seed**, **Peeping Tom**, *The Driller Killer* (1979) and *The Atlanta Child Murders* (TVM 1985). **Jack the Ripper** inspired (but does not appear in) the 1911 novel *The Lodger*, filmed first by Hitchcock in 1926 and by

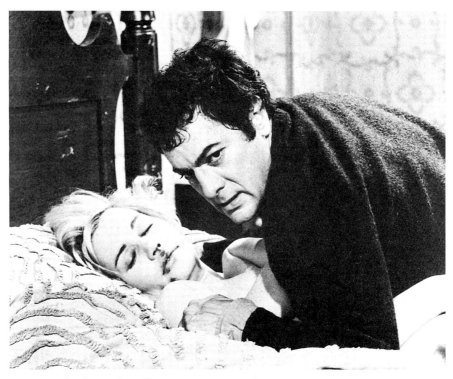

ABOVE Serial Killers: Sally Kellerman, Tony Curtis, *The Boston Strangler*

others in 1932, 1943 and (as *Man in the Attic*) 1953. His exploits are the subject of *Room to Let* (1949), *Jack the Ripper* (1958), *A Study in Terror* (1965), *Der Dirnenmörderer von London/ Jack the Ripper* (1976), and he has appeared as a subsidiary character in *Waxworks* (1924) and many subsequent films. *Lo Squartatore di New York* (1982) and *Jack's Back* (1988) are about modern copycats. Germany's most notorious serial killers, Peter Kurten and Fritz Haarmann, both active in the 20s, inspired **M** and *Die Zärtlichkeit der Wölfe* (1973) respectively. The first film about a modern serial killer is **The Boston Strangler**, based on the life of Albert De Salvo. Other biopics, which multiplied appreciably in the late 80s, include **10 Rillington Place**, *Deranged* (1974), *The Town That Dreaded Sundown* (1977), **Henry Portrait of a Serial Killer**, *Confessions of a Serial Killer* (1987), *The Hillside Stranglers* (TVM 1989), *Cold Light of Day* (1990), *To Catch a Killer* (TVM 1991), *Scramm* (1994), and *Citizen X* (1995). *Aileen Wuornos The Selling of a Serial Killer* (1992) is a documentary about the woman said to be the first female serial killer (seven male victims 1989–91). *Halloween* (1978), about a psychopath who escapes from an asylum to kill (in his view) promiscuous women, instigated the 'slasher' cycle, mostly cheap and sensational B-films aimed at a young audience, which persisted into the 90s despite parodies. The stocks in trade of these films are an invincible, characterless maniac and

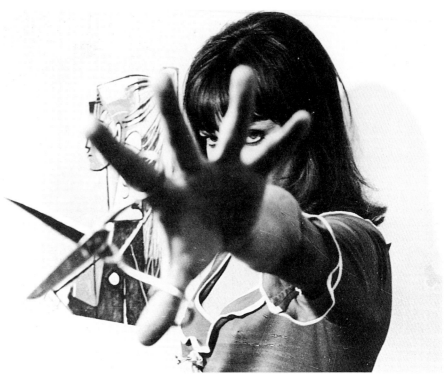

ABOVE *Série Noire*: Anna Karina, *Pierrot le fou*

victims who are either semi-clad women or adolescents having sex. A minority of slashers dwell on rape and other sexual violence, and it was these films that were mainly responsible for the tightening of censorship in several countries. Among titles to arouse critical interest are those that vary the formula and/or make directorial statements. *I Spit on Your Grave* (1980) and **Ms .45** both have female killers avenging rape. *The Slumber Party Massacre* (1982) is directed and written by women. Also of interest are *The House on Sorority Row* (GB: *House of Evil*; 1982); *White of the Eye* (1986); and *The Stepfather* (1987). Recent exploitation pictures have placed serial killers in many other genres. The killers in the *Maniac Cop* television series (1988–92), *The First Power* (1989), *Shocker* (1989), *Night Trap* (1992) and *Ghost in the Machine* (1993) are supernatural. *Peacemaker* (1990) has an extra-terrestrial serial killer. In *Tiger Claws* (1992) the victims are martial artists. Introduced in **Manhunter**, Hannibal the Cannibal made a spectacular impact in **The Silence of the Lambs**, responsible for the latest spate of big-budget serial killer films from major studios. They include *Final Combination* (1993), *Striking Distance* (1993), *Copycat* (1995), *Just Cause* (1995) and **Se7en**. More modest British attempts are *White Angel* (1993) and *Beyond Bedlam* (1993). DM

Serials

The earliest serials, practically all of which are now lost, were intended for adults. The serials of the 30s and 40s, whose clichés

ABOVE Serials: Musidora, *Les Vampires*

have passed into popular culture, were made specifically for children and shown at matinées, typically on Saturday mornings. Consequently the films tended to be cheaply and crudely produced with inexperienced or second-rate actors, or stars past their prime. Although most countries attempted serials, the greatest output (approximately 350 silent films, 231 talkies) came from the USA. The longest serial, *The Hazards of Helen* (1914–17), had 119 episodes or chapters, but most had between ten and twenty. The favourite setting was the Old West. In contemporary detective mysteries the criminals were often madmen bent on world domination.

The first serial was *What Happened to Mary?* (1912). The first with a 'cliff-hanger' was *The Adventures of Kathlyn* (1913). Peril at the tops of cliffs or tall buildings was superseded by entrapment in water- or gas-filled chambers. A common complaint was that the trailer of the following week's episode revealed that the hero survives. The best-known French serials – **Fantômas** (1913), **Les Vampires** (1915) and **Judex** (1916–17), all directed by Louis Feuillade – are now considered superior to American counterparts. No British serial of merit has yet been unearthed. The first was *Boy Scouts, Be*

ABOVE *Série Noire*: Jean-Paul Belmondo, *Borsalino*

ABOVE *Série Noire*: Jean Gabin, René Dary, *Touchez pas au grisbi*

Prepared (1917) in which a troop of Baden-Powell's finest foil a foreign spy. The first serial of the sound era is disputed, but may have been *The Voice from the Sky* (1929).

Famous detectives who made their first screen appearances in serials include **Charlie Chan**, in *House Without a Key* (1926); **Dick Tracy**, who appeared in four serials between 1937 and 1941; Britt Reid alias the Green Hornet, in *The Green Hornet* (1939) and *The Green Hornet Strikes Again* (1944); **The Shadow** in the 1940 film of that name; and Richard Wentworth alias The Spider, in *The Spider's Web* (1938) and *The Spider Returns* (1941). When the serial rights to **Nick Carter** could not be obtained, the result was *Chick Carter, Detective* (1946), a serial about the detective's son. The last serial from a major studio was *Blazing the Overland Trail* (1956); the genre could not sustain itself once its young audience had defected to television. DM

Série Noire

In 1945, shortly after the liberation of France, Marcel Duhamel started for the publisher Gallimard the celebrated *Série Noire* (a title suggested by Jacques Prévert), a series of thrillers and crime novels with distinctive black covers with yellow lettering and no illustration, mostly translated from American crime writers. The first one in the series was a (free) translation of the British writer Peter Cheyney's *Poison Ivy* (1937) as **La Môme vert-de-gris**, which inaugurated the **Lem-**

my Caution series of films. The second volume was *Cet homme est dangereux* (1936), another Lemmy Caution story also filmed later by Bernard Borderie. The third volume was **James Hadley Chase**'s *No Orchids For Miss Blandish* (1939). The series then settled down to introduce genuine American writers, rather than British authors who set their stories in the US, after a long period when American films and novels had been absent from France due to the Nazi occupation. The French editions of **Chandler**, **McBain**, McCoy, **Hammett**, **Burnett**, **Ellin**, **McGivern**, **Woolrich**, **Goodis**, **Himes** and many others followed. The translations by authors such as Boris Vian were often not very faithful, Duhamel preferring to render the material in savoury French whenever possible. The critic Jill Forbes has suggested that: 'In an attempt to render the so-called "hard-boiled" style, the translations evolved a literary argot reminiscent of Céline or Queneau that attempted to be both exotic and relatively comprehensible. The first-person narrative of many such works lent added credibility to the conversational register, the colloquialisms or grammatical solecisms characteristic of such translations.' (*The Cinema in France*, 1992). Soon, a number of French authors joined the series, at first using Anglo pseudonyms: Serge Arcouet became Terry Stewart (1948), Jean Meckert wrote as John Amila (1950) and Boris Vian as Vernon Sullivan. The first openly French author was André Piljean (1951). From the mid-1960s onwards, the

Serpico

Though less distinctive than *Dog Day Afternoon* (1975), his other true-life crime collaboration with Pacino, this is the first of Lumet's obsessive examinations of corruption in the police and legal systems, leading to even darker visions like **Prince of the City**, *The Verdict* (1982), *Daniel* (1983) and *Q & A* (1990). It's based on the career and fate of Detective Frank Serpico (Pacino), a New York undercover cop who became highly unpopular with his colleagues for his stand against the corruption rife in the city, and was finally invalided off the force after being shot in circumstances that suggested collusion between the crooks he was after and the cops who were supposed to be backing him up. Rather than concentrate on the corruption thread, as Serpico gradually learns that the higher up the chain he goes the worse the crookedness is, Lumet adopts a straggling, biopic approach, surrounding the central issues with accounts of Serpico's idealist fervour, strained romantic relationships, in-disguise-as-a-hippie undercover work and semi-vigilante street tactics. KN

1973/129m/De Laurentiis-Artists Entertain-

series was to publish more French authors and, as in most cultural sectors in France, the post-1968 phase of the series saw a brief upsurge of more politically oriented novels (by authors such as Jean-Pierre Manchette). By the 1985, the series had published some 2,000 titles by more than 730 authors, yielding over 130 French films in 30 years. In 1995, the series celebrated its first half-century.

Shortly after the Lemmy Caution films, Albert Simonin's novel **Touchez pas au grisbi** (1953) was filmed by Jacques Becker, which, together with Jules Dassin's film of Auguste Le Breton's **Du rififi chez les hommes** (also 1954), inaugurated a new 'série noire' phase of the French *policier* genre, including a sub-genre of gangster and crime comedies (Georges Lautner's *Les Tontons flingueurs*, 1963). The series provided source material for mainstream as well as New Wave film-makers. For his second feature, **Tirez sur le pianiste**, Truffaut chose a *série noire* novel. In his *Une femme est une femme* (1961), Jean-Luc Godard had an entire dialogue scene consisting of *série noire* titles. His *Pierrot le fou* (1964) and *Bande à part* (1965) were derived from *série noire* novels. After May 1968, the old-style gangsters, with an almost feudal code of honour and for whom male friendship is the most sacred value, represented on the screen by Jean Gabin and by the heroes of Jean-Pierre Melville's films, started giving way to more politically motivated portrayals, although the films derived from the novels could easily

lean towards the opposite political camp from the one favoured by the authors of the books. Claude Chabrol inflected Jean-Patrick Manchette's left-inclined novel *Nada* (1972), about an anarchic terrorist gang, towards the right for his 1973 film, whereas Raf Vallet and Jean Laborde's right-wing tract *Adieu Poulet* (1974) was given a liberal twist by the scenarist Francis Veber, although the nostalgia for a 'strong man' to come and clean up France's rotten politicians can be found in both versions. In the 1970s and 1980s, young directors turned towards the *série noire* for their *polar* (cop) genre movies, both for star vehicles (such as Jacques Deray's films starring Alain Delon, including **Borsalino**, **Le Gang** and **Flic Story**) and for their personal movies (Yves Boisset (**Un Condé**), Bertrand Tavernier). At this time, French crime movies consistently scored well in domestic box-office receipts. The trend soon evolved towards a new phase: in the late 1950s and early 1960s, cinephile directors such as Truffaut and Godard paid tribute to the world of the American crime novel, alongside their visual references to 1940s and 1950s Hollywood. The late 1970s and 1980s film-makers, on the other hand, tended to use the *série noire* to pay tribute to the history of the French thriller genre itself, in the work of Jean-Jacques Beineix (**Diva**), Alain Corneau, Gérard Krawczyk, Claude Miller. PW

RIGHT Cornelia Sharpe, Al Pacino, *Serpico*

ABOVE Brad Pitt, *Se7en*

ment/*p* Martin Bregman/*d* Sidney Lumet/ *s* Waldo Salt, Norman Wexler/*orig* Peter Maas/*c* Arthur J. Ornitz/*m* Mikis Theodorakis/*lp* Al Pacino, John Randolph, Jack Kehoe, Biff McGuire, Tony Roberts.

Se7en

The most commercially successful example to date of a group of thriller movies critically labelled 'neo-noir', *Se7en* features two police detectives in a rain-soaked, unnamed city (grizzled Freeman, reining in headstrong young buck, the rather miscast Pitt) chasing down a serial killer whose crimes are horrific exemplifications of the seven deadly sins. The at times pretentious, but always thoughtful, debut script is shot through with philosophical references, particularly to Dante's *Inferno*, welded to a flashy, jump-cut video style (betraying the director's background) and gothic production design, borrowing heavily from **Blade Runner**, that is overblown yet effective. *Se7en* is thus an atmospheric, gloomy and disturbing movie, half horror, half police procedural, that builds to a guessable but still remarkably shocking denouement. It's anchored perfectly by Freeman as the cynical but deeply feeling cop, enlivened by Paltrow in an underwritten 'nice girl' part and enhanced late on by Spacey as the terrifying killer. Canadian composer Howard Shore's doom-laden orchestral score is an added bonus and the

opening credits are so impressively designed as to make them alone worth the price of admission. AW

1996/127m/New Line/*p* Arnold Kopelson, Phillis Caryle/*d* David Fincher/*s* Andrew Kevin Walker/*c* Darius Khondji/*m* Howard Shore/*lp* Morgan Freeman, Brad Pitt, Kevin Spacey, Gwyneth Paltrow.

The Shadow

A mysterious vigilante in a slouch hat, who emerges from the night with blazing guns to right wrongs, The Shadow originated in 1930 as an unnamed character on a radio series, *Street & Smith's Detective Story Hour*, voiced by James LaCurto and Frank Readick. Acquiring his penumbral cognomen courtesy of writer Harry Engman Charlot, this Shadow was the Rod Serling-style narrator of crime tales dramatised from the pages of *Detective Story*, but the Shadow became so popular that customers seeking the magazine on which the show was based constantly asked for *The Shadow*, prompting Street & Smith to create a magazine with that title, along with a character called the Shadow who then continued on the radio shows. Nearly 300 adventures in the magazine, from *The Living Shadow* (1931) to The *Whispering Eyes* (1949), were written mostly by Walter B. Gibson (a professional magician, hence an emphasis on prestidigitation) under the house name Maxwell Grant.

Gibson revived the Shadow in *Return of the Shadow* (1963) prompting Denis Lynds to take on the Grant name for further paperback originals, from *The Shadow Strikes* (1964) to *The Shadow: Destination: Moon* (1967).

Gibson also created the Shadow's sidekicks Harry Vincent and Margo Lane and an assortment of continuing villains, the most fearsome of whom was the **Fu Manchu**-like Shiwan Khan (introduced in 'The Golden Master', 1939). Most popular on radio – played briefly but indelibly by Orson Welles 1937–8, followed by Bill Johnstone (1938–44), Bret Morrison (1943–4), John Archer (1944–5) and Steve Courtley (1945) – the Shadow was originally the alter ego of wealthy playboy Lamont Cranston, but later developments (revealed in the keystone novella 'The Shadow Unmasks', 1937) suggest Cranston merely lent his identity to the hero, who was really daredevil flier Kent Allard. The radio Shadow was capable of using his powers 'to cloud men's minds' by seeming invisible. Taking a cue from the answer to his catch-phrase 'who knows what evil lurks in the hearts of men?', Lieber and Stoller wrote a song based on the character, 'The Shadow Knows', recorded famously by The Coasters.

A series of six film shorts 1931–2 under the blanket title *Shadow Detective* use the original radio format, having the Shadow narrate after the manner of the later radio and film character the Whistler, recounting ironic crime stories in which fate punishes wrong-doers. Rod La Rocque in *The Shadow Strikes* (1937) and *International Crime* (1937), Victor Jory in the serial *The Shadow* (1940), Kane Richmond in *The Shadow Returns* (1946), *Behind the Mask* (1946) and *The Missing Lady* (1946), Richard Derr in *The Invisible Avenger* (1958) and Alec Baldwin in *The Shadow* (1994) are various versions of the more familiar Shadow. Only hatchet-faced perennial villain Jory, in a rare and apt good guy outing, evokes the character's sinister side. *International Crime*, for instance, depicts the hero as an uncostumed civilian detective. Russell Mulcahy's big-budget 1994 epic returns to pulp roots and features John Lone as Shiwan Khan and Penelope Ann Miller as Margo Lane. KN

Shadow of a Doubt

Hitchcock asked Thornton Wilder to work on this film because he admired Wilder's play *Our Town* (1938). *Shadow of a Doubt* is largely set in a similar small town in middle America, and is another Hitchcock exercise in showing what lies beneath apparent normality. Uncle Charlie (Cotten) is popular with everyone, especially the niece (Wright) with whom he comes to stay. Only gradually does she suspect that he is the man police are hunting for the murder of several widows. As with other Hitchcock villains, Charlie's apparent friendly exterior conceals an arrogant, even fascist, assumption that he has the right to dispose of those deemed unworthy to live ('Useless women. Drinking the money, eating the money, smelling of money.'). As often in Hitchcock, trains are major agents in the plot. Charlie's initial arrival at the town railway station is accompanied by a pall of thick black smoke from the engine. At the end he falls to his death while trying to push his niece under an oncoming train. EB

1942/108m/U/*p* Jack H. Skirball/*d* Alfred Hitchcock/*s* Thornton Wilder, Alma Reville, Sally Benson/*c* Joseph Valentine/*m* Dimitri Tiomkin/*lp* Joseph Cotten, Teresa Wright, MacDonald Carey, Patricia Collinge, Henry Travers.

Shaft

'Who's the black private dick who's a sex machine with all the chicks?' asks Isaac Hayes's Oscar-winning theme song. The answer, pretty obviously, is Shaft. **Cotton Comes to Harlem** set the style for blaxploitation, but *Shaft* was the first big commercial success of the sub-genre, letting loose a flood of imitations. A very conventional and only minimally exciting private-eye movie in the Mickey Spillane tradition, the film finds Shaft hired by a Harlem gangster (Gunn) to enlist the help of a black militant group to rescue the daughter who has been kidnapped by white mafiosi intent on taking over the territory. A major hit, it spawned a couple of less gritty, more James Bondian sequels (Parks's *Shaft's Big Score!*, 1972, John Guillermin's *Shaft in Africa*, 1973) before Roundtree took his act to television for eight 90-minute *Shaft* episodes between 1973 and 1974. Screenwriter Tidyman, who created the character in his novel *Shaft* (1970), wrote his own sequels: *Shaft Among the Jews* (1972), *Shaft's Big Score* (1972), *Shaft Has a Ball* (1973), *Good-bye Mr Shaft* (1973), *Shaft's Carnival of Killers* (1974) and *The Last Shaft* (1977). KN

1971/98m/MGM/*p* Joel Freeman/*d* Gordon Parks Sr/*co-s* John D.F. Black/*orig/co-s* Ernest Tidyman/*c* Urs Furrer/*m* Isaac Hayes/ *lp* Richard Roundtree, Charles Cioffi,

ABOVE Richard Roundtree, *Shaft*

Moses Gunn, Christopher St John, Gwenn Mitchell.

Shallow Grave

A bravura exercise in style, this follows the growing awareness of a trio of would-be upwardly mobile characters that there is no such thing as easy money. Fox, Eccleston and McGregor play the Edinburgh doctor, accountant and journalist respectively who stumble on a suitcase of money when their mysterious new flatmate (Allen) dies of a drug overdose. Thus the grave they dig for Allen is actually their own, as dreams of wealth are shattered by characters from Allen's past (who require new graves), by Stott's prosaic but stubborn policeman, by shifting alliances within the trio, and finally by multiple betrayals which leave the men dead and Fox with a now useless ticket to Rio. The film is superbly photographed by Tufano, who gives an edge to mundane scenes like shopping for spades, and designed with verve by Kave Quinn, who contrasts the opulence of their flat (which is given an oddly distorted quality by being built slightly larger than life-size) with the source of their new-found wealth. Equally superior is the well-honed script that wonderfully eschews British clichés in favour of

an incisive, decidedly Scottish wit as the characters' self-images collapse. All is brought together by Boyle's direction, which perpetually seeks the unusual angle (as when Eccleston takes to living in the ceiling) but never pointlessly. The result is the bleakest of black comedies. Writer, producer and director and several of the cast went on to make the almost surrealistic *Trainspotting* (1996); equally successful but set amongst a group who are mostly downwardly (rather than upwardly) mobile. PH

1994/GB/92m/Figment Films/*p* Andrew Macdonald/*d* Danny Boyle/*s* John Hodge/*c* Brian Tufano/*m* Simon Boswell/*lp* Kerry Fox, Christopher Eccleston, Ewan McGregor, Keith Allen, Colin McCredie, Ken Stott.

Shame

Based on an actual event, this is a powerful story about a small town where a gang of male youths terrorise and rape women with impunity because the respectable citizens turn a blind eye to such youthful exuberance, especially when it concerns a boy from a 'good' family and the daughter of a garage mechanic. Asta Cadell (Furness) is the bike-riding lawyer who encourages the rape victim to bring her attackers to court. PW

1987/Australia/94m/Barron-UAA/*p* Damien Parer, Paul D. Barron/*d* Steve Jodrell/ *s* Beverly Blankenship, Michael Brindley/ *c* Joseph Pickering/*m* Mario Millo/ *lp* Deborra-Lee Furness, Simone Buchanan, Tony Barry, Margaret Ford, Gillian Jones.

Shayne, Michael

Brett Halliday, the pen-name of Davis Dresser (1904–77), introduced red-headed private eye Michael Shayne in *Dividend on Death* (1939), an ordinary mystery notable only for the unusual use of lesbianism as a plot point, with heroine Phyllis Brighton attempting to seduce Shayne to prove her sexuality to herself. Working out of Miami, Shayne continues to romance Phyllis, who has only been bullied by her psychoanalyst into thinking that she might be gay, in further novels, eventually marrying her only to lose her in childbirth after Halliday discovered that a wife was a major plot millstone for a hard-boiled hero. Halliday's sixty-six Shayne novels, some of which contain prefatory material suggesting that Shayne is a real person who has allowed Halliday to be his Boswell, include *The Private Practice of Michael Shayne* (1940), *The Uncomplaining Corpses* (1940), *Murder Wears a Mummer's Mask* (1943), *Murder is My Business* (1945), *A Taste for Violence* (1949), *She Woke to Darkness* (1954, in which Halliday is himself a character), *The Violent World of Michael Shayne* (1965), *Fourth Down to Death* (1970), *At the Point of a .38* (1974) and *Million Dollar Handle* (1976).

ABOVE Lloyd Nolan, Marjorie Weaver, *Michael Shayne Private Detective*

After Dresser's death, the Brett Halliday pseudonym passed on to other hands, notably the team of James Reasoner and Livia Washburn.

Looking to replace their **Mr Moto** series, 20th Century-Fox purchased the rights and cast Lloyd Nolan in seven movies, kicking off with *Michael Shayne Private Detective* (1941). A brisk but ordinary little mystery, the film's major asset is Nolan, a reliable supporting player who does a fine job as the somewhat middle-aged, but still sassy and tough sleuth. *Sleepers West* (1941), *Dressed to Kill* (1941), *Blue, White and Perfect* (1941), *The Man Who Wouldn't Die* (1942), *Just Off Broadway* (1942) and *Time to Kill* (1942) were not based on Halliday's novels, calling instead on the studio's reservoir of bought-and-paid for mysteries, suitable for retailoring to fit any series sleuth. Eugene Forde directed the first three entries, while Herbert I. Leeds took over, with a marked improvement in quality, for the final four. Especially notable are *The Man Who Wouldn't Die*, from Clayton Rawson's *No Coffin for the Corpse* (1942), with premature burial and spiritualism a part of the plot, and *Time to Kill*, a snappy distillation of Raymond Chandler's *The High Window* (1942). When the series resumed with *Murder is My Business* (1946), it was with at the poverty-stricken PRC with the colourless Hugh Beaumont as the detective, his sole character trait being a compulsive addiction to peanuts, presumably more acceptable in a B gumshoe than the heavy drinking of the books. Beaumont returned for three more entries starting with *Larceny in Her Heart* (1946).

Jeff Chandler played Shayne for a 1949 radio season, while Richard Denning starred in *Michael Shayne* (1960–1), a marginally suc-

ABOVE Christopher Eccleston, Kerry Fox, Ewan MacGregor, *Shallow Grave*

cessful TV series shot on Miami locations, with Patricia Donahue and Margie Regan at different times as Lucey Hamilton, Jerry Paris as Tim Rourke and Herbert Rudley as Will Gentry. KN

Sheng Gang Qibing/Long Arm of the Law

Mak's first feature, this was shot in Cantonese with non-professional actors. Illegal immigrants from the neighbouring Giangdong province of China organise themselves into criminal Big Circle gangs and commit several hold ups in Hong Kong, increasing the local residents' animosity towards newly arrived mainlanders who resorted to crime to obtain a share of Hong Kong's capitalist wealth. Mak's picture fills in some of the background details, showing the conditions in China's enterprise zones and the nostalgia for group-cohesion which creates the gangs. The film shows one Big Circle gang plotting a raid across the border to rob a Hong Kong jewellery store. Things go wrong on the return journey and betrayals make the gang members turn on each other. With considerable sentimentality and a style reminiscent of routine TV crime dramas (Mak was a former television director), Mak depicts his gangsters as victims of circumstance contaminated by the ruthlessness of Hong Kong's uninhibited capitalism. *Sheng Gang Qibing 2* (1987), directed by Michael Mak, increases the sadistic violence and exploits the widely held belief that mainland immigrants are murdering misfits. *Sheng Gang Qibing 3* (1989), also by Michael Mak, pushes the anti-PRC propaganda a stage further still, featuring an ex-PLA soldier persecuted by the Communists, and his girl-friend who has been forced into prostitution. PW

1984/Hong Kong/111m/Johnny Mak-Bo Ho/*p*/*d* Johnny Mak [Mai Dangxiong]/ *s* Philip Chan/*c* Koo Kwok-wah/*lp* Wong Yan-tat, Lam Wai, Wong Kin, Yeung Ming, Angela Lau.

Shockproof

The change that *Shockproof* rings on the couple-on-the-run premise is that here the male half of the duo (Wilde) is initially seen as an authority figure, a probation officer who becomes personally implicated in the private life of one of his clients (Knight), and goes on the lam with her after she has shot the crook responsible for inveigling her into crime. The original screenplay by Fuller was evidently tougher in tone that the version subsequently reworked by Deutsch, and

there is a somewhat contrived happy ending (the victim proves to have been merely injured in the affray and finally opts not to press charges). But despite this element of compromise, the film is graced by considerable tension and by a narrative style that is more allusive and 'European' than is the case with most of Sirk's work of the 1950s. The culminating sequence in which the fugitives are (ostensibly) cornered by destiny is particularly striking in its graphic angularity. TP

1949/80m/COL/*p* S. Sylvan Simon, Helen Deutsch/*d* Douglas Sirk/*s* Samuel Fuller, Helen Deutsch/*c* Charles Lawton Jr./ *m* George Duning/*lp* Cornel Wilde, Patricia Knight, John Baragrey, Howard St John, Esther Minciotti.

Shonben Raidda/P.P. Rider

Paul Schrader's brother Leonard wrote the story for this conventional tale scripted in collaboration with the latter's wife. It tells of a group of teenagers facing up to Yokohama gangsters as they try to rescue a kidnapped friend. For his third feature, Somai opts for a long-take style derived from Jancso, but this is all but ruined by shaky hand-held camerawork. The resulting rhythm, further broken by intrusive sound effects, lacks any sense of tension and leaves the viewer with the impression of watching an impossibly gauche attempt at an art movie. Leonard Schrader had collaborated on the script of **The Yakuza** and his co-scenarist had been responsible for the delirious **Gaki Teikoku**, suggesting the intention was to create a ritualistic and somewhat parodistic action film. PW

1984/Japan/122m/Kitty/*p* Hidemori Naga/ *d* Shinji Somai/*s* Takuya Nishioka, Chieka Schrader/*orig* Leonard Schrader/*c* Masaki Tamura, Akihiro Ito/*lp* Tatsuya Fuji, Michiko Kawai, Masatoshi Nagase, Yoshikazu Suzuki, Shinobu Sakagami.

The Sicilian

Based on a novel by Mario Puzo, author of **The Godfather**, this deals with the activities of the bandit Salvatore Giuliano in 1940s Sicily in a would-be operatic manner (far removed from the political analysis of Francesco Rosi's **Salvatore Giuliano**). While the film does not altogether shy away from depicting Giuliano's violent excesses, during a brief career that ironically achieved the feat of uniting Church, state and organised crime in opposing him, the central portrait never comes into dramatic focus.

Lambert's performance is less than commanding, but the undertaking fails not so much due to this as a result of the structural miscalculations and misplaced grandiosity that disfigured Cimino's *Heaven's Gate* (1980). The film was substantially cut for US release but was restored to its full length for UK distribution. TP

1987/146m/Gladden Entertainment Corporation/*p* Michael Cimino, Joann Carelli/*d* Michael Cimino/*s* Steve Shagan/ *c* Alex Thomson/*m* David Mansfield/ *lp* Christopher Lambert, Terence Stamp, Joss Ackland, Barbara Sukowa, John Turturro.

Side Street

Granger and O'Donnell, the star-crossed lovers of **They Live by Night**, are here cast in not dissimilar roles of newly-weds trying to cope with hard times. But while there are trace elements of the earlier film's romantic fatalism, the prevailing emphasis is more external and narrative-centred. The skilfully constructed screenplay by Sydney Boehm (writer also of **The Undercover Man** and **The Big Heat**) adopts the premise of a small-time lawbreaker getting unwittingly embroiled in big-time criminality. A courier (Granger) impulsively steals a parcel of money from premises on his route in a bid to ease the financial burden of his wife's pregnancy, but it turns out to be the proceeds of a conspiracy embracing blackmail and murder. He is caught up willy-nilly in a spiral of events leading to his becoming the quarry of both police and vengeful crooks. However, after matters culminate in an exciting carchase through the dawn streets of New York City, a semi-upbeat ending ensues. Not the least virtue of a compact, gripping film lies in its strength of casting in minor roles, with such iconographic presences as Charles McGraw and Adele Jergens featuring among the assorted gunmen and molls. TP

1949/83m/MGM/*p* Sam Zimbalist/ *d* Anthony Mann/*s* Sydney Boehm/*c* Joseph Ruttenberg/*m* Lennie Hayton/*lp* Farley Granger, Cathy O'Donnell, James Craig, Edmon Ryan, Jean Hagen.

Siegel, Benjamin 'Bugsy' (1906–47)

An extortionist and murderer from an early age, Siegel formed the Bug and Meyer Gang with Meyer Lansky (1902–83) and was a player in the formation of the National Crime Syndicate, executing commissions for Murder, Inc. An ambitious and publicity-hungry figure, Siegel relocated to Hollywood

ABOVE James Craig, Farley Granger, *Side Street*

from his native New York in 1937 and became instrumental in extending organised crime in Los Angeles, all the while associating with stars like George Raft and Jean Harlow. Among his many society and showbiz girl-friends were socialite Contessa DiFrasso, starlet Wendy Barrie and call-girl Virginia Hill. In 1945, Siegel had the idea of building the first hotel-casino in Las Vegas, Nevada, turning a desert backwater where gambling happened to be legal into a major tourist centre. Set-backs and mismanagement impeded the construction of the Flamingo (named for Hill). When the casino was open and operating, Siegel refused to pay back funds invested in the venture by the syndicate and was shot dead presumably on the orders of his long-time friends **Charles 'Lucky' Luciano** and/or Meyer Lansky.

Siegel's showbiz associations and visionary business expansion schemes have made him an often-evoked character in gangster movies. Steve Cochran plays a Siegel equivalent in *The Damned Don't Cry* (1950), with Joan Crawford as a Virginia Hill-based moll; Ray Sharkey builds up the Las Vegas casino business in *The Neon Empire/Gangland: The Las Vegas Story* (1989); and Moe Green (Alex Rocco) of **The Godfather** is also based in part on Siegel, down to the detail of being

fatally shot through the eye. Siegel has been played by Harvey Keitel in *The Virginia Hill Story* (1974), a Joel Schumacher TV movie with Dyan Cannon as Hill, Joe Penny in *The Gangster Chronicles/Gangster Wars* (1981), with Cyril O'Reilly and Mitchell Schorr as the character when younger, Richard Grieco in *Mobsters* (1991), with Patrick Dempsey as

Lansky and Christian Slater as Luciano, Armand Assante in *The Marrying Man* (1990), Greg Evigan in 'What's Up Bugsy' (an episode of *P.S. I Luv U*, 1991) and Warren Beatty in **Bugsy**, with Annette Bening as Hill, F. Murray Abraham as Lansky and Harvey Keitel as Siegel's California associate Mickey Cohen. Though Siegel is not featured in *Billy Bathgate* (1991), the film dramatises the murder of Bo Weinberg (Bruce Willis), historically carried out by Siegel as a favour to Dutch Schultz. Siegel features in the novels *Neon Mirage* (1988) by Max Allan Collins and *Last Call* (1992) by Tim Powers. KN

The Silence of the Lambs

A serial killer, dubbed 'Buffalo Bill' by the press because he skins his female victims, is on the loose. The FBI's behavioural science unit recruits an FBI trainee, Clarice Starling (Foster), to help track him down. This is a desperate manoeuvre to enlist the co-operation of another serial killer, Dr Hannibal Lector [Lecktor in **Manhunter**] (Hopkins), who's a brilliant psychiatrist and psychopath, already serving a life sentence. In exchange for Lector's expertise, Starling reveals details from her childhood. The pressure begins to escalate when Bill kidnaps the daughter of a US senator. Meanwhile Hannibal is plotting his blood-weltering escape. The tension focuses round the duel between Hopkins' icily demented killer, and Foster's insecure but ambitious FBI agent. The film, derived from the novel by Thomas Harris, set off wave of public interest and concern about

'Bugsy' Siegel: Annette Bening, Warren Beatty, *Bugsy*

serial killers. It won a slew of Oscars: Best Picture, Best Actor and Actress, Best Director and Best Adapted Screenplay. MP

1991/118m/Strong Heart Productions-Orion/*p* Edward Saxon, Kenneth Utt, Ron Bozman/*d* Jonathan Demme/*s* Ted Tally/*c* Tak Fujimoto/*m* Howard Shore/*lp* Jodie Foster, Anthony Hopkins, Scott Glenn, Ted Levine, Anthony Heald.

Sleep, My Love

While the narrative – husband plots to drive wealthy wife to suicide in order to claim her fortune, only to be foiled by her new-found admirer – is clearly indebted to **Gaslight**, this is a film of considerable style and vitality, the quality of which tends (like that of **Shockproof**) to be overshadowed by the attention paid to Sirk's later American work. Beginning to great effect *in media res*, with a sequence aboard a night train on which Colbert as the drugged wife awakes to find herself mysteriously a passenger, the storytelling is buoyed up by invention in both setting (the photographic studio where the husband's mistress works as a model) and incident (the visitation of the sinister psychiatrist, actually an impostor, whose subsequent 'disappearance' helps further to unhinge the persecuted wife). Ameche is wittily cast counter to his former genial persona as the husband; Cummings would virtually reprise his role as brash helpmate in *Dial M for Murder* (1954), a later variation on much the same narrative theme. TP

1947/96m/Triangle-UA/*p* Charles Buddy Rogers, Ralph Cohn/*d* Douglas Sirk/*s* Leo Rosten, St Clair McKelway/*c* Joseph Valentine/*m* Rudy Schrager/*lp* Claudette Colbert, Robert Cummings, Don Ameche, George Colouris, Hazel Brooks.

The Sleeping Tiger

The first film Losey made in Britain after being blacklisted in America, *Tiger* introduced the baroque style and thematic concerns that would reach their fulfilment in *The Servant* (1963). Knox is the psychoanalyst who takes Bogarde's young thug of a gunmen into his home as an experiment, only to have his wife (Smith) move swiftly from hate to a devouring love of him. Where others would have attempted to weigh down the melodramatic plot with realistic details and measured direction, Losey delights in the luridness of his material. The end is spectacularly grandiose with Smith driving her car through a poster of the Esso tiger, dying

ABOVE Anthony Hopkins, Jodie Foster, *The Silence of the Lambs*

as it were in its jaws. The central metaphor of the film – indeed of most of Losey's work – is of a rabbit gazing transfixed into the eyes of a snake, while the narrative is a slow dance in which Knox and Smith realise they are the rabbits, not the snakes they thought they were. Thus, slowly Knox's icy smile of reason slips and Smith retreats from the Tudor mansion she has climbed into from the wrong side of the tracks to the haven of a Soho drinking club. PH

1954/GB/89m/Insignia/*p* Victor Hanbury/*d* Joseph Losey/*s* Harold Buchmann, Carl Foreman/*orig* Maurice Moiseiwitsch/*c* Harry Waxman/*m* Malcolm Arnold/*lp* Dirk Bogarde, Alexis Smith, Alexander Knox, Hugh Griffith, Maxine Audley.

Slightly Scarlet

Adapted at considerable remove from **James M. Cain**'s novel *Love's Lovely Counterfeit*, this picture uses Alton's bold Technicolor cinematography to impart a luridly heightened atmosphere to a story-line that crosses the tenets of a syndicate-busting crime yarn with those of (would-be) erotic melodrama. Payne plays the right-hand man to a crime boss (threateningly incarnated by De Corsia), who conceives a scheme to discredit a 'clean-up' politician by exploiting the criminal record of the nymphomaniac sister (Dahl) of his personal assistant (Fleming).

However, Payne's initially dissembling relationship with Fleming gradually brings about his reformation, and despite the complications of Dahl's predatory conduct, he helps, almost at the cost of his life, to bring about his employer's indictment. Dwan spoke of the film as a 'handcuff job' in respect of censorship restrictions on depicting nymphomania. Aside from these considerations, however, the screenplay has a perfunctory quality, which unwittingly serves to assist the picture's appeal on the level of highly wrought kitsch. TP

1955/99m/RKO/*p* Benedict Bogeaus/*d* Allan Dwan/*s* Robert Blees/*c* John Alton/*m* Louis Forbes/*lp* Rhonda Fleming, Arlene Dahl, John Payne, Ted De Corsia, Kent Taylor.

So Dark the Night

Capitalising on the success of the same director's **My Name Is Julia Ross**, this is a B-feature that self-consciously embraces the offbeat, in terms of both narrative content and of style, with elaborate camera movements and depth of focus serving to create an oneiric ambience and to draw attention to themselves in the process. The story-line is suitably bizarre, employing the device, seen more recently in Alan Parker's *Angel Heart* (1987), whereby a detective's investigation leads him inexorably to the realisation that he is himself the guilty party. In this case, the topic is a *crime passionnel*, with a middle-aged police detective (Gcray) on a country holiday becoming infatuated with a younger woman. She and her lover are subsequently found murdered, and as Geray heads the inquiry into their deaths, he is brought face to face with his secret self. The fact that the setting in rural France is denoted by surroundings that would hardly look out of place in a turn-of-the-century operetta makes a presumably unintended contribution to the impression of eccentricity. TP

1946/70m/COL/*p* Ted Richmond/*d* Joseph H. Lewis/*s* Martin Berkeley, Dwight Babcock/*c* Burnett Guffey/*m* Hugo Friedhofer/*lp* Steven Geray, Micheline Cheirel, Eugene Borden, Egon Brecher, Ann Codee.

Socho Tobaku/Buchuiuchi: Socho Tobaku/Gambler Series: The Great Casino/Big Time Gambling Boss/Presidential Gambling/The Big Boss

Yukio Mishima described this picture as a masterpiece, while Japan's leading film critic and historian, Tadao Sato, hailed it as the best of the modern **yakuza** films. The fourth instalment in the Buchuiuchi series is stylistically routine but its script encapsulates all the basic motifs and issues that fuelled the genre. Set in the 30s, it presents the two sides of the yakuza's alleged moral code, loyalty and humanity, as seen in two characters. One, Nakai (Tsuruta), is silent and dutiful while the other Matsuda (Wakayama), his blood brother, is the human and therefore the rebellious one. When their godfather dies, the manipulative Senba (Kaneko) wants to expand the business across South East Asia (as the Japanese military almost succeeded in doing during World War II) and has a puppet godfather put into place. Nakai dutifully serves the new but unworthy boss even to the point of killing his own blood-brother when ordered to do so. In the end, Nakai steps out of line and kills the evil Senba, which is permissible since he is more a businessman than a yakuza. When he is sent to jail, a narrator's voice informs us that he will have to do a life sentence in a tone suggesting this is a major injustice for such a righteous fellow. The conflict between feudal codes and modernity is posed in terms of a tragic inevitability: only life in strict obedience to feudal values and hierarchy is honourable. The ultimate indignity is that businessmen have usurped the place of the feu-

dal despots while their hired thieves and killers, the loyal samurai-yakuza, must resign themselves to a life of lonely suffering, preferably in grim silence. It is against the background of such a film that Seijun Suzuki's critique of yakuza acquires its full subversive impact (**Tokyo Nagaremono** and **Koroshi No Rakuin**). Yamashita's film could even be seen as a desperate attempt to redeem the yakuza from Suzuki's devastating portrayals. PW

1968/Japan/92m/Toei/*p* Koji Shundo/*d* Kosaku Yamashita/*s* Kazuo Kasahara/*c* Nagaki Yamagiahi/*m* Toshiaki Tsushima/*lp* Koji Tsuruta, Junko Fuji, Tomisaburo Wakayama, Nobuo Kaneko, Hiroko Sakuramachi.

Sodoma Reykjavik/Remote Control

The film debut of a former director of pop videos, this is a crime comedy about two rival smuggling gangs. The night-club Sodoma in Reykjavik is run by three gangsters who seek to achieve a monopoly of the smuggling and bootlegging trade by eliminating Moli (Björnsson) and his gang. The hero is Axel (Friibjörnsson), an ineffectual young man living at home with his television-watching mother. Axel seeks to compensate for his inadequacies by driving a flashy American car and seducing his sister's friend, the beautiful Unnur (Eliasdottir).

However, Unnur works for Moli and is kidnapped by the Sodoma gang. Axel rescues her. The film's humour is rather leaden, but it nevertheless prompted the Icelandic foreign minister to declare it the funniest film he had seen for forty years. PW

1992/Iceland/90m/Skifan/*p* Jon Olafsson/*d/s* Oskar Jonasson/*c* Sigurdur Sverrir Palsson/*m* Sigurjon Kjartansson/*lp* Jörundur Friibjörnsson, Helgi Björnsson, Soley Eliasdottir, Eggert Thorleifsson, Margret H. Gustavsdottir.

Le Soleil des voyoux/The Action Man

From the 1960s on, when he didn't play an old police war-horse (as in his next film, Lautner's *Le Pacha*, 1967), Gabin played aged villains who need to do one more big job in order to retire in comfort. Flynn's novel, adapted by crime writer Boudard, tells of Denis (Gabin), running a bar in a small provincial town, who gets a visit from an American friend, Jim (Stack), who is in need of cash as he tries to escape from a drugs gang. Denis, aided by his manageress Betty (Lee) who has become Jim's mistress, takes the opportunity to rob the bank across the street from his bar. Everything goes according to plan until the drug dealers turn up and kidnap Denis's wife (Flon). Betty refuses to hand over the loot and absconds with the

ABOVE Dirk Bogarde, Alexis Smith, *The Sleeping Tiger*

ABOVE AND BELOW Tony Curtis, Jack Lemmon, *Some Like It Hot*

cash; Jim is killed and Denis is arrested as a result of Betty's stupidity. The film's blatant misogyny may be due more to Boudard's contribution: he has claimed never to have met anyone as gynophobic as himself. Stack had become a major star in France as a result of his appearances in the popular television series *The Untouchables*. PW

1967/France, Italy/100m/Copernic-Fida/
p Eric Geiger/*d*/*co-s* Jean Delannoy/
co-s Alphonse Boudard/*orig* Jay M. Flynn *The Action Man* (1961)/*c* Walter Wottitz/
m Francis Lai/*lp* Jean Gabin, Robert Stack, Margaret Lee, Suzanne Flon, Jean Topart.

Solo

François Guerif, the historian of the French *policier*, pointed out that Mocky's films are in dialogue with those of Yves Boisset: 'Whereas Boisset *knows*, like we all do, that society is disgusting, that the politicians are rotten, and so on, Mocky actually experiences this in the core of his being and it makes him angry.' Mocky himself evoked the medieval aspects of the French ruling class who abuse their power in order to appropriate young women whom they subsequently give back to the ordinary people to marry and to have families with, like nice little citizens. This film, made a year after May 1968 when the French state was re-consolidating its power and reverting to old habits, starts with a group of youngsters machine-gunning some 20 people at a high-society orgy in Paris and vowing to kill all the rotten members of the ruling class. The violin player and jewel dealer Vincent Cabral (Mocky, giving himself the name of the Guinea-Bissau revolutionary leader later murdered in 1973) finds that his younger brother, Virgile (Le Guillou) and his girl-friend Annabel (Deleuze) are part of the young terrorist gang, and he is drawn into supporting their actions. Chased by the police, Vincent is eventually gunned down by the cops at the Reims railway station while Virgile and Annabel escape the country by train. PW

1970/France, Belgium/90m/Balzac-Cinevog-Showking/*d* Jean-Pierre Mocky/*s* Jean-Pierre Mocky, Alain Moury/*c* Marcel Weiss/
m Georges Moustaki/*lp* Jean-Pierre Mocky, Denis Le Guillou, Anne Deleuze, Eric Burnelli, Alain Fourez.

Some Like It Hot

Joe (Curtis) and Jerry (Lemmon), two unemployed musicians looking for work, accidentally witness the St Valentine's Day murder, where gangster boss Spats Columbo (Raft) and his gang wipe out several of their opponents. Pursued by the gang, Joe and Jerry take the first job they find which will take them out of town – playing in Sweet Sue's all-girl band. They dress as women, join the train to Florida along with a bevy of female musicians, and both fall in love with the band's singer, Sugar Kane (Monroe). Curtis and Lemmon's drag act avoids camp and is funny. Marilyn Monroe is at her luminous best, without the undertow of pathos that stains her later roles. The gangland bits are a hilarious parody of 50s gangster biopics, and the Curtis impersonation of Cary Grant is a charming blend of tribute and caricature. The whole thing has the light wacky touch of a master, the height of Billy Wilder's comic invention. MP

1959/120m/Ashton/Mirisch/*p*/*d* Billy Wilder/*s* Billy Wilder, I.A.L Diamond/ *c* Charles Lang Jr./*m* Adolph Deutsch/ *lp* Marilyn Monroe, Tony Curtis, Jack Lemmon, George Raft, Pat O'Brien.

Someone to Watch Over Me

This is a romantic police thriller featuring Berenger as a married New York detective who is assigned to protect murder-witness socialite Rogers. The detective falls for the initially frosty woman despite his happy family life. However, a killer is on the track of Rogers and when, due to Berenger's efforts, he fails to get her the killer goes after the detective's wife and son. Director Scott succeeds in effecting a suitably gritty and smoky NY background. TV

1987/106m/COL/*p* Thierry de Ganay, Harold Schneider/*d* Ridley Scott/*s* Howard Franklin/ *c* Steven Poster/*m* Michael Kamen/*lp* Tom Berenger, Mimi Rogers, Lorraine Bracco.

Sonatine

Kitano successfully blends the action of **Sono Otoko, Kyobo Ni Tsuki** with the coolly observed absurdities of *3x4xJugatsu* (1990) and *Anonatsu Ichiban Shizukana Umi* (1991) in this hilarious, stylish and disquieting film featuring a minor but brutally cynical gang-boss, Murakawa (Kitano), on his way to perdition. The Tokyo-based Murakawa is sent by his boss to Okinawa to help defeat a rival gang. The none too bright Murakawa, a long way from his familiar environment, and his subordinate killers soon find themselves overwhelmed and have to seek refuge in a beach house, where they invent silly but at times lethally danger-

ABOVE Takeshi Kitano, *Sonatine*

ous games to kill the time. Their boredom is punctuated by sudden violent execution-style murders. When Murakawa realises he has been used as a pawn, he decides to go out in style, attacking a gathering of clan bosses in a hotel. The final scene shows Kitano at his stylish best: his camera depicts the cataclysmic shoot-out from outside the hotel, looking up at the window of the meeting room, where the flashes of the machine guns are reflected. PW

1993/Japan/94m/Shochiku/*p* Kazuyoshi Okuyama/*d*/*s* Takeshi Kitano/*c* Osamu Sasaki/*m* Joe Hisaishi/*lp* Takeshi Kitano, Aya Kakumai, Tetsu Watanabe, Masanobu Katsumura, Susumu Terashima.

Sono Otoko, Kyobo Ni Tsuki/ Violent Cop

Kitano, better known in the West as Beat Takeshi, played the sergeant in Oshima's *Merry Christmas Mr. Lawrence* (1982). In Japan, he was already a popular cabaret and television star by the time he turned director with this hard-boiled cop movie, starring himself as the taciturn, coolly vicious Ryosuke Wagatsuma, Azuma for short. He is dismissed from the force by the police bureaucrats for excessive violence against a teenage hoodlum in the boy's own home. In order to show that Azuma is really a gentle soul caught in a violent world, the script

gives him an ailing sister to care for. When Azuma's buddy in the vice squad, Iwaki (Hiraizumi), is murdered by a drug-pushing syndicate, the ex-cop finds himself in the same role as the 'repudiated yakuza' figure which was the focus of many films a decade or two earlier, and the plot runs through the same type of action as Azuma, whose sister is forcibly addicted to drugs and raped by the gangsters, defies and eventually kills the big boss, Nindo (Kishibe) and his psychotic gay henchman (Ryu). Takeshi's style of alternating laconically underplayed or slightly absurd scenes with sudden outbursts of violence is already much in evidence. His next film, *3x4xJugatsu* (1990), a gangster comedy where the hero, a down-at-heel baseball player, offends some gangsters and has to invoke the help of a crazy killer (Takeshi) in Okinawa before wreaking revenge on the mobsters with a fuel tanker, develops Kitano's idiosyncratic form of absurd action films a step further, to come to fruition in his best film to date, **Sonatine**. PW

1989/Japan/103m/Bandai-Shochiku Fuji/ *p* Kazuyashi Okuyama/*d* Takeshi Kitano/ *s* Hisashi Nazawa/*c* Yasushi Sakakibara/ *m* Daisuke Kume/*lp* Takeshi Kitano, Haku Ryu, Maiko Kawakami, Shiro Sano, Shigeru Hiraizumi.

Sorry, Wrong Number

This property began life as a brief radio play, much acclaimed when it was first broadcast in 1943, which was in effect a monologue by Agnes Moorehead as a bedridden woman who discovers from a crossed telephone line that she is the subject of a murder plot. For the screen version the original author, Lucille Fletcher, expertly elaborated upon this situation by means of a complex structure of flashbacks, delineating the process whereby the fortune-hunting husband of the intended victim has been ensnared through shady dealings into a scheme to collect on his wife's estate. Stanwyck and Lancaster are ideally cast as the spoiled, demanding wife and her opportunistic partner, and the film, graced by the high production values associated with Hal Wallis, is orchestrated by the director to great effect, whether in deployment of sinister seaboard locations for one of the key flashbacks, or in the build-up to the climactic murder, with the killer's shadow ineluctably mounting the stairs and the victim's screams for help drowned out by the noise of an elevated train. TP

1948/89m/PAR/*p* Hal B. Wallis/*d* Anatole Litvak/*s* Lucille Fletcher/*c* Sol Polito/*m* Franz Waxman/*lp* Barbara Stanwyck, Burt Lancaster, Ann Richards, Wendell Corey, William Conrad.

Spade, Sam

When **Dashiell Hammett** wrote *The Maltese Falcon* (1930), dictates of the plot (the hero had to be a partner in his own business rather than leg-man for a large agency) and character (it is important the detective hero seem shifty and dishonest even if he turns out to be unexpectedly straight in the finale) prevented him from reusing his series character, the Continental Op. Sam Spade, Hammett's replacement private eye, works in San Francisco and tangles with dangerous characters like Kaspar Gutman, Joel Cairo and Wilmer the Gunsel. Even if he doesn't find the real Falcon, Spade at least solves the murder of his partner, Miles Archer, letting his sometime girl, the duplicitous Brigid O'Shaugnessy, take the fall for her crimes.

As with **Nick and Nora Charles**, Hammett did not intend to continue Spade beyond the novel (it's hinted on the last page that he is about to be murdered himself, by Archer's wife), but he was jogged by circumstance to revive, or almost revive, the private eye. A collection entitled *The Adventures of Sam Spade, and Other Stories*

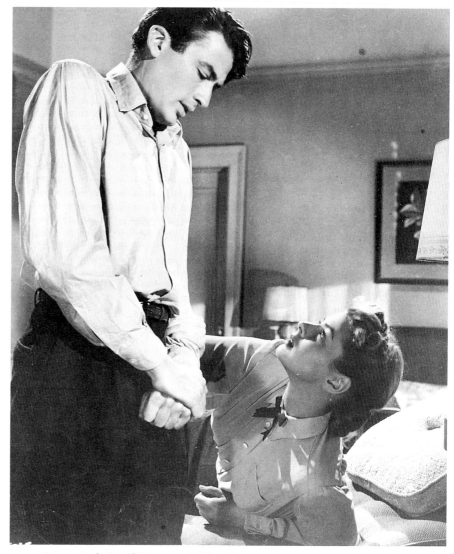

ABOVE Gregory Peck, Ingrid Bergman, *Spellbound*

(1944) consists of three Spade adventures (two of them rewritten versions of earlier non-Spade stories) and four other uncollected pieces.

The **Maltese Falcon** was first filmed in 1931, in a faithful but plodding version also known as *Dangerous Female*, directed by Roy Del Ruth, with Ricardo Cortez overdoing the grinning Satan act as Spade, and an interesting supporting cast including Bebe Daniels as a flapper Brigid, Una Merkel as Effie the secretary, Dudley Digges as Gutman, Thelma Todd as Archer's trampy widow and a twitchy Dwight Frye as Wilmer. Perfectly adequate, it was forgettable enough for Warners to remake it in 1936 as *Satan Met a Lady*, with the falcon turned into the jewelled horn of Roland, Spade renamed Ted Shayne (Warren William) and two female

heavies, in the shape of Bette Davis as Brigid and Alison Skipworth as the equivalent of Gutman. John Huston's classic 1941 adaptation hews remarkably close to the book, down to the use of almost all the dialogue, and immortally casts Humphrey Bogart, Mary Astor, Sydney Greenstreet, Peter Lorre, Elisha Cook Jr and Lee Patrick as Spade, Brigid, Gutman, Cairo, Wilmer and Effie, with memorable bits by Jerome Cowan as Archer and Barton MacLane and Ward Bond as cops. It is this version that has been most often imitated and referenced, notably in David Giler's *The Black Bird* (1975), a sequel with George Segal as Sam Spade Jr and Cook and Patrick in their old roles, and Wim Wenders' **Hammett**, with Frederic Forrest as Hammett embroiled in a plot which supposedly inspired him to write his novel, and with Cook again providing a tangible link to the earlier film.

After the success of *The Maltese Falcon* as a film (and of a radio adaptation of the screenplay broadcast on the anthology show *Academy Award*, with Bogart, Astor and Greenstreet reprising their roles) there was a radio series called *The Adventures of Sam Spade*, starring Howard Duff (1946–50), then Steve Dunne (1950–1). Hammett did nothing but cash royalty cheques, while Bob Tallman and Gil Doud provided wild, semi-humorous scripts, one or two of which were adapted from Hammett's Continental Op stories ('The Fly Paper Chase', 'The Blood Money Caper', 'The Farewell Murders'). The radio programme was harried by suits from Warner Brothers alleging that they, not Hammett, had rights to the character, and further suffered when Hammett became a *persona non grata* jailbird in the McCarthy era, whereupon it was rechristened *The Adventures of Charlie Wild*, though Charlie continued to call upon the services of Sam's secretary, Effie Perrine. *Charlie Wild, Private Detective* (1950–2) was an early TV gumshoe series, with a young Cloris Leachman as Effie, supporting Kevin O'Morrison and then John McQuade as Charlie. Better known was *Richard Diamond, Private Detective*, an imitation Spade played by Dick Powell on radio

(1949–52) and David Janssen on television (1957–60). Diamond's Girl Friday, played on TV as a pair of disembodied legs by Mary Tyler Moore, was called Sam. In a nod of the fedora to this tangle of identities, Neil Simon chose to name his Spade equivalent Sam Diamond in Robert Moore's *Murder By Death* (1976), with Peter Falk and Eileen Brennan providing spot-on parodies of Sam and Effie, though the joke stretched too thin when Simon, Moore, Falk and Brennan reteamed for *The Cheap Detective* (1978), an extended skit on *The Maltese Falcon* and **The Big Sleep**. Among many other retro-romps which play games with Spade and the Falcon are John Huston's *Beat the Devil* (1953), Roger Corman's *Target: Harry* (1968), *The Man With Bogart's Face/Sam Marlow, Private Eye* (1980), the porno *Blonde Heat: The Case of the Maltese Dildo* (1986), the juvenile *Just Ask for Diamond* (1988, from Anthony Horowitz's novel *The Falcon's Malteser*) and the occult-themed *Cast a Deadly Spell* (1991). KN

Spellbound

An attempt to import into the thriller the doctrines of psychoanalysis, then in vogue in Hollywood. Bergman, a doctor in an insane asylum, falls in love with its new Director, Peck, who turns out to be an impostor. Under analysis Peck reveals that he suffers

ABOVE Dorothy McGuire, *The Spiral Staircase*

from a complex over the death of his brother, for which he feels responsible, and also imagines that he has killed the Director whom he is impersonating. Not for the first or last time in Hitchcock, transferred guilt is the motivating factor; people are compelled to feel guilt for crimes they have in fact not committed. (This fascination with guilt is one of the reasons some critics, especially the French, have seen Hitchcock as an essentially Catholic director.) Eventually the real killer is exposed as the previous Director, jealous of his successor. Hitchcock hired the celebrated surrealist Salvador Dali to design the dream sequences symbolising Peck's neurosis. EB

1945/111m/Selznick International/*p* David O. Selznick/*d* Alfred Hitchcock/*s* Ben Hecht/ *c* George Barnes/*m* Miklos Rozsa/*lp* Ingrid Bergman, Gregory Peck, Michael Chekhov, Rhonda Fleming, Leo G. Carroll.

The Spiral Staircase

Set in New England in 1906, during a single (suitably stormy) night, mainly in and around a large and sinister mansion, *The Spiral Staircase* is a bravura exercise in gothic fiction, treating the 'persecuted' heroine

ABOVE *Spellbound*

ABOVE Jane Wyman, *Stage Fright*

Stage Fright

Set in the backstage world of the London theatre, this is perhaps the nearest Hitchcock came to an Agatha Christie-type murder mystery. Todd, hotly pursued by the police, jumps into Wyman's car and relates, in flashback, how Dietrich, a glamorous actress, arrived at his house in bloodstained clothes. She had implored him for help, saying that she has murdered her husband, and wanted him to help destroy the evidence. In the course of doing so, he has himself now been suspected of the crime. Wyman, a RADA student, falls for him and sets out to help him. But at the end of the film we find out that Todd's story is a lie, and that he himself is the criminal. This 'lying flashback' was the subject of much debate for several years. Is Hitchcock unfairly exploiting the unwritten rule that what we see on screen actually happens (unless clearly signalled as 'subjective')? Or are we simply too ready to be led into trusting a seemingly nice young man at the expense of the cynical older woman? EB

1949/GB/110m/ABPC/*p*/*d* Alfred Hitchcock/ *s* Whitfield Cook/*c* Wilkie Cooper/ *m* Leighton Lucas/*lp* Marlene Dietrich, Jane Wyman, Michael Wilding, Richard Todd, Alastair Sim.

Stakeout

Dreyfuss and Estevez are a couple of Seattle detectives assigned to stake out the arrival of an escaped con (Aidan Quinn as a crazy-eyed killer) in this cop-buddy comedy.

theme prevalent in the 1940s. The daring style is set in the opening episode, when as a silent movie (*The Kiss*) plays to piano accompaniment in the hall below, a woman is strangled in her bedroom, her distorted reflection seen in a huge close-up of the murderer's eyeball. The glimpse of *The Kiss* is apposite; since the servant girl heroine has earlier been traumatised into muteness, McGuire's performance takes on something of the quality of silent cinema acting, which in turn contributes to the film's expressionist stylisation. The demented killer, whose next victim McGuire narrowly avoids becoming, proves to be the son (Brent) of her employer (Barrymore); his mission is to eradicate 'imperfection' in the world and he is ultimately shot dead by his mother, so that the drama ends on a fitting note of ritual exorcism. The film as a whole has been aptly described by critic Tom Milne as a 'symphony of shadows'. TP

1945/83m/RKO/*p* Dore Schary/*d* Robert Siodmak/*s* Mel Dinelli/*c* Nicholas Musuraca/ *m* Roy Webb/*lp* Dorothy McGuire, Ethel Barrymore, George Brent, Kent Smith, Rhonda Fleming.

ABOVE Robert Redford, Paul Newman, *The Sting*

Despite its bursts of fast action and clever scenes, the Dreyfuss-Estevez teaming manages somehow to deliver the gung-ho moments expected of this type of story but largely fails to effect the seamless comedy camaraderie established so well in the Mel Gibson-Danny Glover *Lethal Weapon* movies. Quinn's psycho, however, is like a terrifying storm-cloud moving in their direction throughout the picture. The detective pair teamed up again for *Another Stakeout* (1993), also directed by Badham from Kouf's (and others) screenplay. TV

1987/115m/Touchstone-Silver Screen Partners/*p* Jim Kouf, Cathleen Summers/ *d* John Badham/*s* Jim Kouf/*c* John Seale/ *m* Arthur B. Rubinstein/*lp* Richard Dreyfuss, Emilio Estevez, Madeleine Stowe.

Stakeout on Dope Street

This is one of numerous low-budget 'exploitation' pictures of the time which sought to tap the burgeoning youth market. In fact, it is something of a hybrid, combining teenage melodrama with the procedures of the semi-documentary thrillers in vogue a few years earlier and subsequently an influence on television crime series, in a story about a stolen canister of heroin which passes into the hands of three teenage boys. The film is lifted out of the rut by its skilful depiction of the background to the disaffected boys' daily lives. Two sequences are striking: the boys' hunt over the city dump for the canister, presented almost as a jazz ballet (the score is performed by the Hollywood Chamber Jazz Group), and the subjective flashback in which the addicted pusher with whom the heroes make contact relives his experience of 'cold turkey' withdrawal. Kershner's *The Hoodlum Priest* (1961) has something of the same vividness and concludes with a harrowingly detailed account of a gas chamber execution. TP

1958/81m/WB/*p* Andrew J. Fenady/*d* Irvin Kershner/*s* Irwin Schwarz, Irvin Kershner, Andrew J. Fenady/*c* 'Mark Jeffrey' (Haskell Wexler)/*m* Richard Markowitz/*lp* Yale Wexler, Jonathan Haze, Abby Dalton, Allen Kramer, Steven Marlo.

Still of the Night

Hitchcockery is the name of the game here, albeit less in terms of specific allusions (though the central relationship owes a good deal to **Marnie**) than in overall atmosphere. Almendros's luminous cinematography, and the settings of New York auction house and Long Island mansion, go some way to providing a convincing pastiche of Hitchcock, but the content is too pallid, as far as either character or incident is concerned, to engender a sense of involvement. Scheider is a psychiatrist who after the murder of a patient becomes embroiled with the enigmatic blonde (Streep) whom police increasingly suspect is the killer. The perfunctoriness of plotting is borne out by the fact that the concluding twist depends upon information not hitherto vouchsafed to the audience, and the prominence in the narrative scheme of a dream recounted to the psychiatrist by the victim registers as a rather desperate stratagem. TP

1982/91m/MGM-UA/*p* Arlene Donovan/ *d/s* Robert Benton/*c* Nestor Almendros/ *m* John Kander/*lp* Meryl Streep, Roy Scheider, Jessica Tandy, Sara Botsford.

De stilte rond Christine M./ A Question of Silence

A waitress, Annie (Frijda), and an executive secretary, Andrea (Tol), witness housewife Christine (Barends) shoplifting in an Amsterdam boutique. When the stuffy manager apprehends the thief, all three women join in beating and gruesomely butchering the man. The women seem unperturbed by their actions and a psychiatrist, Janine (Habbema), is summoned. Janine gradually begins to sympathise with the women and starts questioning her own life. When at the trial the prosecutor claims that gender has nothing to do with the crime, the three women in the dock burst out laughing, soon joined by Janine and all the other women in the court. The film deploys elaborate cross-cutting between the lives of the three killers, using Janine as the central thread to manipulate the viewer into sympathising with the slaughtering of the manager, while all the men in the story are presented as gross stereotypes. Gorris has claimed that the women's act is analogous to – but the reverse of – the punishment of 'sexually active' women in conventional crime movies and thrillers. However, the film's real analogy is with Hitchcock's *The Birds* (1963), with the women functioning as the creatures usually signifying sweet and lovely nature suddenly pouncing and wreaking a gory revenge on their persecutors. Like the eerie silence which closes Hitchcock's film, and which descends on the women as soon as their crime is mentioned, the laughter at the end of Gorris's signals the women's fundamental 'otherness', their belonging to a realm of nature beyond human rationality and norms. Gorris portrays women as creatures capable of anything at any time at the slightest provocation, as profoundly 'uncultured' in a society where culture is simply coded male. As such, Gorris's film ends up confirming the very view of women propounded by the conventional thrillers, but celebrating women for being beyond human society instead of punishing or killing them for it. PW

1982/Netherlands/96m/Sigma/*p* Matthijs van Heyningen/*d/s* Marleen Gorris/*c* Frans Bromet/*m* Lodewijk de Boer, Martijn Hasebos/*lp* Edda Barends, Nelly Frijda, Henriette Tol, Cox Habbema, Eddy Brugman.

The Sting

A huge box office success, this marries the proven charm of the buddy-buddy teaming of Newman and Redford to a well-constructed con-cum-caper plot-line, dressing the whole package up with pastel-coloured 30s nostalgia and Marvin Hamlisch's repackaging of Scott Joplin's ragtime tunes. When Redford's grifter mentor is murdered by gangster Shaw, he teams up with over-the-hill con-man mastermind Newman, and they construct several puzzles-within-puzzles which dupe the hoodlum *Mission: Impossible*-style, also fooling the audience for a downbeat final turn that suddenly twists towards a happy ending. A pleasurable cultural artefact rather than a movie, paper-thin in essence but substantial in the playing of a large and cunning cast, proven to be a non-repeating phenomenon by the subsequent careers of its producers and writer, not to mention Jeremy Paul Kagan's lamentable *The Sting II* (1983), with Jackie Gleason and Mac Davis taking over from Newman and Redford. Winner of seven Academy Awards including Best Picture, but far less substantial and lasting than 1973's competing nostalgia movies, *American Graffiti*, *Paper Moon* and **Mean Streets**. KN

1973/127m/U/*p* Tony Bill, Michael Phillips, Julia Phillips/*d* George Roy Hill, /*s* David S. Ward/*c* Robert Surtees/*m* Scott Joplin/*lp* Paul Newman, Robert Redford, Robert Shaw, Charles Durning.

The Story of Temple Drake

This version of William Faulkner's 1931 novel, *Sanctuary*, caused a minor storm of protest when Paramount announced it. The

ABOVE Miriam Hopkins, *The Story of Temple Drake*

story of a 'wild' southern belle, Hopkins, who gets mixed up with LaRue's bootlegging outfit and winds up in his big-city brothel was deemed too explosive for its time and the Hays Office censors had advised studios not to film the novel. When Paramount went ahead and made it anyway, the Hays Office warned the studio that no reference must be made to the Faulkner story. The released film was apparently the main reason for the establishing of the Legion of Decency, a Catholic censorship board which urged Catholics to avoid patronising such films. Faulkner's novel was also the source of *Sanctuary* (1961), directed by Tony Richardson. TV

1933/68m/PAR/*p* Emanuel Cohen/*d* Stephen Roberts/*s* Oliver H.P. Garrett/*c* Karl Struss/*lp* Miriam Hopkins, Jack LaRue, William Gargan.

The Story of the Kelly Gang

Only 7 minutes remains of this chronicle of the Kelly brothers' exploits in which Ned and his gang are presented as the heroes and the police as the villains. A major box-office success in Australia and in New Zealand, the film is often claimed to be the first fiction feature in film history. The story, including the undisguised glorification of the gangsters, was reprised a few years later by Harry Southwell in *The Kelly Gang* (1920) and

received an even more glamorised treatment with Mick Jagger in the title role in Tony Richardson's *Ned Kelly* (1970). PW

1906/Australia/45metres/J&N Tait-Johnson & Gibson/*p* John Tait, Nevin Tait, Milliard Johnson, W.A. Gibson/*d/s* Charles Tait/ *c* Milliard Johnson, Orrie Perry, Reg Perry/unknown cast.

Strangers on a Train

Based on a novel by **Patricia Highsmith**, this is one of Hitchcock's most successful demonstrations of the proposition that criminal urges are never far below the surface of even the most respectable of us. Granger plays a tennis pro who meets a fan (Walker) on the train. Walker ingratiates himself, then suggests that Granger kill his father, whom he hates; in exchange Walker will dispose of Granger's wife, who is refusing him the divorce he needs to marry his girl-friend. Granger dismisses the idea, then, when Walker carries out his half of the deal, comes the suspense: is Granger, a decent man, capable of murder in order to prevent Walker telling the police about their 'deal'? One of the film's most famous sequences is the tennis match, with the spectators' heads moving in unison from side to side as the ball crosses the net – all except Walker, whose gaze remains fixed rigidly on Granger. EB

1951/101m/WB/*p/d* Alfred Hitchcock/ *s* Raymond Chandler, Czenzi Ormonde/ *c* Robert Burks/*m* Dimitri Tiomkin/*lp* Farley Granger, Ruth Roman, Robert Walker, Leo G. Carroll, Patricia Hitchcock.

The Sugarland Express

Derived (perhaps rather remotely) from actual events, this is, like Spielberg's preceding *Duel* (1971), a road movie, but also belongs to the 'outlaw couple' sub-genre, exemplified the same year by **Badlands**. The distinctive aspect of *Sugarland* is that its tone is for the most part semi-humorous, even verging on farce. A feckless young woman (Hawn, cleverly used in an oblique variation on her comedienne's persona) persuades her husband (Atherton) to escape from the Texas prison farm where he is nearing the end of his sentence, and head with her for Sugarland to reclaim their baby son, whom welfare authorities are seeking to have adopted. With a bemused hostage in tow, they get under way, gradually pursued by a variety of law officers, and become temporary folk heroes to the crowds who turn

ABOVE Farley Granger, Robert Walker, *Strangers on a Train*

She offers him a job writing her comeback movie, and he's desperate enough to take it in spite of knowing that her dream of a successful return is hopeless. She insists on his staying in the house, and he takes up the role of her gigolo, until he meets another young screenwriter, Betty Schaefer (Olson), begins a hot new screenplay and falls in love. A great and cruel satire on the madness lurking below the surface of the movie industry. Swanson's performance is inspired, crazy and magnificent. The film subsequently was transformed into a musical by Andrew Lloyd Webber. MP

1950/110m/PAR/*p* Charles Brackett/ *d*/*co-s* Billy Wilder/*co-s* Charles Brackett, D.M. Marshman Jr./*c* John Seitz/*m* Franz Waxman/*lp* William Holden, Gloria Swanson, Erich von Stroheim, Nancy Olson, Fred Clark.

Superfly

Gordon Parks Sr's **Shaft**, with its violent black private-eye hero, set box offices alight and offended white liberal sensitivities. *Superfly*, directed by Parks Jr, went even further. Youngblood Priest (O'Neal), the snap-

out to gap at the passing mechanised procession. The action is handled with aplomb, and the film sometimes takes on the air of a live-action cartoon or a pop art painting come alive, while John Williams's punchy, plangent score, with its motif of harmonica solos, helps sustain the offbeat mood. Moreover, the director's control over differing shades of hysteria is such that the concluding declension into tragedy, with events getting out of hand and the husband cut down by police gunfire, contrives not to seem out of kilter with what has gone before. TP

1974/110m/U/*p* Richard D. Zanuck, David Brown/*d* Steven Spielberg/*s* Hal Barwood, Matthew Robbins/*c* Vilmos Zsigmond/ *m* John Williams/*lp* Goldie Hawn, William Atherton, Ben Johnson, Michael Sachs.

Sunset Blvd.

The movie opens with the body of a man floating face down in a swimming pool. In flashback the voice of Joe Gillis (Holden) tells the story. Joe is a screenwriter, broke and desperate. One afternoon he is chased by repo men, and pulls into the driveway of a crumbling Hollywood mansion, where he's conducted by the grim bald-headed butler Max Von Mayerling (von Stroheim) into the presence of Norma Desmond (Swanson).

ABOVE Gloria Swanson, William Holden, *Sunset Blvd.*

pily dressed (wide-brim hat, calf-length coat, gold cross) superstud who karate-chops, fast-talks and screws his way through the movie is a cocaine dealer who is only heroic insofar as his lifestyle (hot babes, a well-appointed apartment, sexually desirable motor vehicles) is enviable. The plot finds him trying for one last score so he can get out of the drugs business, and incidentally pull a scam on 'the Man', the corrupt police commissioner (Shore) who is his biggest rival pusher. Both the film and its score, by Curtis Mayfield, were much imitated, with *The Mack* (1973) and *The Candy Tangerine Man* (1975) doing for the pimp what *Superfly* (the title is slang for cocaine) does for the dealer. Priest returned in *Superfly T.N.T.* (1973), a muddled, pretentious film directed by O'Neal himself from a screenplay by Alex Haley of *Roots* fame, in which the dealer ponders his moneyed retirement in Rome and Africa. The form was amusingly parodied in Keenan Ivory Wayans's *I'm Gonna Git You Sucka* (1988), with Antonio Fargas as 'Flyguy' falling off his platform heels to Mayfield's score, and effectively revived by Mario Van Peebles's *New Jack City* (1991), a more moralistic retread of the theme which takes care to oppose the cool-talking, cool-dressing dealer (Wesley Snipes) with an even cooler and more admirable role model cop (Ice-T). The success of the latter doubtless prompted Sig Shore to produce and direct *The Return of Superfly* (1991), with Nathan Purdee taking over O'Neal's role and Mayfield mixing a little *New Jack City*-style rap into his old soul standards. KN

1972/96m/WB/*p* Sig Shore/*d* Gordon Parks Jr/*s* Phillip Fenty/*c* James Signorelli/*m* Curtis Mayfield/*lp* Ron O'Neal, Carl Lee, Sheila Frazier, Polly Niles, Sig Shore, The Curtis Mayfield Experience.

Suspicion

In his book of interviews with François Truffaut, Hitchcock says that he wanted his film to stick more closely to the plot of the original novel, *Before the Fact* by Francis Iles. In the book, the heroine discovers her husband is poisoning her. Because she loves him she decides to die, but not before writing a letter to alert her mother. In the film, Fontaine only suspects that Grant is trying to murder her, and, perhaps not greatly to our surprise, she turns out to be mistaken. Hitchcock blamed the studio system for preventing him from casting Grant as a murderer, though Truffaut makes a good case for regarding the film version as equally valid. Though one of the earliest films Hitchcock made in America, its middle-class English setting and the presence of a large contingent of British actors show that Hitchcock was not yet ready to desert the tradition of drawing-room crime for more a demotic American milieu. EB

1941/99m/RKO/*p/d* Alfred Hitchcock/ *s* Samson Raphaelson, Joan Harrison, Alma Reville/*c* Harry Stradling/*m* Franz Waxman/ *lp* Cary Grant, Joan Fontaine, Nigel Bruce, Sir Cedric Hardwicke, Dame May Whitty.

Sweet Smell of Success

Sidney Falco (Curtis) is a sleazy PR man dependent on mentions in the column written by J. J. Hunsecker (Lancaster). Falco creeps round Hunsecker, who responds with open contempt. Discovering that his adored younger sister, Susan (Harrison), is involved with a jazz musician, Hunsecker orders Falco to break up the romance. Falco plants a rumour that Dallas (Milner) is a dope-smoking Commie. But Susan breaks her promise to her brother not to see him again and when Hunsecker finds out he sends Falco into action again. This time Falco plants a joint on Dallas and he's beaten up by crooked cop Harry Kello (Meyer). But later on Hunsecker discovers Falco comforting Susan in their apartment, and assuming the worst he sends Kello out after him. Curtis is brilliant, capturing the sleazy, jazzy glamour of 50s Manhattan in a performance which is echoed in Bernstein's score for the Chico Hamilton quintet, and the glassy skin-deep glitter of the interiors. MP

1957/96m/Hecht-Hill-Lancaster/*p* James Hill/*d* Alexander Mackendrick/*s* Clifford Odets, Ernest Lehman/*c* James Wong Howe/*m* Elmer Bernstein/*lp* Burt Lancaster, Tony Curtis, Susan Harrison, Marty Milner, Sam Levene, Emile Meyer.

T

Am Tag als der Regen kam/The Day the Rain Came

Oswald's film, made straight after his version of **Screaming Mimi**, is a respectable contribution to the German 'street films'. In Berlin, a series of hold-ups is committed by black leather-jacketed youngsters led by Werner Maurer (Adorf), the son of a formerly famous surgeon (Fröbe) who became a drunk. A more sensitive teenage gang member, Bob (Wolf), is caught and, supported by his girl-friend Irene (Sommer), decides to help the police. He betrays the gang's next robbery (the bus company) but they escape, taking Bob, who is shot and mortally wounded. Maurer's father is called but he cannot save the boy. Remorseful for having neglected his paternal duties, the old drunk calls the police and his son's gang is arrested.

ABOVE Tony Curtis, Burt Lancaster, *Sweet Smell of Success*

ABOVE *Taiyo No Hakaba*

The plot is sentimental and reflects conservative panic in the face of unruly youngsters asserting their independence, but Oswald achieves bleakly realist imagery that imbues the film with a sense of profound alienation and gloom. PW

1959/Germany/88m/Alfa/*p* Artur Brauner/ *d*/*co-s* Gerd Oswald/*co-s* Heinz Oskar Wuttig, Will Berthold/*c* Carl Loeb/*m* Martin Böttcher/*lp* Mario Adorf, Gerd Fröbe, Elke Sommer, Christian Wolf, Corny Collins.

Taiyo No Hakaba/The Sun's Burial

This, Oshima's third feature, is set in a devastated Kamagasaki, a fetid slum on the outskirts of Osaka, shortly after World War II. To survive, everyone has turned into unscrupulous predators. Hanako (Honoo), the daughter of a junk dealer, runs with a gang led by the smooth Shin (Tsugawa), which trades in birth certificates and operates a blood-bank racket. Subsidiary characters include a ranting political agitator (Ozawa) and an impotent man who hangs himself when he learns of his wife's infidelity. Hanako takes up with a new gang member, Takeshi (Sasaki), who betrays the group to its rivals. When they raid the blood bank, Shin pursues Takeshi across the urban wasteland riddled with holes where houses

used to be and shoots him. As Takeshi agonises on a railway track, he hangs on to his killer's leg until a train tears them both to pieces. Oshima took the conventions of the then popular taiyozoku genre (delinquent movies following on from the success of Shintaro Ishihara's novel, *Taiyo No Kisetsu*, in 1955, filmed by Takumi Furukawa in 1956) to convey a nightmarish world in which callous brutality and sadism are merely means for survival. In this way he strips the gangsters of any semblance of romanticism, portraying them as unmitigated thugs. In this sense, Oshima made an anti-yakuza film which, ironically, shows more respect for the characters than the romanticised versions of yakuza by relating their brutality to a specific environment rather than to an allegedly noble tradition. PW

1960/Japan/87m/Shochiku/*p* Tomio Ikeda/ *d*/*co-s* Nagisa Oshima/*co-s* Toshiro Ishido/ *c* Takashi Kawamata/*m* Riichiro Manabe/ *lp* Kayoko Honoo, Isao Sasaki, Masahiko Tsugawa, Yusuke Kawazu, Junzaburo Ban.

The Taking of Pelham One Two Three

This exciting caper movie about a subway train heist under the streets of Manhattan features a chilling performance from head hijacker Shaw (especially in his microphone exchanges with Matthau's Transit Authority detective) and some splendid above-ground car chases. The film moves at a thrilling pace, intercutting between the hostage and runaway train activities underground and Matthau's control centre surveillance. The title refers to the subway car named for the starting station on the line. TV

1974/104m/UA/*p* Gabriel Katzka, Edgar J. Scherick/*d* Joseph Sargent/*s* Peter Stone/ *c* Owen Roizman/*m* David Shire/*lp* Walter Matthau, Robert Shaw, Martin Balsam.

Tango & Cash

More muscle than mind, this pec-flexing exercise teams Stallone and Russell as a couple of LA detectives (the former as the sophisticated Tango, the latter as the swaggering Cash) who are framed into a tough prison term by big-time drug dealer Palance. Of course, they soon bust loose and set about demolishing Palance's empire as well as everything else within reach or within range of high-calibre gunfire. Albert Magnoli completed the film after Konchalovsky (who had supplied the film with some suitably fiery action sequences) quit in a dispute over the film's ending. TV

1989/98m/WB/*p* Jon Peters, Peter Guber/ *d* Andrei Konchalovsky/*s* Randy Feldman/ *c* Donald E. Thorin/*m* Harold Faltermeyer/ *lp* Sylvester Stallone, Kurt Russell, Teri Hatcher, Jack Palance.

Tangshan Da Xiong/The Big Boss

In the US, Bruce Lee had appeared in TV series and as a slightly ridiculous figure in **Marlowe**, defeated when he becomes hysterical at the suggestion he might be gay. On his return to Hong Kong he became a charismatic star and martial arts expert responsible for the wave of global popularity enjoyed by 'kung fu' films. His first major starring role was in this Mandarin film as Cheng Chaoan, a young Chinese working in his uncle's ice factory in Bangkok. The factory owner turns out to be a triad boss who pushes drugs, runs a prostitution business and doesn't hesitate to kill his workers to keep them into line. Lee, having promised his mother to stay out of trouble, eventually explodes into a frenzy of vengeful violence in defence of his workmates, ending up killing the boss (Han, who is also the film's martial arts instructor) and pounding away at the corpse until his arms are covered in blood up to the elbows. Having given vent to his frustration,

ABOVE Tim O'Kelly, *Targets*

who has discredited the evidence of the sheriff (Carson) of a small California town, is then arraigned by the latter on a trumped-up bribery charge. Stylistically, the film is, as Lawrence Alloway noted, the antithesis of *Touch of Evil*, whose fluidity of movement and depth of field is replaced by the deployment of black-and-white CinemaScope with 'a billboard's emphasis', a procedure Alloway deems 'appropriate to the insistent pattern of conflict in the situation'. Further cross-referencing is provided by *Man in the Shadow* (1957), produced by Zugsmith and directed by Jack Arnold, a modern-day Western in which Chandler plays the upright sheriff of a Texas town and Orson Welles a powerful rancher who regards himself as above the law. TP

1957/93m/U/*p* Albert Zugsmith/*d* Jack Arnold/*s* George Zuckerman/*c* Carl E. Guthrie/*m* Frank Skinner/*lp* Jeff Chandler, Jeanne Crain, Jack Carson, Gail Russell, Edward Andrews.

Taxi Driver

A film that finds a colour 70s equivalent for the monochrome world of 1940s *noir*, with an alienated protagonist, Vietnam veteran Travis Bickle (De Niro), entrapped in a sleazy, neonlit city, cruising in slow motion through steamy slums in his yellow cab while Bernard Herrmann's last score oozes ominousness on the soundtrack. A study in escalating psychosis, the film follows Bickle through various obsessions, as his inarticulate love for a political worker (Shepherd), repulsed when his idea of a date is to take her to a hardcore porno movie, leads to the

he is then persuaded by his sweet cousin (Yi Yi) to turn himself in to the police. The film establishes all the features that would become Lee's trademark, including the facial contortions, shades of self mockery and idiosyncratic fighting stances. He is also seen executing the three-kick movement in mid-air which earned him the nickname Three-Legged Lee. The follow-up, Lo Wei's *Fist Of Fury* (1972), was even more successful, ending with a freeze frame of Lee kicking while jumping, an image that became a popular icon. After a much publicised disagreement, director and star then parted company and Lo Wei, a former actor himself, went on to groom Jackie Chan for stardom. PW

1971/Hong Kong/100m/Golden Harvest/ *p* Raymond Chow [Chou Wen-huai]/*co-s* Lo Wei/*co-s* Ni Kuang/*c* Chen Qingqu/*m* Wang Fuling/*lp* Bruce Lee [Li Xiaolong], Han Yingjie, Maria Yi [Yi Yi], James Tien [Tian Jun], Nora Miao [Miao Kexiu].

Targets

Bogdanovich's chequered career was launched by this picture, which was bankrolled (though he is not credited on screen) by Roger Corman and uses footage from Corman's *The Terror* (1963) in the guise of extracts from the latest work of a veteran horror actor, played by Karloff and closely modelled on the star himself. The almost cosily traditional image of the gothic which

this film-within-a-film projects is contrasted with a starkly modern tale of horror in the intercut account of a well-off young man (O'Kelly) with an obsession with firearms, who unaccountably kills his wife and mother, then starts sniping at passing cars on the freeway. He subsequently takes refuge in a drive-in cinema where Karloff's film is being previewed, and after more mayhem he is cornered by the magisterial figure of Karloff himself. The episodes centred on O'Kelly benefit from precise detail and an avoidance of overt explication, and their effectiveness is pointed by the in-joking manner of the film-making sequences, in which Bogdanovich puts in an appearance as the brash director. TP

1967/90m/Saticoy/*p*/*d*/*s* Peter Bogdanovich/ *c* Laszlo Kovacs/*lp* Boris Karloff, Tim O'Kelly, Nancy Hsueh, James Brown, Peter Bogdanovich.

The Tattered Dress

During his tenure at Universal in the later 1950s, Zugsmith was one of Hollywood's most creative producers, and *The Tattered Dress* anticipates the theme of the relationship between law and justice, developed in the Zugsmith-produced **Touch of Evil**, via a narrative centred upon an unscrupulous attorney (Chandler) with a reputation for always winning an acquittal if the fee is high enough. The ironies mount as the lawyer,

ABOVE Boris Karloff, *Targets*

ABOVE Robert De Niro, *Taxi Driver*

planned assassination of her smooth employer (Harris). Thwarted in this purpose, Bickle transfers his loyalties from Shepherd to twelve-year-old prostitute Iris (Foster), whom, in a reworking of the thematic core of John Ford's *The Searchers* (1956), he rescues from the lowlife by gunning down her pimp (Keitel) and his gang. In direct contrast to the vigilante cycle initiated by **Death Wish**, *Taxi Driver* sees Bickle's one-man crusade against crime as an expression of his essential insanity. A striking combination of the unique talents of Scorsese, Schrader and De Niro, with Schrader's merciless attitudes to urban corruption, as later demonstrated by his paralleling of the story in *Hardcore* (1979), leavening the patter-driven picaresque of Scorsese and De Niro's work on **Mean Streets** (1974) to create a New York inferno. The film created in Travis Bickle an antihero who has entered into popular mythology, his mirror-directed catch-phrase 'You talkin' to me?' quoted in many subsequent films, and his final incarnation as a Mohawk-haired vigilante a seminal influence on the punk movement. KN

1976/113m/COL/*p* Michael Phillips, Julia Phillips/*d* Martin Scorsese/*s* Paul Schrader/ *c* Michael Chapman/*m* Bernard Herrmann/ *lp* Robert De Niro, Harvey Keitel, Cybill Shepherd, Peter Boyle, Jodie Foster, Albert Brooks, Leonard Harris.

10 Rillington Place

Unlike either **Compulsion** or **The Boston Strangler**, which were also directed by Fleischer and depended on differing degrees of melodrama to aid their recreations of complex murders, *10 Rillington Place* hoes to a painstakingly British version of realism in which the right wig (rather than the right theory) is the essential requirement. Filmed in the house next to the actual 10 Rillington Place in London's Notting Hill Gate, it stars Attenborough as multiple murderer John Reginald Christie. Attenborough as an actor-director has shown a predilection for and understanding of the motor forces of the great and the good (*Gandhi*, 1982, *Shadowlands*, 1994). However, as an actor he is equally good at getting into the flesh of the paranoid and the distressed (for example **Brighton Rock** and **Seance on a Wet Afternoon**). His performance in *10 Rillington Place* as the false friend offering kind, but deadly, advice is on a level with that of his impersonation of Pinkie in **Brighton Rock**. Hurt is the innocent (Timothy Evans) who is initially found guilty of Christie's crime. While the film never comes close to explaining Christie, its detailed account of life under the shadow of World War II is powerful and compelling.

1971/GB/111m/COL/*p* Martin Ranshoff, Leslie Linder/*d* Richard Fleischer/*s* Clive Exton/*c* Denys Coop/*m* Johnny Dankworth/ *lp* Richard Attenborough, Judy Geeson, John Hurt, Pat Heywood, Isobel Black, Ray Barron.

ABOVE Richard Attenborough, *10 Rillington Place*

Tengoku No Jigoku/High and Low

The title, literally translated as 'Heaven and Hell', sums up the structure of the movie. The wealthy shoe manufacturer Gondo (Mifune) lives in a mansion on the hill, a constant source of provocation for the poor hospital intern, Takeuchi (Yamazaki), living in the slums below. Takeuchi kidnaps a boy mistakenly believing it to be Gondo's son and demands a huge ransom. The police (Nakadai) persuade Gondo to pay to help catch the criminal. The ransom sequence is a brilliantly handled sequence set on the bullet train, Gondo having to shove the briefcase through the window at a given spot. After an arduous and ingenious investigation, the kidnapper is located thanks to a puff of pink smoke (the only moment of colour in the film). The film's main achievement is to link the suspense and the police procedures to the moral development of the central character, Gondo, who slowly comes to realise his human responsibilities and finally confronts the pathetic criminal in jail where the full implications of a society divided along class lines explode into an emotional scene which, briefly, superimposes the images of the criminal and the businessman onto each other. PW

1963/Japan/143m/Toho/*co-p* Tomoyuki Tanaka/*co-p*/*co-s* Ryuzo Kikushima/*d*/*co-s* Akira Kurosawa/*co-s* Hideo Oguni/*orig* Ed McBain *King's Ransom*/*c* Asakazu Nakai/*m* Masaru Sato/*lp* Toshiro Mifune, Tatsuya Nakadai, Kyoko Kagawa, Takeshi Kato, Tatsuya Mihashi.

Tenkawa Densetsu Satsujin Jikan/The Noh Mask Murders

This is a stylish whodunit set in the milieu of traditional Noh theatre schools. The plot concerns a old Noh-school master (Zaizen) and the problems of finding suitable successor. At the same time pupils at the school are being murdered, their deaths involving a 600-year-old Noh mask symbolising evil. The police investigations, led by Sgt Semba (Kato), are played for comic relief while the investigations of a young traveller (Enoki) are crowned with success. The film is notable mainly for its reliance on parallel cutting between seemingly unrelated events in different parts of the country, a pattern set in the pre-credit sequence. PW

1991/Japan/109m/Kadokaw/*p* Haruki Kadokawa/*d* Kon Ichikawa/*s* Kuri Shitei, Shinya Hidaka, Shinichi Kabuki/*orig* Yasuo Uchida/*c* Yukio Isohata/*m* Fumio Miyashita,

ABOVE Tatsuya Nakadai, *Tengoku No Jigoku*

Kensaku Tanigawa/*lp* Takaki Enoki, Naomi Zaizen, Keiko Kishi, Takeshi Kusaka, Takeshi Kato.

Terrorism

The demonising of terrorism is a comparatively recent phenomenon in the cinema, perhaps because small and underfunded groups using any means available to tackle larger and entrenched forces have always had a certain appeal. Before 1970, many historical, adventure or war films glorified characters who might, in later years, be classed as terrorists: Warner Baxter as Joaquin Murrieta in *The Robin Hood of El Dorado* (1936), Errol Flynn in *The Adventures of Robin Hood* (1938), Tyrone Power in *The Mark of Zorro* (1941), Paul Henreid in *Casablanca* (1943), Sal Mineo in *Exodus* (1960), Chuck Connors in *Geronimo* (1962) and Omar Sharif in *Che!* (1968), not to mention many depictions of the historical IRA (*The Informer*, 1935, *Odd Man Out*, 1947) or Resistance Movements in Nazi-occupied Europe (*Passage to Marseille*, 1943, *The Moon is Down*, 1943, *This Land is Mine*, 1943). Even Barry Jones in *Seven Days to Noon* (1950), a scientist who threatens to detonate an atom bomb in London unless the world agrees to disarm, is seen as sympathetic despite his willingness to slaughter millions of innocent people to prove a point, a lesson not lost on Burt

Lancaster in *Twilight's Last Gleaming* (1977) and Ed Flanders in *Special Bulletin* (1983).

In the 60s and early 70s, due to prevailing sympathy for radical movements, there were respectful depictions of Black Panthers (*The Lost Man*, 1969, **Shaft**) and other underground movements (*The Revolutionary*, 1970, *Katherine*, 1975), though the tide turned with the depictions of neurotic bombers in *Airport* (1970) and *The Mad Bomber* (1972), in which politics take a backseat to psychosis, while *The Day of the Jackal* (1973) introduced the figure of the professional terrorist, a cool hit-man who serves the highest bidder.

ABOVE Terrorism: Omar Sharif, *Che!*

ABOVE Terrorism: Victor McLaglen, *The Informer*

Games (1992). Rare complex terrorists of recent years include Alexis Kanner's troubled academic in *Kings and Desperate Men* (1983), Harvey Keitel's vain insurgent in *Exposed* (1983), and Mickey Rourke's disillusioned ex-IRA gunman in *A Prayer for the Dying* (1987). KN

O tesouro perdido/The Lost Treasure

This is the oldest surviving film of Brazil's classic director Humberto Mauro, most famous for his dramas *Sangue Mineiro* (1929) and **Ganga Bruta** and as a precursor of Cinema Novo. It tells of two orphaned brothers who inherit part of a treasure map. Bandits murder their old relative who possesses the rest of the map and abduct the man's daughter. The younger brother finds the culprits and kills them, being mortally wounded in the process. The elder brother gets rid of his map and marries the liberated girl. Mauro made his mark mainly by shooting on location, achieving a less affected acting style and a quasi-documentary but stylish use of landscape, both inspired by the Hollywood directors he admired, D.W. Griffith and Henry King. PW

1926/Brazil/50m/Phebo Sul America/
p Agenor Cortes de Barros, Homero Cortes Domingues/d/s/co-c Humberto Mauro/
co-c Pedro Comelo/lp Lola Lys, Humberto

Though 60s radicals are still as likely to be the sincere idealists of *Running on Empty* (1988) as the ranting maniacs of *Patty Hearst* (1988), the end of the Vietnam War prompted a wide-scale rethinking of the screen image of terrorism, with Hollywood realigning itself with large and entrenched forces against any small, underfunded groups that might happen along. By the time of *Black Sunday* (1977), the screen image of terrorism had been shaped by the Israeli-Palestine conflict, with the Palestinian terrorists of *21 Hours at Munich* (1976) and *Raid on Entebbe* (1977) depicted in a far less positive light than the Zionist terrorists of *Exodus* had been. *Black Sunday* presents an interesting spectrum of villainy, linking an emotionless German murderess (Marthe Keller) with a deranged Vietnam veteran (Bruce Dern) in a powerful alliance of malevolence and maladjustment, politics and psychosis. Subsequent movie terrorists tend, whether Nazi-style Aryans or swarthy Libyan-Iraqi-Iranian Mid-Easterners, to be flamboyant villains whose causes are not worth arguing and who tend to be mercilessly and justifiably gunned down by square-jawed heroes: witness Klaus Kinski in *Operation Thunderbolt* (1977), Pierce Brosnan in **The Long Good Friday**, Anthony Perkins in *North Sea Hijack/ffolkes* (1980), Rutger Hauer in *Nighthawks* (1981), Judy Davis in *Who Dares Wins/The Final*

Option (1983), Vernon Wells in *Commando* (1985), Richard Lynch in *Invasion USA* (1985), Robert Forster in *The Delta Force* (1986), Gene Simmons in *Wanted: Dead or Alive* (1987), Alan Rickman (posing as a terrorist) in **Die Hard** and Sean Bean in *Patriot*

ABOVE Terrorism: *The Lost Man*

They Drive by Night—They Live by Night

Mauro, Bruno Mauro, Alzira Arruda, Pascoal
Ciodaro.

They Drive by Night

An effective hybrid. The first half is a doom-
laden chase-and-injustice thriller equivalent
to Fritz Lang's early American films, as petty
crook Shorty (Williams), just out of jail, flees
London when circumstantial evidence
makes the police believe him the strangler of
his dance-hall girl-friend. The finale turns to
uneasy comic horror as Shorty and his new
girl (Konstam) are teased and menaced in an
old dark house by Hoover (Thesiger), an
eccentric amateur criminologist and cat-
lover who turns out to be the real murderer.
The crime thriller half is unusually potent for
a British film, blending the *noirish* tone of
American movies with a specifically English
milieu (transport cafés, dance halls, after-
hours clubs, lorry depots, pubs) and revealing an unexpected toughness in a muddy
and rain-swept fight between the hero and a
lecherous lorry driver who has tried to rape
Konstam. With Thesiger's entrance, the film
becomes dominated by his waspish creepy-
camp performance. Produced by Warners'
British sub-division, this was never released
in America because the parent company
decided to appropriate the title for Raoul
Walsh's 1940 truck-driving drama. KN

ABOVE Trevor Howard, Joseph Cotten, Bernard Lee, *The Third Man*

1938/GB/84m/WB/*p* Jerome J. Jackson/
d Arthur Woods/*s* Derek Twist, Paul
Gangelin, James Curtis/*orig* James Curtis/
c Basil Emmott/*lp* Emlyn Williams, Ernest

Thesiger, Anna Konstam, Allan Jeayes,
Jennie Hartley.

They Live by Night

Ray's first film as director, and one which
was very much a personal choice. Ray,
under Houseman's tuition, had completed a
screenplay from Edward Anderson's
Depression novel *Thieves Like Us* (the title
used in Robert Altman's 1974 remake).
Experienced writer Schnee was brought in
by Houseman to give the script a more professional touch, but essentially the film was
as Ray intended it. He presents a pair of star-
crossed lovers, whom the script compares to
Romeo and Juliet, marooned in a world
where fate and evil conspire against them.
Granger is Bowie, a youth whom we first see
involved in a jailbreak with two hardened
crooks, Chicamaw and T-Dub (Da Silva and
Flippen). Bowie's love affair with Keechie
(O'Donnell) provides a brief refuge from a
life of crime which is all he knows; their
hasty marriage, while on the run, at a cheap
motel is a beautifully judged contrast of
innocence and tawdry cynicism. But Bowie
is doomed and, betrayed by the sister of one
of the gang, is gunned down, leaving
Keechie with only her unborn child and a
love letter written moments before his
death. EB

1948/95m/RKO/*p* John Houseman/

ABOVE Farley Granger, Cathy O'Donnell, *They Live by Night*

d Nicholas Ray/*s* Charles Schnee/*c* George E. Diskant/*m* Leigh Harline/*lp* Cathy O'Donnell, Farley Granger, Howard Da Silva, Jay C. Flippen, Helen Craig.

Thieves' Highway

In contrast to earlier thrillers with a truck-driving theme (**They Drive by Night**), *Thieves' Highway* finds the noir sensibility taking on a political ambience. Nick Garcos (Conte) emerges from the war psychologically unscarred only to learn that his father has been crippled by sharp-dealing produce wholesaler Figlia (Cobb). The locus of the trauma which necessarily malforms the *noir* hero is not external like the violence of war but an endemic condition of American society, which forces men to go along with the set of rules imposed by capitalism. When Nick enters a partnership with fellow trucker Ed (Mitchell), he is caught in a trap that becomes obvious as the brightly-lit hometown of the early scenes, where his partner is the stereotypically pretty and pure Polly (Lawrence), gives way to a succession of nighttime nightmares, where Nick is prey to all manner of threats: sleep overcoming him at the wheel, a faulty jack which nearly leaves him crushed under his rig, Figlia's dirty business tricks, hoodlums who steal his money. Only Rica (Cortese), a refugee prostitute, helps him out, finally replacing Polly as his mate, giving him the strength to band together with a pair of other truckers, who have been forced by the system into competing with Nick and Ed (who has been killed in a crash, leaving his apples scattered over a hillside in an unforgettable image), and best the bluff but brutal Figlia. As violent in its climaxes as Dassin's similarly tough **Brute Force** and **Night and the City**, this is a significant, gripping and unusual film. KN

1949/94m/FOX/*p* Robert Bassler/*d* Jules Dassin/*s* A.I. Bezzerides/*orig* A.I. Bezzerides *Thieves' Market*/*c* Norbert Brodine/*m* Alfred Newman/*lp* Richard Conte, Valentina Cortese, Lee J. Cobb, Barbara Lawrence, Jack Oakie, Millard Mitchell.

The Third Man

This highly stylised thriller set in bleak, divided post-war Vienna features Cotten as a naïve writer of Westerns who sets out to find out who killed his friend and ends up killing him himself. Fittingly the film begins with Harry Lime's funeral and ends with his death. Cinematographer Krasker and designer Vincent Korda create a wonderfully evocative Vienna as a mix of once-grand buildings and bomb-sites connected by menacing alleyways (both above and below ground). But it is the taut script and the acting (including such cameos as Hyde White, full of endless bonhomie, and Paul Hoerbiger as an anxious porter) that gives real bite to the film. Welles, who reportedly wrote all his scenes, is all sheen as the racketeer willingly to betray anyone, Cotten is wonderfully energetic, while Howard is the gruff moral centre of the film and Valli is perfect as a mysterious presence. Greene's script is careful to give the characters enough space to breathe but not give the audience enough time to see through them. Similarly, the set pieces, which include Welles's thrilling first appearance in a darkened doorway (an introduction almost as dramatic as John Wayne's in *Stagecoach,* 1939) , Welles 'cuckoo clock' speech, Cotten's lecture on Zane Grey and the modern novel, the chase through the sewers and the final pull-back of the camera are all given real resonance by

ABOVE Orson Welles, *The Third Man*

ABOVE Alan Ladd, Veronica Lake, *This Gun for Hire*

Reed's direction which is both restrained and stylised. The result is not just one of the best British crime films, but one of the best British films ever. 'The Harry Lime Theme' was a million-selling record for its composer Karas, its popularity further boosted by its use as the title music for the 1950 BBC radio series, *The Third Man*, about a much sanitised Harry Lime (played again by Welles). The song was also the theme music to *The Third Man* television series (1959–62) in which Michael Rennie played an even more cleaned-up Harry Lime. Fittingly, in view of the film's story-line, the television series also brought Lime back from the dead (the radio series was set before Lime's death). PH

1949/GB/104m/London Films/*p*/*d* Carol Reed/*s* Graham Greene/*c* Robert Krasker/*m* Anton Karas/*lp* Joseph Cotten, Trevor Howard, Alida Valli, Orson Welles, Bernard Lee, Wilfrid Hyde White, Ernst Deutsch.

This Gun for Hire

'Murder didn't mean much to Raven. It was just a new job,' begins **Graham Greene**'s 1936 novel *A Gun for Sale*, and the feeling is well caught in this film version through the characterisation by Ladd, in his first signifi-

cant screen role, of Raven, the shabby outcast who after being hired for a killing is double-crossed by his fifth-column employers and who sets out to get even with them before the police catch up with him. Greene spoke deprecatingly of the film, making mock of the 'female conjuror' (Lake) who becomes involved with Raven, albeit that the novel's equivalent figure is a chorus girl. While Greene's notations on English provincial life inevitably disappear in the transposition to an American setting, the action is consistently gripping in its own terms, with sharply visualised scenes of pursuit as Raven evades the dragnet the police have set. Moreover, Cregar is noteworthy as the epicene middle man, whose tones become almost voluptuous as he declares, 'I don't want to know,' when the fate of an intended victim is broached. TP

1942/80m/PAR/*p* Richard M. Blumenthal/*d* Frank Tuttle/*s* Albert Maltz, W.R. Burnett/*c* John F. Seitz/*m* David Buttolph/*lp* Alan Ladd, Robert Preston, Veronica Lake, Laird Cregar, Tully Marshall.

The Thomas Crown Affair

As pretty, convoluted, modish, pretentious

and ultimately meaningless as the lyrics of its Oscar-winning theme song ('round like a circle in a spiral, like a wheel within a wheel, never ending or beginning, on an everspinning reel'), *The Thomas Crown Affair* is the heist movie equivalent of such cigarette commercial glossies as *Un Homme et une femme* (1966), *Elvira Madigan* (1967) and *The Graduate* (1967). Jewison, Trustman and usually reliable Wexler fall so in love with their individual set-pieces (a split-screen robbery masterminded by McQueen over the phone, a sophisticatedly sexy game of chess) that they hardly bother with the plot, let alone drama. Boston millionaire Thomas Crown (McQueen), bored with conventional success, plans and executes a perfect bank robbery using a gang of criminals who never meet each other, but finds his interest piqued when the insurance investigator (Dunaway) assigned to the case instinctively suspects his guilt and begins an affair with him. The coolly elegant principles are treated by the camera as beautiful objects, on a par with the furnishings of their tasteful apartments and offices, and the root causes of their amorality never even enter the case. Finally, they are allowed to triumph over the crumpled cops and get away with their stolen loot simply because they are prettier and more chic than the forces of law and order. Though the film's coldness would seem to offer nothing imitable, there have over the years been several variations on the theme: **The Hot Rock/How to Steal a Diamond in Four Uneasy Lessons**, *$*/*The Heist* (1971), *11 Harrowhouse* (1974), *A Man, a Woman and a Bank* (1979) and *How to Beat the High Cost of Living* (1980). KN

1968/102m/UA-Mirisch/*p*/*d* Norman Jewison/*s* Alan R. Trustman/*c* Haskell Wexler/*m* Michel Legrand/*lp* Steve McQueen, Faye Dunaway, Paul Burke, Jack Weston, Yaphet Kotto.

Thompson, Jim (1906–77)

Thompson is possibly the most influential of the American pulp-writers who began publishing during the 40s and 50s. After various jobs in the Texas oil fields of the 20s and a spell in the 30s Federal writers programme in Oklahoma, Thompson published his first novel *Now and On Earth* in 1942. His subsequent career, whilst creatively fertile, was marred by a lack of commercial success and chronic alcoholism. Nevertheless, Thompson's twenty-nine novels such as **The Killer Inside Me** (1952, filmed 1975), **The Get-**

away (1959, filmed 1973) **The Grifters** (1963, filmed 1990) and *Pop. 1280* (1964, filmed 1981)) have left an indelible imprint on the genre. Displaying a pessimistic, satirical and deeply cynical world view, populated by psychopaths, losers and vicious professional criminals, Thompson's lean and mean writing is some of the most innovative and extreme of its era. Thompson worked as a screen writer for Stanley Kubrick on **The Killing** and *Paths Of Glory* (1957) but this was an all too typically short-lived relationship. In the early 1960s Thompson wrote episodes of American TV shows such as *Dr Kildare* and in 1975 had a cameo in a film adaptation of Raymond Chandler's *Farewell, My Lovely*. Some film adaptations of Thompson's work appeared in the 70s and early 80s, including Sam Peckinpah's version of *The Getaway* and Bertrand Tavernier's *Coup de Torchon* (1981, based on *Pop. 1280*). Then, in the late 80s there was a second flurry of Thompson film adaptations, the finest of them being *The Grifters*. AW

Throw Momma from the Train

A black comedy directed by and starring DeVito as a writing student who, in a plot fashioned (quite intentionally) after the murder-exchange idea of Alfred Hitchcock's **Strangers on a Train**, offers his college professor (Crystal) an opportunity to be rid of his shrewish wife in turn for Crystal killing DeVito's surly, overbearing mother (Ramsey). This was DeVito's feature-directing debut. TV

1987/88m/Orion/*p* Larry Brezner/*d* Danny DeVito/*s* Stu Silver/*c* Barry Sonnenfeld/*m* David Newman/*lp* Danny DeVito, Billy Crystal, Anne Ramsey.

Thunderbolt

Sternberg's first sound film took him back to the gangster milieu of **Underworld** and *The Drag Net* (1928), with Bancroft in his fourth leading role for the director. Bancroft (the eponymous 'Thunderbolt') is again a violent gangster, this time in love with Wray. When she falls for respectable young Arlen, Bancroft sets out to kill him, but on the way is arrested for past crimes. The gang frame Arlen for bank robbery and murder, and he and Bancroft face each other on Death Row. Arlen and Wray are married there, Bancroft clears Arlen, but plans to strangle him as he himself goes to the chair. Then, as in *Underworld*, his better self, well submerged thus far, takes over. Although Mankiewicz provided some grittily real dialogue, Sternberg's main concern was to use sound to enhance or counterpoint the visuals. Thus his Death Row is filled with songs, hymns and music, and even comedy, with Marshall's neurotic warden talking lightly of the chair as though it were some delightful feature of a hotel he managed. JL

1929/8571ft/PAR/*p* B. P. Fineman/*d* Josef von Sternberg/*s* Jules Furthman, Herman J. Mankiewicz/*c* Henry Gerrard/*lp* George Bancroft, Fay Wray, Richard Arlen, Tully Marshall, Eugenie Besserer.

Tiger Bay

Polish seaman Bucholtz returns to his Cardiff digs to find his girl-friend with another man and impulsively murders her. The sole witness is a lonely little girl (Mills Jr) who finds herself stuck with the murder weapon and strangely drawn to the hunted man, with whom she hooks up as he is tracked down by a conventional British cinema copper (Mills Sr). Less a crime drama than a study of childhood alienation in line with *Whistle Down the Wind* (1961), which also features Hayley Mills idolising a murderer, or *The Magnet* (1951), this is nevertheless intriguing for its unusual Welsh *noir* setting, with a cross-section of strange characters (smoothly nasty sports reporter Dawson, Indian quack doctor Maitland, chubbily unpleasant choirmaster Griffiths). Thompson, in the brief heyday of his career, draws an excellent and striking performance from Hayley Mills, whose character works far better than the conventionally neurotic murderer, and also establishes a feel for the specific milieu. Interestingly, his other decent film, **Cape Fear**, also involves a girl, an ambiguously menacing murderer and an eponymous provincial setting near water. KN

1959/105m/Rank/*p* Julian Wintle, Leslie Parkyn/*d* J. Lee Thompson/*s* John Hawkesworth, Shelley Smith/*c* Eric Cross/*m* Laurie Johnson/*lp* John Mills, Horst Bucholtz, Hayley Mills, Yvonne Mitchell, Anthony Dawson, Kenneth Griffiths, Marne Maitland.

Tiger in the Smoke

This has the distinction of being one of the few classics of British detective fiction to be faithfully and intelligently translated to the screen. Though let down by the central performance of Wright, the film catches the sense of evil that underpins the novel. Its opening sequence, a gang of embittered war veterans masquerading as a Dickensian set of street musicians tramping through a dreamlike London swathed in fog in search of their former boss – the pointedly named Jack Havoc – is superbly staged, announcing a

ABOVE George Bancroft, Tully Marshall (centre), *Thunderbolt*

Tightrope—Time without Pity

film that is clearly marching towards **Brighton Rock**, even if it never quite gets there. At the centre of the film is stolen war booty which Wright's Havoc has kept from his fellow thieves and which in turn has been kept from him by the officer who led the raid. Hence, the double structure of the story with the gang after Wright, Wright terrorising the officer's widow (Pavlow) and her fiancé (Sinden) attempting to recover the treasure before Wright and the gang, reunited for the second half of the movie. Unfortunately the narrative, which even includes a subplot about Wright escaping from jail and further henchmen, is overly complex but several sequences – Wright's terrorising of Naismith and Pavlow, the hideout of the gang – rise above the naturalism that infects most British films of the period. The prime responsibility for this lies with Baker, who directs with a fine sense of atmosphere, and cinematographer Unsworth. Though the novel featured Allingham's series detective Albert Campion, he does not figure in the film. PH

1956/GB/94m/*p* Leslie Parkyn/*d* Roy Baker/ *s* Anthony Pélissier/*orig* Margery Allingham/ *c* Geoffrey Unsworth/*m* Malcolm Arnold/ *lp* Donald Sinden, Muriel Pavlow, Tony Wright, Bernard Miles, Alec Clunes, Laurence Naismith.

ABOVE Clint Eastwood, *Tightrope*

Tightrope

Eastwood was presumably seeking with this film to renew the box-office potential of the loner cop persona he established in **Dirty Harry** and its sequels, by means of a change of locale to New Orleans, and a scenario which makes its detective hero a divorcé bringing up two young daughters (one of them played by the star's own daughter Alison). The main plot concerns Eastwood tracking down a serial killer, whose victim his girl-friend (Bujold) almost becomes, while the twist is that Eastwood has similar sexual tastes to the killer. The climax is reached with a chase through a railway yard, ending with the murderer being run down by a train and his pursuer left clutching a severed arm which looks as if it might have been remaindered from a joke shop. Surtees's moody camerawork is a minor saving grace. TP

1984/114m/Malpaso-WB/*p* Clint Eastwood, Fritz Manes/*d/s* Richard Tuggle/*c* Bruce Surtees/*m* Lennie Niehaus/*lp* Clint Eastwood, Geneviève Bujold, Dan Hedaya, Alison Eastwood, Jennifer Beck.

Time without Pity

Losey's first completely achieved British film (and the first he made under his own name), *Pity* is driven by a puritanical (American?) sense of morality that is almost hysterical at times. Redgrave is the father who has attempted to stop time with drink who suddenly rouses himself from his torpor with less than 24 hours to spare in a last ditch attempt to prevent his son (McCowen) being hanged for a murder he didn't commit. He races through the film's 88 minutes, forever

ABOVE Alec McCowen, Michael Redgrave, *Time Without Pity*

ABOVE Charles Aznavour (right), *Tirez sur le pianiste*

looking at clocks, and at the end, unable to find enough evidence to secure the conviction of McKern, he commits suicide and makes it look as though McKern murdered him. That said, the tilted camera, the headlong rush of the plot, the lurid references to bullfighting, and the self-loathing of both McKern and Redgrave combine to form, not the basis for a dramatic anti-capital punishment tract in the manner of Fritz Lang's **Beyond a Reasonable Doubt**, but a maddened sense of the moral failure that animates Redgrave. A great film. PH

1957/GB/88m/Harlequin/*p* John Arnold, Anthony Simmons/*d* Joseph Losey/*s* Ben Barzman/*orig* Emlyn Williams *Someone Waiting*/*c* Freddie Francis/*m* Tristram Cary/*lp* Michael Redgrave, Leo McKern, Alec McCowen, Renée Houston, Ann Todd, Peter Cushing.

Tirez sur le pianiste/Shoot the Pianist/Shoot the Piano Player

In the afterglow of his unexpected success with his debut feature, *Les Quatre cents coups* (1959), Truffaut switched from the world of childhood memories to the world of the grown-up cinephile and made this semi-comic tribute to Hollywood *film noir*, using an impressive black and white wide-screen format, at times fragmented by the use of multiple images (with iris effects as in silent films). The story of Goodis's novel is transposed from Philadelphia to a seedy bar in Paris and the hero's name is changed from Eddie to Charlie (the diminutive popular singer Aznavour), although it is revealed later that prior to his degraded existence, the melancholic Charlie was known as a concert pianist called Edouard Saroyan. The change came about when his wife (Berger) committed suicide after sleeping with an impresario. The credits (showing the inside of a piano as it plays the title theme), are followed by a man running at night through the streets, pursued by a car with bright headlights. The chase comes to a stop when the running man knocks himself out against a lamppost and is helped up by someone who insists on talking about his unhappy marriage. Then the chase resumes and Chico (Rémy) joins his brother Charlie in the bar where the pursuing gangsters, a rather comic duo (Boulanger and Mansard), are dealt with by Charlie. The club's singer, Léna (Dubois) is in love with Charlie, to the annoyance of the owner, Plyne (Davri). When the two decide to quit their jobs and to leave, Plyne objects and in the ensuing fight, Charlie kills him. The lovers go on the run and in the end, Charlie and his brothers hole up in the parental home where they confront the pursuing gangsters. In the gun battle, Léna is shot and she very, very slowly sinks to the floor. Charlie returns to his job as a seedy piano player. The film consistently changes moods, mixing comic routines with thriller imagery and situations, interrupted by bleakly romantic flashbacks to Charlie's married life. The film was not a popular success and Truffaut dismissed it as too self-indulgent. However, as a very stylish piece of narrative cinema, the film marked the beginning of an undervalued formalist current in Truffaut's work which would eventually yield some of his most memorable works: *La Nuit américaine* (1973) and **Vivement Dimanche!** During the post-production of *Tirez sur le pianiste*, the editor Decugis was arrested as a political dissident and the work was finished by Bouché. PW

1960/France/85m/Films de la Pléiade/ *p* Pierre Braunberger/*d*/*co-s* François Truffaut/*co-s* Marcel Moussy/*orig* David Goodis *Down There*/*c* Raoul Coutard/ *m* Georges Delerue/*lp* Charles Aznavour, Nicole Berger, Marie Dubois, Albert Rémy, Daniel Boulanger.

T-Men

The success of this film allowed Anthony Mann to graduate from low-budget films to a major studio (MGM). O'Keefe and Ryder play two men from the US Treasury (hence the title) who infiltrate a gang of counterfeit-

ABOVE Dennis O'Keefe, Mary Meade, *T-Men*

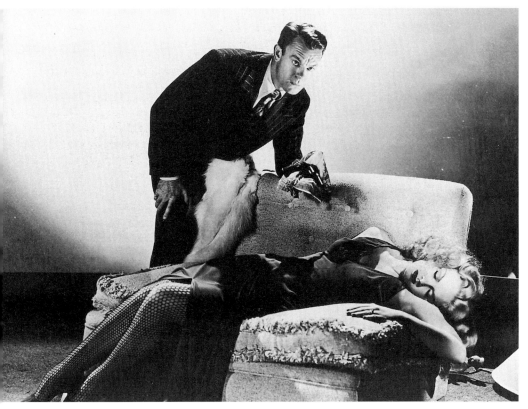

ABOVE Dennis O'Keefe, Mary Meade, *T-Men*

with its criminal plot. The heart of the movie is in the love scenes between Grant and Kelly, which are as powerful as those in **Notorious** with the one difference that Kelly is far less assertive than Ingrid Bergman. Hence the surprise of the first prolonged encounter between Kelly and Grant when, turning at her door to say goodnight, she plants a passionate kiss on his mouth. EB

1955/107m/PAR/*p*/*d* Alfred Hitchcock/ *s* John Michael Hayes/*c* Robert Burks/*m* Lyn Murray/*lp* Cary Grant, Grace Kelly, Charles Vanel, Jessie Royce Landis.

To Kill a Mockingbird

Harper Lee's successful novel of racial prejudice in 1932 Alabama was developed into a chilling observation of life in the deep South by director Mulligan and writer Foote. The gentle merging of two elements in the life of the Peck character, as a quiet-spoken lawyer defending innocent Brock Peters (who is accused of rape) and as the father of two motherless children who are on the verge of moving from childhood to maturity, are dealt with a high degree of compassion and social insight. Foote's literate screenplay and cinematographer Harlan's memorable compositions embellish this gentle yet atmospheric film story. TV

1962/129m/U/*p* Alan J. Pakula/*d* Robert Mulligan/*s* Horton Foote/*c* Russell Harlan/ *m* Elmer Bernstein/*lp* Gregory Peck, Mary Badham, Phillip Alford.

ers. They assume the appearance and mannerisms of gangsters, their true private selves all but lost to view. Eventually the gang grow suspicious of Ryder and, with O'Keefe among them, arrive for a show-down. In one of the most brutal moments in Mann's films, O'Keefe is forced to watch as his partner is shot. Later O'Keefe himself is wounded, but manages to avenge his partner before the Treasury arrive in force. A major contribution to the film is Alton's camerawork which, on a limited budget, achieves wonders of *noir* lighting. Mann and Alton were reunited the next year on **Border Incident**, which has a very similar narrative structure and visual style. EB

1947/92m/Eagle-Lion/*p* Aubrey Schenck/ *d* Anthony Mann/*s* John C. Higgins/*c* John Alton/*m* Paul Sawtell/*lp* Dennis O'Keefe, Alfred Ryder, Mary Meade, Wallace Ford, June Lockhart.

To Catch a Thief

In this slight story Grant is the retired jewel thief who is suspected of a chain of robberies

committed on the French Riviera, who in order to clear his name must find the real thief (Auber). But although the narrative turns on the familiar Hitchcock theme of false accusation, it is not seriously concerned

RIGHT Gregory Peck, Brock Peters, *To Kill a Mockingbird*

Tokyo Nagaremono/Tokyo Drifter

Suzuki rose to prominence with **Yaju No Seishun**. Although he made thrillers, sex and crime movies as well as bitter attacks on militarism (*Kenka Ereji*, 1966), his supreme achievements were his last two yakuza films, this one and **Koroshi No Rakuin**. The hero (Watari) is a gangster who falls foul of his gang and is sent to the country where he is the prey of hired killers. His adventures climax in a night-club where his wife (Matsubara) is performing a schmaltzy song in an impossibly stylised set, with changing colours bathing the shoot-out in different hues as Suzuki flamboyantly displays his contempt for the genre's platitudes. His deadpan irony, occasionally relying on lovely sight gags, revels in a beautifully sensuous formalism recalling the anarchic tendencies in Frank Tashlin or Tex Avery's celebrations of cinema as aesthetic play. The theme song was a popular hit at the time. PW

1966/Japan/83m/Nikkatsu/*p* Tetsuo Nagakawa/*d* Seijun Suzuki/*s* Yasunori Kawauchi/*c* Shigeyoshi Mine/*m* So Tsuburagi/*lp* Tetsuya Watari, Chieko Matsubara, Tsuyoshi Yoshida, Hideaki Nitani, Hideaki Esumi.

Tokyo Wan/Tokyo Bay

Nomura directed many routine police movies for Shochiku (including *Harikomi*, 1957 and *Bokyo To Okite*, 1966) but this is one of his most accomplished efforts. Inspector Sumikawa (Nishimura) investigates a drugs racket and it turns out that his army buddy to whom he owes his life is now a killer in the employ of a notorious boss. As is obligatory in the genre, personal loyalties are made to conflict with institutional allegiances. In the same way the film's style shifts from **yakuza** to thriller movie and back again with consummate ease. The ending is particularly effective: the buddies fight it out on a moving train and then the film cuts to the next morning, two bodies hanging side by side from a railway bridge. PW

1962/Japan/86m/Shochiku/*d* Yoshitaro Nomura/*s* Zenzo Matsuyama, Shosuke Taga/*c* Takashi Kawamata/*m* Yasushi Akutagawa/*lp* Akira Nishimura, Isao Tamagawa, Jiro Ishizaki, Hiromi Sasaki, Kyoko Aoi.

Tony Rome

A slick 1960s private eye thriller, a part of that decade's popular gumshoe revival, which included **Harper** and *Gunn* (1967), starring a wise-guy, Travis McGee-like

ABOVE Tetsuya Watari, *Tokyo Nagaremono*

Sinatra as the title detective hired by a Miami millionaire to look into the private life of his alcoholic daughter. It is not so much the complex mystery plot (based on a novel by Marvin H. Albert) that maintains interest here, but rather Sinatra's flip performance, his smart-aleck dialogue (from scenarist Breen), and the colourful roster of wacky characters he encounters (including Sinatra pals restaurateur Mike Romanoff, boxer Rocky Graziano). The film was successful enough to spawn a sequel, *Lady in Cement* (1968), in which Sinatra retraced his gumshoe steps. TV

1967/110m/FOX/*p* Aaron Rosenberg/*d* Gordon Douglas/*s* Richard L. Breen/*c* Joseph Biroc/*m* Billy May/*lp* Frank Sinatra, Jill St John, Richard Conte, Gena Rowlands, Sue Lyon.

Topkapi

Ten years after **Du Rififi chez les hommes**, Dassin returned to the heist movie and made this item, much more lighthearted than his earlier crime films, an entry in the cycle later typified by such glossy, cosmopolitan dilettante crime movies as *How to Steal a Million* (1966), *Dead Heat on a Merry-Go-Round* (1966) and **The Thomas Crown Affair**. While *Rififi* dilutes its thrills with melancholy sentiment and a Gallic shrug, *Topkapi* gets even further away from Dassin's hard-boiled American roots by milking its

exotic setting for travelogue value, staging the robbery itself as a circus stunt (the gimmick is that the thieves cannot touch the floor of the museum they're robbing without setting off an alarm), and playing crime as a joke. Ustinov gives an Oscar-winningly underbearing performance as the seedy Briton in exile, clinging to shreds of respectability even though he works as an unshaven pimp and petty hustler, but the prevailingly comic, caricaturing tone of his acting shows how far away from 40s or 50s grit Dassin is trying to get. However, like a mediocre musical redeemed by one outstanding production number, the film has a bright spot in the meticulously choreographed robbery, as a team of dedicated stunt-men and tricksters lift a priceless, jewelled dagger from the Topkapi Museum in Istanbul. KN

1964/120m/UA-Filmways/*p*/*d* Jules Dassin/*s* Monja Danischewsky/*orig* Eric Ambler *The Light of Day*/*c* Henri Alekan/*m* Manos Hadjidakis/*lp* Melina Mercouri, Peter Ustinov, Maximilian Schell, Robert Morley, Akim Tamiroff.

Touch of Evil

A car explodes after crossing the US-Mexican border. Mexican narcotics agent Mike Vargas (Heston) begins the investigation with US cop Hank Quinlan (Welles). Quinlan immediately frames a young Mexican, Sanchez (Millan). Vargas doesn't believe he's guilty, and begins digging into Quinlan's past. Adapted by Welles from a script based on *Badge of Evil* by Whit Masterson, the film spawned more of the legends which surround Welles, principally that of the great opening shot which tracks across the Mexican border and ends in a car exploding on the other side. The drama centres on the conflict between Heston's self-righteous investigator, and Welles's monumental portrait of Quinlan as a cop wearied and corrupted by greed and experience. It's also a nightmare journey into a hellish dumping ground of malevolent oddballs, including Marlene Dietrich as the weirdest ever Mexican gypsy. MP

1958/95m/U/*p* Albert Zugsmith/*d* Orson Welles/*s* Orson Welles/*c* Russell Metty/*m* Henry Mancini/*lp* Charlton Heston, Janet Leigh, Orson Welles, Joseph Calleia, Akim Tamiroff, Victor Millan.

Touchez pas au grisbi/Honour among Thieves/Grisbi/Paris Underground

Becker's film proved a turning point in the French *policier* genre, along with Jules Dassin's **Du Rififi chez les hommes**. The story concerns two old-time Montmartre gangsters, Max 'The Liar' (Gabin) and Riton (Dary), who rob a gold shipment at Orly Airport. Riton mentions the heist to his lover, Josy (Moreau), who is also having an affair with another gangster, Angelo (Ventura, in his first screen role), a drug trafficker who resolves to capture the duo and to torture them until they reveal where they stashed the loot. He gets hold of Riton and Max agrees to hand over the money in exchange for his friend. When Angelo nevertheless tries to kill both Max and Riton, a chase ensues and Angelo burns to death in his car. Max escapes but the mortally wounded Riton dies, while the police recover the gold. The film was a massive hit but coolly received by the critics in France. The novelist Simonin, author of the original book, collaborated on the script. His particular contribution was to portray the two thieves as ageing, thoroughly middle-class professionals whose main desire is to retire and to have a quiet life. The novel had engendered many imitations and the film triggered a spate of *Série Noire* adaptations in French cinema. Wiener's theme music became a hit. The enduring reputation of the film as an emblem of post-war French cinema was confirmed when Patrice Rondard alias Patrice Rohmm made a pornographic film starring Brigitte van Meerhaeghe alias Brigitte Lahaie, called *Touchez pas au zizi* (1977). PW

1954/France, Italy/94m/Del Duca Films-Antares/*p* Robert Dorfmann/*d*/*co-s* Jacques Becker/*co-s* Albert Simonin, Maurice Griffe/*orig* A. Simonin/*c* Pierre Montazel/*m* Jean Wiener/*lp* Jean Gabin, René Dary, Jeanne Moreau, Lino Ventura, Dora Doll.

Tracy, Dick

Dick Tracy has been credited with popularising the serial-style mystery-adventure-action newspaper strip. When the detective first appeared in 1931, the Sunday 'funnies' were mainly gag-filled equivalents of the two-reel comedy. Cartoonist-writer Chester Gould (1900–85) pitched a strip called *Plainclothes Tracy* to Captain Joseph Patterson of the *Chicago Tribune*, hoping for national syndication. With a slight name change, Tracy was accepted and, in his first appearance, decides to join the police force because of the murder of his fiancée's father by thugs. Initially down-to-earth and based on actual crimes such as the Lindbergh kidnapping (which Tracy handled much better than his real-life equivalents), *Dick Tracy* gradually evolved along fantastical lines. Tracy, an unglamorous hatchet-nosed hero, began to use science-fictional gadgets (notably his famous two-way wrist radio) in his implacable pursuit of evildoers. The supporting cast – which includes steadfast Tess Trueheart, tousle-haired orphan Junior, crusty Chief Brandon and Dick's sidekicks Pat Patton and Sam Catchem (the first Jewish continuing character in an American comic) – was augmented by more bizarre, comic characters like the odiferous B. O. Plenty, zillionaire Diet Smith and the vainglorious actor Vitamin Flintheart. The villains inflated from simple mobsters to deformed grotesques like Flattop, the Brain, the Brow, Pruneface, Haf-and-Haf, the Blank, BB Eyes, Littleface and the Mole.

Tracy kept up with the times, spending the War fighting home-front Axis agents, and Gould introduced the 'crime-stoppers' feature (anti-crime tips crammed into the heading) to the strip. On a more personal level, in 1949, Tracy finally concluded his engagement and married Tess, whereupon the couple had a child, Bonnie Braids, in 1951. In the 50s, a glamorous lady cop, Lizz,

ABOVE Orson Welles, Janet Leigh, Akim Tamiroff, *Touch of Evil*

ABOVE Jean Gabin, *Touchez pas au grisbi*

joined the team, and the two-way wrist radio was updated to a two-way wrist television. Like **Batman**, whose career parallels Tracy's, the detective took a science fiction detour in the 60s, with the introduction of the super-powered Moon Maid and Tracy tackling a case involving the first gangland rubout in space. When writer Max Allan Collins (also a Batman scripter) and artist Rick Fletcher (Gould's long-time assistant) took over the strip on Gould's retirement in 1977, they pruned away the sci-fi angle, and got back to the basics of crime, detection and bizarre villains, giving Tracy a two-way wrist computer. In recent years, Tracy has tackled up-to-date crimes, foiling video pirate Splitscreen and computer crook Memory Banks, not to mention Freddy Krueger-style dream-stalking hit man the Wraith and yuppie criminal couple Uppward and Trendy Lee-Mobile.

Tracy made his screen debut, played by Ralph Byrd, in *Dick Tracy* (1937), a Republic serial in which the detective transfers from the police force to the FBI and tackles the Lame One, a masked master spy equipped with a streamlined aircraft called the Wing. In *Dick Tracy Returns* (1938), the villain is a male version of **Ma Barker**, Pa Stark (Charles Middleton), and the hero gradually kills his way through the evil Stark brood in an unusually violent scenario. *Dick Tracy's G-Men* (1939) and *Dick Tracy vs Crime Inc* (1941) have even more fantastical villains, Zarnoff

(Irving Pichel), a superspy revived from the dead after his electrocution, and the Ghost (Ralph Morgan), an invisible troublemaker, but are otherwise disappointingly prosaic chapter-plays. Byrd, who has accounted for ninety per cent of the character's screen time, returned for all these serials. *Indiana Jones and the Last Crusade* (1989) repeats exactly a cliff-hanger from *Dick Tracy*, in which a tiny speedboat tries to avoid being crushed between two huge ships. The first serial was directed by Ray Taylor and Alan James, subsequent efforts by stalwarts William Witney and John English.

Prompted by the character's continued popularity on radio (played by Ned Wever, Matt Crowley and Barry Thomson) and in the papers, RKO started a quickie series with William Berke's *Dick Tracy* (1945). Morgan Conway was Dick and Gould's supporting cast – Tess Trueheart (Anne Jeffreys), Pat Patton (Lyle Latell), Junior (Mickey Kuhn) – finally made it to the screen. The Gould-style villain is Splitface, a grotesque thug played by Mike Mazurki (who has a nostalgic bit in the 1990 movie). RKO followed up with Gordon Douglas's *Dick Tracy vs Cueball* (1946), with Conway tackling a bald jewel thief (Dick Wessel). Conway was retired and Byrd lured back for a further pair directed by John Rawlins, *Dick Tracy's Dilemma* (1947), in which the villain is the onehanded Claw (Jack Lambert), and *Dick Tracy Meets Gruesome* (1947), with Boris Karloff as a

gangster who uses a paralysing gas on innocent bystanders. Anne Gwynne and Kay Christopher took over the Tess role, and Ian Keith plays Vitamin Flintheart.

Byrd starred from 1950 to 1952 in a *Dick Tracy* TV series for ABC Television, but it was ended by the actor's death. Subsequently, Tracy appeared in a run of horrendous limited animation cartoons, *The Adventures of Dick Tracy*, in 1961, in which the hero is reduced almost to a minor character. A big-budget movie finally came in **Dick Tracy**, directed by and starring Warren Beatty. Unlike Batman (boosted by the cult TV series and the mega-hit movie), Dick Tracy, though his strip continues, has not become an international icon, but he remains an important American image of the detective. KN

Traffic in Souls

White-slave traffic was a topical subject in 1913. There had been a sensational Rockefeller Report, and an inquiry by New York's District Attorney into the Vice Trust. Lurid plays and exploitative films followed. Most of these were minor outings. *Traffic in Souls* was the only one to open on Broadway and enjoy a lengthy run at a major theatre. The film is fast-moving, confidently juggling three or four sub-plots precisely cut into the basic story. Gail and Grandin are two sisters working in a cake-shop, Moore is the cop who loves Gail, and Welsh is the apparently respectable gentleman who heads a Purity League but runs the slave traffic from the same office. Grandin is kidnapped, Gail stumbles luckily on the crooks' trail and exposes their guilt by some clever work with a dictograph, there is a perfectly orchestrated shoot-out, and a downbeat ending of genuine sadness. The last-minute rescue of Grandin was edited together by Jack Cohen in the parallel-action style invented by D. W. Griffith to great effect. The film, which was largely shot on location in New York, is irresistibly confident and good-humoured, as in the opening shots of Moore and Gail off to work and greeted with a friendly wave from the black window-cleaner next door, and in the police stations scenes, with Tucker and scenarist MacNamara playing bit parts, and their names prominent in the duty roster on the wall. Its success inspired several similar films, the most notable of which was *Inside The White Slave Traffic* (1914), a valuable social document of life in New York's Tenderloin district. JL

1913/6 reels/IMP/*d*/co-s George Loane

Tucker/*co-s* Walter MacNamara/*c* Henry Alden Leach/*lp* Jane Gail, Matt Moore, William Welsh, Howard Crampton, Ethel Grandin, Laura Huntley.

Trancers/Future Cop

The best B of the 80s, this features future cop Jack Deth (Thomerson) sent back through time into the body of his 1980s ancestor with orders to stop a zombie-making guru (Stefani) from killing the ancestors of the rulers of the world and thus revoking their entire lives. A true successor to the gadget-filled sci-fi magazines of the 30s and 40s, this also plays self-aware tricks on its post-**Blade Runner** *noir* feel, with the trench-coated hero bewildered in the twentieth century by a TV cop with an absurd name like Peter Gunn and a heroine smart enough to joke about the villain's supposed omniscience by pretending to find a threat from him inside her fortune cookie. Deth's catch-phrase deserves immortality, 'dry hair is for squids', and there is a cheer-along punchline when the wino baseball player (Manard) whose great-great-great-granddaughter is due to save the world recovers his pitching arm. Inevitably, a run of sequels (reaching *Trancers 5* by 1994) disappoint, as does a related series commenced by Band and Thomerson with Albert Pyun's *Dollman* (1994), about a foot-tall alien cop stranded on Earth. KN

1984/85m/Empire/*p/d* Charles Band/ *s* Danny Bilson, Paul DeMeo/*c* Mac Ahlberg/ *m* Mark Ryder, Phil Davies/*lp* Tim Thomerson, Helen Hunt, Michael Stefani, Art La Fleur, Biff Manard.

Tras el cristal/In a Glass Cage

The Catalonian director and ex-set designer Villaronga's feature debut is a story about a former Nazi child torturer (Meisner) and a boy (Sust) who survived the sadistic abuse and returns to take revenge. The villain is now ensconced in an iron lung and the youth takes full advantage of this to visit the same sexual degradations and sadism on his erstwhile torturer, also murdering the man's wife in a grimly gynophobic scene, and murdering a few more boys. He eventually seduces the Nazi's prepubescent daughter and finally kills Meisner, committing suicide by crawling into the iron lung, victim and torturer having become interchangeable. The claustrophobic film lingers on scenes of homosexual sadism and child abuse, provoking a considerable amount of controversy in Spain at the time. PW

1985/Spain/110m/TEM/*p* Teresa Enrich/ *d/s* Agustin Villaronga/*c* Jaume Peracaula/ *m* Javier Navarrete/*lp* Gunter Meisner, David Sust, Marisa Paredes, Gisela Echevarria.

The Trouble with Harry

In an idyllic countryside setting (glowingly photographed in Technicolor by Burks, Hitchcock's favourite cameraman at the time) a corpse is discovered. It turns out to be that of a man named Harry, whom several people may have wished dead. One is his wife, played by MacLaine. A painter (Forsythe), a retired sea-dog (Gwenn) and others all believe they may have accidentally caused Harry's death. Meanwhile the corpse keeps turning up in odd places. In the end it comes out that Harry has died from natural causes, and Forsythe and MacLaine have started a romance. This is one of Hitchcock's least-known pictures, undeservedly. The story, based on a novel by Jack Trevor Story,

with its contrast between the banality of everyday rural life and the stark reality of the dead man's body, is fundamental to the Hitchcockian oeuvre, especially its more English dimension. EB

1956/99m/PAR/*p/d* Alfred Hitchcock/*s* John Michael Hayes/*c* Robert Burks/*m* Bernard Herrmann/*lp* Edmund Gwenn, John Forsythe, Shirley MacLaine, Mildred Natwick, Jerry Mathers.

True Confessions

Based on the unsolved 'Black Dahlia' murder case of the 40s, this adaptation of Dunne's complex novel reduces the flurry of political and social issues raised by the book's treatment of the case to a simplistic intercutting of the involvement of two brothers – one an ambitious priest (De Niro), the other the pragmatic investigating cop (Duvall) with the affair. The main thrust of Duvall's

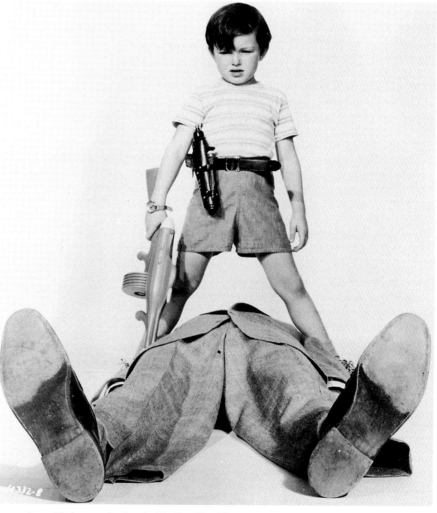

ABOVE Jerry Mathers as the boy in *The Trouble with Harry*

investigation is to pin the crime on the partially-responsible Durning, a gangster trying to expand his legitimate business who is also 'Catholic Layman of the Year' and tied in with the crookeder side of the church, for which De Niro has been tirelessly working. Despite excellent, understated performances, especially from Durning as the glad-handing villain, this sun-struck thriller refuses to take fire. The film lacks directorial focus, and the web of complicity from the novel has been filleted, leaving only a sub-**Chinatown** cynicism. KN

1981/UA/108m/*p* Irwin Winkler/*d* Ulu Grosbard/*co-s* Joan Didion/*co-s*/*orig* John Gregory Dunne/*c* Owen Roizman/*m* Georges Delerue/*lp* Robert De Niro, Robert Duvall, Charles Durning, Burgess Meredith, Cyril Cusack, Kenneth McMillan.

Turner and Hooch

One of sundry 'odd couple' cop movies of the late 1980s (in the manner of **Red Heat**), this is primarily humorous in tone. It puts a fastidious small-town detective in tandem with the obstreperous dog which is the supposed key witness in a drug-connected slaying. Despite (or because of) the large number of credited writers, the comic business deriving from the burgeoning friendship between the two remains largely separate from the rather pedestrian cops-and-robbers narrative, while the latter is marked by gratuitous violence which feels out of place in a supposedly family entertainment. Hanks's charm tends to come off the peg, and it seems like a tactical error to have his canine cohort killed in the climactic affray, even though he has by this stage sired the puppies who provide the 'happy ever after' tag scene. TP

1989/99m/Touchstone/*p* Raymond Wagner/*d* Roger Spottiswoode/*s* Dennis Shryack, Michael Blodgett, Daniel Petrie Jr., Jim Cash, Jack Epps Jr./*c* Adam Greenberg/*m* Charles Gross/*lp* Tom Hanks, Mare Winningham, Craig T. Nelson, Scott Paulin, John McIntire.

The Turning Point

Following the hearings of the Senate Crime Investigating Committee, chaired in 1950 by Senator Estes Kefauver, a large number of early 50s American crime movies dealt with the operations of criminal syndicates. *The Turning Point* covers the operations of a special investigating committee into organised crime in a fictitious US city. The screenplay adopts a traditional strategy of bifurcation

between the upright lawyer (O'Brien) who is heading the proceedings, and his long-time friend (Holden), a cynical journalist who is prepared to use his underworld contacts in the service of personal advancement. In a characteristic subplot, both men are romantically linked to the same woman (Smith), and a further familiar device introduces O'Brien's father (Tully) as a former policeman who proves to have been on the payroll of the mob, and who is murdered to ensure his silence. The film is animated by the theme of democratic responsibility, as demonstrated by Holden's conversion to a principled course of action, and in a 'shock' ending his goading of the syndicate boss (Begley) into betraying himself costs him his life. This climactic sequence, set in a crowded boxing arena, is handled with a graphic energy which typifies the journalistic impact of the film as a whole. TP

1952/85m/PAR/*p* Irving Asher/*d* William Dieterle/*s* Warren Duff/*c* Lionel Lindon/*m* Irving Talbot/*lp* William Holden, Edmond O'Brien, Alexis Smith, Ed Begley, Tom Tully.

U

The Undercover Man

In outline this film can be aligned with a group of post-war movies, of which **T-Men** remains the best known, which dramatise the procedures of one or another branch of law enforcement, in this case, agents of the Internal Revenue Service. In some respects, however, the film looks back to a pre-war context. For one thing, the plot point whereby the agents are seeking to indict a mobster for tax evasion echoes the proceedings against **Al Capone**, and the correspondence is underlined by giving the gangster Capone's sobriquet of the Big Fellow. Moreover, the emphasis on personal feelings, and the sacrifice of personal gratification for the greater good, recalls the romanticised New Deal sympathies evinced in 1930s screenplays by the film's producer, Rossen, though the heightened emotional atmosphere is also consonant with the best work (such as **Gun Crazy**) of director Joseph H. Lewis. The set-pieces are mounted with great dynamism, though perhaps the most striking moment is an intimate one, a love scene between the principal agent (Ford) and his frightened wife (Foch) filmed in an unbroken travelling shot. TP

1949/85m/COL/*p* Robert Rossen/*d* Joseph H.

Lewis/*s* Sydney Boehm/*c* Burnett Guffey/*m* George Duning/*lp* Glenn Ford, Nina Foch, James Whitmore, Barry Kelley, Anthony Caruso.

Undercurrent

Taylor features as the heavy (rather uncharacteristically) in this psychological drama directed by Minnelli. The moody piece deals with the almost-instant marriage of industrialist Taylor and spinster Hepburn, which begins to deteriorate immediately when she develops an obsession over digging into his mysterious past, revealing dark secrets about his missing brother (Mitchum) and a murder. The story builds to a thrilling climax when Taylor turns to getting rid of Hepburn, especially during an exciting cliff-top sequence. TV

1946/114m/MGM/*p* Pandro S. Berman/*d* Vincente Minnelli/*s* Edward Chodorov/*c* Karl Freund/*m* Herbert Stothart/*lp* Katharine Hepburn, Robert Taylor, Robert Mitchum.

Underworld/Paying the Penalty

This was Sternberg's first commercial success. 'Bull' Weed (Bancroft) is a gangster – a tough, heroic, larger-than-life figure at loggerheads with the organised mob. He befriends 'Rolls Royce', a drunken shyster lawyer (Brook), who reforms his habits and

ABOVE Evelyn Brent, *Underworld*

Underworld U.S.A.

The masterpiece among Fuller's crime films, this marries a penetrating analysis of organised crime to the shock-therapy of Fuller's style of direction. Robertson plays Tolly, whose father is beaten to death at the beginning of the film by members of a criminal gang. One by one he tracks them down and avenges his father's death. Tolly is willing to use government help in his crusade, but only on his own terms. He owes loyalty to no one and nothing but his own family. Even Cuddles (Dorn), a woman who falls in love with him, is exploited as a means to an end. Tolly wins the confidence of Conners (Emhardt), the boss of the syndicate, and refuses to turn him in to the government since Conners had no direct part in his father's death. Only when Conners turns against Cuddles does Tolly finally confront him, murdering the grossly fat man by holding him under water in his swimming pool. Fatally wounded, Tolly staggers into an alley and dies among the trash cans, the camera closing on his clenched fist. EB

1960/99m/COL/*p*/*d*/*s* Samuel Fuller/*c* Hal Mohr/*m* Harry Sukman/*lp* Cliff Robertson, Dolores Dorn, Beatrice Kay, Paul Dubov, Robert Emhardt.

The Unholy Wife

Renewing the collaboration between John Farrow and the hard-boiled novelist **Jonathan Latimer**, who had earlier scripted Farrow's **The Big Clock** and **Night Has a Thousand Eyes**, this film, adapted from a television play, represents one of the last entries in the initial *film noir* cycle and is one of the very few movies in that canon to be shot in colour. Ballard's sumptuous, rich-toned camerawork functions in counterpoint to the traditionally sordid aspects of the story, which, utilising a flashback structure, tells how a bar girl (Dors) marries a wealthy wine grower (Steiger), cheats on him, and then plans to murder him under the guise of shooting a prowler. When the wrong man dies in the incident, she contrives to rig matters so that her husband is charged with the killing (a plot manoeuvre reminiscent, though with sex roles reversed, of *Dial M For Murder*, 1954). The concluding passages, with Dors's culpability exposed at the last moment, may be a little strained, but do not detract significantly from the ingenuity of the whole. TP

1957/95m/RKO/*p*/*d* John Farrow/*s* Jonathan Latimer/*c* Lucien Ballard/*m* Daniele Amfitheatrof/*lp* Diana Dors, Rod Steiger, Tom Tryon, Arthur Franz, Marie Windsor.

becomes Bull's brains. Bull suspects an affair between his girl, 'Feathers' (Brent), and Rolls Royce, but before this is cleared up he kills a rival (Kohler) who tries to assault Feathers at a gangsters' ball. He goes to prison, escapes, finds Rolls Royce and Feathers together, is convinced of their love, and stays to be killed by the police while they escape. Aided by three superb performances, and by masterly camerawork from Glennon, most notably at the set-piece of the ball, Sternberg created from this simplistic story an intense study of human emotions bordering on the tragic. But if *Underworld* is about love and loyalty, sacrifice and redemption, characteristic Sternberg themes, the granting of heroic stature to Bull, Feathers and Rolls Royce gave the incipient gangster genre its first true heroes. Hecht won the first Academy Award for 'best original story', a nice irony, for the film had strayed so far from his story that at one point he tried to get his name removed. JL

1927/7643ft/PAR/*p* Hector Turnbull/*d* Josef von Sternberg/*s* Robert N. Lee, Charles Furthman/*orig* Ben Hecht/*c* Bert Glennon/*lp* Clive Brook, Evelyn Brent, George Bancroft, Larry Semon, Fred Kohler.

RIGHT Robert Emhardt, Cliff Robertson, *Underworld U.S.A.*

Marsden as her series detective Adam Dalgliesh. This is from her 1972 private eye novel and Petit handles it in a quietly gothic fashion fans of the authoress found hard to take but which does serve to illuminate the ritual nature of the English Classic Mystery, while presenting in Cordelia, exceptionally played by Guard, an offbeat and credible modern female P.I. Petit has subsequently veered between impenetrably arty mysteries like *Flight to Berlin* (1983) and *Chinese Boxes* (1984) and a professional, solidly BBC Agatha Christie, *A Caribbean Mystery* (1990). KN

1982/GB/94m/Boyd's Co/*p* Michael Relph/*d*/*co-s* Christopher Petit/*co-s* Elizabeth McKay, Brian Scobie/*orig* P.D. James/ *c* Martin Schafer/*m* Chaz Jankel, Philip Bagenal, Pete Van-Hooke/*lp* Pippa Guard, Billie Whitelaw, Paul Freeman, Dominic Guard, Dawn Archibald.

The Untouchables

A lavish period gangster movie based on the book that inspired the 1959–63 teleseries, which makes it a *de facto* remake of Phil Karlson's *The Scarface Mob* (1962), the theatrical version of the first episodes of the teleseries. In Chicago during Prohibition,

Union Station

Based on Thomas Walsh's novel, *Nightmare in Manhattan*, this makes exciting use of the busy railway terminal location. The plot has Olsen witness a kidnapping and convince Holden's chief of railway police that the terminal is to be used as the payoff location. Scenes and settings shift constantly as the investigation gets under way to prove Olsen's story, then the hectic surveillance of the bustling station builds to an exciting underground shoot-out. TV

1950/81m/PAR/*p* Jules Schermer/*d* Rudolph Maté/*s* Sydney Boehm/*c* Daniel L. Fapp/ *m* David Buttolph, Heinz Roemheld/ *lp* William Holden, Nancy Olsen, Barry Fitzgerald.

An Unsuitable Job for a Woman

Cordelia Gray (Guard), an intelligent young woman, inherits a detective agency from her partner-mentor after his suicide, and is hired by a businessman (Freeman) to investigate the supposed suicide-by-hanging of his son. Uncovering a complex back-story involving dubious parentage, sexual perversion and dynastic ambition, Cordelia becomes increas-

ingly fascinated with the dead boy, almost hanging herself while trying to duplicate his last moments. James has been competently served by a series of television versions of her police procedural novels, with Roy

RIGHT Andy Garcia, Sean Connery, Kevin Costner, Charles Martin Smith, *The Untouchables*

uptight treasury agent **Eliot Ness** (Costner) is frustrated by his inability to make a case against the apparently-omnipotent **Al Capone** (De Niro). Under the guidance of a Scots-accented Irish cop (Connery), Ness sets up his own semi-independent task force, 'the Untouchables', to wage war on the boot-legging racketeer. The film is less a historical epic of the origins of the underworld than a further excuse for De Palma to exercise his rampant cinephilia: when Capone bludgeons a black-tie dinner guest with a baseball bat it is not a re-enactment of a historical incident, as it is in **The St. Valentine's Day Massacre**, but a re-enactment of a key moment in Nicholas Ray's **Party Girl**. In addition, De Palma pulls off a mini-Western in a customs raid on a liquor convoy, an Eisenstein tribute in a baroque shoot-out around a bouncing baby carriage in a railway station, and a horror movie set-piece as the prowling camera stalks Connery in his apartment. The film is stolen by De Niro's outlandish Capone, lecturing assembled journalists about his career, crying during *Pagliacci* and making impassioned speeches about Ness, 'I want him *dead*! I want his family *dead*! I want his house *burned to the ground*! And then I want to *piss on his grave*!' KN

1987/119m/PAR/*p* Art Linson/*d* Brian De Palma/*s* David Mamet/*orig* Eliot Ness, Oscar Fraley/*c* Stephen H. Burum/*m* Ennio Morricone/*lp* Kevin Costner, Sean Connery, Charles Martin Smith, Robert De Niro, Andy Garcia.

The Usual Suspects

Taking its title from Claude Rains's memorable command in *Casablanca* (1942) to 'round up the usual suspects', this is a thriller that teases its audience almost unbearably, leading them on through a maze of flashbacks, false trails, sub-plots and mistaken identity. Five men meet in a police identity parade in New York. One, McManus (Baldwin), proposes they join forces and hold up a taxi service run by crooks for corrupt cops. The hold-up is successful and embarrasses the police. But when the gang go to California to launder the money they are embroiled in a dispute with a mysterious Hungarian master-criminal called Keyzer Soze, who through his Japanese lawyer (played with aplomb by British actor Postlethwaite) demands they conciliate him by lifting a drugs consignment from a ship belonging to another gang. When they

ABOVE Stephen Baldwin, Pete Postlethwaite, Gabriel Byrne, *The Usual Suspects*

refuse, one of their number is killed. But when they do raid the ship, no drugs are found, and all of the gang but Kint (Spacey) are killed as the ship explodes. The history of the affair is pieced together by Kujan (Palminteri), a US Customs Agent, through close questioning of Kint. Kujan suspects that the elusive Soze doesn't exist and that it is all an elaborate smokescreen to cover the gang's tracks, but is forced to let Kint go for lack of evidence. After he has walked free Kujan is faxed a likeness of Soze provided by another Hungarian who claims to know him. It looks remarkably like Kint . . . The performances are wonderful and the tension wound as tight as a tourniquet by director Singer's masterly telling of the tale. EB

1995/105m/PolyGram/*p* Bryan Singer, Michael McDonnell/*d* Bryan Singer/*s* Christopher McQuarrie/*c* Newton Thomas Sigel/*m* John Ottman/*lp* Gabriel Byrne, Stephen Baldwin, Chazz Palminteri, Kevin Pollak, Pete Postlethwaite, Kevin Spacey.

V

Vabank

Set in the 30s in Warsaw, this is the tale of a thief's revenge on a banker. Kwinto (Machulski) is a canny burglar who was once double-crossed by Kramer (Pietraszak), a wealthy banker, in an affair that also caused the death of Kwinto's best friend. The thief organises a raid on Kramer's bank and arranges for part of the loot to be found in the banker's villa. The financier's beautiful girl-friend, who could have proved his innocence of that particular crime by providing the man with an alibi, disappears and the banker is arrested and convicted. The film proved so successful that Machulski went on to make *Vabank 2* (1985). In the West, he is best known for the crude sci-fi comedy *Seksmisja* (1984). PW

1982/Poland/110m/PRF Zespoly Filmowe-Kadr-WFF Lodz/*d/s* Juliusz Machulski/*c* Jerzy Lukaszewicz/*m* Henryk Kuzniak/*lp* Jan Machulski, Leonard Pietraszak, Witold Pyrkosz, Jacek Chmielnik, Krzysztof Kiersznowski.

The Valachi Papers/Joe Valachi: i segreti di Cosa Nostra

A docu-drama treatment of Peter Maas's book about the revelations made by **mafia** gangster-turned-Federal-witness Joseph Valachi in the early 1960s. Spanning the period 1929 to 1961, the blood-stained story recounts, via flashback, mafia operations in most every area of activity through the personal experiences of Brooklyn mobster Valachi (Bronson, who gives a powerful performance as the low-on-the-ladder 'soldier'). Ventura's former crime lord Vito Genovese is appropriately menacing, offering an open contract of $100,000 on Valachi from his high-security prison cell. Released hot on the heels of Francis Ford Coppola's blockbuster, **The Godfather**, the De Laurentiis production appears to be something of a rush job, filmed in New York but mostly at the producer's Rome studios (reportedly due in part to actual underworld threats to the production). Unlike the Coppola picture, here the names are unflinchingly named (Lucky Luciano, Murder Inc's Albert Anastasia, Salvatore Marazano, etc.). TV

1972/Italy, France/123m/COL/*p* Dino De Laurentiis/*d* Terence Young/*s* Stephen Geller/*c* Aldo Toni/*m* Riz Ortolani/*lp* Charles Bronson, Lino Ventura, Joseph Wiseman, Jill Ireland.

Les Vampires

Louis Feuillade began work on *Les Vampires*, his masterpiece, shortly after his release from the army, for reasons of health, in July 1915. Whereas the five episodes of **Fantômas** had been separate stories, the ten parts of *Les Vampires* make a continuous, convoluted, whole. The Vampires are a criminal gang, whose guiding spirit is a woman, Irma Vep (an anagram of 'vampire'), played by Musidora with a steely nonchalance. She and her gang, swathed in close-fitting black from head to foot, glide over the walls and rooftops of nocturnal Paris like creatures from some strange world. Set against them are dogged journalist Guérande (Mathé) and a reformed crook Mazamette (Lévesque). Lévesque was a superb comedian. His Mazamette is sardonic, matter-of-fact, a little incompetent, and a perfect balance to the extravagance of the story. The head of the gang mysteriously changes after episode 6. This is because Feuillade lost patience with

ABOVE Musidora, *Les Vampires*

Aymé's lateness on set, and fired him. War shortages, particularly of film stock, also affected the development of the serial. At one point the Grand Vampire tells a story of his grandfather's adventures with Napoleon in Spain. Feuillade had footage of an unfinished movie set there, and it had to be used. JL

1915/France/11000 metres/Gaumont/*d/s* Louis Feuillade/*c* Manichoux/*lp* Edouard Mathé, Marcel Lévesque, Musidora, Jean Aymé, Louis Leubas, Louise Lagrange.

Vance, Philo

Described by critic Julian Symons as 'a monster of snobbish affectation' and summarily dismissed by Ogden Nash in two lines – 'Philo Vance/Needs a kick up the pants' – Philo Vance was the most popular detective in the US in the late 20s and the 30s and one of the few literary detectives to transfer to the screen with any success in his heyday. Vance was the creation of Willard Huntingdon Wright (1888–1939), writing under the pseudonym of S.S. Van Dine, an art and literary critic who turned to writing detective fiction after a lengthy breakdown. An aesthete chock-a-block with esoteric knowledge, Vance was an American cousin to Lord Peter Wimsey and forefather of many later detectives (notably **Ellery Queen**). Although the character now seems stilted to the point of foolishness, in his time Vance revived a flagging genre, broadening the interest in the detective novel with his baroque but very solidly constructed puzzles (in which the murder was more like a work of art and the detective an art critic).

The first novel was *The Benson Murder Case* (1926), but his best novels were *The Greene Murder Case* (1928), in which a series of murders are modelled on killings documented in a library of murder, and *The Bishop Murder Case* (1929), in which all the murders are based on nursery rhymes. In all Dine wrote twelve novels about Vance, the last being *The Winter Murder Case* (1939). The actor

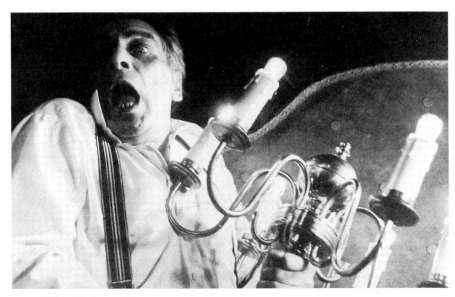

ABOVE Witold Pyrkosz, *Vabank*

ABOVE James Stewart, *Vertigo*

most closely identified with the role of Vance was the urbane William Powell, replete with silk dressing gowns and Egyptian cigarettes; later Powell was to be the even more sophisticated **Nick Charles**. Powell starred in the three films: *The Canary Murder Case* (1929, novel 1927), *The Greene Murder Case* (1929), and *The Benson Murder Case* (1930). These early talkies are somewhat stilted (particularly *Canary*, which was completed as a silent film, then adapted for sound). Eugene Pallette was the sceptical Sergeant Heath and E.H. Calvert the district attorney. Powell's last appearance as Vance was in Warner's *The Kennel Murder Case*, (1933, novel 1931), probably the best film in the series, directed by Michael Curtiz. Prior to this MGM made *The Bishop Murder Case* (1930) with Basil

Rathbone as a more sinister Vance. Rathbone proved to be a better **Sherlock Holmes** than a Vance.

Warren William assumed the role of Vance for *The Dragon Murder Case* (1934, novel 1933) Paul Lukas for *The Casino Murder Case* (1935, novel 1934), and Edmund Lowe in *The Garden Murder Case* (1936, novel 1935). Wilfrid Hyde White starred in a British production *The Scarab Murder Case* (1936, novel 1930). After the lacklustre remake of *The Greene Murder Case* as *Night of Mystery* (1937) with Grant Richards as Vance. Warren William, then starring in Columbia's **Lone Wolf** series, returned for *The Gracie Allen Murder Case* (1939) with Vance in the George Burns role in a story written for the screen by Van Dine. After *Calling Philo Vance*

(1940) a remake of *The Kennel Murder Case* with James Stephenson as a tough Federal agent rather than an effete detective, Vance retired from the screen until 1947. In his three outings for PRC Vance was transformed into a hard-boiled detective Sam Spade look-alike. William Wright starred in *Philo Vance Returns* (1947), Alan Curtis was the deadpan hero in *Philo Vance's Gamble* (1947). Curtis retained the role for *Philo Vance's Secret Mission* (1947) in which he was saddled with Sheila Ryan as a sleuthing girl-friend. PH

La verdad sobre el caso Savolta/The Truth about the Savolta Affair

A political crime thriller set in Barcelona between 1917 and 1923, the story is based on actual events. Antonutti is the unscrupulous munitions manufacturer Savolta who is outfoxed and eventually killed by his French agent, Le Prince (Denner), who takes over the business. The film shows how *pistoleros* were used to keep a factory work force in line and ends with a massacre of strikers shortly before Primo de Rivera became dictator in 1931 and paved the way for Franco. Le Prince is the real villain of the piece, a charming viper ruthlessly pursuing maximum profits. A key scene involves the Frenchman and his disgruntled henchman, Miranda (Montllor). The former charmingly persuading the latter not to kill him and to join him in more profitable enterprises, like eliminating the obstacles to his rise to power. At one point in the film's production the director was fired and some scenes were shot by the Argentinian Diego Santillan; José Maria Forque is also credited as director on poster designs. However, Drove regained control of the film, which has the flavour of a Brechtian morality tale. PW

1980/Spain, France, Italy/80m/Domingo Pedrat-NEF-Filmalpha/*p* Andres Vicente Gomez/*d*/*co-s* Antonio Drove/*co-s* Antonio Larreta/*orig* Eduardo Mendoza/*c* Gilberto Azevedo/*m* Egisto Macchi/*lp* Charles Denner, Jose Luis Lopez Vazquez, Omero Antonutti, Ovidi Montllor, Stefania Sandrelli.

Vertigo

In the view of many this is Hitchcock's masterpiece. Scottie (Stewart) is a policeman who has had to leave the force because of his acute vertigo. He's hired by a former friend to shadow his wife Madeleine (Novak). Gradually Scottie falls in love with her. But she appears to commit suicide by

ABOVE James Stewart, *Vertigo*

Novak, Barbara Bel Geddes, Henry Jones, Tom Helmore.

Victim

Having 'done' the race issue with **Sapphire**, the team of Dearden, Relph and Green turn their attention to **homosexuality**, exploring the then current situation through a comforting police procedural. Indeed, if McEnery's character were a chorus girl, this track-the-blackmailers plot could easily have served, with the same character actors, as an *Edgar Wallace Presents. . .* programmer. Nevertheless, *Victim* is the rare courageous film that, unlike *Sapphire*, is content not merely to attack a generalised wrong but to criticise explicitly a specific unjust law (the 'blackmailer's charter' which criminalised male homosexuality and opened law-abiding individuals to extortion) and have characters supposed unthinkingly to uphold the law (the barrister and the policeman) admit that, in this instance, it is immoral. While Bogarde's screen image is protected by a script that has him confess to homosexual desires but never quite admits he has given in to them, the film – unlike **The Detective**, which attempts much the same with an American gay milieu – presents a cross-section of ordinary gay characters whose only problem is that they are forced to live outside the law. Even such normally swish character actors as Price, Bird and Stock rein in camp mannerisms and try to play ordinary human beings who happen to be gay; while the supposedly 'straight' blackmailers (sneering violent leather-boy Nesbitt with his scooter and goggles, and a repressed spinster who is 'half avenging angel and half peeping tom') are perverted grotesques. KN

1961/GB/100m/Rank-Allied/*p* Michael Relph/*d* Basil Dearden/*s* Janet Green, John McCormick/*c* Otto Heller/*m* Philip Green/*lp* Dirk Bogarde, Sylvia Syms, Dennis Price, Peter McEnery, Derren Nesbitt, Norman Bird.

Vigilantes

A citizen belonging to a 'vigilance committee', an illegal group that intimidated blacks and abolitionists in the southern states of America, was referred to by the Spanish term *vigilante*. Film censors did not approve of plots in which members of the public took the law into their own hands because, at least by implication, official law enforcement authorities were fallible. One of the few films with a contemporary setting to slip through the net was *This Day and Age* (1933), in which schoolboys take revenge on a gangster wrongly acquitted of murder. The rules were bent more often when it came to Westerns, memorably in *The Ox-Bow Incident* (1943), with its story of two innocent cow-

falling from a tower; because of his vertigo he's unable to help her. Much later he meets another young woman who resembles her. In fact it is Madeleine herself. Her original 'suicide' had been staged to disguise the murder of the real wife. When Scottie discovers the truth, he takes her back to the tower to try to get her to confess. She falls to her death. The film is based on a book by **Boileau and Narcejac**, the authors among other works of **Les Diaboliques**. Though the plot revolves around a crime, the film is more of a love story. Stewart's vertigo is symptomatic of his fear of life. Madelcine gives him something to cling to. But ultimately she is an illusion. Once he realises this he is cured of his vertigo. But, the implication is, real life will not hold the same fascination as his obsession. EB

1958/128m/PAR/*p*/*d* Alfred Hitchcock/*s* Alec Coppel, Samuel Taylor/*c* Robert Burks/*m* Bernard Herrmann/*lp* James Stewart, Kim

ABOVE Sylvia Syms, Dirk Bogarde, *Victim*

Violette Nozière

boys hanged by a lynch mob, but also in many less distinguished second features. In Britain the word 'vigilante' was at that time unknown. Accordingly, *The Purple Vigilantes* (1938) had its title changed to *The Purple Riders*, and as late as 1957, when *Utah Blaine* was reviewed, the mysterious word was still in quotation marks.

The situation changed in the late 1960s, when worsening street crime produced a new breed of vigilante whose actions often received tacit approval from the right-wing press. In Britain members of the public with the guts to 'have a go' at tackling criminals were congratulated in Parliament. The first major film to exploit the new dissatisfaction with the police was **Death Wish**. Director Michael Winner reported that each time anti-hero Charles Bronson shot dead a mugger, the audience cheered. The film had a great impact on Hollywood, producing four sequels and a succession of increasingly fantastic and, before censorship curbs, increasingly violent rival productions in which ordinary people, disillusioned ex-cops, Vietnam veterans and downright savages cleaned crime off the streets.

Very few films have treated the subject seriously. In Lina Wertmüller's *Camorra: The Naples Connection* (1985) the mothers of drug-addicted children take on the mafia. A rare Hollywood film that addresses contemporary urban angst is *Falling Down* (1992), in which a white-collar worker goes berserk

and spends a fateful day slaying the thugs who cross his path. The best variation on the *Death Wish* scenario is Abel Ferarra's **Ms .45**, in which Zoe Tamerlis is an anti-sexist vigilante who stalks the city at night, killing any man who harasses her

The most slavish *Death Wish* imitations are evident even from their titles: *Trackdown* (1976), *The Exterminator* (1980), *Fighting Back* (1982), *Vigilante* (1982), *Exterminator 2* (1984), and the television film *The Gladiator* (1986). Women are vigilantes in *Savage Streets* (1984), the television film *The Ladies' Club* (1984) and *Assault of the Killer Bimbos* (1989). In *Young Warriors* (1982) and *Dangerously Close* (1986) the vigilantes are students. In *Ten to Midnight* (1983) the *Death Wish* formula is repeated, complete with Charles Bronson (as a different character).

Attempts to ring the changes were made in *Citizens Band* (1977) with a sequence in which a CB radio enthusiast roots out troublemakers misusing the airwaves; *Defiance* (1979), a B-Western transposed to present-day New York; *Siege* (1982) in which rednecks raid the local gay bars; and Barry Levinson's quirky satire *Jimmy Hollywood* (1994) with a tour-de-force by Joe Pesci as a would-be tough-guy actor turned vigilante. The television film *Keeper of the City* (1991) tackles within the thriller format the moral issues involved in the idolising of a killer, no matter how despicable his victims. Vigilante movies remain popular with the grassroots

ABOVE Vigilantes: Michael Douglas, *Falling Down*

audience, watching on video and via satellite, who may still feel that the most antisocial crimes demand rough justice. DM

Violette Nozière

In Paris in 1933, the teenage Violette (Huppert), living with her train-driver father Baptiste (Carmet) and her mother Germaine (Audran), escapes her oppressive home to lead a secret, promiscuous life in the students' quarter bars. She claims to get the money required from blackmailing her natural father, a Mr Emile whom we never meet. Having contracted syphilis, she first poisons her mother, who recovers, and later, madly in love with the wastrel Dabin (Garreaud), she poisons her father as well. Accused of the murder, Violette claims she had been raped as a child by Baptiste. She is condemned, her sentence being alleviated under the collaborationist regime of Marshal Pétain. Violette marries the prison clerk's son shortly before her death in 1963. Chabrol's rather sensuous period piece seems more interested in the social circumstances and reverberations of the case than in the question of guilt or innocence, as Violette's actions are exploited by newspapers allied to varying political tendencies but never really elucidated. As for Chabrol, the film's strongest moments come when he portrays the stridently bickering students enjoying the night-life of 30s Paris and lingers on the everyday horrors of family life: the hypocrisies, betrayals and brutalities that accompany daily meals and other domestic rituals. PW

ABOVE Vigilantes: Henry Fonda, Paul Burns, Frank Conroy, *The Ox-Bow Incident*

1977/France, Canada/122m/ Filmel-Fr 3-
Cinévidéo/*p* Eugène Lepicier, Denis Héroux/
d Claude Chabrol/*s* Odile Barski, Hervé
Bromberger, Frédéric Grendel/*orig* Jean-
Marie Fitère/*c* Jean Rabier/*m* Pierre Jansen/
lp Isabelle Huppert, Stéphane Audran, Jean
Carmet, Bernadette Lafont, Jean-François
Garreaud.

Vivement Dimanche!/Finally Sunday/Confidentially Yours

Truffaut's last feature showed that he was
still a master of the peculiar mix of suspense
and humour which he had learnt from
Hitchcock. The film returns with even
greater mastery to the atmosphere of **Tirez
sur le pianiste**. Shooting almost exclusively
in bars, night-clubs, domestic interiors and a
cinema, at night and often in the pouring
rain, the story of love and betrayal derived
from Charles Williams's novel acquires an
almost hallucinatory character. In the end,
the plot makes way for a wondrous celebration of the kind of delight in cinephilia
which, by the early 1980s, had become a
nostalgic memory. Barbara Becker (Ardant),
the secretary of estate agent Julien Vercel
(Trintignant), investigates the murders of
which her beloved boss has been accused,
including the killing of his unfaithful wife's
(Sihol) lover. Barbara conducts the action
while Julien hides in the cellar, wistfully
looking at the legs of the women who pass
by the tiny street-level window. After many
chases and narrow escapes from the police,
she discovers that the culprit is a solicitor,
Clément (Laudenbach), who commits suicide. The film is a compendium of Truffaut's
most beloved scenes, with many quotes from
his favourite directors and 40s and 50s
Hollywood thrillers, with special attention
paid to the stunningly photographed (in
beautifully graded black and white) Fanny
Ardant. With *La nuit américaine* (*Day for
Night,* 1973), *Vivement Dimanche!* encapsulates Truffaut's philosophy of cinema as well
as conveying his intense delight in film-making itself. PW

1983/France/111m/Les Films du Carrosse-
A2-Soprofilms/*p/d/co-s* François Truffaut/
co-s Suzanne Schiffman, Jean Aurel/
orig Charles Williams *The Long Saturday Night*
(1962)/*c* Nestor Almendros/*m* Georges
Delerue/*lp* Fanny Ardant, Jean-Louis
Trintignant, Jean-Pierre Kalfon, Philippe
Laudenbach.

ABOVE Jean-Louis Trintignant, Fanny Ardant, *Vivement Dimanche!*

W

Wallace, [Richard Horatio] Edgar
(1875–1932)

Incredibly prolific and concomitantly slap-
dash, Edgar Wallace poured forth novels,
plays, revue sketches, screenplays, stories
and articles, peaking in the last decade of his
life when shrewd promotion and sheer
industry made him the foremost best-seller
of his age. Though at least 136 films, starting
with *Nurse and Martyr* (1915), have been
adapted from the 183 books published by
Wallace in his lifetime, his major contributions lie outside the mystery field with
which he is most often associated. His most
lasting credits are classic adventures with
jungle themes: Ernest B. Schoedsack and
Merian C. Cooper's *King Kong* (1930), for
which Wallace co-authored the screen treatment, and Zoltan Korda's *Sanders of the River*
(1935) with Paul Robeson and Leslie Banks,
based on the 1911 short story collection.
Besides *King Kong*, and *Red Aces* (1929) and
The Squeaker (1930), which he also directed,
Wallace wrote screenplays for *The Ringer*
(1926), *Nurse and Martyr* (1928), *Valley of the
Ghosts* (1928), *The Forger* (1928), *Should a
Doctor Tell?* (1930), *The Hound of the
Baskervilles* (1931) and *The Old Man* (1931).

The bulk of the filmed Wallace is in the

thriller genre, with his most popular works
yielding multiple adaptations: six films of *The
Gaunt Stranger* (1925), better known under
the title of its stage version *The Ringer*
(1926), five of *The Crimson Circle* (1922) and
Terror Keep (1927), better known under the
title of its stage version *The Terror* (1929),
and four of *The Squeaker/The Squealer/Sign of
the Leopard* (1927) and *The Case of the
Frightened Lady/Criminal at Large* (1932), and
three apiece of *The Four Just Men* (1905), *The
Green Archer* (1923), *The Fellowship of the Frog*
(1925), *The Clue of the New Pin* (1923), *The
Flying Squad* (1928), *The Traitor's Gate* (1927)
and *Dark Eyes of London* (1924).

The overwhelming majority of Wallace
films are British or German, but there are
significant American items. *The Terror*
(1928), which used the full gamut of spooky
sound effects: whistling wind, driving rain,
creaking doors, screaming girls, the sinister
midnight organ-playing of the hooded fiend,
the croak of an evil toad, was the second all-
talking picture. The film prompted a sequel,
Return of the Terror (1934), with Mary Astor
and Lyle Talbot, and a British remake, *The
Terror* (1938). Two German versions followed in the 60s, *Der unheimliche Mönch*
(1965) and *Der Mönch mit der Peitsche* (1967).

In the 30s, a loosely connected series of
British films was based on Wallace's most

popular novels. Well cast and produced by British standards (frequently luring directors or actors from Hollywood to add international flavour), these do not stand with the best contemporary American product, or even equal the first rank British thrillers of Alfred Hitchcock. Though William K. Howard's *The Squeaker* (1937) was an Alexander Korda production, it is typical of the Wallace films, with imported Edmund Lowe as a disgraced detective on the trail of a fence-cum-informer and Alastair Sim as a strained Scots newsman in a tinny, makeshift but still somewhat endearing quickie. Like *The Squeaker, The Ringer* was made several times, most notably by Walter Forde in 1938 as *The Gaunt Stranger*, with Wilfrid Lawson again the dastard, Alexander Knox as the avenging vigilante and outrageously melodramatic dialogue ('this is the room in which he broke his sister's heart!'). Forde also directed *The Four Just Men* (1939), with Hugh Sinclair, Francis L. Sullivan, Frank Lawton and Griffith Jones diverging wildly from the source novel by playing Wallace's righteous villains as outlaw heroes. Its British fascism (the heroes' activities include murdering a Member of Parliament whose policies they disagree with) is typical of the megalomaniac, above-the-law tone that creeps often into Wallace's work and makes him today an even harder read than the similarly anti-semitic, anti-communist Sapper.

The Just Men, whom Wallace himself turned into heroes in sequels (*The Council of Justice*, 1908, *The Just Men of Cordova*, 1917, *The Three Just Men*, 1925), are played by Dan Dailey, Jack Hawkins, Vittorio De Sica and Richard Conte in a 1959–60 British TV series. Wallace's most famous detective, Mr J.G. Reeder, introduced in *The Mind of Mr J.G. Reeder* (1925), is played by Leslie Perrins in *Mr Reeder in Room 13*, but the mild-mannered sleuth's contribution to the case was considered so negligible that he is written out of the German remake *Zimmer 13* (1963) and replaced with two-fisted Joachim Berger. Reeder is badly impersonated by Scots comedian Will Fyffe in two 1939 outings, *The Mind of Mr Reeder* and *The Missing People*, but Hugh Burden is ideally cast in a British television series, *The Mind of Mr J.G. Reeder* (1969–71). The most enjoyably daft 30s British Wallace mystery is Walter Summers' *Dark Eyes of London* (1939) in which Bela Lugosi plays a crooked insurance executive with a grudge against the world who lives a double life as the benevolent head of a home for the blind that serves as a

ABOVE Edgar Wallace directing *Red Aces* in 1929

cover for his nefarious scheme to murder all his policy-holders and dump their bodies in the Thames. It was remade twice by the Germans, as *Die toten Augen von London* (1961), with the inevitable Klaus Kinski, and as *Der Bucklige von Soho* (1966).

There was a Wallace revival in the 60s. In Britain *Edgar Wallace Presents. . .* became the prefatory title, complete with a Hitchcockian smoking silhouette of the author, for a slew of hour-long features that were ubiquitous on the bottom half of double bills, including *On the Run* (1962), *Time to Remember* (1963), *Return to Sender* (1963), *Incident at Midnight* (1963), *The Partner* (1963), *Who Was Maddox?* (1964), and *Face of a Stranger* (1964). At best these were solid little mysteries with convoluted plots and at worst dialogue-heavy bores. At the same time from Germany came a further series of Wallace films. These

RIGHT *Warui Yatsu Hodo Yoku Nemuru*

included *Die Bande des Schreckens* (1960), *Der schwarze Abt* (1963), *Das Ratsel des Silbernen Dreiecks* (1967, from *Again the Three Just Men*, 1928) and *Die Tote aus der Thamse* (1971). More horrific than the prosaic British films, they took place in a fantasised London somewhere between *The Threepenny Opera* (1928) and **The Blue Lamp**, often featuring large doses of sex, sadism and the bizarre. Just as the German Karl May Westerns were important precursors of the spaghetti Western boom of the late 60s, so these Wallace programmers were a major influence on the Italian *giallo* genre popularised by Mario Bava and Dario Argento

Freddie Francis's *Traitor's Gate* (1964) is a rare crossbreed, a German production made in Britain with a British crew and a German supporting cast, while Cyril Frankel's *The Trygon Factor* (1967) attempts to wrestle Wallace into the Bondian 60s with Stewart Granger as a two-fisted Scotland Yard man in a trendy setting. Since the end of these series, Wallace has been as forgotten in the cinema as he is in publishing, his last big screen credit being as co-provider of the source story for the remake of *King Kong* (1976), though the BBC did produce a nostalgic *The Case of the Frightened Lady* (1983). KN

Wambaugh, Joseph [Aloysius]
(1937–)

Generally regarded as the first cop to become a successful novelist, Wambaugh's novels of life among Los Angeles police department's finest appear more as police activities than police procedurals. All of his works to date have been filmed for television or features, beginning with his first novel *The New Centurions* (1972) which presented the psy-

chological juxtaposition of the veteran and rookie cop. The 1973 TV mini-series of *The Blue Knight*, featuring a superbly-cast William Holden as an ageing LA street cop, inspired a follow-up TV movie and short-run series (starring George Kennedy). Wambaugh adapted his own screenplay for *The Onion Field* (1979), a truly grim yet gripping story of a cop who cracks up after his partner is murdered, a triumph in its sharp perception of human psychology and emotion under stress. On a lighter note, *The Choirboys* (1978) observes a group of LA cops as they relieve their work pressures by behaving off-duty like psychopathic children, while **The Black Marble** presents another veteran cop, whose female partner helps him through the daily grind of police work. The Wambaugh-created TV anthology *Police Story* (1973–7), with its scripts derived from interviews with real LA cops, was a refreshing revision of the department-approved Dragnet 'case histories' police drama. TV

Warui Yatsu Hodo Yoku Nemuru/ The Bad Sleep Well/The Rose in the Mud

For his first independent production, Kurosawa used a revenge plot to expose corruption and murder in big business. Nishi (Mifune), the secretary of a massive construction company, marries the boss's crippled daughter (Kagawa) and sets out to avenge the death of his father, driven to suicide or killed by the company management. On the point of succeeding, his growing love

ABOVE Hugh Williams, Bela Lugosi, *Dark Eyes of London* from the book by Edgar Wallace

ABOVE Richard Beymer, George Chakiris, Russ Tamblyn, *West Side Story*

nile elements (the 'rumble', the switchblade, the aggressive local cop, etc.). In essence, a powerful culmination of the 1950s juvenile street gang films, which included *City Across the River* (1949), *Teen-age Crime Wave* (1955), *Rumble on the Docks* (1956), *The Delinquents* (1956), *The Cool and the Crazy* (1958). TV

1961/153m/UA/*p*/*co-d* Robert Wise/
co-d Jerome Robbins/*s* Ernest Lehman/
c Daniel L. Fapp/*m* Leonard Bernstein/
lp Natalie Wood, Richard Beymer, Russ Tamblyn, Rita Moreno, George Chakiris.

The Western

Almost all Westerns are crime films in the strict sense that they deal with the violation and enforcement of the law. The opposed figures of the outlaw and the lawman are central to both genres, and there are obvious cross-overs between the lawman Western (*Dodge City*, 1939, *High Noon*, 1950, *Rio Bravo*, 1958) and the cop movie, and between the outlaw Western (*Jesse James*, 1939, *Butch Cassidy and the Sundance Kid*, 1969, *Pat Garrett & Billy the Kid*, 1973) and the gangster film. This reflective kinship is made explicit in those crime movies which take on Western iconography to underline a point (usually about the out-of-time stature of a protagonist), as in the cowboy overtones given the loner cops of **Dirty Harry**, *Walking Tall* (1973), *Lone Wolf McQuade* (1983) and *Extreme Prejudice* (1987) or the Wild West frills given to twentieth-century bandits in **Gun Crazy**, *Bobbie Jo and the Outlaw* (1976),

for his wife proves his undoing and the unscrupulous boss (Mori) has him killed. The bleak film, superbly scored by Sato, reveals how aristocratic ritual and bourgeois respectability provide a facade for a kind of corporate culture that regards human decency as a fatal flaw. Kurosawa's opening sequences of the marriage ceremony culminating in the wheeling in of a gigantic cake in the shape of a building (to remind the boss of past crimes), is a model of narrative control, enhanced by striking urban settings and superbly composed, high-contrast black and white wide-screen imagery. PW

1960/Japan/151m/Toho/*co-p*/*d*/*co-s* Akira Kurosawa/*co-p* Tomoyuki Tanaka/
co-s Shinobu Hashimoto, Hideo Oguni, Ryuzo Kikushima, Eijiro Hisaita/*c* Yuzuru Aizawa/*m* Masaru Sato/*lp* Toshiro Mifune, Takashi Shimura, Takeshi Kato, Masayuki Mori, Akira Nishimura.

West Side Story

This is a superbly produced and handsomely mounted *Romeo and Juliet* musical story of racial and social tensions incorporating stylised street-gang violence (stunningly choreographed by Robbins), romantic interludes between forbidden lovers Wood and

Beymer, and some high-energy ensemble dance numbers performed on the actual locations of upper West Side Manhattan. The main focus is on the territorial gang warfare between Tamblyn's street outfit, the 'Jets', and Chakiris's Puerto Rican gang, the 'Sharks'; which includes all the 1950s juve-

ABOVE The Western: *Assault on Precinct 13*

ABOVE The Western: Jon Voight, *Midnight Cowboy*

The Great Texas Dynamite Chase/Dynamite Women (1978) and *Convoy* (1978).

Western-gangster hybrids were quite common in the 30s, with movies like *Gun Smoke* (1931), *Broadway to Cheyenne* (1932), *Crossfire* (1933) and *Public Cowboy No. 1* (1937) demonstrating that straight-shooting range riders can see off any big city tommy-guns who try to muscle in on the ranges, and a whole cycle of Westerns (*Yellow Sky*, 1948, *3 Godfathers*, 1948, *The Professionals*, 1966, *Sam Whiskey*, 1969) spun off from the heist-caper school of crime films. The most interesting cross-breed is Don Siegel's **Coogan's Bluff**, which casts bi-genre icon Clint Eastwood as an Arizona deputy who comes to New York to haul back a suspect and wanders, like Jon Voight in *Midnight Cowboy* (1969), through a disorienting and degraded urban landscape longing for the wide open spaces.

However, as is suggested by the fantasised archetypal settings adopted by such attempted 'modern-day Westerns' as *Billy Jack* (1971), **Assault on Precinct 13** and *Road House* (1988), the historical context of the Western makes it a genre unto itself, with rules that have to be considerably stretched in order to slot into a contemporary setting, replacing marauding Indians with a zombie street gang or rethinking the Shane-style lone hired gun as a night-club bouncer played by Patrick Swayze. There are isolated instances of crime films remade as Westerns (**High Sierra** as *Colorado Territory*, 1949; **Kiss of Death** as *The Fiend Who Walked the West*, 1958; *House of Strangers*, 1949, as *Broken Lance*, 1954; **The Asphalt Jungle** as *The Badlanders*, 1958) and W.R. Burnett's Western novel *Saint Johnson* (1931) was simultaneously adapted as a gangster movie (*Beast of the City*, 1931) and a Western (*Law and Order*, 1932), while Dashiell Hammett's crime masterpiece *Red Harvest* (1929) is far better served by the Western *Per un pugno di dollari/A Fistful of Dollars* (1964), filtered through the samurai movie *Yojimbo* (1961), than by the 'official' adaptation *Roadhouse Nights* (1930). But the issues under question in *My Darling Clementine* (1947) and *The Wild Bunch* (1969), to select two outstanding examples from among thousands, have little to do with the concerns of the crime film, embodying instead a debate about the nature of America, violence, individuality and civilisation that remains at the core of the Western. KN

Wetherby

One of the best British films of the 80s, *Wetherby* is the most successful of writer-director Hare's politically-themed thrillers. The lives of a group of middle-class friends are shattered when McInnerny's unhinged youth commits suicide in front of Redgrave. In the manner of **An Inspector Calls** – but lacking that film's moral certainty; even the investigating officer in *Wetherby* is in turmoil – Wilson is the policeman who unravels the lives of quiet desperation that bind the characters together. At the centre is Redgrave, hostess of the dinner party that sets the action in motion. She is momentarily attracted to Morgan but put off by his anguished passion, which brings back to the surface her repressed memories of her youthful affair which ended when she succumbed to parental pressure. But all the characters lead powerless, self-deceiving lives in which all they can do is watch. Thus Redgrave is powerless to stop one of her bright pupils quitting school, and Downie, McInnerny's 'girlfriend' who comes to stay with Redgrave after his suicide, is even more inert, almost gripped with a terminal passivity. What gives the film such resonance – as well as the superior performances from Redgrave and Wilson – is Hare's studiedly formal direction, which tweaks out the underlying atmosphere, foregrounding what normally would be merely background. PH

1985/GB/102m/Greenpoint-Zenith/*p* Simon Relph/*d/s*David Hare/*c* Stuart Harris/*m* Nick Bicat/*lp* Vanessa Redgrave, Ian Holm, Judi Dench, Penny Downie, Tim McInnerny, Stuart Wilson.

ABOVE Vanessa Redgrave, *Wetherby*

Where the Sidewalk Ends

Andrews is the tough New York cop given to beating confessions out of his suspects. He finds himself involved in killing a man by accident. In trying to cover up the accidental killing, he fakes evidence so that it points to mobster Merrill, but events spin out of his control and the police pick up an innocent cab driver (Tom Tully) who happens to be the father of Tierney, the dead man's wife and the woman Andrews has fallen in love with. Despite the plot's well-crafted twists and incidental turns, it is a swiftly-paced monochrome drama of the type that Fox were adept at producing around this time (**Night and the City**, **Panic in the Streets**, **Whirlpool**). The fluid screenplay was adapted from the 1948 novel *Night Cry* by William L. Stuart. TV

1950/95m/FOX/*p/d* Otto Preminger/*s* Ben Hecht, Victor Trivas, Frank P. Rosenberg, Robert E. Kent/*c* Joseph La Shelle/*m* Cyril J. Mockridge/*lp* Dana Andrews, Gene Tierney, Gary Merrill.

While the City Sleeps

Question for a movie buff quiz: which American film other than *Citizen Kane* begins with the death of a media tycoon whose corporate logo is the letter K? Answer: *While the City Sleeps*, Lang's penultimate Hollywood film and one of the director's own preferred works. The scenario contains elements of the then popular 'boardroom' genre, exemplified by such films as *Executive Suite* (1954), in the contest, launched by the corporation's heir apparent (Price), among a quartet of contenders for a top post in the new regime. However, this is based upon a race to crack the case of the 'lipstick killer', a serial murderer (Barrymore), whose plea of 'catch me before I kill again' summons up a memory of Lang's **M**. The critic Jean Domarchi has aptly spoken of the film's 'icy detachment'; at the same time, though, the screenplay's touches of sardonic humour and the presence of such distinctive players as Sanders and Lupino make the film less Euclidean than its successor, **Beyond a Reasonable Doubt**. The climax, with the killer run to ground in a subway tunnel and struggling vainly to escape through a manhole, utilises a quasi-religious patterning of darkness and light which recalls the symbolism of Lang's early German work. TP

1956/99m/RKO/*p* Bert E. Friedlob/*d* Fritz Lang/*s* Casey Robinson/*c* Ernest Laszlo/*m* Herschel Burke Gilbert/*lp* Dana Andrews, Rhonda Fleming, George Sanders, Ida Lupino, Vincent Price, John Barrymore Jr.

Whirlpool

The principle that animates *Whirlpool* is the Hitchcockian one of orderly, complacent living fissured by a force of malignancy. The heroine (Tierney) is the wife of a fashionable psychiatrist (Conte). At the outset she succumbs to kleptomania in a department store, and is extricated from an embarrassing situation by a hypnotist (Ferrer) who persuades her to become his patient. His implicitly supernatural powers are such that he is able to send her in a trance to the scene of the crime after he has murdered the ex-mistress he has been swindling. Moreover, to commit the deed he has hypnotised himself into leaving the hospital bed where by way of an alibi he is recovering from an appendix operation. The exposition is a masterly demonstration of Preminger's narrative finesse, expertly catching the spectator up in Tierney's predicament while still preserving a measured detachment. However, the latter stages of the story, with the husband and the detective on the case (Bickford) conspiring to unmask Ferrer, lapse into predictability. TP

1949/97m/FOX/*p/d* Otto Preminger/*s* Ben Hecht, Andrew Solt/*c* Arthur Miller/*m* David Raksin/*lp* José Ferrer, Gene Tierney, Richard Conte, Charles Bickford, Barbara O'Neil.

White Heat

Policeman Hank Fallon (O'Brien) goes undercover as convict Vic Pardo, to share a cell with Cody Jarrett (Cagney), a psychotic gangster prone to murderous rages, blinding headaches and crippling seizures. Out of prison Pardo joins Jarrett's gang, now led by Ma (Wycherly). Cody's wife, Verna (Mayo), is playing around with Big Ed (Cochran), a game that Cody squashes. But after his recapture Cody hears that Big Ed has shot Ma Jarrett dead. He breaks out and embarks on a trail of mayhem which can only end in his death. The definitive, iconic Cagney role, full of invention: for instance, having Cody rest in Ma's lap while she soothes his headache away was Cagney's idea. He even exploits his perky, dancer's grace in the celebrated mess hall scene, where he staggers along in a precisely choreographed rhythm, slugging warders as he goes. The result is electrifying visual drama, especially the climax on top of an oil refinery where Cody blows himself out of existence. MP

1949/114m/WB/*p* Louis F. Edelman/*d* Raoul Walsh/*s* Ivan Goff, Ben Roberts/*c* Sid Hickox/*m* Max Steiner/*lp* James Cagney, Virginia Mayo, Edmond O'Brien, Margaret Wycherly, Steve Cochran.

Who Framed Roger Rabbit

A superb technical achievement in integrating animation and live action, this is based on Gary K. Wolf's book *Who Censored Roger*

ABOVE Bob Hoskins, *Who Framed Roger Rabbit*

Rabbit? In a spoof 1940s thriller setting where humans co-exist with cartoon characters, a Toon character (as in cartoon), Roger Rabbit (voiced by Charles Fleischer), is aided by dishevelled private eye Hoskins to beat a framed murder rap and be reunited with his Toon wife, the sultry Jessica (voice by Kathleen Turner). A stunning production in all special effects departments, with particular credit to British animation director Richard Williams (the film was produced primarily in London). TV

1988/103m/Buena Vista/*p* Robert Watts, Frank Marshall/*d* Robert Zemeckis/*s* Jeffrey Price, Peter S. Seaman/*c* Dean Cundey/ *m* Alan Silvestri/*lp* Bob Hoskins, Christopher Lloyd, Joanna Cassidy.

The Wild One

Inspired via a magazine article by a 1947 incident in which the Californian town of Hollister was 'invaded' by bikers, *The Wild One* is both an extension of the post-war movement of social issue movies (such as the Kramer-produced *Home of the Brave*, 1948) and an indirect harbinger of the exploitation youth movies which would shortly flood from the minor Hollywood companies. The first half of the film, with its pointed observation of the rising tide of petty aggression among the rival motor-cycle gangs who pour into an unsuspecting small town one weekend, is orchestrated to commanding effect. Subsequently, with the citizenry's resort to vigilantism and the accidental death this provokes, the narrative becomes somewhat contrived and fragmented. Even here, though, the expressive quality of Brando's playing as the dominant gang's leader, especially in the sensitively written scenes of his tentative relationship with a local girl (Murphy), ensures that the picture retains considerable impact. In the UK the film was initially banned by the censors and though seen at club showings was not certified for public screening until 1968. TP

1953/79m/COL/*p* Stanley Kramer/*d* Laslo Benedek/*s* John Paxton/*c* Hal Mohr/*m* Leith Stevens/*lp* Marlon Brando, Mary Murphy, Lee Marvin, Robert Keith, Ray Teal.

Williams, Charles (1909–75)

Most of the mystery in Williams's stories centres on a woman, usually one with a past, while the plot is narrated by a man who becomes the victim of the *femme fatale*'s scheme. His early novels were back-country bayou dramas with a somewhat similar feel-

ABOVE Marlon Brando, *The Wild One*

ing to the later works of **James M. Cain**, with their manipulative, scheming women and easily-seduced fall guys (with film versions *Peau de banane*, 1963; *La Fille des collines*, 1990; *The Hot Spot*, 1990). Moving slightly away from the back-water settings but still retaining the scheming woman and fall guy conned-into-a-murder plotting (*The 3rd Voice*, 1960; *Le Gros Coup*, 1964; *Fantasia chez les ploucs*, 1971), Williams's later novels emphasised his romance with the sea and with most things of a nautical nature. Phillip Noyce's **Dead Calm** remains a fine filmed example of Williams's innocents who are not only up against the dangers of their immediate environment (the sea) but also the human terror that visits them (*L'Arme à gauche/Guns for the Dictator*, 1965; *The Man*

Who Would Not Die, 1975). Unfortunately, Williams's compelling narrative construction has been cast adrift in most of the screen adaptations. TV

The Window

'Daringly filmed on New York's teeming East Side', proclaimed the posters, and the adroit matching of location footage with studio interiors lends the film's tenement milieu a persuasive sense of authenticity. *The Window* can in fact be annexed to a group of post-war American films, encompassing both thrillers and works in other genres, like the love story *From This Day Forward* (1946), which were concerned to paint a sympathetically realistic portrait of everyday urban living. This context points up the effectiveness

ABOVE Kelly McGillis, Harrison Ford, *Witness*

of a narrative, derived from a story by **Cornell Woolrich**, which is founded on paranoia. A small boy is known for telling tall tales, so that nobody will believe him when he says he has witnessed a murder – except the killer and his wife, who then attempt to do away with him. While Driscoll's playing of the boy may be a shade histrionic, Hale and Kennedy are naturalistically muted as the parents, and Stewart makes the murderer fittingly frightening. TP

1949/73m/RKO/*p* Frederic Ullman Jr./*d* Ted Tetzlaff/*s* Mel Dinelli/*c* William Steiner/*m* Roy Webb/*lp* Bobby Driscoll, Barbara Hale, Arthur Kennedy, Paul Stewart, Ruth Roman.

Witness

Australian director Weir's first film with an American setting, this well-made drama is actually a love story (between Ford's streetwise detective and McGillis' widowed housewife) set in a fascinating setting (a Pennsylvania Amish community). The threat of violence that hangs over the film is of particular interest, given the seventeenth-century lifestyle and pacifism of the Amish. Weir plays it honestly when he finally introduces violence to the peaceful setting (unlike Ernest Borgnine's pitchfork-wielding Amish farmer in Richard Fleischer's *Violent Saturday*, 1955). TV

1985/112m/PAR/*p* Edward S. Feldman/*d* Peter Weir/*s* Earl W. Wallace, William Kelley/*c* John Seale/*m* Maurice Jarre/*lp* Harrison Ford, Kelly McGillis, Josef Sommer.

The Woman in the Window

Ostensibly this is a parable on the perils of straying from the straight and narrow. Robinson plays a comfortably-off professional man who, while his wife and family are in the country, meets a beautiful woman (Bennett) whose portrait he sees in an art gallery. She invites him home; while they are having an innocent drink, her jealous boyfriend arrives and attacks Robinson. They fight and, with the woman's assistance, Robinson kills the other man. They dump the body; but the victim's accomplice suspects the crime and blackmails the pair. Fearful of the shame of discovery, Robinson poisons himself. The camera then tracks back to reveal it was merely a dream; he has fallen asleep in his club. This is one of Lang's more sardonic essays on the power of fate and on the thin line between the moral world of respectability and the depths to which any of us, with one slip, might fall. The debt to Freud, whose work was fashionable in Hollywood at the time, is directly acknowledged in one of Robinson's own speeches. Lang's **Scarlet Street**, made the same year, has a very similar story and the same leading actors, only this time there is no wakening from the nightmare. EB

1944/99m/International Pictures/*p/s* Nunnally Johnson/*d* Fritz Lang/*c* Milton Krasner/*m* Arthur Lange/*lp* Edward G. Robinson, Joan Bennett, Raymond Massey, Edmund Breon, Dan Duryea.

The Woman in White

This costume melodrama based on the famous 1860 mystery novel by **Wilkie Collins** concerns a scheme by unscrupulous Greenstreet and accomplice (John Emery) to seize young Parker's fortune through marriage. The eerie production moves gracefully between the mystery melodrama and the 1940s horror genres. The title derives from the mystery figure (Parker in a dual role) who appears at intervals to warn of Greenstreet's scheme. Four silent film versions of the novel precede this entry. TV

1948/109m/WB/*p* Henry Blanke/*d* Peter Godfrey/*s* Stephen Morehouse Avery/*c* Carl Guthrie/*m* Max Steiner/*lp* Eleanor Parker, Alexis Smith, Sydney Greenstreet, Gig Young.

Woolrich, Cornell [George Hopley-] (1903–68)

Woolrich, who also wrote as George Hopley and William Irish, was the master of the dark, pessimistic mood, of doom-laden characters. Implicit in the novels was the belief that diabolical powers prey upon the lost and the lonely. His novels and short stories, clichéd as they are at times, are a virtual storehouse of the characters, themes and elements that many of the narrative components of 1940s thrillers were drawn from: the race against time and death themes of **Phantom Lady**, *Black Angel* (1946), and *Deadline at Dawn* (1946), where everything contrives to delay the helpless characters; alternatively, the feverish rush toward an unavoidable doom in **Night Has a Thousand Eyes** presents other terrors. The malignant powers that appear to prevent a witness's story from being believed, as experienced in *Fear in the Night* (1947), **The Window**, *Nightmare* (1956; a remake of *Fear in the Night*, 1947), and, perhaps his most famous story, Hitchcock's **Rear Window**, in which most of the above elements come into play. A victim of amnesia or simply an innocent victim of switched identities becomes a victim of fate in *Street of Chance* (1942) and *No Man of Her Own* (1950). Woolrich was a brilliant if not haunted poet of the tormented and the self-destructive, related to an almost autobiographical fatalism. TV

The Wrong Man

Fonda gives a brilliant performance as a small-time musician who's arrested for a

ABOVE Henry Fonda, Vera Miles, *The Wrong Man*

robbery he didn't commit. When he's convicted of the crime his wife (Miles) literally goes out of her mind with worry. Although, by mere chance, the real criminal is caught and Fonda is released, there's no certainty his wife will recover. Hitchcock portrays the details of police procedures and prison life with quasi-documentary realism (in his interviews with Truffaut he claimed the film was based on an actual case), while also using a subjective camera to make us feel through Fonda's eyes. Though innocent, he feels a criminal's shame as he is fingerprinted and put through the humiliating rituals of incarceration. The law has ways of making even the innocent feel guilty. And Fonda's eventual vindication is small compensation for the ruination of his wife's sanity. EB

1956/105m/WB/*p/d* Alfred Hitchcock/ *s* Maxwell Anderson, Angus McPhail/ *c* Robert Burks/*m* Bernard Herrmann/ *lp* Henry Fonda, Vera Miles, Anthony Quayle, Harold J. Stone, Charles Cooper.

X/Y/Z

Xing Gui/Hang Gui/The System

Trained by James Wong Howe, cinematographer Yung in his first feature shows a remarkable mastery of quasi-documentary location shooting. A police inspector (Pak) is on the trail of a heroin syndicate's boss (Lam) with the reluctant help of a hood (Shek) he blackmailed into becoming an informer. Although at times this is close to a US TV crime drama, the story and above all the pictorial style come alive when the differences between police, informers, undercover cops and gangsters begin to get blurred, each of them caught in larger, overlapping and linked institutional systems operating as mercilessly as impersonal machines. In the end, the police inspector breaks the gang only to find he has now become the target of a rival syndicate. Some of the elaborate surveillance scenes shot in crowded Hong Kong streets convey a genuine sense of place, with everyone perpetually in transit and lacking any sense of stability. Yung directed with flair and the acting is convincingly low-key, giving the film an edge over the second 'realist' gangster movie to emerge from the British colony's 'new wave', Alex Cheung's *Bianyuan Ren*. PW

1979/Hong Kong/87m/Trinity Asia/*p/d/ co-s/co-c* Peter Yung [Yong Weiquan]/*co-s* Lee Sien/*co-c* Tom Lau/*m* Wong Shan/*lp* Pak Ying [Pai Ying], Shek Kin [Shih Kien], Chiao Chiao, Ching Chi-keung, Lam Wai-kei.

Yaju No Seishun/Wild Youth

Suzuki's irreverent attitude towards gang-sters is fully in evidence in this ironic film. The conventions of the genre, including the **yakuza**'s so-called code of honour (ninkyo-do) are rendered comic though no less violent by pushing stylisation to the point where they are revealed as hollow artifice. The film starts with the discovery of a cop in the arms of a woman in a sordid hotel, both dead. A yakuza (Shishido) eventually uncovers that it is the cop's wife who arranged the killing when her husband came too close to finding out that she was the local narcotics boss. Sarcastically, but with a straight face, Suzuki shows that the yakuza image is a romanticised version of an already idealised version of the samurai figure, the main difference being that the aristocrat who employed samurai to murder, terrorise and steal on his behalf has been replaced by urban entrepreneurs. Suzuki's masterpiece, **Tokyo Nagaremono** pushes these aspects to surreal heights. PW

1963/Japan/90m/Nikkatsu/*p* Keinosuke Bubo/*d* Seijun Suzuki/*s* Ichiro Ikeda, Tadaki Yamazaki/*orig* Haruhiko Oyabu/*c* Katsue Nagatsuka/*m* Hajime Okumura/*lp* Jo Shishido, Akira Kobayashi, Kinzo Shin, Hideaki Esumi, Tamio Kawaji.

Yakuza

The yakuza is a member of a major crime syndicate in Japan. Since the 1960s, this figure has become the focus of an entire genre of action-crime movies in Japan, spawning imitations in Hollywood (such as Sydney Pollack's **The Yakuza** and Ridley Scott's **Black Rain**) and, more recently, in Hong Kong (the films of John Woo). The film genre and its conventions are rooted in films of the 1920s, when Tsumasaburo Bando started playing what were called 'nihilistic outlaws', mainly roving samurais alienated from society, although their antecedents went further back in the theatre and in popular literature. These figures evolved into the protagonists of the sword-fight movies (*chambara*). In the 1930s, under increasing military repression, the liberal scenarist Shintaro Mimura adapted the yakuza figure to reflect his disenchantment with the prevailing social order. His characters (petty criminals, gamblers, wandering samurai, and so on) were set in the period 1630–1850 but addressed the situation in the 1930s. Mimura's yakuza, contrary to the samurai, were not ruled by the *giri-ninyo* code which bound subordinates to their feudal masters and implied a complex ethical code for hon-

The Yakuza

ourable macho behaviour. Mimura's figures were anarchists and malcontents. The subgenre of films featuring wandering gamblers, which also fed into the yakuza genre, derived from novels by Shin Hasegawa and Kan Shimozawa, which featured 'free spirits' on the run after performing some Robin Hood-like deed.

In the 40s, films derived from Eiji Yoshikawa's newspaper serial about the hero Musashi Miyamoto introduced a new element. Yoshikawa's hero embodied the proposition that refinement and expertise in the handling of lethal weapons was a sign of moral nobility. Miyamoto perfects his fighting skills as an art for its own sake, confident that spiritual qualities will follow automatically. After World War II, historical films were forbidden by the American occupying forces. Nevertheless, in 1947, Daisuke Ito, the main director of pre-war *chambara* films, made *Suronin Makaritoru* (*The Paltry Ronin Forces his Way Through*), and the yakuza genre re-emerged with heroes who, although ostensibly critical of feudalism, incarnated the spirit of the way of the warrior, known as *bushido*: figures analogous to the noble, loyal and devoted knights of nineteenth-century European romances set in the middle ages. The yakuza, historically, are dispossessed farmers and artisans who become outlaws, and they could not care less about the feudal chivalric code of *ninkyodo* attributed to the fictional yakuza. According to the critic Tadao Sato, this chivalric code is often confused with bushido, but is actually

quite different. Whereas bushido is based on unquestioning loyalty, the yakuza code is based on the concepts of *giri* (duty) balanced by *ninjo* (humaneness).

From 1963 onwards, the yakuza genre received a new impetus with films set in the twentieth century chronicling a conflict between one old-fashioned and honourable gang of gamblers and a bunch of newcomers who do not abide by the old rules and commit robberies and murders. The boss of the 'modern' gang usually has his HQ in an office block and is closely tied to modern industries. Quickly, these tensions evolved into another type of conflict: the ruthlessly 'modern' gang in cahoots with big business versus equally modernised gangsters who nevertheless incarnate older, feudal (village) values and oppose big corporations. This development engendered the lonely, tragic yakuza figure facing overwhelming odds but bravely going to his death because that is the honourable thing to do. This figure was best incarnated by a real-life yakuza turned film actor in the 1960s, Noboru Ando, who constructed the template of the cool, fearless, fatalistic yakuza hero later played by, for instance, Koji Tsuruta (Kosaku Yamashita's *Bakuchiuchi-Socho Bakuto* (1968) and Ken Takakura.

Excluding the historical sword-fighting movies, the genre can roughly be divided into two strands: the gambling films and the modern urban gangster films. Among the most innovative series in the gambling genre is the *Hibotan Bakuto* series (1968–72), fea-

turing the Red Peony, played by Junko Fuji, which followed on from another series featuring fighting-gambling heroines, the *Onna Tobakushi* series (starting in 1966). The contemporary urban gangster genre flourished in a number of Japanese studios, but the most memorable examples are those directed by Kinji Fukasaku at Toei, especially his *Jingi Naki Tatakai* series (from 1973 onwards) and his *Jingi no Hakaba* series (from 1975). The former featured Bunta Sugawara and was based on stories written by the yakuza Koichi Iiboshi, while Noboru Ando acted as advisor. The latter starred the yakuza Rikio Ishikawa, who fought both the police and the gangster milieu at the same time, eventually committing suicide by jumping off the roof of a Tokyo prison. Fukasaku's films are hysterically violent and push the myth of the yakuza beyond its limits, exposing the political and moral corruption at the heart of organised crime. The masterpieces of the genre, however, were produced at Nikkatsu by Seijun Suzuki, starting with *Yaju No Seishun/The Beast Must Die/Wild Youth* (1963) and culminating in the extraordinary **Tokyo Nagaremono** and *Koroshi No Rakuin/ Branded To Kill* (1967). PW

The Yakuza

An ambitious but listless attempt to fuse American and Japanese genres, as a hardboiled private eye (Mitchum) is sent by a friend (Keith) to Japan to rescue a daughter who has been kidnapped by the **yakuza**, the traditional Japanese mafia, and has to forge an alliance with a man-of-honour ex-yakuza (Takakura) to rescue the girl. Mitchum and Takakura, icons on either side of the Pacific whose teaming makes this the action movie equivalent of *King Kong vs Godzilla* (1964), are impressive presences but work at halfthrottle. John Frankenheimer's *The Challenge* (1982) and Ridley Scott's **Black Rain**, the latter also with Takakura holding up the Japanese end, also try for an American-Japanese thriller crossbreed. The effect always seems to be that entirely ordinary elements of American pot-boiler are overwhelmed by the conventions of the yakuza movie, with their incomprehensible feuds and honourable finger-severings, but that the Japanese genre never finds its way in an international dilution. KN

1975/112m/WB/*p/d* Sydney Pollack/*s* Paul Schrader, Robert Towne/*orig* Leonard Schrader/*c* Okazaki Kozo, Duke Callaghan/ *m* Dave Grusin/*lp* Robert Mitchum, Ken

ABOVE Yakuza: *Sonatine*

ABOVE *Year of the Dragon*

Takakura, Brian Keith, Herb Edelman, Richard Jordan, Kishi Keiko.

Year of the Dragon

Rourke is the lone renegade cop who is assigned to clear up a street-gang problem in New York's Chinatown but instead begins a useless one-man crusade in cleaning up the community's age-old underworld culture. His main target is Lone's young crime-lord who (in quite a fascinating side plot of its own) has his own problems and power-plays in trying to modernise the ancient drug racket. Some excellent action moments fail to develop this rather overlong story and the Rourke character appears to have achieved very little by the end. The NYC Chinatown setting was recreated at producer De Laurentiis' North Carolina studios. TV

1985/136m/MGM-UA/*p* Dino De Laurentiis/ *d* Michael Cimino/*s* Oliver Stone, Michael Cimino/*c* Alex Thomson/*m* David Mansfield/ *lp* Mickey Rourke, John Lone, Ariane.

Yoidore Tenshi/Drunken Angel

Although the released version of this film was cut by almost a full hour, Kurosawa still claimed it to be his first truly personal film. Mifune, who became identified with Kurosawa's films over the next 20 years, here enters the director's world as a small-time gangster, Matsunaga, suffering from TB in a devastated Tokyo. The dominant image is that of a fetid pool of water in the midst of a bombed out cityscape around which the love-hate relationship between Matsunaga and the alcoholic slum doctor (beautifully played by Shimura) is played out. The gangster eventually consents to being treated but his former boss (Yamamoto) returns from prison, signified through an impressive shot of a menacing figure reflected in the dirty pool, and triggers a tragic ending. The resonant imagery, enhanced by the masterfully orchestrated camera movements and lighting effects, evokes the complex situation in a post-war Japan struggling to shake off a diseased past. There are a few clumsy passages, such as an overly symbolic dream sequence and a superfluous cabaret number. PW

1948/Japan/150m/Toho/*p* Sojiro Motoki/ *d*/*co-s* Akira Kurosawa/*co-s* Keinosuke Uegusa/*c* Takeo Ito/*m* Fumio Hayasaka/*lp* Takashi Shimura, Toshiro Mifune, Reisaburo Yamamoto, Chieko Nakakita, Michiyo Kogure.

You and Me

Lang's third American picture, *You and Me* can be seen as the concluding part of a social trilogy in which **Fury** and **You Only Live Once** are the preceding instalments, with Sidney the leading lady of all three. The difference is that *You and Me* is ultimately optimistic in tenor, providing its social victims with the prospect of a positive future. The premise is, in fact, reminiscent of a contemporary 'fantasy of goodwill' by Frank Capra, involving a philanthropist tycoon who gives paroled convicts a second chance by way of employment in his department store. The film was, however, considered a failure in its own time and has received little subsequent attention (Lang himself later described the project as 'jinxed'). The problem seems to be that while the film contains a couple of songs and some non-realist aspects, the elements of comedy and stylisation have generally been subordinated to a more conventional dramaturgy, with a somewhat novelettish result. All the same, a rewarding curio. TP

1938/90m/PAR/*p*/*d* Fritz Lang/*s* Virginia Van Upp/*c* Charles Lang/*m* Kurt Weill/*lp* Sylvia Sidney, George Raft, Barton MacLane, Harry Carey, Robert Cummings.

You Only Live Once

Three-time loser Eddie Taylor (Fonda) emerges from prison vowing to fiancée Jo (Sidney) that he intends to go straight. However, his struggle ends when old associates commit a bank robbery and leave evidence suggesting Eddie was involved. Unjustly imprisoned and sentenced to death for the killing of a bank employee, Eddie becomes deeply embittered and, with Jo's

ABOVE Toshiro Mifune, *Yoidore Tenshi*

351

help, makes an escape. Ironic fate conspires to unearth evidence that he is innocent just as he guns down the chaplain (Gargan) who has been trying to help him, and the couple make a doomed dash for Canada, achieving a final transcendence as they are together shot dead by unseen marksmen as they cross the border. Like **Fury**, this finds Lang's style increasing in confidence as he blends the semi-gothic fatalism of his German films with a distinctively American, grittily realist insight into the workings of crime. The robbery sequence, incidental to the plot, is a miniature of the heist workings of **The Asphalt Jungle**, with masked figures invading a bank through swirling gas that allows for neo-expressionist visual effects. The casting of Fonda, even in 1937 the image of American integrity, as the loser hero is a powerful suggestion that Eddie

Taylor's fate is not of his own making and demonstrates a deep and ineradicable flaw in the society that dooms him. *You Only Live Once* stands as the first masterpiece of Lang's American career. KN

1937/87m/UA/*p* Walter Wanger/*d* Fritz Lang/*s* Gene Towne, Graham Baker/*c* Leon Shamroy/*m* Alfred Newman/*lp* Sylvia Sidney, Henry Fonda, Barton MacLane, Jean Dixon, William Gargan.

Zapis zbrodni/Chronology of a Crime

This was one of the first Polish films to address the issue of teenage crime in a quasi-documentary fiction. Kazek and Bogdan (Hryniewicz and Radecki) are cynical and frustrated youngsters from a village near Lodz. They attack a cab driver in an episode

that foreshadows the murder of a cab driver in Kieslowski's better known **Krotki film o zabijaniu**. They go on to rob a carpenter, taking his wife's gold wedding ring off her finger. On the run and alienated from their former village mates, they become social outcasts. The duo are arrested on a train by a diligent cop, but Kazek escapes only to give himself up a little later, exhausted and at the end of his tether. PW

1974/Poland/87m/PRF Zespoly Filmowe-Kadr-WFD/*d*/*co-s* Andrzej R. Trzos-Rastawiecki/ *co-s* Maciej Krasicki/*c* Zygmunt Samosiuk/*m* Henryk Kuzniak, Jerzy Maksymiuk/*lp* Mieczyslaw Hryniewicz, Waclaw Radecki, Jerzy Bonczak, Wojciech Gorniak, Tomasz Neuman.

ABOVE Guinn Williams, Henry Fonda, *You Only Live Once*